Leszek A. Utracki

# POLYMER ALLOYS AND BLENDS

# Leszek A. Utracki

# POLYMER ALLOYS AND BLENDS

## Thermodynamics and Rheology

Hanser Publishers, Munich Vienna New York

Distributed in the United States of America by Oxford University Press, New York
and in Canada by Oxford University Press, Canada

The Author:
Dr. Leszek A. Utracki, Associate Director, National Research Council of Canada, Industrial Materials Research Institute, Boucherville, Quebec, Canada

Distributed in USA by
Oxford University Press
200 Madison Avenue, New York, N. Y. 10016

Distributed in Canada by
Oxford University Press, Canada
70 Wynford Drive, Don Mills, Ontario M3C IJ9

Distributed in all other countries by
Carl Hanser Verlag
Kolbergerstr. 22
D-8000 München 80

The use of general descriptive names, trademarks, etc, in this publication, even if the former are not especially identified, is not to be taken as a sign that such names, as understood by the Trade Marks and Merchandise Marks Act, may accordingly be used freely by anyone.

While the advice and information in this book are believed to be true and accurate at the date of going to press, neither the authors nor the editors nor the publisher can accept any legal responsibility for any errors or omissions that may be made. The publisher makes no warranty, express or implied, with respect to the material contained herein.

*CIP-Titelaufnahme der Deutschen Bibliothek*

**Utracki, Leszek A.:** Polymer alloys and blends : thermodynamics and rheology / Leszek A. Utracki. – Munich ; Vienna ; New York : Hanser, 1989
ISBN 3-446-14200-2

ISBN 3-446-14200-2 Carl Hanser Verlag, Munich, Vienna, New York
ISBN 0-19-520796-3 Oxford University Press, New York

Printed in the Federal Republic of Germany by C. H. Beck'sche Buchdruckerei, Nördlingen

# PREAMBLE

Persuaded by the eloquence of a Hanser Editor, this "12 to 18 months" project started in 1983. It is safe to say that we were overly optimistic. However, there was a good objective reason for the delay. The literature on polymer alloys and blends, PAB, has assumed avalanche proportions. Recognizing the commercial importance of these materials, everyone feels obliged to contribute; annually there are about 4,500 patents and at least ten times as many technical publications on the subject. Writing a monograph on PAB, one can not afford to ignore these developments. The science and technology of PAB is being created now. Every month, every week, a new important element is added.

In this volume I tried to construct as complete an image of PAB fundamentals as possible. However, on the one hand some of the information could not be verified and on the other, by the time the volume reaches readers' hands, new discoveries will have been made. Sorry, but only Rama was a perfect man.

There are two types of scientists: the analysts and the synthesists. A good friend of mine, who has been working for over 20 years in polymer engineering, collected about 120 references and considered everything else trash. As this text certifies, my own approach is different. Trying to build a consistent image of the current status of PAB science, I have read about 20,000 patents and papers and spoken with hundreds of industrial and academic researchers and engineers. After critical evaluation, there remained over a thousand references that I felt it necessary to cite in the text. My aim was to provide an outline with enough information for the interested reader to expand on. The text should be used as a guide to this exponentially growing science and technology.

The data published in scientific literature are honest. However, there are instances when the cited reports seem to contradict each other. In many cases after a careful analysis the reason for the contradiction becomes apparent: a difference in molecular parameters, compounding, specimen preparation or method of measurements may lead to wide differences in experimental results. One may say that this is inherent in the nature of PAB's! Frequently one can learn more from these "contradictions" than from papers "confirming" the published data. However, it takes time and effort to make the comparison and then confirm the conclusions.

Initially the text was intended to cover the whole area of PAB science and technology; the fundamental aspects (thermodynamics and rheology) as well as the technological ones (compounding, forming and properties) were to be treated. However due to the time factor and the growing volume of information only the developments in thermodynamics and rheology are being presently published. Furthermore, the main emphasis of the latter aspect is the melt flow, with only a short chapter dedicated to the dynamic methods of PAB analysis in solid state within a range of the linear viscoelastic behavior. This seemed necessary in order to discuss the effects of miscibility and morphology.

Even though most of the cited references are in English, the literature search was conducted „sans prejudice". If some important contribution has been omitted please blame my poor judgement... or the abstracting services. I am certain that in spite of all the efforts there are omissions and mistakes in the text. My apologies - please let me know where I erred, and how the text should be corrected, supplemented or changed. Besides the two main parts on thermodynamics and rheology, several appendices provide a source for more general information.

The introductory Part I is written in a form of a general review referring to more specific information in the other parts of the book. It is in a sense a "poor man's compendium", outlining reasons for blending, properties, economy and markets as well as providing a list of steps for developing new PAB's. This "how to" approach is based on succesfully tested industrial procedures, developed to replace more common trial-and-error methods.

Polymer alloys and blends are one of the most dynamic sectors of the polymer industry. In particular the annual growth rate of engineering PAB's has been systematically outstripping that of the industry as a whole by a factor of 4 to 5. The main reason for the popularity of PAB is the ever increasing cost of development of new materials. In 1986 one of the major resin suppliers disclosed that development of its new polymer cost nearly US $ 15 million for research and development and an additional US $ 150 million in capital costs for a pilot plant. Blending is quicker and less expensive. The cost of development of a new PAB seldom exceeds a few million dollars with little if any capital investment for efficient compounding. With present knowledge and industrial know-how there are fewer dead-ends in the development of PAB than of new resins. The blend properties can be "tuned" to satisfy a spectrum of customer demands. On the other hand, blend properties are combinations of properties of the components, with rare cases of mild synergism. To generate new properties, new polymers are still needed.

In 1986 consumption of the high value engineering PAB's exceeded 1.4 million tons (1.4 Mt). Nearly a quarter of this was absorbed by the transport industry and this share is expected to grow to a third by 1997. The new engineering PAB's compete favorably with aluminum alloys as far as both the continuous use temperature and specific mechanical properties are concerned. Without any fundamental change in car design the plastics consumption in the automobile industry will reach 1.9 Mt by 1990. However, most of the automakers are actively working on all-plastics cars. When the design and test phase is completed the demand for engineering PAB's will see a quantum jump. Already blends based on polyphenyleneether or polycarbonate are being used for body panels, bumpers, instrument panels, etc.

There are three areas of PAB technology which need further development prior to expected wider use of polymeric mixtures in automobile industry: (i) development of reliable methods for part testing, especially under cyclic loading, (ii) examination of the long term performance and weatherability, and (iii) recycling. The importance of fatigue testing for automobile part is easy to comprehend. Unfortunately, the subject literature is limited and understanding is still lacking of how the composition and processing affect it. Weatherability plays a vital part in the esthetics and performance of exterior panels.

The world production of automobiles and small track is about 50 million units per year; the problem of what to do with so many scrapped plastic automobiles is both a technical and socio-political one which must be solved. The annual volume of plastics scrap in the USA is already sufficient to pave the New York - Los Angeles four lane (15 m wide) highway with a layer 37 cm thick. Recycle we must!

The earliest blends were prepared by exploiting the natural miscibility of the components. Good examples are blends of polyvinylchloride with acrylonitrile rubber or polyphenyleneether with high impact polystyrene. The miscibility was the main criterion for blending. During the next stage miscibility still was king. New blends of immiscible polymers were developed using graft, or preferably block, copolymer having one part interacting with one polymer and another with the other. The third stage was chemical modification of immiscible polymers to ensure their miscibility via e.g. ionic interactions. The latest additions to these still very much used methods are reactive processing, reactive compounding, reactive impact modification, etc.

Reactive processing during the compounding or forming stage assures a controlled chemical reaction between the components. The reaction can be direct or by the intervention of a third ingredient. This technology not only opens up new possibilities for old products but also allows preparation of blends which could not be economically made before. Furthermore, it makes some simple polymers more attractive for blending. For example, from the point of view of the polymer properties polyoxymethylene (POM), and polycarbonate (PC), are comparable, with some mechanical properties of POM being better than those of PC. However, excepting the toughened POM blends, this resin is seldom used in high performance alloys. The reason is the simplicity of the POM macromolecular chain which does not provide for similar variety of specific interactions as that of PC. The reactive processing may change this; it allows POM to be blended with any polymer. Interest in and consumption of POM for blending purposes should significantly increase.

In the latest stage blends are increasingly being used as a base for either foams or composites. A better control of multicomponent interfacial properties either via sophisticated chemistry or reactive processing makes this step possible. Foamed PAB are being used for computer housings, hospital or office furniture, automobile parts, etc. Reinforced grades of PAB are becoming standard on the list of product brochures (e.g. see Appendix I).

Not only PAB science is young. The technology is also undergoing a rapid evolution. It is my hope that this volume will further stimulate interest in these formidable materials and accelerate the progress of their technology.

Finally, I wish to express my thanks and appreciation to many without whom this book could not been written. First of all to my wife who for several years patiently saw me spending evenings and weekends behind a wall of papers. I am deeply indebted to Director of the Institute, Mr. G.L. Bata for encouragement as well as for permission to use the Institute's resources in preparing this text. Thanks to my mentor, friend and inspiration, Robert Simha, for numerous discussions and comments on parts of this text. My warmest thank you to Donald Patterson, Ron Koningsveld, Jan Noolandi, Jorgen Lyngaae-Jorgensen, Pierre Carreau, Musa Kamal, Michel Dumoulin, Andrzej Plochocki, Lloyd Robeson and others who sacrificed their time reading the manuscript, helping to weed out the errors. Special thanks to two ladies who translated my handwritten notes into manuscript: Mesdames Marcelle Duguay and Colette Bussières Desmarais. My thanks to many good friends from the Shushrusha hospital in Bombay who somehow managed to bring me back to finish this work. I also want to express my profound gratitude to Drs. S. Ganguly and J.S. Anand as well as numerous other colleagues from the Indian Petrochemicals Corporation Ltd. and N.C.L. for the interest in this work and their extraordinary hospitality.

Montreal 1983 - Bombay 1988

# TABLE OF CONTENTS

# Part 1

# INTRODUCTION TO POLYMER ALLOYS AND BLENDS

## 1.1    Historical Outline of the Industrial Development of Polymer Alloys and Blends

The contemporary reader of polymer blend literature may be under the impression that blending is a recent development. When asked to name the first polymer blend an audience usually casts about 70% of its votes for "Noryl", 25% for ABS, with the remaining 5% for various blends listed in Table 1.2 later in the text.

This lack of historical perspective on the commercial development of polymer alloys and blends, PAB, is due to their rapid growth in importance during the 1980's. For example, in 1987, it was estimated that 60 to 70% of polyolefins and 23% of other polymers were sold as blends (but not necessarily identified as such). Furthermore, while during the late 80's the annual growth rate (AGR), of the plastics industry was 2 to 4%, that of PAB was 9 to 11% while the AGR of engineering blends was 13 to 17%. Clearly, the plastics industry is moving toward more complex systems. Whereas the use of polymers in composites and filled plastics is nearly 29%, the use of unmodified neat resin has shrunk to less than 50%. The future will bring a further increase of complexity in the form of multicomponent/multifunctional blends, foamed and reinforced PAB with more emphasis on enhanced optimization of material performance through processing.

### 1.1.1    Definitions

In the context of this volume the following terminology will be used:

  (i) *polymer,* polymeric material or resin with linear, branched or crosslinked structure whose degree of polymerization exceeds 50 to 70.
  (ii) *copolymer,* polymeric material synthesized from more than a single monomer.
  (iii) *engineering polymer (EP),* a processable polymeric material, capable of being formed to precise and stable dimensions, exhibiting high performance at the continuous use temperature above 100°C, and having tensile strength in excess of 40 MPa.
  (iv) *polymer blend (PB),* a mixture of at least two polymers or copolymers.

   *(v) homologous polymer blend (HPB),* a mixture of two homologous polymers, usually narrow molecular weight distribution fractions of the same polymer.

   *(vi) miscible polymer blend (MPB),* polymer blend homogenous down to the molecular level, associated with the negative value of the free energy of mixing; $\Delta G_m \simeq \Delta H_m \leq 0$.

   *(vii) immiscible polymer blend,* any PB whose $\Delta G_m \simeq \Delta H_m > 0$.

   *(viii) compatible polymer blend,* a utilitarian term indicating a commercially attractive polymer mixture, normally homogenous to the eye, frequently with enhanced physical properties over the constituent polymers.

   *(ix) polymer alloy (PA),* an immiscible PB having a modified interface and/or morphology.

   *(x) compatibilization,* a process of modification of interfacial properties of an immiscible polymer blend, leading to the creation of a polymer alloy.

   *(xi) engineering polymer blend (EPB),* a PB or PA either containing or having properties of the EP.

   It is clear that the miscibility of PB, being defined in terms of the equilibrium thermodynamics, must be considered only within the range of independent variables (temperature, pressure, molecular weight, chain structure, etc.) under which the free energy of mixing is negative. Note that observed miscibility of a given polymer pair is insufficient for generalization of such behavior to other pairs of the same polymers or to another set of physical conditions.

   As will be discussed in Part 2, the condition for $\Delta G_m < 0$ can exist only if the binary polymer-polymer interaction coefficient, $\chi_{12}$, is negative. There are three contributions to $\chi_{12}$: dispersion forces, free volume and the specific interactions. Their relative magnitude and the temperature dependence is shown schematically in Fig. 1.1. In the Figure the dependency on the left is most frequently observed in low molecular weight solutions, while that on the right in polymer blends. The UCST and LCST indicate the upper and the lower critical solution temperature respectively. For UCST < T < LCST the mixture is miscible, i.e. for PAB the miscibility vanishes on heating above the LCST. In consequence, blending PB above LCST leads to a state of miscibility in the finished product which depends on the kinetics of phase separation during the post-processing cooling stage.

   The rate at which the thermodynamic equilibrium can be achieved depends on the driving thermodynamic force, i.e. the polymer-polymer interaction coefficient, and the resisting rheological forces, i.e. the diffusivity. For example, it can be calculated that for polyolefin blends, where the interaction coefficient $\chi_{12} \rightarrow 0$, the time for thermodynamic equilibrium, depends on the low self diffusion coefficient. As a result the polyolefin blends prepared in a common solvent may show miscibility, whereas those prepared by mechanical mixing apparent immiscibility. Only detailed studies of the tendency of these blends to mix or to separate over a long period of time can answer the question of their true thermodynamic miscibility. However, miscible or not, most polyolefin blends are compatible, with an enhancement of their physical performance responsible for the predominance of blending in the polyethylene industry.

   Another term which needs further explanation is polymer alloy (PA). The general relation between blends and alloys is shown in Fig. 1.2. PA constitutes a specific sub-class of PB. Virtually all high performance engineering blends are alloys. For practical reason PA can be subdivided into two categories: (A) those in which the compatibilization leads to very fine (usually sub-micron) dispersion so the molded part will show neither streaking nor excessive weld-line weakening, and (B) those where some compatibilizer is added in order to facilitate the formation of the desired morphology in a subsequent processing step. Most PA's belong to category A (e.g. BASF Ultranyl polyphenyleneether/polyamide blend). DuPont Selar-PA polyamide/ ionomer blend (to be added to polyolefin and then blow molded) can serve as an example of category B. The methods of detecting polymer-polymer miscibility are

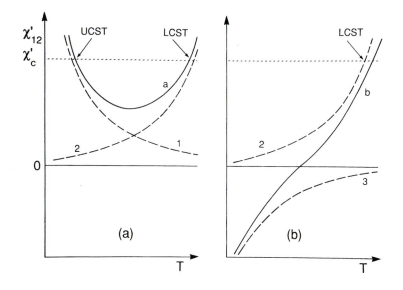

Fig. 1.1 Schematic representation of the temperature variation of the interaction parameter, $\chi'_{12}$ (solid line) and its components: 1. dispersion forces, 2. free volume, and 3. specific interactions. The resulting graph (a) represents interactions encountered mostly in solutions with upper and lower solution temperatures, UCST and LCST respectively, whereas graph (b) is more typical of polymer blends where only LCST is visible. (*Patterson* and *Robard*, 1978).

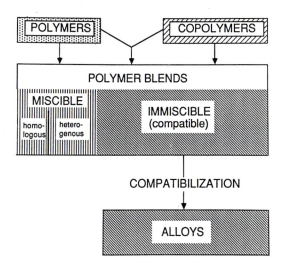

Fig. 1.2 Interrelations in polymer blend nomenclature.

discussed in Part 2.6. In most cases, since these do not allow for direct determination of either phase diagram, $\Delta G_m$, $\Delta H_m$ or $\chi_{12}$, they can only be taken as measures of apparent miscibility. The most popular of these is a plot of the compositional dependency of the glass transition temperature, $T_g$. The presence of two $T_g$'s is taken as an indication of immiscibility. In fact, detection of a single concentration dependent $T_g$ only signifies that the size of the blend domains is below 15 nm. In Fig. 1.3 low frequency storage modulus is plotted as a function of temperature. The broken lines represent the behavior of neat polymers, the solid of 50:50 blend. The sudden drop of a modulus is associated with onset of molecular thermal motions in the region of $T_g$. The four schematics illustrate: 1. miscible, 2. immiscible, 3. partially miscible, and 4 immiscible blend with fine dispersion and broad glass transition region.

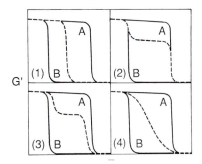

Fig. 1.3 Schematic representation of temperature dependence of storage shear modulus for polymer A, polymer B (solid lines) and their 50:50 mixture (broken line). Case (1) A and B are miscible, Case (2) A and B are immiscible, Case (3) The miscibility is limited to low concentration of A in B and B in A, Case (4) Blend with fine dispersion (compatibilized).

### 1.1.2    Development of Commercial Alloys and Blends

In Table 1.1 the dates of commercialization of major thermoplastics are listed. The table is intended to highlight main steps in development of plastics industry. The interested readers will find more exhaustive information in monographs on the subject (*Winding* and *Hiat*, 1961; *Mason*, 1972; *Schwartz* and *Goodman*, 1982; *Seymour*, 1982; *Morawetz*, 1985). Table 1.2 provides a more complete listing of commercial polymer blends. Blending of rubbers predates that of thermoplastics by nearly a century. The original idea of gaining extra performance by blending must be credited to Thomas Hancock, who by mixing natural rubber with gutta percha obtained a mixture which was easily applied for waterproofing cloth.

Polyvinylchloride has been known in laboratories since 1872 but became commercial only in 1927 after the advantage of plasticization was discovered. However, development of acrylonitrile rubber (NBR), and in 1942 the discovery of its ability to permanently plasticize PVC spurred rapid penetration of the market. The PVC/NBR blend was the first commercial thermoplastics blend in the modern sense of the word. In the same year, 1942, Dow Chemical Co. introduced Styralloy-22 (a precursor of interpenetrating polymer network materials, IPN), of polystyrene and polybutadiene. Thus the term "alloy" for the first time was used in reference to a polymeric mixture. In 1942 development of mechanical mixtures of NBR with poly(styrene-co-acrylonitrile), SAN, (known as ABS type A) was an important step in starting a flood of polymer alloys and blends. As one may note in the lists of

TABLE 1.1 Commercialization Dates of Selected Synthetic Polymers

| Year | Code | Polymer | Producer |
|------|------|---------|----------|
| 1927 | PVC | Polyvinylchloride | B. F. Goodrich |
| 1929 | GRS/SBR | Styrene-butadiene rubber | I.G. Farben |
| 1930 | PS | Polystyrene | I. G. Farben/Dow |
| 1936 | PMMA | Polymethylmethacrylate | Rohm and Haas |
| 1936 | PA-6,6 | Polyamide-6,6 | DuPont |
| 1939 | LDPE | Low density polyethylene | ICI |
| 1943 | PDMS | Polydimethylsiloxane | Dow Corning |
| 1946 | PTFE | Polytetrafluoroethylene | DuPont |
| 1948 | ABS | Acrylonitrile-butadiene-styrene copolymer | Rohm and Haas/ I. G. Farben |
| 1954 | PU | Polyurethanes | Bayer/DuPont |
| 1954 | HDPE | High density polyethylene | Hoechst |
| 1954 | PET | Polyethyleneterephthalate | ICI |
| 1956 | PA-6 | Poly-ε-caprolactam (Polyamide-6) | Allied |
| 1957 | PP | Isotactic Polypropylene | Phillips Petrol. |
| 1958 | PC | Polycarbonate of bisphenol-A | GEC/Bayer |
| 1958 | SMM | Poly(styrene-co-methymethacrylate) | Rohm and Haas |
| 1958 | POM | Polyoxymethylene, (Acetal) | DuPont |
| 1959 | LLDPE | Linear low density polyethylene | DuPont-Canada |
| 1960 | Aramid | Aromatic polyamide | DuPont |
| 1962 | Phenoxy | Polyhydroxyether | Union Carbide |
| 1963 | PI | Polyimides | DuPont |
| 1964 | -- | Ionomers | DuPont |
| 1965 | PPE | Polyphenyleneether | GEC |
| 1965 | P4MP | Poly-4-methyl pentene-1 | ICI |
| 1965 | SBS | Poly(styrene-b-butadiene) | Shell |
| 1965 | PAI | Polyamide-imide | Amoco |
| 1965 | PSO | Polysulfone | Union Carbide/3M |
| 1969 | -- | Amorphous, aromatic polyamides | Dynamit Nobel |
| 1969 | PBT | Polybutyleneterephthalate | Celanese |
| 1972 | PPS | Polyphenylenesulfide | Phillips Petrol. |
| 1972 | LCP | Polymeric liquid crystal | Carborundum |
| 1978 | PES | Polyethersulfone | ICI |
| 1978 | PEEK | Polyetheretherketone | ICI |
| 1982 | PEI | Polyetherimide | GEC |
| 1985 | PAE | Polyarylether | Union Carbide |
| 1986 | PISO | Polyimidesulfone | Celanese |
| 1986 | APEC | Aromatic polyestercarbonate | Bayer |
| 1987 | PPMB | Poly-p-methylenebenzoate | Amoco |
| 1987 | PA-4,6 | Polyamide 4,6 | DSM |
| 1987 | -- | Sulfone based "super engineering" polymer (Amoroon) | Dainippon Ink & Chem. |

commercial PAB's (see Appendix I) over 25% of them contain ABS. In fact the ABS-type blends dominate the blend market; in 1986 they amounted to 74% of all PAB sales in Europe, 77% in Japan and 69% in the North America. The dynamism of the market is such that annually about 80 new grades of ABS are introduced to the USA market alone.

The year 1960 was most important for modern engineering PAB's. During that year an addition of polystyrene (PS), to poly-2,6-dimethyl-1,4-phenyleneether (PPE), was found to allow processing of this new resin. Blends of PPE/PS are miscible. Their density is higher

TABLE 1.2  Historical Brief on Development of Polymer Alloys and Blends

| No. | Year | Event | Reference |
|---|---|---|---|
| 1. | 1846 | First patenting of polymer blend: natural rubber with gutta percha | T. Hancock, Engl. Pat. No. 11,147 |
| 2. | 1929 | Copolymerization of butadiene with styrene leads to styrene rubber, Buna-S, GRS or SBR. Commercial production starts in 1934. | W. Bock and E. Tschunkur, U.S. Pat. No. 1,938,731 (1933) to I.G. Farben |
| 3. | 1934 | Patenting of acrylonitrile rubber, Buna-N or NBR. | E. Konrad and E. Tschunkur, U.S. Pat. No. 1,973,000 (1934) to I.G. Farben |
| 4. | 1942 | First patent on thermoplastic polymer blends: polyvinyl chloride, PVC, with NBR as a permanent semi-soluble polymeric plasticizer. (Plasticization of PVC was invented 16 years earlier). | E. Badum, U.S. Pat. No. 2,297,194 (1942); D. E. Henderson, U.S. Pat. No. 2,330,353 (1943) to B.F. Goodrich Co. W. L. Semon, U.S. Pat. No. 1,929,453 of 10 Oct. 1933. |
| 5. | 1942 | First use of the term alloy in reference to thermoplastic: "Styralloy-22" commercialized by Dow Chem. Co. interpenetrating polymer network (IPN) of styrene and butadiene. | R. F. Boyer, in "History of Polymer Science and Technology, R. B. Seymour, Ed., M. Dekker, New York (1982). |
| 6. | 1944 | R. F. Boyer polymerizes styrene in the presence of soluble GRS what leads to development of high impact PS (HIPS); commercial production starts in 1948. | (see above); J. L. Amos, O. R. McIntyre and J. L. McCurdy, U.S. Pat. No. 2,694,692 (1954) assigned to Dow Chem. Co. |
| 7. | 1946 | Developing ABS-type A, a mechanical mixture of NBR with poly(styrene-co-acrylonitrile), SAN. | L. E. Daly, U.S. Pat. No. 2,439,202 (1948) to US Rubber Co. |
| 8. | 1946 | Introduction of polyurethanes (PU) – a family of copolymers leading to heterogenous polymeric structures. | C. S. Schollenberger, H. Scott and G. R. Moore, Rubber World, *137*, 549 (1958). |
| 9. | 1947 | Miscibility of 35 polymer pairs was studied; three miscible ones: nitrocellulose (NC) with polyvinylacetate (PVAc) or with polymethylmethacrylate (PMMA) and benzyl cellulose (BC) with polystyrene (PS). | A. Dobry and F. Boyer-Kawenoki, J. Polym. Sci., *2*, 90 (1947). |
| 10. | 1951 | Discovery of crystalline polypropylene (i-PP), followed in 50's with work on low temperature impact improvements by blending with polyethylene or co-polymerizing with ethylene. | J. P. Hogan and R. L. Banks, U. S. Pat. Appl. No. 333,576; filed 27 Jan. 1953 on behalf of Phillips Petroleum Co. |
| 11. | 1960 | Discovery of miscibility of PS with polyphenylene ether (PPE) invented in late 50's by A. S. Hay, (JACS, *81*, 6335 (1959)) lead to a whole family of Noryl blends commercialized in 1965. | E. M. Boldebuck, U. S. Pat. No. 3,063,851 (1962); E. P. Cizek, U. S. Pat. No. 3, 383, 4435 (1968) to General Electric Co. |
| 12. | 1962 | Commercial introduction of ethylene-propylene rubbers, (EPR) and ethylene-propylene-diene rubber (EPDM); the ingredients used frequently in PAB for impact improvement. | W. F. Gresham and M. Hunt, U. S. Pat. No. 2,933,480, Apr. 10, 1960 to DuPont. |
| 13. | 1962 | Blends of ABS with poly(α-methylstyrene-co-acrylonitrile), "High-heat ABS" | H. H. Irving, U. S. Pat. No. 3,010,936 (1961) to Borg Warner. |
| 14. | 1965 | Patenting of styrene-butadiene-styrene block copolymers | G. Holden and R. Milkovich, U. S. Pat. No. 3,265,766 (1965) to Shell. |

| No. | Year | Event | Reference |
|-----|------|-------|-----------|
| 15. | 1969 | Commercialization by Borg Warner of ABS/PVC blend under trade name Cycovin. | Modern Plast., Feb. 1969, pg. 77. |
| 16. | 1969 | Discovery of PP/EPDM blend by Coran and Patel commercialized by Monsanto under the trade name of Santoprene. | A. Y. Coran and R. Patel, Rubber Chem. Technol., 53, 141, 781 (1980); 54, 91, 892 (1981); 56, 210 (1983); R. Patel and D. Williams, Rubber Chem. Technol., 54, 116 (1981); 55, 1063 (1982). |
| 17. | 1975 | Development at DuPont of "super tough nylon", Zytel-ST, followed by toughening of polyethylen-eterephthalate (PET) by addition of small quantity of polyolefinic elastomer. | "Nylon-ST super tough Nylon Resin" bulletin E29250 by DuPont. |
| 18. | 1976 | Development of PET/polybutyleneterephthalate (PBT), blends (Valox 800 series) by General Electric Co. | J. A. Vaccarl, Product Eng., 39, Febr. |
| 19. | 1977 | Mobay starts production of Bayblend containing polycarbonate (PC) and ABS on license from Borg Warner who simultaneously introduced ABS/PC blend under trade name Cycoloy. | J. J. Gasparich, "CANPLAST-'81", Montreal, Que., Canada, Oct. 25, 1981. |
| 20. | 1979 | General Electric introduced impact modified blend of PC with polybutyleneterephthalate and/or polyethyleneterephthalate under trade name Xenoy. | M. D. Bertolucci and D. E. De-Laney, Soc. Plast. Eng. NATEC, Sept. 20-27, 1983. |
| 21. | 1980 | Toughened blends of elastomer with PBT (Celanex 500) and polyoxymethylene (POM) (Celcon C-400) introduced by Celanese. | "Celanex – Thermoplastic Polyester", Bulletin JIA, Celanese Corp., Febr. 1984. |
| 22. | 1980 | Introduction by Union Carbide of Mindel, blend of ABS and polysulfone (PSO) with improved processability. (First ABS/PSO blend was Arylon-T from Uniroyal). | Mater. Eng., 93 (2), 18 (1981); 93 (3) 21, (1981); 93 (7), 16 (1981). |
| 23. | 1981 | Borg Warner enters the market with new PPE-copolyether/PS blend, Prevex. | Plast. Focus, March 2, 1981, p. 3. |
| 24. | 1981 | New blends of poly(styrene-co-maleic anhydride) (SMA), with ABS (Cadon) and with PC (Arloy) introduced respectively by Monsanto and Arco. | Mater. Eng., 93 (6), 22 (1981); Plast. Focus, May 1983, p. 1. |
| 25. | 1982 | DuPont introduces Selar, modified and compatibilized, amorphous polyamide to be used as additive to polyolefin to reduce permeability. | "Selar Barrier Resins", Bulletins E73971, E73973, E73974 by DuPont. |
| 26. | 1983 | Polyarylate blend, Ardel D-240, introduced by Union Carbide Corp. | Polym. News, Jan. 1984, p. 188; Modern Plast., 61 (3), 60 (1984). |
| 27. | 1983 | Noryl GTX, blend of PPE with polyamide (PA) starts a new family of high performance GEC blends, Noryl Plus. | Chem. Weeks, Nov. 27, 1985, p. 108. |
| 28. | 1983 | ATOCHEM introduces two blends based on its proprietary polyetherblockamide, PEBA: Orgater = PBT/EVA/PEBA and Rilsan PA/PEBA for powder coating. | J.-L. Arraou, Caoutch. Plast., Juin-Juil., 1986, p. 79. |
| 29. | 1984 | Mobay Chem. Corp. developed polyurethane elastomer/PC blend, Texin, for use in automobile industry. | J. Commerce, June 13, 1985, p. 2113. |

TABLE 1.2 continued

| No. | Year | Event | Reference |
|-----|------|-------|-----------|
| 30. | 1984 | Borg Warner developed ABS/PA blend, Elemid, for automobile body panel. | Plast. Focus, Mars 11, 1985, p. 3. |
| 31. | 1984 | Mobay developed Macroblend, PC/PBT/Elastomer, for automobile use. Some grades of Macroblend use PET. | Plas. Buss. News, April 23, 1984, p. 6 |
| 32. | 1985 | Badische Corp. introduced Terblend-S, blend of PC with poly(acrylate-co-styrene-co-acrylonitrile) (ASA). | Plast. World, Dec. 1985, p. 66. |
| 33. | 1986 | New blends for car interior, Pulse, PC/ABS type, developed by Dow Chem. Co. | Plast. Technolog., April 1986, p. 103. |

than that expected from additivity of specific volumes. As a result, several mechanical properties of these blends (such as modulus or yield stress) showed a significant synergistic behavior (*McCarthy* and *Rogers,* 1987). The densification of the PPE/PS blends could also be taken as an indication of specific interactions which in turn increased blend viscosity above the log-normal additivity rule. In 1964 Richardson Co. commercialized PPS blended with "crystal" PS. In 1965 General Electric Co. introduced a family of toughened PPE/PS under the trade name Noryl. Twenty years later the annual sales value of these blends exceeded one billion dollars. After expiry of the original patent several major polymer producers (e.g. BASF, Hüls, Borg-Warner, Asahi, Engineering Plastics Ltd., Mitsubishi) commenced sales of their own blends based on polyphenyleneether or its copolymers with PS and/or PS-copolymers. It must be stressed that the miscibility of PPE with PS opened a whole spectrum of possible modification of properties. It is sufficient for a copolymer to have a styrenic part in order to impart the desired properties to the mixture (e.g. toughening, flame resistance, solvent resistance). However, in spite of PPE/PS miscibility, no single phase blend is on the market.

Blends of ABS have been already mentioned. However due to the broad range of properties and commercial importance the blends of ABS with polyvinylchloride (PVC), marketed since 1969 by Borg Warner under the name of Cycovin, and those with polycarbonate (PC), sold under the name of Cycoloy deserve special mention.

In 1975 DuPont de Nemours introduced new supertough polyamide (PA), Zytel-ST. The importance of this event extends beyond PA. The observation that addition of a small amount of finely dispersed polyolefin or rubber dramatically changes the fracture behavior of PA led to improvement of impact properties not only this but also other engineering resins: polycarbonate, polyesters, polyoxymethylene, etc.

While in the past blending relied mostly on mechanical incorporation of the ingredients (e.g. about ten-fold improvement of notched Izod strength was achieved by addition of 5 wt% of immiscible high density polyethylene to polycarbonate; US Pat. No. 4,335,032) newer technology introduces another degree of sophistication – reactive blending. As shown in Appendix II several patents on PA toughening already require addition of a reactive ingredient: ionomers, adducts of maleic or fumaric acids (or their anhydrides), succinic copolymers etc. During the last few years the importance of combined effects of chemistry, physics and engineering on performance of PAB's was particularly noticeable. Reactive blending of engineering polymers with maleated block copolymer provide a direct method of impact modification (*Gelles,* 1987).

In 1979 the toughened blends of polycarbonate (PC), with thermoplastic polyesters, TPEs, were introduced by GEC-Europe under the name of Xenoy. Preparation of these blends involved a careful control of the exchange reaction between the ingredients. Control of miscibility can also be achieved by judicious selection of a reactive impact modifier (see Fig. 1.4). Noryl-GTX is a blend of PPE with PA, introduced by General Electric Co. in 1983. By contrast with all other Noryls where PS acted as a PPE-soluble binder between PPE and an immiscible ingredient, here both PPE and PA (usually polyamide-6,6) are antagonistically immiscible. The schematic of the alloy preparation is similar to that shown in Fig. 1.4. The compositions claimed usually cover 30 to 70% of each of the main ingredients with additionally up to 4 parts of such modifier as: polycarboxylic acid, trimellitic anhydride acid chloride, quinone, oxidized polyolefin wax, etc. In most cases PA forms a matrix with spherical inclusions of PPE acting as compatibilized low density filler.

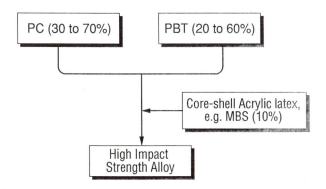

Fig. 1.4 Schematic of preparation of polycarbonate/polybutyleneterephthalate blend.

### 1.1.3   Patentability

Annually about 4,500 PAB patents are published world-wide. The selected recent USA and European patents on engineering polymer alloys and blends are listed in six parts of Appendix II, the first five concerning the five principal engineering polymers and the sixth that of the high performance speciality resins. The order of presentation was based on the world consumption of EP given in Table 1.3.

TABLE 1.3  World Demand for Engineering Resins* (kt)

| No. | Polymer | Code | Demand 1985 | Demand 1995 | % Change |
|-----|---------|------|------|------|----------|
| 1. | Polyamides | PA | 500 | 900 | 80 |
| 2. | Polycarbonate | PC | 300 | 810 | 170 |
| 3. | Polyoxymethylene | POM | 220 | 360 | 64 |
| 4. | Polyphenyleneether | PPE | 180 | 470 | 161 |
| 5. | Thermoplastic polyesters | TPE | 133 | 400 | 200 |
| 6. | Specialty resins | Spec. | 19 | 118 | 520 |

* after: Zimmer Market Research, 1987

The first ten companies who received the largest patent protection are:

| No. | Company | Number of PAB Patents Relative to DuPonts' |
|---|---|---|
| 1 | DuPont | 100% |
| 2 | Asahi | 88 |
| 3 | BASF | 82 |
| 4 | Bayer | 66 |
| 5 | Teijin | 65 |
| 6 | General Electric Co. | 65 |
| 7 | Monsanto | 51 |
| 8 | ICI | 44 |
| 9 | Dow Chem. | 44 |
| 10 | Union Carbide | 40 |

During the years 1981-4 the number of patents issued for polybutyleneterephthalate (PBT), blends was 597, those for polyethyleneterephthalate (PET), 468, whereas the blends with polyamide-6,6, PA-6,6, were patented 431, PC 390, PPE 360 and POM 242 times. Comparing these numbers with the world demand data in Appendix I one notes a disproportionate patenting activity for TPE's, auguring a wider use of these blends in e.g. the automobile industry.

Reading the patents listed in Appendix II one may attempt to identify the reasons for blending and the means by which these goals were achieved. In Table 1.4 the most sought after properties for engineering PAB are listed. It is apparent that toughening and processability are of major concern (51% total). The second group of importance (27%) includes: the strength, modulus and heat deflection temperature. The third group (14%) concerns flammability, solvent resistance as well as thermal and dimensional stability. Other properties, such as: elongation, gloss, etc. are seldom mentioned (8%).

TABLE 1.4  Principal Properties Claimed in PAB Patents

| No. | Property | Frequency % |
|---|---|---|
| 1. | High impact strength | 38 |
| 2. | Processability (including weld line) | 18 |
| 3. | Tensile strength | 11 |
| 4. | Rigidity/modulus | 8 |
| 5. | Heat deflection temperature | 8 |
| 6. | Flammability | 4 |
| 7. | Solvent resistance | 4 |
| 8. | Thermal stability | 3 |
| 9. | Dimensional stability | 3 |
| 10. | Elongation | 2 |
| 11. | Gloss | 2 |
| 12. | Others | 4 |

The patent literature also provides information on means for achieving these goals. As the data in Table 1.5 indicate, in most cases the blending effect is non-specific, e.g. addition of an elastomer to any engineering resin will improve its impact strength, (see Fig. 1.5), or addition of a high modulus material to the lower modulus matrix will increase rigidity, etc.

TABLE 1.5  How to Modify Properties by Blending

| No. | Property | Matrix Resin | Modifying Polymer |
|---|---|---|---|
| 1. | Impact strength | PVC, PP, PE, PC, PA, PPE, TPE | ABS, ASA, SBS, EPR, EPDM, PBR, SAN, SMA, MBA, Poly-olefin, HIPS |
| 2. | HDT, stiffness | PC, PA<br>ABS, SAN | TPEs, PEI, PPE<br>PC, PSO |
| 3. | Flame retardancy | ABS, Acrylics<br>PA, PC | PVC, CPE<br>Aromatic-PA, PSO, copolysil-oxanes or phosphazanes |
| 4. | Chemical/solvent resistance | PC, PA, PPE | TPEs, copolysiloxanes polyphos-phates |
| 5. | Barrier properties | Polyolefins | PA, EVOH, $PVCl_2$ |
| 6. | Processability | PPE<br>HT thermoplastics<br>PET, PA, PC<br>PVC<br>PSO<br>PO | Styrenics<br>LCP, TPU<br>PE, PBR, MBS, EVOH<br>CPE, Acrylics<br>PA<br>PTFE, SI |

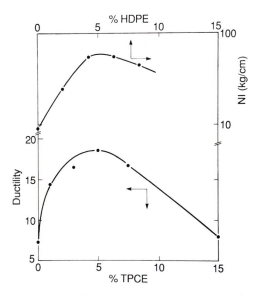

Fig. 1.5 Concentration dependence of (top) notched Izod impact strength at room temperature of polycarbonate/high density polyethylene blend (Rosenquist, 1982) and (bottom) ductility of acrylonit-rile-butadiene-styrene copolymer (ABS) with thermoplastic copolyether ester elastomer (*Dufour* and *Jones*, 1985).

On the other hand there are numerous specific responses accounting for the fact that e.g. the size of dispersed elastomer phase can generate significant variation of impact perform-ance. It was also observed that multicore latex elastomers (*Schlund* and *Lambla*, 1985) provide additional improvement of performance. Optimization of performance must involve a multivariable analysis where the molecular parameters of the ingredients, the interphase and morphology interact. This obviously can not be gleaned from the data in Table 1.5. The Table should only be considered a general guide to blending. The fact that two polymers with desired properties are immiscible should not be a deterrent. The modern compatibilization and reactive processing methods can overcome this problem.

In some cases the blend properties are truly exceptional beyond expectation. One of these rare cases is presented in Fig. 1.6 where the room temperature notched Izod impact strength, NIRT, is plotted as a function of composition for PBT/PC/copolymer (SAN-EPDM) system (*Wefer*, 1985). Addition to PBT of either PC or a copolymer of styrene-acrylonitrile grafted on ethylene-propylene-diene (EPDM) resulted only in a small improvement of NIRT. However, blending PBT with a preblend of 80% PC and 20% copolymer improved the impact properties by 1.5 decades. Since each ingredient of the pre-blend showed only a small effect this large improvement of impact strength must be due to three pairwise interaction coefficients: PC-PBT, PBT-SAN and SAN-PC. A "window of miscibility" (see Part 2.3.6) may be responsible for the effect.

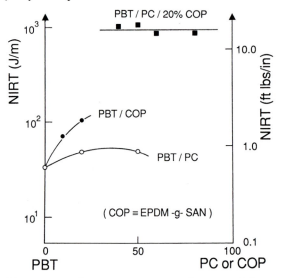

Fig. 1.6 Notched Izod impact strength at room temperature for two and three component blends of polybuteneterephthalate (PBT) with polycarbonate (PC) and/or styrene-acrylonitrile grafted on ethylene-propylene-ethylidene-norbornene copolymer (*Wefer*, 1985).

To illustrate the effects of blending the comparative properties of few blends and those of neat resins are listed in Table 1.6.

TABLE 1.6 Selected Properties of Unfilled Engineering Resins and Blends

| No. | Resin or Blend | Commercial Name | Elong. % | Flex. Mod. (GPa) | Tens. Str. (MPa) | Notched Impact Str. (J/m) 23°C | HDT (1.82MPa, °C) |
|-----|----------------|-----------------|----------|------------------|------------------|-------------------------------|-------------------|
| 1.0 | PC | Lexan | 90 | 2.20 | 56 | 640 | 132 |
| 1.1 | PC/ABS | Bayblend | 50 | 2.20 | 45 | 640 | 105 |
| 1.2 | PC/ABS | Pulse | 100 | 2.59 | 53 | 530 | 96 |
| 1.3 | PC/SMA | Arloy | 80 | 2.20 | 45 | 640 | 121 |
| 1.4 | PC/PET | Macroblend | 165 | 2.07 | 52 | 970 | 88 |
| 1.5 | PC/PBT | Xenoy | 130 | 2.07 | 56 | 854 | 121 |
| 1.6 | PC/SEBS | Pat.4,122,131 | – | – | 61 | 910 | 139 |

| No. | Resin or Blend | Commercial Name | Elong. % | Flex. Mod. (GPa) | Tens. Str. (MPa) | Notched Impact Str. (J/m) 23°C | HDT (1.82MPa, °C) |
|---|---|---|---|---|---|---|---|
| 2.0 | PA-6,6 | Zytel | 60 | 2.83 | 83 | 53 | 90 |
| 2.1 | PA/PO | Zytel-ST | 60 | 1.72 | 52 | 907 | 71 |
| 2.2 | PA/PPS | Pat.4,292,416 | 90 | 2.18 | 65 | 186 | 88 |
| 2.3 | PA/CPA | Pat.4,383,084 | 77 | 3.07 | 77 | 171 | 119 |
| 2.4 | PA/Ionomer | Pat.4,404,325 | 252 | 1.80 | 45 | 955 | – |
| 2.5 | PA-6,6/PPO/ | Noryl-GTX | 60 | 2.14 | 60 | 215 | 143 |
|  | HIPS | " | 8 | 7.66 | 159 | 105 | 235 |
| 2.6 | PA-6,6/Elast. | Bexloy | 120 | 2.07 | 62 | 1030 | 115 |
| 2.7 | PA-6/ABS | Elemid | – | 2.07 | 48 | 998 | 200 |
| 3.0 | PSF | Udel | 60 | 2.69 | 70 | 69 | 174 |
| 3.1 | PSF/PC | Pat.4,489,181 | 14 | 2.46 | 62 | 390 | 180 |
| 3.2 | PSF/PBT with glass fiber | Mindel | 2.9 | 2.41 | 115 | 88 | 166 |
| 4.0 | POM | Delrin | 40 | 2.83 | 48 | 75 | 136 |
| 4.1 | POM Copolymer | Celcon | 75 | 2.59 | 43 | 75 | 110 |
| 4.2 | POM/Elastomer | Duraloy | 220 | 1.04 | 37 | <220 | 60 |
| 4.3 | POM/Elastomer | Delrin | 75 | 2.62 | 69 | 123 | 136 |

## 1.2    The Reasons For and Methods of Blending

There is no doubt that the main reason for blending, compounding and reinforcing is economy. If a material can be generated at a lower cost with properties meeting specification the manufacturer must use it to remain competitive. In general the following economy-related reasons can be listed:

1. Extending engineering resin performance by diluting it with a low cost polymer.
2. Developing materials with a full set of desired properties.
3. Forming a high performance blend from synergistically interacting polymers.
4. Adjusting the composition of the blend to customer specifications.
5. Recycling industrial and/or municipal plastics scrap.

About 65% of polymer alloys and blends are produced by the resin manufacturers, about 25% by compounding companies and the remaining by the transformers. In Table 1.7 a list of major engineering polymer blend producers in the USA is given.

### 1.2.1    How to Select Blend Components

While extension of EP performance constitutes the largest part of PAB production volume, the main and most difficult task is development of materials with a full set of desired properties. This has been achieved by selecting blend components in such a way that the principal advantages of the first polymer will compensate for deficiencies of the second and vice versa. For example, in Table 1.8 the disadvantages of PPE (processability and impact strength) are compensated by advantageous properties of either PA or HIPS. Due to PPE/PS miscibility the original Noryls were formulated around the PPE/HIPS pair. Only the more recent reactive methods of compatibilization allowed the second generation Noryl GTX (based on PA/PPE pair) to be developed.

TABLE 1.7  Major Suppliers of Engineering-Resin Blends

| Supplier | Basic Position | Blend |
| --- | --- | --- |
| Allied | Polyamide | Polyamide/elastomer |
| ARCO | SMA | Polycarbonate/SMA |
| Amoco Chem. | Polysulfone | ABS/polysulfone, polysulfone/PET |
| | Polyarylate | Polyester/polyacrylate |
| Borg-Warner | ABS | ABS/polycarbonate |
| | | Polyphenyl ether/polystyrene |
| Celanese | Acetal | Acetal/elastomer |
| | Polyamide | Polyamide/elastomer |
| | PBT | PBT/PET, PBT/elastomer |
| Dow Chem. Co. | ABS | Polycarbonate/ABS, TPU/ABS |
| | Polycarbonate | |
| Du Pont | Acetal | Acetal/elastomer |
| | Polyamide | Polyamide/elastomer, |
| | | Polyamide/polyethylene |
| | PET | PET/elastomer |
| Emser | Polyamide | Polyamide/elastomer |
| GAF | PBT | PBT/PET, PBT/elastomer |
| General Electric | PBT | PBT/PET, PBT/elastomer |
| | Polycarbonate | Polycarbonate/polyethylene |
| | | Polycarbonate/PBT |
| | Polyphenyleneether | Polyphenyleneether/polystyrene |
| | Copolyester elastomers | Polycarbonate/copolyester elastomers |
| | Polyetherimide | Polyetherimide/Thermoplastics |
| LNP | – | Polyamide/elastomer |
| Mobay | Polycarbonate | Polycarbonate/ABS, polycarbonate/ polyethylene, polycarbonate/PET |
| Nycoa | Polyamide | Polyamide/elastomer |
| Thermofil | – | Polycarbonate/PET |
| Wilson-Fiberfil | – | Polyamide/elastomer |

Similarly, PC weaknesses are the stress cracking and chemical sensitivity. Stress cracking can be treated as a part of impact properties; addition of ABS or ASA provides a simple solution. On the other hand, to enhance the solvent resistance, the property particularly important in automobile applications, a semi-crystalline polymer should be added. From Table 1.8 it is apparent that TPEs could provide that property, but on the other hand TPEs also lack the impact strength and warp resistance. In consequence, the ideal blend for automobile application based on PC and TPEs blend should also be impact modified with e.g. acrylic latex copolymer (see Fig. 1.3).

The semicrystalline polyoxymethylene has excellent mechanical properties but poor impact strength. Due to the simplicity of its monomeric structure the non-reactive blending has been limited to a few basic elastomeric impact modifiers; e.g. polybutadiene or poly- urethane. However, with the advances in reactive processing the means are being found for chemically bonding the impact modifier e.g. via unsaturated carboxylic acid groups as in maleated linear low density polyethylene. More POM blends should soon become available.

As exemplified by PC/TPE/latex system modern blends increasingly have to play multi- ple roles; mechanical properties, chemical/solvent resistance, dimensional stability, painta- bility, weatherability and of course economy are simultaneously required. Such a complex balance of properties is usually achieved by multicomponent blending with frequent unav- oidable compromises.

TABLE 1.8  Advantages and Disadvantages of Some Engineering Polymers and Modifiers

| No. | Polymer | Code | Principal Advantages | Principal Disadvantages |
|-----|---------|------|---------------------|------------------------|
| 1. | Polyamide | PA | processability, impact strength, crystallinity | water absorption, HDT |
| 2. | Polycarbonate | PC | low-temperature toughness, HDT | stress-crack sensitivity, solvent and chemical resistance |
| 3. | Polyoxymethylene | POM | tensile strength, modulus | stress-crack sensitivity, impact strength |
| 4. | Polyphenylene ether | PPE | HDT, rigidity, flame retardancy | processability, impact strength |
| 5. | Thermoplastic polyesters | PET, PBT | chemical and solvent resistance | shrinkage, low temperature toughness, processability |
| 6. | High impact polystyrene | HIPS | processability, impact strength | HDT |
| 7. | Acrylonitrile-butadiene-styrene copolymer | ABS (or ASA) | impact strength, processability, weatherability | HDT |

## 1.2.2  Economy of Blending

The principal cost of PAB depends on the price of the main polymeric components and the interface modifier, as well as compounding costs:

$$C = w_1C_1 + w_2C_2 + w_3C_3 + K \tag{1.1}$$

where $w_i$ and $C_i$ are weight fraction and cost in dollars per kilogram of ingredient i, and K is the compounding cost per kilogram of blend. Usually $w_3 \simeq 0.01$ to $0.04$ and $C_3$, depending on the type, can be either comparable to $C_1$ and $C_2$ or (for a special tapered block copolymers) about ten-fold higher. The value of K depends on the scale of operation; $K \simeq \$0.6$ for 5 tons/hr but $K \simeq 0.08$ for a larger scale production (*Utracki*, 1982).

For commodity resins the economic justification for blending may be as small as a fraction of one cent per kilogram (*Hamielec*, 1986). For engineering materials the calculation of economy are more complex taking into account not only price of the replaced material but also the difference in fabrication cost, maintenance, longevity, recyclability, etc. For example, the weight reduction, ease of fabrication as well as lack of corrosion make a replacement of metal fenders by PAB attractive in spite of higher cost of Xenoy than steel. Evaluating the economy of PAB one must also take into account difference in cost of testing both the raw material and the finished parts.

Due to the multiphase nature of PAB most standard tests developed for homopolymers are invalid for polymer blends. As an example (see Part 3), the melt index or even the steady state capillary flow tests are unsuitable for most PAB. This situation leads to a profusion of conflicting "company tests" varying from one supplier to another. The user in turn is forced to establish his or her own test procedures, further adding to the confusion and total material cost. Since establishment of a viable method of evaluation provides a commercial organization with a competitive edge there is unfortunate reluctance by blend manufacturers to cooperate toward international standards.

## 1.2.3    The Methods of Blending

Preparation of polymer blends can be accomplished by:
 (i) mechanical mixing,
 (ii) dissolution in co-solvent then film casting, freeze or spray drying
(iii) latex blending (e.g. SAN + AB → ABS),
(iv) fine powders mixing,
 (v) use of monomer(s) as solvent for another blend component then polymerization as in
        IPN's or HIPS, manufacture,
(vi) diverse other methods of IPN technology.

For economic reasons mechanical blending predominates. It is important that the size of the dispersed phase is optimized considering the final performance of the blend. In order to avoid streaking and delamination peeling during injection molding the size of the dispersed phase is normally reduced to a sub-micron. The optimization of HIPS impact strength requires d = 1 to 3 μm of the elastomeric phase; smaller particles are required for ABS, PVC and tough matrix resins. On the other hand for generating lamellar or fibrillar structures relatively large drops are needed.

Before discussing methods of compounding, the compatibilization process should be considered. The role of compatibilizer is similar to that of an emulsifier in classical emulsion technology; compatibilizer should migrate to the interface causing reduction of dispersed phase dimensions and stabilization of PAB morphology. The details of compatibilization will be discussed in Part 2.7.

The most common compatibilizers are block or graft copolymers and polymeric co-solvents. These are either synthesized, carefully optimizing their structure, then added to the polymer mixture (*Fayt et al.*, 1986; *Teyssié et al.*, 1988), or they can be generated during compounding by means of controlled reactive processing. The first method involves sophisticated chemistry and an extensive research program. As a result the price of the interfacial agent is high but only a small quantity, 1 to 2%, is required. The second method, the reactive compatibilization, is a chemical engineering process requiring closed loop control. For large continuous compounding line it is cost effective. By contrast with the first method the degree of optimization is not as high and usually larger quantities of compatibilizer are required. There are instances when a low molecular weight immiscible "compatibilizer" acts as an adhesive for the pair of mutually immiscible polymers.

In some cases, as for example in polycarbonate/polybutyleneterephthalate (PC/PBT) systems, the ester exchange seems to be the easiest compatibilization method. Unfortunately, since crystallinity of PBT is of utmost importance, the method is neither easy to control nor of apparent advantage.

Reactive processing can also be used as a method of functionalization of one polymer, which upon addition of the other forms an alloy. Alternatively a preblend of polymer A with functionalized interphase polymer is prepared then polymer B is added. This method can be used to compatibilize PPE with numerous polymers by preblending PPE with oxazoline modified polystyrene. Compatibilization via incorporation of hydrogen bonding or ionic groups have been long known by the industry.

Finally, it is worth mentioning a somewhat reversed approach to blending; instead of adding a compatibilizer in order to reduce droplet size and stabilize the morphology, the method requires an efficient, intensive mechanical dispersion of immiscible blend components, then interlocking them into a stable, desired morphology. The stabilization can be achieved either by chemical (e.g. crosslinking by electron beam irradiation) or physical means (e.g. by controlled crystallization).

Recyclability should be of major concern while designing new blends. As the automobile industry moves closer to all-plastics car it is inconceivable that the volume of polymer used in millions of vehicles per year can be buried or turned into smoke. In 1984 only 1% of the total 133 million tons of plastics waste was recycled (*Franklin Associates Ltd.,* 1988). At the moment recycling is limited to but a few polymers: high density polyethylene, polyethylene terephthalate, PET, and in some cases industrial or municipal plastics waste.

The bright sign on the horizon is a serious effort on the part of General Electric's marketing division toward integrated flow of engineering materials. It is proposed that a polymer will be reused sequentially in fewer and fewer critical applications. General Electric also demonstrated that such engineering materials as PPE, PC or PBT from automobiles can successfully be recycled after 10 years of weathering.

The requirements for an ideal PAB compounder/mixer are simple: (i) uniformity of shear and elongational stress field, (ii) flexible control of uniform temperature, pressure and residence time, (iii) capability for homogenization of liquids with large differences in rheological properties, (iv) efficient homogenization before onset of degradation, and (v) flexibility for change of mixing parameters in a controllable manner. Unfortunately, as the requirements are simple the designing of a mixer to fulfill them is difficult. Most of the patented work on PAB was done using either an internal mixer or a single screw extruder. In a standard configuration the single screw extruder is a poor mixer, inadequate for PAB preparation. However, there are several mixing screw designs, barrel groves and add-on mixing devices such as motionless or RAPRA's CTM mixers (see Fig. 1.7) which facilitate blend preparation, particularly in systems containing a large quantity of a compatibilizer. The run-to-run reproducibility of PAB prepared in single screw extruders usually is poor. Due to "dead spaces" the single screw extruders are inherently unsuitable for reactive blending.

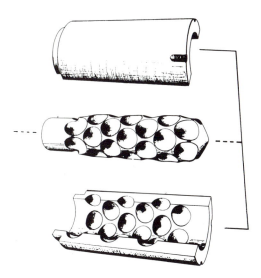

Fig. 1.7 RAPRA's Cavity Transfer Mixer, CTM (*Hindmarch* and *Gale,* 1982).

More expensive but easier to control is the twin screw extruder. Due to modular design, with many types of elements fulfilling different functions, the twin screw extruder can be optimized for specific polymeric system. The ratio of dispersive to distributive mixing can be adjusted and the width of the residence time can be controlled. As a result, the blend quality and run-to-run reproducibility are satisfactory.

TABLE 1.9  PAB Compounders

| No. | Machine | Function |
|-----|---------|----------|
| *I. Continuous Mixers* | | |
| I.1 | Twin-screw extruder | primary PAB compounder |
| I.2 | Twin-shaft intensive mixers | primary PAB compounder |
| I.3 | Disk extruder | adaptable for PAB compounding |
| I.4 | Single screw extruder | second choice |
| I.5 | Single shaft mixer | second choice |
| I.6 | Motionless mixer | add-on |
| I.7 | RAPRA CTM-mixer | add-on |
| I.8 | Dynamic melt mixer | add-on |
| *II. Batch Mixers* | | |
| II.1 | Roll mills | laboratory or short runs |
| II.2 | Internal sigma-blade mixers | laboratory or short runs |
| II.3 | Kinetic energy mixers | speciality or short runs |
| *III. Special Machines* | | |
| III.1 | Plastificator Patfoort | blending or recycling |
| III.2 | Reverser | recycling |
| III.3 | Multi-stage systems | large volume, primary |

In Table 1.9 a list of PAB compounders is given. In the column "Function" the first and secondary choices are indicated, some add-on mixing devices and batch as well as special compounders are listed. The advantages and disadvantages of typical machines are listed in Table 1.10.

TABLE 1.10  Advantages and Disadvantages of Some PAB Mixers

| No. | Machine | Advantages | Disadvantages |
|-----|---------|-----------|---------------|
| I.1 | Twin-screw extruder | Uniform high shear stress flow, short residence time, self-cleaning, flexibility and ease of change | Capital cost |
| I.4 | Single-screw extruder | Cost, availability, flexibility for modification of screws and add-ons | Poor control, low rate of shearing, long residence time, dead-spaces |
| II.2 | Internal mixer | Uniformity of stress history, control | Capital and operational cost, long cycle, batch to batch variation |
| III.3 | Multi-stages system | Flexibility, control, uniformity | Capital cost (for large diameter machine the uniformity of temperature can be poor) |

There are several devices particularly well suited for preparation of PAB. One of these is the Maxwell normal stress extruder (*Maxwell* and *Scalora*, 1959). Its operation is schematically shown in Fig. 1.8. As shown in Fig. 1.9 the principle of Maxwell extruder is an integral part of the Patfoort Plastificator (*Patfoort*, 1969, 1981). In the latter device a short screw, with a length-to-diameter ratio of five, is grooved only in the anterior part. The tree-start grooves are designed for transport of solids. The material is melted by shearing it between the barrel and the smooth cylindrical part of the screw. Finally, the flat-end part of the screw act as a pump forcing the molten, blended material out by the Maxwell normal stress extruder. The distribution of residence times is fairly narrow, with an average value of 10 to 20 sec. Furthermore, since the axial position of the screw can be adjusted by a large thrust bearing, the gap in the Maxwell extruder can be controlled allowing for modification of the degree of dispersion in the blend. The plastificator seems to be particularly suitable for preparing co-continuous mixtures with a high volume fraction of the disperse phase $0.35 < \phi < 0.65$. Currently the main use of the machine is for recycling industrial and municipal plastics waste.

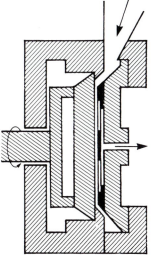

Fig. 1.8 Schematics of Maxwell normal stress extruder (*Maxwell* and *Scalora, 1959*).

The quality of the compounded blend shows up in processing and performance stages. Layering and poor weld lines in injection molding, skin-core extrudate structure (resulting in low notched Izod impact strength) all indicate poor quality of the compound. One must realize that preparation of PAB generates new, different problems than those encountered in standard polymer compounding operations. For example, mixing batches to match specifications is well accepted in the plastics industry. At present a large number of alloys are prepared by reactive processing. However attempting to blend two batches of the same PAB with different degree of co-reaction may lead to disaster; a small variation in the extend of reaction makes them behave as two immiscible polymers leading to poor impact strength, expecially at the weld lines. The mixed PAB lot may pass standard tests and still yield an unacceptable product.

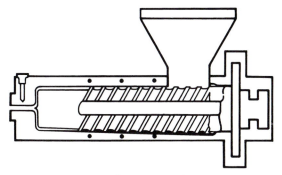

Fig. 1.9 Patfoort Plastificator/mixer-extruder (*Patfoort, 1969*).

## 1.3    Fundamental Principles for Development of Polymer Alloys and Blends

PAB's are in a marvelous, intricate world of their own. The more one learns about them, the more their scope and hidden potentials become apparent. In discussing the processing aspect little was said about the basic principles of polymer blending: the equilibrium and non-equilibrium thermodynamics, microrheology, rheology, morphology, part formation and solidification.

Part 2 in this volume deals with the thermodynamics of phase separation, interface, interactions, etc. while Part 3 first summarizes the basic principles of experimental rheology, then discusses the flow of model fluids and finally that of PAB. In Part 3 there is an emphasis on microrheology as its principles to a large extent are responsible for structure development in PAB melt. Flow induced morphology as well as viscoelasticity (in solid and molten state) are also presented. A schematic representation of interrelations between these themes is shown in Fig. 1.10.

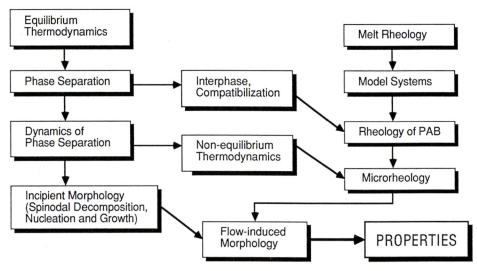

Fig. 1.10 Interrelations between different branches of science important in development of polymer alloys and blends.

Parts 2 and 3 provide a fundamental basis for understanding PAB processing as well as the resulting morphology and properties. An effort was made to isolate the effects of one variable at a time on blending, dispersing or flow behavior. For example, in discussing the flow properties, the effects of large and small (dynamic) shear strains are presented separately in an attempt to contrast the PAB behavior under these conditions and draw general conclusions.

Unfortunately in any commercial process, compounding or forming, the material undergoes deformation under superimposed diverse types of stress and strain fields. In different processing equipment the proportions of these fields vary. By interactive modeling and flow analysis one can identify the principal controlling variable. The basic knowledge of PAB behavior under well described flow condition is necessary as an input into such analysis of the process. To complete the picture the information provided in this volume should be supplemented with that dealing specifically with compounding, forming, morphology and finished part properties and behavior.

### 1.3.1   Miscibility and Phase Equilibria

Starting with the classical Huggins-Flory relation for polymer solutions, it follows that for PB the configurational entropy is vanishingly small and the free energy of mixing can be expressed as:

$$\Delta G_m/RTV \simeq \chi'_{12}\phi_1\phi_2 \tag{1.2}$$

where R, T, V, $\phi_i$ are respectively: the gas constant, temperature, (molar) volume of the system and the volume fraction of component i = 1,2. The polymer-polymer interaction parameter, $\chi'_{12}$, contains both the enthalpic and entropic parts. According to *Koningsveld* et al., (1980) in the simplest form it can be expressed as:

$$\chi'_{12} = (a_0 + a_1/T + a_2T)(b_0 + b_1\phi_2 + b_2\phi_2^2) \tag{1.3}$$

In short, $\chi'_{12}$ is a function of both T and $\phi$ as reported in Fig. 2.10 (p. 51). Determination of $\chi'_{12}$ in the whole range of composition is a tedious and seldom carried out experiment.

Eq (1.2) states that for miscibility of PAB $\chi'_{12} < 0$ is required. This condition can be achieved either by the presence of specific interations between the polymer pair (see Table 1.11) or strong repulsive forces between segments in one polymer, $\chi'_{AB} > 0$, larger than those between its segments A and B and the second polymer C (see Part 2.3.6).

TABLE 1.11  Example of Miscible Polymer Pairs

| No. | Polymer 1 | No. | Polymer 2 |
|---|---|---|---|
| I | Polystyrene, PS<br><br>$-CH_2-CH-$ (with phenyl ring) | 1. | Polyvinylmethylether, PVME<br><br>$-CH_2-CH-$<br>      $\vert$<br>      $O-CH_3$ |
|  |  | 2. | Poly(2,6 di-alkyl phenylene ethers), PPE<br><br>$R_i = -CH_3, -C_2H_5, -C_3H_7$<br><br>(phenylene ring with $R_1$, $-O-$, $R_2$) |
| II | Polyvinylchloride, PVC<br><br>$-CH_2-CH-$<br>        $\vert$<br>        $Cl$ | 1. | Polyester<br><br>$-O-\overset{\displaystyle}{\underset{\displaystyle O}{C}}-(CH_2)_n-$ |
|  |  | 2. | Polybutyleneterephthalate, PBT<br><br>$-O-\overset{O}{C}-$ (benzene ring) $-\overset{O}{C}-O-(CH_2)_4-$ |

| No. | Polymer 1 | No. | Polymer 2 |
|---|---|---|---|
| III | Polyethyleneoxide, PEO<br><br>$—CH_2—CH_2—O—$ | 1. | Polyacrylic acid, PAA<br><br>$—CH_2—CH—$<br>$\mid$<br>$C{=}O$<br>$\mid$<br>$OH$ |
| | | 2. | Polymethacrylic acid, PMA<br><br>$CH_3$<br>$\mid$<br>$—CH_2—C—$<br>$\mid$<br>$HO—C{=}O$ |
| IV | Poly(sodium styrene sulfonate)<br><br>$—CH_2—CH—$<br><br>(phenyl ring)<br><br>$\dot{S}O_3\,Na^+$ | 1. | Poly(vinylbenzyltrimethyl amonium chloride)<br><br>$—CH_2—CH—$<br><br>(phenyl ring)<br><br>$N(CH_3)_3^+Cl^-$ |
| V | Polybutylene-1, PB<br><br>$—CH_2—CH—$<br>$\mid$<br>$CH_2—CH_3$ | 1. | Polypropylene, PP<br><br>$—CH_2—CH—$<br>$\mid$<br>$CH_3$ |
| VI | Phenoxy<br><br>$CH_3$ ... $OH$<br>(bisphenol A structure) $—CH_2—CH$<br>$CH_3$ ... $CH_2$<br>$O—$ | 1.<br>2. | PVME<br>PEO |
| VII | PVC | 1.<br><br>2. | Poly(butadiene-co-acrylonitrile) with 30 to 40% acrylonitrile content.<br>Poly(ethylene-co-vinyl acetate) with 60 to 75% vinyl acetate content. |

The main reason for wanting to know the extent of polymer-polymer miscibility is not necessarily to produce miscible commercial blends, but rather to devise methods for blend modification, to enhance such properties as impact, modulus, HDT, etc. The miscibility provides a simpler means of accomplishing this than other types of compatibilization methods.

In systems where the phase separation occurs within an accessible range of variables, e.g. temperature, pressure, concentration of co-solvent, processing with a particular attention to miscibility may lead to a highly successful product. "Deep quenching" (see Part 2.4.2) can result in a three-dimensional co-continuous network structure even at a concentration of minor phase as low as $\phi = 0.1$ to $0.15$. The three-dimensionality allows the blend to simultaneously show the best performance of each component nearly unaffected by the presence of the other polymer, e.g. blends with high initial modulus and high yield strength may at the same time show large values of the maximum strain at break (*Inoue* et al., 1984, 1985, 1987).

An important part of the thermodynamics of PAB's deals with properties of the interphase. In a simple approach, addition of the third ingredient is similarly treated as that of surfactant to oil/water mixture. Since the equilibrium thermodynamics considers neither dynamics of dispersion nor size of the phases, the way one may estimate the compatibilizer effect is to assume its crossectional area at the interphase and then compute the total interface area. It is not surprising that for polymeric compatibilizers the method rarely works. There are several reason for this: polydispersity of all three ingredients affects the miscibility of the compatibilizer, its micellization is frequently observed inside one of the phases, and the rate of equilibration is very slow in comparison to that of the low molecular weight surfactant. The theory which provides good description of compatibilization using diblock copolymers is that developed by Noolandi and his collaborators (Part 2.3.7); it predicts the degree of dispersion, thickness of the interphase as well as the interfacial tension coefficient. Examples of compatibilized systems are listed in Table 2.16 (p. 125).

The thermodynamics of polymer blends leads one to expect two types of morphology. The first originates in the dynamics of phase separation and exists for a short time before phase ripening takes over (see Part 2.4). The second type of morphology is controlled by the equilibrium thermodynamics where the size and shape of the phase is determined by minimization of the total free energy of the system, including that of the interface.

## 1.3.2   Flow and Flow-Induced Morphology

The Part 3 starts with a brief summary of the experimental rheology then reviews the flow behavior of the PAB model systems. It is of utmost importance to map-out the known behavior of diverse liquid systems, to recognize the established principles behind corellations in classical multiphase rheology, before moving on to the unknown territory of PAB's. It is useful to recapitulate what has been learned over the years from those systems that may be considered PAB models.

Excellent models of the miscible blends are solvent mixtures or blends of polymeric fractions (homologous polymer blends). For immiscible blends with low viscosity of the dispersed phase the emulsions or foams, for those with high viscosity the suspensions can be used as model. Furthermore, the flow of compatibilized blends is well simulated by that of block copolymers.

In the single phase binary mixtures, the thermodynamics plays an important role. Both, the free volume additivity in non-interacting system, and the energetic interaction parameters in others similarly affect the viscosity–composition, $\eta$–$\phi$, dependence generating slightly higher viscosities than those predicted by the simple log-additivity rule (see Part 3.2.1).

The emulsion and suspension flows both suggest that the viscosity must increase with the volume fraction of the dispersed phase. Since in blends, at the two ends of the concentration scale, the roles of dispersed/matrix polymer are reversed, the simplest emulsion model lead one to expect that for PAB, $\eta$–$\phi$ dependence will show a positive deviation from the log-additivity rule (or PDB for short). On the other hand *Lees'* (1900) model of additivity of components' fluidity, as well as the one proposed by *Lin* (1979) for telescopic flow of liquid mixtures, lead one to expect negative deviation from the log-additivity rule (or NDB behavior). This type of flow has been frequently observed in antagonistically immiscible polymer blends. In capillary flow the slip surfaces are most often concentric, created within the cylindrical volume of the low viscosity phase.

Block polymers are instructive models, as here the flow properties undergo drastic changes at the three temperatures: at the glass transitions of phases 1 and 2, $T_{g1}$ and $T_{g2}$, as well as at the block polymer dissolution temperature, $T_s$ (above which the system is homogeneous). An analysis of shear stress influence on $T_s$ lead to the discovery of a simple law with a direct implication for PAB, Eq (3.145).

The fact that emulsions, suspensions and block polymers are a model for polymer blends also implies that in PAB one should expect the presence of an apparent yield stress, $\sigma_y$. Whereas in classical systems $\sigma_y$ is a known phenomenon with established methods of determination and incorporation into the general rheological behavior, in PAB $\sigma_y$ plays that as well as a more subtle role: it controls the micro-rheological behavior.

On the basis of these model systems one expects that in immiscible PAB's on one hand, the morphology should affect the flow behavior and, on the other, the flow changes the conditions for phase separation i.e. the morphology. The rheology is not only affected by morphology but it also has a profound reciprocal effect on the PAB structure. The key for understanding these effects is the microrheology (see Part 3.5).

Of primary concern to microrheology is the deformation of the dispersed phase under steady state large strains as well as the dynamics of change of the thus generated structures. Three principal quantities are used: (i) the relative viscosity, $\lambda = \eta_{dispersed}/\eta_{matrix}$, (ii) the ratio of the rheological to interfacial forces, $\varkappa = \sigma d/\nu$ (where $\sigma$ is the stress, d is the initial droplet diameter and $\nu$ is the interfacial tension coefficient), and (iii) time, t. Both $\lambda$ and $\varkappa$ enter the classical Taylor Equation (3.123) derived for the linear range of Newtonian liquids droplet deformability. Use of this dependence for interpretation of large strain deformability of PAB systems has no sense; note that for $0 > \lambda > \infty$ the drop deformability D may change by less than 19% by contrast with the data (for Newtonian and non-Newtonian dispersions) presented in Fig. 3.18 (p. 164). Similarly $\varkappa$ in Eq (3.123) provides the proper equivalence between the rheological and interfacial forces, but it should not be used outside the range of linearity (small deformation).

At this point it is worth mentioning the controversy surrounding $\nu$. There are several experimental methods for its determination, some of which require days of heating the viscous commercial polymers before the equilibrium drop shape can be obtained. The two further complications arise from polydispersity and migration of low molecular weight component to the interphase. Furthermore, there is a relation between $\nu$ and the melt elasticity, e.g. as expressed by Eq (3.174). In short, since $\nu = \nu$ (t, MWD, $\sigma$, ...) it is quite difficult to be certain to what extent the equivalence between $\sigma d$ and $\nu$ implied by the constancy of $\varkappa$ is valid. In both, the steady state shear and extensional flows, thread-like structures develop; upon cessation of motion they disintegrate into small droplets. The time factor is particularly important for describing kinetics of thread diisintegration by means of Taylor instability. The time scale also determines the distribution of droplet size for low values of $\lambda$ (see Fig. 3.18), i.e. the proportion of those created by tip-spinning to those broken by shear. Furthermore, even at low concentration of the dispersed phase, $\phi > 0.1$, the drops exists in a state of dynamic equilibrium between broken and coalesced; here again the time factor comes into account.

It is in the process of thread disintegration where the yield stress, $\sigma_y$, plays a major role; viz. Eq (3.172). In case when $\sigma_y$ exceeds a critical value the thread will not disintegrate. Thus by varying the apparent yield stress (e.g. by interfacial agents) one may greatly affect the morphology of PAB's; when fine dispersion is desired $\sigma_y \rightarrow 0$ should be generated, but when fiber reinforcement is preferred $\sigma_y$ should obey Inequality (3.172). The thread formation has been observed in the steady state Couette as well as in extensional flows. Fiber reinforcements with high aspect ratio, high strength fibrillas is one of the frequent goal of blending for industrial monofilament applications.

The theory, Eq (3.182), predicts that drop deformability in extensional flow is about 4 times as large as in shear. Furthermore, as indicated in Fig. 3.18 here the deformability is more regular in a wider range of $\lambda$, exceeding the critical value for shear flow, $\lambda = 3.7$, above which no drop breakup is possible. For example, the convergent flow to the die provides powerful elongational field with stresses sufficient for deformation and fibrillation of semi-crystalline polymers even far below the melting point (Fig. 3.45, p. 209).

The problem of drop deformability is important not only because of fibrillation (which in case of fiber spinning may significantly improve the performance) but also in applications such as blow molding where bi-axial stretching should allow the droplets to form randomly dispersed lamellas for controlling the diffusivity and permeability of gases or liquids. The microrheology forms the basis for understanding the observations presented in Figs. 3.21 (p. 166), 3.30 (p. 187) and 3.31 (p. 188).

There are several theoretical and experimental indications of drastic changes of rheological behavior in the vicinity of phase separation. Near the spinodal there is a particularly strong coupling between flow and conditions for phase separation. In most cases the flow enhances miscibility while the rheological responses (e.g. $\eta^*$) dramatically increase in the vicinity of phase separation (see Figs. 3.24 to 3.26 and 3.46).

### 1.3.3   Rheology of Polymer Alloys and Blends

As discussed in the previous paragraphs there is a reciprocal relation between the morphology and flow. However, one may also ask what, if any, information can be inferred from the rheological test data regarding the miscibility or morphology of the system. Directly, the rheology can say very little about the degree of phase separation.

During high strain steady state shear or elongational flow, the morphology of the initial material undergoes a severe change. For example, in pipe flow of blends with $\lambda < 1$ the dispersed phase migrates toward the wall, determining the total pressure drop. As a result the capillary flow of PAB is controlled by the low viscosity component. In extensional flow, the two phases form parallel strands with the total response being close to the additivity of parallel fibers. However, *the initial response* in shear or elongation contains the information on morphology modification and properly analyzed may provide an insight into the miscibility/structure problem. Unfortunately analysis of these transients is not simple.

The most appropriate method of testing for information on PAB miscibility is the small strain dynamic flow. Here the sample is examined within range of the linear viscoelastic response, which means that the structure remains largely unaffected. Over the years a large volume of information has been collected on the effects of composition of homologous polymer blends on the dynamic response. Presently one can extend this approach to PAB. When the relaxation spectrum computed assuming miscibility of components agrees with the experimental data, there is a basis for suspecting blend miscibility. This method seems to be quite sensitive. However, the frequently used shortcut by means of the Cole-Cole dependence ($\eta''$ vs. $\eta'$) can be misleading. These and other methods relating the rheological response to miscibility are discussed in Parts 3.6 to 3.10.

## 1.4   How to Design a Polymer Blend

On many occasions I have been asked how fundamental information can help development of a better blend. The question is both naively simple and severely challenging. Are we in a position not only to observe and interpret, but also to provide guidance? Due to diversity of types and uses of PAB it is impossible to provide a generally valid answer to the initial question. However, it is eminently possible to propose a flow chart, a step diagram, which on one hand is general enough and on the other may prevent waste of time in searching in dead alleys by the trial-and-error approach for the elusive goal of an ideal blend:

Step  1. Define the physical and chemical properties the ideal blend should have.
Step  2. From a list of resin properties select those polymers which may provide some of the required behavior. Usually a wider range of desired properties requires several types of potential candidates.
Step  3. Tabulate the advantages and disadvantages of the selected resins in a form resembling Table 1.8. There must be alternative candidates capable of providing each of the required properties.
Step  4. From the list of candidates select a set of resins which assures the most suitable complementarity of properties.
Step  5. Determine the miscibility of the selected resins and/or a method of making them compatible.
Step  6. Examine the economics, including cost of resin, compatibilization and compounding as well as the effect on forming, maintenance, longevity, etc. If the cost is prohibitive return to Step 4 and select another set of resins.
Step  7. Define the ideal morphology which will assure the optimum performance of the finished product.
Step  8. Select the rheological properties of the blend components (molecular weights, compounding parameters, etc.), concentration of ingredients, amount of compatibilizer and type and intensity of the deformation field needed for generating the precursor morphology.
Step  9. Determine the method of stabilization of morphology, e.g. by controlled cooling rate, crystallization, chemical reaction, irradiation, etc.
Step 10. Select the optimum fabrication method which will assure formation of the final morphology. If the morphology does not agree with that required for optimization, return to step 8.

Steps 8 to 10 are crucial. Frequently, the customer will impose the fabrication method (Step 10) unwilling to bear the capital cost required for modernization of technology. In this case the optimization must be accomplished in Steps 8 and 9, usually with a compromise as far as optimization of morphology is concerned. In most cases, under these circumstances the preferred solution seems to be the generation of a fine and reproducible dispersion which allows the customer to use the PAB in a manner similar to that of a homopolymer. This approach permits the blend manufacturer to provide several fabricators with, on one hand, a non-specific, problem-free material but on the other without the benefits optimized morphology could bring.

Generation of a fine dispersion is relatively simple if the following four principles are observed: (i) the viscosity ratio of the two polymers $1/3 > \lambda > 1$, (ii) the yield stress $\sigma_y \to 0$, (iii) the interfacial tension coefficient $v \to 0$ and (iv) the rate of cooling slow enough for Taylor instabilities to break the dispersed liquid threads but insufficient for the coarsening to take place. It is worth noting that $\lambda$ in (i) refers to viscosity under the type of deformation, temperature, pressure and stress level dominant in the mixer. The $\sigma_y$ in (ii) is not $\sigma_y$ of the blend but rather of the dispersed liquid with the interphase. For a very broad molecular weight distribution the value of the zero-shear viscosity may be so high that the big disparity between $\eta_0$(disp) and $\eta_0$(matrix) may effectively play the role of an apparent yield stress. The principal means of $v$-control in (iii) is compatibilization. A less specific compatibilizer may have to be used in such a large amount that it may adversely affect final properites. On the other hand an optimized, specific compatibilizer such as a tapered di-block copolymer is expensive. The reactive compatibilization is strongly affected by the processing step and its parameters. Finally, the time for breaking the thread may be shortened by initiating the process with a mechanically imposed standing wave (see Part 3.5).

The effects of elasticity (to be considered in Step 8) are discussed in Part 3.8. In accord with Eq 3.174 at a constant concentration of dispersed phase the resulting morphology depends (between other factors) on the relative magnitude of the first normal stress difference, $N_1$, of the two liquids; when $N_1$ of the dispersed phase is larger than that of matrix, $N_{1,1} > N_{1,2}$, the drops are formed, in opposite case the co-continuous morphology is expected. Since on the two ends of the blend composition the role of the two polymers reverses, this rule is sometimes called "van Oene complementarity principle". Due to numerous complicating factors the "principle" is not universal, but it holds for a number of polymer pairs.

The last comment regarding the selection of the rheological properties (Step 8) refers to phase inversion (see Part 3.4.5). In classical emulsions the concentration at which the dispersed and matrix liquids invert their role is determined by concentration, type of surfactant and method of emulsion preparation. By comparison, PAB technology is primitive. Due to simultaneous mixing of all ingredients, non-specificity of the compatibilizer and non-uniformity of deformational field, a complex morphology is usually generated. Even at low concentration of polymer A in polymer B the drops of A frequently contain small droplets of the matrix polymer B. However, in a similar manner to emulsions, above a critical concentration of phase A in the mixture, $\phi_A > \phi_i$, the phase inversion takes place - now A becomes the matrix and B the dispersed phase. In emulsion $\phi_i$ is narrowly defined and varies little with the direction of concentration changes. In PAB $\phi_i$ represents a mid-range value of a broad concentration range at which the two phases are co-continous (see Fig. 3.50, p. 217). Theoretically $\phi_i$ depends on $\lambda$ (see Part 3.4.5).

In the above discussions the effect of polymer crystallinity was omitted. The crystallinity is examined to some extent in Parts 2 and 3. The implications can readily be incorporated into Steps 8 to 10. There is a large body of knowledge of how to supress, enhance or modify crystal morphology (*Wunderlich;* 1976, 1980) and thus affect the properties of the finished part.

## 1.5    Final Comments

This volume provides the fundamental information on thermodynamics and rheology with only a short introduction dealing with economy and methods of PAB preparation. In addition to these, the compounding, forming, morphology of the finished part and performance should be examined. These subjects will hopefully be discussed in a later volume.

The information on the analysis of compounding equipment is rather sparse. Little is known about the stress fields, proportion of the dispersive to distributive mixing, the distribution of residence times and relation of these variables to blend morphology. Active research is being carried out on these subjects in various parts of the world and in a few years the situation should dramatically improve. Recently, the blending capability of six principal compounders (in standard configuration) was examined. For this purpose the manufacturers were supplied with the same dry mixed immiscible polymers and the resulting blends were analyzed for particle size distribution. Surprisingly, only small differences were observed (*Plochocki,* 1986). In general the dispersion was poor with a wide distribution of droplet diameters. Some of the blame can be placed on uncontrollable post-blending coalescence, but the most likely reason is the nonuniformity of the deformational fields in the machines in their standard configuration. Obviously, optimization of compounder geometry and its processing parameters is not simple; it should be based on theoretical analysis of the machine operation and properties of the PAB constituents. Without this an experimental optimization is a long and wasteful process. The information on thermodynamics and rheology provides a logical basis for this analytical process.

# Part 2

# POLYMER/POLYMER MISCIBILITY

## 2.1   Introduction

Thermodynamics is the key to understanding the behavior and propereties of PAB. Miscibility defines the flow behavoir and orientation effects, i.e. the performance of the finished article. However, due to the low value of the self-diffusion coefficient for macromolecules, equilibrium thermodynamic conditions are frequently difficult to achieve. Furthermore, even when near-equilibrium conditions are obtained in the processing equipment, e.g. extruder or injection molding machine, they are not necessarily preserved in the extruded or molded part.

There is also another danger in the direct use of the literature data on solubility in industrial practice. Due to the experimental difficulties in mixing and measuring highly viscous polymer blends, it is a frequent laboratory practice to attain intimate mixing by dissolving the two polymers in a common solvent then drying them. However, the morphology of PAB prepared by solvent casting depends on the solvent, temperature, time, concentration etc. To diminish these effects the solution-prepared sample should be melt-blended in a manner similar to that intended for commercial production. Only in this way may one learn what properties are to be expected from ideally mixed (dispersed) PAB. The problems associated with producing PAB under far-from-equilibrium conditions can be severe. During the product's lifetime its properties drift toward the equilibrium. For poorly mixed homogeneous polymer blends this may not be detrimental; it may even lead to an improvement of properties. However, for heterogeneous polymer blends, the phase ripening and deterioration of mechanical properties may lead to disastrous results.

Today no single theory is able to predict details of the phase equilibria of commercially attractive systems. There are numerous groups working toward this ideal goal and progress is being made. The most difficult parameter for a theory to take into account is molecular polydispersity – by itself rather difficult to determine experimentally. In addition, commercial systems can seldom be represented by a single chemical species. Modification of composition provides the desired flexibility for the manufacturer but at the same time may significantly affect the "compatibility" of a given resin with others.

In this Part 2 the current status of the theoretical work, the methods of miscibility measurement, characterization and control will be summarized. It is recognized that polymer/polymer miscibility is determined by a delicate balance of enthalpic and entropic forces, significantly smaller than those observed in small molecule liquid mixtures (solutions). In particular the combinatorial entropy term, which to a great extent is responsible for miscibility of solvents and in polymer solutions, is negligibly small in high molecular weight polymer blends. The polymer/polymer miscibility is primarily due to the negative heat of mixing, i. e. to specific interactions between the two types of macromolecules.

Another characteristic feature of the PAB phase diagram is that for most homogeneous systems an increase of the temperature leads to phase separation, i.e. the existence of the lower critical solution temperature, LCST. The upper critical solution temperature, UCST, which predominates in the systems containing solvent is a less frequent phenomenon in PAB. For example, UCST was observed in blends of polystyrene with polybutene, polyisoprene, polybutadiene, poly-ε-caprolactone, polymethylphenylsiloxane and poly(butadiene-co-methylstyrene), both UCST and LCST were reported in systems: polymethylmethacrylate/chlorinated polyethylenes, as well as for polystyrene with either poly-2,6-dimethyl-1,4 phenylene ether, polyvinylmethylether or poly-o-chlorostyrene, while LCST in blends of polyvinylchloride with polymethacrylates, polyvinylidenefluoride with polyacrylates or polymethacrylates, poly-ε-caprolactone with styrene-acrylonitrile copolymer, polycarbonate or polyvinylmethylether (*Nishi*, 1985; *Kuleznev* et al., 1985; *Cong* et al., 1986; *Ougizawa* et al., 1985, 1986). A few examples of UCST and LCST blends are listed in Table 2.1.

## 2.2   General Principles of Phase Equilibria Calculation
   *(Tompa, 1956)*

The total energy of the system, U, can be expressed as the difference between the heat content, H, and the compressive energy, PV: U = H-PV. Note that for closed system where U is constant any change in enthalpy is compensated by an increase of either pressure, P, or volume V:

$$dH = PdV + VdP; \qquad U = \text{const.} \tag{2.1}$$

At equilibrium the Gibbs free energy is given by: G = H - TS where: S and T are entropy and absolute temperature respectively. The change in G can be written as:

$$dG = VdP - SdT + \Sigma_i \, \mu_i dn_i; \qquad \mu_i = (\partial G/\partial n_i)_{P,T,n_j} \tag{2.2}$$

where: $n_i$ represents the number of moles of the substance i having the chemical potential $\mu_i$. The free energy, enthalpy, entropy and chemical potential of mixing are respectively defined as a difference:

$$\Delta F_m = F - F_0; \qquad F \equiv G, H, S, \mu_i \tag{2.3}$$

where F and $F_0$ represent the mixture and pure state respectively. The conditions of miscibility in a binary system are described in terms of binodal:

$$\Delta \mu_i' = \Delta \mu_i''; \qquad i = 1,2 \tag{2.4}$$

(where the superscripts ′ and ″ indicate the two phases), spinodal:

$$D \equiv (\partial^2 \Delta G_m/\partial x_2^2)_{P,T} = 0 \tag{2.5}$$

and the critical point:

$$CST \equiv (\partial^3 \Delta G_m/\partial x_2^3)_{P,T} = D' = 0 \tag{2.6}$$

where $x_2$ is the mole fraction of component 2. The dependencies (2.4) to (2.6) are illustrated in Fig. 2.1; the upper part shows the isothermal and isobaric variation of $\Delta G_m$ with $x_2$

TABLE 2.1 Phase Diagrams for Polymer Blends

| System | Polymer A | | Polymer B | | LCST (L) or UCST (U) (°C) | Comments |
|---|---|---|---|---|---|---|
| | Code | $M_w/M_n$ (kg/mol) | Code | $M_w/M_n$ (kg/mol) | | |
| 1. | PS | 237/78 | PVME | 13.3/7.7 | L 120 | Small variation of $T_c$ with $M_w > 30$ |
| 2. | SAN | 223/88.6 | PMMA | 92/45.6 | L 150 | Azeotropic SAN with 28% AN |
| 3. | SAN | " | PCL | 35/2.2 | L 90 | PCL: $T_m = 57$ °C |
| 4. | PS | (commercial) | 4MPC | ($T_g \simeq$ 200 °C) | L < 220 | Processing at 220 °C |
| 5. | PVDF | 100/? | i-PEMA | 332/? | L 200 | PVDF: $T_m = 155$, $T_c = 141$ °C |
| 6. | PS | 29/26 82.9/80.8 | PoClS | ?/? 169/77.7 | L 350 U 100 | PoClS – laboratory sample |
| 7. | αMSAN | 160/57 | PMMA | 126/56 | L 185 | Commercial resins |
| 8. | PMMA | 42/10.4 | CPE (50% Cl) | 190/22 | L 100 | Experimental polymers |
| 9. | PMMA | 80/36 | PVC | 55/30 | L 190 | Commercial resins |
| 10. | PES | (commercial) | PEO | 20 to 200 | L 80 | PES: $T_g = 226$ °C |
| 11. | PS | 22/20 | P(S-co-4-BrS) | (similar to PS) | U 218 | Copolymer obtained by bromination of PS |
| 12. | PVC | 160/76 | NBR (26% AN) | 340/119 | (controversial) | Commercial blends contain a plasticizer |
| 13. | PS | 10/9 | PMPS | 2.8/1.8 | U 103 | $T_g$ (PMPS) = −50 °C |
| 14. | BR | 390/180 | SBR-45 | 480/160 | U 140 | Commercial rubbers |
| 15. | SAN (25% AN) | 194/68.4 | NBR-40 (40% AN) | 297/91.3 | U 140 L 52 | Commercial resins, $T_g$(SAN) = 107 °C |

*Code for polymer:*

PS – polystyrene
SAN – poly(styrene-co-acrylonitrile)
PCL – poly-ε-caprolactone
PVDF – polyvinylidenefluoride
PoClS – poly-ortho-chlorostyrene
CPE – chlorinated polyethylene
PES – polyethersulfone (Victrex)
P(S-co-4BrS) – poly(styrene-co-4bromostyrene)
PMPS – polymethylphenylsiloxane
SBR – poly(butadiene-co-styrene)

PVME – polyvinylmethylether
PMMA – polymethylmethacrylate
4MPC – 4-methyl-bis-phenol-A-polycarbonate
i-PEMA – isotactic polyethylmethacrylate
αMSAN – poly(α-methylstyrene-co-acrylonitrile)
PVC – polyvinylchloride
PEO – polyethyleneoxide
NBR – poly(acrylonitrile-co-butadiene)
BR – polybutadiene

*References:* System 1. *T. Nishi* and *T. K. Kwei,* 1975; *D. D. Davis* and *T. K. Kwei,* 1980; *I. C. Sanchez,* 1983; *J. Kumaki* and *T. Hashimoto,* 1986; *J. M. Ubrich* et al., 1986; *S. Reich,* 1986; *I. G. Voigt-Martin* et al, 1986. System 2. *L. P. McMaster,* 1975; *W. A. Kruse* et al., 1976; *K. Naito* et al., 1978; *V. J. McBrierty* et al., 1978. System 3. *L. P. McMaster,* 1973; *L. P. McMaster* and *O. Olabisi,* 1975. System 4. *M. T. Shaw,* 1974. System 5. *E. Roerdink* and *G. Challa,* 1980; *G. ten Brinke* et al., 1981, 1982; *H. Saito* et al., 1987; *B. R. Hahn* et al., 1987. System 6. *H. N. Gilmer* et al., 1982; *S. L. Zacharius* et al., 1983; *M. S. Takahashi* et al., 1985. System 7. *S. H. Goh* et al., 1982. System 8. *D. J. Walsh* et al., 1982. System 9. *H. Jagger* et al., 1983. System 10. *D. J. Walsh* and *V. B. Singh,* 1984; *D. J. Walsh* and *S. Rostami,* 1985. System 11. *G. R. Strobl* et al., 1986. System 12. *D. E. Henderson,* 1943; *M. C. Reed,* 1949; *O. Olabisi,* et al., 1979; *T. Inoue* et al., 1985. System 13. *S. Nojima* et al., 1982; *M. H. Takahashi* et al., 1986. System 14. *T. Ougizawa* et al., 1985; *T. Izumitani* and *T. Hashimoto,* 1985. System 15. *T. Ougizawa* and *T. Inoue,* 1986.

whereas the lower part represents the isobaric phase diagram for binary mixtures with the upper critical solution temperature, UCST. Note that the equilibrium variation of $\Delta G_m$ with $x_2$ follows the solid line, i.e. the line b'b", which corresponds to Eq (2.4). The points of contact define the limiting conditions for miscible system, $x_2 < b'$ or $x_2 > b''$. The inflection points, s' and s", define the spinodal conditions, i.e. for $s' < x_2 < s''$ the system is phase-separated. Within the concentration range between the b and s curves the system is meta-stable.

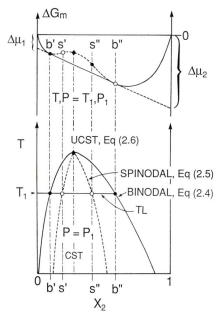

Fig. 2.1 Upper part: Gibbs free energy of mixing as a function of concentration in a binary liquid system at constant temperature and pressure, $T,P = T_1,P_1$. Lower part: phase diagram at $P = P_1$. The points marked b, s and CST represents binodal, spinodal and critical solubility temperature, respectively.

In polymer blends two other types of phase diagrams, illustrated in Fig. 2.2, are also observed; the LCST, is more frequent than UCST. An elegant demonstration of a continuous transformation of phase separation behaviour upon increase of molecular weight, MW, is shown in Fig. 2.3 (*Patterson, 1982*).

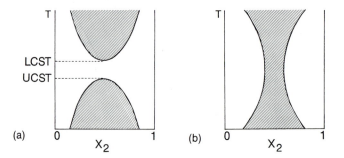

Fig. 2.2 Schematic phase diagrams, T vs. $x_2$, for polymer/polymer systems; shaded areas represent two phases. In figure (a) the lower and upper critical solution temperatures are indicated. Diagram (a) or (b) can be generated by varying either the interaction parameter or molecular weight of the ingredients.

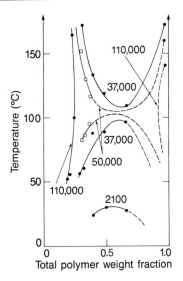

Fig. 2.3 Cloud point temperatures for mixtures of equal weights of PVME and PS of indicated molecular weights in trichloroethene as a function of the weight fraction of total polymer in the mixture. Molecular weight of PVME = 10 kg/mol (*Patterson, 1982*).

The above considerations are general. In order to apply them to a given system one has to:

1. Select an appropriate expression:

$$\Delta G_m = f(P, T, x_i, \ldots), \tag{2.7}$$

2. determine the value of the characteristic material parameter(s) in Equation (2.7),
3. solve Equations (2.4) - (2.6) for Equation (2.7).

The most important step is the selection of the theoretical model, i.e. the form of Equation (2.7). The balance between the complexity of its form and the adequacy of description of the experimental behaviour must be preserved.

In the following part a historical synopsis on the development of the theories will be given. Mainly the lattice-type approach will be discussed. There has been continuous progress in the ability of the theories to describe the observed phenomena. The complexity of the mathematical formulas has increased, but the availability of computers makes these easier to solve than the "simple" dependencies in past decades. To secure good knowledge of the phenomena one has to concentrate on the experimental part: precise characterization of the polymers, especially their molecular weight averages and structure, stabilization of the system and precise and rapid measurements of the equilibrium phase separation. Only with precise experimental data can the adequacies of the theoretical treatment be judged.

## 2.3    Theories of Liquid Mixtures Containing Polymer

### 2.3.1    Huggins-Flory Theory

In 1941, independently, *Huggins* and *Flory* proposed the first thermodynamic description of a binary mixture containing polymer:

$$\Delta G_m^R \equiv \Delta G_m / RTV = \Sigma(\phi_i \ln\phi_i)/V_i + \chi'_{ij}\phi_i\,\phi_j \tag{2.8}$$

where i,j = 1,2. Differentiation of this relation leads to the chemical potential:

$$\Delta\mu_1^0/RT = \ln\phi_1 + (1-r_2^{-1})\,\phi_2 + \chi_{12}\,\phi_2^2 \tag{2.9}$$

where $\phi_i$, $V_i$ are respectively the volume fraction and the molar volume of component i, $r_2 = V_2/V_1$ and $\chi'_{12}$ is the binary interaction parameter:

$$\chi'_{12} \equiv \chi_{12}/V_1 = z\Delta w_{12}r_1/k_B TV_1 \tag{2.10}$$

where: z is the lattice coordination number, $\Delta w_{12}$ is the energy change due to formation of the 1-2 contact pair:

$$\Delta w_{12} = w_{12} - (w_{11} + w_{22})/2 \tag{2.11}$$

$r_1$ is an effective number of segments of component 1 and $k_B$ is the Boltzman constant. Parameter $\chi'_{12}$ is considered to be independent of concentration and as predicted by Equation (2.10) it increases with P and decreases with T. In the original treatment, $\chi'_{12}$ was purely enthalpic, written in terms of the solubility parameter difference:

$$\chi'_{12} = (\delta_1 - \delta_2)^2/RT > 0 \tag{2.12}$$

while the entropic term in Eqs (2.8) and (2.9) was negative, i.e. the Huggins-Flory theory predicted that the solubility can be achieved only by the effect of the combinatorial entropy.

In the thermodynamics of polymeric systems it is customary to assign subscript 1 to solvent, and 2, 3.... to polymers. Accordingly, since the molar volume of a solvent and monomer are comparable, $V_2$ in Eq (2.9) represents a degree of polymerization. From Eqs (2.5),(2.6) and (2.8) the critical values are:

$$\phi_{2,\,crit} = 1/[1 + (V_2/V_1)^{\frac{1}{2}}] \tag{2.13}$$

and    $$2\chi_{12,\,crit} = \phi_{1,crit}^{-2}$$

$$\chi'_{12,\,crit} = (V_1^{-\frac{1}{2}} + V_2^{-\frac{1}{2}})^2/2 \tag{2.14}$$

can be found. For solvent mixtures where $V_1 \simeq V_2$, $\chi'_{12,\,crit} \simeq 2/V_1$; for polymer solutions:

$$\chi'_{12,\,crit} = (1 + r_2^{-\frac{1}{2}})^2/2V_1 \simeq 1/2V_1$$

and for polymer/polymer systems $\chi'_{12,\,crit} \to 0$.

Qualitatively, Eq (2.8) has two shortcomings: it is incapable of predicting LCST ($d\chi_{12}/dT < 0$) and polymer/polymer miscibility. Two early refinements (*Flory*, 1953) - incorporation of the excluded volume effect and assumption that $\chi'_{12}$ is both enthalpic and entropic in nature lead to some improvements, but without eliminating the above shortcomings.

*Maron* (1959) should be credited with the introduction of the concept of volume changes on mixing. His theory has been extended to ternary systems by *Utracki* (1962) who found it to be satisfactory for toluene/ethanol/PS mixtures (see Figure 2.4). Incorporation of the volume coefficients provided a means of predicting LCST before it was discovered (*Freeman* and *Rowlinson*, 1960).

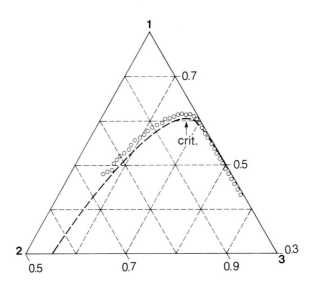

Fig. 2.4 Ternary phase diagram for toluene(1)/polystyrene(2)/ethanol(3). Line – Maron's theory; point – turbidity measurements; crit. - indicates location of the theoretical critical point (*Utracki*, 1962).

### 2.3.2    Equation of State Theories

The second generation theories were developed by *Flory, Patterson, Sanchez* and their coworkers (*Flory* et al., 1964; *Eichinger* and *Flory*, 1968; *Patterson*, 1969, 1982; *Patterson* and *Robard*, 1978; *Sanchez* and *Lacombe*, 1976, 1977; *Sanchez*, 1983, 1984). These are based on the equation of state.

In Flory et al. treatment $\chi_{12}$, as defined by Eqs (2.8–2.10), is modified to read:

$$\chi_{12}\phi^2 = X_{12}(r_1 V_1^* \tilde{\varrho} \Theta_2^2) + r_1 E^* \{\tilde{\varrho}_1 - \tilde{\varrho} + \tilde{P}_1(\tilde{V} - \tilde{V}_1)$$
$$+ 3\tilde{T}_1 \ln[(\tilde{V}_1^{1/3} - 1)/(\tilde{V}^{1/3} - 1)]\}  \tag{2.15}$$

where $V_1^*$ is the hard core molar volume of the substance "1", $\tilde{\varrho}_1 = V_1^*/V_1$, $\Theta_2 = \phi_2 s_2/s$ (s the average number of interactions per segment; $s_1$ is the same in pure i = 1 substance), and

$$\tilde{F} \equiv F/F^*; \qquad F = P, T, V  \tag{2.16}$$

are the reduced pressure, temperature and specific volume respectively. The symbols without subscripts represent the mixture parameters. The interaction term, $X_{12}$, in Eq (2.15) contains both the enthalpic and entropic contributions. The second and third expression on the right hand side (RHS) of this equation represents the "equation of state" contribution; for a mixture of liquids having the same reduced specific volume, $\tilde{V}_1 \simeq \tilde{V}_2 \simeq \tilde{V}$, these terms vanish. For systems in which the difference between $V_1$ and $V_2$ increases, $\chi_{12}$ increases with it. Furthermore, Eq (2.15) predicts that pressure affects $\chi_{12}$ differently, depending on the sign of the $(\tilde{V} - \tilde{V}_1)$ term; in contracting systems, $V < V_1$, an increase of P causes a decrease of $\chi_{12}$, i.e. enhances miscibility, in dilating systems it reduces it. On the other hand the temperature, $\tilde{T}_1$, is a multiplication factor of largely negative term and its increase reduces $\chi_{12}$, i.e. increases miscibility.

*Patterson* and *Robard* (1978) demonstrated the usefulness of the simplified form of Eq (2.15), namely:

$$\frac{\chi_{12}}{M_1 V_1^{*}} = \frac{P_1^{*}}{RT_1^{*}}\left[\frac{\tilde{V}_1^{1/3}}{(\tilde{V}_1^{1/3}-1)}\frac{X_{12}}{P_1^{*}} + \frac{\tilde{V}_1^{1/3}}{2(4/3 - \tilde{V}_1^{1/3})}\tau^2\right] \tag{2.17}$$

where the first term on the RHS represents the interactional and the second the "free volume" contribution, respectively. In Eq (2.17): $3 < 3\tilde{V}_1^{1/3} < 4$, and:

$$\tau = 1 - T_1^{*}/T_2^{*} \tag{2.18}$$

In *Sanchez* et al.'s treatment the combinatorial free energy is again expressed as that in Eq (2.8). The non-combinatorial part differs from that given by *Flory* et al.:

$$\Delta \equiv [(\Delta G_{\tilde{m}c}(\text{Sanchez}) - \Delta G_{\tilde{m}c}(\text{Flory})]/k_B T = [(1 - \tilde{\varrho})\ln(1 - \tilde{\varrho}) + (\tilde{\varrho}\ln\tilde{\varrho})/r]/\tilde{\varrho}$$
$$+ 3c\ln(\tilde{\varrho}^{-1/3}-1) \tag{2.19}$$

where $3c$ is the number of external degrees of freedom per segment:

$$ck_B T^{*} = P^{*}V^{*} \tag{2.20}$$

It can be seen that for polymeric mixtures $r \rightarrow 1$, $3c \rightarrow 2$ and:

$$\Delta = (\tilde{\varrho}^{-1}-1)\ln(1-\tilde{\varrho}) + 2\ln(\tilde{\varrho}^{1/3}-1) \tag{2.21}$$

In Fig. 2.5 the difference, $\Delta$, is plotted as a function of $\tilde{\varrho}$. Excepting the region $\tilde{\varrho} > 0.9$ the difference is small, of the order of $-1/2$ kJ/mole. In short, Sanchez's theory predicts lower values of $\Delta G_m$, i.e. in general a better solubility in polymeric systems than both the Huggins-Flory and the revised Flory et al. theories.

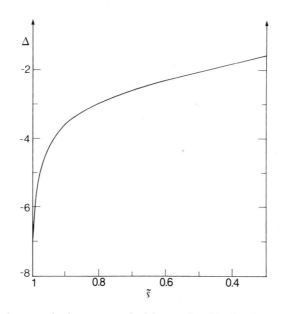

Fig. 2.5 Difference between the free energy of mixing predicted by Sanchez and Flory theories as a function of the reduced density.

### 2.3.3   Gas-Lattice Model

The examples of phase diagram in Figs. 2.1 and 2.2 are characterized by a single critical point, the UCST or LCST, per curve. However, multi-peak spinodals were reported for an anionically prepared oligostyrene/oligoisoprene blend (*McIntyre*, 1969; *Koningsveld* et al., 1974). Later data (*Koningsveld* and *Kleindjens*, 1977; *Koningsveld* et al., 1980, 1982) indicated that this behaviour is rather a frequent occurrence. It can be shown that the theories discussed on the previous pages cannot predict such a phenomenon.

In a purely empirical manner *Koningsveld* et al. (1974) expressed $\chi'_{12}$ in Eq (2.9) as a power series in $\phi_2$:

$$\chi'_{12} = \sum_{i=0}^{n} a_i \phi_2^i; \qquad n \le 2; \qquad a_i = \sum_{j=-1}^{m} a_{ij} T^j; \qquad m \le 1 \tag{2.22}$$

Equation (1.3) is a simplest form of the above relation. With such modification the multi-peak spinodals could be calculated from Eq (2.8). As *Koningsveld* et al. (1980) pointed out, the modified *Huggins* theory (1976) also provides for such a curve. In the derivation of that theory *Huggins* assumed concentration and orientation dependent surface interaction parameters. The assumption led to:

$$-\chi'_{12} = \ln \left[1 + k_1 (1 - \gamma)\phi_2 Q\right]/\phi_2 + \ln[1 + k_2\phi_1 Q]/\phi_1 \tag{2.23}$$

where $\gamma = 1 - s_1/s_2$ ($s_i$ are the interacting segment surfaces), $Q = 1/(1-\gamma\phi_2)$ and $k_i$ are parameters. The Equations (2.22) and (2.23) provide enough flexibility for description of even complex phase diagram (*Strobl* et al., 1986).

*Koningsveld* and co-workers (*Kleintjens* et al., 1980; *Nies* et al., 1983) proposed a lattice-gas model. The model considers a pure liquid as a binary mixture of randomly distributed, occupied and vacant sites. P and T can change the concentration of holes, but not their size. A molecule may occupy m sites. As in Huggins' approach, the interaction occurs per unit contact area. Binary liquid mixtures are treated as ternary systems of 2 liquids (subscripts "$_1$" and "$_2$") with holes (subscripts "$_0$"). The derived simple equations described surprisingly well the vapor-liquid equilibrium of n-alkanes and predicted rather well the phase separation of n-alkanes/polyethylene systems, even when drastic simplifications in the selection of the equation parameters were used. The lattice-gas model gives the non-combinatorial free energy as:

$$\chi_{12} = \chi_{01}^{L}\phi_0/\phi_2 + \chi_{02}^{L} \phi_0/\phi_1 + \chi_{12}^{L} \tag{2.24}$$

where the superscript L indicates the interaction parameters in the framework of the lattice-gas model:

$$\chi_{0i}^{L} = \alpha_i + \chi_{ii}^{L} (1-\gamma_i) / (1-\gamma_1\phi_1-\gamma_2\phi_2); \qquad i = 1,2 \tag{2.25}$$

$$\chi_{12}^{L} = \alpha_m + \chi_m (1-\gamma_2) / (1-\gamma_1\phi_1 - \gamma_2\phi_2) \tag{2.26}$$

In these relations:

$$\gamma_i = 1 - s_i / s_0; \qquad i = 1,2 \tag{2.27}$$

$\alpha_i$, $\chi_{ii}$ and their analogs $\alpha_m$, $\chi_m$ are parameters – $\alpha$'s numerical and $\chi$'s dependent on T only:

$$\chi_{ii}^{L}, \chi_m = \sum_{i=0}^{n} a_i T^{-i}; \qquad n \le 2 \tag{2.28}$$

All but two parameters are determined from the P-V-T dependence of pure substances. The two, $\alpha_m$ and $\chi_m$, describe the interactions within the same rigid lattice structure. For branched polymers or copolymers the above equations can also be used, redefining the surface interaction parameters $\gamma_i$ for each molecular structure (*Nies* et al., 1983a).

The derivation is strictly valid for monodispersed liquids. For polymers, the polydispersity enters the spinodal equation as the weight-average $V_{iw}$. If $\chi_{12}$ is considered to be independent of concentration, molecular weight and polydispersity Eqs (2.13) and (2.14) may be replaced respectively by:

$$\phi_{2,\,crit} = 1 / [1 + r_{wz}] \qquad (2.13a)$$

$$\chi'_{12,\,crit} = (1 + r_{wz}) / [1 + (V_{2z} / V_{1z})^{\frac{1}{2}}] / 2V_{2w} \qquad (2.14a)$$

where $r_{wz} \equiv (V_{2w} / V_{1w}) (V_{1z} / V_{2z})^{\frac{1}{2}}$

For monodisperse systems with $V_{iz} = V_{iw} = V_i$ Eqs (2.13) and (2.14) are recovered (*Koningsveld*, 1986).

In conclusion, there are four factors determining the polymer/polymer miscibility (*Koningsveld* et al., 1982): 1. interacting surface areas of the various types of segments; 2. coil dimensions as a function of temperature, molar mass and concentration; 3. molar mass distribution whether or not in connection with 2; 4. free volume. While the first three elements provide the proper shape of the phase equilibrium diagram, the fourth, free volume, indicates primarily whether the critical point will be of the LCST or UCST type. However, since miscibility of high polymers requires that specific interactions occur and these may alter the $\Delta S_m$, one should not consider the free volume to be the sole influence on the type of separation of the phases. An alternative mechanism will be discussed in Part 2.3.6.

### 2.3.4   Simha's Cell-Hole Theory

During the last twenty years Simha and his collaborators have been pursuing the thermodynamic description of polymeric systems from a slightly different perspective. On the basis of the cell-hole model *Simha* and *Somcynsky* (1969) derived a set of coupled equations, which over the years have been found to be successful in describing the P-V-T relationship for low-molecular weight as well as polymeric liquids (*Mc Kinney* and *Simha*, 1976; *Olabisi* and *Simha*, 1977; *Simha* and *Jain*, 1984b). Since these equations provide an explicit relation between the free volume and P and T, they were also used to interpret the aging of glass (*Curro* et al., 1982; *Simha* et al., 1984a) as well as to predict the variation of liquid viscosity with P and T (*Utracki*, 1985b, 1986c). Recently (*Jain* and *Simha*, 1980, 1981, 1982, 1984) the theory has been extended to a full thermodynamic description of multicomponent systems. The derived relations were tested on the P-V-T dependencies of solutions and blends. Other work has further extended this treatment into the domain of gas-liquid and liquid-liquid phase equilibria (*Stroeks* and *Nies*, 1988).

For a two component system the Helmholtz free energy of the mixture is given by (*Jain* and *Simha*, 1984):

$$\Delta F_m / RT = x_1 \ln x_1 + x_2 \ln x_2 - (\bar{s}-1)\ln [(z-1) / e] + \ln(y/\bar{s})$$
$$+ \bar{s}y^{-1} (1-y)\ln(1-y) - \bar{c} \{\ln[(\bar{M}_0 V^* / N_A)Q^{-1}(1-\eta)^3$$
$$\cdot (2\pi\bar{M}_0 k_B T/N_A h^2)^{3/2}] - (y/2\bar{T})Q^2(A_1 Q^2 - A_2)\} \qquad (2.29)$$

where $x_i$ is the mole fraction, s is the average number of statistical segments in the systems ($s_i M_{oi} = nM_o$, repetitive), z is the coordination number, 3c is the effective number of the external degrees of freedom, $Q = (yV)^{-1}$; $\eta = 2^{-1/6}yQ^{1/3}$; $A_1 = 1.011$; $A_2 = 2.409$. Here $M_{0i}$ is the molecular weight of a segment, $v_i = V_i M_{0i}/N_A$ its repulsive volume, with $V_i$ the corresponding specific volume, and $h = 1-y$ the fraction of vacant sites in the quasi-lattice spanning the fluid. The tildes indicate reduced variables and the scaling parameters are derived by superposition of the experimental and reduced theoretical equation of state. The symbols with bar are averages. From Eq (2.29) one can derive the appropriate chemical potentials, recognizing that:

$$G \quad = F + PV \tag{2.30}$$

$$\Delta G_m \ = G_m - \Sigma x_i \, G_i; \qquad i = 1,2 \tag{2.31}$$

$$\Delta \mu_1 \ = \Delta G_m - x_2 \, (\partial \Delta G_m / \partial x_2)_{P,T} \tag{2.32}$$

$$\Delta \mu_2 \ = \Delta G_m + x_1 \, (\partial \Delta G_m / \partial x_2)_{P,T}$$

Due to the complexity of the expression (2.29) it is not practical to write the phase equilibria relations: binodal, spinodal and critical point. Instead Eqs (2.29-2.32) can be numerically solved by using the definitions in Eqs (2.4) to (2.6).

The advantage of this treatment is its generality - once the characteristic parameters of the system are known one can predict P-V-T, free volume fraction, gas-liquid and liquid-liquid equilibria as functions of composition, P and T. The disadvantage is the difficulty in extending this treatment to polydispersed systems and that arising from the demand of high accuracy of the scaling parameters, especially P*, which are difficult to compute in a non-ambiguous manner (*Utracki*, 1985b, 1986c). Recently accuracy of the scaling parameters determination has been greatly improved by developing a computer program which simultaneously optimizes the fit between the full set of experimental PVT data and the theoretical predictions, adjusting the values of P*, V* and T* (*Nies* et al., 1983b; *Hartmann* and *Haque*, 1985; *Hartmann* et al., 1987; *Stroeks* and *Nies*, 1988). It is expected that this treatment will lead to a both precise and intellectually satisfying thermodynamic description of polymer blends.

### 2.3.5   Strong Interactions Model

A new directional-specific model of segmental interactions was proposed by *Walker* and *Vause* (1982) and applied to polymer blends by *ten Brinke* and *Karasz* (1984). The treatment results in the following expression for the interaction parameter which replaces the one in the original Huggins-Flory Eq (2.8):

$$\chi_{12} = U_2 / k_B T + \ln(1-\lambda) + \ln(1+q^{-1}) \tag{2.33}$$

where: $\lambda = 1/[1+q \exp\{(U_1-U_2)/kT\}]$

$U_1$ and $U_2$ are the attractive and repulsive energy respectively, and q is the degeneracy number.

The interaction parameter, $\chi_{12}$ as given by Eq (2.35), can be divided into enthalpic and entropic parts:

$$\chi_h = -\partial \chi / \partial \ln T; \qquad \chi_s = \partial T \chi / \partial T \tag{2.34}$$

The parameters $U_1$, $U_2$ and q are adjustable. It can be seen that, depending on the relative value of $U_1$ and $U_2$, the $(\partial \chi / \partial T)$ can be negative or positive, predicting respectively UCST or LCST:

$$- (\partial \chi_{12} / \partial T) \, k_B T^2 = U_2 + (U_1 - U_2) \, \lambda^{-3} \tag{2.35}$$

Since: $0 \leq \lambda \leq 1$, $\lambda^{-3}$ acts as an intensity factor of the interactional forces.

In summary, the model provides an alternative explanation for LCST, particularly attractive in cases of incompressible systems having strong interactions, such as the acid-base type.

### 2.3.6   Heat of Mixing Approach

Since the configurational entropy in PAB plays a minor role, Paul and Barlow demonstrated the usefulness of adiabatic calorimetry in predicting polymer/polymer miscibility from the heat of mixing of low molecular weight analogues (*Cruz* et al., 1979). The experimental success directed these researchers to concentrate their theoretical work on $\Delta H_m$. The first outcome was redefinition of i and j in the enthalpic term of Eq (2.8); the authors now identify i and j with the structural units, which may or may not correlate with mers (*Paul* and *Barlow;* 1984; *Barlow* and *Paul,* 1987). The concept is natural for explanation of the "miscibility window" for polymer/copolymer blends (*Balazs* et al., 1985; *Fernandes,* 1986; *Fernandes* et al., 1986; *Goh* and *Lee,* 1987) or for blends of two copolymers with a common monomer (*Shiomi* et al., 1986). However, it has been also useful for explaining the "miscibility window" in series of polymer blends, e.g. polyamide blends (*Ellis,* 1989), polyesters with either polyvinylchloride (*Woo* et al., 1985), or polyhydroxyether of bisphenol-A (Phenoxy) (*Harris* et al., 1983). In the latter case polyester is assumed to consist of two structural units: ester carbonyl ($CH_2COO$-) and paraffinic (-$CH_2$- or -$CH_3$). The method has been extended to ternary blends as well (*Shah* et al., 1986).

The phase behavior of random copolymer/homopolymer blends has been considered by *Bauer* (1985), *Kammer* (1986) as well as *Suess* et al. (1987). The concept of the repulsion between copolymer segments lead to computation of phase diagrams in satisfactory agreement with the experimental data (*ten Brinke* et al., 1983).

A logical next step within the framework of the heat of mixing approach is an extension of the quasichemical group contribution method to polymeric systems (*Guggenheim,* 1952; *Panayiotou* and *Vera,* 1980), recently proposed by *Barlow* and *Paul* (1987). In this concept:

$$\chi'_{ij} = S\ \Gamma_{ij}\ \Delta E_{ij} \tag{2.36}$$

where S is number of contact sites per unit volume of the mixture, $\Gamma_{ij}$ is a non-randomness parameter for placement of i and j segments in the mixture, and $\Delta E_{ij} = E_{ij} - (E_{ii} + E_{jj})/2$ is the exchange energy of i-j contact. Each pair contact is characterized by two parameters: $\Delta E_{ij}$, $A_{ij}$, where $A_{ij}$ is a preexponential intensity factor, and $\Gamma_{ij} = f(\Delta E_{ij}, A_{ij})$. Once the contact parameters are tabulated the polymer/polymer miscibility can be predicted. So far ($\Delta E_{ij}$, $A_{ij}$)-values are known for $CH_2/CH_2COO$, $CH_2/CH_2Cl$ and $CH_2Cl/CH_2COO$. These were used to compute $\chi'_{12}$ with an error of less than 20% and the "miscibility window" for polyvinylchloride/polyesters which approximated fairly well to the experimental results.

The heat of mixing approach is a result of a conscientious drive to strike a balance between simplicity and precision of the theoretical description. Note that in the three discussed versions of this approach $\chi'_{ij}$ has been treated as independent of concentration, pressure, macromolecular structure (e.g. stereospecificity), molecular weight, molecular weight distribution, etc. Even more surprisingly, in the first two approaches the temperature effects were also neglected, while in the third only the quasichemical factor, $\exp\{-2\Delta E_{ij}/k_BT\}$, was assumed to affect the randomness of the contacts. Considering the severity of these assumptions, the success of the heat of mixing approach is remarkable. It is evident that this method will not be succesful in generating the phase diagram, but for estimating the blend miscibility it serves its purpose well.

### 2.3.7   Theory of Block Copolymer-Homopolymer Blends

In homopolymer/block polymer blends the usual mean field assumption breaks down. The system is phase-separated with thermodynamically defined microstructure and interphase region. To facilitate theoretical derivation, the free energy is usually calculated with reference to an arbitrary state, e.g. to that given by Huggins-Flory Eq (2.8) (*Hong* and *Noolandi*, 1981a). The theory allows calculation of the interfacial tension (*Hong* and *Noolandi*, 1981b,c; *Noolandi* and *Hong* 1982a), the structure and periodicity of microdomains as well as the phase diagrams (*Noolandi* and *Hong*, 1982b; *Noolandi*, 1984, 1985; *Whitmore* and *Noolandi*, 1985).

The free energy is expressed as:

$$G/RT = \frac{1}{2} \Sigma \frac{\chi_{ij}}{\varrho_{0j}} \int d^3r \varrho_i(r)\varrho_j(r) \quad - \frac{1}{12} \Sigma \frac{\sigma_{ij}^2}{\varrho_{0j}} \int d^3r \nabla \varrho_i(r) \nabla \varrho_j(r)$$

$$- \Sigma \int d^3r \varrho_i(r)\omega_i(r) \quad + \Sigma \frac{N_i}{Z_i} \ln \left( \frac{N_i}{Z_i L_i[\omega_i]} \right); \tag{2.37}$$

with    $L_i[\omega_i] = \int\int d^3r d^3r_0 Q_i(r,Z_i \mid r_0)$

where $\varrho_i(r)$ is the density of component i at point r, with $\varrho_{0i}$ the density of the neat component, and $\sigma_{ij}$ is the short-range interaction parameter. The first two terms in Eq (2.37) originate from, respectively, the local interactions between segments, as well as the short-range gradient. In the third term $\omega_i(r)$, represents conformational entropy changes in the interfacial regions. The last term accounts for the contribution to the configurational entropy. The number of polymer chains and the degree of polymerization are respectively denoted by $N_i$ and $Z_i$, Q is the polymer distribution function; for a homopolymer of type A, $Q_A(r,l \mid r_0)$ gives the probability of a polymer of length l with ends at $r_0$ and r.

The block copolymer/homopolymer blend phase diagram computed from Eq (2.37) (*Noolandi*, 1985) was in excellent qualitative agreement with the experimental observation (*Roe* and *Zin*, 1984; *Roe*, 1985) presented later in the text (Fig. 2.26, p. 73).

## 2.3.8  Summary

The lattice-model theories are most frequently used to interpret and to predict the phase equilibria in multicomponent systems containing polymers. There are others.

Since the early '80's the continuous thermodynamics of multicomponent systems has been making inroads into the discussion of the properties of PAB's (*Kehlen* and *Ratzsch*, 1983, 1984; *Ratzsch* et al., 1985). The advantage of the method is its inherent ability to consider polydisperse systems. As the later paper demonstrated (*Ratzsch* et al., 1986) the method allows prediction of several thermodynamic quantities from a single experimental function, viz. binodal. The polymer-polymer interaction parameter, $\chi'_{12}$, used by these authors is assumed to depend on both $\phi_2$ and T:

$$\chi'_{12} = (1+a_0\phi_2)(a_1+a_2/T) \tag{2.38}$$

The similarity of this relation to Eq (2.22) is to be noted; in both $\chi'_{12}$ is assumed to be independent of molecular weight (MW), and molecular weight distribution (MWD). With these assumptions the continuous thermodynamics allows e.g. the computation of MWD of both blend components in the two phases. An extensive review of the theory was published recently (*Ratzsch* and *Kehlen*, 1989).

The other theoretical approach has been used by *De Gennes* (1971, 1979), *Joanny* (1978), *Moore* (1977) and *Lifschitz* et al. (1978). These authors considered the thermodynamics of binary systems from the point of view of the dynamics of a single macromolecule. The work led to analysis of the critical fluctuation of concentration near the critical point, spinodal decomposition, dynamics of chain motion, the "coil-globule transition" and other fundamental aspects of the phase separation behaviour.

To summarize the lattice models of the liquid-liquid phase equilibria it should be noted that the Huggins-Flory Equation (2.8), in which $\chi'_{12}$ is considered constant, enthalpic in origin and as such non-negative, has a limited applicability to non-specific hydrocarbon solutions. Due to its inability to predict either LCST or the multi-critical point binodals its value for polymer blends must be judged as poor.

In polymer blends the combinatorial entropy is small and the miscibility is determined by the interactional term, $\chi'_{12}\phi_1\phi_2$ in Eq (2.8). In a sense the last forty years have been spent searching for the most suitable expression for $\chi'_{12}$. Theoretical derivations by *Maron, Flory, Patterson* and *Robard, Sanchez* and *Lacombe, Kleintjens* and *Koningsveld* provided explicit relations for $\chi'_{12}$, the one by *Simha* and *Jain* gives the equations from which $\chi'_{12}$ can be computed.

*Koningsveld* et al. (1974) noted that from the experimental point of view $\chi'_{12}$ must be a function of $\phi_2$ at least up to the $\phi_2^2$ term (in order to allow for multi-critical point phase separation curves), and it must decrease with T at a lower, and increase with T at a higher, range of temperature (to allow for UCST and LCST). These considerations lead to the empirical Eq (2.22). The need for incorporation of $\phi_2$ and T into the expression for $\chi'_{23}$ has been frequently demonstrated; e.g. *Chalykh* and *Avdeyev* (1985) found that in polyethylene/polydimethylsiloxane blends $\chi'_{23} \simeq -0.01 + 16.7 \; (2.8+\phi_1)/T$. Similar strong dependence on $\phi_2$ and a weaker one on T was reported by *Zhang* and *Prud'homme* (1987) for blends of caprolactone with copolymers of vinylchloride.

The influence of pressure, P, on phase separation is less well known. The pressure effects on the critical phenomena have been discussed by *Patterson* and *Robard* (1978), *Sanchez* (1978) and by *Jain* and *Simha* (1984). For non-aqueous systems with $\Delta H_m < 0$ the data indicated increase of miscibility with P whereas for those with $\Delta H_m > 0$, a decrease; $\partial T/\partial P$ at LCST was about ten times larger than that at UCST (*Rostami* and *Walsh*, 1984, 1985; *Walsh* and *Rostami*, 1985). For blends of poly-2,6-dimethyl-1,4-phenylene ether with a random copolymer of o- and p-fluorostyrene the gradient d(UCST)/dT $\simeq$ 64 to 108°C/GPa, depending on the copolymer composition (*Maeda* et al., 1986). For polystyrene/polyvinyl-methyl ether the gradient d(LCST)/dP = 300°C/GPa was reported (*Hiramatsu* et al., 1983). The authors observed that while spinodal decomposition is similar at low and high pressure the gradient it is lower the latter case.

The pressure effect on the phase diagram of polyethylacrylate/polyvinyl- fluoride blend (with LCST) was studied by *Suzuki* et al. (1982). The authors reported a complex dependence of the cloud point on P, T and composition, probably engendered by variation of $\chi'_{12}$ with $\phi_2$. *Walsh* and *Zoller* (1987) using pressure dilatometer determined phase diagram of polyethersulfone/polyethyleneoxide in a range of P $\leq$ 200 MPa. The phase separation was found to be accompanied by volume expansion. Both the LCST and the spinodal temperature, $T_s$, increased with P.

Using the listed empirical criteria it is evident that none of the existing theories directly satisfies all of them. The most promising are the gas-lattice model proposed by *Koningsveld* and his colleagues, and the one developed by *Simha* and his collaborators. In the first, only the concentration dependence is explicitly given, whereas both P and T effects are hidden in the $\alpha_i$, $\gamma_i$ and $\chi_{ii}^L$ parameters calculable from the P-V-T relation of pure substance i. In the latter, the pressure effect enters directly through the equation of state. To describe a two component mixture the theory requires information about the pure components (accessible from PVT-data) and two interaction parameters: energetic and volumetric. Once these are known the theory provides spectacular predictions, e.g. a phase diagram with LCST and UCST within a few degrees of the experimental (*Stroeks* and *Nies*, 1988). The most recent efforts are directed toward incorporation of the polydispersity factors.

# 2.4   Mechanisms of Phase Separation

As shown in Fig. 2.1, there are three regions of phase separation of a binary (or polydis-persed pseudo-binary) system: miscible, metastable and immiscible. Phase separation occurs in the two latter systems although by different mechanisms. In the metastable region bet-ween binodal and spinodal some form of activation mechanism must trigger the phase separation. In the immiscible region such a triggering is not needed – the phases separate spontaneously. Due to fluctuation of density within the metastable region the spinodal is a diffuse boundary – the need for activation rapidly vanishes as the conditions move from binodal to spinodal. The phase separation phenomena were reviewed by *Kwei* and *Wang* (1978), by *Olabisi, Robeson* and *Shaw* (1979), *Herkt-Maetzky* (1984), *Aifantis* (1986, 1987), *Hashimoto* (1987), *Nose* (1987), *Binder* (1987), *Hashimoto* (1988) and *Han* (1988). Only a brief description and resumé of the latest developments in the area will be given here.

Theories of dynamic phase separation are based on a mean field approach developed for metallurgical application by *Cahn* and *Hilliard* (1958), *Cahn* (1978). In this theory two types of quenching from a homogenous state have to be distinguished: (i) to the metastable, and (ii) to the spinodal region.

Consider for example, the phase diagram presented in the lower part of Fig. 2.1. Lower-ing the temperature from above the binodal into the metastable region (enclosed between the binodal and spinodal) provides for the first type of quench. Here, the initial evolution of the phase separation takes place by localized fluctuation of concentration (or density) and the mechanism responsible for phase separation is known as nucleation and growth, or NG. On the other hand, rapidly lowering the temperature from above the binodal through the metastable into the spinodal region (enclosed by the spinodal) provides for the latter type of quench. In the spinodal region the concentration fluctuations are delocalized, leading to long range spontaneous phase separation by what is known as the spinodal decomposition mechanism, or SD. The mean-field theory is not adequate to describe the phase dynamics of small molecule liquids, especially near the critical point. However, owing to large chain dimension and slow diffusion rates of macromolecules the theory is quite successful in describing the phase separation in polymer blends. The linearized theory was recently extended to polydisperse systems (*Schichtel* and *Binder,* 1987).

## 2.4.1   Nucleation and Growth (NG)

The metastable regions are located on the convex part of the $\Delta G_m$ vs. $x_2$ curve (Fig. 2.1), within the phase separation zone, i. e. where:

$$(\partial^2 \Delta G_m / \partial x^2)_{P,T} > 0 \qquad (2.39)$$

or where (*Sanchez,* 1983):

$$(\partial^2 \Delta G_m / \partial x^2)_v > v\beta \, (\partial^2 \Delta G_m / \partial x \partial v)^2_{P,T} \qquad (2.40)$$

(v is the specific volume of mixture and $\beta$ is the compressibility). For the phase separation to occur a "jump" has to be executed across to the other part of the $\Delta G_m$ vs. x curve along the tie-line located above the tangential line in Fig. 2.1, which defines the two binodal points at T, P = const. Such a "jump" requires an initial expenditure of energy, the activation energy of nucleation. Further separation into two phases (with composition defined by binodal) is spontaneous.

Nucleation is initiated by local fluctuations of density. The activation energy of nuclea-tion, $\delta E_N$, depends on the value of the interface energy required to create a nucleus, i.e. a product of the interfacial tension coefficient v and the surface of the nucleus, S. Following the nucleation the droplet grows by diffusion of macromolecules into the nucleated domains. The rate of this process can be approximated by the *Ostwald* (1900) ripening equation:

$$dV_d / dt \propto vx_e V_m D_t / RT \quad \text{or} \quad d \propto t^{1/n_c} \tag{2.41}$$

where $n_c \simeq 3$ is the coarsening exponent, d and $V_d$ are respectively the droplet diameter and volume, $x_e = b'$ or $b''$ is the equilibrium concentration, $V_m$ is the molar volume of the droplet phase and $D_t$ is the diffusion coefficient. Note (Fig. 2.6) that in NG region $x_e = $ const, independent of time. The diffusion stage of the droplet growth is followed by the coalescence coarsening, determined by the interphase energy balance (*Hashimoto* et al., 1986a; *Hashimoto*, 1988).

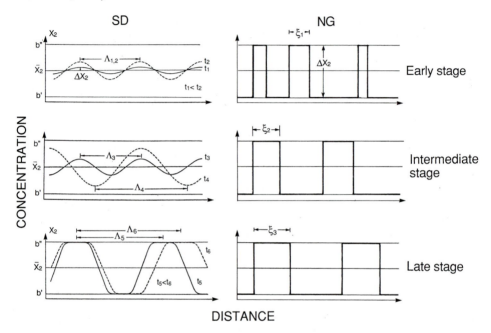

Fig. 2.6 A schematic representation of the early (top), intermediate and late (bottom) stage of phase separation for spinodal decomposition (SD, left) and nucleation and growth (NG, right) mechanism. Note that for SD at early stages the wavelength of concentration fluctuation $\Lambda(t_1) = \Lambda(t_2)$, but at the late stages $\Lambda(t_3) < \Lambda(t_4)$, where the phase separation times: $t_1 < t_2 \ll t_3 < t_4$.

The natural form of phase separation via the NG-mechanism is the droplet/matrix type, in the full range of concentration. Stabilization of the nucleated meta-stable system will determine the size of the droplet at equilibrium but not the form of phase separation.

As mentioned before, nucleation depends on the local density fluctuation which can be expressed in terms of the energy or concentration waves. The amplitude of these fluctuations depends on the distance from the critical conditions. As a consequence near the spinodal the distinction between the metastable and immiscible (spinodal) regions becomes diffused and phase separation can occur either by the NG mechanism or by spinodal decomposition, SD (*Langer*, 1977, 1980).

### 2.4.2    Spinodal Decomposition (SD)

As indicated in Fig. 2.1 the phase separation at $T_1$ leads to two phases with equilibrium composition $x_e = b'$ and $b''$, independently if the initial composition of quenched liquid is within the unstable SD region, $s' < x_2 < s''$, or within the metastable (NG) one, $b_1 \leqslant x_2 \leqslant s'$ or $s'' \leqslant x_2 \leqslant b''$. However, the mechanism of the early stage of phase separation in SD is quite different from that in the NG region. While in NG the composition of the separated domains, $x_e = b'$ or $b''$, is constant, with only the size and size distribution of nucleated drops changing with time, in SD both the composition and size depend on t (see Fig. 2.6). The time-dependent probability distribution function for concentration can be determined directly by digital image analysis method. For polystyrene/polyvinylmethylether (PS/PVME) blend the function changes with time from a sharp Gaussian to bimodal (*Tanaka* and *Nishi,* 1987).

In SD three stages of size growth can be identified (*Siggia,* 1979): diffusion, liquid flow and coalescence. The diffusion stage follows the Ostwald equation (2.41) and is limited to the earliest period with $d_0 \leqslant d \leqslant 5d_0$, where $d_0$, the initial diameter of the segregated region, decreases with increase of the quench depth $\Delta T = |T-T_c|$; for PS/PVME systems, the values of $d_0 = 9$, 3 and 2 nm at 82, 85 and 94°C respectively were estimated by *Voigt-Martin* et al. (1986). The authors also reported that the flow region is dominant, extending for $5d_0 \leqslant d = 0.9tv/\eta \leqslant 1\mu m \simeq d_{max}$ where $\eta$ is the viscosity of dispersed liquid (*Tomotika,* 1935). The values of $d_0$ and $d_{max}$ are not general but depend on molecular parameters. It is expected that the probability distribution function, Gaussian within the diffusion region, loses its regularity within the flow region and becomes bimodal within the last, the coalescence stage of SD. An example of the morphology developing during SD is shown in Fig. 2.7. The importance of the coarsening flow mechanism is quite evident. In micrographs 6 to 8 coarsening due to coalescence takes place (*Reich,* 1986). The author observed that when the time axis is reversed the process resembles a phenomenon of creation of infinite clusters, successfully treated by the percolation theory.

Fig. 2.7 Development of morphology in polymer blends following SD (after *Reich,* 1986).

Description of the dynamics of phase separation within the SD domain starts with balance between the thermodynamics and material flux. *Cahn* and *Hilliard* (1958) are credited for solving the dynamic flux equation. They obtained the diffusion equation:

$$\partial\phi / \partial t = M(\partial^2 G / \partial\phi^2) \nabla^2\phi - 2MK\nabla^4\phi + \dots \tag{2.42}$$

where M is the mobility constant and K is the energy gradient term. For negative values of $\partial^2 G / \partial\phi^2$ the solution of Eq (2.42) is inherently unstable. Truncating the relation after the second term and integrating leads to:

$$\phi - \bar\phi = \sum_\beta \{ \exp[R(\beta)t] \} [A\cos(\beta r) + B\sin(\beta r)] \tag{2.43}$$

where $\bar\phi = x_2$ is the average, uniform concentration, $\beta$ is the wave number of the sinusoidal composition fluctuation, r is the position variable, A and B are $\beta$-dependent parameters and

$$R(\beta) = -M\beta^2 [D + 2K\beta^2] \tag{2.44}$$

is the Rayleigh kinetic growth factor, which can be thought of as a first-order rate constant describing the SD. In Eq (2.44) D is the second derivative of the free energy of mixing given by Eq (2.5). There are two magnitudes of the scattering vector $\beta$ for R to vanish: $\beta_1 = 0$ and $\beta_2 = (-D/2K)^{\frac{1}{2}}$. Because of the exponential form of Eq (2.43) the phase separation process is dominated by the fluctuations with the wave vector $\beta$, defined by setting the first derivative of Eq (2.44) to zero:

$$\beta_m = (-D/4K)^{\frac{1}{2}} ; R_m = -MD\beta_m^2/2 \tag{2.45}$$

with the product $MD \equiv D^C$ being the Cahn-Hilliard diffusion constant. Both D and M are temperature dependent. For deuterated PS/PVME $D \propto (1/T - 1/T_s)$, whereas $d\ln M/d(1/T) = -155kJ/mol$ was reported by *Sato* and *Han* (1988).

It can be seen that from the nature of Eqs (2.43)-(2.44) outside the spinodal region $D > 0$, $R < 0$ and concentration fluctuations are rapidly damped. At the spinodal $\beta = \beta_m$ and $R_m = D = 0$. The plot of $R_m = R_m(T)$ or $D = D(T)$ is used to define the spinodal temperature, $T_s$.

For the one-dimensional case Eq (2.43) can be approximated by:

$$\phi - \bar\phi \doteq \exp\{R(\beta_m)t\} A(\beta_m) \cos(\vec\beta_m r) \tag{2.43a}$$

In short, the *Cahn* and *Hilliard* approach provides a qualitatively correct description of SD. However, it over-emphasizes the difference in the mechanism of phase separation at the spinodal boundary. Infinitesimal changes in concentration or temperature which cause change of sign of $(\partial^2 G_m/\partial\phi^2) \equiv D$ would cause a dramatic change of behaviour – for $D > 0$ the meta-stable system would not phase-separate (at least not by the SD-mechanism), whereas for $D < 0$ the system would spontaneously decompose. In nature such a discontinuity of behaviour is rarely observed. In the case of polymer blends the "diffuseness" of the spinodal is a well-known phenomenon (*Snyder* et al., 1983). The "diffuseness" may originate in polydispersity and/or thermal fluctuations.

The most frequently used method of studying the kinetics of phase separation involves time-resolved scattering techniques, with light, neutrons or other irradiation sources. There is a direct relation between the compositional wavenumber $\beta$ and the q-vector measured in scattering experiment:

$$\beta = q = (4\pi/\lambda) \sin(\theta/2) \tag{2.46}$$

where $\lambda$ is the wavelength and $\vartheta$ the scattering angle. The scattering intensity ratio:

$$I(q,t)/I(q,t_0) = \exp\{2R(q)t\} \tag{2.47}$$

From Eqs (2.44) and (2.47)

$$- (\partial^2 \Delta G_m/\partial x^2) = \lim_{q \to 0} (R(q)/M(q)^2) \tag{2.48}$$

allowing for direct correlation between the scattering variables and thermodynamic quantities such as interaction parameter, concentration fluctuations, etc., usually expressed in terms of the ratios $\phi/\phi_s$ or $T/T_s$ (the subscript s refers to spinodal). As demonstrated in several publications (*Izutimani* and *Hashimoto*, 1985; *Kumaki* and *Hashimoto*, 1986; *Hashimoto*, 1987) in the early stage of phase separation and for small values of $q \lesssim q_m \simeq$ 10 mm$^{-1}$ the Cahn-Hilliard relations provide a good description and an easy method of determining the molecular parameters for the diversity of polymeric systems.

Similar conclusions were reported earlier on the basis of Monte Carlo simulations (*Heermann*, 1984a). The author reported that the onset of non-linearity depends on concentration. The theory breaks down in the immediate vicinity of the spinodal. Numerical simulation of the region between NG and SD (*Heermann*, 1984b, 1985) allowed a dynamic spinodal with a transient percolating structure to be postulated. The divergence between the classical mean-field definition of spinodal and its dynamic analog decreases with increase of the interaction range. The simulation also revealed that in the early stage of phase separation the coarsening exponent $n_c$ in Eq (2.41) does not necessarily equal 3, as postulated by *Ostwald* (1900), *Lifschitz* and *Slyozov* (1961) or *Wagner* (1961). *Ratke* and *Thieringer* (1985) calculated that only for particle growth (coarsening) in stationary fluid is $n_c = 3$, whilst it decreases in the presence of flow:

$$(\bar{d}/d_o)^{n_c} = 1 + K_c t \tag{2.41a}$$

where $\bar{d}$ is the average droplet diameter. The coarsening exponent varied from $n_c = 5/2$ to $3/2$ depending on the flow type. $K_c$, the coarsening rate constant, was found to increase strongly with volume fraction of the dispersed phase (*Ardell*, 1972).

Both *Cook* (1970) and *Langer* et al. (1974, 1975) incorporated the heat fluctuation into the initial flux equation. The truncated relation derived by the first author improved the accuracy for describing the initial stage of SD, but did not allow for the observed coarsening process ed the latter stage. The relation derived by *Langer* et al. was rather complex and had to be solved numerically. It had proper bounds; it predicted the initial SD well but failed at longer times (*Snyder* and *Meakin*, 1985). The mode-coupling hydrodynamic effects were included by *Kawasaki* and *Ohta* (1978), by *Ohta* and *Kawasaki* (1978) as well as by *Siggia* (1979). The dependencies were found to be adequate to describe SD in the later stages of separation.

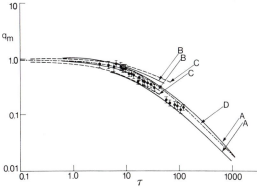

Fig. 2.8 Comparison of $q_m$ vs. $\tau$ behavior found in small molecule systems (A), inorganic glasses (B), metallic alloys (C) and high molecular weight polymer blends (points). Also shown is dependence predicted by Equation (2.50) (D); after *Suyder* and *Meakin* (1983).

The generality of the initial SD behaviour for metallic alloys, inorganic glasses, small molecular systems, and polymer blends was observed by *Snyder* and *Meakin* (1983). The authors reported that for all these systems $q_m$ is a single parameter function of $\tau$, where $\tau$ is the reduced time:

$$q_m = \zeta_0 \, \beta_m; \qquad \tau = tD_0^c/\zeta_0^2 \qquad\qquad (2.49)$$

where $D_0^c$ and $\zeta_0$ are respectively the diffusion coefficient and the concentration correlation length at the quench time, t=0.

The empirical relation illustrated in Fig. 2.8 has the form:

$$\ln q_m = -\ln(1+a\tau) \qquad\qquad (2.50)$$

with the numerical constant taken as a = 0.05. Similarly, the maximum scattering intensity was found to scale with $\tau$. It should be noted that $D_0$ for these systems vary within 7.5 decades! The observed general validity of Eq (2.49) indicates that SD is surprisingly insensitive to the molecular nature of the liquids, although there are indications that it may be limited to liquids with low degree of entanglement (*Hashimoto* et al., 1986b; *Hashimoto*, 1988). Note that Cahn-Hilliard linear theory was found to be valid for $\tau \leqslant 2.7$ (*Izumitani* and *Hashimoto*, 1985).

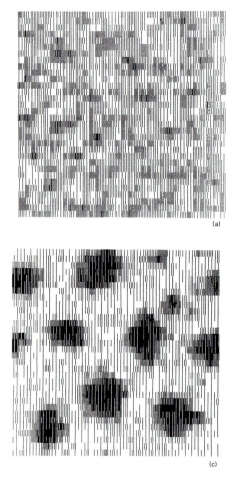

(a)

(b)

(c)

Fig. 2.9a Computer simulated concentration distribution during early stage by spinodal decomposition. The degree of darkness is proportional to concentration. The Figs. (a), (b), and (c) represent the concentration distribution at the times $10\tau_0$, $56\tau_0$ and $223\tau_0$ respectively, after the quench.

The SD was computer simulated using finite-difference in time and space, Runge-Kutta and Monte Carlo with a Hamiltonian methods (*Petschek* and *Metiu,* 1983; *Meakin* and *Reich,* 1982; *Meakin* et al., 1983). The prime reason for simulation has been the uncertainty of, on one hand, the validity of various assumptions made in developing the SD theories, and on the other, the reliability and precision of the scattering methods used to validate them. Both simulation methods were found to be equivalent (*Meakin* et al., 1983), provided that the Monte Carlo number of attempts, N, was properly related to the real time appearing in the Runge-Kutta integration, $t = N(\delta\psi_{max})^2/12$, where $\delta\psi_{max}$ is the Monte Carlo time evolution step size. In deriving this dependence small step sizes and high Langevin friction coefficient were assumed. The results of the simulation (*Petschek* and *Metiu,* 1983) are presented in Figs. 2.9a and b as concentration patterns in the NG and SD regions, respectively.

It is evident that modern theories of polymer dynamics reproduce the observed pattern of phase separation in both regions. The NG and SD mechanisms are two features of the liquid/liquid kinetics of phase behaviour moderated by the thermodynamics of phase equilibrium. The unity of the phase separation dynamics on both sides of the spinodal has been emphasized by *Leibler* (1980) and *Yerukhimovich* (1982). In the theoretical treatment by the latter author the wave number β was expressed in terms of the structural matrix of the system. The matrix contained information on the macromolecular architecture, polydisper-

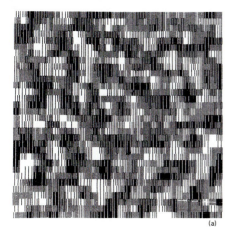

(a)

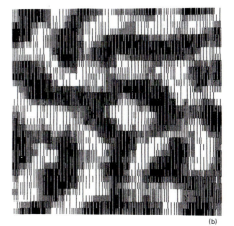

(b)

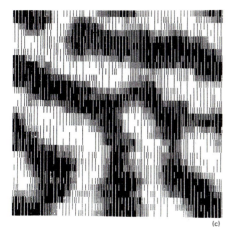

(c)

Fig. 2.9b Same as Fig. 2.9a but for an off-critical NG quench (*Peschek* and *Metiŭ,* 1983).

sity and composition. The difference in SD for block, graft and random copolymers was demonstrated numerically. The theory was found to correlate quite well with the experimental results of the spinodal temperature dependence on molecular structure.

The difference in concentration pattern evolution for NG and SD regions originates in the differences of early stages of separation shown in Fig. 2.6. Provided that the concentration of the minor phase is above 10 to 15%, the SD occurs via rapid growth of regularly spaced interpenetrated structures. Neglecting the fine structure of the dispersed phase the phase separation by NG and SD mechanism for low concentration of the minor phase looks similar. At the latter stages in both regions the Ostwald ripening as well as other mechanisms generate a droplet/matrix morphology (*Hasegawa* et al., 1988).

The dynamics of concentration fluctuation and SD were studied by *de Gennes* (1979, 1980), *Joanny* (1978), *Joanny* and *Brochard* (1981), *Brochard* and *de Gennes* (1983), and *Pincus* (1981). The starting point was the extension of the Huggins-Flory Equation (2.8) by adding the third, kinetic term:

$$\Delta = \langle r^2 \rangle \, (\nabla \phi)^2 \, / \, 36 \phi_1 \phi_2 \tag{2.51}$$

where $\langle r^2 \rangle = Na^2$ is the mean square end-to-end distance of the macromolecular coil, N = $N_1 = N_2$ is the degree of polymerization and $\nabla \phi$ allows for fluctuation of $\phi$. The motion of macromolecules was treated according to the reptation concept. The authors derived the relaxation spectrum in terms of $\chi'_{12, \phi}$ and $\langle r^2 \rangle$. They concluded that the wavelength of the unstable mode of SD near the spinodal is comparable to $\langle r_\Theta^2 \rangle^{\frac{1}{2}}$ (unperturbed dimension), i.e. it should scale as $N^{\frac{1}{2}}$, whereas the growth rate being proportional to the reptation diffusion constant should scale as $N^{-2}$. However, for very deep quenching within the spinodal region the separation may occur on the scale $N_e^{\frac{1}{2}}$ where $2N_e$ is the entanglement degree of polymerization.

*Gelles* and *Frank* (1983) extended this treatment to the unsymmetrical molecular weight case $N_1 \neq N_2$, deriving for the growth rate of concentration fluctuations with wavenumber $\beta$ the following dependence:

$$1/\tau(b_m) \propto (T\mu_0 N_e/a^2) \, \phi_1 \phi_2 \, (\chi_{12} - \chi_{12, s})^2$$
$$\times (\phi_1 N_1 + \phi_2 N_2) \, / \, [\chi_{12, s} \, N_1 N_2 (\phi_1 N_2 + \phi_2 N_1)] \tag{2.52}$$

where $\mu_0$ is the microscopic mobility (assumed to be the same for both polymers) and $\chi_{12, s}$ is the interaction parameter evaluated at the spinodal. The authors found that the growth rate of the dominant concentration fluctuation (during initial stage of decomposition) increases with $N_1$ as predicted by Eq (2.52) but its absolute magnitude is about four times smaller than theoretically predicted.

*Herkt-Maetzky* and *Schelten* (1983) as well as *Herkt-Maetzky* (1984) examined the correlation between the mean-field SD theories and experimental results. They found that in general the predictions provided good approximation of the general behaviour of polymer blends with the scaling parameters for the correlation length and the susceptibility in agreement with the theory. However, the fundamental assumption of the theory that $\chi_{12}$ does not depend on $\phi$ was found to be incorrect (see Fig. 2.10); similar results were previously reported by other authors both for polymer blends (*Wendorff*, 1980) and polymer solutions (*Kamide* and *Miyazaki*, 1981).

The Monte Carlo simulation has been used to study details of SD. The rate of quenching was found to have very large effect on $R(\beta)$ (*Carmesin* et al, 1986). The SD in two dimensions was found to follow a non-exponential kinetics (*Baumgärtner* and *Heermann*, 1986), at variance with the Cahn-Hilliard prediction for three-dimensional systems.

By contrast with the preoccupation with the kinetics of phase separation, the studies of phase dissolution are less popular (*Piglowski* et al. 1986). Since most PAB's show a LCST behavior, the dissolution of the separated phase upon cooling has direct implications in

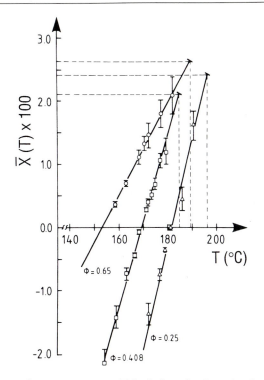

Fig. 2.10 An average interaction parameter $\bar{\chi}$ vs. T for indicated volume fractions of PVME blended with deuterated PS. Dotted lines represent the spinodal conditions (after *Herkt-Maetzky* and *Schelten* (1983).

industrial practice. The dissolution of both SD and NG morphologies present in unstable and metastable phase regions, respectively, was found to be the same (*Kumaki* and *Hashimoto, 1986*) with $R(q)/q^2 \simeq$ constant as given by Eq (2.48) for phase separation.

The above discussion concentrated on the effect of temperature on phase equilibrium in binary polymer mixtures. However, one should not forget that in industrial practice the other independent variables may be of equal importance. For example, the previously discussed effect of pressure on phase separation behavior is being used to control the morphology of PAB's (*Kleintjens*, 1986). The imposition of stress also affects the phase equilibrium. Use of simple shear stress to generate either NG or SD morphology at constant T,P has been experimentally demonstrated (*Lyngaae-Jorgensen* and *Sondergard*, 1987). When polymer blends are cast from a common solvent, the type of solvent, solution concentration, temperature and method of casting may dramatically affect the blend morphology and its final performance. It was shown that the interconnected SD morphology leads to high modulus, typical of one of the components, and high maximum strain at break, characteristic of the other (*Inoue* et al., 1985, 1987). Flash evaporation seems to provide means of extending this method to commercial applications other than assymetric cast-film (*Nauman* et al., 1986).

The SD leads to three-dimensional co-continuous PAB morphology responsible for the outstanding, synergistic performance of blends, e.g. chemical resistance or mechanical properties. In principle, any variable which affects the phase diagram can be used for generation of such a structure. P, T, $\phi$, and stress field have already been already mentioned. Compatibilization by means of a co-solvent provides another possibility.

Co-continuity can also be obtained near the phase inversion concentration without aid of SD. There are three basic differences between these two mechanisms: (i) SD originates in a homogenous, miscible system via quenching to the spinodal region, whereas inversion is a change of morphology in an immiscible blend, (ii) SD occurs at any concentration whereas the inversion is usually restricted to a higher range (see Part 3), and (iii) SD generates fine morphology, initially in the nanometer size range, whereas phase inversion leads to much coarser structures of the order of 0.1 to 10 μm. In short, SD provides finer control of properties in a wider range of concentrations than does inversion, but is restricted to systems which can be made miscible (viz. Table 1.2). On the other hand phase inversion is a general phenomenon in immiscible blends usually taking place at high concentrations. Toughening thermoplastics by addition of a compatible elastomer has been known since its first incorporation into PS in the early 40's (Table 1.2). More recently engineering resins, e.g. polyamides, have been toughened by the addition of hydrocarbon rubber (*S. Wu*, 1983), poly-(ethylene-g-maleic anhydride) (*Hobbs* et al., 1983), partially hydrollzed poly(ethylene-co-vinylacetate) (*Han* and *Chuang,* 1985), etc.

New toughened polyamide/acrylonitrile-butadiene-styrene copolymer blends were commercialized by Monsanto Chem. Co. under the trade name Triax (*Lavengood* and *Silver,* 1987). These materials show excellent toughness, chemical resistance and resistance to multiaxial stress, engendered by fine three-dimensional co-continuous structure with submicron dimensions. The performance is particularly good for compositions near 50:50 vol%, where the co-continuity seems to be at its best. Usually an acidic compatibilizer (e.g. styrene-acrylonitrile-maleic anhydride copolymer) is required to ensure fine dispersion (*Lavengood* et al., 1986; *Lavengood* and *Padwa,* 1988).

## 2.5    Semi-Crystalline Polymer Blends

### 2.5.1    General Types of Polymer Blends

In the preceding parts only the liquid/liquid phase separation was considered. However, from the commercial point of view, the semi-crystalline polymers are of prime importance. Suffice it to point out that of the four commodity resins: polyethylene (35 wt% of the market), polystyrene (14%), polyvinyl chloride (13%) and polypropylene (9%), constituting 71 wt% of all polymers (the remaining 29% of the market is shared between all other thermoplastics - 17% and thermosets - 12%) only polystyrene is non-crystalline.

In formulating polymer blends a serious consideration must be given to three factors: (1) are the resins semi-crystalline, C, or amorphous, A, (2) will they be compounded and processed in the liquid state, and (3) will properties of the blend prepared under a given set of conditions be stable under another set imposed by the product use? It is known that most substances tend to crystallize pure. The additives are normally expelled from the growing crystal. For polymer blends this frequently means that, independently of miscibility in the liquid state, there is phase segregation at crystallization temperatures. Some polymers have a melting point higher than the customary compounding and/or processing temperature. A typical example is polyvinylchloride, PVC. If the second polymer forms very strong specific interactions with PVC, then the crystals may be dissolved or not, depending on the actual blend and blending conditions. Lastly, even in a pair of amorphous polymer blends the system may be miscible during processing (e.g. extrusion) and immiscible at ambient conditions, or vice-versa.

On the previous pages the sensitivity of the phase equilibria was discussed. One can expect that all factors affecting the molecular weight and molecular weight distribution may have a profound effect on phase separation in polymer blends, viz. degradation, branching, crosslinking, oxidation, dehydrochlorination, etc. In short, one should not expect that statements such as: "polymers A and B form homogeneous blends" will be universally true. Immiscibility occurs so much more frequently that miscibility should be treated as an exception observed only under a precisely defined set of conditions. One of the most serious problems facing the polymer blend industry is stabilization of the desired properties (i.e. elimination of residual stresses and stabilization of the process-generated morphology) at conditions of normal use of the manufactured part.

In amorphous polymer blends, A/A, the miscibility phenomena should be considered only within one phase: liquid or glass. Considering the whole range of experimental conditions A/A may be miscible, m, immiscible, im, or partially miscible, pm, i.e. miscible within one zone of conditions and immiscible in another.

In an amorphous resin blend with a semi-crystalline one, A/C, the situation is more complex. If processing occurs above the glass transition of A, i.e. $T_{proc} > T_g(A)$, and above the melting point of C, $T_{proc} > T_m(C)$, both the phase equilibrium at $T_{proc}$ and crystallization upon cooling must be considered. In this case: at $T_{proc}$ the system is either m or im, but at T $< T_m$ the semi-crystalline resin may supercool or crystallize. Supercooling allows consideration of A/C as A/A, i.e. three possibilities would exist: m, im and pm. On the other hand crystallization generates two states: amorphous, a, and crystalline, c, within the A/C system, increasing the number of possibilities to six: A/C(a): m, im, pm, each with two possible versions of the crystalline phase: A/C(c):m, im, where A/C(c)m indicate a thermodynamic interaction between A and crystals of C.

This discussion can readily be extended to blends of two semi-crystalline resins, C/C. Considering that by virtue of the NG and SD mechanisms the phase separation may lead to different morphologies which will be reflected in the morphology of a and c phases, it is apparent that the phase separation in binary blends can be rather complex. In industrial applications the situation is further complicated not only because of the multicomponent nature of industrial formulas, but also because $T_{proc}$ may be below $T_m$ of some of these and the equilibrium thermodynamic condition is never reached.

The phase equilibria in semi-crystalline polymer blends have been discussed (*MacKnight* et al., 1978; *Olabisi* et al., 1979). In the following part a brief outline of polymer crystallization will be given. Interested readers should consult the subject literature (*Wunderlich*, 1976, 1980). Recent developments in crystallization of "miscible polymer blends" will be discussed in the latter part of this chapter.

### 2.5.2   Polymer Crystallization

The discussion on the crystallization of neat polymers can be directly applied to immiscible polymer blends, where the crystallization takes place within a domain of nearly pure resin, largely unaffected by the presence of other macromolecules. A study of the crystallization behavior can provide valuable information on the miscibility, interactions between the ingredients and even on degree of dispersion.

Crystallization from the melt takes place when the system is cooled below the equilibrium melting point, $T_m°$, i.e. to the crystallization temperature $T_c \leq T_m°$. The difference $\Delta_c = T_m°$ $- T_c$ is a measure of supercooling, which in turn depends on the cooling rate and nucleation mechanisms. There are three mechanisms: (i) spontaneous homogeneous nucleation which occurs (rarely) in the supercooled homogeneous melt, (ii) orientation induced nucleation caused by alignment of macromolecules and spontaneous crystallization, and (iii) heterogeneous nucleation on the surface of a foreign phase. In preparation of thermoplastic blends the mechanisms (ii) and (iii) are most important. Shear crystallization of polyolefins is known to occur at temperatures 20-30°C higher than $T_m$ (*Dumoulin* et al, 1984a,b). The heterogeneous nucleation due to the presence of the other crystalline polymer in the blend was found to virtually prevent the possibility of supercooling of polyethyleneterephthalate (PET) into an amorphous state (*Kamal* et al., 1982, 1983; *Pillon* and *Utracki*, 1984, 1985, 1986).

A simple but informative method of analysis, proposed years ago (*Hoffman* and *Weeks*, 1962) is illustrated in Fig. 2.11. A plot of the observable melting and crystallization temperatures, $T_m$ vs. $T_c$, where $T_c$ is obtained from a static (isothermal) or dynamic (scanning) experiment, allows determination of the equilibrium melting point, $T_m^\circ = T_c^\circ$, of a given polymer. The absence of linearity provides information on the inclusion of defects into the crystalline network. The graph gives direct information on the degree of supercooling, $\Delta_c$, and allows the lamellar thickness to be determined. The plot was found to be valid for PAB as well (*Eshuis* et al., 1982; *Martuscelli* et al., 1982, 1984).

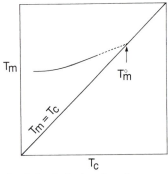

Fig. 2.11 Hoffman-Weeks plot for defect inclusions in polymer crystals at low $T_c$ (high crystallization rate). The equilibrium melting point, $T_m^0$ is also indicated.

The crystallization proceeds through a series of stages: melt, nucleation, lamellar growth, spherulitic growth, aggregate growth. Depending on the crystallization conditions, i.e. nucleation mechanism, the rate and extent of crystallization, various types of morphology can be obtained, viz. single lamellar crystals, axialities, dendrites, extended chain, fibrillar, epitaxial, etc. Furthermore in some polymers, depending on the conditions (e.g. pressure, composition or strain), more than one type of crystalline lattice structure can be generated (*Zoller* and *Bolli*, 1980; Yip, 1981; *Chow*, 1981; *Nishi*, 1985).

The rate of nucleation can be expressed as (*Turnbull* and *Fisher*, 1949):

$$N = N_0 \exp\left\{-(E_0 + \Delta G_0^*)/RT\right\} \tag{2.53}$$

where $N_0$ is a measure of the concentration of the polymer segments, $E_0$ is the energy of activation for transport across the liquid-nucleus interface and $\Delta G_0^*$ is the free energy for forming a nucleus. Equation (2.53) has been modified by *Hoffman* and *Lauritzen* (1961) by replacing the $\Delta G_0^*/RT$ term with a modified segmental jump rate term: $U^*/(T-T_\infty)$. In the latter expression $U^*$ represents the activation energy for transport of crystallizable segment through the melt to the crystallization side and $T_\infty$ is a hypothetical temperature at which viscous flow ceases: $T_\infty = T_g - C$, where $C \simeq 50^\circ C$ is a constant. The Hoffman-Lauritzen equation can be written as

$$-\ln(N/N_0) = K_g/\Delta_c Tf + U^*/(T-T_\infty) \tag{2.54}$$

where on the right hand side the first term is equal to $E_0/RT$ in Eq (2.53). The parameter f = $2T/(T_m^\circ + T)$ corrects the bulk free energy difference between the supercooled liquid and the crystal at large $\Delta_c$. The parameter $K_g$ can be expressed as (*Lauritzen* and *Hoffman*, 1973):

$$K_g = n_a\, b_0\, \nu\, \nu_e\, T_m^\circ/k_B\Delta H_f \tag{2.55}$$

where $n_a = 4$ or 2 for respectively the regime I or II kinetics (in I formation of surface nucleus is followed by rapid completion of the substrate, whereas in II the nuclei form on the substrate), $b_0$ is the crystallite plane monomolecular thickness, $v$ and $v_e$ are respectively the side and end interfacial energies, $k_B$ is the Boltzmann constant and $\Delta H_f$ is the heat of fusion. The overall rate of crystallization (G) is proportional to the rate of nucleation and the rate of growth around the nucleus. The formation of the primary nucleus, as discussed above, creates stresses in its immediate vicinity, which in turn are responsible for secondary nucleation. The secondary nucleation is often the primary mechanism of crystal growth. Under steady state growth the rate determining step is the primary nucleation and the overall rate of crystallization as given by Eqs (2.53) and (2.54) in which N and $N_0$ are replaced by G and $G_0$ respectively and T is taken as the crystallization temperature, $T_c$.

The macroscopic crystallization is frequently analyzed in terms of the empirical *Avrami* (1939, 1940) equation:

$$\ln \phi_a = -K_A(t-t_0)n_A \qquad (2.56)$$

where $\phi_a$ is the volume fraction of the amorphous phase ($\phi_a + \phi_c = 1$), $t_0$ is the induction time, while $K_A$ and $n_A$ are Avrami parameters; $t_0$ and $n_A$ are shear sensitive (*Sherwood et al.*, 1978). The parameter $n_A$ is frequently refered to as dimensionality. Concise but comprehensive reviews of Eq (2.56) are given by *Wunderlich* (1976, 1980) and *Hay* (1979).

The direct assignment of the physical meaning to $K_A$ and $n_A$ can be obtained by comparing the Avrami equation with either the rate Equations (2.53), (2.54) or with the computational results of the Witten-Sander model of diffusion limited aggregation (*Witten and Sander*, 1981). In the first case the rate constant $K_A$ can be expressed directly in terms of the rate theory parameters, $E_0$ and $\Delta G_0^*$. In the second $n_A$ can be correlated with the exponent $\beta$, defined by the relation:

$$\phi_c \propto t^\beta \qquad (2.57)$$

For three-dimensional growth $\beta$ changes from 5/3 (low concentration of aggregated particles) to 3 (high concentration). The results were computed by *Meakin* and *Deutch* (1984) using the Monte Carlo simulation for constant nucleation density. The method is powerful and can be extended to two-dimensional aggregation, non-stationary nucleation and other cases. Its particular value is on the one hand the exact correlation between $\beta$ and the Hansdorff dimensionality and on the other the ability to clearly separate various influences on the overall crystallization process.

Extension of the Hoffman-Lauritzen theory predicts the variation of the melting point, $T_m$, with the thickness of the lamella, L:

$$T_m = T_m^{\circ}(1-2v_e/\Delta H_f L) \qquad (2.58)$$

where $T_m^{\circ}$ is the maximum value of $T_m$ determined for the equilibrium crystal having the maximum lamellar thickness, $L_{max}$. The interfacial energy, $v_e$, plays the role of a magnifying parameter for this effect, i.e. the variation in L will have a particularly strong effect on $T_m$ in multicomponent systems.

The initial lamella thickness is given by:

$$L^* = 2 v_e T_m^{\circ}/\Delta H_f \Delta_c + k_B T/v\, b_0 \qquad (2.59)$$

with the first term usually the dominant one.

The pressure dependence of $T_m$ can be calculated from the Clausius-Clapeyron equation:

$$\ln T_m = \ln T_{m,0} + \int_0^P (\Delta v/\Delta H_f)\, dP \qquad (2.60)$$

where $T_{m,0} = T_m(P = 0)$, and $\Delta v$ is a difference in specific volume between amorphous and crystalline phases. Within a narrow range of P the slowly varying ratio can be replaced by its average:

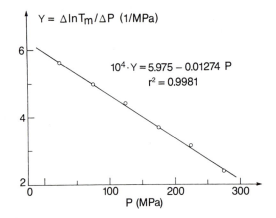

Fig. 2.12 Pressure dependence of $T_m$ for aliphatic polyester-6,6; (data from *Aylwin* and *Boyd*, 1984).

$$\Delta v/\Delta H_f \simeq \overline{\Delta v/\Delta H_f} \tag{2.61}$$

Under these conditions a plot of $\ln T_m$ vs. P would be linear. In Fig. 2.12 the data reported for poly-2,5-hexamethyleneadipate by *Aylwin* and *Boyd* (1984) are replotted as:

$$Y \equiv (\Delta \ln T_m/\Delta P) = \overline{\Delta v/\Delta H_f} \tag{2.62}$$

vs. the pressure. The least squares analysis yields:

$$Y \cdot 10^4 = 5.975 - 0.01274 \, P \, (MPa) \tag{2.63}$$

with the correlation coefficient squared $r^2 = 0.9981$. The value of Y at P = 0 is: $Y_0 \cdot 10^4 = 5.975$, which agrees with those calculated from independent thermodynamic measurements: $Y_0 \cdot 10^4 = 5.63$ to $6.23$. This encouraging result indicates that Eqs (2.60)–(2.63) can be used to determine the pressure variation of $\Delta H_f$, provided that the compressibility of the material is known (*Harrison* and *Runt, 1980; Runt* et al., 1980).

The morphology of the semi-crystalline polymers, the molecular ordering within the crystal and the structure of the crystal/amorphous phase interface are of continual interest and controversy. For steady state crystallization from melt the lamellar model with pre-adjacent reentry is favored by theoretical arguments (*Dimarzio* and *Guttman, 1980; Dimar-zio* et al., 1980), as well as experimental results (*Reault* et al., 1980; *Robelin* et al., 1980). A quantitative model for flow induced crystallization was proposed by *McHugh* (1982).

The above discussion is limited to the pure case of a kinetically controlled process. In industry the crystallization is frequently limited by heat flux. It is important to recognize that for a general case both these effects must be simultaneously taken into account. The non-isothermal crystallization has been theoretically treated by *Ziabicki* (1974). The theory was found to well describe the crystallization of polyoxyethylene in its blends with polymethyl-methacrylate (*Addonizio* et al., 1987).

A mathematical model for crystallization from the melt was developed by *Illin* et al. (1983). The authors incorporated the Avrami-Hoffman-Lauritzen kinetics into the Fourier heat conduction equation. The resulting differential equations could be analytically solved only for limited applications. The finite-difference computations indicated an excellent agreement between theory and experiment.

Crystallization during injection molding of semi-crystalline polymers is of great practical interest. The problem has been successfully treated by *Kamal* and collaborators (*Kenig* and *Kamal,* 1970; *Kamal* and *Lafleur,* 1984, 1986; *Lafleur* and *Kamal,* 1986).

To close this section on polymer crystallization it is worth pointing out a new method for studying the crystallization process with great potential for providing detailed information on kinetics and phase mobility in crystallizing PAB (*Tanaka* and *Nishi*, 1986). Real-time pulsed nuclear magnetic resonance, RTP-NMR allows measurement of both spin-spin relaxation time, $T_2$, and spin-lattice relaxation time in the rotating frame, $T_{1,\varrho}$, as the crystallization progresses. From these the content as well as the mobility (relaxation times) in the crystalline, intermediate and amorphous phase can be determined. Four crystallization time periods were identified: I. induction, II. nucleation, III. steady state crystallization, and IV. secondary crystallization. During I, $T_2$ of the amorphous and intermediate phases slightly decreased. In II the amount of the crystalline and intermediate phase increased, $T_2$ of these two phases decreased while that of the amorphous one was constant. In III, $T_2$ of the crystalline and intermediate phase reached their final value. Finally in IV, there was a slow, continuous decrease of $T_2$ and the content of the amorphous phase; the volume of the interface region decreased as well.

The results indicate that crystallization generates an ordered structure not only in the crystalline phase, but (to a lesser extent!) in the amorphous phase as well. This ordering (deduced from the decrease of $T_2$ by a factor of two) must be related to a change of density of the amorphous phase. As a consequence, RTP-NMR raises serious questions regarding validity of the dilatometric method to studies of the polymer crystallization. For example when RTP-NMR results were analyzed in terms of the Avrami Equation (2.56) $n_A = 2.5$ (related to formation of lamellae) was found; dilatometry gave $n_A = 3.17$, too large to be considered a measure of dimensionality.

### 2.5.3   Crystallization in Miscible Polymer Blends

The crystallization kinetics of neat polymer, as discussed in the preceeding Part 2.5.2, is directly applicable to crystallization of immiscible blends. Here the other limiting case, that of miscible blends, will be considered. The starting point is a single phase melt from which one component crystallizes out. As demonstrated by *Nishi* and *Wang* (1975, 1977) the melting point of the crystals $(T_m)$ can be related to that of neat polymer $T_m^{(0)}$ by the relation:

$$(1/T_m) - (1/T_m^{(0)}) = -(RV_{2u}/\Delta H_{2u}V_{1u})\left[(\ln\phi_2)/m_2 + (m_2^{-1} - m_1^{-1})\phi_1 + \chi_{12}\phi_1^2\right] \quad (2.64)$$

where subscripts 1 and 2 indicate polymer and diluent respectively, subscript u indicates the value per mole of polymeric units, m is the number of units in the molecule (degree of polymerization), V is the molar volume, $\Delta H = \Delta H_f$, and $\chi_{12}$ is the polymer-polymer interaction parameter.

For polymer blends $m_1 \simeq m_2 \rightarrow \infty$, and Eq (2.64) can be simplified to read:

$$T_m/T_m^{(0)} = 1 + B(V_{2u}/\Delta H_{2u})\phi_1^2 \quad (2.65)$$

where B is a measure of the characteristic interaction density for the polymer pair:

$$B = \chi_{12} RT/V_{1u} \quad at \quad T = T_m \quad (2.66)$$

Comparing Eq (2.65) with Lauritzen and Hoffmann Eq (2.58) it is important to note that B $\propto \nu_e$. The Eqs (2.65)–(2.66) are frequently used to evaluate miscibility in crystallizable polymer blends. An example of numerical data is shown in Fig. 2.13 (*Riedl* and *Prud'homme*, 1984).

The above relations are valid as long as: (i) crystals are at equilibrium, (ii) the melting is conducted under close to equilibrium conditions, (iii) the presence of the second component does not induce change in the crystal system, its lattice spacing, or lamellar thickness, and (iv) the second component does not undergo a phase transition within the investigated range of variables. Unfortunately, these conditions are rarely considered and seldom met. Interpo-

lation of the measured data must be done with utmost care. *Wunderlich* wrote: "For derivation of the equation (i.e. Eq (2.64)) one assumes equilibrium, which is not normally
achieved. The main difficulty lies with the need to work with crystals which all have the same
lamellar size and crystal perfection at the maximum experimental melting temperature ..."
(*Wunderlich*, 1976).

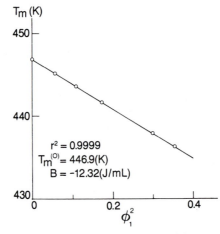

Fig. 2.13 Melting point of polyvinylidenefluoride as a function of the square of the polymethylmethacrylate volume fraction (data from *Riedl* and *Prud'homme*, 1984).

In Fig. 2.14 melting temperatures are plotted as functions of the high density polyethylene (HDPE) content in its blends with low density polyethylene (LDPE) (*Remizova* et al.,
1983). The influence of composition on the $T_m$ of both components is quite strong. However, from the thermodynamics point of view $v_e$ should be insensitive to composition, i.e.
the observed variations of $T_m$ must originate in geometrical factors, such as crystal imperfec-
tions, lamellar sizes, etc. *Walsh* and *Singh* (1984) reported $\chi_{23} = -0.20$ to $-0.23$ for
polyethyleneoxide/polyethersulfone blends, cautioning about a large inherent error in the
$\Delta T_m$ method.

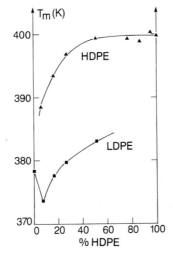

Fig. 2.14 Melting temperatures in blends of low density polyethylene (LDPE) with high density polyethylene (HDPE) (*Remizova* et al., 1983).

The change in the crystal system of polypropylene (PP) from monoclinic to smectic on addition of thermoplastic rubber was reported by *Yip* (1981). Here again Eq (2.65) should not be used. The influence of the second polymer on morphology of the first must be expected from the known effects of low molecular weight additives on crystalline structure (*Horikiri* and *Kodera*, 1973). The presence of HDPE (*Noel* and *Carley*, 1984) or LLDPE (*Dumoulin*, 1988; *Dumoulin* et al., 1987) in blends with PP has a disruptive effect on the regularity of the crystalline structure of the latter polymer. *Morra* and *Stein* (1982, 1984) demonstrated that polyvinylidenefluoride ($PVF_2$), blended with polymethylmethacrylate (PMMA) develops a variety of crystalline morphologies at low undercooling; three $T_m$'s were recorded for $PVF_2$.

A modification of Eq (2.65) was proposed by *Plans* et al. (1984). The authors noted that annealing $PVF_2$/PMMA blends at higher temperatures causes formation of three types of crystals: $\alpha$, $\gamma$ and $\gamma'$, with $\gamma$ and $\gamma'$ having much higher $T_m$ than that of $\alpha$. Contrary to the prediction of Eq (2.65) the plot of $T_m(\alpha)$ vs. $\phi_1^2 \equiv \phi_{PMMA}^2$ was found to be non-linear. However, when the authors corrected $\phi_1$, noting that the $\gamma$ and $\gamma'$ phases do not actively participate in the thermodynamic melt/$\alpha$-crystal equilibrium, e.i.:

$$\phi_{1,corr} \equiv \phi_1/(1-\phi_{\gamma,\gamma'}) \tag{2.67}$$

the linearity of $T_m$ vs. $\phi_{1,corr}^2$ was obtained. Such a correction applies only to systems in which the kinetics of crystalline phase transformation, e.g. $\gamma' \to \alpha$, is relatively slow near the considered melting point $T_m(\alpha)$.

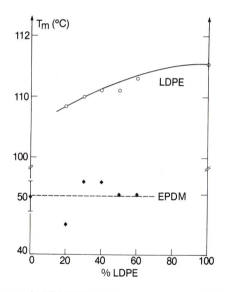

Fig. 2.15 Melting temperatures in LDPE/EPDM blends; curves Eq (2.65) (data from *Starkweather*, 1980).

Another example of systems in which relation (2.65) should not be used is presented in Fig. 2.15. Here $T_m$'s of blends of LDPE with polyethylene-co-propylene-co-1,4-hexadiene (EPDM) are plotted as functions of composition (*Starkweather*, 1980). Without any additional information the dependencies could be approximated by Eq (2.65) with B = −15 (J/ml) calculated for LDPE. However, there are two things wrong with this analysis: (a) as the author reported, on addition of EPDM the unit cell of LDPE was expanded and its spherulitic growth disturbed, and (b) the two polymers were found to cocrystallize. The conclusion based only on the calorimetric results would indicate strong interactions between LDPE and

EPDM, unexpected from the chemical nature of these two polymers. Only crystallographic analysis provided information on the true reasons for the observed variation of LDPE melting point with composition.

From the thermodynamic point of view crystallization lowers the total free energy of the system:

$$\Delta G_c = -\varrho_c \Delta H_0^f \Delta_c / T_m^0 \qquad (2.68)$$

where $\varrho_c$ is the density of the crystalline phase. It can be seen that the free energy change on crystallization is proportional to the degree of supercooling, $\Delta_c$, provided that $T > T_{gi}$, $i = 1,2$. The total free energy of the system can be expressed as:

$$\Delta G = \Delta G_m + \Delta G_c \phi_c \qquad (2.69)$$

where $\phi_c$ is the volume fraction of the crystal and $\Delta G_m$ represents the free energy of mixing as computed from Eq (2.8) correcting $\phi_i$ for the presence of the crystals. It is clear that crystallization will take place only if the conditions of Eq (2.68) and $\Delta G < 0$ are simultaneously fulfilled. *Paul* and *Barlow* (1979) identified five patterns of crystallinity development upon addition $\phi_1$ of a crystallizable diluent:

(1) the diluent does not affect crystallization,
(2) the diluent retards the crystallization rate,
(3) the diluent prevents crystallization at its high loading,
(4) the diluent accelerates crystallization,
(5) the diluent provides enough thermal mobility to cause crystallization of normally non-crystalline polymer.

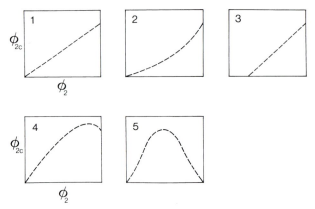

Fig. 2.16 Five patterns of crystallization in polymer blends containing semi-crystalline polymer-2 (after *Paul* and *Barlow*, 1979).

The examples of blends crystallizing in each of these five patterns are presented in Fig. 2.16, where the crystalline fraction, $\phi_{2c}$, of polymer-2 is plotted as a function of the total polymer-2 fraction, $\phi_2$, in the blend. With the exception of pattern (1) the presence of the diluent significantly alters the kinetics of crystallization.

Detailed studies of poly-ε-caprolactone (PCL) crystallization from blends with polystyrene (PS) and/or polyvinylmethylether (PVME) were conducted by *Tanaka* and *Nishi* (1983, 1986) and *Tanaka* et al. (1986). Blend PCL/PS shows UCST, while PS/PVME and PCL/PVME show LCST. The ternary blends PCL/PS/PVME are miscible. Strong influences of PS and/or PVME on crystallization of PCL were reported (*Tanaka* and *Nishi*, 1983, 1986). Crystallization of polyvinylidenefluoride in its blends with polymethylmethacrylate was investigated by *Morra* and *Stein* (1984) as well as by *Tekeley* et al. (1985). Presence of polyvinylmethylether was found to enhance the spherulitic growth rate of poly-styrene (*Martuscelli* et al., 1985). By contrast polymethylmethacrylate was observed to slow down the spherulitic growth rate of polyethyleneoxide (*Addonizio* et al., 1987; *Bartczak* and *Martuscelli*, 1987). The difference in rate originated in a difference of miscibility at the crystallization temperature. While i-PS/PVME blend showed only partial miscibility, with PVME acting as a plasticizer, the PEO/PMMA blend was miscible. In the latter system PMMA depressed the melting point of PEO reducing the crystallization rate.

In Fig. 2.17 data for Kodar-A150 with polycarbonate (PC) (*Barnum*, 1981) are plotted according to Avrami Equation (2.56). Kodar-A150 is a linear copolyester of 1,4-cyclohex-anedimethanol with a mixture of iso- and terephthalic acids. It is obvious that the two-parameter Avrami equation ($t_0 = 0$ was assumed) cannot cope with the system, classified by Paul and Barlow as belonging to the crystallization pattern (2). At shorter times ($t < 13$ min) addition of PC increased the total crystallinity above that observed for the neat copoly-mer but at longer times the crystallinity remained unaffected. The neat resin curve can be linearized by setting up: $t_0 = 2.12$ min. The increase in crystallinity of the blend can be caused either by enhanced nucleation or increased chain mobility (*Harris* and *Robeson*, 1987).

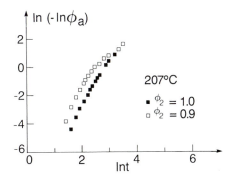

Fig. 2.17 Avrami plot of neat Kodar-A150 and its blend containing 10% of PC (data from *Barnum*, 1981).

When the crystallization rate, G of homopolymers, is plotted as a function of tempera-ture, T, the dependence is approximately parabolic with $G = 0$ at $T_g$ and at $T_m$ while at $T_{max} = (T_g + T_m)/2$ it reaches the maximum value, $G_{max}$. The presence of a second ingredient may affect the absolute value of $T_g$ and/or $T_m$ of the semi-crystalline ingredient, causing either an increase or decrease of G depending on the absolute value of the difference between the isothermal crystallization temperature, $T_i$, and $T_{max}$; if the absolute value $|T_i - T_{max}|$ increases with addition of the second ingredient G will decrease, if $|T_i - T_{max}|$ decreases then the rate of crystallization will increase. Since $T_g$ and $T_m$ are primarily affected by soluble ingredients the modification of crystallization rates is especially important for the (at least partially) miscible blends.

Blends containing two semicrystalline polymers are particularly common between poly-olefins. Most of the newest member of the polyethylene (PE) family, the linear low density polyethylene (LLDPE) is sold blended with other polyolefins. Blends of isotactic polypropy-lene (PP) with PE have been commercially available for over 20 years (*Plochocki*, 1966). The blends are immiscible with the thickness of the interphase layer, $\Delta l \simeq 1.5$ to 2.8 nm (*Letz*, 1979). The crystallization and the resulting morphology strongly depend on the crystallization conditions. Structures with larger spherulites encapsulating the smaller ones are relatively common (*Wenig* and *Meyer*, 1980; *Nakafuku*, 1983; *Bartczak* et al., 1986;

*Bartczak* and *Galeski,* 1986; *Dumoulin,* 1988). In blends of PP with polybutene-1 an enhancement of PB-1 crystallinity was reported (*Lee* and *Chen,* 1987). By contrast, the total crystallinity in PE/polyphenylenesulfide blends was lower than that of neat resins (*Nadkarni* and *Jog,* 1986). However, the rate of isothermal crystallization of PPS vs. composition was found to be a non-linear; an initial acceleration with a local maximum at about 35 wt% PE, followed by a sharp decrease to below the level observed for the neat resin. On the other hand the rate of PE crystallization increased linearly with PPS content.

Crystallinity in PE blends: LLDPE with low density PE, LDPE, was studied by several techniques (*Kyu* et al., 1987; *Ree* et al., 1987). It has been demonstrated that LDPE crystallizes in a secondary step within the LLDPE spherulites. There was a slight depression of LLDPE melting point, but virtually no effect of that polymer on $T_m$ of LDPE. The total blend crystallinity was found to be independent of composition. On the other hand the spherulite radius was recorded to be systematically larger by about 50% than the additivity rule would predict.

Melting and crystallization of several binary PE blends were studied by *Ree* (1987). Under the isothermal conditions LDPE blended either with HDPE or LLDPE crystallized separately whereas the ultrahigh molecular weight PE, UHMWPE, cocrystallized with these two polymers forming isomorphic crystals. The LDPE/HDPE (or LLDPE) blends were found to crystallize as volume-filled with either HDPE or LLDPE providing the primary crystals. The secondary LDPE crystallization followed the Avrami Equation (2.56) with exponent $n_A = 1.0$. A much higher value of the exponent, $n_A = 3$ to 4, was observed for the UHMWPE blends.

When two components of the blend are semicrystalline Eq (2.65) ought to predict the variation of $T_m$ of both polymers: $T_{m,1}$, of polymer-1, treating polymer-2 as a diluent, and $T_{m,2}$ of polymer-2, considering polymer-1 as an additive. Note that, according to that relationship, in both cases B should be constant, independent of concentration. An algebraic rearrangement of these two dependencies allows prediction of the eutectic point, $T_e \equiv T_{m,1} = T_{m,2}$, and eutectic concentration, $\phi_e$ (*Nishi* 1978, 1980, 1985). These calculations have not been experimentally verified.

The cocrystallization of two polymers into isomorphic crystalline cells is a rare phenomenon reported for a few pairs, e.g. for polyvinylfluoride/ polyvinylidenefluoride (Natta et al., 1965), poly-4-methylpentene/poly-4-methylhexene and poly-isopropylvinylether/poly-sec-butylvinylether (*Natta* et al., 1965, 1969), poly-p-phenyloxide/poly-p-phenoxyphenylmethane (*Montaudu* et al., 1973), LLDPE/HDPE (*Hu* et al., 1987); UHMWPE/HDPE or LLDPE (*Ree,* 1987) and recently for blends of polyaryletherketones (*Harris* and *Robeson,* 1987).

The isomorphic polymer blends are miscible in both molten and crystalline states, and in consequence they exhibit a single glass transition temperature, $T_g$, and a single melting point, $T_m$. Furthermore, it has been noted that, in variance with random copolymers, where $T_m$ is a linear function of composition, this dependence for isomorphic blends has a strong positive variation; in fact $T_m$ for compositions up to about 50% of the higher melting component is virtually constant, what in terms of Eq (2.65) would indicate a vanishingly small value of the interaction parameter B. However, when considering the other concentration range a steep increase of $T_m$ is found, suggesting large value of B. *Harris* and *Robeson* (1987) using the Huggins-Flory Eq (2.8) derived an expression for compositional variation of $T_m$ for isomorphic systems. The theory agrees quite well with the experimental observations. Physically, since the maximum extent of crystallinity (determined by chain mobility) is about 50%, during cooling the isomorphic blend with high content of the higher melting ingredient crystallizes first, leading to a substantial difference in composition of the amorphous and crystalline phase after solidification. When the complementary blend composition is crystallized, the minor component with high-$T_m$ crystallizes first following the low-$T_m$ one. In both cases composition of the isomorphic crystalline phase determines $T_m$ of the blend.

It is evident that in semicrystalline polymer blends the phase equilibria, the kinetics of crystallization and the morphologies are more complex. Complexity means that interpretation of results is more difficult. In fact, there are numerous theoretical possibilities not explored as yet in published literature. On the other hand the complexity, the multi-parameter dependence of the morphology and resulting properties, provides greater flexibility for the design engineer.

### 2.5.4. Influence of Liquid/Liquid Phase Separation on the Crystallization and Morphology

The crystallization kinetics of macroscopically segregated PAB melt can be described in terms of theories developed for neat polymers. The morphology frequently depends on the structure of the coarsened liquid (*Schaaf* et al., 1987). Crystallization from the miscible system was discussed in the preceeding part. What is happening between these two limiting cases?

For simplicity let us assume that $T_1$ in Fig. 2.1 represents the melting point of polymer-1 (independent of $x_2$) and only the right hand side of the diagram ($x_2 > 0.5$) is considered. The morphology of the blend cooled from $T > T_c$ will depend on $T - T_1$, on concentration, as well as on the degree and the rate of undercooling. For $x_2 > b''$ crystallization from homogeneous melt takes place, for slow cooled systems with $x_2 < b''$ crystallization occurs from coarsened binary phase liquid. The most intriguing are the structures (and properties) of blends quenchend within the NG ($s'' \leqslant x_2 \leqslant b''$) and SD ($x_2 < s''$) concentration regions.

The crystallization of polycaprolactone in its blends with polystyrene was reported occurring when the concentration of the crystallizable polymer exceeded 50% (*Tanaka* and *Nishi*, 1985). If prior to crystallization the system had separated by the SD mechanism, the solidification preserved the liquid structure, with the periodicity $\Lambda$ as indicated in Fig. 2.6. During the process the second polymer was expelled from the growing spherulites, forming a skin-layer around it (see Fig. 2.18) . In polyvinylidenefluoride/polymethylmethacrylate blends the thickness of this layer was found to be about 2.5 nm (*Hahn* et al., 1987). Since the spherulite diameter ($D_s$), does not depend on phase separation time but $\Lambda$ does, there are two types of structures possible: (i) $D_s \leqslant \Lambda$, i.e. crystallization following the co-continuous lines of composition illustrated in Figs. 2.7 and 2.9, and (ii) $D_s > \Lambda$, where the spinodal structure is embedded in the spherulite (*Inaba* et al., 1986).

Fig. 2.18 Excretion of PS during crystallization of PCL from polystyrene/polycaprolactone (30/70) system at 50 °C (after *Tanaka* and *Nishi,* 1985).

Even more complex morphologies can be generated (and stabilized by crystallization) making use of the kinetics of phase separation at different temperatures. A blend of polyvinylidenefluoride ($T_m \simeq 180°C$) with polyethylacrylate has UCST $\simeq 150°C$ (*Endres et al.*, 1985). When the blend is allowed to phase separate and coarsen at 200°C, then taken up to 210°C and immediately quenched below $T_m$, there is a secondary phase separation within the phase separated domains creating the crystallization stabilized "salami" structure.

## 2.6    Determination of Polymer/Polymer Miscibility

In thermodynamics "miscibility" means single phase down to molecular level. In a pragmatic sense miscibility means that the system appears to be homogeneous in the type of test applied in the study, i.e. it is defined in terms of degree of dispersion. As a result, in the literature one finds conflicting reports on "miscibility" of a given polymer/polymer blend.

The methods used to study blend miscibility will be divided into three groups: phase equilibria methods, measurements of $\chi_{ij}$, and indirect compatibility tests. This division, as with almost all systems of classification, is far from being without fault. Placing methods like neutron scattering or a fluorescence probe into the latter category does not negate their precision, reliability and universality. Approximate limits of useful ranges of these techniques to study the blend morphology are shown in Fig. 2.19.

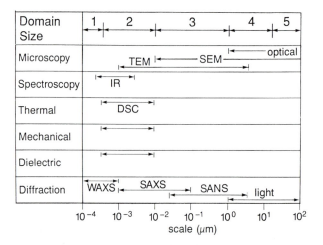

Fig. 2.19 Approximate ranges of experimental techniques to study blend morphology of: (1) interatomic; (2) molecular, spherulites; (3) filler aggregates, compatibilized blends; (4) reinforcements, noncompatible blends; (5) voids.

### 2.6.1    Phase Equilibria Methods

For commercially important high molecular weight polymer blends the combinatorial entropy of mixing is negligibly small and the free volume contribution further increases the free energy of mixing. As a result, the miscibility depends either on specific interactions or on intramolecular repulsions. Examples of miscible polymer blends based on different types of specific interactions are listed in Table 2.2.

TABLE 2.2 Examples of Miscible Polymer Blends with Different Types of Specific Interactions

| No. | Polymer 1 | Polymer 2 | Specific interactions | References |
|-----|-----------|-----------|----------------------|------------|
| 1 | PS | PPE | π-hydrogen bond between π-orbitals in PS aromatic rings and Me-groups in PPO | Djordjevic and Porter, 1981–3 |
| 2 | PS | PVME | between hydrogen of the PS CH group and the ether group in PVME | Garcia, 1987 |
| 3 | PVC | PCL | between hydrogen of ClCH and the ester group | Riedl and Prud'homme, 1986 |
| 4 | PMMA | PVF$_2$ | = CO stretching in PMMA and overall reduction of C-mobility | Douglass and McBrierty, 1978 Saito et al., 1987 |
| 5 | Phenoxy | PCL, PVME | direct hydrogen bonding | Garton, 1984 a |
| 6 | PMHCM | PHENBM | electron-donor-acceptor complexing | Rodriguez-Parada and Percec, 1986 |
| 7 | PEO | PAA, PPO, | direct hydrogen bonding | Paul and Barlow, 1980 |
| 8 | PSS$^-$ Na$^+$ | PSNH$_4^+$Cl$^-$ | ionic interactions | Smith et al., 1987 |
| 9 | PB-1 | PP | non-specific interactions | |

Notes: PS = polystyrene; PPE = poly(2,6-dimethyl-1,4-phenyleneether); PVME = polyvinylmethylether; PVC = polyvinylchloride; PCL – poly-ε-caprolactone; PMMA = polymethylmethacrylate; PVF$_2$ = polyvinylidenefluoride; Phenoxy = poly(hydroxyether of bis-phenol-A); PMHCM = poly(methyl-3-hydroxymethylcarbazoylyl methacrylate); PHENBM = poly(β-hydroxyethyl-3,5-dinitrobenzoylmethacrylate); PEO = polyethyleneoxide; PAA – polyacrylicacid, PPO = polypropyleneoxide; PSS$^-$N$^+$ = sodium parasulfonated PS; PSNH$_4^+$Cl$^-$ = chloro p-quaternary aminated PS; PB-1 = poly-1-butylene; PP = polypropylene; PVAc = polyvinyl acetate; PMA = polymethylacrylate.

There are over 400 polymer blends cited as "miscible" (*Robeson*, 1980; *Paul* and *Barlow*, 1980; *Robeson*, 1989). Various types of specific interactions are responsible for miscibility: hydrogen bonding, dipolar interactions, phenyl group coupling, charge transfer complex formation (*Tsuchida* et al., 1980), Lewis acid-base interaction (*Fowkes* et al., 1984) or ionic (*Smith* et al., 1987). They all contribute to the negative heat of mixing:

$$\Delta H_m / \phi_1 \phi_2 \doteq B < 0 \qquad (2.70)$$

As mentioned in Part 2.3.6 a simple calorimetric scan of low molecular weight analoges has been used to predict the miscibility of polymer blends (*Paul*, 1981; *Barlow* and *Paul*, 1981; *Harris* et al., 1983; *Paul* and *Barlow*, 1982). The value of the parameter B determined in the "analog calorimetry" method was shown to agree reasonably well with those values measured (by other methods) for high molecular weight polymeric pairs. The method is quick and easy to use, interpret and extend to wide ranges of T and P conditions. It is particularly useful for identifying new miscible, or at least compatible, polymer alloys and blends. However, it cannot be substituted for the phase equilibria maps. Analog calorimetry cannot take into account the effects of the molecular weight, molecular weight distribution, short and long chain branching, stereoisomerism and distribution of isomeric sequences. Furthermore, the temperature influence on B is most often neglected. To know if the pair is miscible one has to determine the conditions of miscibility, i. e. study the phase equilibria.

Differential scanning calorimetry, DSC, of several miscible polymer blends, viz. polystyrene/polyvinylmethylether, polyvinylchloride/polycaprolactone, and polyacryloyl-2'-hydroxyethyl-3,5-dinitrobenzoate/poly-N-methyl-3-hydroxymethylcabazolylacrylate all showed an exothermic effect of "decomplexation" resulting from demixing of components (*Natansohn, 1985*). For example, when PS/PVME miscible blend was scanned from −100°C to 250°C a single glass transition at −12°C and an exothermic peak at 214°C were recorded. Rescanning the sample after quenching indicated two glass transition temperatures at −25 and 70°C corresponding to the depressed glass transitions of PVME (−31°C) and PS (78°C). DSC indicated miscibility of polymethylmethacrylate/polybutylmethacrylate blends (*Piglowski* and *Kozlowski, 1987*).

## 2.6.1.1 Turbidity Measurements

This is the oldest method of determination of phase relationships. It consists of preparation of a series of mixtures near the phase separation condition then causing the separation to occur. The precipitation is observed by onset of turbidity either visually or in a photoelectric cell. The method has been used to study the phase separation in polymer solutions (*Flory, 1953; Tompa, 1956; Utracki, 1962; Koningsveld* and *Staverman, 1968*). The ensemble of the turbidity (or cloud) points defines the cloud-point curves, CPC. For strictly binary mixtures at equilibrium, CPC should follow the binodal equation. To complete the description of the system, mixtures deep within the immiscibility region should be prepared and the composition of the separated phases analyzed, generating the tie-lines and locating the critical point, e.g. by plotting the phase volume ratio as a function of temperature. The spinodals can also be determined in a series of quenching experiments.

A partial list of polymer-1/polymer-2 systems investigated by this method is listed in Table 2.3. Other examples can be found in *Olabisi* et al., monograph (1979).In systems Nos. 1, 3 and 12 the upper critical solution temperature, UCST, was observed. In systems Nos. 4, 6 to 11 and 13 to 16 the lower critical solution temperature, LCST, was reported. In system No. 3, not the effect of temperature but that of the third ingredient was considered. In system No. 5, on first heating the cast films cleared at 60 to 80°C. The initial clearing took up to 24 hrs, depending on the temperature and sample thickness. This diffusion controlled dissolution of domains left over from the solvent evaporation should not be confused with the liquid/liquid phase equilibrium. On further heating the LCST was observed at T ⩾ 140°C.

As shown in Figs. 2.20 and 2.21 in systems 6 and 14 (respectively) both liquid/liquid and liquid/solid transitions were observed. The effect of molecular weight of PEMA on the size of the miscibility region should be noted. In Fig. 2.21 the concentration dependence of the glass transition temperature ($T_g$), is also shown.

The pressure (P), effect on CPC was reported for system No. 8. It was observed that in accord with predictions of the equation of state theories, on increase of P from 15 to 290 MPa the LCST increased from about 120 to 160°C. To determine CPC for systems Nos. 15 and 16 a specially designed light scattering turbidimeter (with photodiode at 45°) was used (*Walsh* et al., 1981, 1982, 1983; *Rostami* and *Walsh, 1984*).

Experimentally CPC can be determined in a number of ways. The principle is to prepare films of the blend under conditions of miscibility, by mechanical mixing or by use of a co-solvent. Usually a series of compositions is prepared. The films are heated or cooled through the cloud point. Depending on the rate, type of system, and polydispersity the difference between CPC on heating and cooling can be significant; spread in excess of 10°C was reported by *McMaster* (1973).

It is preferable to use a programmable hot stage with the heating rate not exceeding 0.1°C/min. The sample can be illuminated with white light, laser beam or UV source. The variation of turbidity is observed either directly, under microscope with a naked eye, or with a photoelectric detector, e.g. a light dependent resistor placed in the focal point of an optical microscope tube. The UV-visible spectro-photometer has also been used (*Shih* and *Beatty, 1981*). As is to be expected the cloud point was found to depend on the wavelength used.

TABLE 2.3 Cloud-Point Curves Reported for Polymer Blends

| No. | Polymer 1 | Polymer 2 | Method | Ref. |
|---|---|---|---|---|
| 1 | Polyisobutene, PIB; M = 0.25 kg/mol | Polydimethylsiloxane, PDMS; M = 0.85 and 17 | Turbid. | 1 |
| 2 | Polyisoprene, PI; $M_n$ = 2.7 | Polystyrene, PS; $M_n$ = 2.1 and 2.7 | Turbid. | 2 3 |
| 3 | Polyisoprene, PI; $M_w$ = 17 to 270 | Polystyrene, PS; $M_w$ = 24 to 420 | Turbid. | 4 |
| | (with and without block polymer PI-PS) | | | |
| 4 | Polystyrene, PS; $M_n$ = 2.1 to 2000 | Polyvinylmethylether, PVME; $M_w$ = 51.5 | Turbid. | 5 |
| 5 | Polystyrene $M_n$ = 2.2 to 63 | Polyvinylmethylether, PVME, ($M_w$ about 50) | Turbid., DSC | 6 |
| 6 | Polyvinylidenefluoride, $PVF_2$; $M_w$ = 100 | iso-Polyethylmethacrylate, PEMA; $M_v$ = 4 to 172 | Turbid., DSC | 7 to 9 |
| 7 | Poly(α-ethylstyrene-coacrylonitrile), $M_w$ = 160 | Polyacrylates and Polymethacrylates $M_w$ = 20 to 1000 | Turbid., DSC | 10 |
| 8 | Polystyrene; $M_n$ = 16.7 to 422 | Polyvinylmethylether; $M_n$ = 46.5 | Turbid. | 11 |
| 9 | Polyvinylchloride; $M_n$ = 30 | Polyacrylates and Polymethacrylates | Dynamic, Turbid. | 12 |
| 10 | Polyvinylchloride; $M_v$ = 16 to 55 | Polymethylmethacrylate; $M_v$ = 2.6 to 80 | Turbid. | 13 |
| 11 | Polystyrene; $M_w$ = 60 | Polyvinylmethylether; $M_w$ = 62.7 | Turbid., Light Sc. | 14 |
| 12 | Polystyrene-b-butadiene; di-block, $M_w$ = 28, 25% styrene | (a) Polybutadiene $M_w$ = 26 (b) Polystyrene; $M_w$ = 2.4 and 3.5 (c) Polystyrene-r-butadiene; $M_w$ = 29,   25% styrene | Turbid., Light Sc., SAXS | 15 to 17 |
| 13 | Polyneopentylglycoladipate | (a) Poly(epichlorhydrin-coethylene oxide) (b) Chlorinated polyethylenes | Turbid., DSC | 18 |
| 14 | Poly-ε-coprolactone; | Polystyrene-co-acrylonitrile, SAN; AN content 5.53 to 36.35% $M_w$ = 341 to 433 | Turbid., Dynamic, DSC | 19 |
| 15 | Polymethylmethacrylate, PMMA; $M_n$ = 434 to 29,000 | Chlorinated polyethylene, CPE; $M_n$ = 0.395 to 25.3 degree of chlorination 27.4 to 53.1 | L.Sc.Int., Dynamic | 20 21 |
| 16 | Poly(ethylene-co-vinyl acetate) EVA; $M_w$= 130 to 256 | Chlorinated polyethylene, CPE; $M_w$ = 120 to 188 | L.Sc.Int., DTA, Dynamic, Inv. GPC | 22 to 24 |

*References: 1. G. Allen et al., 1961; 2. R. Koningsveld et al., 1974; 3. R. Koningsveld and L. A. Kleintjens, 1977; 4. J. Kohler et al., 1968; 5. T. Nishi and T. K. Kwei, 1975; 6. D. D. Davis and T. K. Kwei, 1980; 7. E. Roerdink and G. Challa, 1980; 8. G. ten Brinke et al., 1981; 9. G. ten Brinke et al., 1982; 10. S. H. Goh et al., 1982; 11. H. Hiramatsu et al., 1983; 12. D. J. Walsh and J. G. McKeon, 1980; 13. H. Jager et al., 1983; 14. H. L. Snyder et al., 1983; 15. W.-Ch. Zin, 1983; 16. W.-Ch. Zin and R.-J. Roe, 1984; 17. R.-J. Roe and W.-Ch. Zin, 1984; 18. S. H. Goh et al., 1984; 19. Ch. Shao-Cheng, 1981; 20. D. J. Walsh et al., 1981; 21. D. J. Walsh et al., 1982; 22. D. J. Walsh et al., 1983a; 23. D. J. Walsh et al., 1983b; 24. S. Rostami and D. J. Walsh, 1984.*

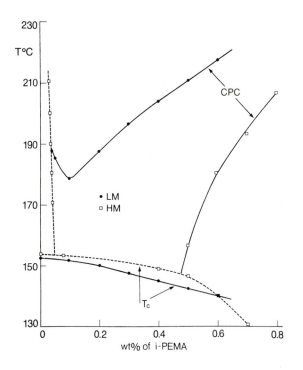

Fig. 2.20 Phase equilibria in blends of polyvinylidenefluoride, $M_w = 100$ kg/mol, with i-polyethyl-methacrylate; open points $M_w = 4$, solid points $M_v = 115$ or 172 kg/mol. In upper part the CPC's and in lower part the crystallization curves are shown (after *Roerdink* and *Challa*, 1980; *ten Brinke* et al., 1981).

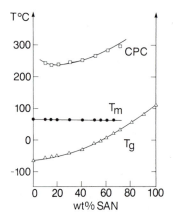

Fig. 2.21 Phase diagram for poly-ε-caprolactone/polystyrene-co-acrylonitrile with $M_w = 40.4$ and 446 kg/mol respectively. CPC-cloudpoint curve, $T_m$ – melting temperatures of PCL, $T_g$ – glass transition temperature of the amorphous phase (after *Shao-Cheng*, 1981).

For a two phase system the scattering invariant can be written as:

$$Q_L \propto (n_1-n_2)^2 \, \phi_1' \phi_2' \tag{2.71}$$

where: $\phi_i'$ is the volume fraction of the phase i with the refractive index $n_i$. Obviously when $n_1 = n_2$ the scattering method cannot be used. Furthermore, according to Bragg's law the characteristic dimension of the separating phase, $D_m$, is related to the wavelength, $\lambda$, and the scattering angle $\theta$:

$$D_m = \lambda/2 \sin (\theta/2) \tag{2.72}$$

Under standard conditions used to observe the turbidity, $\theta = 90$ to $45°$, $D_m$ and $\lambda$ are of comparable size. Eq (2.72) is strictly valid for monodispersed particle suspension.

The use of diverse optical and thermooptical techniques to study dispersions in polymeric systems has been recently discussed (*Cielo* et al., 1986, 1987; *Krapez* et al., 1987). As an example it was reported that size polydispersity usually reduces the angular scattering whereas the spectral turbidimetry can provide means for incorporating the size and size distribution of scatterers into the optical examination of phase separation.

In short, the turbidity method suffers from a number of experimental problems. In addition there is no direct theoretical link between CPC and the thermodynamically defined phase separation curves, spinodal and binodal.

An interesting version of the turbidity measurements was proposed by Shaw and Somani (*Somani* and *Shaw*, 1981; *Somani*, 1981; *Shaw*, 1982; *Shaw* and *Somani*, 1984) under the name of the melt titration technique, MTT. The authors used an extruder equipped with a special die, optical detector, traced return tube and a syringe-pump. The schematic is presented in Fig. 2.22. Briefly, the test starts with the major component circulating through the system. The second polymer, dissolved in a volatile solvent, is added continuously from a syringe-pump to the hopper of the extruders. The presence of a second phase in the mixture is detected by a sudden increase in scattered light intensity. Solubility of the second

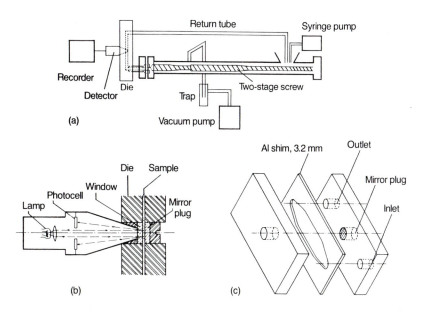

Fig. 2.22 Melt titration technique: (a) schematic of the method, (b) cross section through the die showing the optical detector, and (c) expanded view of die (*Somani*, 1981).

polymer in the major component is calculated from the initial mass of the circulating component, and that of the dissolved polymer added up to the moment of the increase of light scattering intensity.

The method is applicable to systems of marginal miscibility such as those listed in Table 2.4. The solubility limits listed in the Table were established at 150°C and at constant but unknown pressure. The results were found not to correlate with the theoretical calculations based on Flory or Sanchez-Lacombe theories.

TABLE 2.4  Solubility of Polymers by Melt Titration Technique

| No. | Major Component | | Minor Component | | Solubility of minor component (ppm) at 150 °C | Ref. |
|---|---|---|---|---|---|---|
| | Polymer | $M_w$ (kg/mol) | Polymer | $M_w$ (kg/mol) | | |
| 1 | Polystyrene | 500 | Polydimethylsiloxane | 71.8 | 4 | 1, 2 |
| 2 | Polystyrene | 520 | Polymethylacrylate | 200 | 38 | 1, 2 |
| 3 | Polystyrene | 520 | Polyethylacrylate | 125 | 86 | 1, 2 |
| 4 | Polystyrene | 520 | Polybutylacrylate | 119 | 78 | 1, 2 |
| 5 | Polystyrene | 520 | Polyn-butylmethacrylate | 320 | 50 | 1, 2 |
| 6 | Polystyrene | 520 | Polymethylmethacrylate | 160 | 3.9 | 1, 2 |
| 7 | Polystyrene | 520 | Polydimethylsiloxane | 71.8 | 3.9 | 1, 2 |
| 8 | Polystyrene | 520 | Polymethylmethacrylate | 75 | 8.6 | 1, 3 |

*References:* 1. *R. H. Somani, 1981; 2. R. H. Somani and M. T. Shaw, 1981; 3. M. T. Shaw and R. H. Somani, 1984.*

## 2.6.1.2 Light Scattering Methods

The turbidity method can be extended to rigorous studies of the phase separation. It suffices to note that the scattered intensity of light due to concentration fluctuation, $R_\theta^c$, extrapolated to zero scattering angle is inversely proportional to the second derivative of $\Delta G_m$, defined in Eq (2.4). A plot of $(1/R^c)_{\Theta=0}$ vs. T is linear, allowing extrapolation to the spinodal conditions:

$$\left.\begin{array}{c} (\partial^2 \Delta G_m / \partial \phi_1 \partial \phi_2)_{P,T} = 0 \\ \\ (1/R^c)_{\Theta=0} = 0 \end{array}\right\} \quad T = T_S \qquad (2.73)$$

where $T_s$ indicates the spinodal temperature. The technique is applicable only to homogeneous systems, i.e. at temperatures $T < T_s$ for systems having LCST, or at $T > T_s$ for those having UCST. The method has been used mainly to study the phase equilibria in polymer solutions.

In Fig. 2.23 the region accessible to the conventional light scattering method is indicated by arrow $a_1$; the data are collected at $T < T_B$ and extrapolation performed to $T_s$. Since away from the critical point the difference between $T_s$ and $T_B$ can be as large as 40°C, (*Snyder* et al., 1983), it is desirable to extend the measurements closer to the spinodal i.e. into the meta-stable region; PICS does precisely that.

PICS stands for pulse-induced critical scattering, an elegant method of measurements for a small mass of liquid mixture very rapidly heated or cooled into the meta-stable region. The laser light scattering intensity is measured after the thermal equilibrium is reached, but before the system can phase-separate, then the mixture is brought out into the homogeneous

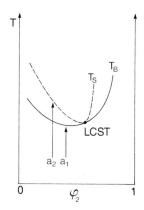

Fig. 2.23 Schematic phase diagram for binary liquid system with lower critical solution temperature (LCST). Binodal, $T_B$, and spinodal, $T_s$, temperatures as function of composition are indicated. The two arrows $a_1$ and $a_2$, indicate respectively regions accessible to conventional light scattering and pulse-induced critical scattering (PICS).

region and the cycle repeated (*Gordon* et al., 1973; *Derham* et al., 1974; *Kennedy* et al., 1975). The temperature change can be accomplished in milliseconds, the time of one cycle is less than one minute. The region of T accessible to PICS is marked by arrow $a_2$ in Fig. 2.23.

One of the most serious obstacles in the phase equilibria studies of polymer blends is the viscosity of the system. At temperatures limited by the degradation the self-diffusion coefficient of macromolecules is of the order of magnitude $10^{-14}$ to $10^{-16}$ m$^2$/s (*Klein* et al., 1983; *Fleischer*, 1987; *Kausch* and *Tirrell*, 1989). As a result the phase separation is slow; it may never reach completion. To accelerate the process *Rietveld* (1974) constructed a low speed centrifuge with Schlieren optics allowing observation of the accelerated phase separation process during rotation. Even with this improvement determination of the critical point would take about two weeks (*Gordon* et al., 1978).

Further amelioration was incorporated into the "centrifugal homogenizer", CH, by *Gordon* and *Ready* (1978). The principle of CH operation is presented in Fig. 2.24. During the

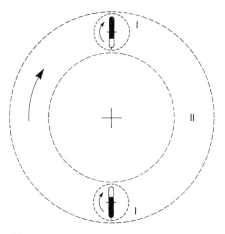

Fig. 2.24 Principle of the centrifugal homogenizer. Five PICS capillaries are mounted in each of the four holders I (only two shown) rotating on the track II which can be thermostated at T ≤ 200 °C. For mixing the holders can rotate in the indicated direction, thus superposing a planetary motion on the rotation of track II. For accelerated phase separation rotation of the holders is halted.

last few years the machine has been significantly upgraded within the cooperative program between the University of Essex, UK, and DSM in Geleen, Netherlands (*Onclin* et al., 1979, 1980; *Kleintjens* et al., 1980; *Koningsveld* et al., 1982). CH allows the phase diagram to be determined 10 times faster than the Rietveld centrifuge. Furthermore, profiting from the homogenizing mode of the CH planetary rotation of specimen tubes, the machine can be used with PICS. In short, centrifugation within the immiscibility zone permits determination of binodal and critical points, while use of the PICS mode allows location of the spinodal.

### 2.6.1.3 SAXS and SANS

The principle of light scattering can be extended to other sources of radiation, in particular X-rays and neutrons. In order to follow the fluctuation of density in the sub-micron region, the $\theta$ in Equation (2.72) must be small. Small angle X-ray scattering, SAXS, and small angle neutron scattering, SANS, are used with increasing frequency to study polymer blend structure. The range of application of these techniques was illustrated in Fig. 2.19. Since the light, X-ray and neutron scattering depend on differences in refractive indices, electron densities and atomic number respectively, these techniques complement each other. The methods can be used for systems in liquid, glassy or crystalline states to study the molecular weight and molecular sizes of polymer as well as particle or crystalline morphology.

*Zin* and *Roe* (*Zin*, 1983; *Zin* and *Roe*, 1984; *Roe* and *Zin*, 1984) investigated the phase equilibria in systems containing poly(styrene-b-butadiene) di-block polymer, SB, mixed either with a homopolymer or random copolymer. By plotting the reciprocal of the intensity of the main SAXS peak as a function of $1/T$ (see Fig. 2.25) the authors determined the spinodal, $T_s$, and binodal, $T_B$, temperatures. The complex phase diagram presented in Fig. 2.26 is a result of CPC and SAXS measurements. As mentioned in Part 2.3.7 the Noolandi-Hong theory allows phase diagrams of such complexity to be computed.

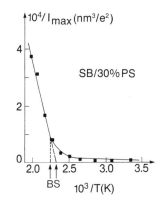

Fig. 2.25 SAXS for SB with 30 wt% PS. B and S indicate position of $T_B$ and $T_s$, respectively.

SAXS has been used by Stein and his coworkers to study the morphology of polymer blends in the solid state (*Khambatta*, 1976; *Russel*, 1979; *Russel* and *Stein*, 1982, 1983). The authors concluded that in the interlamellar regions of poly-$\varepsilon$-caprolactone (PCL) blend with polyvinylchloride (PVC) the system is miscible on a molecular scale. Addition of PVC impedes crystallization of PCL. At high PVC concentration PCL remains in solution with the radius of gyration, $R_g$, larger than that under unperturbed conditions, $R_g(\Theta)$, in spite of the fact that at the same time the second virial coefficient, $A_2$, is virtually zero. Blends: poly-o-iodostyrene (PoIS) with polystyrene (PS) poly-o-chlorostyrene (PoClS) with PS, PoClS with poly-2,6-dimethyl-1,4- phenyleneether (PPE), poly-p-chlorostyrene (PpClS) with PPE, PpClS with PS (*Russel*, 1979), atactic PS with isotactic PS, and polymethylmethacrylate (PMMA) with polyvinylidenefluoride (PVF$_2$) (*Stein* et al., 1981) were also studied. The latter system was also investigated by *Wendorff* (1980, 1982) using SAXS and SANS methods. In Fig. 2.27 the values of the interaction parameter $\chi_{12}$ of the Huggins-Flory Eq (2.8), are plotted vs. PVF$_2$ content. The data were linearized by means of Eq (2.24).

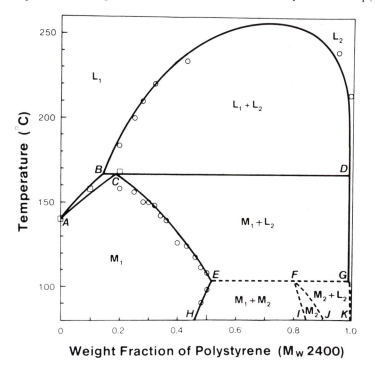

**Weight Fraction of Polystyrene (M$_W$ 2400)**

Fig. 2.26 Phase diagram of the mixture containing styrene-butadiene diblock copolymer and polystyrene (M$_w$ = 2.4 kg/mol) drawn to agree with the observed cloud points (circles) and the block copolymer transition temperatures (squares) determined by SAXS. The liquid phases L$_1$ and L$_2$ consist of the disordered block copolymer and the polystyrene. Mesophase M$_1$ consists of ordered microdomains of the block copolymer swollen with polystyrene. Mesophase M$_2$ contains micellar aggregates of the block copolymer suspended in the polystyrene medium. The two lines AB and AC coalesce into a single line representing the transition temperature between the ordered and disordered structure. The features on the lower right, drawn in broken lines, are speculative (*Zin*, 1983).

SAXS was used to study the morphology of a low density (LDPE) blended with high density polyethylene (HDPE) (*Reckinger* et al., 1984-5). Effects of blend composition and crystallization rate were investigated. It was found that segregation of different chains during crystallization takes place even during quenching at about 100°C/min; at these rates the segregation distance was comparable to coil dimension in the melt.

Small angle neutron scattering (SANS) has been used to determine the phase diagram in polyvinylmethylether/deuterated polystyrene (*Schwahn* et al., 1987). In the vicinity of the critical region the non-mean field behavior (Ising) was observed.

SANS is one of the most important tools for studying macromolecular sizes, conformation and morphology. The method has been used to study a single or multicomponent system in its molten or solid state. For the test one has to replace the hydrogen atoms in a

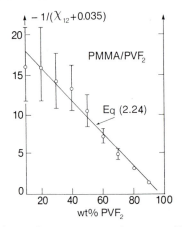

Fig. 2.27 Linearization of the interaction parameter $\chi_{12}$ by means of Eq 2.24. Values from SAXS for polymethylmethacrylate/polyvinylidenefluoride (*Wendorff, 1982*).

part of the molecule by deuterium atoms. The deuterated polymer is then dissolved in a non-deuterated matrix at a concentration usually about or below 0.1%, or the reverse - the non-deuterated molecules are dispersed in the deuterated matrix. The data are treated via the modified relation derived for conventional light scattering:

$$Kc_2/R(q) = [1/M_2P(q)] + 2A_2c_2 + \dots \tag{2.74}$$

where $q = 4R/\lambda \sin\theta$ is the scattering parameter, $c_2$, $M_2$, and $A_2$ are respectively the concentration, molecular weight, and the second virial coefficient of the polymer component present in the lower concentration, $R(q)$ is the ratio between the scattered and the incident intensities. $P(q)$ is Debye's one-particle scatter function, $\lambda$ is the neutron wavelength and $\theta$ is the scattering half-angle. The constant K contains the scattering distances of hydrogen and deuterium as the most important quantities. The average scattering radius, $\langle r^2 \rangle$, of the polymer is calculated from $P(q)$ with the aid of:

$$P(q) = 1 - \langle r^2 \rangle_z q/3 + \dots \tag{2.75}$$

The conversion of $\langle r^2 \rangle$ into the weight-average scattering radius of gyration $R_g$ is done in the usual way, on the assumption of a Schulz-Flory distribution. According to Zimm one plots $Kc_2/R(q)$ against the sum of the concentration of polymer-2 and the square of the scatter parameter q. Extrapolation to $c_2 = 0$ and $q = 0$ gives $P(q)$ and $A_2$, respectively. The intercept with the ordinate gives the reciprocal of $M_2$.

A review of SANS application in the characterization of polymer conformation and morphology was published by *Sperling* (1984) while that on the use of neutron scattering in the characterization of crystalline polymers by *Keller* (1983). SANS has also been used to support SAXS data discussed previously (*Russel, 1979; Stein et al., 1981; Wendorff, 1980, 1982*).

In the series of papers (*Kirste and Lehnen, 1976; Krause, 1986; Smith and Kirste, 1978; Jelenic et al., 1979, 1984; Wignall et al., 1980; Kambour et al., 1980; Schmitt, 1979; Schmitt et al., 1980; Hadziioannou et al., 1983; Ree, 1987*) the $R_g$ and $A_2$ were measured for macromolecules in polymer blends. An example of the Zimm plot for deuterated polystyrene (DPS) dissolved in PS/PPE blend is given in Fig. 2.28 (*Maconnachie et al, 1984*).

Knowing $A_2$ allows calculation of the chemical potential, $\Delta\mu_i$, of the polymeric component-1 ("solvent") present in the higher concentration:

$$\Delta\mu_i = -RT[(V_1c_2/M_2) + A_2V_1c_2^2 + \dots \tag{2.76}$$

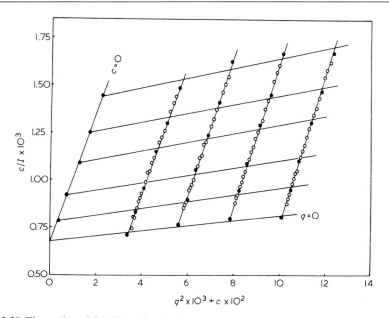

Fig. 2.28 Zimm plot of SANS results for deuterated polystyrene dissolved in polystyrene/poly-2,6-dimethyl-1,4phenylene oxide = 50:50 blend (*Maconnachie et al., 1984*).

where $V_1$ is the partial molar volume of component-1. When the chemical potential and the composition of the mixture are known, integration of $\Delta\mu_1$ gives $\Delta G_m$. One should note that Eq (2.76) is valid only for $c_2 \to 0$. The interaction parameter $\chi'_{12}$ can be obtained from $A_2$ using the relation:

$$\chi'_{12} = \chi'_{12}/V_{ref} = (2v_1M_1)^{-1} - A_2v_2^2 \tag{2.77}$$

where $V_{ref}$ is taken as the molar volume of the "solvent", $v_i$ are partial specific volumes of the components i = 1 and 2 respectively and $M_1$ is the molecular weight of the "solvent".

Examples of SANS results for PAB are given in Table 2.5. These can be summarized as:

(i) the $M_w$(sol) agrees with $M_w$(SANS); the average ratio $M_w$(sol)/$M_w$(SANS) = 1.02 ± 0.14,

(ii) on increase of temperature the second virial coefficient, $A_2$, decreases, indicating universality of the LCST for the systems studied,

(iii) the radius of gyration, $R_g$, of the probe specimen decreases on increase of $M_w$ of the matrix of the same chemical character,

(iv) the coil expansion coefficient $\alpha = 1$ for specimen molecules dissolved in a matrix of the same chemical character and molecular weight,

(v) in a given system $\alpha$ increases with $A_2$,

(vi) in a given system $A_2$ decreases with $M_w$,

(vii) even when $A_2 < 0$, $M_w$(SANS) does not show aggregation,

(viii) in blends: PMMA/PSAN, PVC/PMMA, PPE/PS and PMVE/PS the second virial coefficient, $A_2$, is positive, indicating miscibility,

(ix) within each of these systems $R_g$ is proportional to $M_w^n$, where the exponent n equals about $\frac{1}{2}$; n = 0.57 and 0.52 at 25 and 120°C respectively for PS in PMVE, n = 0.55 for PPE in PS, n = 0.5 for PS in PS and PMMA in PMMA, n = 0.60 and n = 0.64 for PMMA in PSAN-19 or vice-versa, respectively,

(x) none of the investigated systems is very far from the unperturbed state.

TABLE 2.5  Summary of SANS Results for Polymer Blends

| No. | Matrix (i = 1) | | Probe (i = 2) | | | T (°C) | $A_2 \cdot 10^4$ | $R_g$ | α | Ref. |
|---|---|---|---|---|---|---|---|---|---|---|
| | Polymer code | $M_w$ (kg/mol) | Polymer code | $M_w$ (sol.) | (SANS) | | (ml/g²mol) | (nm) | | |
| 1 | d-PDMS | 250[a] | PDMS | 200[a] | 186 | 20 | −0.22 | 11.4 | 1.02 | 1 |
| 2 | d-PDMS | 50 | PDMS | 200[a] | 226 | 20 | 0.54 | 13.0 | 1.16 | 1 |
| 3 | d-PDMS | 9.6 | PDMS | 200[a] | 200 | 20 | 0.87 | 13.5 | 1.21 | 1 |
| 4 | d-PDMS | 3.0 | PDMS | 200[a] | 217 | 20 | 2.8 | 16.6 | 1.48 | 1 |
| 5 | d-PDMS | 0.18 | PDMS | 200[a] | 173 | 20 | 4.6 | 19.0 | 1.70 | 1 |
| 6 | d-PMMA | 260[b] | PSAN-19 | 133[b] | 180 | 25 | 1.2 | 11.4 | 1.03 | 2 |
| | d-PMMA | 260[b] | PSAN-19 | 133[b] | 180 | 130 | 1.13 | 11.1 | 1.00 | 3 |
| 7 | d-PMMA | 260[b] | PSAN-19 | 260 | 270 | 25 | 1.2 | 14.7 | 1.07 | 2 |
| | d-PMMA | 260[b] | PSAN-19 | 260 | 270 | 130 | 0.93 | 14.2 | 1.03 | 3 |
| 8 | d-PMMA | 260[b] | PSAN-19 | 443 | 440 | 25 | 1.08 | 20.2 | 1.17 | 2 |
| | d-PMMA | 260[b] | PSAN-19 | 443 | 440 | 130 | 0.89 | 19.2 | 1.11 | 3 |
| 9 | d-PMMA | 260[b] | PSAN-10 | 62 | 70 | 25 | −1.00 | 7.4 | | 2 |
| | d-PMMA | 260[b] | PSAN-10 | 62 | 70 | 130 | −1.10 | 7.0 | | 3 |
| 10 | d-PMMA | 260[b] | PSAN-28.7 | 242 | 200 | 25 | 0.67 | 14.0 | | 2 |
| | d-PMMA | 260[b] | PSAN-28.7 | 242 | 200 | 130 | −0.20 | 12.0 | | 3 |
| 11 | PSAN-17 | 210 | d-PSAN-19 | 290 | 320 | 25 | −0.10 | 13.7 | 0.99 | 4 |
| | PSAN-19 | 210 | d-PSAN-19 | 290 | 280 | 25 | 0 | 13.8 | 1.00 | 4 |
| | PSAN-21.9 | 150 | d-PSAN-19 | 290 | 280 | 25 | −0.22 | 13.6 | 0.99 | 4 |
| 12 | d-PMMA | 260 | PSAN-19 | 260 | 270 | 25 | 1.17 | 14.9 | 1.08 | 4 |
| 13 | PSAN-19 | 210 | d-PMMA | 490 | 510 | 25 | 0.8 | 20.9 | 1.13 | 4 |
| 14 | PVC | 58 | d-PMMA | 490 | 510 | 25 | 0.3 | 20.8 | 1.12 | 4 |
| 15 | PPE | 580 | d-PS | 460 | 470 | 25 | 0.13 | 24.4 | 1.30 | 4 |
| 16 | PPE | 46.4 | d-PS(6.1%) | 97[a] | 70±15 | amb? | 0.05 | 9.8 ± 2 | | 5 |
| | PPE | 46.4 | d-PS(4.2%) | 97[a] | 70±15 | amb? | to | 10 ± 2 | | 5 |
| | PPE | 46.4 | d-PS(1.3%) | 97[a] | 70±15 | amb? | 0.75 | 10 ± 2 | | 5 |
| 17 | PS | ? | d-PS | 97 | 70±15 | amb? | ? | 8.5-9.0 | | 5 |
| 18 | PS/PPE(91%) | 33/35 | d-PS | 29 | | amb? | 3.7 | 4.8 ± 0.4 | | 6 |
| 19 | PSAN-15.5 | 130 | d-PSAN-19 | 290 | 285 | 25 | −0.65 | 12.8 | 0.93 | 7 |
| | PSAN-15.5 | 130 | d-PSAN-19 | 290 | 285 | 130 | −0.63 | 12.9 | 0.93 | 7 |
| 20 | PSAN-20.5 | 190 | d-PSAN-19 | 290 | 280 | 25 | −0.15 | 13.7 | 0.99 | 7 |
| | PSAN-20.5 | 190 | d-PSAN-19 | 290 | 280 | 130 | −0.10 | 13.5 | 0.98 | 7 |
| 21 | PSAN-21.9 | 150 | d-PSAN-19 | 290 | 280 | 130 | −0.22 | 13.4 | 0.97 | 7 |
| 22 | PSAN-25 | 155 | d-PSAN-19 | 290 | 280 | 25 | −0.22 | 13.4 | 0.97 | 7 |
| 23 | PSAN-26.8 | 110 | d-PSAN-19 | 290 | (1120) | 25 | phase separation | | ---- | 7 |
| 24 | PMVE | 10 | d-PS | 25 | 22 | 25 | 1.6 | 3.6 | 0.88 | 8 |
| | PMVE | 10 | d-PS | 25 | 22 | 120 | 0.26 | 3.6 | 0.88 | 8 |
| 25 | PMVE | 10 | d-PS | 63 | 60 | 25 | 1.2 | 6.9 | 1.03 | 8 |
| | PMVE | 10 | d-PS | 63 | 68 | 120 | 0.1 | 6.2 | 0.93 | 8 |
| 26 | PMVE | 10 | d-PS | 188 | 187 | 25 | 1.34 | 12.4 | 1.05 | 8 |
| | PMVE | 10 | d-PS | 188 | 214 | 120 | 0 | 11.3 | 0.96 | 8 |
| 27 | PMVE | 10 | d-PS | 465 | 460 | 25 | 1.0 | 19.7 | 1.07 | 8 |
| | PMVE | 10 | d-PS | 465 | 426 | 120 | −0.28 | 16.8 | 0.91 | 8 |

| No. | Matrix (i = 1) Polymer code | $M_w$ (kg/mol) | Probe (i = 2) Polymer code | $M_w$ (sol.) | (SANS) | T (°C) | $A_2 \cdot 10^4$ (ml/g²mol) | $R_g$ (nm) | α | Ref. |
|-----|------|------|------|------|------|------|------|------|------|------|
| 28 | PPE | 36 | d-PS | 25 | 29 | 25 | 1.15 | 3.92 | 0.9 | 8 |
| 29 | PPE | 36 | d-PS | 63 | 76 | 25 | 0.74 | 6.83 | 0.99 | 8 |
| 30 | PPE | 36 | d-PS | 188 | 168 | 25 | 0.4 | 12.23 | 1.03 | 8 |
| 31 | PPE | 36 | d-PS | 465 | 470 | 25 | 0.19 | 22.5 | 1.20 | 8 |
| 32 | PSAN-19 | 211 | d-PMMA | 87 | 83 | 25 | 1.0 | 7.3 | 0.94 | 8 |
| 33 | PSAN-19 | 211 | d-PMMA | 183 | 201 | 25 | 1.0 | 12.5 | 1.11 | 8 |
| 34 | PSAN-19 | 211 | d-PMMA | 634 | 631 | 25 | 0.47 | 25.0 | 1.18 | 8 |
| 35 | PSAN-13 | 200 | d-PMMA | 213 | 182 | 25 | 0.23 | 11.3 | 0.93 | 8 |
| 36 | i-PMMA | 200 | d-PSAN-19 | 316 | 312 | 25 | 0.24 | 16.0 | 1.11 | 8 |
| 37 | PVC | 58 | d-PMMA | 87 | 83 | 25 | −1.78 | 9.1 | 1.17 | 8 |
|    | PVC | 58 | d-PMMA | 87 | 90 | 85 | −2.0 | 8.2 | 1.01 | |
| 38 | PVC | 58 | d-PMMA | 183 | 189 | 25 | −0.47 | 14.2 | 1.26 | 8 |
|    | PVC | 58 | d-PMMA | 183 | 185 | 185 | −0.8 | 8.4 | 0.75 | |
| 39 | PVC | 58 | d-PMMA | 213 | 210 | 25 | 0.09 | 15.0 | 1.23 | 8 |
|    | PVC | 58 | d-PMMA | 213 | 196 | 85 | 0 | 12.7 | 1.00 | |
| 40 | PVC | 58 | d-PMMA | 490 | 510 | 85 | 0.05 | 18.7 | 0.98 | 8 |
|    | PVC | 58 | d-PMMA | 490 | 480 | 185 | −0.4 | 10.4 | 0.56 | |
| 41 | PVC | 58 | d-PMMA | 634 | 694 | 25 | 0.15 | 26.0 | 1.23 | 8 |
| 42 | PPE | 37 | d-PS | 23 | ---- | amb? | 1.51 ± 0.2 | 4.4 | 1.16 | 9 |
| 43 | PPE/PS=1:1 | ---- | d-PS | 23 | ---- | amb? | 0.32 ± 0.15 | 3.7 | 0.97 | 9 |
| 44 | PS | 31.5 | d-PS | 23 | ---- | amb? | 0 | 3.8 | 1.00 | 9 |
| 45 | PPE(B=0.84) /PS=1:1 | ---- | d-PS | 23 | ---- | amb? | 0.033 ± 0.7 | 3.3 | 0.87 | 9 |
| 46 | PP/EP | ---- | d-PP | ---- | ---- | amb. and 200 | immiscible for E 8wt% in EP | ---- | ---- | 10 |

$M_w$  = "sol." and "SANS" indicate the method of determination in solution and by SANS, respectively. Within "sol." "a" from GPC "b" from light scattering

T     = "amb.?", temperature not specified by the authors; probably ambient

$R_g$  = $\langle r_w^2 \rangle^{1/2}$ is the weight average radius of gyration and α is the ratio of $R_g$ to its value at the unperturbed state = $(\langle r^2 \rangle / \langle r_w^2 \rangle)^{1/2}$

d     = in front of the polymer code indicates deuteration

Code  = PDMS: polydimethylsiloxane; PMMA: polymethylmethacrylate; PSAN-X: poly(styrene-co-acrylonitrile), with X indicating the weight percent of acrylonitrile in the random copolymer; PVC: polyvinylchloride; PP: polypropylene; EP: ethylene-propylene copolymer; PPE: poly-2,6-dimethyl-1,4-phenyleneether; PS: polystyrene; PMVE: polymethylvinylether; i-PMMA: isotactic PMMA; PPO(B=0.84): 0.84 mole of Br per monomer unit of PPE; PPE/PS:1: indicate weight ratio of the two polymers in the blend.

*References:* 1. R. G. Kirste and B. R. Lehnen, 1976; 2. Kruse et al., 1976; 3. B. J. Schmitt, 1979; 4. J. Jelenic et al., 1979; 5. G. D. Wignall et al., 1980; 6. R. P. Kambour et al., 1980; 7. B. J. Schmitt et al., 1980; 8. J. Jelenic et al., 1984; 9. A. Maconnachie et al., 1984; 10. D. J. Lohse, 1986.

The important, although seldom stated, assumption is that deuteration alters neither the conformation of macromolecules nor their solubility behavior. The data presented in Table 2.5 seem to corroborate the assumption. However, evidence is accumulating that this is not always so. The theoretical calculations allow one to expect phase separation (with UCST) for a blend of hydrogenated with deuterated polymer (*Buckingham* and *Hentschel, 1980; Edwards, 1983*), i.e. isotopic labelling may alter many physical properties of polymeric systems. The experimental evidence of phase separation of poly-1,4-butadiene with its deuterated analog (*Bates* et al., 1985, 1986; *Bates* and *Wignall, 1986*) or change in the value of $T_c$ upon deuteration (*Schelten* et al., 1977; *Yang* et al., 1983; *Atkin* et al., 1984) demonstrate this quite convincingly. Furthermore, measurements of the interaction parameter $\chi_{12}$ of a deuterated polydimethylsiloxane, PDMS, in its hydrogenated analog lead to $\chi_{12} \cdot 10^3 = 1.7 \pm 0.2$, i.e. a non-negligible value indicating immiscibility (*Lapp* et al., 1985). The latter paper is also worth noting for its theoretical derivation of the relation between the apparent radius of gyration, $R_g$, of the mixture and $\chi_{12}$ in polydispersed, miscible blends. The method of determination of $R_{gz}$ and $\chi_{12}$ which follow from it is general. The isotopic effect in PS/PVME blends was ingeniously exploited for demonstrating that solubility originates in the specific interaction between benzene ring of PS and the ether group of PVME (*Larbi* et al., 1986).

*Green* and *Doyle* (1986, 1987) investigated the mutual diffusion coefficient, $D(\theta)$, in PS-deuterated PS blends. $D(\theta)$ was found to be strongly dependent on composition going through a local minimum, the "thermodynamic slowing down", in the vicinity of the critical concentration for phase separation $\phi_c \simeq 1/2$ at $T_c$. The obtained experimental values of the interaction parameter $\chi_{12} \cdot 10^4 = 0.22(\pm 0.06)/T - 3.2(\pm 2.1)$ were in excellent agreement with *Bates* and *Wignall*'s (1986) data calculated from SANS measurements.

The theoretical basis for compensation of the isotopic segregation effects in SANS have been developed by *W. Wu* (1983). The author provided correcting formulas for $M_w$ as well as for $\langle r^2 \rangle$.

The reports on alteration of physical properties by isotopic labeling seems to contradict the data listed in Table 2.4. Apparently, there are three effects which play a role: (i) position of the isotope; (ii) conditions for SANS measurements and (iii) difference in segmental volume upon deuteration. Regarding (i), PS and polyphenyltrideuteroethylene showed very similar miscibility with PVME, whereas polypentadeuterophenylethylene was quite different (*Larbi* et al., 1986). Regarding (ii), when the measurements were carried out at 100 to 180°C in system with UCST $\simeq -73°C$ the isotopic effect was unimportant (*Yang* et al., 1986). Regarding (iii), the theory indicates importance of the segmental volume for phase relations; it can be inferred that the isotope effect will be stronger for polybutadiene $\Delta V(D/H) \simeq 0.33\%$ than for polystyrene $\Delta V(D/H) \simeq 0.21\%$.

In conclusion, SANS is an excellent method for determination of molecular size and intermolecular interaction in polymer blends provided that the isotopic effects are either absent or appropriately corrected for. It allows precise measurement of the effects of molecular weight, molecular structure, chemical substituents and additives as well as the independent variables, P, T, deformation, etc. Its use in studies of the complex multicomponent systems has but begun.

### 2.6.1.4 Fluorescence Techniques

Scattering techniques are applicable only at relatively high concentration of the scattering ingredient as well as are not being specific enough regarding the nature of the polymer/polymer interface. Fluorescence techniques show promise in overcoming these disadvantages. The application of these methods to characterize polymer blends has been discussed in several reviews (*Frank, 1981; Morawetz, 1983; Winnik, 1984; Egan* and *Winnik, 1986*).

The term "fluorescence techniques" is applied to four steady state and three transient test methods listed in Table 2.6. The excitation can be induced either in a bimolecular process (such as energy transfer), in excimer or in exciplex formation (*Winnik, 1984; Winnik* et al., 1988). Of these, excitation fluorescence, EF, is most commonly used in studies of blend structures (*Frank* et al., 1980; *Semerak* and *Frank*, 1981, 1984; *Gelles* and *Frank*, 1983; *Gashgari*, 1983; *Semerak*, 1983; *Menzheres* and *Moisya*, 1983) and only this method will be discussed here.

TABLE 2.6 Fluorescence Techniques (after M. A. Winnik, 1984)

| A. Techniques | | | | |
|---|---|---|---|---|
| No. | Steady State Measurements | No. | Transient Techniques | Time Scale |
| 1 | fluorescence spectra | 5 | fluorescence decay | ns |
| 2 | phosphorescence spectra | 6 | phosphorescence decay | ns to s |
| 3 | polarization | 7 | polarization decay | ns to s |
| 4 | excitation spectra | | | |

| B. Bimolecular Processes | | |
|---|---|---|
| Reaction | Observation | Spatial Scale (nm) |
| A | energy transfer $A^* + B \to B^* + A$ | emission from B | 1 to 8 |
| B | excimer and exciplex formation $A^* + A \to (AA)^*$ $A^* + D \to (AD)^*$ | new emission from $(AA)^*$ or $(AD)^*$ | 0.5 |
| C | quenching, self-quenching $A^* + Q \leftarrow A + Q$ $A^* + A \leftarrow 2A$ | decreased emission intensity; shorter decay time | 0.5 to 1.5 |

In order to measure EF a system containing an excimer is required, i. e. an electronically excited molecular complex formed from two identical π-systems sharing the same quantum of excitation energy. In practice, the excimers are naturally generated in polymers containing aromatic hydrocarbon rings, viz. polystyrene, polyvinyl-di-benzyl, polyvinylnaphthalene, by grafting the excimer group to the macromolecular chain or by simply adding "probe" molecules (e.g. anthracene) to the polymer blend. In order to form the excimer the aromatic rings must form a coplanar sandwich.

In aromatic vinyl polymers there are three possibilities for rings to form excimers: intramolecular adjacent and non-adjacent as well as inter-molecular types. Each of these is sensitive to different aspects of chain conformation and environment. The most important of these for studies of polymer blends is the intermolecular, usually identified from concentration measurements.

Most frequently, the EF of a quenched film is measured using a steady-state illumination method. It is convenient to express the excimer emission intensity as a ratio $I_D/I_m$ where $I_D$ and $I_M$ are the intensities of emission of the excimer and monomer (e.g. isolated aromatic ring) bands. An example of the results is shown in Fig. 2.29. Here $I_D/I_M$ is plotted as a function of annealing time at 150°C for a blend containing 10% of polystyrene ($M_w$ = 1800 kg/mol) and polyvinylmethylether ($M_v$ = 44.6). The increase of $I_D/I_m$ is caused by separation of phases. EF can also provide quantitative information on the development of phase composition even at a very early stage of phase separation, thus allowing definition of both spinodal and binodal. The method can be equally well applied to study the effect of the annealing temperature, molecular weight of the ingredients, etc. (*Gelles* and *Frank*, 1983).

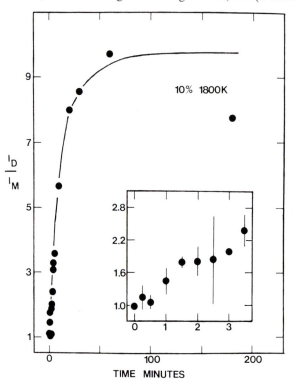

Fig. 2.29 Effect of annealing time on corrected fluorescence ratio for blend containing 10 wt% of polystyrene ($M_w$ = 1800 kg/mol) and 90 wt% of polyvinylmethylether. Annealing temperature was 150 °C (*Gelles* and *Frank*, 1983).

Morawetz is credited with introducing *Förster*'s (1959) method of nonradiative energy transfer (NRET) to polymer blends (*Morawetz* and *Amrani*, 1978; *Nagata*, 1980; *Nagata* and *Morawetz*, 1981). In NRET the energy is transferred from donor to receptor chromophores if the distance between them is of the order of 2 to 5 nm. Carbazolyl- (or naphthyl-) and anthryl- chromophores were incorporated in the two constituents of the blends. Phase separation was evident from a decrease of the chromophore energy transfer (*Morawetz* and *Amrani*, 1978; *Morawetz*, 1980, 1981, 1983; *Amrani* et al., 1980; *Mikes* et al., 1980). NRET allowed it to be concluded that polymethylmethacrylate (PMMA) has poor miscibility with copolymer of methylmethacrylate and either ethyl or butylmethacrylate. For systems containing from zero to about 60% of ethyl (or butyl) methacrylate a continuous decrease of energy transfer was observed, while at 60% the phases separated. The "miscibility windows" for polyethylmethacrylate or polypropylmethacrylate blends with polymethyl-co-butylmethacrylate as well as that of PMMA blend with polystyrene-co-acrylonitrile, SAN, were determined as well (*Amrani* et al., 1980).

The detailed study of PVC blend miscibility by NRET were carried out. Good miscibility of methylethylketone cast film of PVC blended with PMMA was observed. PVC/SAN

miscibility in PVC/PMMA system with PMMA molecular weight was investigated as well (*Albert* et al., 1986).

Miscibility of homopolymers and block copolymer blends were also studied by NRET. Here interpretation of the data was more complex. In these systems the energy transfer, to start with, depends on the morphology of phase separated block polymer. Data on PS or poly-α-methylstyrene, PMS, with PS-MS copolymer, PS or PMS or poly-tertbutylstyrene, PBS, and PS + PBS with PS-BS copolymer were examined (*Mikes* et al., 1984). NRET requires about 1 to 2 mol % of each chromophore, which, considering their high molecular weight seems to be a lot, but so far there is no evidence that grafting chromophores onto polymers affects the macromolecular miscibility. However, use of this technique for measurement of the polymer diffusion coefficient lead to the conclusion that chromophores do slow down the process (*Shiah* and *Morawetz*, 1984; *Antonietti* et al., 1984). The effect may be less important in solutions, where NRET was successfully used to define three ranges of concentration, C, for PS coil interpenetration: (i) $0 < C[\eta] < 1$ no interpenetration, (ii) $1 \leqslant C[\eta] \leqslant 3$ increasing interpenetration, and (iii) $C[\eta] > 3$ interpenetration remains constant. Using the intrinsic viscosity, $[\eta]$, as a scaleup parameter eliminated influence of the solvent (*Chang* and *Morawetz*, 1987).

A summary of systems recently studied by fluorescence techniques is given in Table 2.7. It is rather unexpected to see correlation between the solubility parameter difference [viz. Eq (2.12)] and the miscibility reported for polyvinylaromatics blended with polyalkylmethacrylates. The EF has also been used in studies of the fine structure of latex particles, polymethylmethacrylate swelling kinetics and temperature and environment dependent segmental mobilities (*Winnik*, 1984; *Loufty*, 1984; *Winnik* et al, 1988). The phase separation in blends of polystyrene/polyvinylmethylether was studied by *Naito* and *Kwei* (1979) by means of the chemiluminescence method.

TABLE 2.7 Polymer Blends Studied by Fluorescence Techniques

| No. | Polymer 1 | Polymer 2 | Observation | Ref. |
|---|---|---|---|---|
| 1 | Polyvinylnaphthalene | polyalkylmethacrylates polystyrene, polyvinyl acetate | miscibility was found to decrease with increase of the difference in solubility parameters | 1 |
| 2 | Polyacenaphthalene | same as No. 1 | | 2 |
| 3 | Polyvinylbiphenyl | same as No. 1 | | 3 |
| 4 | Polyvinylnaphtalene $M_w$ = 21, 70 and 365 kg/mol | polystyrene; $M_w$ = 2.2, 4, 9, 17.5, 35, 100, 158 and 233 | phase separation enhanced by increase in $M_w$ | 4 5 |
| 5 | Polyoxymethylene | low and high density polyethylenes | anthracene probe added | 6 |
| 6 | Polyvinylnaphthalene $M_w$'s same as in No. 4 | polymethacrylate $M_n$ = 1, 2.3, 12, 20, 54, 79, 92, 180 and 350 kg/mol | $\chi_{12}$ calculated from critical conditions | 5 7 |
| 7 | Polymethylmethacrylate | poly(methyl methacrylate-co-butyl methacrylate) | tagged with naphthyl-donor and anthryl-acceptor respectively | 8 |
| 8 | Polymethylmethacrylate | poly(styrene-co-acrylonitrile) | tagged with anthryl and carbazolyl groups | 9, 10 |
| 9 | Polyethylmethacrylate or polypropylmethacrylate | poly(methylmethacrytateco-butylmethacrylate) | maximum miscibility defined by minimum in ratio of donor to acceptor fluorescence | 10 |

| No. | Polymer 1 | Polymer 2 | Observation | Ref. |
|-----|-----------|-----------|-------------|------|
| 10 | Polymethylmethacrylate | polybenzylmethacrylate | temp. and conc. effects on miscibility were studied | 11 |
| 11 | Polystyrene | poly-t-butylstyrene | effect of block copolymer on miscibility was studied | 12 |
| 12 | Polyvinylchloride | polymethylmethacrylate or polycaprolactone or poly-(styrene-co-acrylonitrile) | anthracene and naphthalene labelled | 13 |
| 13 | Polystyrene | polystyrene | coil interpenetration was studied | 14 |

*References:* 1. *C. W. Frank*, 1981; 2. *C. W. Frank*, et al., 1980; 3. *M.-A. D. Gashgari*, 1983; 4. *S. N. Semerak* and *C. W. Frank*, 1981; 5. *S. Semerak*, 1983; 6. *A. Y. Menzheres* and *E. G. Moisya*, 1983; 7. *S. N. Semerak* and *C. W. Frank*, 1984; 8. *H. Morawetz* and *F. Amrani*, 1978; 9. *H. Morawetz*, 1980; 10. *F. Amrani* et al., 1980; 11. *H. Morawetz*, 1983; 12. *F. Mikes* et al., 1984; 13. *B. Albert* et al., 1986a, b; 14. *L. P. Chang* and *H. Morawetz*, 1987.

## 2.6.1.5 Ultrasonic Velocity

Sound waves provide a useful tool for investigation of the molecular and macroscopic polymer structures in liquid (*Sakiadis* and *Coates*, 1954; *Pethrick*, 1973) or solid state (*Phillips* and *Pethrick*, 1977–8; *Hartmann*, 1984). Two types of waves, longitudinal (compressive), $V_L$, and transversal (shear), $V_S$, can be used, allowing determination of, the compressive as well as shear elastic properties. The test usually involves measurement of sound velocity and sound absorption.

For low molecular weight liquids empirically: $d\ln V_L/dT = A\, d\ln\varrho/dT$ (*Rao*, 1940), where $A \approx 3$. For polymers the relationship in a generalized version (*Schuyer*, 1959):

$$d\ln V_L/dT = A\, d\ln\varrho/dT - [v_p/(1-v_p^2)]\, d\ln v_p/dT \qquad (2.78)$$

also holds ($\varrho$ is the density and $v_p$ is the Poisson ratio). Since $v_p = v_p(\varrho)$ the measurement of $V_L$ provides a method of rapid and precise determination of $\varrho$ in semi-crystalline polymers (*Schuyer*, 1959; *Davidse* et al., 1962; *Sharma*, 1981; *Piché*, 1984).

Assuming $A = 3$ in Eq (2.78) and integrating lead to definition of the "Rao constant":

$$R_R = V_L^{1/3}(M/\varrho)\,[(1+v_p)/3\,(1-v_p)]^{1/6} \qquad (2.79)$$

where M is the molecular weight and $R_R$ has a unique, characteristic value for each liquid. It is important to note that $R_R$ is an additive constant, whose value can be calculated from tabulated group contributions (*Rao*, 1941, 1946). For low molecular weight liquids M is well defined and $R_R$ can be calculated with high precision on the basis of the molecular structure. For polymers, the situation is more complex; in the case of simple linear macromolecules $R_R$ can be calculated (with error below 10%) assuming disconnected mers, e.g. polyethylene = $-CH_2-CH_2-$, polyoxymethylene = $-CH_2-O-$, etc. Interestingly enough this approach works also for more complex macromolecules such as polyamides, polycarbonate or polyarylsulfone, but it gives false results for associating liquids (*Reddy* et al., 1981; *Bagchi* and *Singh*, 1982). Apparently the method is self consistent; as long as the value of M in Eq (2.79) is consistent with the assumed structure for group additivity calculation, the results are surprisingly good. However, if in the liquid there are associations, immobilizations (due to transitions) or specific interactions, then the experimental $R_R$-values differ from those calculated from the additivity rule.

One can extend this concept a step further. Knowing that bulk modulus:

$$K = \varrho V_L^2 \tag{2.80}$$

and that $V_L$ can be calculated from Eq (2.79) with $R_R$ obtained by group additivity, it is possible to estimate elastic constants for any polymer by means of the "Rao constant" (*McCrum* et al., 1967; *Beyer* and *Letcher*, 1969; *Van Krevelen* and *Hoftyzer*, 1976; *Read* and *Dean*, 1978). For solutions a simple mixing rule is obeyed:

$$R_{Rm} = \Sigma R_{Ri} x_i \tag{2.81}$$

where $R_{Ri}$ is the Rao constant calculated per polymer or a solvent molecule and $x_i$ is the molar fraction of ingredient i. Again lack of agreement usually can be traced to associations, e.g. due to hydrogen bonding (*Singh* et al., 1980; *Das* et al., 1980; *Ekka* et al., 1980; *Reddy* and *Singh*, 1980; *Reddy* et al., 1981; *Gupta* et al., 1982). Eqs. (2.79) and (2.81) should be applicable to miscible mixtures in full range of temperature, including miscible polymer blends in solid or liquid state. It can be expected that immiscibility by virtue of the interface will introduce discontinuity into the sound wave propagation, i.e. enhanced absorbance and deviation from the additivity expressed by Eq (2.81).

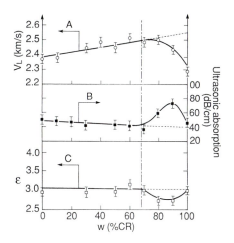

Fig. 2.30 Miscibility study of polyvinylchloride/chlorinated polyisoprene (CR) blends; plot of : A. compressional velocity ($V_L$ at 6 MHz), B. ultrasonic absorption and C. dielectric constant ($\varepsilon$ at 1.592 kHz) vs. CR content. Onset of phase separation is indicated by a vertical chain line at $w(CR) \simeq 68$ wt% (*Suresh* et al., 1984).

The compressive sound velocity at 6MHz at room temperature was used to investigate the ultrasonic behavior of cast film blends of: polymethylmethacrylate/polyvinylacetate (PMMA/PVAc), PMMA/polystyrene (PMMA/PS), and polyvinylchloride/chlorinated poly-isoprene (PVC/CR), (*Singh* and *Singh*, 1983a; *Suresh* et al., 1984). Indeed, as expected, miscibility resulted in linear correlation between $V_L$ and composition, whereas immiscibility (as in PMMA/PS blends) in a highly irregular dependence. It was also observed that in miscible PMMA/PVAc system, due to a morphological change at about w = 70 wt% of PMMA, the correlation was made of two intersecting straight lines. For PVC/CR the $V_L$ vs. w plot showed good straight line dependence up to w = 70 wt % of CR. However, the plot of the ultrasonic absorption vs · composition gave much stronger evidence of immiscibility at high rubber content (Fig. 2.30). PS/ethylenepropylene diene rubber blends were also investigated by the ultrasonic method (*Shaw* and *Singh*, 1987).

Explanation for the non-linearity in $V_L$ and ultrasonic absorption vs. composition dependence in immiscible polymer blends can be found in work by *Arman* et al., (1983, 1986). The authors reported that the experimental plot of attenuations vs. concentration can be theoretically reproduced assuming that excess attenuation (over the linear dependence) is due to the presence of voids at the interface between the two immiscible polymers. In the calculations the measured decrease of average density of blended samples were used. If this explanation has general validity, one may expect that any method which determines density with adequate precision can provide indication of miscibility. However, even if this were the whole story, it is worth recalling that ultrasonics have great advantage for rapidly detecting the density fluctuation via attenuation mapping over large surfaces (*Piché*, 1984; *Arman* et al., 1986). Thus the ultrasonics can be used as a screening method for optimization of processing and its pamareters.

Ultrasonics have been successfully used to study the phase behavior in polyurethanes. The observed $V_L$ vs. T dependence was characteristic for composition and method of preparation (*Volkova*, 1981). The miscibility of polymer blend solutions has also been studied by ultrasonics (*Singh* and *Singh*, 1983b, 1984).

## 2.6.2    Measurement of the Polymer/Polymer Interaction Parameter, $\chi_{ij}$

Of the three types of radiation scattering techniques only light and X-ray have been directly used in determining the phase equilibria. So far SANS has not been analyzed by Eq (2.73) to define the spinodal. Instead, the method found its application for measurements of $M_w$, $R_g$ and $A_2$, i.e. $\chi_{12}$ in the most direct manner. SAXS was also used to determine $\chi_{12}$ (*Wendorff*, 1980, 1982).

In the text the term "direct" is used to separate the methods of $\chi_{ij}$ measurements into two groups: those which do not require addition of a test medium, i.e. where $\chi_{ij} = \chi_{12}$ is measured directly in polymer/polymer blends and those where a test medium (usually a low molecular weight liquid) is needed to calculate indirectly the polymer/polymer interaction coefficient, $\chi_{ij} = \chi_{23}$. A reasonable agreement between $\chi_{23}$ measured by different methods was obtained (*Harris* et al., 1983; *Riedl* and *Prud'homme*, 1984; *Barlow* and *Paul*, 1987).

### 2.6.2.1 Direct methods

SANS and SAXS methods have already been discussed. Here the depression of the melting point, $T_m$, will be of particular interest. The method is based on the Nishi and Wang Equation (2.64). It is worth recalling that on one hand $T_m$ depends on the crystalline type and size (viz. Part 2.5), and on the other that $\chi_{12}$ or B are functions of the independent variables: T, P, $\phi$. To measure $T_m$ is simple, but to measure it with all the necessary care required for subsequent calculation of the interaction parameter is considerably more difficult; it should be a part of the crystallographic studies where, to start with, the unit cell spacing and lamellar sizes are determined. An example of the data is presented in Table 2.8. In system No. 4 a strong concentration effect was noted. In systems Nos. 9 and 19 the variation in crystalline structure precluded calculation of $\chi_{12}$. In system No. 10 the interaction parameter was calculated for the $\alpha$-form of polyvinylidenefluoride. Recently these data were reanalyzed (*Plans* et al., 1984) subtracting the $\gamma$ and $\gamma'$ crystal volumes from the calculations. A good review of the field and careful analysis of the data can be found in *Rim*'s thesis (1983).

Frequently, to support the general conclusions, the $T_m$ depression is taken as one of the signs of "compatibility". Summary of these results is given in Table 2.9. Presence of a compatible, amorphous polymer in the blend usually slows down or even prevents crystallization of the semi-crystalline resin at higher dilutions (*Slagowski* et al., 1981; *Ting*, 1980;

TABLE 2.8 Polymer-Polymer Interaction Parameters Calculated from the Melting Point Depression

| No. | Polymer 1 | Polymer 2 | T (°C) | −B (J/cm³) | −χ'₁₂ | Ref. |
|-----|-----------|-----------|--------|------------|-------|------|
| 1 | Polymethylmethacrylate | Polyvinylidenefluoride | 160 | 12.5 | 0.30 | 1 |
| 2 | Polymethylmethacrylate | Polyvinylidenefluoride | 160 | 12.0 | 0.34 | 2 |
| 3 | Polymethylmethacrylate | Polyvinylidenefluoride | 160 | 13.3 | ----- | 3 |
| 4 | Poly(2,6-dimethyl-1,4 phenylene oxide) | isotactic polystyrene | 240 | 12-26 | ----- | 4 |
| 5 | Polyvinylchloride | Poly(methyl-n-propyl propiolactone) | 90 | ----- | 0.29 | 5 |
| 6 | Polyvinylchloride | Polypivalolactone | 250 | ----- | 0.05 | 5 |
| 7 | cis-Polyisoprene | trans-Polyisoprene | 69 | 0 | 0 | 6 |
| 8 | Polymethylmethacrylate | Polyvinylidenefluoride | 200 | ----- | 0.15 | 7 |
| 9 | Polymethylmethacrylate | Polyvinylidenefluoride | 160 | ? | ----- | 8 |
| 10 | Polymethylmethacrylate | Polyvinylidenefluoride | 170 | 8.83 | ----- | 9 |
| 11 | Polycaprolactone | Saran[a] | 67 | ----- | 0.02 | 10 |
| 12 | Saran[a] | Polycaprolactone | 175 | ----- | 0.21 | 10 |
| 13 | Polycaprolactone | Poly(vinylidene chloride-covinyl acetate) | 67 | ----- | 0.01 | 10 |
| 14 | Poly(vinylidene chloride-co-vinyl acetate) | Polycaprolactone | 175 | ----- | 0.28 | 10 |
| 15 | iso-Polymethylmethacrylate | Polyvinylidenefluoride | 175 | ----- | 0.13 | 11 |
| 16 | syndio-Polymethylmethacrylate | Polyvinylidenefluoride | 175 | ----- | 0.06 | 11 |
| 17 | atactic-Polymethylmethacrylate | Polyvinylidenefluoride | 175 | ----- | 0.10 | 11 |
| 18 | Polycarbonate | Polyarylate | 245 | 6.98 | 0.48 | 12 |
| 19 | Polycaprolactone | Poly(styrene-coacrylonitryle) | 64 | ? | ----- | 13 |
| 20 | Poly-1,4-butylene adipate | Phenoxy[b] | 61 | 16.2 | ----- | 14 |
| 21 | Polyethyleneadipate | Phenoxy[b] | 49 | 9.7 | ----- | 14 |
| 22 | Polycaprolactone | Phenoxy | 56 | 8.5 | ----- | 14 |

Notes: (a) Poly(vinylchloride-co-vinylidenechloride), (b) Poly(hydroxypropylether of bisphenol-A)

*References:* 1. *T. Nishi* and *T. T. Wang, 1977*; 2. *T. K. Kwei* et al, 1976; 3. *R. L. Imken* et al., 1976; 4. *E. B. Wilusz, 1976*; 5. *M. Aubin* and *R. E. Prud'homme, 1980*; 6. *C.-C. E. Kuo, 1981*; 7. *J. H. Wendorff, 1980, 1982*; 8. *Y. Hirata* and *T. Kotaka, 1981*; 9. *B. S. Morra* and *R. S. Stein, 1982*; 10. *M. Aubin* et al., 1983; 11. *E. Roerdink* and *G. Challa, 1978, 1980*; 12. *I. Mondragon, 1983*; 13. *P. B. Rim, 1983*; 14. *J. E. Harris* et al., 1982.

*Pillon* and *Utracki, 1984, 1985, 1986*). However, the opposite effect, i.e. enhancement of crystallinity and increase in $T_m$ has also been observed (*Wang* and *Chen, 1980, 1981*; *Kalfoglu, 1982*; *Harris* and *Robeson, 1987*; *Dumoulin* et al., 1987). It is well known that the method of preparation of blends (mechanical mixing, solvent casting, etc.) have serious effects on blend properties (*Shao-Cheng, 1981*). *Baitoul* et al. (1981) showed that, depending on the type of the mixing equipment, the thermograms of crystallization of LDPE in PS may vary; the melting peak at $T_m \simeq 71°C$ was particularly strongly affected. This peak has not been observed in blends of LDPE/HDPE or LLDPE/HDPE (*Datta* and *Birley, 1982*). The latter blends were found to be "compatible". As shown in Fig. 2.31, $T_m$ is a continuous-,monotonic function of composition.

TABLE 2.9 Melting Point Depression in Polymer Blends

| No. | Polymer 1 | Polymer 2 | T (°C) | Observation | Ref. |
|---|---|---|---|---|---|
| 1 | Polybutyleneterephthalate | Aromatic polyester, CP-350 | 218–226 | Miscible | 1 |
| 2 | Polyethyleneoxide | Styrene copolymers | 50–58 | Miscibility decreases with concentration of-OH in copolymer. | 2 |
| 3 | Polyamide | Epoxy | 140–153 | Three phases | 3 |
| 4 | Polyvinylchloride and Poly-(vinyl chloride-co-vinylidene chloride), 35% vinylchloride (Saran) | Poly(acrylonitrile-co-buta-diene) 30 and 40% of acrylo-nitrile, AN | 140–152 | Miscible ternary blends containing 40% AN; partially miscible for 30%AN | 3 |
| 5 | Poly-ε-caprolactone | Poly(styrene-co-acrylonitrile) | 55, 64 | Miscible for 8.45 AN(wt%) 29.6 | 4 5 |
| 6 | Polyethylene (low density, LDPE) | Polystyrene, PS | 71, 101 | Two melting peaks located at temperatures dependent on mixing method immiscible | 6 |
| 7 | Polyethyleneoxide | Polyvinylacetate | 39–68 | $\chi_{12} = -0.18$ at 65 °C limited miscibility | 6 |
| 8 | Polyethylene (low density and linear low density, or LDPE and LLDPE, respectively) | Polyethylene (high density, HDPE) | 109–134 | Blend HDPE/LLDPE compatible, that with LDPE incompatible. | 8 |
| 9 | Aromatic polyether-ester-amide | Poly-ε-caprolactam | 215–220 | Miscible, strong mutual effects of these polymers on kinetics of crystallization. | 8 |
| 10 | Aromatic polyesters | Chlorinated polymers | 125–268 | Miscibility window in terms or the chlorine content vs. number of $CH_2$-per-COO-group was defined. | 9 |

*References:* 1. *E. L. Slagowski* et al., 1981; 2. *S.-P. Ting* et al., 1980; 3. *Y.-Y. Wang* and *S.-A. Chen*, 1980, 1981; 4. *Ch. Shao-Cheng*, 1981; 5. *S.-Ch. Chiu* and *T. G. Smith*, 1984; 6. *N. K. Kalfoglou*, 1982; 7. *N. K. Datta* and *A. W. Birley*, 1982; 8. *E. Biagini* et al., 1983; 9. *M. Aubin* and *R. E. Prud'homme'* 1984.

An effect of semi-crystalline components of a blend on kinetics of crystallization is expected and has been observed; addition of 10 to 20% of polyetheresteramide to poly-ε-caprolactam nearly doubled its crystallization rate (*Biagini* et al., 1983).

A thorough analysis of crystallization of polyethyleneoxide in blends with polymethyl-methacrylate by *Martuscelli* et al. (1984) led to the conclusion that the system is miscible with $\chi_{23} = -0.35$. The Hoffman-Weeks plot indicated concentration dependent morphology. The entropic effects of mixing were found to be non negligible. For blends of homologous series of aliphatic polyesters with either polyvinylchloride or Phenoxy the importance of the $CH_2$/COO ratio for miscibility has been reported (*Aubin* and *Prud'homme,* 1980, 1984; *Prud'homme,* 1982; *Harris* et al., 1983; *Aubin* et al., 1983). The "window of miscibility" ought to be defined in terms of relative content of interacting groups, e.g. CHCl vs. $CH_2$/COO ratio. The melting point depression correlates with this observation quite well.

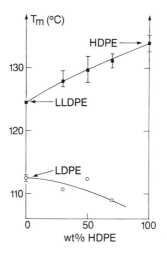

Fig. 2.31 Melting point of high density polyethylene blends with low density (LDPE) and linear low density (LLDPE) polyethylenes (after *Datta* and *Birley*, 1982).

Finally a word of caution. To determine $\chi_{12}$ from the melting point depression: (i) *all* samples must be treated in an identical way, (ii) the molecular parameters, i.e. MW and MWD, must not depend on composition, and (iii) possible chemical reaction between the two polymers should be prevented. Frequently, for practical reasons, the neat resins are tested "as received", whereas blends undergo intensive compounding (*Golovoy,* 1987); it is obvious that such a set of samples would be inappropriate for determination of $\chi_{12}$. It has been noted that blending may enhance shear or thermal degradation of polymers; for example, degradation of polypropylene, PP, upon addition of linear low density polyethylene, LLDPE, has recently been reported (*Dumoulin,* 1988). Ester exchange between two polyesters (*Hanrahan* et al., 1985, 1986) or polyester and polyamide (*Pillon* and *Utracki,* 1984, 1985, 1986; *Hanrahan* et al., 1985, 1986) has been frequently observed and does affect the crystallizability.

The interaction parameter can also be calculated from the P-V-T data on polymer blends (*Jain* et al., 1982; *Privalko* et al., 1985). However, due to the need for subtraction of two large numbers, the computed $\chi_{12}$ values are quite erratic. Instead, it seems that a simpler and more viable method could be computation of the reducing parameters, P*, V* and T*. For miscible systems the dependence of these values on composition can be easily calculated. Usually these compare quite well with the experimental data; immiscibility causes large variation from the monotonic dependence.

An interesting observation of the exothermic effects associated with phase separation of the LCST-type polymer blends was reported by *Natansohn* (1985). The author observed that the magnitude of this effect correlates with the interactions between the components. No effort was made to calculate $\chi_{23}$.

Finally, the analog calorimetry method should be again mentioned (*Cruz* et al., 1979). The enthalpic interaction parameter determined for low molecular analogs via direct measurements of $\Delta H_m$ was found to correlate well with $\chi_{23}$ determined by other methods (*Barlow* and *Paul,* 1987). The disadvantage of the method is its obvious inability to account for structural and or polydispersity effects observed in polymers. A "half way" method is a determination of $\Delta H_m$ for low viscosity oligomeric mixtures (*Zhikuan* et al., 1983; *Zhikuan* and *Walsh,* 1983; *Rostami* and *Walsh,* 1984; *Walsh* et al., 1982, 1985; *Singh* and *Walsh,* 1986).

## 2.6.2.2 Ternary Systems Containing Solvent

For three component systems Eq (2.8) can be written as:

$$\Delta G_m^R = \sum_{i=1}^{3} (\phi_i \ln\phi_i)/V_i + \chi_{12}' \phi_1\phi_2 + \chi_{13}' \phi_1\phi_3 + \chi_{23}' \phi_2\phi_3 \tag{2.82}$$

where $\Sigma\phi_i = 1$, and according to convention, subscript $i = 1$ refers to the solvent and $i = 2, 3$ to the two polymers in the blend. Any method which allows measurements of $\Delta G_m$ or its derivative should in principle yield $\chi_{23}$. Of course, in such a treatment all inadequacies of the Huggins-Flory Eq (2.8) are reflected in variability of $\chi_{23}'$, treated here not as a theoretical parameter of the equation but as an empirical function; viz. Eqs (2.24)–(2.28).

From Eqs (2.2) and (2.82) the osmotic pressure, $\pi = -\Delta\mu_1/V_1$, can be expressed in terms of $\chi_{ij}$. Measurements of $\pi$ provide one of the most direct methods of $\chi_{23}$ determination. It was used by *Shiomi* et al. (1985) to characterize polystyrene(2)/polyvinylmethylether(3) system. In toluene(1): $\chi_{12} = 0.424$, $\chi_{13} \simeq 0.301$ whereas $\chi_{23}$ was found to vary with PS/PVME composition from $-0.044$ to $+0.0093$. In ethylbenzene(1): $\chi_{13} = 0.311$ and $\chi_{23}$ again tend to increase with PVME content varying from $-0.060$ to $0.027$. Elimination of the solvent effects gives: $\chi_{23}' = \chi_{23}/V_1 = 10^{-4}(-7.41 + 11.01\phi_3)$.

The osmotic pressure has also been used to study $\chi_{23}$ between polystyrene and poly-p-chlorostyrene in toluene, 2-butanone and cumene (*Ogawa* et al., 1986). In this case: $\chi_{23} = 0.070 \pm 0.016$. For the same system $\chi_{23} = 0.087 \pm 0.12$ was calculated from the intrinsic viscosity measurements.

The second method of this category is vapor sorption. *Saeki* et al. (1986) investigated the phase separation of polystyrene/poly-α-methylstyrene system using piezoelectric vapor sorption instrument (*Saeki* et al., 1981). The values of $\chi_{23} > 0$ were found to depend on T as well as on polymer concentration. The system was found to be immiscible with UCST above 100°C.

The other method is based on the principle of the Hess cycle, which states that the change $\Delta$ in any thermodynamic state function depends only on the initial and final states, not on the path between them. For example, starting with a solvent and two polymers, the state function F of the blend solution can be calculated either as:

I.      $\Delta F(2,3) = \Delta F_m(2) + \Delta F_m(3) + \Delta F \text{ (solution)}$         (2.83)

or:

II.     $\Delta F(2,3) = \Delta F(\text{blend}) + \Delta F_m(2+3)$          (2.84)

In case I, polymers were dissolved separately ($\Delta F_m(2) + \Delta F_m(3)$), then mixed together ($\Delta F$ (solution) $\simeq 0$). In case II, polymers were first blended together ($\Delta F$ (blend)), then dissolved ($\Delta F_m(2+3)$). From Eqs (2.83) and (2.84):

$$\Delta F(\text{blend}) \simeq \Delta F_m(2) + \Delta F_m(3) - \Delta F_m(2+3) \tag{2.85}$$

Usually, in calorimetric studies the enthalpy is measured, i.e. $\Delta F = \Delta H$. Hence, by measuring heats of dissolution of the two polymers and their blends one can determine the heat of mixing of these two polymers, $\Delta H_m$, and calculate the enthalpic part of the interaction parameter:

$$\chi_h = \Delta H_m/RT\phi_1\phi_2 = -(\partial\chi_{23}/\partial\ln T)_{P,n} \tag{2.86}$$

It is important to recognize that $\Delta H_m$ is the heat of mixing between liquid polymers at the blending temperature $T > T_m > T_g$. If the heats of dissolution, $\Delta H_m$, are determined at temperatures lower than the transition temperatures, $T_m$ and $T_g$, the excess heat of transition, $\Delta H_T$, must be taken into account, i.:

$$\Delta H_m(2) = \Delta H_m^s - \Delta H_T \qquad (2.87)$$

The above treatment would provide reliable results for polymer blends if the data, $\Delta H_m$ or $\chi_h$, could be extrapolated to $\phi_1 = 0$, $\phi_2 + \phi_3 = 1$ condition. Since, usually, $\Delta H_m$ is measured in dilute solutions and extrapolation to melt is impractical, the ternary system methods should be used with caution (*Koningsveld* et al., 1974). The following dependence was proposed (*Kamide* and *Miyazaki*, 1981):

$$\chi_{12} = \chi^0 \, (1 + a_1/m) \, (1 + a_2\phi_2) \qquad (2.88)$$

where: $\chi^0$ is a constant independent of polymer molecular weight and concentration, m is the molar volume ratio of polymer to solvent, $a_1$ and $a_2$ are the molecular weight and concentration dependent coefficients. Eq (2.22) or Eq (2.88) can be used as a guide in the extrapolation procedure.

The early works on $\Delta H_m$ measurements are reviewed in the cited literature. More recently $\Delta H_m$ (at unspecified dilution) of halogenated polystyrenes and copolymers blended with poly-2,4-dimethyl-1,6-phenyleneether (PPE), and with polystyrene (PS) was measured (*Weeks* et al. 1977, *Ryan*, 1979; *Karasz* and *MacKnight*, 1980; *Zacharius* et al., 1983). The results can be summarized as follows:

(i) at 34.8°C the heat of mixing of PS/PPE blend is small and negative: $\Delta H_m / w_2 w_3 = -20 \pm 4$ J/g, where $w_i$ stands for weight fraction of the two polymers, i = 2,3; it seems that in the solutions of PS/PPE there are weak specific interactions between the two polymers;

(ii) in PS/poly-2-chlorostyrene $\Delta H_m = 0 \pm 2$ J/g, i.e. very small, slightly dependent on molecular weight and temperature,

(iii) for PS/poly(2-chlorostyrene-co-4-chlorostyrene) $\Delta H_m = 0 \pm 1$ J/g was found in the full range of copolymer composition; data were taken at 34.8°C using 50/50 by weight of PS/copolymer in the blends,

(iv) by contrast with (iii) in a PPE/copolymer system $\Delta H_m$ plotted vs copolymer composition indicated rapid changes within the range of $\pm 7$ J/g.

The next method of determination of the polymer/polymer interaction parameter in three component systems containing solvent is the ever popular inverse gas chromatography or IGC, method. The method is well described in *Olabisi, Robeson* and *Shaw* (1979) monograph.

IGC has been in vogue since its first description by *Guillet* (1973). The method uses a standard gas chromatograph (GC). In the first step the blend of polymers is deposited on the surface of an inert support, e.g. 60 to 8 mesh polytetrafluoroethylene powder. Next the dry powder is loaded into a GC column and the retention volume, $V_g$, is measured. Finally $\chi_{23}$ is calculated:

$$\chi_1(2,3) = \ln[RT(w_2v_2 + w_3v_3)/P_1^0 V_g V_1] - (1 - V_1/V_2)\phi_2 - (1 - V_1/V_3)\phi_3$$
$$- P_1^0 \, (B_{11} - V_1)/RT \qquad (2.89)$$

where: $\chi_1(2,3) = \chi_{12}\phi_2 + \chi_{13} \, \phi_3 - \chi'_{23}\phi_2\phi_3$ and $\chi'_{23} = \chi_{23} \, V_1/V_2$ with:

$\phi_i$, $w_i$, $v_i$ and $V_i$, respectively, the volume fraction, weight fraction, specific volume and molar volume of the solvent (i = 1) and the two polymers, i = 2, 3, $P_1^0$ the vapor pressure in the column, and $B_{11}$ is the second virial coefficient of the solvent probe. The two interaction coefficients $\chi_{12}$ and $\chi_{13}$ are measured analogously as $\chi_1(2,3)$.

The concentration and temperature dependence of $\chi_{23}$ for blends of cellulose acetate/polyoxymethylene (polyacetal) (*Lipatov* et al., 1979a) is shown in Fig. 2.32. The form of this dependence was reflected in the flow properties. In the following publication the crystallinity and the enthalpy of mixing in low density polyethylene/polyoxymethylene was reported. A complex boundary layer migration in these incompatible systems was postulated (*Lipatov* et al., 1979b).

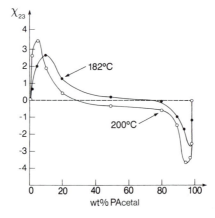

Fig. 2.32 Concentration dependence of the interaction parameter $\chi_{23}$ at 182 and 200 °C for cellulose acetate/polyoxymethylene (polyacetal) blends (*Lipatov* et al., 1979 b).

*Walsh* and *McKeown* (1980) tabulated $\chi_{23}$ at 120°C for blends containing 50/50 by weight of polyvinylchloride (PVC), with any of the following polymers: polyethylmethacrylate, poly-n-propylmethacrylate, poly-n-butylmethacrylate, poly-n-pentylacrylate, poly-n-propylacrylate and poly-n-butylacrylate. As a control the following solvents were used: hexane, butane-2-one, acetonitrile, chloroform, n-propanol, acetone and ethyl acetate. The absolute values of $\chi_{23}$ were relatively large and widely different for each polyacrylate/solvent combination; e.g. for PVC/poly-n-pentylmethacrylate $\chi_{23}$ varied from $-1,97$ (acetonitrile) to $+0.65$ (n-propanol), with the average value $\chi_{23} = -0.36 \pm 0.97$. Miscibility of chlorinated polyethylene (chlorine content 62.1 wt%) with polyethylmethacrylate or polybutylmethacrylate was studied by IGC (*Zhikuan* and *Walsh*, 1983). In the first case the decreasing negativity of $\chi_{23}$ with increase of T ($\chi_{23} = -1.58, -0.50$ and $+0.80$ at T = 80, 100 and 120°C, respectively) indicated expected LCST phase separation behavior. For the second case $\chi_{23}$ were found to be positive, decreasing with T. The behavior was proven to originate in phase separation during the coating process. Under these circumstances Eq (2.89) is not applicable and the values generated by its blind use do not reflect reality.

*DiPaola-Baranyi* and collaborators (1981-5) investigated solubility of several PAB's in the full range of concentration. For blend polystyrene/poly-n-butyl methacrylate at 140°C the following solvents were used: n-octane, 2,2,4-trimethylpentane, n-decane, 3,4,5-trimethylheptane, cyclohexane, benzene, carbon tetrachloride, chloroform, 2-pentanone, 1-butanol, n-butyl acetate. The authors observed that $\chi'_{23}$, calculated from Eq (2.89), had smaller specimen-to-specimen variation than those obtained for $\chi_{23}$. The average values are shown in Fig. 2.33. To check the generality of this observation the previously discussed $\chi_{23}$ values for PVC/polyacrylates (*Walsh* and *McKeown*, 1980) were converted to $\chi'_{23}$. However, in this case no reduction of scatter was obtained.

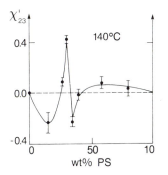

Fig. 2.33 Composition dependence of $\chi_{23}$ at 140 °C for blends of polystyrene (PS), with poly-n-butylmethacrylate; data : *DiPaola-Baranyi* and *Degré* (1981).

The compositional variation of $\chi_{23}$ for the systems: cellulose acetobutyrate/ polyoxymethylene, polystyrene/polycarbonate, polyethylene/poly(ethylene-co-vinylacetate), polyethylene/polyoxymethylene was reported (*Lipatov* et al., 1982; *Gorbatenko* et al., 1982). In all cases the plot resembled that shown in Fig. 2.32; large changes in $\chi_{23}$ at low concentrations were observed. The data at higher temperature were higher, possibly indicating LCST behaviour.

For polyethyleneoxide/polymethylmethacrylate blends at 150°C $\chi_{23}$ was found to be negative and quite sensitive to the type of solvent; i.e. at 51.9 wt% of PEO $\chi_{23} = 0.015$ was calculated from data with CHCl$_3$, whereas $\chi_{23} = -0.077$ from results with benzene (*Elorza* et al., 1984).

Variability of $\chi_{23}$ in IGC determination is a recognized phenomenon. Besides difficulties in controlling experimental sources (e.g. such as thickness of the blend layer on the support particle, casting-solvent dependent morphology) the variability related to the chemical nature of the solvent is universally observed. Some of the reported differences are shockingly large, viz. $\chi_{23} = +7.25$ vs. $-3.84$ reported for polyvinylchloride/polyethylmethacrylate using respectively hexane and CHCl$_3$ (*Walsh* and *McKeown*, 1980). There is no satisfactory explanation. The possible sources of these variabilities include: (i) non-random distribution of polymers combined with a preferential affinity of solvents with one or another polymer in the blend, (ii) different depth of penetration of samples leading to variation of the tested mass of polymer blend, (iii) differences in the concentration of solvent molecules, $\phi_1$, resulting in determination of $\chi_{23} = f(\phi_1)$ at different dilution, etc. It should be recognized that IGC is a diffusion controlled process treated via the equilibrium thermodynamics. It is a surprise when $\chi_{23}$ determined by IGC is in qualitative agreement with values measured by other methods (*Nishi* and *Wang*, 1975, 1977; *Di Paola-Baranyi* and *Degre*, 1981).

*Murakami* et al. (1983) and *Lipatov* et al. (1986) used IGC to study effects of inorganic solid particles on phase equilibrium in polymer/polymer system. As expected, irreversible selective adsorption has been observed; from polyethyleneoxide/polystyrene blends SiO$_2$ or Al$_2$O$_3$ adsorbed preferentially PEO, whereas active carbon PS. The adsorption depended not only on the specific surface area of the inorganic solids but also on the pore size. Since the high molecular weight macromolecules were preferentially adsorbed the addition of solids generally improved the "miscibility". As a corollary, it should be noted that preferential adsorption changes the effective values of $\phi_i$ in Eq (2.89). Since there is no simple method to determine the true $\phi_i$ in IGC experiment the adsorption leads to undeterminable $\chi_{23}$.

For polymethylacrylate/polyvinylacetate blends IGC allowed determination of $\chi_{23}$ vs. composition dependence (*Nandi* et al., 1985); upon increase of PVAc content $\chi_{23}$ decreased from 0.214 at w = 25 wt% to $-0.018$ at w = 75 wt%. The authors reported lack of specific interactions in the system and virtual independence of $\chi_{23}$ from molecular weight.

*Riedl* and *Prud'homme* (1986) determined $\chi_{23}$ at 120°C as a function of the composition of polyvinylchloride blends with seven aliphatic polyesters where the $CH_2/COO$ molar ratio varied from $R_n = 1$ to 7. Depending on the $R_n$ $\chi_{23}$ increased or decreased with PVC concentration in the blend, $\phi_2$. Plot of $\chi_{23}$ (at $\phi_2$=const.) vs. $R_n$ indicated a shallow minimum at $R_n \simeq 5$. The results were discussed in terms of binary interactions between $CH_2$, COO and CHCl groups.

The polymer-polymer interaction parameter can also be calculated from binodal composition in ternary solutions:

$$\chi_{23} = [(1/m_3)\ln(\phi_3''/\phi_3') - (1/m_2)\ln(\phi_2''/\phi_2') -$$
$$(\chi_{13}-\chi_{12})\,(\phi_1'-\phi_1'')]/(\phi_3''-\phi_3'+\phi_2'-\phi_2'') \qquad (2.90)$$

Size exclusion chromatography (SEC) has been used for determination of polymer-polymer interaction coefficient in three component systems: solvent/polymer/polymer (*Narasimhan* et al., 1979, 1983, 1984). The authors demonstrated that SEC gives more precise and thermodynamically more significant data than those determined by turbidity. SEC with a dual detection system allowed determination of the equilibrium composition of separated phases yielding tie-lines, critical points and $\chi_{23}$. In Fig. 2.34 an example of the results is presented. Strong solvent concentration dependence of $\chi_{23}$ is to be noted. The phase diagram for toluene/polymethylmethacrylate/polystyrene systems was reported by *Lau* et al. (1984, 1985). Unexpectedly $\chi_{23}$ was found to be higher for the lower molecular weight polymer pair than for the higher pair; $\chi_{23} = 0.0393$ for PS(37)/PMMA(29) whereas $\chi_{23} = 0.0235$ for PS(100)/PMMA(180).

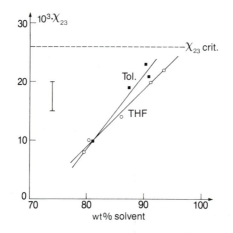

Fig. 2.34 Polystyrene ($M_w = 100$ kg/mol)/polybutadiene ($M_w = 170$) interaction parameter in three component systems containing toluene (top) and tetrahydrofuran at 23 °C. The error bar ± 0.005 and the critical value of $\chi_{23}$ are indicated (*Narasimhan* et al., 1983).

The determination of $\chi_{23}$ is of dubious value for predicting polymer/polymer miscibility. One must recognize the unpredictable variation of $\chi_{ij}$ with T and $\phi$; $\chi_{12}$ and $\chi_{13}$ in Eq (2.90) are not numerical constants; even if they were, extrapolation of $\chi_{23}$ to $\phi_1 = 0$ (see Fig. 2.34) is not obvious. The above comment is pertinent to any of the ternary solvent methods of $\chi_{23}$ determination. These include vapor sorption, equilibrium swelling and other tests (*Olabisi* et al., 1979; *Masi* et al., 1982; *Morel* and *Paul,* 1982; *Harris,* 1981; *Harris* et al., 1982, 1983, 1984).

### 2.6.3   Indirect Methods

Here the methods which provide neither the binodal/spinodal composition nor the numerical value of the interaction parameter will be discussed. In the previous part it was already pointed out that $T_m$ can be used either to calculate $\chi_{12}$ or simply as an indicator of miscibility. Consequently, in the following text the remaining methods of determination of polymer/polymer miscibility will be divided into three parts: 1. Glass transition temperature, 2. Spectroscopy, and 3. Microscopy.

### 2.6.3.1 Glass Transition Temperature ($T_g$)

Glass transition is the generalized Ehrenfest type second order transition existing between glass and a liquid supercooled below its melting point (*Rehage* and *Borchard,* 1973). The generalization involves specifying definite values of the structure parameter, which in turn has a kinetic character. In short, the glass transition is not a pure thermodynamic phenomenon. The change in the extensive thermodynamic functions during glassification of liquid depends not only on the initial and final set of T and P, but also on the way the change has been accomplished. The transition is associated with an increase of the density fluctuation, resulting in a discontinuous jump of the first derivatives dF/dT and dF/dP, where T and P are temperature and pressure, respectively, and F stands for any thermodynamic quantity, e.g. G, S, H or V. The temperature at which the transition occurs is the glass transition temperature, $T_g$, dependent on: sample preparation, rate of scanning, pressure, frequency, additives (plasticizers as well as fillers), molecular parameters (molecular weight and its distribution, tacticity, branching), crystallinity, etc. It can be determined in nearly any physical test, viz. dilatometric, calorimetric, spectroscopic, diffractional, rheological, dielectric or electric.

The values of $T_g$ are quoted either "as measured", i.e. bearing the imprint of all the experimental conditions (i.e. sample size and method of preparation, scanning rate, testing frequency), or reduced to standard conditions taken as equilibrium liquid quenched deep into sub-$T_g$ region, scanned at a rate of (or extrapolated to) below 1°C/min and tested at (or extrapolated to) frequencies in the range: $10^{-2}$ to $10^{-3}$ Hz. In spite of temperatures sometimes quoted with a precision of 1/100°C, the accuracy of $T_g$ measurements is rarely better than ±2°C.

In polymers the glass transition is related to cooperative segmental motion. *Boyer* (1966) suggested that $T_g$ involves 50 to 100 backbone chain carbon atoms, i.e. a domain with diameter $d_d = 2-3$ nm. In agreement with this *Warfield* and *Hartman* (1980) calculated that in the glass transition of amorphous thermoplastics there are 15 to 30 statistical segments (not mers) involved. Much larger values $d_d = 15$ and from 10 to less than 5 nm were assigned respectively by *Kaplan* (1976) and by *Bair* and *Warren* (1981).

The use of $T_g$ in determination of polymer/polymer miscibility is based on the premise that a single $T_g$ indicates that the domain size is below $d_d$, where $2 \leq d_d \leq 15$ nm. Confirmation of this can be found in several publications on $T_g$ of multiphase systems; e.g. *Frisch* et al. (1982) observed two $T_g$'s in interpenetrating polymer network systems, IPN's, and blends having the domain size of 10 to 50nm large. It should be noted that, since the $T_g$ of a copolymer depends on the sequence distribution (*Bonardelli* et al., 1986), the morphology of IPN is expected to influence its $T_g$ behavior.

It is important to recognize that a single $T_g$ *is not a measure of miscibility* (as defined in thermodynamic terms in Part 1.1.1) but only of the state of dispersion. This was clearly demonstrated in a work by *Shultz* and *Young* (1980). The authors dissolved polystyrene (PS) and polymethylmethacrylate (PMMA), in naphthalene, sublimated the solvent out and measured $T_g$ of the blends using differential scanning calorimetry (DSC). The plots of $T_g$ vs. PMMA content for the first and the third scans were different – in the first a single $T_g$ was observed changing linearly with wt% of PMMA, while in the third, as well as subsequent tests performed on annealed samples, two $T_g$'s, typical for PS and PMMA, were observed. Apparently in freeze-dried samples PS and PMMA molecules existed in domains smaller than 15 nm. On annealing the domains coarsened, leading to two distinctive glass transition temperatures characteristic of PS and PMMA.

The correlations between phase equilibria, miscibility under processing conditions and $T_g$ are elusive. $T_g$ is a good tool to for obtaining information, but as any tool, it must be used properly. The glass contains the slowly dissipating memories of the previous treatment of the system, viz. mixing and cooling. Since both the way the blend is prepared and the rate with which it is brought to the initial test condition affect the morphologies and stress distribution, different conclusions can be drawn for the same blend composition, depending on the sample treatments. Table 2.10 lists some of the systems investigated by the DSC method.

In Fig. 2.35 a plot of $T_g$ vs. composition for: immiscible (No. 1), partially miscible (No. 2) and totally miscible (No. 3) blends is presented (*Fried* et al., 1978). There are several equations relating $T_g$ to composition. *Couchman* (1978) proposed the following:

$$\ln T_g = \left[ \sum_i w_i \Delta C_{pi} \ln T_{gi} \right] / \left[ \sum_i w_i \Delta C_{pi} \right] \tag{2.91}$$

where $w_i$, and $T_{gi}$ are respectively weight fraction and glass transition temperature of polymer i in the blend. The symbol $\Delta C_{pi}$ designates the glass transition increment of the heat capacity the of specimen, originally assumed to be independent of T. *Lau* et al. (1982) demonstrated that removing this assumption resulted in a better agreement with the experimental data for polystyrene/poly-α-methylstyrene. Eq (2.91) was derived for intimately miscible blends considering the entropic contribution of pure components and neglecting the enthalpy of mixing. From this relationship several empirical formulas can be recovered:

(i) *Gordon-Taylor* (1952) equation, rederived by *Wood* (1958):

$$\sum_i w_i \Delta C_{pi} (T_{gi} - T_g) = 0 \tag{2.92}$$

For two component systems Eq (2.92) is frequently written in the form:

$$w_1(T_{g1} - T_g) + k w_2 (T_{g2} - T_g) = 0 \tag{2.93}$$

where k (formally equal $\Delta C_{p2} / \Delta C_{p1}$) can be used as an empirical parameter – a measure of miscibility.

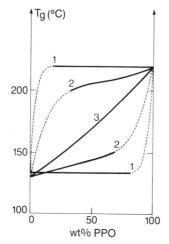

Fig. 2.35 Glass transition temperature vs. poly-2,6-dimethyl-1,4 phenylene ether content for its blends with (1) poly-4-chlorostyrene, (2) poly(styrene-r-4-chlorostyrene) containing 68.6 mol % of 4-chlorostyrene, and (3) as in (2) but 58.5 mol % of 4-chlorostyrene (*Ryan*, 1979).

TABLE 2.10  Glass Transition of Thermoplastic Blends as Measured by Differential Scanning Calorimetry, DSC, or Differential Thermal Analysis, DTA

| No. | Polymer 1 | Polymer 2 | $T_g$ | Observation | Ref. |
|---|---|---|---|---|---|
| 1 | Poly-2.6 dimethyl-1,4 phe-nylene oxide (PPE) $M_w = 34.8$ kg/mol | Poly(styrene-r-4-chloro sty-rene) $M_w = 82$ to 487 | 1 or 2 | Miscible up to 67.1 mole % of 4-chloro-styrene in the copo-lymer. | 1 |
| 2 | PPE | Polystyrene, PS | 1 | | 2 |
| | PPE | Poly(styrene-r-4-chloro-styrene) | | LCST | |
| | PPE | Poly(styrene-r-2-chloro-styrene) | | LCST | |
| | PPE | Poly(4-chlorostyrene-r-2-chlorostyrene) | | LCST | |
| | PPE | Poly-4-chlorostyrene | 2 | | |
| | PS | Poly-2-chlorostyrene | 1 | | |
| | PS | Poly-4-chlorostyrene | 2 | | |
| | PPE | Poly-2-chlorostyrene | | | |
| 3 | PPE | PS | 1 | miscible | 3 |
| | PS | Poly-2-chlorostyrene | 1 | miscible | |
| | PPE | Poly(4-fluoro-r-2-fluoro sty-rene); mole fraction of 4-fluoro: | | | |
| | | X ≤ 0.375 | 1 | miscible | |
| | PPE | X ≥ 0.428 | 2 | immiscible | |
| | PPE | Poly(4-chloro styrene-r-sty-rene) | | | |
| | | X(4-chloro) ≤ 0.679 | 1 | miscible | |
| | PPE | X(4-chloro) ≥ 0.759 | 2 | immiscible | |
| | PPE | Poly(4-bromo-styrene-r-sty-rene) | | | |
| | | X(4-bromo) ≤ 0.520 | 1 | miscible | |
| | | X(4-bromo) ≥ 0.576 | 2 | immiscible | |
| | PPE | Poly(4-methyl styrene) | 1 | miscible | |
| | PPE | Poly(2-bromostyrene-r-sty-rene) | | | |
| | | X(2-bromo) = 0.125 | 1 | miscible | |
| | | X(2-bromo) ≥ 0.313 | 2 | immiscible | |
| | PPE | Poly(4-bromostyrene-r-2 bromo styrene) | 2 | immiscible | |
| 4 | Polyvinyl chloride (PVC) | Polymethyl methacrylate (PMMA) | 1&2 | UCST above 180 °C postulated. | 4 |
| 5 | Chlorinated polyethylene (CPE) degree of chlorina-tion 62% | PMMA | 1&2 | UCST above 180 °C postulated. | 5 |
| 6 | Polybutyleneterephthalate (PBT) | CP-350 aromatic co-poly-ester | 1 | miscibility confirmed in dynamic tests. | 6 |
| 7 | Polyethyleneoxide (PEO) $M_w = 100$ | Poly(styrene-co-4-vinyl phenol) | 1 | miscible | 7 |
| | PEO | Poly(styrene-co-4-vinyl phenyl trifluoromethyl car-binol) | 1&2 | miscible up to 50% PEO | |

| No. | Polymer 1 | Polymer 2 | $T_g$ | Observation | Ref. |
|---|---|---|---|---|---|
| | PEO | Poly(styrene-co-vinyl hexa-fluorodimethyl carbinol) | 1&2 | miscible up to 50% PEO | 7 |
| | PEO | Poly(styrene-co-vinylphenyl trifluoromethyl carbinol) | 1&2 | miscible up to 33% PEO | |
| | PEO | Poly(styrene-co-vinylphenyl methyl carbinol) | 1&2 | miscible up to 11% PEO | |
| | PEO | (PS) | 2 | immiscible | |
| 8 | Poly-ε-caprolactone (PCL) $M_w = 40,400$ | Poly(styrene-co-acryloni-trile), SAN-X, where X is wt % of AN | 2 | immiscible for X ≤ 6 and X ≥ 30 | 8, 9 |
| | PCL | Poly(styrene-co-acryloni-trile), SAN-X, where X is wt % of AN | 1 | miscible for 8 ≤ X ≤ 28 as confirmed in dynamic tests | |
| 9 | Poly(acrylonitrile-co-butadiene) 30 and 40 wt% AN, NBR | PVC | 1&2 | miscible with NBR 40, immiscible with NBR 30 | 10 |
| | Poly(acrylonitrile-co-butadiene) 30 and 40 wt% AN, NBR | Poly(vinylidene chloride-co-vinyl chloride); 65% viny-lidene chloride; P(VC-VC₂), Saran | 2 | immiscible, confirmed in dynamic tests | |
| | PVC | P(VC-VC₂) | 2 | immiscible | |
| | PVC | P(VC-VC₂) + NBR | 1 | miscible | |
| 10 | Poly(styrene-co-4(2-hydroxyl-hexafluoroisopropyl) styrene) MPS-X, where X is mole % of OH | Polyvinylmethylether, or polyvinylacetate, or polyethylmethacrylate, or polybutylmethacrylate or | 1 | miscible for X = 9.7 | 11 |
| | MPS-X | PPO aromatic polyesters (poly-carbonate, polyethy-leneterephthalate, poly-buthyleneterephthalate) aromatic polyamide | 1&2 | partially miscible at X ≤ 17, miscible above | |
| | MPS-X | polyphenylsulfone | 2 | partial miscibility at X = 87 | |
| | MPS-X | polydimethylsiloxane | 2 | incompatible | |
| 11 | PS | Poly(styrene-co-n-butyl methacrylate); X is the wt % of styrene, (COP) | 1 or 2 | compatible for X = 80 up to 15% COP; for X = 64 up to 10% COP | |
| 12 | Poly(α-methyl-n-propyl-β-propiolactone); (PMPPL) | PVC | 1 | miscibility confirmed in dynamic mechani-cal and dielectric tests | 13 14 15 |
| 13 | PMMA | Poly(4-methacryloyloxy-butyl-pentamethyldisiloxane) (P(MBPD)) | 2 | incompatible | 16 |
| | P(MMA-co-MBPO) | PMMA or P(MBPD) | 1 | miscible | |
| 14 | PCL | Chlorinated PVC, or poly-ethylene or polyvinylbromide | 1 | miscible | 17, 18, 19 |
| 15 | Polyurethane | Polyacrylate | 2 | immiscible | 20 |
| 16 | PEO | Polyvinylacetate | 1&2 | partial miscibility ap-parent in dynamic tests | 21 |

| No. | Polymer 1 | Polymer 2 | $T_g$ | Observation | Ref. |
|---|---|---|---|---|---|
| 17 | PS<br>$M_w = 37$, $10^2$ and $10^4$<br>or L, M and H | Poly-α-methylstyrene, PαMS<br>$M_w = 19$, 90 and 510<br>or L, M and H | 1<br>or<br>2 | only PS-L/<br>PαMS-M<br>miscible | 22 |
| 18 | PS | PMS | 1<br>or<br>2 | miscibility depends on<br>the type of solvent<br>used to prepare<br>blends, $M_w$'s and<br>composition | 23 |
| 19 | Polycarbonate (PC) | Poly(ethylene glycol-co-<br>1,4cyclohexane dimethanol<br>teraphthalate) with X mole<br>% of glycol | 1<br>or<br>2 | miscible up to X=54,<br>immiscible above this<br>value | 25 |
| 20 | PBT, M= 45 kg/mol<br>PBT<br>Polyhexamethylenetereph-<br>thalate; $M_w = 30$ | CPE<br>PVC<br>Chlorinated PVC | 2<br>1<br>1<br>or<br>2 | immiscible<br>miscible<br>miscible if cast from<br>toluene, immiscible<br>from 1,4-dioxane | 25 |
| 21 | Polyethyleneterephthalate,<br>PET; $M_w = 40.5$ | Polyestercarbonate,<br>PEC; $M_w = 21.8$ | 1 | miscible | 26 |
| 22 | PBT | Poly(bisphenol-A-phthalate) | 1 | miscible | 27 |
| 23 | PET; $M_w = 81$ | Poly(bisphenol-A-phtha-<br>late), PAr; | 2 | immiscible but misci-<br>bility can be achieved<br>by transesterification | 28 |
| 24 | PAr; $M_w = 51.4$<br>PAr, $M_w = 51.4$ | PET, PBT, PC<br>PEO, SAN, PCL, PMMA<br>cellulose propionate, poly-<br>vinylacetate, polyvinylbuty-<br>rate, Phenoxy | 1<br>2 | miscible<br>immiscible | 29 |
| 25 | Poly(styrene-co-vinyl phenyl<br>hexafluoro dimethyl carbinol)<br>PS | PC or PPE or poly(n-butyl<br>methacrylate)<br>PPE | 1<br><br>1 | miscible<br><br>miscible | 30 |
| 26 | Polyvinylidenefluoride,<br>$PVF_2$; $M_w = 100$ kg/mol | Polyethylmethacrylate<br>isotactic, $M_v = 115$<br>syndiotactic, $M_v = 93$ | <br>2<br>1 | <br>immiscible<br>miscible | 31 |
| 27 | Phenoxy (Poly-hydroxyether<br>of bisphenol-A) | Poly(1,4 butylene adipate),<br>or polyethyleneadipate, or<br>poly(dimethyl-1,3-propylene<br>succinate), or poly(1,4 di-<br>methyl cyclohexane succi-<br>nate) or poly(dimethyl-1,3-<br>propylene adipate), or PCL | 1 | miscible | 32 |
| | Phenoxy | Polyhexamethylenesebacate<br>or polyethylenesuccinate | 2 | immiscible | |
| 28 | PC | Poly(1,4-cyclohaxane di-<br>methylene phthalate)<br>(Kodar) | 1 | miscibility confirmed<br>in dynamic tests | 33<br>34<br>35 |
| 29 | Polyneopenthylglycol adipate | PVC or polyepichlorhydrin | 1 | miscible | 36 |
| 30 | PS | Oligomeric liquid crystals | 1 | miscible | 37 |
| 31 | Poly(styrene-b-α-methyl sty-<br>rene) di-block polymer<br>$M_v = 155$ | PS, $M_v = 355$<br>PαMS, $M_v = 152$ | 2<br>1 | immiscible<br>miscible | 38 |

| No. | Polymer 1 | Polymer 2 | $T_g$ | Observation | Ref. |
|-----|-----------|-----------|-------|-------------|------|
|     | poly(p-tert-butyl styrene) (PtBS) $M_w = 380$ | PS, $M_w = 355$ | 2 | immiscible also in energy transfer tests immiscible | |
|     | PtBS, $M_v = 172$ | PαMS, $M_v = 152$ | 2 | | |
|     | PtBS, $M_w = 58$ | PS, $M_w = 80$ | 2 | | |
| 32  | Polypropylene | Polybutylene | 2 | immiscible but compatible | 39 40 |
| 33  | PS | PMMA | 2 | immiscible | 41 |

*References: 1. J. R. Fried et al., 1978; 2. P. S. Alexandrovich, 1978; 3. Ch. L. Ryan, Jr., 1979; 4. A. Y. Chalynkh et al., 1979; 5. A. Y. Chalynkh and I. N. Sopozhnikova, 1983; 6. E. L. Slagowski et al., 1981; 7. S.-P. Ting, 1980; 8. Ch. Shao-Cheng, 1981; 9. S.-Ch. Chiu and T. G. Smith, 1984; 10. Y.-Y. Wang and S.-A. Chen, 1980, 1981; 11. B. Y. Min and E. M. Pearce, 1981; 12. Y. Baba et al., 1981; 13. R. E. Prud'homme, 1982; 14. T. M. Malik and R. E. Prud'homme, 1984; 15. T. M. Malik and R. E. Prud'homme, 1983; 16. T. F. Blahovici et al., 1982; 17. R. E. Prud'homme, 1982b; 18. P. Cousin and R. E. Prud'homme, 1982; 19. G. Belorgey and R. E. Prud'homme, 1982; 20. K. C. Frisch et al., 1982; 21. N. K. Kalfoglou, 1982; 22. S.-F. Lau et al., 1982; 23. S. Saeki et al., 1983; 24. Anon., 1983; 25. M. Aubin and R. E. Prud'homme 1984; 26. S. M. Aharoni, 1983–1984; 27. M. Kimura et al., 1983; 28. M. Kimura et al., 1984; 29. J. I. Eguizabal, et al., 1984; 30. S. P. Ting et al., 1980; 31. G. ten Brinke et al., 1982; 32. J.E Harris et al., 1982; 33. P. Masi et al., 1980, 1982; 34. E. A. Joseph et al., 1982; 35. D. R. Paul and J. W. Barlow, 1981; 36. S. H. Goh et al., 1982; W. Huh et al., 1983; 38. F. Mikes et al., 1984; 39. Ph. Berticat et al., 1980; 40. G. Boiteux et al., 1980; 41. B. A. Thornton et al., 1980.*

(ii) *Fox* equation (1956):

$$\sum_i w_1(1 - T_g/T_{gi}) = 0 \tag{2.94}$$

(iii) *Utracki* and *Jukes* equation (1984):

$$(\ln T_g)/T_g = \sum_i (w_i \ln T_{gi})/T_{gi} \tag{2.95}$$

The last relation was derived assuming $T_{gi}\Delta C_{pi} = $ const. (*Simha* and *Boyer*, 1962). Detailed examination of the product indicated that for most linear polymers $T_g\Delta C_p = 114 \pm 2(J/g)$ (*Utracki*, 1985b). However, for series of halogenated polystyrenes (*Ryan*, 1979): poly(styrene-co-4-chlorostyrene) and poly(4-fluorostyrene-co-2-fluorostyrene) $T_g\Delta C_p$ was found to decrease with increase of the halogen content from $114 \pm 2$ to $91.2 \pm 5.2$ and $79.4 \pm 5.7$, respectively. It is evident that there are exceptions to the Simha-Boyer rule. Furthermore, since polymer/polymer miscibility (originating from specific interactions) frequently leads to volume reduction, also the assumption of $\Delta C_p$ additivity, $\Delta C_p = \Sigma w_i \Delta C_{pi}$, is not expected to be generally valid.

Eq. (2.95) was found to follow the $T_g$ vs. $w_i$ dependencies for miscible blends (e.g. PPE/PS) as well as plasticized systems (e.g. polyvinylchloride/ di-2-ethylhexylphthalate). However, in blends showing limited miscibility (viz. system No. 2 in Fig. 2.35) it was necessary to introduce an empirical parameter describing deviation from the assumed negligibility of the entropy of mixing. For a two component system:

$$w_1 \ln(T_g/T_{g1}) + kw_2 \ln(T_g/T_{g2}) = 0 \tag{2.96}$$

The dependencies predicted by this relation for different values of k are illustrated in Fig. 2.36. It is apparent that the results presented in Fig. 2.35 can be described by Eq (2.96). It is interesting to note that due to the logarithmic form of this equation for k = 1, a small

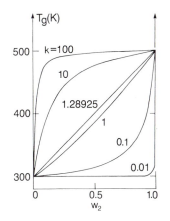

Fig. 2.36 $T_g$-composition dependence as predicted by Eq (2.96) for the indicated values of k. $T_{g1} = 300$ and $T_{g2} = 500K$ were assumed. Note that linearity requires that k = 1.28925.

negative deviation from linear additivity is obtained in qualitative agreement with observations for miscible blends.

Since Eq (2.91) was derived for miscible blends, outside this range the relation (2.96) must be considered empirical, with the parameter k losing its theoretical meaning. Indeed, k calculated from the experimental $T_g$ vs. w dependence gives a measure of miscibility; for k close to one the blends are miscible, for those much larger (or smaller) than one, blends are immiscible. Since as in Eq (2.93) the formal meaning of k is the ratio $\Delta C_{p2}/\Delta C_{p1}$ it is appropriate to ask if proximity of $\Delta C_{pi}$'s can be used as an indication of their miscibility. *Ryan*'s (1979) data dispels such a notion. If $\Delta C_p$ were to be a measure of miscibility, PPE would be miscible with poly(2-fluorostyrene) and immiscible with polystyrene, contrary to the observed behavior. It seems that in the blend, $\Delta C_{pi}$ changes as a result of specific interactions between the two polymers and the parameter k assumes values different from those calculated from the properties of neat resins. In short, k should be considered an adjustable parameter of both Eqs (2.93) and (2.96). Note that since assignment of the subscript i is arbitrary each value of k must be replicated in $k^* \equiv 1/k$.

Eq (2.91) predicts a monotonic variation of log $T_g$ between the two limiting values log $T_{g1}$ and log $T_{g2}$. Consequently the secondary dependencies (2.92) to (2.96) do not permit extremum on the $T_g = T_g(w_i)$ function. On the other hand, the experiment (e.g. *Rodriguez-Parada* and *Percec*, 1986) indicate the existence of miscible blends with higher $T_g$ than that of either of the components. This suggests a reduction of molecular miscibility and that of the free volume fraction caused by strong intermolecular interactions.

For strongly interacting miscible polymer blends the volume can be written as:

$$v = (1 + w_1 w_2 K) v_1^{w_1} v_2^{w_2} \tag{2.97}$$

where K is a measure of the interaction. From the point of view of statistical thermodynamics $T_g$ corresponds to the temperature at which on cooling a certain degree of freedom of motion (or a certain part of the free volume fraction) becomes lost (*Simha*, 1977). From Eq (2.97), expressing v as a function of T and equating the volume of glass and liquid leads to:

$$T_g = (1 + K^* w_1 w_2)(w_1 T_{g1}^{3/2} + w_2 T_{g2}^{3/2})^{2/3} \tag{2.98}$$

where $K^*$ is a material parameter. In Fig. 2.37 $T_g$ is plotted vs. weight percent of poly(N-alkyl-3-hydroxymethyl carbozoylylmethacrylate), N=1 or 2, blended with poly(β-hydroxyethyl-3,5-dinitro benzoylmethacrylate) (*Rodriguez-Parada* and *Percec*, 1986). The polymers

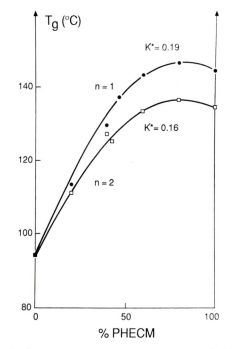

Fig. 2.37 The glass transition temperature for strongly interacting miscible blends forming electron donor-acceptor complex. Data (points) from *Rodriguez-Parada* and *Percec* (1986); lines Eq (2.98) with the indicated value of K*.

form strong electron-donor-acceptor (EDA), complexes with single $T_g$. The single parameter Eq (2.98) describes the dependence quite well, giving correct coordinates of the maximum. The lower value of the interaction parameter K* upon increasing length of the alkyl group is to be noted.

Recently a two-parameters empirical relation was proposed (*Kwei,* 1984; *Kwei* et al., 1987):

$$T_g = (w_1T_{g1}+kw_2T_{g2})/(w_1+kw_2)+qw_1w_2 \tag{2.99}$$

The first term on the right hand side of Eq (2.99) is equivalent to *Gordon-Taylor* Eq (2.93), whereas the second one represents the polymer-polymer interaction contributions. According to the authors the values of the interaction parameter can be correlated with the intermolecular forces originating in polymer structure.

Several authors have stressed the importance of the width of the glass transition, TW, for evaluation of the blend miscibility. For example TW = 6°C was determined (*Fried* et al., 1978) for pure polymers, TW = 10°C for miscible blends and TW $\geq$ 32°C for blends approaching immiscibility. *Alexandrovich* (1978) reported that for miscible blends TW also depends on composition, as illustrated in Fig. 2.38. By molding or annealing the blended samples at different temperatures the author was able to define the location of the LCST (at constant PPE loading) as a function of the copolymer composition, Fig. 2.39. These studies were extended by *Ryan* (1979) to PPE blends with fluorinated and brominated polystyrenes.

*Casper* and *Morbitzer* (1977) studied miscibility of polystyrene/poly(tetra methylbisphenol-A-carbonate), polyvinylchloride/poly(α-methylstyrene-co-methylmethacrylate-co-acrylonitrile) and poly (butadiene-g-acrylonitrile/polyethylene-co-vinylacetate) blends. For

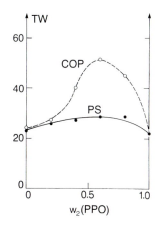

Fig. 2.38 Width of the glass transition temperature for poly-2,6-dimethyl-1,4 phenyleneether blends with polystyrene (PS) or poly(4-chloro-styrene-r-2-chloro-styrene) (COP) containing 36 mole % of 4-chlorostyrene (data *Alexandrovich*, 1978).

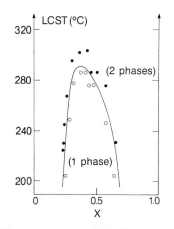

Fig. 2.39 Lower critical solubility temperature of blends containing 60 wt% poly-2,6-dimethyl-1,4-phenyleneether and poly(4-chlorostyrene-r-2-chlorostyrene) in which X, the mole fraction of 4-chloros-tyrene varies. Solid and open points indicate the annealing temperature which generated respectively two $T_g$'s or one $T_g$ (after *Alexandrovich*, 1978).

constructing the phase diagram the blends were annealed at a temperature of interest, then quenched and either scanned in DSC or examined either in a thermo-mechanical analyzer or a torsion pendulum instrument. All three methods allowed determination of $T_g$ from which it was concluded whether at the annealing temperature the blend was phase separated or not. This probably was the first publication on the use of $T_g$ for constructing phase diagrams in complex blends.

In works by *Ting* (1980), *Robeson* et al. (1981), *Min* and *Pearce* (1981), *Macchi* et al. (1986) or by *Goh* and *Lee* (1987) the effect of hydrogen bonding on miscibility of polymers was demonstrated. The effect of molecular weight, i.e. of combinatorial entropy, was discussed (*Lau* et al., 1982; *Saeki* et al., 1983). Compatibility of polylactones with chlorinated polymers was discussed by Prud'homme and collaborators (*Prud'homme*, 1982; *Belorgey* and *Prud'homme*, 1982; *Malik* and *Prud'homme*, 1984). A proof that the old alchemists' rule "simili similibus solvantur" (like dissolves like) is (sometimes) valid for polymer blends

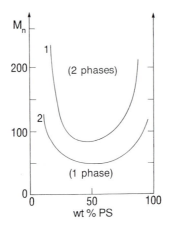

Fig. 2.40 Miscibility gap for polystyrene/poly-α-methylstyrene film cast from toluene (curve 1) or from propylene oxide (curve 2). $M_n$ refers to either polymer (after *Saeki* et al., 1983).

can be found in several publications (*Baba* et al., 1981; *Anon.*, 1983; *Lehr*, 1985). Compatibilization via transesterification of aromatic polyesters was also reported (*Kimura* et al., 1984; *Birley* and *Chen*, 1984; *Hanrahan* et al., 1986).

In work by *Aubin* and *Prud'homme* (1984) as well as by *Saeki* et al. (1983) the authors observed that miscibility depends on the type of solvent used to cast the film. For polyhexamethyleneterephthalate/polyvinylchloride blends toluene yielded a single $T_g$, whereas 1,4-dioxane two $T_g$'s. The results for polystyrene/poly-α-methylstyrene are illustrated in Fig. 2.40 (*Sakei* et al., 1983); it is apparent that films cast from toluene have finer domain size than those cast from propyleneoxide. The $T_g$ behavior of polycarbonate/polyethyleneterephthalate as well as of that polystyrene/polypropylene were reported by *Mucha* (1982, 1986).

To conclude this discussion on DSC/DTA determined $T_g$ of polymer blends it is appropriate to add that for immiscible blends very seldom were two $T_g$'s recorded for compositions containing less than 10 to 20 wt% of the dispersed phase. This experimental range of resolution depends on the difference between $T_g$ of the two polymers; $\Delta T_g = T_{g1} - T_{g2}$. In addition, since the width of the glass transition, TW, can be as large as 40°C (for systems approaching immiscibility), $T_g$ as a method of assessment of miscibility should not be used for systems with $\Delta T_g \leq TW/2 \simeq 20$°C.

To close on a positive note, a double glass transition was obtained for systems in which the energy transfer tests indicated immiscibility, and a single $T_g$ in those where energy transfer showed miscibility (*Mikes* et al., 1984). Furthermore, two $T_g$ and broadening of glass transition region were observed for polycaprolactone/chlorinated polymer blends before the sample became cloudy (*Cousin* and *Prud'homme*, 1982) and in polystyrene/polystyrene-co-n-butylmethacrylate (*Baba* et al., 1981) before a drop in transmittance indicated onset of phase separation. The phase diagram for polystyrene/poly(tetramethylbisphenol-A-carbonate) were constructed using the $T_g$ (*Casper* and *Morbitzer*, 1977; *Illers* et al., 1984).

While, due to the accessibility of relatively inexpensive equipment and ease of operation, DSC/DTA is the most popular method of $T_g$ determination, a close second in popularity is a group of dynamic tests: dielectric, shear, bending or tensile. Since these tests will be discussed in more detail in Parts 3.2 and 3.11, only the conclusions regarding the miscibility of additional systems, not considered on the previous pages, will be presented here. The summary is provided in Table 2.11.

TABLE 2.11 Evaluation of Polymer Blend Miscibility by Dynamic Methods

| N-o. | Polymer 1 | Polymer 2 | Method | Observations | Ref. |
|---|---|---|---|---|---|
| 1 | Polyvinylchloride (PVC) | Polymethylmethacrylate, or Polyethylmethacrylate, or Poly-n-propylmethacrylate, or Poly-n-butylmethacrylate, or Poly-n-hexylmethacrylate, or Poly-n-propylacrylate or Poly-n-butylacrylate | tensile | miscible, film clear | 1 |
|  | PVC | Poly-n-pentylacrylate | tensile | immiscible but film clear | |
|  | PVC | Polymethylacrylate, or Polyethylacrylate | tensile | immiscible, films cloudy | |
| 2 | Polyvinylidenefluoride (PVF$_2$) | Polymethylmethacrylate (PMMA) | tensile | LCST 200°C | 2 |
| 3 | Polystyrene (PS) sulfonated – (PS) containing X mol% of $-SO_3H$ | Polyethylacrylate, or polyisoprene, Poly-(ethylacrylate-co-4-vinyl pyridine), containing X mol% of vinyl pyridine | torsion torsion | immiscible miscible for X $\geq$ 5 | 3 |
|  | Sulfonated polyisoprene, containing X mol% of -SO$_3$H | Poly(styrene-co-4-vinyl pyridine), containing X mol% of vinyl pyridine | torsion | miscible for X $\geq$ 5 | |
|  | Poly(styrene-co-methacrylic acid) | Poly(ethyl acrylate-co-acrylic acid) | torsion | immiscible | |
| 4 | PVC | Poly(butadiene-co-acrylonitrile); NBR -40, containing 40% of acrylonitrile | tensile | single E″ peak in whole range of composition | 4 |
| 5 | Poly-ε-caprolactone, PCL | Polycarbonate, PC, or poly(styrene-co-acrylonitrile), with 28% acrylonitrile | tensile | miscible | 5 |
| 6 | Polyethyleneterephthalate | Polytetramethyleneterephthalate | bending | miscible | 6 |
| 7 | Polymethylmethacrylate, PMMA | Polycarbonate, PC | tensile | partial miscibility confirmed by DSC and SEM | 7 |

*References:* 1. *D. J. Walsh* and *J. G. McKeon*, 1980; 2. *Y. Hirata* and *T. Kotaka*, 1981; 3. *A. Eisenberg* et al., 1982; 4. *C.-Y. Chen* and *S.-A. Chen*, 1982; 5. *G. Groeninckx* and *M. Vandermarliere*, 1984; 6. *H.-M. Li* and *A. H. Wong*, 1982; 7. *Z. G. Garlund*, 1984.

The reasons for using the dynamic methods are much broader than the determination of $T_g$. Knowledge of moduli (or complex dielectric parameters) are essential for proper application of any material. In addition, dynamic spectra allow calculation of the relaxation times providing the basic information about the mobility of affected segments.

In most mechanical or dielectric spectrometers the directly measured properties are the storage modulus, $F'$, (or dielectric constant, $\varepsilon'$) and "damping factor", "phase shift" or the loss tangent, $\tan\delta = F''/F'$, where F stands for shear ($F \equiv G$), bulk ($F \equiv K$), tensile or Young's ($F \equiv E$) modulus or dielectric parameter ($F \equiv \varepsilon$) and ' indicates storage or in-phase quantity while " indicates loss or out-of-phase quantity. While the damping factor has a direct use for some engineering applications (e.g. selection of materials for anechoic rooms) it only expresses the ratio of lost to stored energy. The loss tangent does not have a direct molecular meaning and it should not be used as a measure of $T_g$. It is quite obvious that since in the proximity of this transition both parts of the complex moduli, $F'$ and $F''$, change rapidly the location of the peak position of $F''$ is different from that of $\tan\delta$.

The dynamic data are collected in two ways: (1) more often as a temperature scan at constant frequency, or (2) as the isothermal frequency scans. Due to the "invasion" of computers into test control and evaluation, several instruments provide multiple frequency sweeps during a single temperature scan. For homogeneous, single phase systems methods 1 and 2 generate the same information; for multiphase systems this is seldom the case.

There are numerous reports indicating good, qualitative agreement between DSC/DTA and dynamic mechanical results (*Masi* et al., 1982, *Wang* and *Chen*, 1980, 1981; *Paul* and *Barlow*, 1981; *Shao-Cheng*, 1981; *Slagowski* et al., 1981; *Joseph* et al., 1982; *Prud'homme*, 1982; *Malik* and *Prud'homme*, 1983, 1984; *Chiu* and *Smith*, 1984; *Garlund*, 1984). On the other hand there are some indications of conflict. For polypropylene/polybutylene blends there were two $T_g$'s detected by DSC, whereas only one by dielectric scan (*Boiteux* et al., 1980). Similarly, for polyvinylchloride/poly(butadiene-co-acrylonitrile), PVC/NBR-40, only one $E''$ peak was observed (Fig. 2.41), but detailed analysis of the time-temperature shift parameter, $a_T$, as well as vapor sorption indicated immiscibility (*Chen* and *Chen*, 1982). Due to polymerization sequencing and mismatch of the reactivity ratios the poly(butadiene-co-acrylonitrile) copolymers often show a two phase behavior. Detection of a single $T_g$ in PVC/NBR blends does not preclude existence of small polybutadiene domains with $d \leqslant$ 15 nm.

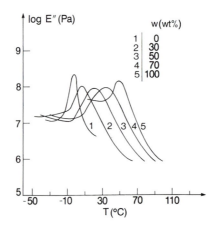

Fig. 2.41 Tensile loss modulus at 35Hz for poly(butadiene-co-acrylonitrile) with w(wt%) of polyvinyl-chloride (*Chen* and *Chen*, 1982).

Of the other methods of $T_g$ determination dilatometry should be mentioned. The method can be easily adapted to test blend miscibility under the pressure expected during processing (*Zoller* and *Hoehn*, 1982; *Jain* et al., 1982; *Walsh* and *Zoller*, 1987). The first authors reported that in poly-2,6-dimethyl-1,4-phenylene ether/polystyrene blends the gradient s ≡ $T_g/P$ changes with the PPE content from 4.3 to 8.2 °C/GPa. Experimentally, the gradient is known to decrease with P: s = $\Sigma s_i P^{i-1}$ (*Dalal* and *Phillips*, 1983). The $T_g$-P dependence has been considered by *Couchman* (1987) and *Couchman* et al. (1984). The following relation was proposed:

$$T_g = s_1 P + s_2 + s_3/[1 + (s_4 P)^2] \qquad (2.100)$$

where $s_i$, i = 1, ..., 4, are material parameters. The authors demonstrated that $T_g$ as well as the melting point and total crystallinity of the polymethylmethacrylate/polyvinylidene-fluoride blends strongly depend on P.

### 2.6.3.2 Nuclear Magnetic Resonance

In the previous sections the miscibility and its influence on the first and second order transitions were treated from a macroscopic point of view. With progress in the fundamental understanding of macromolecular dynamics and rapid developments of instrumentation one can directly trace the sources of the macroscopic transitions to the individual modes of vibrations of specific atoms and their chemical bonds. The spectroscopic methods which are of growing importance for studies of interactions in polymer blends include: (1) nuclear magnetic resonance (NMR), and (2) infrared spectroscopy (IR).

In recent years the developments in NMR have been particularly spectacular (*Ivin*, 1976; *Nishi*, 1978; *Garroway* et al., 1978, 1979; *Callaghan* et al., 1980; *Levy*, 1982; *Tekely*, 1982; *Akitt*, 1983; *Lin*, 1983; *Randall*, 1984; *Caravatti* et al., 1985, 1986; *Blum*, 1986; *Coleman* et al., 1988; *Painter* et al., 1988). High resolution spectra in solution as well as in solid state can be obtained for proton, $^1H$, carbon-13, $^{13}C$, and other common nuclei: $^2D$, $^3T$, $^{11}B$, $^{15}N$, $^{17}O$, $^{19}F$, $^{27}Al$, $^{29}Si$, $^{31}P$, $^{33}Si$, $^{35}Cl$, $^{79}Br$. The broad line NMR, while less popular, still finds its use in studies of slower molecular motion (v = $10^4 - 10^5$ Hz) of e.g. side groups, conformational reorientation of main chain, $T_g$ − related changes in mobility, and studies of morphology.

The early papers on application of NMR methods to studies of polymer blends were reviewed by *Olabisi* et al. (1979) and by *Robeson* (1980). In these papers as well as in the majority of the later publications (*Douglas* and *McBrietry*, 1978; *McBrierty* et al., 1978, 1980; *Kaplan* and *O'Malley*, 1981; *Schaefer* et al., 1981; *Stejskal* et al., 1981; *Kosfeld* and *Zumkley*, 1982; *Derinovskii* et al., 1982; *Jelinski* et al., 1982; *Martuscelli* et al., 1983; *Kaplan*, 1984) the parameters used in determination of polymer/polymer miscibility are mainly the half-life of the spin relaxation times: $T_1$, the spin-lattice, $T_2$, the spin-spin, and $T_{1\varrho}$, the spin-lattice in the rotating frame. The relaxation usually occurs exponentially:

$$\Delta n = \Delta n_0 \exp\{-t/T_i\}; \qquad i = 1, 2 \qquad (2.101)$$

where $\Delta n$ and $\Delta n_0$ indicate the population of perturbed states at time t and t = 0, respectively. In the $T_1$-process the energy difference is transferred to neighboring atoms either of the same molecule or those of the solvent whereas in $T_2$ the energy is transferred to neighboring nuclei.

In Fig. 2.42 the temperature dependence of $T_i$ for polyvinylidenefluoride, $PVF_2$, polymethylmethacrylate, PMMA, and their 3:1 blend is presented. On the relaxation map (a) the Roman numerals, I and II, refer to crystalline chain rotation (or oscillation) and motion of folds, while III and IV to general and restricted motions of amorphous chains, respectively. Similarly in (c) I and II indicate the glass transition and ester side group motion, III motion of − $CH_3$ in the main chain, IV motion of −$CH_3$ in side chains and V torsional

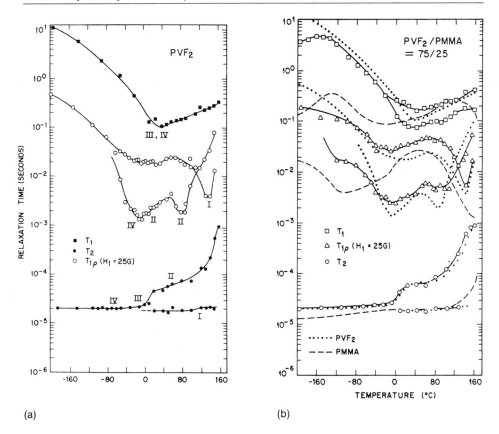

(a)                                                    (b)

motion of the main chain, respectively. The spectral map (b) shows the data obtained for PVF$_2$/PMMA 3:1 blend. Here the results obtained for pure polymers are also denoted. It can be seen that T$_2$ of PVF$_2$ is hardly affected, but both T$_1$ and especially T$_{1\varrho}$ show a remarkable sensitivity to the change of composition. This is a result of the nearest-neighbour proximity of PMMA/amorphous PVF$_2$ segments.

There is a direct relation between the relaxation time and line width – shorter it is, broader it becomes. For solid samples the lines are broad, for liquids and solution they are narrow. The position of the lines, i.e. the precessional frequency of the nucleus, depends on its chemical environment, spatial configuration and interactions. The position of the peak or the so-called "chemical shift" (usually quoted as δ in parts-per-million, ppm) is a reflection of the energetic state of the nucleus, while the line intensity is that of its population.

The modern methods of taking NMR spectra involve use of very short radio frequency pulses (of variable duration from 1 to 200μs) instead of a continuous signal as in older NMR. This requires full automatization of the test, the Fourier transform analysis, data storage and multiple scan capability. With the scalar (low power, about 4kHz) and dipolar (about 45 kHz) decoupling, "magic angle" spinning and cross polarization methods one can obtain spectra of solid samples with resolution similar to those known for liquids. The spectra provide precise information on the local environment of selected nuclei, configuration, interactions and sample morphology.

In Tables 2.12 and 2.13 the summary of more recent works on polymer blends in "solid state" and in solution respectively are presented. The term "solid state" is used to indicate absence of a solvent. The polymer/polymer blends are usually investigated at a wide range of

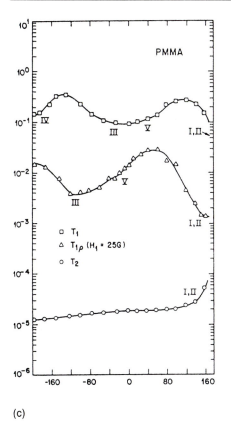

Fig. 2.42 $^{19}$FNMR. $T_1$, $T_{1\varrho}$ and $T_2$ relaxation times as functions of temperature for (a) polyvinylidenefluoride, (b) 3:1 blend of polyvinylidenefluoride with polymethylmethacrylate, the dotted and broken lines indicate the responses of the two pure polymers, and (c) polymethylmethacrylate. The Roman numerals refer to the molecular process discussed in the text (*Douglass* and *McBrierty*, 1978).

(c)

temperatures spanning the crystalline, vitreous and liquid states. Depending on the type of material and the range of temperature the relaxation could be described by a single exponential of the type given by Eq (2.101), or by a more complex type (*Derinovskii* et al., 1982):

$$A/A_0 = \Delta n_1 \exp\{-t/T_{2,1}\} + \Delta n_2 \exp\{-t/T_{2,2}\}$$

$$+ \Delta n_3 \exp\{-\pi(2t/T_{2,3})^2\} + \ldots$$

(2.102)

where A and $A_0$ are the observed signals at time t and t = 0 respectively, and $\Delta n_i$ is the population of nuclei each undergoing spin-spin relaxation with $T_{2,i}$ constant.

The interactions between polyvinylidenefluoride (PVF$_2$), and polymethylmethacrylate (PMMA), polyvinylacetate (PVAc), or polyvinylmethylether (PVME), were studied by dipolar-dipolar decoupling, cross-polarization, magic angle spinning, high resolution $^{13}$CNMR (*Lin*, 1983; *Lin* and *Ward*, 1983; *Ward* and *Lin*, 1984). In Fig. 2.43 the signal intensity attenuations of PMMA and its 50:50 blends with PVF$_2$ are shown. Clear peak assignment for each carbon can be made and peak intensities measured. On blending, the polymer/polymer interaction has relatively little effect on the peak frequency but a very significant one on its intensity. Defining the attenuation $A_t$ (in %) as a ratio of observed to expected (from pure component) intensities the authors reported that for PVF$_2$: PMMA = 50:50 blends cast from dimethyl formamide $A_t$ = 100% (indicating immiscibility), cast from methyl ether ketone $A_t$ = 60 to 75%, and extruded $A_t$ = 26 to 49%. The range quoted does not indicate experimental error (reported to be 5 to 10%) but rather the difference in the

TABLE 2.12  Summary of Solid State NMR Studies of Polymer Blends

| No. | Polymer 1 | Polymer 2 | Method | Observations | Ref. |
|---|---|---|---|---|---|
| 1 | Polystyrene, PS; $M_w = 200$ kg/mol | Polyvinylmethyl ether, PVME; $M_v = 51.5$ | $T_1$ and $T_2$ vs temperature $-200$ to $+170$ °C pulsed $^1$HNMR | miscible but microheterogeneous on segmental scale. LCST $\simeq 84$ °C | 1 2 18 |
| 2 | Polyvinylchloride, PVC; $M_w = 83$ | Poly(ethylene-co-vinyl acetate), EVA; 95 wt% VA, | wide line pulsed line $^1$HNMR; $T_1$ and line width, at $-53$ and 177 °C | semi compatible; co-precipitated blends phase separate at 120 °C | 3 |
| 3 | Polyvinylidenefluoride, PVF$_2$; $M_w = 400$ | Polymethylmethacrylate PMMA; $M_w = 92$ | $T_1$, $T_{1e}$ and $T_2$ at $-200$ to 160 °C pulsed $^1$HNMR and $^{19}$FNMR, cross-relaxation, line intensity | miscible in amorphous phase PVF$_2$ crystals premelting | 4 5 |
|   | Same | Polyethylmethacrylate (PEMA); $M_v = 400$ | same | similar to PVF$_2$/PMMA | 4 |
| 4 | PMMA; | Poly(styrene-co-acrylonitrile) (SAN) | pulsed $^1$HNMR at $-150$ to 160 °C $T_1$, $T_{1e}$ and $T_2$ | inhomogenities on 2 to 15 nm scale | 6 |
| 5 | High density polyethylene (HDPE); $M_w = 1000$ | Polypropylene (PP) $M_w = 4,000$ | pulsed $^1$HNMR at $-200$ to 130 °C $T_1$, $T_{1P}$ and $T_2$ | mixed crystalline regions in "surface grown" fibers | 7 |
| 6 | Poly(styrene-b-ethylene oxide) (PS-PEO) di-block 39.3 wt% PS; $M_n = 20$ and 13 for PEO and PS resp | --- | pulsed $^1$HNMR at $-133$ to 227 °C $T_1$ and $T_2$ | in melt 23% PS is plasticized by PEO, PEO crystallinity lowered by PS | 8 |
| 7 | PS – perdeuterated – d$_8$ | Poly(styrene-b-butadiene), (SB) di-block polymer, or PS | magic angle $^{13}$CNMR $T_1$, line intensity | unstructured interfacial region around rubber domains | 9 |
| 8 | Poly(2,6 dimethyl–1,4-phenylene ether) (PPE); $M_w = 37.5$ | PS; $M_w = 246$, or $M_w = 35$, or isotactic polystyrene (i-PS); $M_w = 335$ | same line shape | miscible, but small regions of undispersed atactic PS | 10 |
| 9 | Low density polyethylene (LDPE) | Polyamide-6, PA-6 | pulsed $^1$HNMR at 20 to 100 °C $T_2$ by free induction decay (FID) | "distinctly incompatible" | 11 |

| No. | Polymer 1 | Polymer 2 | Method | Observations | Ref. |
|-----|-----------|-----------|--------|--------------|------|
| 10 | Epoxy (diglycidyl ether or resorcinol) | Rubber (polyester urethane type) | pulsed $^1$HNMR at $-95$ to $160\ °C$ $T_1$ and $T_2$ (FID) | direct evidence of miscibility from segmental mobility | 12 |
| 11 | Poly(butylene terephthalate-tetramethyleneoxy-terephthalate), with 0.8 to 0.96 mole fraction of "hard" PBT segments (HYTREL's) | ----- | $^{13}$CNMR with scalar and dipolar decoupling, cross polarization, magic angle spinning, nuclear overhauser enhancement (NOE). $T_{1e}$ | separation of phases mobility of "soft" segments is not affected by "hard" | 13 |
| 12 | PMMA; $M_w = 116$ | Polyethyleneoxide, (PEO); $M_w = 20$ | $^{13}$CNMR at 60 and 90 °C $T_1$ from NOE line width | at 90 °C blends are miscible, at 60 °C excessive broadening of PMMA peaks indicates low mobility in miscible blends | 14 |
| 13 | HDPE; $M_n = 50$ | Polytetrafluoroethylene, (PTFE); $M_n = 12$ | $^1$HNMR and $^{19}$FNMR broad line | molecular interaction on interface between PE and PTFE | 15 |
| 14 | PVF$_2$; $M_w = 100$ | Polyvinylacetate, PVAc; $M_w = 70$ or PMMA; $M_w = 800$ or PVME; $M_w = 18$ | $^{13}$CNMR, magic angle spinning, dipolar decoupling, cross polarization, $^{19}$FNMR | different specific interactions for different carbons. Variation of the extend of mixing on method of preparation | 16 17 |

*References:* 1. *T. K. Kwei* et al., 1974; 2. *T. Nishi* et al., 1975; 3. *C. Elmquist,* 1977; 4. *D. C. Douglass* and *V. J. McBrierty,* 1978; 5. *D. C. Douglass,* 1979; 6. *V. J. McBrierty* et al., 1978; 7. *V. J. McBrierty* et al., 1980; 8. *S. Kaplan* and *J. J. O'Malley,* 1979, 1981; 9. *J. Schaefer* et al., 1981; 10. *E. O. Stejskal* et al., 1981; 11. *R. Kosfeld* and *L. Zumkley,* 1982; 12. *V. S. Derinovskii* et al., 1982; 13. *L. W. Jelinski* et al., 1982; 14. *E. Martuscelli* et al., 1983; 15. *S. Nagarajan* and *Z. H. Stachurski,* 1982; 16. *T. S. Lin* and *T. C. Ward,* 1983; 17. *T. C. Ward* and *T. S. Lin,* 1984; 18. *S. Kaplan,* 1984.

TABLE 2.13 Summary of Solution NMR Studies of Polymer Blends

| No. | Polymer 1 | Polymer 2 | Method | Observations | Ref. |
|---|---|---|---|---|---|
| 1 | Polyethyleneoxide | Polypropyleneoxide | $^1$HNMR, amb. temp in CCl$_4$ | determined composition with ± 4% max error | 1 |
| 2 | Polyethyleneterephthalate $M_w = 55$ kg/mol | Polyamide-6,6 $M_w = 36$ | $^1$HNMR and $^{13}$CNMR of trifluoro acetic acid/ chloroform solutions at 40 to 50 °C | determined extend of ester-amide exchange reaction | 2 3 |
| 3 | Poly-2,6 dimethyl-1,4 phenylene ether (PPE) (low mol. weight analogue) | Polystyrene (PS) (low mol. weight analog) | $^{13}$CNMR solution in differents solvents | PPE – methyl group interacts with benzene ring of PS; oxygen is not directly involved | 4 |
| 4 | Polyvinylmethylether (PVME) | PS | same | mechanism of interaction and that causing change of morphology during solvent casting | 5 |
| 5 | Poly-ε-caprolactone (PCL) and low molecular weight analogues | Polyvinylchloride (PVC) low molecular weight models | $^{13}$CNMR at 20 °C, 2500 to 3000 scans averaged, binary solvent mixtures | Association with ester group decrease in a sequence: α, β, hydrogenated chlorocarbons, CCl$_4$, heptane | 6 |
| 6 | Polyesters | Polyvinylbromide or PVC | same | same | 7 |

*References:* 1. *R. Janik* and *J. Plucinski,* 1980; 2. *L. Z. Pillon* and *L. A. Utracki,* 1984; 3. *L. Z. Pillon* and *L. A. Utracki,* 1986; 4. *M. B. Djordjevic* and *R. S. Porter,* 1981, 1983; 5. *M. B. Djordjevic* and *R. S. Porter,* 1982; 6. *A. Garton* et al., 1983; 7. *P. Cousin* and *R. E. Prud'homme,* 1984.

intensity of interaction of particular carbons; the interactions with methoxy were found to be the strongest, while that with α-methyl the weakest. The intermolecular distances $^{13}$C − $^{19}$F were in the range of 0.3 to 0.4 nm.

The use of the variable temperature cross-polarized magic angle spinning method for solid state $^{13}$CNMR spectroscopy adds another dimension to the capabilities of this powerful technique (*Fleming* et al., 1984).

High resolution NMR of polymer solutions has been used to determine the composition and structure of macromolecules, resulting e.g. from co-reaction between two polymers in the blend (*Janik* and *Plucinski,* 1980; *Pillon* and *Utracki,* 1984-6). Another use of this method is to determine the solvent induced changes in chemical shift, or SIS. *Rummens* (1975, 1976) as well as *Rumens* and *Moritz* (1977) demonstrated that for weak, dispersive interactions SIS is proportional to $g^2$, where g is defined as:

$$g = (n_1^2 - 1)/(n_1^2 + 1) \tag{2.103}$$

with $n_1$ being the refractive index of the solvent. The specific intermolecular interactions, IMI, are apparent as deviations from the straight line dependence for a specific group

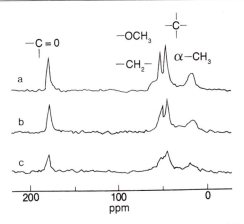

Fig. 2.43 Signal attenuation intensities of: (a) polymethylmethacrylate and its 50:50 blends with poly-vinylidenefluoride cast from methyl ethyl ketone (b) and then remelted and quenched (c). The spectrum was taken using solid state $^{13}$CNMR at 15MHz with dipolar decoupling, cross-polarization and magic angle spinning (*Lin*, 1983).

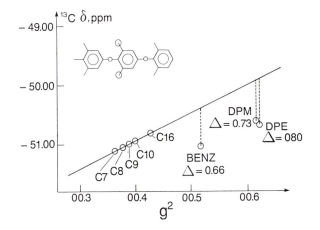

Fig. 2.44 Rummen's plot of $^{13}$CNMR chemical shifts for methyl carbon on the middle segment of 2,6DMP trimer in n-alkanes and aromatic solvents (*Djordjevic* and *Porter*, 1983).

vibration. In Fig. 2.44 the δ vs. $g^2$ plot is shown for a model of polyphenyleneether (PPE), a trimer of 2,6-dimethylphenol (2,6DMP) in n-alkanes, $C_7$ to $C_{10}$, benzene, diphenyl methane (DPM) and diphenyl ether (DPE). The broken lines indicate the IMI effect. From a series of tests on solutions of polymers (or oligomers) in different solvents one can determine not only the source of the specific polymer/polymer interaction, but also its relative magnitude (*Djordjevic* and *Porter*, 1981-3). The data in Fig. 2.44 indicate that the driving force for PPE/PS miscibility is the π-hydrogen bond, between the electrodeficient methyl groups in PPE and π-orbitals in PS (*Djordjevic* and *Porter*, 1983).

The third method of application of solution NMR to polymer blends involves dissolution of a polymer (or a model substance) in a binary mixture of interacting and non-interacting solvents. From the magnitude of δ displacement one can calculate the relative strength of interaction between a specific group of the solute and the two solvents. The information is then used to explain the interaction mechanism in polymer blends (*Garton* et al., 1983; *Cousin* and *Prud'homme*, 1984).

Proton spin-diffusion NMR provides information on the short distance spatial proximity of different segments of molecules. These techniques allow fine characterization of blends. In polystyrene/polyvinylmethylether films cast from chloroform or toluene the method yields information on: blend composition, fraction of interacting groups (phenyl from PS with ether from PVME) and group mobility within each of the three domains (PS, PVME and PS-PVME). In a film cast from chloroform no mixed PS/PVME domains were found, i.e. a phase separated system was concluded. In a film cast from toluene 79% of polymers existed in a mixed phase made of 64 wt% PS and 36 wt% PVME. PS-pure phase contained 8.5 wt% and PVME-pure phase or 12.5 wt% of the total polymer mass. It was observed that group mobilities in the mixed and pure phases were essentially identical (*Caravatti* et al., 1985, 1986).

## 2.6.3.3 Infrared Spectroscopy

Application of infrared spectroscopy in characterization of polymer blends is extensive. There are literally hundreds of papers on the subject. The previous work was reviewed (*Olabisi* et al., 1979; *Robeson*, 1980; *Coleman* et al., 1981; *Coleman* and *Painter*, 1984). Here only selected papers, printed after 1979, will be mentioned. An introductory text to various modern spectroscopic methods for polymeric systems was published by *Klopffer* (1984). The applicability of each of these methods was clearly presented. The fundamental aspects as well as principles of experimentation using infrared dispersive double beam spectrophotometer (IR) or computerized Fourier transform interferometers (FTIR) were discussed.

FTIR was used to study hydrogen bonding in polymer blends (*Ting*, 1980; *Ting* et al., 1980; *Cangelosi*, 1982; *Moskala*, 1984; *Moskala* et al., 1985; *Pennacchia*, 1986; *Coleman* et al., 1988; *Painter* et al., 1988). These interactions not only affected the –OH absorption region (3500 to 3600cm$^{-1}$) but also the =CO stretching (1737 cm$^{-1}$), the –CH$_2$– symmetric stretching (2886 cm$^{-1}$) as well as the finger-printing frequency region (1300 to 650 cm$^{-1}$) and others. The results indicate that macromolecular conformation in hydrogen bonding blends is affected.

In a series of articles *Coleman* and collaborators discussed the interactions in blends of polyesters with chlorinated polymers (*Coleman* and *Varnell*, 1980; *Varnell* and *Coleman*, 1981; *Varnell*, 1982; *Coleman* et al., 1983; *Varnell* et al., 1983). Within the polyester group poly-β-propiolactone, poly-ε-caprolactone and poly(ethylene-co-vinylacetate) were used. The chlorinated polymers were: polyvinylchloride, polyvinylidene chloride and poly(vinyl-chloride-co-vinylidene chloride). Similar systems were also studied by others (*Prud'homme*, 1982; *Garton* et al., 1983; *Iskandar* et al., 1983; *Leonard* et al., 1983; *Morra* and *Stein*, 1984; *Albert* et al., 1986b). Shift of the polyesters carbonyl stretching absorption (1700 to 1775 cm$^{-1}$) was observed in miscible blends and its absence in macroscopically immiscible ones. There is still a question regarding the precise mechanism responsible for miscibility. Hydrogen bonding between C=O and α- or β-hydrogen were proposed as well as a dipolar C=O with C–Cl interactions. There is some indication that mechanisms may vary from system to system within the polyester/ chlorinated polymer group.

FTIR was used for identification of the mechanism of specific interaction in blends of polyvinylidenefluoride/polymethylmethacrylate (*Saito* et al., 1987). Only a small effect of blending was observed in the carbonyl stretching frequency region around 1735 cm$^{-1}$. However, since the system shows UCST there is no reason to expect strong interactions of this type.

Blends of poly-2,6-dimethyl-1,4-phenyleneether (PPE) with polystyrene (PS) are of continuing interest. FTIR, using 1030/700 cm$^{-1}$ peak ratio, can provide a reasonably accurate ($\pm$ 3%) and rapid method of determination of blend composition (*Mukherji* et al., 1980). The factor analysis of the FTIR spectrum at T $\leqslant$ 200 °C indicates the presence of three components: PPE, PS and interacted PPE/PS specimens. The interaction was found to be the highest for 30% PPE in the blends. In the immiscible PPE/poly-p-chlorostyrene blends only two components, PPE and PpClS, were detected (*Koenig* and *Tovar-Rodriguez*, 1981). FTIR was also found to be useful in characterizing the differential orientation of macromolecular chains in solid-state co-extruded blends (*Wang* and *Porter*, 1983).

The amorphous phases of polybisphenol-A-carbonate (PC) blends with poly-ε-caprolactone (PCL) (*Varnell* et al., 1981; *Coleman* et al., 1984c) and with polybutyleneterephthalate (PBT) (*Birley* and *Chen*, 1984) are miscible. Due to the presence of the crystalline phase it was impossible to assign the specific mechanism responsible for miscibility.

Blends of polyhydroxyether of bisphenol-A, Phenoxy, with PCL (*Coleman* and *Moskala*, 1983; *Garton*, 1984), with polyvinylethylether (PVEE), and polyvinylisobutylether (PVBE), (*Moskala* and *Coleman*, 1983) as well as with model compounds (*Garton*, 1983) were studied by FTIR. Direct evidence of hydrogen bonding between the phenoxy -OH group (3400 to 3450 cm$^{-1}$):

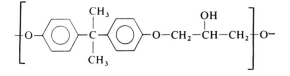

and C=O of PCL was reported; due to steric restrictions only about 50% of C=O groups participated in the process. By contrast, no such interactions were detected in the immiscible blends with PVEE and PVBE.

The homogeneous and heterogeneous blends of polystyrene (PS), with polyvinyl methylether (PVME), prepared by film casting technique from toluene and from chloroform or trichloroethane respectively were studied by FTIR (*Burchell* et al., 1982; *Burchell* and *Hsu*, 1983; *Lu* et al., 1983; *Hsu* et al., 1984). Since the conditions of the phase equilibrium for this system are well known the blend was particularly useful in studying the source of changes introduced by miscibility to FTIR and Raman spectra. The most sensitive vibrations to changes in molecular environment were found to be: in PS the out-of-plane CH, and in PVME the COCH$_3$ at 700 and 1100 cm$^{-1}$, respectively (*Garcia*, 1987).

IR, FTIR and calorimetry were used (*Fahrenholtz* and *Kwei*, 1981; *Coleman* and *Varnell*, 1982; *Fahrenholtz*, 1982) to study compatibility of phenol-formaldehyde (Novolac) resins with polystyrene (PS), poly(styrene-co-acrylonitrile) (PSAN), polyethylacrylate (PEA), polyvinylacetate (PVA), polyethylmethacrylate (PEMA), polymethylmethacrylate (PMMA), poly-2-methyl-1- pentenesulfone (PMPS), polybisphenol-A-carbonate, and polyvinylmethylether (PVME). Large frequency shifts (by about 20 cm$^{-1}$) in CO vibration from 1774 to 1752 cm$^{-1}$ were assigned to hydrogen bonding in miscible blends.

FTIR has been used to study the molecular interactions in blends of poly-4-vinylphenylhexafluorodimethylcarbinol (*Kwei* et al., 1982) polyvinyl alcohol (*Miya* et al., 1984) and polyethyleneterephthalate (*Balizer* and *Talaat*, 1983). The ester exchange has also been studied by FTIR: polyethylene terephthalate/polycarbonate by *Huang* and *Wang* (1986), that of polyethyleneterephthalate/polyamide-6,6 (*Pillon* and *Utracki*, 1986).

FTIR has been used to characterize the interphase region in polymer composites (*Garton*, 1984; *Garton* and *Daly*, 1984). The method can be extended to immiscible polymer blends. The internal reflection spectroscopy (IRS), principle was used. The total depth of penetration varied from 300 to 500 nm. In one of several possible variants of the method a sandwich of two polymers was placed on the IRS element, with the first polymer about 100 to 200 µm thick. For several pairs the first polymer had large enough "windows" in the IR spectrum through which the characteristic bands of the second one could be observed. Comparison of these for neat polymer and for the sandwiched one gave information on the interactions (*Koenig, 1983*).

There are a few publications on the use of other spectroscopic techniques such as: Brillouin scattering (*Patterson, 1979*), photoacoustic (*Balizer* and *Talaat, 1983*) and Raman (*Lu* et al., 1983b, *Coleman* et al., 1984b) spectroscopy. The primary application of these has been to study the heterogeneities in polymer blends, viz. crystallization or phase separation.

### 2.6.3.4 Microscopy

Modern electron microscopy using vacuum tunneling technique allows resolution better than 1Å (*Quate, 1986*). In polymer blends the main application of microscopy is not so much to determine miscibility but rather to study their morphology.

For convenience, as shown in Table 2.14, the microscopic methods can be divided into three categories: optical or light microscopy (OM), scanning electron microscopy (SEM), and transmission electron microscopy (TEM). In most cases some mode of sample preparation has to be used: viz. staining, swelling, fracturing or etching.

In optical microscopy staining with the Smith mixture of two dyes (methylene blue and Sudan III) (*Newman, 1962*), osmium tetroxide (*Kato, 1966, 1967*) or via a proprietary technique developed at CRIF for selective coloring of e.g. polystyrene and polyvinylchloride (*Frederix* et al., 1981) are used. Staining is the preferred method of identification and observation of phases in OM. In the descending order of reliability and convenience the other techniques that have been used are: phase contrast, polarized light, reflected and transmitted light (*Karger-Kocsis* et al., 1984; *Dumoulin* et al., 1984). Etching, grafting and selective swelling are sometimes used to enhance the phase contrast. However, these are dangerous steps which can introduce morphological changes to the blends.

SEM is becoming the most popular method of observation of polymer blends. The great advantages of this technique are: rapidity, range of readily accessible magnifications, depth of field and, almost universal for modern machines, the ability to perform back scattered electron imaging and X-ray elemental analysis of the observed surface. In many cases the latter capabilities eliminate the need for sample preparation. Several reviews on advances of SEM in polymer characterization have been published (*Thomas, 1977*; *Roche* and *Thomas, 1981*; *Vesely* and *Lindberg, 1982*; *Michler, 1984*; *White* and *Thomas, 1984*; *Shaw, 1985*).

Etching of polyamide blends with polyethylenes (*Kamal* et al., 1984b; *Dumoulin* et al., 1985; *Utracki* et al., 1986) and with polyethyleneterephthalate (*Pillon* and *Utracki, 1985, 1986*) not only allowed clear identification of the composition and shape of the dispersed phase (rods vs. spheres) but also demonstrated the physical presence of a block polymer, generated in exchange reaction between the two components of the blend. Polymerizing butyleneterephthalate in the presence of poly(ethylene-co-vinylacetate) resulted in partial transesterification. The SEM was used to investigate adhesion between EVA particles and the PBT matrix (*Pilati* and *Pezzin, 1984*). *Carlin* (1984) used SEM to study the morphology of polymethylmethacrylate/poly(bis-phenol-A-carbonate) blends. Polypropylene blends with polyethylene (*Noel* and *Carley, 1984*), poly(styrene-b-butadiene) teleblock polymer (*Karger-Kocsis* et al., 1984) and with ethylene-propylene rubber (*Yang* et al., 1984) were also observed under SEM; freeze fracture with or without n-heptane etching was used. The use of selective chemical staining techniques was shown to reduce artifacts, enhance contrast and facilitate identification via back-scattering (*Hobbs* and *Watkins, 1982*).

TABLE 2.14 Microscopic Methods

| No. | Parameter | Units | Optical Microscopy (OM) | Scanning Microscopy (SEM) | Transmission Microscopy (TEM) |
|-----|-----------|-------|-------------------------|---------------------------|-------------------------------|
| 1 | Magnification | (times) x | 1 to 500 | 10 to $10^5$ | $10^2$ to $5.10^6$ |
| 2 | Resolution | nm | 500 to 1000 | 5 to 10 | 0.1 to 0.2 |
| 3 | Dimensionality | -- | 2 to 3 | 3 | 2 |
| 4 | Field depth | $\mu$m | ~ 1 (at high magn.) | 10 to 100 | ~1 |
| 5 | Field size | $\mu$m | $10^3$ to $10^5$ | 1 to $10^4$ | 0.1 to 100 |
| 6 | Specimen | -- | solid or liquid | solid | solid |

Notes: No. 1 total range of available magnification within each category;
No. 2 finest detail the microscope can resolve;
No. 3 nearly planar vision (2 dimensions) in TEM and at high resolution OM;
No. 4 ability to discern details perpendicular to the field direction;
No. 5 the diagonal size of field under observation;
No. 6 only OM allows observation of liquid/liquid phase changes.

The effects of concentration, compatibilization and annealing for polyamide blended with either polystyrene or polyethylene were studied by SEM (*Chen* et al., 1988). As the compatibilizer either polypropylene grafted with maleic anhydride or poly(styrene-co-maleic anhydride), SMA, were used at 5 wt% level. Addition of these ingredients reduced the diameter of dispersed phase by a factor of ten and stabilized the system against coalescence at the annealing temperature (T = 200 to 230 °C) for at least 1.5 h.

*Favis* and *Chalifoux* (1988) reported that SEM/OM analysis of polycarbonate/polypropylene blends indicates presence of log-normal distribution of particle size with the particle diameter increasing toward the concentration of phase inversion. The authors also reported that in the vicinity of the phase inversion the droplets adopt a complex, "salami-type" morphology. The diameter of the droplet was found to be proportional to the volume fraction of the dispersed phase, $d \propto \phi^{2/3}$, which may indicate that coalescence is the mechanism responsible for concentration-dependent growth of d.

Influence of process variables on resulting morphology in model polystyrene/polyethylene blends was also investigated by SEM (*Elemans* et al., 1988; *Meijer* et al., 1988; *Valsamis* et al., 1988) polymer viscosity ratio, $\lambda$, resin concentration, type of compounding equipment, processing conditions and compatibilization methods were varied.

Preparation of samples for observation under TEM is more tedious and exacting. The specimens have to be hardened and stained with $Br_2$, $OsO_4$, or $RuO_4$, microtomed into thin ($\geq 20\mu$m) slices, mounted on a grid and polymeric film support and measured. The surface morphology can also be observed under TEM by cryogenic shadow casting and/or replication methods. Here also etching is frequently used to enhance the morphological details (*Rybnikar*, 1985; *Eastmond* and *Phillips*, 1985).

Microscopic methods are frequently used in parallel, the SEM/TEM pair being the most frequent. In all cases microscopy is considered but one method of characterization of polymer blends. (*Lars* et al., 1983; *Yang* et al., 1984; *Karger-Kocsis* and *Kiss*, 1987; *Kyotani* and *Kanetsuna*, 1987; *Hsu* and *Geil*, 1987).

The morphology of polyurethane/polyvinylchloride, PVC, and poly(butadiene-co- acrylonitrile)/PVC blends was studied under TEM by *Wang* (1982). Blends of PS with poly(styrene-g-butadiene) (*Jiang* et al., 1983), as well as those containing poly(p-phenylene terephthalamide) with ABS (*Karger-Kocsis* et al., 1984) were also investigated by this technique.

$RuO_4$ – stained samples of polycarbonate/styrene-maleic anhydride copolymer at several concentrations were analyzed in TEM by *Kita* et al. (1984). TEM was also used in morphological studies of polycarbonate/polybutyleneterephthalate blends (*Delmoy* et al., 1988). Ruthenium tetroxide staining of ultrathin sections revealed partial compatibility in the molten state. Crystallization of PBT from PC solution was observed. The commercial Xenoy CL100 blend (PC/PBT/MBS) was also studied.

There is extensive literature on morphology of rubber-modified thermoplastics. The major publications by *Echte* (1977), *Keskkula* (1979), *Riess* et al. (1980), *Haaf* et al., (1981) and *Paul* et al. (1985) discuss numerous morphological forms observed using several electron microscopy methods. It is of no surprise that the main system of these discussions is rubber modified polystyrene. Using different styrene-butadiene block copolymers lead to variety of morphologies (Fig. 2.45) with imaginative names, e.g. "salami", "onion", "labyrinth", "scalpings", "heap of sticks", "heap of balls", "core-shell", etc. The second system which often is modified to improve its impact strength is polypropylene. Here crystallization complicates the morphological analysis. In the presence of elastomeric particles the spherulitic growth of PP is reduced. The elastomer, although primarily concentrated in the amorphous phase, is also entrapped within the spherulites. The microscopic methods used are:

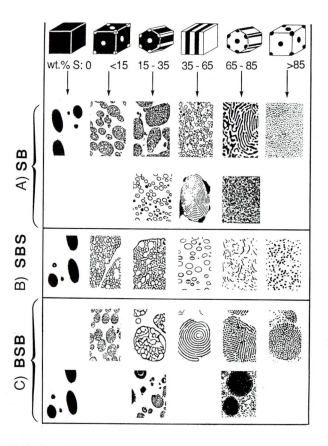

Fig. 2.45 Morphologies of homopolymer/block polymer blends; A) polystyrene/poly(styrene-b-butadiene), B) polystyrene/poly(styrene-b-butadiene-b-styrene) and C) polystyrene/poly(butadiene-b-styrene-b-butadiene).

polarized optical microscopy (*Bartczak* et al., 1984; *Coppola* et al., 1987), transmission electron microscopy (*Karger-Kocsis* et al., 1984; *Hsu* and *Geil*, 1987) and scanning electron microscopy (*Fortelny* et al., 1985; *Karger-Kocsis* and *Csikai*, 1987; *Dumoulin*, 1988; *Dumoulin* et al., 1987).

There are numerous sources of possible errors and for introduction of artifacts in electron microscopy (*Roche* and *Thomas*, 1981; *White* and *Thomas*, 1984). In particular, metallization in SEM and $OsO_4$ staining in TEM may introduce an artificial grain structure observed under greater magnification. Serious errors can be made in cases where the size of the deposit and expected size of the domains are comparable (*Handlin* et al., 1980). Hardening of liquid blend samples is another source of artifacts. Here, experience with biological specimens or with emulsions (*Tung* and *Jones*, 1981) can be of particular value. Staining and hardening may also engender chemical changes in the system, which in turn can be expected to promote phase separation.

Recently two new highly advantageous techniques were introduced to studies of polymer blends: Scanning-transmission electron microscopy, STEM, and low voltage scanning electron microscopy (0.1 to 2 kV accelerating voltage), LVSEM.

STEM uses ultrathin ($\simeq$ 200 nm thick) hardened and stained cast films. The method allows for three techniques of image enhancement which lead to a few nanometers resolution (*Vesely* and *Finch*, 1988). The authors reported phase separation in blends of polyvinylchloride (PVC), with either poly(styrene-co-acrylonitrile) (SAN), polymethylmethacrylate (PMMA), or polyoxymethylene, POM. The PVC/PMMA blends indicated concentration-dependent miscibility; at w $\leqslant$ 40% one phase but at w = 80 wt% PMMA two phases were observed with droplet diameter d $\simeq$ 10 nm. POM/PMMA blends were also found to be immiscible. The method allowed estimation of the interphase interactions.

The advantage of LVSEM is the about ten-fold increased image contrast (in comparison to conventional SEM) with almost no charging problem (*Berry*, 1988). Due to the high value of the secondary electron coefficient even small compositional changes show up in the image. Owing to shallow sampling depth and low energy of the secondary electrons, conductive coating is not required. The method uses flat, ultramicrotomed specimens. Blends of polyestercarbonate/polyphenylene sulfide, polyethylene/poly(vinylchloride-co-vinylidene chloride), polycarbonate/polystyrene, poly(styrene-co-acrylonitrile)/polybutyleneterephthalate, polyethylene/polyamide, polyethylene/polystyrene, polycarbonate/ABS and polybutyleneterephthalate/ABS were investigated. The quality of LVSEM was found to be comparable to that of TEM.

## 2.7    Interphase, Diffusion and Compatibility

From the commercial point of view the properties of the manufactured articles must be reproducible and stable. The variability of morphology with the processing conditions and the phase ripening on aging are two characteristics of heterogeneous blends which deter wider penetration of blends into the market. To be on the safe side, both the resin manufacturer and the processor are looking for a PAB that can tolerate process variability, handling and storing: in short a material which will behave as a homopolymer. One obvious solution is to look for miscible blends with superior properties in processing and/or in performance. While there are more than 400 known miscible blends (*Robeson*, 1980, 1989), this number represents but a fraction of the immiscible ones. Furthermore, from the practical point of view the hetero-phased systems are advantageous; the dispersed phase improves the toughness of brittle polymers or has a reinforcing effect (*Bucknall*, 1977; *Bucknall* and *Stevens*, 1980; *Bucknall* and *Page*, 1982; *Juliano*, 1984; *Bucknall* and *Partridge*, 1985). In short, it is advantageous to produce heterogeneous blends which will be as easy to handle and as stable and reproducible as homopolymers. The way to obtain such systems is by stabilization of the phases, by "compatibilization" or alloying.

The ultimate method of stabilization is by chemical or physical crosslinking of the multiphase system, as is done in the rubber industry (*Bauer*, 1982). Temporary or reversible crosslinking can be achieved by block polymerization (*Krause*, 1981) or by introduction of ionic interactions (*Eisenberg* et al., 1982; *Eisenberg* and *Hara*, 1984; *Smith* et al., 1987). Another way is to generate various types of interpenetrating polymer networks (*Siegfried*, 1980; *Sperling*, 1981; *Siegfried* et al., 1981; *Djomo* et al., 1981; *Adachi* et al., 1982; *Frisch* et al., 1982; *Sperling* and *Widmaier*, 1983; *Yeo* et al., 1983; *Sperling* et al., 1983; *Hage*, 1983; *Lipatov* et al., 1986). However, the prevailing methods of stabilization, compatibilization or alloying, involve addition or generation of an agent which will modify the interfacial properties in polymer systems. In this part first the theory and properties of the interphase region will be discussed, then the current methods of compatibilization will be reviewed.

### 2.7.1    Role of the Interfacial Phenomena in Polymer Blends

When analyzing the composition as a function of linear dimension, l, in immiscible blends one finds that between a domain of polymer A and that of polymer B there exists an interfacial layer of a final thickness $\Delta l$. The value of $\Delta l$ as determined e.g. by SAXS can be as large as 4 nm and contain up to 60% of polymers (*Shilov* et al., 1984). It is reasonable to consider the interfacial region as an "interphase", a third phase in the immiscible blends with its own characteristic properties. In several commercial polymer alloys stabilization of the interphase (e.g. via selective radiation crosslinking) results in reproducibility of performance, processability and recyclability.

Classical thermodynamics specifies the conditions of phase separation, but it is not helpful in determining the size of dispersed phases nor the concentration gradient, g*, existing between them. In the melt, the interface is not a mathematical plane separating the two phases, but as schematically indicated in Fig. 2.46 , a region of interdiffusion of the two types of macromolecules, which can be defined either in terms of:

$$^*g = |\partial \phi_i / \partial l|_{T, P} = \Delta l^{-1} \tag{2.104}$$

or the volume fraction of the interphase. In general, the segmental mobility within the interphase is lower (*Lipatov*, 1978; *Wu*, 1978), as evidenced by increased $T_g$. The relation between $T_g$ and $\Delta l$ is non-monotonic, as are the packing density, surface tension, and the free energy of mixing. The thickness of the interphase layer depends on the thermodynamic interactions, macromolecular segment size, concentration and phase conditions. As a result, the interphase is not a homogeneous diffused layer, but a complex entity with micro- and macro-heterogeneities in orthogonal directions. For this reason neither the measurement nor the interpretation of data pertaining to this layer is straightforward.

There are two important parameters which characterize the interphase: (i) the interfacial tension coefficient, $v$, and (ii) the domain adhesion. The interfacial tension between polymers 1 and 2 can be defined as:

$$v_{1,2} = \int_{-\infty}^{\infty} \Delta F(\phi) dl \tag{2.105}$$

where $\Delta F(\phi)$ represents the profile of the Helmholtz free energy change across the interphase, i.e. $\Delta F(\phi) = F(\phi) - F(\phi = 0)$ and l is the linear dimension perpendicular to the interface. In Eq (2.105) the details of the interphase are incorporated into the profile: $F = F(\phi)$. The equation predicts that $v_{1,2}$ will depend not only on the limiting values: $F(0)$ and

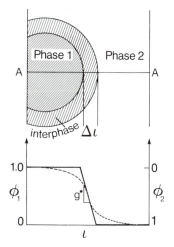

Fig. 2.46 Schematic representation of the interphase region with the concentration gradient g* along the A-A line. The broken line represents Eq (2.106).

F(1), which are determined by the properties of pure resins, but also on the form of the free energy profile across the interphase. In general $v_{1,2}$ is inversely proportional to $\Delta l$.

For a reversible process the interface adhesion can be predicted from values of the interface and surface tensions. However, reversibility is rare. In most cases the separation of two phases will result in energy losses due to plastic deformation, light emission, electric charge dissipation etc.; these losses can be three orders of magnitude larger than the surface energy balance. The adhesion increases with the size and deformability of the interphase.

An exact theory of interfacial tension for two and three component systems (polymers 1 and 2 with their copolymer) near the consolute point has been proposed (*Joanny* and *Leibler, 1978; Leibler, 1982*). The concentration profile of polymer 2 in the interphase can be written as:

$$\phi_2 = \tanh{(l/l_0)} \tag{2.106}$$

where l varies from minus to plus infinity and the reference distance:

$$l_0 = 2L_{\frac{1}{2}}/\ln3 \tag{2.107}$$

with $L_{\frac{1}{2}}$ defined as a distance at which $\phi_2 = 1/2$. It was shown that for three component systems the interfacial tension may be separated into two parts:

$$v_{1,2} = v_{1,2}{}^{(0)} - v_{1,2}{}^{(1)} \tag{2.108}$$

where the first and the second terms respectively represent the polymer and copolymer contributions:

$$v_{1,2}{}^{(0)} = v_0 \{1-[1+\chi^2/8 + 3x/2(\chi-2)]\phi_{12}\} \text{ and } v_{1,2}{}^{(1)} = 3v_{1,2}{}^{(1)}\phi_{12}/2$$

In these equations $v_0 \equiv v_{1,2}{}^{(0)}$ at $\phi_{12} = 0$, $\chi$ is the interaction parameter, and N the degree of polymerization taken here as $N = N_1 = N_2$ and $\phi_{12}$ is the copolymer concentration. Nearly compatible cases with $\chi N = 2$ to 4 were considered. Since $v > 0$, the maximum copolymer concentration $\phi_{12}{}^m - \phi_{12}{}^c = 1-2/\chi N$, where $\phi_{12}{}^c$ is the critical copolymer content. This indicates that Eq (2.108) is only valid at low copolymer concentration. The emulsifying effect of block polymers was recently discussed by *Leibler* (1988). The theoretical analysis indicated that the most favorable case is adsorption of symmetrical block copolymer on large drop surface in highly incompatible blends.

The interfacial tension theory can be based either on the generalized van der Waals or density gradient theory (*Poser* and *Sanchez*, 1981). The latter authors attempted to extend their earlier surface tension theory (*Poser* and *Sanchez*, 1979) to multicomponent low and high molecular weight mixtures. The extension was successful for low molecular weight mixtures, where the profile of $v_{1,2}$ as a function of $v_2$ was computed with less than 5% error. Calculation of the surface tension of polymer solution required use of $\chi$ as an adjustable parameter. For the interfacial tension in polymer blends the treatment was only a crude approximation. Assumption of incompressibility and omission of the macromolecular conformational effects were cited as reasons for the variance. As shown by the authors the older theory (*Helfand* and *Tagami*, 1971; *Helfand* and *Sapse*, 1975) on average provided better agreement. This older theory led to the following expression:

$$v_{1,2} = (2kT\chi'^{\frac{1}{2}}/3) \, [(\beta_1^3-\beta_2^3)/(\beta_1^2-\beta_2^2)]$$

$$\text{(2.109)}$$

where $\beta_i \equiv \varrho_{0i} \langle r^2 \rangle_i / 6N_i$

with $\varrho_{0,i}$ being the number density and $\langle r^2 \rangle_i$ the end-to-end distance of polymer i.

The mutual diffusion (or interdiffusion) coefficient, $D_M$, controls the rate of disappearance of a gradient in inhomogenous system toward homogeneity. Using the Huggins-Flory Equation (2.8) the following dependence can be derived (*Brochard* et al., 1983):

$$D_M = 2\phi_1\phi_2(\chi_s-\chi) \, (N_1D_1^*\phi_2 + N_2D_2^*\phi_1)$$

$$\text{(2.110)}$$

where $\phi_i$, $D_i$ and $N_i$ (i = 1, 2) are respectively volume fraction, tracer diffusion coefficient and polymerization index. The value of the interaction parameter $\chi$ at the spinodal is indicated by $\chi_s = (1/\phi_1N_1 + 1/\phi_2N_2)/2$. An excellent review of the polymer interdiffusion was recently published by *Kausch* and *Tirrell* (1989).

The mutual diffusion coefficient in polystyrene ($M_w$ = 20,000 kg/mol)/ polystyrene ($M_w$ = 110) was measured by Rutherford backscattering spectrometry; here $D_M = D_2(\phi_1 + \phi_2N_2/N_1)^2$. At T = 150°C and $\phi_2 \to 0$ $D_M \to D_2^* \simeq 3 \cdot 10^{-13}$ cm²/s (*Kramer* et al., 1984). $D_M \simeq 5.5 \cdot 10^{-10}$ cm²/s was determined at 176°C for saturated polybutadiene ($M_w$ = 32 kg/mol) diffusing into its high molecular weight homologue (*Jordan* et al., 1988). In miscible polyvinylchloride/polycaprolactone blends $D_M = 10^{-11}$ to $10^{-9}$ cm²/s, with the highest values observed for about 50:50 composition (*Parker* and *Vesely*, 1986; *Jones* et al., 1986). In polyphenyleneether/polystyrene blends $D_M$ values were used to calculate the temperature dependence of the interaction parameter: $\chi_{12} = 0.112 - 62/T$, predicting LCST $\simeq 280$°C (*Composto* et al., 1986, 1988).

Only recently the $D_M$ measurements were used for studying the interface formation in partially miscible polymer blends (*Rafailovich* et al., 1988). The authors measured $D_M$ of the solution chlorinated polyethylene (66% Cl, $M_w$ = 1009 kg/mol) blended with polymethylmethacrylate ($M_w$ = 107) as a function of T. Starting at $T_g$(PMMA) $\simeq 105$°C the diffusion coefficient increased sharply by 4 decades reaching a maximum at T $\simeq 145$°C, then decreasing in a qualitative agreement with Eq (2.110). At 181.5°C $D_M$ achieved a level of $10^{-15}$ cm²/s, comparable to that at $T_g$, i.e. under the phase separation conditions the mutual diffusion virtually stops.

In recent reviews *Sanchez* (1983, 1984) puts forward strong arguments for wider use of *Cahn*'s (1978) approach in theoretical description of the interphase region in two or multicomponent systems.

Noolandi and Hong (*Hong* and *Noolandi*, 1981; *Noolandi* and *Hong*, 1982; *Noolandi*, 1984) developed the most comprehensive theory to date of the interphase region in two and three component systems containing block copolymers. The theory is based on the lattice fluid model with mean-field approximation. For comparison with the Poser and Sanchez calculations the authors also used the equation of state notation. Their computation of the surface tension, $v_i$, of polymer melts took into account the (neglected by *Poser* and *Sanchez*) conformational entropy effects. At low values, the theoretically predicted $v_i$ (no adjustable

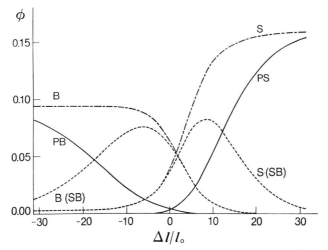

Fig. 2.47 Computed concentration profiles at the interface of polystyrene/poly(styrene-b-butadiene)/polybutadiene; compatibilized blend, PS/SB/PB (*Noolandi* and *Hong, 1982*).

parameters) was in excellent agreement with experimental data. However, as the value increased the theoretical predictions were found to be by up to 20% larger than experimental. It is worth recalling that the Poser and Sanchez theory underestimated $v_i$.

The Noolandi and Hong theory is particularly useful in describing the interphase of systems containing block copolymers. Here a systematic discussion of the interfacial tension, size and structure of the interphase layer is provided. In Fig. 2.47 the computed concentration profiles within the interphase region of a three component system: polystyrene (PS), polybutadiene (PB) and the poly(styrene-b-butadiene) diblock (SB) polymer is presented. There are six curves representing: homopolymer concentrations (PS) and (PB), styrene and butadiene concentrations in SB, S(SB) and B(SB), and finally the total concentration of styrene and butadiene mers. The infinite molecular weight of homopolymers was assumed and N(S)-N(B) = 500-1000 in SB (*Noolandi* and *Hong, 1982*). Computation of the interphase size, tension and concentration profiles via numerical integration requires information on concentrations, $\phi_i$, binary interaction parameters, $\chi_{ij}$, short-range parameters, $\sigma_{ij}$, and degrees of polymerization $N_i$. It can be shown that as the molecular weight of block polymer increases so does its efficiency in decreasing the interface tension. This efficiency is at maximum near the critical-micelle-concentration, CMC. At CMC there is a saturation of block polymer at the interface – any additional amount will form micelles within the homopolymer phases, which do not participate in the behaviour of the interphase region. Variation of CMC with the total degree of polymerization N(SBS) is shown in Fig. 2.48 (see "Discussion" following the *Noolandi* (1984) paper).

More recently *Ronca* and *Russel* (1985) theoretically re-examined the phase equilibrium in two component systems. Their calculations for $\Delta l$ near the critical point, $T_c$, indicated that the interphase thickness can be expressed as:

$$\Delta l^2 \propto MT_c Q/(T_c - T) \qquad (2.111)$$

where, M is the molecular weight. $Q = Q(M, T_c)$ is constant when the three interaction parameters: $\chi_{11}$, $\chi_{22}$, $x_{12}$ have the same temperature dependence. Furthermore the interfacial tension, $v$, was derived to depend on: $\Delta l$, M and Q:

$$v/RT \propto \Delta l^{-3} MQ^2 \qquad (2.112)$$

Note that theoretically $\Delta l \neq 0$.

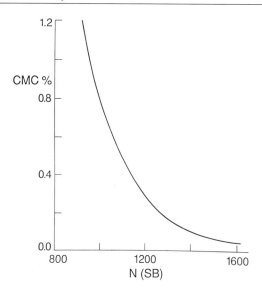

Fig. 2.48 Critical micelle concentration of SB as a function of its total degree of polymerization in PS/SB/PB blend (*Noolandi* and *Hong,* 1982).

There are several experimental methods for determination of v. Of these the sessile drop, pendant drop and spinning drop are the most successful.

In the sessile drop method the equilibrium shape of the stationary droplet of polymer with higher density immersed in the melt of the second polymer is observed. Usually a small cube of the denser material is first placed on the bottom of quartz container then filled with grains of the less dense one. After melting (usually under a blanket of inert gas) formation of an equilibrium droplet is recorded. The equilibration involves flow of polymer melt under the influence of the interfacial forces. Since viscosity of most commercial resins at processing temperatures are $\eta \geqslant 1$ kPa·s and the interfacial tension coefficient usually $v \leqslant 0.4$ Pa·cm the equilibration time can be of the order of hours or days (*Miles,* 1986). From the equilibrium droplet shape, the interfacial tension coefficient is calculated from the *Bashforth* and *Adams* (1882) equation:

$$(a^2 \Delta \varrho g / v) \, (z/a) + 2 = (r/a)^{-1} + \sin\phi / (x/a) \tag{2.113}$$

where x and z are coordinates of the drop shape envelope, r and a are respectively the radius of curvature at the point (x, z), and at the drop apex, $\Delta \varrho$ is the difference of density between the two liquids, g is the gravitational constant and $\phi$ is the angle between a tangent to the drop profile and the horizontal axis. Since the only expression in the first parentheses on the left hand side of Eq (2.113) contains the material parameters, for general use the relation has been numerically solved and tabulated (*Padday,* 1969).

The pendant drop method has been frequently used in academic and industrial laboratories around the world. Unfortunately, for polymer blends the results are usually disapointing. There are several experimental difficulties which make the final equilibrium shape of the droplet rather difficult to detect. On the other hand since here the gravitational forces play a bigger role than in the sessile drop method the equilibrium occurs sooner. During the last few years *Koberstein* and his coworkers developed a computerized method of recording the pendant droplet shape (*Anastasiadis* et al., 1986). The data acquisition allows a continuous analysis of the droplet form and comparison with the theoretical prediction of Eq (2.113), which in turn offers the capability of monitoring attainment of equilibrium. For blends of oligodimethylsiloxane, ODMS, with oligobutadiene, OBD, the authors reported that $v$ decreases with MW of both components as well as with the temperature:

$$v = a_0 + a_1/T \tag{2.114}$$

where $a_0$ and $a_1$ are empirical parameters. Numerically $a_1$ seems to depend on $M_n$ of OBD, whereas $a_0$ to that of ODMS.

According to *Helfand* and *Tagami* (1972):

$$v = \varrho_0 RT(\chi'_{23} \langle R_g^2 \rangle /N)^{\frac{1}{2}} \tag{2.115}$$

where $\varrho_0$ is an average segment density, $\langle R^2 \rangle /N$ is the average radius of gyration per statistical segment and $\chi'_{23}$ is the polymer-polymer interaction coefficient. The empirical Eq (2.115) suggests that variations of $v$ originate in $\chi'_{23}$; i.e. that $v$ must be affected by both enthalpic and entropic effects.

The third is the spinning drop method of $v$-measurements (*Vonnegut*, 1942):

$$v = \Delta\varrho\omega^2 d^3/32 \tag{2.116}$$

where $\Delta\varrho$ is the density difference between the matrix and droplet diameter, $\omega$ is the rotational speed and d is the equilibrium droplet diameter (it must be at least 4 times smaller than its length). Measurements of $v$ is reduced to determination of d at several $\omega$ and averaging the results (*Elmendorp* and *de Vos*, 1986). This method can be used for industrial polymer blends. Not only can the high rate of spinning accelerate the equilibration of droplet shape (reducing the problems associated with thermal degradation) but also it can be used for systems with yield stress.

An interesting method is based on Tomotika's equation for fiber distortion by the capillarity forces. The method is outlined in Part 3.4.4.

Examples of the interfacial tension coefficient determined by various methods are listed in Table 2.15. More complete information on $v$ can be found in the review and monograph published by *Wu* (1978, 1979).

Due to differences in thermal fluctuations within the adjacent phases there are spontaneous capillary waves (amplitude 0.3 to 1 nm, wavelength about 100 μm) on the interface (*Kelvin*, 1871). As predicted by the Navier-Stokes equation their velocity is controlled by the interfacial tension and their damping by the dynamic shear and extensional viscoelastic characteristics of the interphase (*Hansen* and *Mann*, 1964). Using the dynamic laser light scattering from the capillary waves one can probe the interphase with much higher precision than previously available by the more standard methods (*Langevin*, 1981). The method allows one to measure interfacial viscosity, elasticity and tension coefficient with precision better than ± 10% (*Sano* et al., 1986; *Sauer* et al., 1987; *Chen* et al., 1987) at a different concentration level. From this information the molecular packing on the interface can be deduced. So far the method has not been applied to polymer blends.

Since $v$ is inversely proportional to the cube of the interphase thickness, Eq (2.112), there have been serious efforts to determine $\Delta l$. By direct TEM of microtomed polystyrene/polymethylmethacrylate $\Delta l \simeq 5$nm was determined (*van Oene* and *Plummer*, 1977). SAXS has also been used to determine $\Delta l$ (*Koberstein* et al., 1980). As pointed out by *Shilov* et al. (1984), SAXS systematically leads to smaller values, $0.5 \leqslant \Delta l(nm) \leqslant 4$, than other methods.

TABLE 2.15 Interfacial Tension Values Determinded by Different Methods

| No. | System | T(°C) | Interfacial Tension Coefficient (mN/m) | | | Ref. |
|---|---|---|---|---|---|---|
| | | | Spinning Drop | du Nuoy Ring | Pendant Drop | |
| 1 | Water/air | RT | 71.8 | 73.0 | – | 1 |
| 2 | Water/toluene | RT | 29.6 | 28.5 | – | 1 |
| 3 | Silicone oil/castor oil | RT | 4.6 | 4.3 | – | 1 |
| 4 | PMMA/air | 200 | 28.6 | – | 30.7 | 1 |
| 5 | HDPE/air | 200 | 23.6 | – | 22.9 | 1 |
| 6 | PE/PS | 200 | 4.4 | – | 4.7 | 1 |
| 7 | PE/PA-6 | 250 | 10.7 | – | – | 1 |
| 8 | PE/PMMA | 200 | 10.0 | – | 8.8 | 1 |
| 9 | PS/PMMA | 200 | 1.26 | – | 0.94 | 1 |
| | | | | | 1.7 | 2 |
| 10 | LLDPE/PC | 285 | – | – | 8 to 9[a] | 3 |

Notes: Nomenclature: RT – room temperature; PMMA – polymethylmethacrylate; HDPE, high density polyethylene; PE – polyethylene; PS – polystyrene; PA-6 – polyamide-6; LLDPE – linear low density polyethylene; PC – polycarbonate. (a) estimated from sessile drop results on low viscosity analogs.

*References: 1. J. J. Elmendrop, 1986; 2. S. Wu, 1978; 3. I. S. Miles, 1986.*

## 2.7.2   Compatibilization Methods

The goal of compatibilization is to obtain a stable and reproducible dispersion which would lead to the desired morphology and properties. Compatibilization has been achieved by:

1. addition of linear or star-shaped block polymers,
2. addition of graft or random copolymer,
3. co-reaction within the blend to generate in-situ either copolymers or interacting polymers.
4. using IPN technology,
5. crosslinking the blend ingredients,
6. modification of homopolymers, e.g. through incorporation of acid/base groups, hydrogen bonding groups, charge-transfer complexes, ionic groups, etc.
7. addition of co-solvent
8. high stress shearing
9. other means.

*Paul* (1978) and *Barlow* and *Paul* (1984) reviewed the use of block polymers and copolymers to compatibilize immiscible polymer blends. The beneficial effects of Kraton 1652G (tri-block polymer: 15% polystyrene - 70% central block - 15% polystyrene, where the central block is like a random copolymer of ethylene and butene) or Epcar 847 (ethylene-propylene-ethylidene norborene copolymer with relatively long ethylene blocks, sufficient to crystallize) are of particular interest; addition of one or another of these materials to polyethyleneterephthalate/high density polyethylene blends variously affected the different physical properties, viz. modulus and yield strength (*Traugott* et al., 1983). Ethylene-propylene copolymers, with or without diene mers, are frequently used as compatibilizers. Their properties depend not only on composition and "blockiness" but also on a finer molecular structure introduced by the use of different catalysts (*Starkweather*, 1980; *Galli* et al., 1984).

A summary of recent work on compatibilization is given in Table 2.16. Use of block polymers of the same chemical nature as the two homopolymers is an obvious choice which, once optimized, will lead to enhancement of properties. The disadvantage of this method is, on one hand, their inaccessibility and the price, on the other, the lack of flexibility in tuning the properties to specific applications. For these reasons the compatibilizer successfully used in commercial application is frequently a commercial multicomponent and/or multiphase material (*Ghaffar* et al., 1981; *Sadrmohaghegh* et al., 1983; *Baker* and *Catani*, 1984; *Jiang* et al., 1985; *Del Giudice* et al., 1985; *Albert* et al., 1986; *Ouhadi* et al., 1986). Their utility varies from system to system, not only as a function of compatibilizing efficiency but also in relation to the overall performance of the final product, including e.g. the weathering. The thermodynamics can again serve a guiding role. Calculations (*Leibler,* 1981) indicated that multi-block polymers should be more efficient than di-block, which seems to be confirmed by the results of *Trostyanskaya* et al. (1983). On the other hand there is also strong theoretical argument for symmetrical diblocks (*Leibler,* 1988).

*Paul* and *Barlow* (1984) considered the macromolecular chain of polymer or copolymer as a sequence of interacting segments characterized by a value of the intra-molecular interaction parameter $\chi_{ij}$. The miscibility in a two component system was assumed to result from a complex balance of interacting forces. Depending not on a sign but on the relative magnitude of various individual $\chi_{ij}$ the overall interaction parameter, $\chi_{12}$, in a blend could be positive, zero or negative, even when $\chi_{ij}$ were all negative or all positive. For details see part 2.3.6. The concept is useful in fine tuning of PAB miscibility by slight variation of copolymer composition or a degree of coreaction during reactive processing. In particular blends

TABLE 2.16 Compatibilization

| No. | Polymer 1 | Polymer 2 | Compatibilizer | | Ref. |
|---|---|---|---|---|---|
| 1 | Polyisoprene, PI | Polybutadiene, PB | Poly(cis-1,4-isoprene-b-1,4 butadiene); di-block | | 1 |
| 2 | Low density Polyethylene, LDPE | Polystyrene, PS | Poly(styrene-b-ethylene); di-block | | 2 |
| 3 | LDPE | PS, or polyvinylchloride, PVC, or polypropylene, PP | (i) EPDM | (ethylene-propylene-diene copolymer) – Enjay-4608 | 3 |
| | | | (ii) NR | (natural rubber) | 4 |
| | | | (iii) BR | (butyl rubber) | |
| | | | (iv) ABS | (acrylonitrile-butadiene-styrene copolymer) – Lustran | |
| | | | (v) SBS | (styrene-butadiene-styrene block polymer) – Kraton | |
| | | | (vi) CPE | (chlorinated polyethylene) – DGU 5320 or CI | |
| | | | (vii) ACS | (acrylonitrile – chlorinated polyethylene – styrene) – Showa Denko Ltd | |
| | | | (viii) HIPS | (high impact PS) – Carinex | |
| | | | (ix) PU | (polyurethane) | |

| No. | Polymer 1 | Polymer 2 | Compatibilizer | Ref. |
|---|---|---|---|---|
| 4 | Poly-1,2-butadiene | Poly-1,4-butadiene | Poly(1,2 butadiene-b-1,4 butadiene), di-block polymers | 5 6 |
| 5 | Polycarbonate (PC) | Polydimethylsiloxane (PDMS) | Poly(carbonate-s-dimethyl siloxane) sequenced multiblocks | 7 |
| 6 | Polyarylate (PAr) | Phenoxy | exchange reaction | 8 |
| 7 | PAr | Polyethyleneterephtalate (PET) | transesterification | 9 |
| 8 | Polyamide-6,6 (PA) | PET | catalyzed amide-ester exchange reaction during extrusion | 10 11 12 |
| 9 | Polyvinylchloride, PVC | Polyethylacrylate (PEA) | IPN technology | 13 |
| 10 | PVC | Polybutylacrylate (PBA) | IPN technology | 14 |
| 11 | LDPE | PP | irradiation | 15 |
| 12 | PET | PP | crystallization of oriented fibers | 16 |
| 13 | PET | PA | crystallization of oriented fibers | 17 18 19 |
| 14 | PS containing 5 mol % of $-SO_3H$ | Poly(ethylacrylate-co-4-vinyl pyridine) with 5 mol % of vinyl pyridine (VP) | ionic interactions | 19 20 |
| 15 | PI containing 5 mol % of $-SO_3H$ | Poly(styrene-co-4-vinyl pyridine) with 5 mol % VP | ionic interactions | 21 |
| 16 | PS containing 3.8 mol % of $-SO_3H$ | Polyurethane (PU) | ionic interactions between $-SO_3H$ and amine groups in hard segments of PU | 22 |
| 17 | Poly(styrene-co-lithium methacrylate) containing 9.5 mole % $Li^+$ | Polyalkyleneoxides, where alkylene = ethylene, propylene, PVC or polycaprolactone, . . . | ion – dipole interactions | 23 24 25 |
| 18 | Polyarylethers (PAE) | Poly(styrene-co-methyl methacrylate-co-acrylonitrile)'s | by attaching nitrile and/or ester group to PAE | 26 |
| 19 | Polyvinylidenefluoride, $PVF_2$ | Polyvinylalcohol (PVAl) | by hydrolysis of $PVF_2$ / polyvinylacetate blend | 27 |

*References:* 1. *R. E. Cohen* and *A. R. Ramos,* 1979; 2. *W. J. Coumans* et al., 1980; 3. *A. Ghaffar* et al., 1981; 4. *C. Sadrmohaghegh* et al., 1983; 5. *R. E. Cohen* and *D. E. Wilfond,* 1982; 6. *M. A. Hartney* and *R. E. Cohen,* 1983; 7. *E. B. Trostyanskaya* et al., 1983; 8. *J. I. Eguiazabal* et al., 1984; 9. *M. Kimura* et al., 1983; 10. *L. Z. Pillon* and *L. A. Utracki,* 1984; 11. *L. Z. Pillon* and *L. A. Utracki,* 1986; 12. *L. Z. Pillon* and *L. A. Utracki,* 1985; 13. *D. J. Walsh* and *G. L. Cheng,* 1984; 14. *J. M. Liegois* and *F. Terreur,* 1984; 15. *G. Rizzo* et al., 1983; 16. *A. Rudin* et al., 1980; 17. *M. R. Kamal* et al., 1983; 18. *M. R. Kamal* et al., 1982; 19. *P. Smith* and *A. Eisenberg,* 1983; 20. *A. Eisenberg* et al., 1982; 21. *Z.-L. Zhou* and *A. Eisenberg,* 1983; 22. *M. Rutkowska* and *A. Eisenberg,* 1984; 23. *A. Eisenberg* and *M. Hara,* 1985; 24. *M. Hara* et al., 1984; 25. *M. Hara* and *A. Eisenberg,* 1984; 26. *O. Olabisi* and *A. G. Farhnam,* 1979; 27. *I. Cabasso,* 1979.

containing styrene-acrylonitrile copolymer can be successfully analyzed with this approach (*Mendelson*, 1985; *Fowler*, 1986; *Fowler* et al., 1987; *Goh* et al., 1987; *Wu*, 1987).

In several commercial polymer blends "modifiers" are used (see Appendix II). The modifier is usually a copolymer containing a rubbery component with interactive one(s). Acrylic-based copolymers, chlorinated polyolefins, ethylene-propylene-diene, poly(ethylene-co-vinylacetate), etc. are frequently used. These play a dual role, compatibilizing and toughening the blend. For this reason they are used at much higher loading than pure compatibilizers; while 1 to 2 wt% of the latter is usually sufficient 20 to 40 wt% of a modifier may be needed (*Chuang* and *Han*, 1984; *Utracki*, 1987, 1988; *Hobbs* et al., 1988).

Co-reaction of blends to improve the performance has for decades been a practice in the rubber industry (*Coran* et al., 1985). In high-shear mixers some of the chains in rubbers are broken and re-formed by the free-radical mechanism. A similar phenomenon occurs during intensive mixing of polyolefins. To enhance this process sometimes a source of free radicals, e.g. peroxides, can be added (*Paul* and *Newman*, 1978).

Compatibilizations of polyesters and polyamides via an exchange reaction have been reported as well. Transesterification has been used for years to manufacture polyesters (*Utracki*, 1972) or to modify the properties of miscible polyester blends (*Kimura* and *Porter*, 1981; *Devaux* et al., 1982; *Eguizabal* et al., 1984; *Robeson*, 1985; *Calahorra* et al., 1987). Compatibilization via co-reaction between polyarylate and phenoxy also was reported (*Eguizabal* et al., 1984). *Devaux* et al. (1982, 1984) observed that at the initial stage of transesterification between polycarbonate and polybutyleneterephthalate block polymers with reduced solubility are produced. At a later stage, soluble random copolymers are formed. Significant changes of properties on transesterification between polyethyleneterephthalate and polyarylate were reported (*Kimura* et al., 1983). Particularly interesting is the catalyzed exchange between polyamide-6,6 and polyethyleneterephthalate conducted during a standard processing operation, i.e. extrusion or injection molding (*Pillon* and *Utracki*, 1984, 1985, 1986). Due to the small interface area in these immiscible blends, previously the exchange reaction had to be conducted by heating the mixtures for 5 to 30 hours at 220 to 290°C. Use of organic phosphites to enhance coreaction between amine hydroxyl terminated macromolecules (polyamides or polyesters) was reported by *Aharoni* (1985).

The interpenetrating polymer network, IPN, is a diverse, rapidly developing branch of polymer blends technology. The principle is to combine two polymers into a stable interpenetrating network. At least one of these polymers is synthesized and/or crosslinked in the immediate presence of the other. The crosslinking in thermoplastic IPN can be of a physical nature: hard blocks, ion clusters, crystalline region (*Sperling*, 1981). Most of the IPN's can be classified as compatibilized, immiscible polymer blends or alloys. Controlling kinetics of phase separation during the formation of the IPN (or the semi-interpenetrating polymer networks, SIN's) provide the method of generation of desired properties (*Lipatov* et al., 1986). The main disadvantage of IPN's is their non-recyclability.

Single phase IPN are also known. Polymerization of vinyl chloride (VC) in the presence of polyethylacrylate, PEA, resulted in a homogenous system, whereas the physical blending of polyvinylchloride (PVC) with PEA produce immiscible blends (*Walsh* and *Cheng*, 1984). Similarly, VC was polymerized in the presence of polybutylacrylate (PBA) (*Liégeois* and *Terreur*, 1984). In dynamic tests the resulting PVC/PBA blends behaved as a single phase system in spite of the observed microheterogeneity (standard blends of these two polymers are immiscible).

Crosslinking via irradiation of e.g. low density polyethylene/polypropylene blends (*Rizzo* et al., 1983; *Brooks*, 1983) follows on earlier works where vulcanization has been used to stabilize polymer blends (e.g. *Kuleznev* et al., 1975). Irradiative crosslinking is a free radical process resulting in a similar structure to that created by chemical crosslinking or vulcanization (*Nakamura* et al., 1987). The aim of the process is first to generate the compatibilizing copolymer which then provides the desired morphology. The continuous crosslinking stabilizes the system. For best results the crosslinking should preferentially affect the interphase. The irradiative processing improves the mechanical strength, thermal stability low temperature toughness, maximum strain at break, abrasion and solvent resistance. Controlled crosslinking of the interphase in dispersed PAB leads to a recyclable product. Crosslinking of one phase results in IPN-type materials.

Physical crosslinking via crystallization of oriented blends is another method used to fix the performance of polyethyleneterephthalate/polypropylene (*Rudin* et al., 1980) and poly-ethyleneterephthalate/polyamide-6,6) (*Utracki* and *Bata*, 1982; *Kamal* et al., 1982; *Utracki* et al., 1982; *Kamal* et al., 1983) blends.

Compatibilization by incorporation of ionic groups in polymers has been the method propagated by Eisenberg and coworkers (*Eisenberg* et al., 1982; *Smith* and *Eisenberg*, 1983; *Zhou* and *Eisenberg*, 1983; *Hara* et al., 1984; *Rutkowska* and *Eisenberg*, 1984; *Hara* and *Eisenberg*, 1984; *Smith* et al., 1987; *Agarwal* et al., 1987; *Natansohn* et al., 1987). Attaching about 5 mol% of $-SO_3H$ groups to polystyrene and copolymerizing about 5 mol% of vinyl pyridine with ethyl acrylate then mixing these two polymers resulted in a compatible blend. Similar results were obtained by blending sulfonated polyisoprene with styrene copolymerized with 5 mol % of vinyl pyridine (*Eisenberg* et al., 1982). Recently it was demonstrated that compatibilization can be obtained by securing ion-dipole interaction, as in poly(styrene-co-lithium methacrylate), containing 9.5 mol% of ionic groups, with polyalkyleneoxides (*Eisenberg* and *Hara*, 1984).

There is a special class of PAB in which the miscibility originates from the electron donor-acceptor complexation, EDA. Polymerization or copolymerization of e.g. (donor) N-(2-hydroxyethyl)carbozolylmethacrylate with (acceptor) methacryloyl-β-hydroxyethyl-3,5-dinitrobenzoate resulted in total or partial miscibility (*Schneider* et al., 1982, 1984). In miscible blends the complexation lead to reduction of free volume and, as illustrated in Fig. 2.37, to increase of $T_g$ above the additivity (*Rodriguez-Parada* and *Percec*, 1986). Since complexation is one of several types of specific interactions, the phase separation of these systems occurs with LCST (*Pugh* et al., 1986; *Rodriguez-Parada* and *Percec*, 1986). The EDA complexing groups can also be used for compatibilization in a similar manner as ionic groups. However, since the latter ones are stronger one should expect that more EDA than ionic groups will be required to generate similar level of miscibility. Indeed to achieve miscibility in poly-2,6-dimethyl-1,4-phenyleneether/polyepichlorhydrin system at least 25% of structural units had to contain EDA complexing groups, e.g. N-carbazolyl acetate, N-carbazolyl propianate or 3.5 dinitrobenzoacetate (*Pugh* and *Percec*, 1986).

*Olabisi* and *Farnham* (1979) attached nitrile and/or ester groups to polyaryl ether's to achieve miscibility with poly-α-methylstyrene-co-methyl methacrylate-co-acrylonitrile interpolymers. Numerous blends with a single $T_g$ were reported by the authors.

A different method of achieving compatibility via chemical reactions was used by *Cabasso* (1979). Polyvinylidenefluoride/polyvinylalcohol ($PVF_2/PVAl$) normally form immiscible blends. On the other hand polyvinylidene fluoride/ polyvinylacetate are miscible. Hydrolyzing the latter blend led to a homogeneous $PVF_2/PVAl$ system.

Co-solvent can also be used to generate compatible blends. Frequently two immiscible polymers will form a true solution in a common solvent. After its removal (e.g. by sublimation, freeze-drying, etc.) the interfacial area is so large that even very weak polymer/polymer interactions will sufficiently stabilize such a pseudo-homogeneous system. This method works particularly well in systems with weak hydrogen bonding (*Cangelosi*, 1982). Another application of a co-solvent principle is an addition of co-miscible oligomeric plasticizer. This method can be quite advantageous in rigid-chain polymer blends (*Helminiak*, 1978; *Hay* et al., 1979; *Holste* et al., 1980). Observation of the single phase in solution blended HDPE/LLDPE and UHDPE/LLDPE by SANS while at the same time measuring $\chi_{23} > 0$ also indicated non-equilibrium compatibilization (*Ree*, 1987).

The other method of compatibilization, by high shear mixing, has been reported by *Maxwell* and coworkers (*Thornton* et al., 1980; *Maxwell* et al., 1982; *Maxwell* and *Jasso*, 1983). The authors blended immiscible polymers in an elastic melt extruder (otherwise known as "Maxwell normal stress extruder") generating blends of two continuous-phase morphologies. Polystyrene (PS) polymethylmethacrylate (PMMA) and polyethylene (PE) were blended each with another. Extraction by a selective solvent indicated a three-dimensional intertwined network of homopolymeric strands with diameter 1 to 50μm. While the blends are known to be immiscible the generated structure was found to be surprisingly stable, e.g. PMMA/PE was largely unaffected by annealing for one hour at 200°C. Since, by definition, compatibilization means generation of a stable structure, the high shear mixing of immiscible blends must fall into this category. As indicated in Part 1.2.3 the principle of Maxwell normal stress extruder has been incorporated into the commercial high speed plastifying compounder-extruder (*Patfoort*, 1969; *Frederix* et al., 1981).

There is a large and untapped potential in the generation of compatibilized polymer blends using polyurethanes (PU) or the newer class of polyetherblockamides (PEBA). Properly formulated, PU can form miscible or compatible systems with numerous polymers, viz. eighteen different types of mixtures listed by *Yoshida* and *Tsunekawa* (1981). Blends of PU with polyvinyl chloride are of particular interest. Appropriate selection of PU can generate the degree of dispersion desired for a specific application (*Gifford* et al., 1980; *Rahimian*, 1982; *Szulenyi* and *Mokry*, 1983). PEBA has a similar potential. Currently the material is used in its neat form or as a component of polymer blends with acrylonitrile-butadiene-styrene copolymer, polyamides, etc.

It is clear that in most cases compatibilization is a form of locally induced miscibility. The miscible systems provide important source of information on the possible methods of compatibilization (*Robeson*, 1980; *Paul* and *Barlow*, 1980; *Olabisi*, 1982; *Fox* et al., 1985; *Walsh* and *Rostami*, 1985; *Krause*, 1986). As the recent publications on miscibility of polymethylmethacrylate with polyethyleneoxide (*Silvestre* et al., 1987) or with polycarbonate (*Chiou* et al., 1987) demonstrated the miscibility sometimes can be difficult to ascertain. In addition to several factors discussed in Part 2.6 the miscibility depends on tacticity and the method of preparation. For polymers the self diffusion coefficient, D, is very low. As an example, for polystyrene $D^*(cm^2/s) = 5.05 \cdot 10^{-3}/M_w^2$ (*Green* et al., 1986; *Fleischer*, 1987). For two component blends the mutual diffusion coefficient, $D_M$, can be calculated from Eq (2.110). Near the spinodal conditions where $\chi \to \chi_s$ the interdiffusion stops and the generated morphology tends to remain stable.

This terminates the discussion on the compatibilization, but hardly exhausts the methods used to achieve this goal. Diverse and relatively stable morphologies can be obtained by other means as well. Out of these, the whole domain of reactive processing (*Lambla*, 1988) and solid state formation is where rapid technological progress must be expected (*Ward*, 1982; 1985).

# Part 3

# RHEOLOGY OF POLYMER ALLOYS AND BLENDS

## 3.1 Introduction

Rheology is the science of deformation and flow, of the interrelations between the force and its effects. Polymer rheology is a well investigated subject in its fundamental and experimental aspects. Selected monographs are listed in Appendix IV A. However, the rheology of polymer alloys and blends is still in an early stage of development (*Han*, 1981; *White* et al., 1981; *Han* et al., 1983; *Utracki*, 1987a, 1988, 1989).

The term "multiphase system" refers to any mixture of solid, liquid and gas, e.g. composites, suspensions, blends, emulsions, aerosols, foams etc. In the following text only the melt flow of PAB and the viscoelastic behavior of these materials will be discussed. However, to introduce the subject the behavior of better known "models" (viz. solutions, suspensions and emulsions) will be summarized.

Selected list of rheological terms can be found in Appendix IV B. The symbols used in the text follow the recommendation of the Society of Rheology (*Dealy*, 1984).

The feature common to all multiphase systems is the presence of phases. For the simplest case of dilute dispersion of one phase in another, one may ask: (1) how the presence of the dispersed phase affects the continuous phase, (ii) how stress and deformation rate gradients affect the distribution, shape and orientation of the dispersed phase, (iii) what is the effect of the interface, and (iv) what is the net effect of the influences (i) to (iii) on the measured response of the material. Only for the simplest cases may one find answers to these questions. However, to understand what the measured quantity of a function means, an attempt must be made to postulate a reasonable answer to all four.

Most of the rheological equations of state were derived assuming the material to be (1) a continuum, with no discontinuity from one point to another, (2) homogeneous, i.e. without a concentration gradient, and (3) isotropic, i.e. whose properties are independent on orientation. There is obviously a dichotomy between the theoretical assumptions for continuum theories and the observed behavior of most multiphase systems. In some cases the assumptions do not seem critical, i.e. dispersion of small spherical particles flowing through a large conduit can be analyzed in terms of continuum theories, but this is seldom so for blends with deformable droplets.

In rheometry: I. the steady state shear, II. the dynamic linear viscoelastic shear and, III. the extensional flows are most frequently used. These can be classified, according to strain, $\gamma$, vorticity, $\Omega$, uniformity of stress and uniformity of strain rate. A summary is given in Table 3.1, referring mainly to steady state behavior. For small strain testing in dynamic field, steady state is limited to the linear viscoelastic zone of low strain and frequency.

TABLE 3.1 Classification of Rheological Methods of Measurements

| No. | Method | Strain | Vorticity | Uniformity of | | Comment |
|---|---|---|---|---|---|---|
| | | | | Stress | Strain rate | |
| I. | **Steady State Shear** | large | yes | | | |
| I.1 | Sliding Plate (drag) | | | homogeneous | homogeneous | in small gap, $\eta$ |
| I.2 | Poiseuille (capillary or slit) | | | variable with radius and length | not uniform | needs large L/d |
| I.3 | Rotational Couette | | | linear with gap | not uniform | in small gap, $\Delta r$ |
| I.4 | Rotational Cone-and-Plate | | | homogeneous | homogeneous | cone angle < 4° |
| I.5 | Rotational Parallel Plates | | | linear with radius | linear with radius | for small gap and shear rates |
| II. | **Dynamic Shear** | small | yes | | | |
| II.1 | Couette | | | variable | variable | gap dependent |
| II.2 | Cone-and-Plate | | | uniform | uniform | for small angles |
| II.3 | Parallel Plates | | | linear | linear | at optimized gap |
| III. | **Extensional Flows** | moderate | irrotational | | | |
| III.1 | Uniaxial | | | homogeneous | homogeneous | beware of end effects |
| III.2 | Biaxial | | | homogeneous | homogeneous | |

In multiphase systems the large and the small strain measurements lead to distinctly different morphologies. By contrast with the rheometry of homogeneous, single phase liquids, here the selection of the deformation mode according to the four classification criteria in Table 3.1 provides different response. For example, in capillary flow of PAB the fibrillation of deformable dispersed phase, shear-segregation and redispersion/coalescence have been observed. If the testing is carried out to generate data for e.g. die flow modeling, the measurements must be carried out not only duplicating the processing variables: temperatures (T), pressure (P), shear rate ($\dot{\gamma}$), but also replicating the flow geometry, especially as far as the convergence in the entrance region is concerned.

Stretching flow, with its moderate strains, is a special case; here it is assumed that steady state can be achieved at relatively low strains, so the properties are measured under homogeneous, nonrotational conditions. However, this situation exists only for low molecular weight simple liquids. For high molecular weight polymeric fluids, strain hardening is the rule and steady state conditions can seldom be achieved in available commercial instruments. The situation is further complicated for multiphase systems. During flow start-up, anisometric particles align with principal stress direction, i.e. just as large strain shear flow, steady state extension does not provide information on rheological behavior or the original specimen but rather on its oriented version.

It thereby follows that to characterize multiphase materials steady state dynamic testing should be used. In principle, the information on the original specimen as well as it modification by shear or extension is part of the start-up or transitory flows. It is hoped that theoretical developments will soon allow these deformations to be more thoroughly explored.

## 3.2    Basic Relations

It is convenient to use the stress, $\sigma_{ij}$, strain, $\gamma$, and rate of strain $\dot\gamma_{ij}$, defined with orthogonal indices, i,j = 1,2,3, where customarily i identifies the plane perpendicular to one of the orthogonal axis whereas j indicates the direction of stress or rate of strain (see Fig. 3.1). In tensor notation the total stress is:

$$\sigma' = \sigma - p\,\mathbf{1} \tag{3.1}$$

where $\sigma$ is the extra-stress tensor related to flow, p is the isotropic scalar quantity, usually associated with the hydrostatic pressure and $\mathbf{1}$ is the unit tensor. The elements of tensor matrices $\sigma'$ and $\sigma$ are related:

$$\sigma'_{ij} = \sigma_{ij} - p \quad \text{and} \quad \sigma'_{ij} - \sigma'_{ji} = \sigma_{ij} - \sigma_{ji}$$

In the text only $\sigma$ will be considered. The stress and strain tensors can be written as:

$$\sigma = \begin{vmatrix} \sigma_{11} & \sigma_{12} & \sigma_{13} \\ \sigma_{21} & \sigma_{22} & \sigma_{23} \\ \sigma_{31} & \sigma_{32} & \sigma_{33} \end{vmatrix} \quad ; \quad \gamma = \begin{vmatrix} \gamma_{11} & \gamma_{12} & \gamma_{13} \\ \gamma_{21} & \gamma_{22} & \gamma_{23} \\ \gamma_{31} & \gamma_{32} & \gamma_{33} \end{vmatrix} \tag{3.2}$$

The rate of strain tensor $\dot\gamma = d\gamma/dt$ can be expressed in terms of the velocity 1 gradients:

$$d\gamma_{ij}/dt = \dot\gamma_{ij} \equiv \dot\gamma_{xy} = \partial v_x/\partial y + \partial v_y/\partial x \tag{3.3}$$

where $v_x$ indicates velocity in the direction i = x. Due to the symmetry principle: $\sigma_{ij} = \sigma_{ji}$ and $\gamma_{ij} = \gamma_{ji}$ the matrices (3.2) can be simplified. Furthermore, in shear $I_0 \equiv \sigma_{11} + \sigma_{22} + \sigma_{33} = 0$. From Eq (3.3) it follows that the symmetry principle extends to the elements of the rate of deformation matrix.

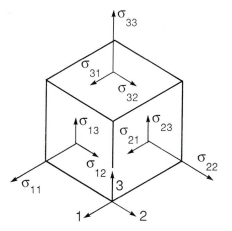

Fig. 3.1 Notation used for stress, $\sigma_{ij}$, or strain $\gamma_{ij}$.

### 3.2.1.  Melt Flow

### 3.2.1.1 Steady State Shear

Further simplification is possible considering specific cases. For example, for an isotropic material in simple shear $\sigma_{31} = \sigma_{13} = \sigma_{32} = \sigma_{23} = 0$ and all elements of the rate of deformation matrix, with the exception of $\dot{\gamma}_{12} = \dot{\gamma}_{21} = \dot{\gamma}$, are zero. Consequently one can define the *shear viscosity*, $\eta$, the *first* and the *second normal stresses*, $N_1$ and $N_2$, as well as their coefficients, $\psi_1$ and $\psi_2$:

$$\eta = \sigma_{12}/\dot{\gamma} \tag{3.4}$$

$$N_1 = \sigma_{11} - \sigma_{22}; \quad \psi_1 = N_1/\dot{\gamma}^2 \tag{3.5}$$

$$N_2 = \sigma_{22} - \sigma_{33}; \quad \psi_2 = N_2/\dot{\gamma}^2 \tag{3.6}$$

### 3.2.1.2 Dynamic Flow

When a liquid undergoes sinusoidal deformation with *frequency*, $\omega$, the response is expressed in terms of in-phase or *storage*, $G'$, and 90° out-of-phase or *loss*, $G''$, moduli. The complex modulus is given by:

$$G^* = (G'^2 + G''^2)^{\frac{1}{2}} \tag{3.7}$$

Correspondingly, the three functions can be defined:

$$\eta' = G''/\omega \; ; \; \eta'' = G'/\omega \; ; \; \eta^* = G^*/\omega \tag{3.8}$$

called respectively: dynamic, out-of-phase, and complex viscosity.

For parallel-plate geometry, using the cylindrical coordinates (angle of oscillation $\Theta$, radius r, and height z) the flow velocities are (*Bird* et al., 1987):

$$V_\Theta = r \, \text{Re}\{f(z)e^{i\omega t}\}, \quad v_r = v_z = 0 \tag{3.9}$$

where Re is the real part of complex function of z. The components of the stress tensors are:

$$\sigma_{\Theta z} = \sigma_{z\Theta} = - r\text{Re}\{\eta^*f'(z)e^{i\omega t}\} \tag{3.10}$$

with all others $\sigma_{ij} = 0$

### 3.2.1.3 Extension

For isotropic materials in uniaxial elongational flow the *strain* and the *elongational rate of straining* are defined as:

$$\varepsilon = \ln L/L_0; \quad \dot{\varepsilon} = d\varepsilon/dt = d\ln L/dt \tag{3.11}$$

where $L_0$ and L are initial and after time, t, length of the specimen. The *stress growth function* and its equilibrium value are defined as:

$$\eta_E^+ = \sigma_{11}^+/\dot{\varepsilon}; \quad \eta_E(\dot{\varepsilon}) = \lim_{t \to \infty} \eta_E^+(\dot{\varepsilon}) \tag{3.12}$$

It can be shown that here all off-diagonal elements of the stress tensor, $\sigma_{ij} = 0$ and that $\sigma_{11} \neq \sigma_{22} = \sigma_{33} = 0$. Similarly, the elements of the rate of deformation tensor are zero with the exception of $\dot{\varepsilon}_{11} = \dot{\varepsilon}, \dot{\varepsilon}_{22} = \dot{\varepsilon}_{33} = - \dot{\varepsilon}/2$.

From Eq (3.3) for Newtonian liquids in shear:

$$\sigma_{ij} = \eta_0\dot{\gamma}_{ij} = \eta_0(\partial v_x/\partial y + \partial v_y/\partial x) \tag{3.13}$$

and in uniaxial extension:

$$\sigma_{11} = \sigma_{11} - \sigma_{22} = \eta_{E,0}\dot\epsilon = 2\eta_0(\partial v_1/\partial x - \partial v_2/\partial y) \qquad (3.14)$$

From Eqs (3.13) and (3.14) it follows that:

$$\eta_{E,0} = 3\eta_0 \qquad (3.15)$$

The first derivation of Eq (3.15) is credited to *Trouton* (1906). The liquids which follow this dependence are sometimes called "Troutonian". At low deformation rate, $\dot\gamma = \omega = \dot\epsilon \to 0$, the single phase neat polymeric liquids (without yield stress) behave as Newtonian:

$$\eta_0 = \lim_{\dot\gamma \to 0} \eta = \lim_{\omega \to 0} \eta' = \lim_{\dot\epsilon \to 0} \eta_E/3 \qquad (3.16)$$

with:

$$N_{1,0} = N_{2,0} = G_0' = 0$$

where the subscript "$_0$" indicates zero deformation rate. It is convenient to define the Trouton ratio for any liquid as:

$$R_T \equiv \eta_E/3\eta \quad \text{at} \quad \dot\epsilon = \dot\gamma$$

In accord with Eqs (3.15) and (3.16) at vanishingly small deformation rates, $\dot\epsilon = \dot\gamma = \omega \to 0$, $R_T \to 1$.

### 3.2.1.4 Time Effects

Outside the range of infinitely small deformation rates most polymeric liquids show *non-Newtonian* and/or non-Troutonian behavior. The term refers to either time, t, or rate of deformation dependencies. If the sheared system shows an increase of $\eta$ with t it is called *thixotropic*. If there is a decrease it is either *anti-thixotropic* or *rheopectic*. Historically, the terms referred to non-elastic liquids, e.g. suspensions or emulsions in low molecular weight media (*Schalek* and *Szegwary*, 1923; *Mill*, 1959; *Sherman*, 1963, 1968; *Jeffrey* and *Acrivos*, 1976; *Mewis*, 1979). The simplest, single-exponential thixotropic relation is:

$$\eta - \eta_\infty^t = (\eta_\infty^t) \exp\{-t/\tau^*\} \qquad (3.18)$$

where $\eta_0$ and $\eta_\infty$ refer to initial and final values of viscosity, t is the shearing time, and $\tau^*$ the relaxation time, dependent on $\phi$, T, and $\dot\gamma$.

### 3.2.1.5 Rate of Deformation Effects

3.2.1.5.1 Pseudoplasticity. The non-Newtonian system whose $\eta$ increases with $\dot\gamma$ is called *dilatant* (or shear thickening) and when $\eta$ decreases *pseudoplastic* (or shear thinning). The dilatancy is rare, usually observed in multiphase systems at high volume fraction, $\phi$.

Pseudoplasticity is dominant in polymeric systems. Several semi-empirical equations have been used to describe the pseudoplastic behavior. The relations can be cast in a common form:

$$\eta = \eta_\infty + (\eta_0 - \eta_\infty)/f(\dot\gamma) \qquad (3.19)$$

where $\eta_0$ and $\eta_\infty$ are the plateau values for the upper and lower Newtonian viscosities, respectively. For unfilled systems $\eta_\infty \to 0$. Examples of $f(\dot\gamma)$ with one, two or three parameters are:

*Williamson* (1930):

$$f(\dot{\gamma}) = 1 + a_w\sigma_{12} \tag{3.20}$$

*Krieger* and *Dougherty* (1959):

$$f(\dot{\gamma}) = 1 + \sigma_{12}/\sigma_c \tag{3.21}$$

*Cross* (1965):

$$f(\dot{\gamma}) = 1 + a\dot{\gamma}^b \tag{3.22}$$

*Williams* (1966):

$$f(\dot{\gamma}) = [1 + 2(\tau\dot{\gamma})^2]^m \tag{3.23}$$

*Carreau* (1972):

$$f(\dot{\gamma}) = [1 + (\tau\dot{\gamma})^2]^{(1-n)/2} \tag{3.24}$$

*Yasuda* (1979):

$$f(\dot{\gamma}) = [1 + (\tau\dot{\gamma})^a]^{(1-n)/2} \tag{3.25}$$

*Elbirli* and *Shaw* (1978), *Utracki* (1984a):

$$f(\dot{\gamma}) = [1 + (\tau\dot{\gamma})^{m_1}]^{m_2} \tag{3.26}$$

In these relations $\tau$ is the relaxation time, while the other parameters are constants.
    For polymeric liquids at high deformation rates the "power law" relation:

$$\sigma_{12} = \sigma_{12}^0\dot{\gamma}^n; \quad \sigma_{12}^0 \equiv \sigma_{12}(\dot{\gamma} = 1) \tag{3.27}$$

provides a good approximation. Setting $\tau\dot{\gamma} \gg 1$ in Eqs (3.22) to (3.26) the power-law exponent can be written as: $n = 1 - b$, $1 - 2m$, $n$, $n$, and $1 - m_1m_2$, respectively. Note the equivalence of relations: (3.20) and (3.21), (3.23) and (3.24), (3.25) and (3.26).


3.2.1.5.2 Dilatancy. A disruption of ordered flow of layered particles above a critical value of the shear rate is an accepted explanation for dilatant behavior (*Hoffman*, 1972, 1974; *Tomita* et al. 1983; *Tomita* and *van de Ven*, 1984). Optical methods allow precise determination of the pseudo-lattice spacing in flowing systems as a function of $\dot{\gamma}$. In some systems such a disruption of flow pattern leads to "fusing" of particles, i.e. to shear coagulation (*Utracki*, 1973). Dilatancy most frequently was reported for concentrated suspensions, e.g. of polyvinylchloride latex particles (*Gillespie*, 1966; *Hoffman*, 1972, 1974; *Utracki*, 1973), mineral powders ($TiO_2$: *Metzner* and *Whitlock*, 1958; *Trapeznikov* et al., 1967; $Fe_2O_3$: *Morgan*, 1968; $SiO_2$: *Pivinski*, 1973), red blood cells (*Barbee*, 1973), polystyrene latexes (*Krieger*, 1972; *Tomita* and *van de Ven*, 1984) and others.
    The dilatancy depends on multiple factors: concentration, particle shape and size as well as their distribution, type and intensity of the inter-particle interactions, flow characteristics, etc. For these reasons it is very difficult to derive a general form of $f(\dot{\gamma})$. Two dependencies can be used; (*Gillespie*, 1966):

$$f(\dot{\gamma}) = (1 + x)^2/[1 + a_0x/(a_1 + x)] \tag{3.28}$$

where $x \equiv a_2\tau\dot{\gamma}$ and $a_i$ are parameters, or:

$$f(\dot{\gamma}) = [1 + (\tau\dot{\gamma})^{m_1}]^{m_2}/[1 + b_0\exp\{(\tau\dot{\gamma}-b_1)^{2b_2}\}] \tag{3.29}$$

based on Eq (3.26) with $b_i$ being the parameters. The functions in the second bracket of Eqs (3.28) or (3.29) determine the shape of the flow curve in the dilatant region. For $a_0 \to 0$ or $b_0 \to 0$ the pseudoplastic form of $f(\dot{\gamma})$ is recovered.

3.2.1.5.3 Yield Stress. For liquids with a structure due to: association (e.g. hydrogen bonding), temporary crosslinking (e.g. in liquid crystal polymers or block polymers), addition of solid particles or dispersing another liquid, the *yield stress*, $\sigma_y$, is to be expected. In this case the measured stresses are augmented by $\sigma_y$, which in principle is a constant, characteristic parameter of the system.

For these systems Eqs (3.19) to (3.29) may also be used provided that $\eta$ is redefined (*Bingham* and *Green*, 1919) as:

$$\eta = (\sigma_{app} - \sigma_y)/\dot{\gamma} \tag{3.30}$$

where $\sigma_{app}$ is the measured, apparent shear stress.

The fundamental mechanism causing variation of $\eta$ with $\dot{\gamma}$ are the changes of structure of the flowing liquid under the influence of shear rate. Behind the relations (3.20) to (3.29) there are different models predicting how the structure varies with $\sigma_{12}$ or $\dot{\gamma}$. For example, the constant a in *Cross* Eq (3.22) is related to the ratio of kinetic constants for formation and rupture of interparticle linkages. Due to the diversity of mechanisms responsible for structural variation as well as complexity of polymeric systems (e.g. polydispersity, additives) frequently only the more flexible relations, such as those in Eqs (3.25) or (3.26), can reproduce the flow curve.

Strictly speaking Eq (3.30) requires that the system with yield stress undergo an instantaneous change of structure from that of solid-like at $\sigma_{12} \lesssim \sigma_y$ to a fluid-like behavior above this limit. Such an assumption is not always realistic, expecially in those systems in which $\sigma_y$ has only an apparent character, observed on the time scale of laboratory measurements or processing operations. In these systems $\sigma_y = \sigma_y(t) = \sigma_y(\dot{\gamma})$ (time of measurement is inversely proportional to the deformation rate: $\dot{\gamma}$, $\omega$ or $\dot{\epsilon}$), there is a multitude of $\sigma_y$'s. Here, the flow curve can be quite complex as schematically illustrated in Fig. 3.2. The two zero-shear viscosity regions, (see curve 2) are related to two regions without yield stress, in the first one the test is slow enough for the dynamic three-dimensional structures to continuously rebuild under stress, i. e. for the apparent absence of the yield stress. In the second region the stress $\sigma_{12} \gg \sigma_y$ and the three-dimensional structure no longer exists. The curves in Fig. 3.2. have been generated assuming that the apparent shear stress:

$$\sigma_{app} = \sigma_{12} + \sigma_y(\dot{\gamma}) \tag{3.31}$$

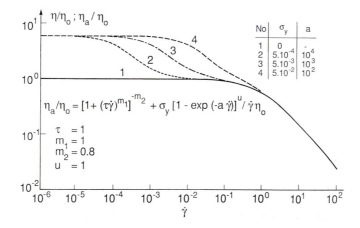

Fig. 3.2 Calculated flow curve for fluid with time dependent apparent yield stress given by Eqs (3.26), (3.31) and (3.32).

in which $\sigma_{12} = \eta\dot{\gamma}$ was computed from Eqs (3.19) and (3.26), whereas the dynamic yield stress from:

$$\sigma_y(\dot{\gamma}) = \sigma_y[1 - \exp(-\tau_y\dot{\gamma})]^u \qquad (3.32)$$

in which $\sigma_y$ is the apparent yield stress measured at high rate of deformation, u = 0.2 to 1.0 is an exponent, and $\tau_y$ is the characteristic time for disassociation/association of the three-dimensional structure; a measure of the relative rapidity for reformation of network. Fig. 3.3 shows the flow curve for 10% of poly(styrene-co-divinylbenzene) particles with diameter 100 nm, suspended in 10% polystyrene solution in diethylphthalate (*Onogi and Matsumoto, 1981*). The data are well represented by Eqs (3.19), (3.26) and (3.32) with u = 1.0. The original investigators reported that in the system at $\dot{\gamma} < 0.3\,(s^{-1})$, in agreement with the computed value, a well defined $\sigma_y \simeq 5Pa$ was observed, but for $\dot{\gamma}$ decreasing below this value, the $\sigma_y \rightarrow 0$. It is worth noting that, while the principal relaxation time for the flow of polystyrene solution is 1.5 ms, for association/disassociation complexes it is 26,000 times longer. The wide separation of these material parameters is responsible for the appearance of the two plateaux of shear-rate independent viscosity.

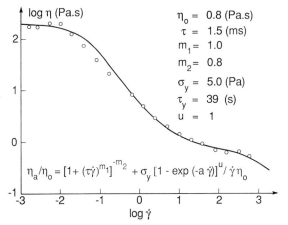

Fig. 3.3 Viscosity of 10% crosslinked polystyrene spheres suspended in polystyrene solution. Points – experimental (Onogi and Matsumoto, 1981); line – Eqs (3.26), (3.31) and (3.32) with listed parameter values.

There are several methods for determining $\sigma_y$. Among these is the modified *Casson* (1959) equation:

$$\sigma_{12}^{\frac{1}{2}} = k_0 + k_1(\eta_a\dot{\gamma}/\eta_0)^{\frac{1}{2}} \qquad (3.33)$$

where $k_0$ and $k_1$ are constants, $\eta_0$ and $\eta_a$ are zero shear and apparent viscosity of the dispersing liquid, respectively. Eq (3.33) can be written as (*Utracki and Kamal, 1982*):

$$F^{\frac{1}{2}} = F_y^{\frac{1}{2}} + aF_m^{\frac{1}{2}} \qquad (3.34)$$

where F may be shear stress, $\sigma_{12}$, elongational stress, $\sigma_E$, shear storage, G', or loss modulus, G'', etc., $F_y$ indicates the yield value of F, $F_m$ is the F-value of pure matrix liquid at the same deformation rate as F and "a" is a measure of the relative value of F. For instance, if F = $\sigma_{12}$ then $F_y$ is the yield stress in shear, $\sigma_y$, and $a^2 = \eta_r$, i.e., Equation (3.34) predicts a straight line dependence only for those liquids with yield for which the relative viscosity, $\eta_r = \eta_r(\dot{\gamma})$.

The concentration dependence of $\sigma_y$ can either be expressed as (*Utracki and Kamal, 1982, Utracki* et al., 1984):

$$\sigma_y = K(\phi - \phi_0)^n \qquad (3.35)$$

or

$$\sigma_y = A_1 \exp\{A_2\varphi\} \qquad (3.36)$$

In these equations, K, $\varphi_0$, n, A and $A_2$ are adjustable parameters.

There are three important effects of the yield stress on the flow behavior:

1. in any flow field with a stress gradient, e.g. in a tube, there is plug flow, i.e. within the region where $\sigma_{12} < \sigma_y$ the material behaves as a "solid plug"; only the skin region where $\sigma_{12} > \sigma_y$ undergoes deformation.

2. The extrudate swell for systems with yield is reduced. There are two reasons for this; in plug flow only a portion of the extrudate undergoes deformation, and the swelling occurs in the skin region if and only if the residual stresses are larger than $\sigma_y$.

3. As will be discussed in Part 3.5, $\sigma_y$ has a profound effect on flow-induced morphology.

Plug flow can be treated as a wall slip phenomenon. Following the early theoretical treatment (*Reiner*, 1931) for power-law liquid flowing through a capillary the wall shear rate can be expressed as:

$$\dot{\gamma} = \dot{\gamma}_N(3 + 1/n)/4 - (s/R)[n^* + 3] \qquad (3.37)$$

where:

$$n^* \equiv \mathrm{dlns/dln\sigma_{12}},$$

s is the effective slip velocity, R is the capillary radius and $\dot{\gamma}_N$ is the rate of shear of Newtonian liquid flowing through the capillary under analogous conditions. For n = 1 and s = 0 the shear rate: $\dot{\gamma} = \dot{\gamma}_N$ as it should. The slip velocity depends on shear stress:

$$s = s_0(\sigma_{app} - \sigma_y)^{s_1} \qquad (3.38)$$

where $s_0$ and $s_1$ are parameters. Analysis of flow with slip allows four cases to be identified: (i) $s_1 = 0$, i.e. s = const.; (ii) $\sigma_y = 0$ and $s \propto \sigma_{12}$; (iii) when $s_0$, $s_1$ and $\sigma_y$ are on-zero, than s = 0 for $\sigma_{app} < \sigma_y$ and $s \neq 0$ for $\sigma_{app} > \sigma_y$; and (iv) the relation between s and $\sigma_{12}$ is more complex due to flow induced changes in morphology. In Fig. 3.4 the slip velocity for capillary flow of rigid polyvinylchloride formulation G (for properties see: *Utracki* et al.,

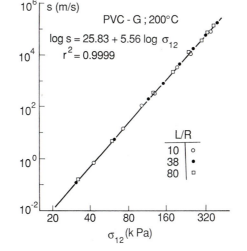

Fig. 3.4 Slip velocity on capillary wall for rigid polyvinylchloride vs. shear stress at 200 °C. Three sets of capillaries were used with length-to-radius ratios L/R = 10, 38 and 80.

1975) is shown. The data originated from three sets of capillaries, each of length-to-radius ratio L/R = 10, 38 and 80, and several R in each set. The data follow Eq (3.38) with $s_0$(m/s) = $1.466.10^{-26}$, and $s_1$ = 5.557 indicating high sensitivity of the slip phenomenon to $\sigma_{12}$. Within the investigated range of shear stress $\sigma_{12}$ > 20kPa the yield stress can be neglected, i. e. $\sigma_y \simeq 0$. The correlation coefficient square was computed as $r^2$ = 0.9999.

There are several direct methods of slip velocity measurements, such as flow visualization, laser-Doppler-velocimetry or hot-film probes (*Atwood, 1982*).

### 3.2.2   Viscoelasticity

Dynamic testing of polymers in solid or in molten state is becoming the preferred method of characterization. With modern instruments the reproducibility within ± 2% can be obtained between runs spaced by several years. Excellent agreement between dynamic data in round-robin international tests for polymers, blends and alloys has been reported (*Utracki, 1988*). At low sinusoidal deformation the test introduces minimal modification of sample morphology.

The viscoelastic behavior is divided into linear and non-linear. Linear viscoelastic materials are those in which stress is proportional to strain, e. g. in stress relaxation experiments:

$$\sigma(t)/\gamma = G_\infty + G(t) \tag{3.39}$$

in which neither the shear stress relaxation modulus, $G(t)$, nor its residual, $G(\infty)$, depend on strain, $\gamma$. In short, linear viscoelasticity is observed at small stresses, strains and/or rates of strain. For example, usually the molten single phase polymers show strain independence of $G'$ and $G''$ within $\gamma \leqslant 20\%$, while composite melts may be linear only for $\gamma \leqslant 1\%$. In solid state testing the polymers may behave as linear viscoelastic bodies only at strains as low as 0.001%. While in dynamic testing the strain range can be limited to the linear region, this is impossible to do in processing as well as in those rheological tests simulating the process (viz. capillary or extensional flow). There is also a growing tendency to extend dynamic testing to the high strain, non-linear region (*La Mantia, 1977; Powell* and *Schwarz, 1979; Onogi* and *Matsumoto, 1981; Booij* and *Palmen, 1982; Giacomin* and *Dealy, 1986*). While the instruments can be constructed to provide strains of 1000% and more, the theory, the way the data are presented and even their significance are still open to question (*Soong, 1981; Leblans, 1985*).

### 3.2.2.1 Transition Map

Within the linear viscoelastic region the storage and loss moduli depend on the structure. The simplified variation of $G'$ vs. temperature, T, for amorphous, semi-crystalline and crosslinked polystyrene is shown in Fig. 3.5. Note that the same behavior can be expected if $G'$ is plotted as a function of test time, $t = 2\pi/\omega$. As the temperature or test time increases the polymer behavior changes from the glassy to rubbery and then to liquid. When the material is crosslinked the rubbery plateau extends up to the decomposition temperature; when it is semicrystalline the behavior above the glass transition temperature, $T_g$, resembles that of either filled rubber or a suspension (of crystals) in viscous liquid; only above the melting point, $T_m$, is the behavior of amorphous and semicrystalline polymer similar, dependent on molecular weight.

It is useful to identify the absolute values of moduli in the glassy and rubbery region: $G'_g \simeq 1$ GPa and $G'_r \simeq 100$ kPa, respectively. Presence of "additives" can significantly alter $G'_r$; filler or crystallinity may push it up by two orders of magnitude while solvent or plasticizer lower it by a similar amount.

As shown in Fig. 3.6, the loss modulus shows greater sensitivity to transitions in the material below and above $T_g$ than does the storage modulus. These transitions are frequency dependent, with the activation energy:

$$E_i = R \, \partial \ln \omega_i / \partial (1/T), \quad i = \alpha, \beta, \gamma \ldots \qquad (3.40)$$

increasing with the transition temperature $T_i$. Plot of the frequency, $\omega_i$, vs. $T_i$ is called the "transition map"; an example is shown in Fig. 3.7. The map details the frequency dependence of the transition temperatures, providing direct evidence of equivalence between the time (or frequency) and temperature (or pressure).

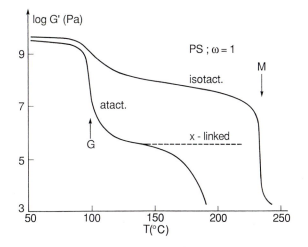

Fig. 3.5 Temperature dependence of the dynamic storage modulus at $\omega = 1$ rad/sec for three polystyrenes: isotactic (semicrystalline), atactic-amorphous and atactic-crosslinked. Arrows G and M indicate the glass transition and melting temperature region, respectively.

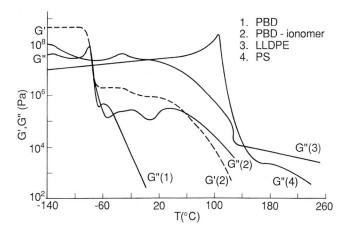

Fig. 3.6 Loss shear modulus, G″, (solid lines) at $\omega = 1$ (rad/s) vs. temperature for: (1) polybutadiene, (2) sodium carboxylated polybutadiene, (3) linear low density polyethylene, and (4) polystyrene. The broken line represents the storage shear modulus, G′, for system (2).

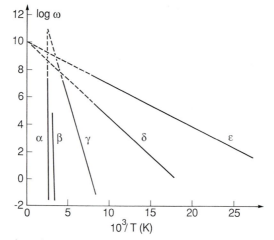

Fig. 3.7 Transition map for polystyrene. Solid lines – experimental, broken line – extrapolation. α, β, γ, σ and ε indicate five transitions in the order of descending temperature; α is the principal, glass transition (after *Yano* and *Wada*, 1971).

### 3.2.2.2 Interrelations

Interrelations between rheological functions in the linear viscoelastic region. For *isotropic viscoelastic body* at equilibrium:

$$E = 9GK/(G + 3K) = 2G(1 + \mu) \tag{3.41}$$

where: E, G and K are respectively tensile (Young), shear and bulk modulus, and the Poisson's ratio:

$$\mu = \varepsilon_{22}/\varepsilon_{11} \tag{3.42}$$

with ε being the linear strain: $\varepsilon = \Delta L/L_0$. Each of these four functions, F = E, G, K or μ, can be written in a complex form:

$$F^* = F' - iF'' = (F'^2 + F''^2)^{\frac{1}{2}} \tag{3.43}$$

From Eqs (3.41) and (3.43) it follows that e.g.:

$$E' = 2[(1 + \mu')G' + \mu''G'']; \qquad E'' = 2[(1 + \mu')G'' - \mu''G']; \tag{3.44}$$

$$\text{or} \quad E' = 3[(1 - 2\mu')K' - 2\mu''K'']; \qquad E'' = 3[(1 - 2\mu')K'' + 2\mu''K']; \tag{3.45}$$

In short, the small deformations of isotropic body provide equivalent information in tension, compression and shear (*Yee* and *Takemori*, 1982).

The mechanical models of viscoelastic bodies built from a spring and dashpot (in series – *Maxwell*, in parallel – *Voigt*) have been used to express the viscoelastic functions in terms of modulus and viscosity, the spring and dashpot constants, respectively. *Wapner* and *Forsman* (1971) demonstrated that both models can be conveniently incorporated into linear viscoelasticity formulated in a Fourier transform space:

$$\sigma(\omega) = E^*(\omega)\varepsilon(\omega) \tag{3.46}$$

$$\sigma(\omega) = \int_{-\infty}^{+\infty} \sigma(t)\exp\{-i\omega t\}\, dt \tag{3.47}$$

$$\varepsilon(\omega) = \int_{-\infty}^{+\infty} \varepsilon(t)\exp\{-i\omega t\}\, dt \tag{3.48}$$

where $E^*$ is the complex modulus whereas $\sigma(\omega)$ and $\varepsilon(\omega)$ are Fourier transforms of stress and strain histories, $\omega$ is the frequency and t is the time. Using the bead and spring model *Rouse* (1953) and *Zimm* (1956) extended the mechanical model into closer proximity of molecular theory. For undiluted polymers the modified Rouse theory (*Ferry*, 1980) gives:

$$G' = (\varrho RT/M) \sum_p (\omega\tau_p)^2/[1 + (\omega\tau_p)^2] \tag{3.49}$$

$$G'' = (\varrho RT/M) \sum_p (\omega\tau_p)/[1 + (\omega\tau_p)^2] \tag{3.50}$$

$$G(t) = (\varrho RT/M) \sum_p e^{-t/\tau_p} \tag{3.51}$$

where the relaxation time:

$$\tau_p = 6\eta_0 M/\pi^2 p^2 \varrho RT \tag{3.52}$$

with $\varrho$ – the polymer density at the temperature T, R – gas constant, M – molecular weight, and $\eta_0$ – zero shear viscosity. The relations (3.49) to (3.52) have been derived for idealized monomolecular homopolymers and since $\tau_p \equiv \tau_1/p^2$ there is a rapid decrease of importance of relaxation tiemes higher than $p = 1$ ($\tau_1$ is frequently called the principal relaxation time, $\tau$). For polydisperse systems it is convenient to introduce the concept of the spectrum of relaxation times, $H(\tau)$, or that of frequency, $H_G(\omega)$, (*Gross*, 1968). In terms of these functions Eq (3.51) can be expressed as:

$$G(t) = G_e + \int_{-\infty}^{+\infty} H(\tau)e^{-t/\tau}d\ln\tau \tag{3.53}$$

$$G(t) = G_e + \int_{-\infty}^{+\infty} H_G(s)e^{-st}ds \tag{3.54}$$

where $G_e$ is the equilibrium shear modulus at $t\to\infty$. For viscoelastic liquids $G_e = 0$. The relaxation spectra can be calculated from:

$$H(\tau) = \pm (1/\pi)\mathrm{Im}G^*(\omega e^{\pm i\pi}) \tag{3.55}$$

$$H_G(\omega) = \pm (1/\omega\pi)\mathrm{Im}G^*(\omega e^{\pm i\pi}) = (2/\omega\pi)\mathrm{Re}G''(\omega e^{\pm i\pi/2}) \tag{3.56}$$

where Im and Re indicate the imaginary and real part of the indicated complex function, respectively.

The components of the complex shear modulus in Ferry's notation are given by:

$$G' = G_e + \int_{-\infty}^{+\infty} [H(\tau)\omega^2\tau^2/(1 + \omega^2\tau^2)]d\ln\tau \tag{3.57}$$

$$G'' = \int_{-\infty}^{+\infty} [H(\tau)\omega\tau/(1 + \omega^2\tau^2)]d\ln\tau \tag{3.58}$$

Using Gross's relaxation spectrum:

$$G'(\omega) = G_e + \int_{-\infty}^{+\infty} \{sH_G(s)/[1 + (s/\omega)^2]\}d\ln s \tag{3.59}$$

and

$$G''(\omega) = \int_{-\infty}^{+\infty} \{\omega H_G(s)/[1 + (\omega/s)^2]\}d\ln s \tag{3.60}$$

The advantage of studying the linear viscoelastic functions is that once one of them is known, the relaxation spectrum can be calculated in principle and then all the other linear viscoelastic dependencies can be computed from the exact analytical expressions; e.g.

Eqs (3.53), (3.54), (3.57)-(3.60). Since there is an exact mathematical relation between the relaxation and retardation spectra:

$$L(t) = H(\tau)/\{[G_e + \int_{-\infty}^{+\infty} (H(u)/(\tau/u - 1))d\ln u]^2 + \pi^2 H^2\} \tag{3.61}$$

knowledge of H or $H_G$ allows computation also of those functions usually expressed in terms of the retardation spectrum, L(t), such as creep, dynamic compliance, etc.

Introduction of $G'' = \eta'\omega$ into Eq (3.56) leads to an analytical form of $H_G$. From Eqs (3.19) and (3.26) for viscoelastic liquids:

$$\eta' \equiv G''(\omega)/\omega = \eta_0[1 + (\omega\tau^*)^{m_1}]^{-m_2} \tag{3.62}$$

Use of this relation lead to (*Utracki*, 1987; *Utracki* and *Schlund*, 1987):

$$\tilde{H}_G(\omega) \equiv H_G(\omega)/\eta_0 = (2/\pi)r^{-m_2}\sin(m_2\theta) \tag{3.63}$$

where $\eta_0$ is the zero shear viscosity and:

$$r \equiv [1 + 2(\omega\tau^*)^{m_1}\cos(m_1\pi/2) + (\omega\tau^*)^{2m_1}]^{\frac{1}{2}} \tag{3.64}$$

$$\theta \equiv \text{arc sin}\{(\omega\tau^*)^{m_1}r^{-1}\sin((m_1\pi/2)\} \tag{3.65}$$

By definition:

$$\int_{+\infty}^{+\infty} \tilde{H}(\omega)d\ln\omega = 1 \tag{3.66}$$

As a result one may expect that the coordinates of the maximum ($\omega_{max}$, $\tilde{H}_{G,max} \equiv \tilde{H}_G(\omega_{max})$) relate to the molecular parameters: $\omega_{max}$ to molecular weight or $\eta_0$ and $\tilde{H}_{G,max}$ to polydispersity. Differentiation of Eq (3.63) provides the conditions for the maximum:

$$\tan(m_2\theta) = \sin(m_1\pi/2)/[\cos(m_1\pi/2) + (\omega\tau^*)^{m_1}]|_{\omega = \omega_{max}} \tag{3.67}$$

From this and Eq (3.63) ($\omega_{max}$, $\tilde{H}_{G,max}$) can be computed. Numerical integration of Eq (3.59) with $H_G$ calculated from Eqs (3.63) to (3.65) provided a good agreement with direct observations (see Fig. 3.8). Another consequence of Eq (3.66) is that the blending rules for $\eta_0$ and $H_G(\omega)$ must be identical; once the effect of composition on e.g. $\eta_0$ is known, that for any other linear viscoelastic function can be calculated (*Watanabe* and *Kotaka*, 1984; *Bersted*, 1986; *Utracki*, 1989).

### 3.2.2.3 Time-Temperature-Pressure Superposition

The moduli G(t), G'($\omega$) and G''($\omega$) in Eqs (3.49) to (3.51) depend on three variables: M, $\omega$ and T. The molecular dependence in accord with network theories is restricted to $M \leq M_e$, where $M_e$ is the entanglement molecular weight. The two remaining variables, $\omega$ and T, as experiments indicate seems to be related. The question to ask is how to eliminate one of them in an attempt to generate a master equation?

The answer is particularly simple if, guided by the theoretical form of e.g. the G' dependence (3.49), one tries to reduce all isothermal scans to a single reference temperature, $T_R$. It can be seen that multiplying G' by a factor:

$$b_T \equiv \varrho_R T_R/\varrho T \tag{3.68}$$

eliminates the temperature variation of the pre-summation expression. Furthermore, since $\omega$ always enters as a product with $\tau_p$ given by Eq (3.52), then multiplying $\omega$ by a factor:

$$a_T = \eta_0\varrho_R T_R/\eta_{0R}\varrho T = b_T\eta_0/\eta_{0R} \tag{3.69}$$

should also elminate the temperature effect from the independent variable.

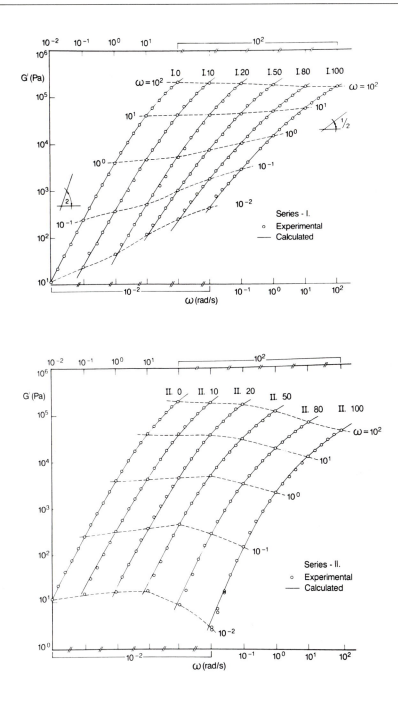

Fig. 3.8 Frequency dependent storage shear modulus at 150 °C for a linear low density polyethylene blend with low density polyethylene (immiscible, Series I) or with another linear low density polyethylene (miscible, Series II). Points – experimental, solid lines – computed from relaxation spectrum, broken lines – isohoric data.

Turning to definitions involving the relaxation or retardation spectrum it is evident that the superposition can only be achieved if the variation of the temperature affects the same way all the frequencies, i. e. if the same spectrum $H_G(\omega_R)$ can be generated at any temperature, T, by multiplying the frequency by $a_T$ defined in Eq (3.69). Another way to express this is to say that the structure of the viscoelastic body must not be altered by variation of the temperature. It is obvious that melting affects the structure, changing the population of vibrating units, not necessarily in a linear manner, and as a result the time-temperature superposition in the vicinity of $T_m$ is expected not to be obeyed; when experimentally obtained it must be considered a miraculous event, most likely engendered by a narrow frequency scans.

A similar argument can be raised about the $T_g$ region. Is the structure of glass and liquid similarly affected by T and $\omega$? Since the transition is kinetic in nature obviously this is not so. Due to physical aging of glass its structure changes with time, its free volume and mobility at constant temperature decreases over a period of time. In short, one may expect the time-temperature superposition to be valid only within a given structure of viscoelastic body, i. e. within limits of the transition map regions.

The selection of $a_T$ and $b_T$ reducing parameters as proposed above is not unique. For $\eta^* = \eta^*(\omega)$ the $a_T = \eta_0 = 1/b_T$ was proposed by *Vinogradov* and *Malkin* (1977). For the terminal plateau region *Graessley* and *Edwards* (1981) derived:

$$b_T = (\varrho^2 T \langle r_\theta^2 \rangle)_{ref}/\varrho^2 T \langle r_\theta^2 \rangle \tag{3.70}$$

where $\langle r_\theta^2 \rangle$ is mean square unperturbed end-to-end distance of the macromolecule.

However, irrespective of which set of reducing parameters is selected, due to linear shifting of the relaxation spectrum ($\omega \rightarrow \omega a_T$) all linear viscoelastic functions must generate a master curve when plotted as: $Fb_T = f(\omega a_T)$. It is impossible to accept a notion that one set of ($a_T$, $b_T$) parameters is required for $G'$, another for $G''$, and a third for their ratio, $\tan\delta \equiv G''/G'$, etc.

The free volume concept provides a unifying basis for simultaneous consideration of superposition principles of time, temperature *and* pressure effects. Two approaches have been proposed. In the first, the experimental double shifting generates a set of temperature and pressure reducing parameters:

$$a_{Tp} = -C_1^{00} T_p/(C_2^{00} - T_p) \tag{3.71}$$

where $\quad T_p \equiv T - T_0 - \theta(P) \tag{3.72}$

$$\theta(P) = C_3^0 \ln[(1+C_4^0 P)/(1+C_4^0 P_0)] - C_5^0 \ln[(1+C_6^0 P)/(1+C_6^0 P_0)] \tag{3.73}$$

the $C_i$ are equation constants related to the free volume theory (*Moonan* and *Tschoegl*, 1984).

The second approach is based directly on the statistical thermodynamic theory discussed in Part 2.3.4 (*Simha* and *Somcynsky*, 1969). The effects of variation of T, P, or both, are converted into a free volume argument:

$$Y_S = 1/(f + \Delta) \tag{3.74}$$

where the free volume fraction $f = f(T,P)$ is computed from the hole theory and $\Delta$ is a numerical constant (*Utracki*, 1983, 1985b, c, 1986b, c). Successful time-temperature-pressure superposition of $\eta_0$ by means of Eq (3.74) is shown in Fig. 3.9 (*Utracki*, 1986b, c).

As in the case of temperature, the time-temperature-pressure shifting should be limited to a range of variables under which the structure of the viscoelastic body remains unchanged.

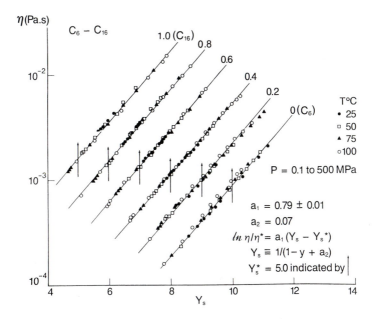

Fig. 3.9 Pressure, P, and temperature, T, dependent viscosity of hexane/hexadecane mixtures linearized by the theoretical free volume Eq (3.74). Points – experimental data at P = 0 to 500 MPa and T = 25 to 100 °C; lines – computed. For clarity, the data for constant composition were displaced horizontally, each by one $Y_s$-unit. The position of $Y_s^* = 5$ is indicated by an arrow (*Utracki*, 1986c).

## 3.3.    Model Systems

The flow behavior of PAB is quite complex. It is influenced by equilibrium thermodynamics, by dynamics of phase separation, by morphology, by a host of independent variables and even by flow geometry. To sort out these and others influences, to begin understanding the rheology of PAB, the subject must be approached from the perspective of known systems.

As discussed in Part 2, from the thermodynamics point of view, polymer blends can be classified as miscible and immiscible, although a third category should be considered as well – blends whose phase separation takes place in the proximity of the conditions of processing, i. e. those blends which, influenced by small variation in composition, temperature, pressure or stress, may be either miscible or not.

Two systems can be used as models for miscible polymer blends: (i) mixture of low molecular weight liquids, i. e. a solution, and (ii) mixtures of polymer fractions or homologous polymer blends. The systems: (iii) suspensions, (iv) emulsions and (v) block copolymers can serve as models for immiscible PAB; suspension for blends with a low concentration of more viscous polymer, emulsions as a general model of blends with dispersed morphology, and block copolymers for well compatibilized blends and/or PAB with co-continuous morphology. The last model to discuss is (vi) solution of two liquids near the critical point of phase separation; it provides information on PAB flow behavior near the spinodal. All six model systems will be discussed briefly in the following chapters.

### 3.3.1　Solution of Low Molecular Weight Liquids

In the absence of strong interactions, $\chi_{12} \simeq 0$, the statistical thermodynamic treatment of free volume, f, provides a most direct approach. During the last few years the equation of state derived for a single component (*Simha* and *Somcynsky*, 1969) has been extended to homologous mixtures (*Jain* and *Simha*, 1980; *Simha*, 1982; *Simha* and *Jain*, 1984b). The extension was rigorous, following two assumptions: (i) that the size of holes and occupied sites is the same in single and multicomponent liquids, and (ii) that segment placement is random, i.e., there are no specific interactions between the statistical segments of unlike molecules in the mixture. With the above assumptions the equations:

$$\tilde{P}\,\tilde{V}/\tilde{T} = [1-2^{-1/6}y\phi^{1/3}]^{-1} + (2y/\tilde{T})\phi^2[1.011\ \phi^2-1.2045] \tag{3.75}$$

and

$$[(s-1)/s+y^{-1}\ln(1-y)]/u = (y/6\tilde{T})\phi^2[2.409-3.033\phi^2]$$
$$+[2^{-1/6}y\phi^{1/3}-1/3][1-2^{-1/6}y\phi^{1/3}]^{-1} \tag{3.76}$$

derived for single component liquids, can be formally used for mixtures replacing the parameters c,s, and $M_0$ by their arithmetic averages. In these equations $\tilde{F} \equiv F/F^*$ where F = P, V or T, and $F^*$ is the reducing value of F, y = 1−f, u ≡ 3c/s and $\phi \equiv 1/(y\tilde{V})$. Furthermore,

$$(P^*V^*/T^*)M_0 = (c/s)R \tag{3.77}$$

where the gas constant R = 8.31432 (J/molK), s stands for the number of statistical chainmers, each of molecular weight $M_0$ (i.e., $M = sM_0 = rM_r$ where r is the degree of polymerization and $M_r$ is the molecular weight of a mer), and 3c is the number of external effective degree of freedom. For liquid mixtures the molecular parameters are replaced by the averages:

$$\langle M_0 \rangle = \Sigma x_i s_i M_{0i}/\Sigma x_i s_i; \quad \langle c \rangle = \Sigma x_i c_i; \quad \langle s \rangle = \Sigma x_i s_i \tag{3.78}$$

where $x_i$ is the mole fraction of component i. In short, to be able to compute y, the following information is required: molecular parameters of the pure liquids ($s_i$, $c_i$, $M_{0i}$), composition ($x_i$), and the reducing (or scaling) parameters of the mixtures ($\langle P^* \rangle$, $\langle V^* \rangle$, and $\langle T^* \rangle$). For the linear, single component, flexible chain molecules:

$$3c = s + 3 \tag{3.79}$$

The P-V-T-$\eta_0$ data for hexane, $C_6$, hexadecane, $C_{16}$, and their mixtures, ($C_6/C_{16}$) were measured by *Dymond* et al. (1980, 1981) at T = 25 to 100 °C and P = 0.1 to 500 MPa. Using these data f = f(P,T, composition) was computed from Eqs (3.75) to (3.79) assuming $\Delta$ = 0. The result is shown in Fig. 3.9. The isobaric plot of f and $\ln\eta_0$ as a function of composition at T = 25 and 100°C is shown in Fig. 3.10. It is evident that for homologous $C_6/$ $C_{16}$ blends the free volume shows a negative deviation from additivity while $\eta_0$ the positive. Note that the method successfully predicts variation of $\eta$, in the full range of P, T and $x_2$.

For solutions in which $\chi_{12} \neq 0$ (*Glasstone* et al., 1941; *Bondi*, 1967):

$$\log(V\eta_0) = \underset{i}{\Sigma}\ x_i \log(V_i\eta_{0i}) + \log(V\eta)^E \tag{3.80}$$

where $V_i$ is the molar volume, $x_i$ is the mole fraction and the "excess" term can be written as:

$$\log(V\eta)^E = -\Pi\, x_i\Delta H_m/2.45\ RT \tag{3.81}$$

Equations (3.80) and (3.81) formulate the Eyring's mirror image rule. Eq (3.80) can be written as a sum of log-terms of V and $\eta_0$. It can be demonstrated that for most organic systems the volume contraction due to intermolecular interactions is small in comparison to changes in $\eta_0$ (which depends on variations of f!). If so Eq (3.80) can be approximated by:

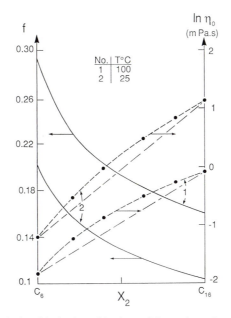

Fig. 3.10 Theoretically calculated isobaric and isothermal free volume fraction, f, as well as computed (lines) and measured (points) zero shear viscosity, $\eta_0$, at T = 25 and 100 °C for hexane/hexadecane mixtures.

$$\log\eta_0 = \sum_i x_i \log\eta_{0i} + \log\eta^E \tag{3.82}$$

known as an Arrhenius rule of mixing. For $\eta^E \rightarrow 0$ Eq (3.82) represents the widely used "log-additivity rule". When applied to polymer blends this relation is used replacing the mole function $x_i$ by the weight fraction, $w_i$, or the volume fraction, $\phi_i$.

Turning back to Fig. 3.10 it is worth noting that for homologous $C_6/C_{16}$ mixtures the free volume is less than average while log $\eta_0$ is more than average, i.e. these solutions show a positive deviation from the log-additivity rule, PDB.

A slightly different emphasis emerges from Eqs (3.80) and (3.81). Here for $\Delta H_m = 0$ a log-additivity is anticipated. In systems with $\Delta H_m < 0$ a positive deviation, i.e. PDB is expected while in those with $\Delta H_m > 0$ the negative deviation, the NDB. An example of this "mirror image" dependence is shown in Fig. 3.11 for aniline/chlorobenzene solutions (*Meyer* et al., 1971; *Katz* et al., 1971). As discussed in Part 2 the miscibility in polymer blends can take place only if $\Delta H_m \simeq \Delta G_m < 0$, i.e. PDB would be expected for miscible polymer blends. This indeed has been reported for melts of poly-2,6-dimethylphenyleneether/poly-styrene (PPE/PS) (*Prest* and *Porter*, 1972), polypropylene/polybutene-1 (PP/PB-1) (*Geni-lon* and *May*, 1978) or cis-1,4-polyisoprene/polyvinylethylene (PIP/PVE) (*Roland*, 1988) blends. The normal stress coefficient, $\psi_1$, or the storage modulus, $G'$, for these blends was also found to show positive deviation.

Several blending rules for solution viscosity have been proposed (*Bondi*, 1967). Recently the one derived by *McAllister* (1960) enjoyed enthusiastic but somewhat confusing attention (*Carley* and *Crossan*, 1980, 1981; *Plochocki*, 1986):

$$\ln v_B = x_1^3 \ln v_1 + x_2^3 \ln v_2 + 3x_1^2 x_2 \ln v_{12} + 3x_1 x_2^2 \ln v_{21}$$
$$+ 3x_1^2 x_2 \ln[(2M_1 + M_2)/3] + 3x_1 x_2^2 \ln[(M_1 + 2M_2)/3]$$
$$+ x_1^3 \ln M_1 + x_2^3 \ln M_2 - \ln(x_1 M_1 + x_2 M_2) \tag{3.83}$$

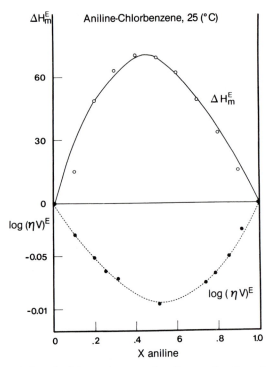

Fig. 3.11 Excess enthalpy of mixing and excess viscosity as a function of mole fraction of aniline in chlorobenzene at 25 °C (*Meyer* et al., 1971).

where $v_i$ is the kinematic viscosity, $M_i$ the molecular weight and the two kinematic viscosities with double subscripts are the empirical interaction viscosities. Eq (3.83) was derived from a three-body model of a miscible mixture of two low molecular weight liquids with two interaction viscosities. Use of this formula for immiscible systems negates the physical sense of its parameters, and reduces its significance to an empirical one. A third order polynomial ($y = \Sigma a_n x^n$; $n = 0$ to 3 with $y = \log\eta$ vs. $x = \phi$) provides at least as good a description of $\eta = \eta(\phi)$ dependence and being an algebraic relation can be used to describe any function one may wish without abusing the fundamental principles (*Carley* and *Crossan*, 1980, 1981; *Carley*, 1985).

The McAllister relation indicates that depending on the values of $v_{12}$ and $v_{21}$ the solution viscosity may show either PDB, NDB or a mixed positive-negative deviation from the log-additivity rule, PNDB, characterized by local minimum and local maximum on the $\ln v_{13}$ vs. $x_2$ plot. Similar dependence may be expected for miscible polymer blends. However, the mechanism responsible for variation of $v_{ij}$ is obscure.

Both, the free volume theory for homologous mixtures without specific interactions, and the Eyring mirror image rule based on thermodynamic argument indicate that PDB should be expected for miscible polymer blends.

### 3.3.2   Homologous macromolecular blends

Since on one hand the free volume-viscosity correlation established through use of Eqs (3.74) to (3.77) was found to be valid for solvents as well as for polymers (*Utracki*, 1974, 1980, 1982 b, 1983, 1985 b, c; *Utracki* and *Ghijsels*, 1987) and on another it was found applicable for predicting flow behavior of n-paraffin mixtures (*Utracki, 1986c*) one would expect the method to be suitable for describing the behavior of homologous macromolecular blends. On the basis of data presented in Fig. 3.10 a PDB dependence between $\eta_0$ and composition is expected.

There are numerous blending rules proposed in the literature (*Vinogradov* and *Malkin*, 1977; *Shenoy* et al., 1984; *Bird* et al., 1987). Large number of these can be written as (*Friedman* and *Porter*, 1975):

$$\eta_0^e = \Sigma \, E_i\eta_{0i}^e \tag{3.84}$$

where e is a parameter and $E_i$ a function of composition and molecular weight. Both e and $E_i$ are specified by given blending rule. For narrow molecular weight distribution polymers:

$$\eta_0 = KM_w^{\alpha} \tag{3.85}$$

where $\alpha \simeq 1$ for $M < M_e$ and $\alpha \simeq 3.4$ for $M > M_e$ (*Fox*, 1965). For broad molecular weight distribution, $M_w/M_n > 4$, the weight average in Eq (3.85) has to be replaced by a higher average. For log-normal distribution of linear low density polyethylenes this average can be expressed as (*Utracki* and *Schlund*, 1987):

$$M_a = \left[ \int_0^\infty M_w^a(M)dM \right]^{1/a} = M_z \, (M_w/M_n)^{1/5} \tag{3.86}$$

If $M_a$ of a homologous blend can be approximated by:

$$M_a \simeq \Sigma_i \, w_iM_{ai} \tag{3.87}$$

then from (3.87), assuming that Eq (3.85) is valid for fractions as well as for broad molecular weight polymers:

$$\eta_0 \simeq [\Sigma w_i\eta_{0i}^{1/a}]^a \tag{3.88}$$

Equation (3.88) is a successful approximate formula used over the years with $w_i$ standing either for weight or for volume fraction, and considered an empirical parameter most often divorced from its original meaning in Eq (3.85).

It can be easily demonstrated that for two component systems with constant $a \geqslant 0$:

$$d^2ln\eta_0/dw_2^2 = -a(\eta_{02}^{1/a} - \eta_{01}^{1/a})^2/\eta_0^{2/a} < 0 \tag{3.89}$$

i.e. a binary mixture of homologous polymers is expected to show a positive deviation from the log-additivity rule, PDB. Experimentally the data for homologous polymer blends have been fitted with the parameter: $1 \leqslant a \leqslant 100$ (*Montfort* et al., 1978; *Christov* et al., 1978; *Liu* et al., 1983; *Franck* and *Meissner*, 1984; *Bersted*, 1986). In Fig. 3.12 the dependence (3.88) is illustrated for different values of a.

*Wisniewski* et al. (1985) generalized Doolittle equation assuming additivity of f and of the pre-exponential factor:

$$ln\eta_0 = ln \, \Sigma a_{0i}\phi_i + a_1/\Sigma\phi_if_i \tag{3.90}$$

but if:     $a_{0i} = \eta_{0i}exp \, \{-a_1/f_i\} \tag{3.91}$

for a two component system assuming $a_1 \simeq 1$:

$$\partial^2ln\eta_0/\partial\phi_2^2 = -[(a_{02}-a_{01})/(\phi_2a_{02}+\phi_1a_{01})]^2 +$$
$$2(f_2-f_1)^2/(f_2\phi_2+f_1\phi_1)^3 \tag{3.92}$$

predicting PDB for most cases with a possibility of a small negative deviation from the log-additivity rule, NDB.

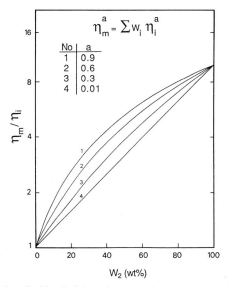

Fig. 3.12 Relative viscosity of a blend of homologous polymers as a function of the weight fraction of the second component. The curves calculated from Eq (3.88) assuming $\eta_2 = 10\eta_1$, and the four values of a = 1.1, 1.7, 3.3 and 100 for curve No. 1 to 4, respectively.

There is a mounting evidence that PDB is not the rule for miscible PAB. Depending on the system and method of preparation $\eta_0 = \eta_0(\phi)$ can be PDB, additive or NDB (*Suprun* and *Romankevich*, 1984; *Martuscelli*, 1984; *Singh* and *Singh*, 1984; *Aoki*, 1984). From the free volume theory NDB ought to be associated with an extra free volume generated on mixing. This effect may be due either to $\Delta H_m > 0$ or to less efficient packing in the mixture caused by specific interaction (i.e. $\Delta H_m < 0$) which resulted in an increase in stereo-restrictions and reduction of the entropy of mixing.

### 3.3.3    Viscosity of Suspensions

For immiscible blends suspension, emulsions and block copolymers can serve as models. Viscosities of these systems are expressed in terms of relative viscosity, $\eta_r$, defined as a ratio of suspension or emulsion viscosity to that of the medium. The hydrodynamic volume of the suspended particle or droplet is proportional to the intrinsic viscosity:

$$[\eta] \equiv \lim_{\phi \to 0} (\eta_r - 1)/\phi \qquad (3.93)$$

The uniform, hard sphere suspension in Newtonian liquids has been the subject of ongoing theoretical and experimental attention. Early works have been reviewed by *Frish* and *Simha* (1956), *Rutgers* (1962) and *Thomas* (1965), with more recent contributions by *Utracki* (1982b, 1984b, 1987a), *Utracki* and *Fisa* (1982), *Mewis* (1980), *Metzner* (1985) and others. Quite unique in depth and scope are reviews of microrheology of dispersions by *Goldsmith* and *Mason* (1967) and by *Brenner* (1974).

Theories derive from three assumptions: (i) the diameter of rigid particles is large compared to that of suspending medium molecules, but small compared to the smallest dimension of the rheometer, (ii) flow is at steady state, without inertial, concentration gradient or wall slip effects, and (iii) the medium liquid adheres perfectly to particles. Depending on the theory, there may be also be a fourth assumption for inter-particle interaction.

A multitude of relations have been proposed between $\eta_r$ and $\phi$ for the monodisperse hard sphere suspensions. Of these, the following two were found to provide the best description (*Utracki* and *Fisa*, 1982). The first is the semi-empirical formula proposed by *Mooney* (1951):

$$\ln\eta_0 = [n]_s\phi/(1-\phi/\phi_m) \tag{3.94}$$

while the second is the theoretical dependence derived by *Simha* (1952):

$$\eta_r = 1 + [\eta]_s\lambda\phi \tag{3.95}$$

with    $\lambda = 4(1 - Y^7)/[4(1 + Y^{10}) - 25Y^3(1 + Y^4) + 42Y^5]$

$Y \equiv [2(\phi_m/\phi)^{1/3} - 1]^{-1}$

In these relations $[\eta]_s$ indicates intrinsic viscosity of hard spheres and $\phi_m$ is the maximum packing volume fraction. The $\eta_r$ is taken at $\dot{\gamma} \rightarrow 0$. Mooney's Eq (3.94) can be derived from the free volume theory (*Utracki*, 1980; *Utracki* and *Simha*, 1981). In Fig. 3.13 the dependencies predicted by these relations are compared with the experimental data evaluated by *Thomas* (1965): $[\eta]_s = 2.5$, $\phi_m = 0.91$ and $[\eta]_s = 2.5$, $\phi_m = 0.78$ were respectively used in Eqs (3.94) and (3.95). Note the more realistic set of parameters required by the latter dependence.

The relative viscosity of suspensions expressed by a general formula:

$$\eta_r^0 = [1 + \alpha\phi]^\beta \tag{3.96}$$

with $\alpha$ and $\beta$ parameters, was used by *Einstein* (1905, 1906, 1911, 1920) for very dilute suspensions ($\alpha = 2.5$, $\beta = 1$). If $\beta < 0$ the Eq (3.96) becomes any of the "relative fluidity"

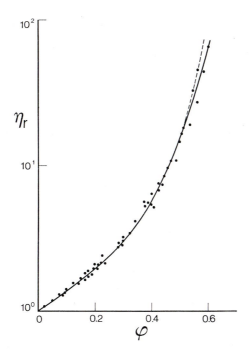

Fig. 3.13 Relative viscosity of hard sphere suspensions. Points – data from *Thomas* (1965), solid and broken lines – Eqs (3.94) and (3.95), respectively.

equations discussed in the literature since 1920. *Hess* (1920) and later *Vand* (1954) proposed $\alpha = -2.5$ and $\beta = -1$ for concentrations in excess of 50 vol%. *De Bruijn* (1942) obtained better results using $\alpha = -1.73$ and $\beta = -2$. Eq (3.96) with the later value of $\beta$ was rederived several times, e.g. by *Maron* and *Pierce* (1956) or by *Quemada* (1977). In spite of "wrong" limits (note that for $\beta < 0$, $\phi_m = -1/\alpha$, but then for $\phi \to 0$ $\eta^0 \simeq 1 + (2/\phi_m)\phi$ which reduces to Einstein's equation only if $\phi_m = 0.8$!) Eq (3.96) with $\beta = -2$ continuously finds its advocates (*Metzner*, 1985). There is almost as much support for $\beta = -2.5$ (*Brinkman*, 1952; *Roscoe*, 1952; *Landel* et al., 1963). An interesting solution to this problem was taken by *Krieger* and *Daugherty* (1959) who derived Eq (3.96) with $\alpha = -1/\phi_m$ and $\beta = -[\eta]_s\phi_m$. Note that these constants give not only the correct low and high values but also sufficient flexibility to accommodate systems with different numerical values of $[\eta]_s$ and $\phi_m$. Recently *Bedeaux* (1983, 1987) has proposed a new theory for effective viscosity in two-phase flow.

There are several ways to pack even the monodisperse, hard spheres resulting in a large variation of $\phi_m$ (viz. Table 3.2 and *Cumberland* and *Crawford*, 1987).

TABLE 3.2   Maximum Packing Volume Fraction in Suspensions of Uniform Hard Spheres

| No. | Arrangement | $\phi_m \cdot 10^3$ | Ref. | Comments |
|-----|-------------|---------------------|------|----------|
| I.1 | Cubical | 523.6 | 1 | Theoretical |
| I.2 | Single-staggered (cubical tetrahedral) | 604.5 | 1 | Theoretical |
| I.3 | Double-staggered | 698.0 | 1 | Theoretical |
| I.4 | Pyramidal, face-centered | 740.5 | 1 | Theoretical |
| I.5 | Hexagonal, close-packed | 740.5 | 1 | Theoretical |
| I.6 | Random-loose | 601 | 2 | Experimental limits for |
| I.7 | Random-dense | 637 | 2 | steel spheres |
| I.8 | Random-loose | 596 | 3 | Experimental limits for |
| I.9 | Random-dense | 641 | 3 | nylon spheres |
| I.10 | Average random-loose | 598 ± 4 | 4 | Average of published |
| I.11 | Average random-dense | 639 ± 3 | 4 | experimental data |
| I.12 | Most probable random | 620 | – | Experimental average |

*References:* 1. *H. E. White* and *S. F. Walton*, 1937; 2. *C. D. Scott*, 1960; 3. *R. Rutgers*, 1962; 4. *D. I. Lee*, 1970.

Eqs (3.94)-(3.96) predict that $\eta_r$ should be independent of diameter, d. However, it was recognized early that properties of suspensions of small particles with $d \ll 1\mu m$ should show higher $\eta_r^0$ than theoretically predicted by a hydrodynamic argument. There are three reasons for this:

1. the low mobility of liquid molecules adsorbed on the particle surface (*Smoluchowski*, 1916)
2. the contribution due to thermal (Brownian) motion, and
3. effects of colloidal aggregation of particles (*de Bruijn*, 1951).

The data from 16 laboratories were examined by *Thomas* (1965). After correcting the diameter for these effects the author obtained good superposition of data (see Fig. 3.13) onto an empirical curve:

$$\eta_r^0 = 1 + 2.5\phi + 10.05\phi^2 + 0.00273 \exp (16.6\phi) \tag{3.97}$$

Another set of complicating effects in uniform hard sphere suspensions is due to orientation or structure formation under flow conditions (*Manley* and *Mason*, 1952). In the limiting region of dilute suspensions where the linear relation derived by Einstein holds, the only shape dependent parameter: $[\eta]_s = 2.5$ is independent of polydispersity. The effect becomes important only at $\phi \geqslant 0.2$ (*Rutgers*, 1962); below this limit, blending two generations of spheres with the diameter ratio:

$$R_d = d_1/d_2 \tag{3.98}$$

resulted in a small depression of $\eta_r$ (*Eveson*, 1959; *Goto* and *Kuno*, 1982, 1984). The importance of particle size distribution for rheological behavior is most conveniently discussed in terms of the maximum packing volume fraction. Most of the relations between $\eta_r$ and reduced concentration, $\tilde{\phi}$, can be cast in terms of reduced variables:

$$\tilde{\eta}_0 = \tilde{\eta}_0(\tilde{\phi}) \tag{3.99}$$

where: $\quad \tilde{\eta}_0 \equiv (\eta_r - 1)/\phi[\eta]_s \quad$ and $\quad \tilde{\phi} \equiv \phi/\phi_m$

Accordingly, any increase in $\phi_m$ reduces $\tilde{\phi}$ and effectively lowers $\eta_r$ at constant value of $\phi$.

The problem of maximization of $\phi_m$ by designing appropriate mixtures of particles with specific diameter ratios and specific concentrations has been critical to numerous industries. The need to maximize $\phi_m$ originates not only in its ability to reduce $\eta_r$ but also in generating higher modulus of organic or inorganic composites, improving the hiding power of paint, obtaining more energetic propellents or explosives, etc. Several approaches have been used to increase $\phi_m$.

1. *McGeary* (1961) data for maximum values of $\phi_{m,2}$ (subscript "2" indicates a binary mixture obtained by blending two generations of uniform diameter hard spheres) with diameter ratio $R_d$ is shown in Fig. 3.14. There is a simple relation between $\phi_{m,2}(R_d = 1) = \phi_m$ and $\phi_{m,2}(R_d \to \infty) = \phi_{m,2}(\infty)$:

$$\phi_{m,2}(\infty) = \phi_m + [1 - \phi_m]\phi_m \tag{3.100}$$

which can easily be generalized for N generations of spheres, each with $R^N \to \infty$:

$$\phi_{m,N}(\infty) = \phi_{m,N-1}(\infty) + [1 - \phi_{m,N-1}(\infty)]\phi_{m,N-1}(\infty) \tag{3.101}$$

From Eq (3.101), assuming $\phi_m = 0.625$, since only at $R_d > 100$ are the conditions for $R \to \infty$ approached, and since the smallest diameter should not be below $0.1\mu m$, this method can generate binary or ternary mixtures with expected $\phi_m \leqslant 0.980$.

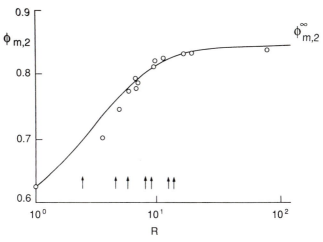

Fig. 3.14 Maximum packing volume fraction as a function of particle diameter ratio. Points – experimental (*McGeary*, 1961), solid line – Eq (3.102). The arrows indicate $R_d$ values fitting into interstices of hexagonally closed packed spheres.

For random packing of binary spheres the dependence $\phi_{m,2} + \phi_{m,2}(R)$ can be expressed in the form of the nested growth function:

$$\phi_{m,2} = \phi_{m,2}(\infty)[1 - \exp\{a_0 + a_1 \exp(-a_2 R_d)\}] \tag{3.102}$$

where $a_i$'s are parameters. Taking $\phi_m = 0.625$, i.e. $\phi_{m,2}(\infty) = 0.859$, $a_0 = -4.2$, $a_1 = 3.2$ and $a_2 = 0.1$ the curve in Fig. 3.14 was generated. In spite of the approximate nature of selected parameters, a reasonable fit to McGeary's data was obtained.

2. Another method of designing multimodal suspensions of spheres with high $\phi_m$ starts by assuming a crystal-like arrangement to uniform spheres, then calculating the maximum diameter of the second generation of spheres to go into spaces left between the first generation, then the third generation to go into new spaces, etc. These calculations have been carried out several times (*Horsfield*, 1934; *White* and *Walton*, 1937; *Utracki*, 1970, 1971; *Kausch* and *Tschoegl*, 1986) assuming either hexagonal or cubic structure. An example is shown in Table 3.3. The arrows in Fig. 3.14 indicate the space filling values of $R_d$. Note that addition of the second generation spheres with $R_d < 2.42$ has a deleterious effect – it disrupts the close packing, decreasing $\phi_m$.

TABLE 3.3  Calculated Space Filling Distribution for Hexagonal Hard Sphere Arrays

| n | $R_d$ | N | $\phi_i \times 10^3$ | $\phi_m \times 10^3$ |
|---|---|---|---|---|
| 1 | 1 | 1 | 740.5 | 740.5 |
| 2 | 2.42 | 1 | 52.6 | 790.3 |
| 3 | 4.44 | 2 | 16.8 | 809.9 |
| 4 | 5.65 | 8 | 32.6 | 842.5 |
| 5 | 8.06 | 8 | 11.3 | 853.8 |
| 6 | 9.01 | 4 | 4.0 | 857.8 |
| 7 | 12.4 | 12 | 4.7 | 862.5 |
| 8 | 12.5 | 12 | 4.5 | 867.0 |
| 9 | 13.9 | 24 | 6.6 | 873.6 |

Note: n is the sphere generation number; $R_d$ is the diameter ratio of the spheres, $R_d \equiv d_i/d_1$; N is the number of spheres of i-th generation per one sphere of the first generation; $\phi_i$ is the volume fraction of the i-th generation, and $\phi_m = \Sigma \phi_i$ is the total volume fraction of spheres up to i = n-th generation.

3. Still another method uses the log-normal distribution as the desired final result. This method has been applied both to uniform and random packing of nearly spherical particles. Setting $R_N$ and $\phi_N$ as the diameter ratio and the volume fraction of N-th generation particles, the method requires that:

$$R_N = A^{1-N}; \qquad \phi_N = \phi_m/R_N; \qquad \sum_1^\infty V_N = 1 \tag{3.103}$$

where A is a parameter. For five generations of particles with $R_N = 100$ $\phi_m \simeq 0.94$ was obtained.

4. In some applications not only high $\phi_m$ but also uniform porosity and ease of handling are important. For such applications *Ritter*'s (1971) method for non-segregating mixtures seems to be most suitable (*Lord*, 1971). Four generations of particles are required with the diameter ratios $1 : 3 \pm 0.4 : 9 \pm 2 : 17 \pm 3$ at respective volume fractions 0.4, 0.1, 0.1 and 0.4. Experimentally $\phi_m = 0.78$ and uniform porosity were obtained. Higher $\phi_m$ were reported for other compositions, but the small particles tended to settle at the bottom and the porosities were not as good.

5. In order to achieve the lowest $\eta_r$ in systems containing the same total volume fraction of solids, *Farris* (1968) derived the following relation for polydisperse systems:

$$\eta_r = \Pi \, \eta_{r,i}(\Phi_i) \tag{3.104}$$

Farris' calculations require that:

$$\Phi_i = V_i / \underset{i}{\Sigma} \, V_i = \text{const.} \tag{3.105}$$

where $V_i$ is the volume of the i-th generation of spheres. It is customary to assign the subscript $i = 0$ to the liquid and $i = 1$ to either the smallest or the largest particles.

From Eqs (3.94) and (3.104) the following relation was derived (*Parkinson* et al., 1970):

$$\eta_r = \Pi_i \, \exp\{2.5 \, \phi_i / (1 - k_i \phi_i)\} \tag{3.106}$$

where for monodisperse suspensions $k_i = 1/\phi_{mi}$. Empirically:

$$k_i = 0.168 \, d_i^{-1 \cdot 0072} \tag{3.107}$$

To conclude this discussion on suspensions containing spherical particles, it is worth stressing that so far only the behavior at $\dot{\gamma} \to 0$ have been considered. As $\phi$ increases, the association and clustering of spheres increases leading to non-Newtonian behavior. These effects will be discussed later, after the Newtonian flow of suspensions with anisometric particles is reviewed.

At the onset of shearing, the anisometric particle begins to rotate with the period:

$$t_p = 2\pi(p + p^{-1})/\dot{\gamma} \tag{3.108}$$

where p is the aspect ratio: $p \equiv a_{max}/a_{min}$ ($a_{max}$ and $a_{min}$ are respectively the maximum and minimum particle dimension). In microrheology the aspect ratio of a particle in orthogonal coordinates is usually defined as $p^* = a/b$, where a is the spheroidal particle half axis in the polar direction and b is the larger one of the two equatorial semi axes. Thus for fibers and prolate elipsoids $p^* > 1$, for spheres $p^* = 1$ and for discs or oblate elipsoids $p^* < 1$. Note that Eq (3.108) is valid for either definition of the aspect ratio, p or $p^*$.

The rate of rotation goes through a periodic acceleration for rods at times $t = 0$, $t_p/2$ and $t_p$, and for disks at $t = t_p/4$ and $3t_p/4$. Due to these orientation effects $[\eta]$ is a periodic function of time, gradually dumped to reach constant value (e.g. see Fig. 3.15). Under

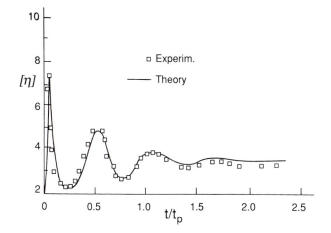

Fig. 3.15 Experimental (points) and theoretical (line) variation of intrinsic viscosity for suspensions of initially aligned fibers; after *Ivanov* et al. (1982) see also *Ivanov and van de Ven* (1982).

steady state shearing, the particles continue to rotate. For small ones the rotary Brownian motion becomes important at Péclet numbers:

$$Pe = \dot{\gamma}/D_r \tag{3.109}$$

$Pe < 1$ ($D_r$ is the rotary diffusion coefficient). Thus the flow depends on p and Pe resulting in non-Newtonian behavior. These aspects will be discussed later in Part 3.3 (*Goldsmith* and *Mason*, 1967; *Brenner*, 1974; *van de Ven*, 1985).

Since rheological effects are related to particle orientation, the theoretical description must combine the kinetics of motion with rheology. Furthermore, since orientation is determined by the deformation tensor there is no direct, general correlation between rheological responses of these suspensions tested under different modes of deformation. For suspensions of anisometric particles there is no equation, $\eta_r = \eta_r(\phi,p)$, that ist valid for the full range of $\phi$. There are two reasons for this: (i) severe theoretical difficulties, an (2) relatively low limit of independent variables, such as $\phi$, $\dot{\gamma}$, $\varrho$, etc. For infinite dilutions one may define the intrinsic viscosity of anisometric particle, $[\eta]_a$, either in steady-state or time-dependent form. For rigid dumbbells (*Simha*, 1940, 1949, 1950):

$$[\eta]_a = 3(L/d)^2/4 \tag{3.110}$$

(L is the sphere's separation distance and d their diameter). For ellipsoids of rotation and rigid rods (*Simha*, 1945):

$$[\eta]_a = \frac{14}{15} + \frac{p^2}{5}\left[\frac{1}{3(\ln 2p - \sigma)} + \frac{1}{\ln 2p - \sigma + 1}\right] \tag{3.111}$$

where $\sigma$ is the numerical constant. For ellipsoids of rotation, $\sigma = 1.5$, and for rigid rods, $\sigma = 1.8$. Equation (3.111) holds for $p > 20$. It provides the upper bounds for freely rotating particles. For time averaged optimum orientation (*Goldsmith* and *Mason*, 1967):

$$[\eta]_a = p^3/[3(\ln 2p - \sigma)(p + 1)^2] \tag{3.112}$$

For low aspect ratio particles the tabulated values of $[\eta]_a$ (*Scheraga*, 1955) or a general theory for triaxially anisometric ellipsoids (*Haber* and *Brenner* 1984) should be used.

In the region of infinite dilution the particle rotates freely without being affected by the presence of others. Accordingly, $[\eta]_a$ is a measure of particle hydrodynamic volume defined by its geometry. The customary definition of the dilute region is that where particles are not restricted in their motion, i.e. to $\phi < p^{-2}$. Outside this region the two-body interactions have to be taken into assount. One can postulate that this can be done using a power series expression:

$$\tilde{\eta}_0 = 1 + k_H[\eta]_a\phi + \ldots \tag{3.113}$$

where, by analogy with polymer solutions, the Huggins' constant, $k_H$, expresses the particle-particle interactions. Its value is theoretically known for hard-sphere suspensions; Equation (3.95) gives $k_H = 5/16\,\phi_m \approx 0.5$. For anisometric particles $k_H$ depends on the type of flow, on shape and on orientation. For rigid rods or dumbbells flowing through pipes, experimentally $k_H = 0.7 \pm 0.2$. Within the diluted region the period of rotation, given by Equation (3.108), increases with $\phi$. At the limit, due to crowding, no free rotation is possible.

In the semi-concentrated region, $p^{-2} < \phi < p^{-1}$, movement is possible only in two-dimensions. Rheologically, this results in a reduction of the apparent hydrodynamic volume of the particles, observed as a decrease in the rate with which $\eta_r$ increases with $\phi$ as shown in Fig. 3.16 (*Fisa* and *Utracki*, 1984).

*Utracki* (1984a) proposed that the effect of crowding on $[\eta]_a$ be considered as similar in its limit to that induced by high strain rates. For rods (*Brenner* and *Condiff*, 1979):

$$[\eta]_0/[\eta]_\infty = p/1.17 \tag{3.114}$$

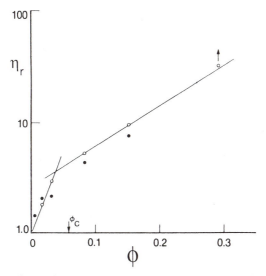

Fig. 3.16 Semi-log dependence of relative viscosity vs. volume fraction for mica flakes in polyethylene (*Fisa* and *Utracki*, 1984).

where subscripts $"_0"$ and $"_\infty"$ indicate limits: $\dot{\gamma} \to 0$ and $\dot{\gamma} \to \infty$, respectively. For disks the numerical factor of 1.17 ought to be changed to 3.31. *Doi* and *Edwards* (1978) predicted that for rods $\eta_r \propto \phi^3$.

Within the concentrated region, $\phi > 1/p$, as $\phi$ approaches the maximum packing value, theoretically $\phi_r$ should increase toward infinity. Experimentally, a series of complicating factors, (to be discussed in later sections) are observed. Invariably, all these lead to non-Newtonian behavior and the zero-shear viscosity can be extracted only after a series of correcting procedures.

Alternatively, one can use a pragmatic approach and describe $\eta - \phi$ dependence in a wide range of concentration by a hard-sphere Equation (3.94) or (3.95) taking $[\eta]_s$ and $\phi_m$ as adjustable. Due to the aforementioned orientation effects, usually the dilute region of freely tumbling particles has to be treated separately from semiconcentrated and concentrated ones. The limiting concentration is easy to calculate from the encompassed volume of freely rotating rods or plates. The relation between $[\eta]_a$ and $\phi_m$ on aspect ratio p for disks and rods can be approximated by:

$$[\eta]_a, \, 1/\phi_m = a_0 + a_1 p^{a_2} \tag{3.115}$$

with $a_i$'s being parameters. An example of their values is given in Table 3.4.

TABLE 3.4  Experimental Values of Parameters $a_i$ of Equation (3.115)

| No. | Particle | Y | $P_m$ | $a_0$ | $a_1$ | $a_2$ | Ref. |
|-----|----------|-----|-----|------|--------|-----|------|
| 1 | Disks | $[\eta]$ | 50 | 2.51 | 0.1127 | 1 | 1 |
| 2 | Disks | $1/\phi_m$ | 50 | 1.29 | 0.0598 | 1 | 2 |
| 3 | Rods | $[\eta]$ | 50 | 2.34 | 0.1636 | 1 | 2 |
| 4 | Rods | $1/\phi_m$ | 150 | 1.38 | 0.0376 | 1.4 | 3 |

Note: $P_2$ indicate the maximum value of the aspect ratio used to determine the parameters $a_i$.

*References.*: 1. *L. A. Utracki* et al., 1984; 2. *L. A. Utracki*, 1987a; 3. *M. M. Cross* et al., 1983.

The value of $[\eta]_a$ is an average one. Since the particle continue to rotate in the shear flow its effective hydrodynamic volume depends on time, t. In Fig. 3.15 the $[\eta]_a$ vs. t is shown for suspensions of fibers initially aligned in electrical field (*Ivanov* et al., 1982). The oscillations predicted by Eq (3.108) are slowly dumped to converge to an average theoretically predicted value of $[\eta]_a = 3.4$ (*Scheraga*, 1955; *Okagawa* et al., 1973; *Zuzovsky* et al., 1980).

As the data in Table 3.4 indicate $\phi_m$ is a strong function of p; e.g. for p = 50 the maximum packing of freely rotating fibers is $\phi_m = 0.10$ ($[\eta]_a = 10.52$). As a consequence the fibers can rotate only at loading $\phi < \phi_m$; above this value only a limited freedom of movement can be expected, i.e. an abrupt change of effective hydrodynamic volume of anisometric particles is expected in the vicinity of $\phi_m$. (Note that this effect is quite different from that expected for hard sphere suspension where near $\phi_m$ the viscosity $\eta_r \to \infty$). This behavior is illustrated in Fig. 3.16 with $\eta_r$ vs. $\phi$ for mica-polyethylene system (*Fisa* and *Utracki,* 1984). The data are plotted in terms of Kraemer equation:

$$\ln \eta_r = [\eta]_a\phi + k_k[\eta]_a^2\phi^2 + \dots \tag{3.116}$$

allowing a direct measure of the local value of the intrinsic viscosity:

$$[\eta]_{a,\phi_i} = \lim_{\phi \to \phi_i} (\partial\ln\eta_r/\partial\phi) \tag{3.117}$$

Concluding this part one may note that: 1. addition of rigid particles increases $\eta$; polydispersity of sizes reduces this effect while anisometry increases it; 2. the particles rotate under shear; and 3. both the concentration and anisometry cause non-Newtonian behavior.

Translating these observations into the behavior expected for PAB's it is apparent that dispersing a more viscous polymer in a less viscous one should result in an increase of $\eta$. By contrast with single phase systems here $\eta$ depends not only on $\phi$, but also on: (i) interfacial properties which may change the effective volume of the dispersed phase, (ii) polydispersity of droplets, (iii) the geometry of dispersed phase and (iv) association. In general the suspension model allows prediction of the PDB.

Suspensions are also valuable models for flow segregation and microrheological behavior of PAB's, as well as the non-Newtonian behavior of these systems.

### 3.3.4    Rheology of Emulsions (Two Newtonian Liquids)

Early works have been summarized by *Sherman* (1963, 1968), *Barry* (1977) *Nielsen* (1977) and *Rallison* (1984). The rheology of emulsion has also been discussed as a model for flow of polymer blends and alloys by *Han* (1981), *Utracki* and *Bata* (1982), *Utracki* and *Kamal* (1982) and *Utracki* (1983a, 1987a).

For infinite dilution, neglecting the influence of the interphase, *Taylor* (1932, 1934) expressed the intrinsic viscosity of the liquid droplets as:

$$[\eta]_E = 2.5(\eta_p + 2\eta_m/5)/(\eta_p + \eta_m) \tag{3.118}$$

where subscripts "E", "p" and "m" indicate respectively emulsion, droplet and medium. For $\eta_p \gg \eta_m$, Einstein's limit is recovered. At low concentration, and for $\eta_p \geqslant \eta_m$, Equation (3.118) is well obeyed (*Nawab* and *Mason,* 1985). The effect of the interphase on relative viscosity of emulsion was reconsidered by *Oldroyd* (1953, 1955), who wrote:

$$[\eta]_{E,d} = 2.5(\eta_p + 2\eta_m/5 + \eta_i/5d)/(\eta_p + \eta_m + \eta_i/5d) \tag{3.119}$$

where $\eta_i = 2\eta_{si} + 3\eta_{ei}$ expresses the shear, $\eta_{si}$, and extensional, $\eta_{ei}$, viscosities of the interface. Defining parameter $\Lambda$ as:

$$\Lambda = (\eta_p + \eta_i/5d)/\eta_m \tag{3.120}$$

the dependence $[\eta]_{E,d}$ vs. $\Lambda$, shown in Fig. 3.17 was computed. For $\Lambda \to 0$ the solution value of the intrinsic viscosity is obtained while for $K \to \infty$ the hard sphere suspension value of the intrinsic viscosity is recovered. Eq (3.119) was found to be valid for a wide range of $\Lambda \geq 1.3$.

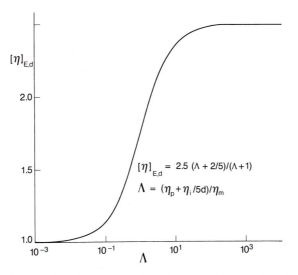

Fig. 3.17 Intrinsic viscosity of emulsion vs. $\Lambda$, where $\Lambda$ combines the influence of relative viscosity of the two liquids, droplet diameter and shear as well as extensional properties of the interface (*Oldroyd*, 1953, 1955).

For hard-sphere suspension, Equations (3.94) or (3.95) are valid over the full range of concentrations. For emulsions, in the absence of deformation and coalescence, they can be used as well, provided $[\eta]_E$ and $\phi_m$ are treated as adjustable parameters, dependent primarily on the interphase (*Matsumoto* and *Sherman*, 1969) and viscosity ratio (*Oldroyd*, 1955). This pragmatic approach has been successfully used to describe $\eta - \phi$ variation for such complex systems as industrial lattices (at various stages of conversion), plastisols and organosols (*Utracki*, 1970, 1971).

Emulsions are usually prepared as concentrated systems; industrial emulsions are formulated at $\phi \leq 0.99$. Due to interface interactions and deformability of droplets these systems behave like elastic, soft solids. Between the highly concentrated and diluted regions there is a wide zone of structural changes reflected in a spectrum of non-Newtonian behavior.

A dilute emulsion under low deformation rate behaves like a suspension of hard spheres. The difference becomes apparent when the concentration and stress field increase. Even in the dilute region emulsion droplets rarely exist individually (*Goldsmith* and *Mason*, 1967). In most cases, droplets are polydisperse in size, forming string-like structures or aggregates. Two types can be distinguished: (a) formed by the shear field (e.g., skin-core structures in long tube flows), and (b) those formed by interactions. The structures (a) are at non-equilibrium but by various methods of morphology stabilization they can be fixed in order to enhance performance of the product. The structure (b) in principle leads to morphology determined by the simple formula: the interface area = surface which can be protected by a surfactant.

Structures of type (a) are subject of microrheological studies. They are responsible for the non-Newtonian effects. Knowledge of these is essential for correct interpretation of flow behavior (*Brandt* and *Gugliarello*, 1966; *Goldsmith* and *Mason*, 1967; *Utracki*, 1973; *Okagawa* and *Mason*, 1975; *Harris* and *Pittman*, 1976; *Elmendorp*, 1986). Knowledge of (b)-type structures is the key for utilization of emulsion rheology in processing (*Smith,* 1972). Since the effective volume fraction of dispersed particles increases with increase of association, $\eta_r$ is strongly affected. In general, $\eta_r$ of these systems depends on shear history (*Zosel,* 1982).

By contrast with polymer blends, emulsions are prepared by carefully designing the interface system and then sequential addition of the ingredients. Both elements are essential when 99 vol% of one liquid must be dispersed in 1% of another. If, due to interactions with emulsifier, the continuous phase becomes viscoelastic, the emulsion has a high consistency, or a "body". There is gradual passage of structures from rotating doublets in dilute systems to entrapment of the dispersed phase in a continuous network of interacting interphases. Consequently, emulsions do possess both a purely Newtonian character as well as a complex thixotropic and viscoelastic one (*Barry,* 1977; *Nielsen,* 1977).

*Cox* and *Mason* (1971) and *Leal* (1980) reviewed the theoretical treatment of flow of two phase systems. The shear flow of dilute emulsions is controlled by two parameters:

$$\lambda \equiv \eta_1/\eta_2 \tag{3.121}$$

where $\eta_1$ indicates the viscosity of dispersed and $\eta_2$ that of the matrix liquid, and:

$$\varkappa \equiv \sigma_{12}d/v \tag{3.122}$$

where $\sigma_{12}$, d and v are respectively shear stress, droplet diameter and interfacial tension coeficient. Both $\lambda$ and $\varkappa$ are dimensionless. In the literature occasionally $1/\varkappa$ is titled the Taylor number, $N_T$, while $\varkappa$ the Weber number, We. However, since in chemical engineering $N_T$ and We express other dimensionless groups it is better to avoid these terms. Using the $\lambda$ and $\varkappa$ parameters the droplet deformability can be expressed as (*Taylor,* 1932, 1934):

$$D \equiv (d_1 - d_2)/(d_1 + d_2) \simeq \varkappa(19\lambda/16 + 1)/2(\lambda + 1) \equiv E_T \tag{3.123}$$

where $d_1$ and $d_2$ are major and minor axes of the deformed ellipsoid. For small deformations Eq (3.123) predicts the conditions when the drop will burst (*Goldsmith* and *Mason,* 1967):

$$\sigma_{12}(19\lambda + 16)/16(\lambda + 1) > v/d \tag{3.124}$$

(equivalent to $d_1 > 3d_2$), the rate of droplet migration away from the wall (*Cox* and *Mason,* 1971):

$$U = (33Dvd^3/4480y_0^2)(79\lambda^2 + 77\lambda + 54)/(\lambda + 1)^2 \tag{3.125}$$

(where $y_0$ is the distance of the droplet from the wall), or the first normal stress difference (*Schowalter* et al., 1968):

$$N_1 = \phi d(\sigma_{12}D\varkappa)^2/40v \tag{3.126}$$

Equations (3.123) to (3.126) are strictly valid for dilute emulsions of monodisperse droplets with the interphase characterized only by the interfacial tension. On the basis of this simple model Oldroyd derived an expression for the relaxation time:

$$\tau^* = d\eta_2 \, D\varkappa(2\lambda + 3)/40v \tag{3.127}$$

In Oldroyd's model the interphase was considered as a thin membrane, characterized by four parameters: shear and tensile moduli and viscosities. In another model (*Sakanishi* and *Takano,* 1974) the interphase is treated as the third component with two interfacial tension coefficients, $v_1$ and $v_2$, for the inner and outer interfaces. Both these models predict two relaxation times, observed by *Oosterbroek* et al. (1980).

*Cox* (1969) extended Taylor's work on drop deformation to time dependent flow fields. For small deformation of Newtonian drops in shear flow he obtained:

$$D_c = \varkappa(19\lambda/16+1)/2(\lambda+1)[(1.9\lambda/\varkappa)^2+1]^{\frac{1}{2}} \tag{3.123a}$$

which at a limit $\lambda/\varkappa \to 0$, or $\nu \to 0$, leads to Taylor's solution, Eq (3.123). As it can be seen the Cox Equation predicts smaller deformation than Taylor's:

$$D_c = E_T[1+(1.9\lambda/\varkappa)^2]^{-\frac{1}{2}} \tag{3.123b}$$

with $E_T$ defined in Eq (3.123).

Theoretical studies of deformation and breakup of single droplet under extensional, hyperbolic and shear field lead to approximate numerical solution (*Acrivos* and *Lo*, 1978; *Hinch* and *Acrivos*, 1979):

$$\tilde{\lambda} \equiv 2L\lambda^{1/3}/d \simeq 3.50\tilde{\gamma}^{\frac{1}{2}}; \qquad \text{for } \tilde{\gamma} \equiv \varkappa\lambda^{2/3}/2 < 0.045 \tag{3.128}$$

$$\tilde{\lambda} \simeq 261\tilde{\gamma}^2 + 0.0231/\tilde{\gamma}; \qquad \text{for } \tilde{\gamma} > 0.05$$

where $\tilde{\lambda}$ and $\tilde{\gamma}$ are the dimensionless half length of a drop and non-dimensional shear rate with L being the droplet length. The theoretical prediction for droplet breakup, $\tilde{\gamma} = 0.0541$, agrees with the experimental data by *Grace* (1971) for droplet breakup due to fracture:

$$\varkappa\lambda^{0.55} = 0.34 \tag{3.130}$$

Grace also reported that droplet breakup due to droplet tip streaming occurred at $\varkappa = 1.12$.

The shear stress dependence of dilute emulsion viscosity at small deformation was derived by *Barthes-Biesel* and *Acrivos* (1973):

$$\eta_r = 1 + [(5\lambda+2)/2(\lambda+1) - f(\lambda)(\sigma_{12}/\Delta_E)^2 + 0(\sigma_{12}^3)]\phi \tag{3.131}$$

where $f(\lambda) > 0$ is a rational function of $\lambda$. The relation predicts a decrease of $\eta_r$ with the square of the shear stress. The effect of stress is moderated by interphase elasticity expressed as $\Delta_E$. The theory was experimentally verified using emulsions with crosslinkable interphase; varying the degree of crosslinking changed the value of $\Delta_E$ (*Bredimas* et al., 1983). *Esmukhanov* et al. (1985) examined the rheological behavior of dilute systems with dispersed deformable particles, characterized by viscoelastic memory functions. The theory, originally written for ellipsoidal molecular clusters of polymer chain in a poor solvent without Brownian motion, can also describe the rheological behavior of dilute emulsions.

Semi-concentrated emulsions in the linear viscoelastic region were studied theoretically as well as experimentally (*Oesterbrock* and *Mellema*, 1981; *Oesterbrock* et al., 1981; *Eshuis* and *Mellema*, 1984). The authors considered two models: (i) a two dimensional viscoelastic film and (ii) the interphase of final thickness. Both models led to at least two relaxation times. The experimental results of dynamic testing in kHz region for ionic emulsions could equally well be interpreted in terms of either model. However, since the thickness of the interface was monomolecular, model (i) was considered a better reflection of the physical reality. The mechanism responsible for emulsion elasticity was found to originate in droplet deformation. For non-ionic emulsions only one relaxation time was observed. These later results were interpreted in terms of the second Oldroyd's model. Two retardation time processes were observed by *Gladwell* et al. (1986).

The structural theory of concentrated emulsions and foams (*Princen*, 1983, 1985) predicts that at low strains the system behaves as a solid body. The stress increases linearly, $\sigma = G\gamma$, up to its yield value, $\sigma_y$, then catastrophically drops to negative values. The reason for the latter behavior is the creation of an energetically unstable (at that $\gamma$) cell structure. The theory lead to the following dependencies:

$$G = a_0\nu\phi^{a_i}/d_{vs} \tag{3.132}$$

$$\sigma_y = a_2 G \tilde{F}_{max}(\phi) \tag{3.133}$$

where $a_i$ are numerical parameters, and $d_{vs}$ is the average volume-to-surface diameter. For the three-dimensional case $a_1 = 1/3$. The function $F(\phi)$ is the concentration dependent dimensionless contribution to stress per drop; $F_{max}$ is taken at the yield point. The theory was verified using concentrated oil-in-water emulsions.

The shear flow of emulsions is quite different within the three concentration regions: at $\phi < 0.3$, it is nearly-Newtonian, at $0.3 \leq \phi \leq \phi_m$ pseudoplastic and at $\phi_m \leq \phi \leq 1.0$ it exhibits solid-like properties with modulus and yield. Obviously the difference originates in the stress dependent structure. Before discussing the mechanisms responsible for this behavior it is useful to consider how the structure of an emulsion varies with $\lambda$, $\varkappa$ and $\phi$.

Equations (3.123) or (3.123a) seem to predict that deformability is proportional to $\varkappa$, while Eq (3.124) gives conditions for its break up. It should be noted that according to this formula for any value of $v$, $d$ and $\lambda$ there is a level of shear stress which leads to droplet burst. However, both Taylor's and Cox's Equations have been derived for small deformations defined by proportionality $D \propto \sigma_{12}$, insufficient for droplet break. *Rumscheidt* and *Mason* (1961) demonstrated that in shear flow there are four regions of drop deformability: (i) for $\lambda < 0.2$ small drops are shed off from two tips of original drop which assumed a sigmoidal shape; (ii) for $0.2 < \lambda < 0.7$ Taylor's relation (3.125) is obeyed; (iii) for $0.7 < \lambda < 3.7$ the drops elongate into threads which may break by a capillary instability mechanism; and (iv) for $\lambda > 3.7$ the drops deform into prolate elipsoids but do not break. Since deformability depends on several material parameters as well as experimental conditions, the cited limits are only approximate. A variation of d with $\lambda$ is schematically indicated in Fig. 3.18. Deformability in hyperbolic flow fields is also indicated.

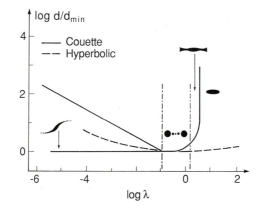

Fig. 3.18 Reduced droplet diameter vs. viscosity ratio, $\lambda$, in shear and extensional flows. The type of shear drop deformation within each of the four zones of $\lambda$ is indicated (*Grace, 1982*).

*Grace* (1982) reported that the linearity between D and $\dot{\gamma}_d$ is observed up to $D_L \simeq 0.4$, i. e. for $d_1/d_2 \leq 2.3$, while the break up at $D_b \simeq 0.8$ for $d_1/d_2 \simeq 9$. For $\lambda = 10^{-6}$ to 950 and $v = 1$ to 25 he observed that the relation shown in Fig. 3.18 was obeyed when, according to Eq (3.123), the initial drop diameter is scaled by $E_T/d = \sigma_{12}(19\lambda+16)/32v(\lambda+1)$. Two other reduced functions were found for these systems: 1. draw ratio defined as the length of a drop required for breakup divided by the original diameter, $DR = d_{1B}/d$, and 2. the reduced time to burst, $\tilde{t}_B = t_B v/d\eta_2$. These are schematically shown in Fig. 3.19.

Filming a single drop burst at mild rates of shearing, *Rumscheidt* and *Mason* (1961) observed formation of satellite smaller drops, i. e. breaking one drop resulted in the formation of five or more secondary ones. *Grace* (1982) for $\lambda \leq 0.107$ observed that the number of the secondary drops depends on the ratio $E_T/E_{TB}$ ($E_{TB}$ is the critical $E_T$-value required for break; see Eq (3.123)) and can be as high as $10^4$! This "bursting" of a drop into fragments changes the concept of droplet deformation and break (see Part 3.5).

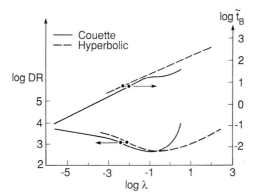

Fig. 3.19 Effect of viscosity ratio, $\lambda$, on critical draw ratio, DR = $d_B/d$, and burst time $\tilde{t}_B = t_B v/d\eta_2$ in Couette and hyperbolic flow (*Grace*, 1982).

The above discussion on the effects of $\lambda$ on droplet deformability concerns individual drops in the sea of matrix liquid. As the concentration increases from that of infinitely dilute emulsion the recombination or coalescence of droplets needs to be considered. Coalescence is a dynamic process. Its critical parameter is the critical coalescence time, $t_c$. *Elmendorp* (1986) considered this aspect, deriving the following relation for systems with mobile interface:

$$t_c = (3\varkappa/4\dot\gamma)\ln(d/4h_c) \tag{3.134}$$

where $h_c$ is the critical separation distance. The relation between d and $\sigma_{12}/v$ predicted by Taylor and Elmendorp treatments is shown in Fig. 3.20. Taylor's criterion is taken as

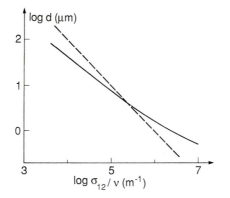

Fig. 3.20 Taylor (broken line) and Elmendorp (solid line) relation between drop diameter and ratio of the shear stress to interfacial tension coefficient.

predicting the smallest drops which can be broken, while Elmendorp's the largest drops which can coalesce. It is expected that drops with diameter located between these two dependencies exist in real systems. Since Eq (3.134) has been derived considering isolated pair of drops as a result independent on $\phi$ $t_c$ should be valid in dilute emulsions. Since $t_c \geq 0$, $h_c \leq d/4$ is independent of $\phi$ the entrapment distance between colliding spheres. A simplified theory of coagulation at higher $\phi$ lead to the following dependencies (*Utracki*, 1973):

$$t_c = KE^+d^3/\varrho_1(1+N^+/N_0)\phi^{8/3}\dot\gamma^2 \tag{3.135}$$

or $\qquad t_c = 2.940E^+(\phi_m-\phi)/\eta_2(V_x/V)\phi^{8/3}\dot\gamma^2 \tag{3.136}$

where K is a numerical parameter, $E^+$ is a threshold energy of coagulation, $N_0 > N^+$ is the number of coagulating drops, initially and at $t = t_c$, and $(V_x/V)$ represents the volume fraction of emulsion undergoing uniform shearing. Experimentally $t_c$ was taken as the time for the onset of coagulation. The proportionality $t_c \propto \dot{\gamma}^{-2}$ was experimentally verified. For polydisperse systems $\phi$ should be replaced by $\tilde{\phi} \equiv \phi/\phi_m$ and from Eq (3.136) $\partial t_c/\partial \tilde{\phi} = (5\tilde{\phi}-8)/3\tilde{\phi}^{11/3}$, i.e. the coagulation is expected to increase with the emulsion concentration. The theory also predicts that owing to coalescence the average-droplet diameter, $\bar{d}$, should increase with concentration as $\bar{d} \propto \phi^{2/3}$.

Returning to the discussion of the $\eta$ vs. $\dot{\gamma}$ dependence it is evident that emulsions in shear flow are quite complex. In the region of $\phi < 0.3$, where usually $\eta$ is independent of $\dot{\gamma}$ there is a dynamic shear stress dependent on equilibrium between shear breaking and coagulation of droplets. The relatively low interaction between the sheared layers of the drops is responsible for the Newtonian behavior. In the intermediate range, $0.3 \le \phi \le \phi_m$, in most cases the flow is pseudoplastic with or without yielding (*Pal* et al., 1986). Upon increase of $\dot{\gamma}$ the drops are elongated (see Fig. 3.21), the layers become more compacted, but the distance between them increases. Coagulation in this range plays an important role. Not only does it affect the droplet size distribution, but it also may destroy the emulsion generating a layered liquid structure, or globular coagulated clusters; in the latter case a dilatant behavior was observed (*Utracki, 1973; Kuznetsov* et al., 1985). At $\phi > \phi_m$ the drops are compressed and at low $\dot{\gamma}$ they respond as solids. At high strains the behavior depends on $\dot{\gamma}$; at low values the structure can re-form, at high values a plug, lubricated flow predominates.

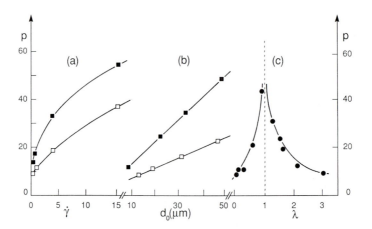

Fig. 3.21 Drop axial ratio as a function of: (a) shear rate, (b) initial diameter, and (c) viscosity ratio for polyvinyl alcohol/gelatine/H₂0 (solid points) and dextran/gelatine/H₂0 (open squares) at 32.5 °C (data *Tolstoguzov* et al., 1974).

Most theoretical treatments assume monodispersity of droplet size. Experimentally the distribution was found to follow the gamma function (*Djakovic* et al., 1976) for surface distribution:

$$n_i s_i/S = [a^{aD+3}/\Gamma(aD+3)]d_i^{aD+2}e^{-aD} \qquad (3.137)$$

where $n_i$ is number of particles each having surface $s_i$ and diameter, $d_i$, a is the rate of homogenization constant and D is the most probable diameter. The average drop diameter, $\bar{d}$, is related to specific surface, S:

$$\bar{d} = D + 3/a = 6/S \qquad (3.138)$$

It is usually defined as surface mean average droplet diameter (sometimes called the volume-to-surface average) given by:

$$\bar{d} = d_{v/s} = \Sigma n_i d_i^3 / \Sigma n_i d_i^2 \tag{3.139}$$

For liquid-liquid systems upon increase of $\phi$ a phase inversion takes place; suddenly the dispersed and continuous liquid exchange roles. In most cases the inversion is associated with a local maximum on the $\eta$ vs. $\phi$ curve. However, as shown in Fig. 3.22, a transition with a minimum is also possible. The phase inversion in PAB will be discussed in Part 3.4.5.

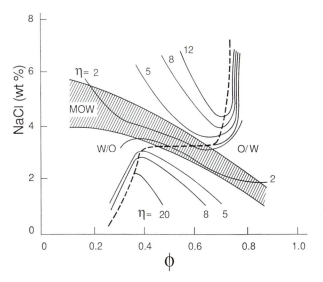

Fig. 3.22 Iso-viscosity contour map (solid lines) for oil/water/sodium dodecyl sulfate system at 25 °C; MOW, W/O and O/W respectively stand for: multiple oil in water microemulsion, water-in-oil and oil-in-water emulsions; the numbers refer to viscosity in mPa·s. The broken line indicates phase inversion (*Salager* et al., 1983; *Minana-Perez* et al., 1986).

### 3.3.5   Block Copolymers

The subject has been well discussed in several books and reviews (e.g. *Allport* and *Jones*, 1973; *Noshay* and *McGrath*, 1977; *Folkes*, 1985). The melt rheology of block copolymers was recently discussed by *Lyngaae-Jorgensen* (1985) and that for copolymer solutions by *Kotaka* and *Watanabe* (1987). The following summary will stress the common aspects of block copolymer and PAB flow.

Very rarely are the components of a block copolymer (BC) soluble in one another. BC is purposely designed as a two-phase system with "rigid" and "soft" domains. The concentration and molecular weights are selected to provide interconnection between the domains. The existence of a dispersed rigid phase in an elastomeric matrix is responsible for its "thermoplastic elastomer" behavior.

In considering melt flow of BC, it is usually assumed that the test temperature, $T > T_{gc}$, where $T_{gc}$ stands for glass transition temperature, $T_g$, of the continuous phase. At $T_{gc} < T < T_{gd}$ ($T_{gd}$ is $T_g$ of the dispersed phase) the system behaves as a crosslinked rubber with strong viscoelastic character. At $T > T_{gd}$ the viscosity of BC is much greater than would be expected on the basis of the total molecular weight and composition (*Kraus* and *Gruver*, 1967; *Holden* et al., 1969; *Estes* et al., 1970; *Arnold* and *Meier*, 1970; *Chii* et al., 1975;

*Cogswell* and *Hanson,* 1975; *Chung* and *Gale,* 1976). The reason for this behavior is a need to deform the domain structure and pull filaments of one polymer through domains of the other. Viscosity increase with immiscibility of the BC components (*Pico* and *Williams,* 1976; *Henderson* and *Williams,* 1979) is similar to that caused by increase of the interfacial tension coefficient in concentrated emulsions.

Frequently, BC exhibits yield stress (*Liu* et al., 1983; *Yoshimura* and *Richards,* 1987). *Bates* (1984) studied poly(1,2-butadiene-b-1,4-polybutadiene) di-block with UCST $\simeq$ 110 °C. The author reported that at T > UCST, the system behaved as a homopolymer, but below UCST the phase-separated ordered melt, showed unusual rheological behavior, e.g. at low frequency $G'' \propto \omega^{\frac{1}{2}}$ instead of the usual linear dependency. This may be due to dynamic yielding with a specific disassociation/association kinetics. For poly(styrene-b-butadiene-b-styrene) tri-block SBS polymers the $\sigma_{12}$ vs. $\dot{\gamma}$ dependence indicated presence of either true $\sigma_y$, its dynamic analog (as defined by Eq (3.32)) or both (*Hansen* and *Williams,* 1987). The yield stress was found to depend on the total molecular weight and polystyrene content (see Fig. 3.23). The yield stress in SBS solutions was directly measured by a quasi-static plate technique (*De Kee* et al., 1986).

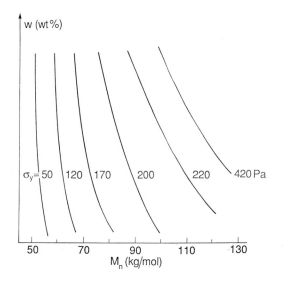

Fig. 3.23 Map of the yield stress dependence of poly(styrene-b-butadiene-b-styrene) SBS block copolymer on its molecular weight and styrene content (*Hansen* and *Williams,* 1987).

An explanation for $\sigma_y$ can be found in earlier work by *Wildemuth* and *Williams* (1984). The authors assumed that $\phi_m$ depends on $\sigma_{12}$. Defining $\phi_{m,0}$ and $\phi_{m,\infty}$ as the values of $\phi_m$ at normalized shear stress $\tilde{\sigma}_{12} \equiv \sigma_{12}/M \to 0$ and $\tilde{\sigma}_{12} \to \infty$, respectively, the authors derived the relation:

$$\phi_m = (\phi_{m,0} + \phi_{m,\infty}\tilde{\sigma}_{12}{}^m)/(1 + \tilde{\sigma}_{12}{}^m) \tag{3.140}$$

where M and m $\simeq$ 1.0 to 1.17 are parameters. When m, $\phi_{m,0}$ and $\phi_{m,\infty}$ are known, the relation (3.140) can be used to predict yield stress, $\tilde{\sigma}_y$:

$$\tilde{\sigma}_y = [(\phi - \phi_{m,0})/(\phi_{m,\infty} - \phi)]^{1/m} \tag{3.141}$$

where $\phi_{m,\infty} < \phi < \phi_{m,0}$ is volume fraction of the interacting phase equal to $\phi_m$ under given value of shear stress.

An equation which is capable of describing multiple phenomena: yield, upper and lower Newtonian plateaux, pseudoplasticity, stress growth and overshoot, thixotropicity, hysteresis, etc. was proposed by *Liu* et al. (1983):

$$\sigma_{12}(t) = \sigma_y + \eta_0\dot\gamma\{\beta + [(1-\beta)/(1+b\dot\gamma^m)][1+b\dot\gamma^m\exp\{-kt(1+b\dot\gamma^m)/b\}]\} \qquad (3.142)$$

where $\beta$ represents the relative residual viscous dissipation parameter, b and m are parameters originating from the structural breakdown and reformation of structure and k is the loss-rate constant. For $\dot\gamma \to \infty$, $\sigma_{12}/\dot\gamma \to \eta_0\beta = \eta_\infty$.

The multiplicity of rheological phenomena observed in BC is related to the sensitivity of the melt structure to molecular and rheological variables. The structure, as indicated in Eq (3.142), is time and rate of deformation dependent, varying with molecular weight, macromolecular architecture and concentration. For example, for SBS the activation energy of flow $\Delta E_\eta = 80$ or 160kJ/mole for compositions containing respectively less or more than 31 vol% of styrene. The difference originates in the structure; it is dispersed below 31% and interconnected above (*Arnold* and *Meier*, 1970). There is also a regular variation of morphology with composition (from spheres, to cylinders to lamellas) controlled by equilibrium thermodynamics.

Effects of molecular parameters and composition were reviewed by *Holden* (1973) who expressed the temperature dependence of shear viscosity for BC in terms of *Fulcher's* (1925) relation:

$$1n_\eta = a_0 + a_1/(T-T_\infty) \qquad (3.143)$$

where by definition $T_\infty$ is the temperature at which $\eta \to \infty$. Differentiating Eq (3.143) one obtains an expression for the temperature dependent activation energy of flow:

$$\Delta E_\eta = a_1R[T/(T-T_\infty)]^2 \qquad (3.144)$$

Experimentally, $T_\infty$ is not far away from the glass transition temperature, $T_\infty \simeq T_g - 50\,°C$, but the curvature in $\Delta E_\eta$ vs. T plot is frequently greater than would be expected from WLF theory (*Williams, Landel* and *Ferry*, 1955); the temperature dependent solubility of components is the most probable explanation for this augmentation.

On the basis of statistical thermodynamics *Leary* and *Williams* (1970, 1973, 1974) introduced a concept of a separation temperature, $T_s$, at which $\Delta G_m = 0$. Since, in the model, the volume of the interphase depends on geometry (spheres, cylinders, lamelli), $T_s$ is also a function of morphology.

At $T > T_s$ BC is a homogeneous liquid, below $T_s$ two phases coexist. However, it follows from *Lyngaae-Jorgensen* (1985) work that at $T \le T_s$ there is a possibility of homogenization if $\sigma_{12} \ge \sigma_{cr}$, where:

$$\sigma_{cr}^2 = a_0T(T_s-T); \qquad T \le T_s \qquad (3.145)$$

For SBS $T_s \simeq 425K$ and at $T = 396K$ $\sigma_{cr} \simeq 55kPa$ which gives the value of the proportionality factor: $a_0 = 0.263(kPa/K)^2$.

The BC structure depends on the nature of the casting solvent. Correspondingly, the rheological response as well as $T_s$ are affected. SBS structure breakup was studied by *Sivashinsky* et al. (1983) by stress growth and relaxation methods. Detailed studies on the nature of structural changes introduced by solvent nature, concentration, temperature and deformation were carried out (*Watanabe* and *Kotaka*, 1983, 1984; *Kotaka* and *Watanabe*, 1987). The authors found the dynamic tests to be particularly suitable. The storage and loss moduli, G' and G'', vs. frequency, $\omega$, as well as the relaxation spectrum provided a detailed image of structural changes. The results were interpreted in terms of the "tube renewal" model.

Block polymers, due to the tendency for formation of regular structures tailored by molecular design, are ideal models for PAB. As will be evident later, PAB show similar rheological phenomena, e. g. yield, pseudoplasticity, thixotropy, structural rearrangements, etc., but since PAB morphology is more difficult to control, the interpretation of data presents more serious problems. Comparison with better understood systems: solutions, suspensions, emulsions and block copolymers serves as a guide.

### 3.3.6  Lessons From the Models

Solutions and homologous blends of polymeric fractions were used as models for miscible blends. The discussion focussed primarily on the effects of composition. On the basis of free volume as well as the heat of mixing arguments, the solution model leads one to expect that $\eta_0$ (as well as other rheological functions related to $\eta_0$ through the linear viscoelastic behavior) should be PDB type, i.e. larger for the blends than predicted from the log-additivity rule. Similar conclusion can be reached from theoretical and experimental studies of homologous blends. However, there are cited documents that in miscible blends PDB is not always observed. In principle McAllister's Eq (3.83) can be used to describe the found dependencies, but it does not provide a mechanism to explain it. It seems that, at this stage, volume dilatation on blending is the most likely explanation.

At the opposite end of the spectrum, there are suspensions as one model of immiscible blends in which $\lambda \gg 1$. Suspensions allow one to expect variation of rheological functions with concentration, polydispersity, shape, the uncorrelability of data from one type of flow to another, diverse rheological effects such as yield stress, pseudoplasticity, dilatancy, time effects and, related to all these, the flow induced changes of structure.

Emulsions brought in another important element, the deformability of drops, their dispersion and coalescence in flow as well as the aspects of microrheology. However, in spite of these new effects, both suspensions and emulsion have several elements in common, e. g. the concentration dependence of $\eta_r$, viscoelastic behavior, yield stress, flow induced morphological changes, etc.

The final model, that of block polymers, brings the models closer to the world of PAB's. In fact, block polymers form a natural bridge – on one hand, depending on T, they can be seen as either suspensions or emulsions, but on the other they are a special class of immiscible, compatibilized polymer blends. Block polymers provided an opportunity to introduce the concept of shear induced miscibility and that of concentration dependent structures. Again, the viscoelastic character as well as yield stress and flow induced morphologies are apparent.

The rheological consequences of phase separation have not been yet discussed. Increasing concentration through binodal and spinodal region leads to phase separation and change of $\eta$. One may expect that if the viscosity of two polymeric liquids is similar, $\lambda \simeq 1$, then in the vicinity of the spinodal composition the PAB viscosity of the PAB should increase due to creation of a "polymeric emulsion". However, experiments with low molecular weight liquids (*Brunet* and *Gubbins*, 1969; *Doan* and *Brunet*, 1972) as well as those with oligomers (*Kirianov* et al., 1975) demonstrated a local maximum on the $\eta$ vs. composition curve, *prior* to any apparent phase separation. This is illustrated in Fig. 3.24. After the phase separation, the viscosity usually decreases. Note that the viscosity increases slowly in the region where the volume fraction of the dispersed phase $\phi < 0.3$. At higher $\phi$ the viscosity is expected to increase more strongly. Such an expectation does not take into account the polydisperse character of the blend components. By analogy with solution fractionation (e.g. see *Cantow*, 1967) the dispersed phase contains the high molecular weight portion of the phase separated polymer, while the low molecular weight macromolecules play a role of plasticizer depressing the viscosity of the matrix polymer. Since the world is symmetrical (with the awful exception of time) the disperse phase is plasticized by low molecular weight functions of the continuous phase polymer. These variations of composition play a decisive role on $\eta$ vs. $\phi$ dependence near the phase separation region.

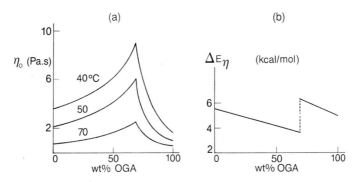

Fig. 3.24 Flow of oligoethyleneglycoladipate/oligobutadienediol mixture near the phase separation; (a) zero shear viscosity as a function of composition at 40, 50 and 70 °C; (b) activation energy vs. oligoethyleneglycoladipate, OGA, content. (*Kirianov* et al., 1975).

# 3.4    Newtonian Flow of Polymer Blends

Equilibrium thermodynamics distinguishes three regions of miscibility: (i) miscible, on the outside of binodal, (ii) metastable between binodal and spinodal and (iii) immiscible, inside the spinodal. In rheology also it is convenient to introduce the three regions of phase behavior: (i) miscible single-phase systems, (ii) critical region near the phase separation, and (iii) immiscible two-phase systems. However, by contrast with the precise thermodynamic definitions of boundaries, the phase separation region in the rheological sense is rather illdefined.

### 3.4.1   Miscible Blends

Miscible blends have been modeled with solutions of low molecular weight liquids and homologous blends of polymeric fractions. Both models allowed one to expect a positive deviation from the log-additivity rule, PDB (viz. Parts 3.3.1 and 3.3.2).

There are several reports in which indeed PDB has been observed for miscible polymer blends, e.g., polyphenylenether/polystyrene (*Prest* and *Porter*, 1972), polyisoprene/polyvinylethylene (*Roland*, 1988), polymethylmethacrylate/poly(styrene-co-acrylonitrile) (*Wu*, 1987). The latter author proposed that specific interactions between dissimilar macromolecules force their alignment resulting in stiffening of the chains, a higher degree of entanglement and higher viscosity. Correcting the data for constant level of entanglement indeed resulted in log additivity dependence for some systems. The high density polyethylene/poly(ethylene-co-vinylacetate) blends were also reported miscible with PDB dependence (*Fujimura* and *Iwakura*, 1970, 1974), although EVA clearly formed fine domains in the PE matrix, and by definition in Part 1.1.1, the systems should be considered immiscible.

Blends of linear polybutadienes also showed PDB when $\eta_0$ was plotted versus volume (*Struglinski* and *Graessley*, 1985) or weight fraction (*Tsenoglu* and *Bhakuni*, 1987). The interpretation of data was based on the relation:

$$\eta = \int_0^\infty [\Sigma_i \, \phi_i G_i^{\frac{1}{2}}(t)]^2 dt \qquad (3.146)$$

where $G_i$ is the shear stress relaxation modulus of blend components (*Tsenoglou,* 1985). For two-component mixtures, assuming a single exponential form of G(t), integration of Eq (3.146) gives:

$$\eta = \phi_1^2 \eta_1 + \phi_2^2 \eta_2 + 4F(G) \phi_1\phi_2 \qquad (3.147)$$

where, in the absence of specific interactions:

$$F(G) = (G_1^0 G_2^0)^{\frac{1}{2}} \eta_1\eta_2/(G_1^0\eta_2 + G_2^0\eta_1) \qquad (3.148)$$

with $G^0$ the plateau modulus. Equation (3.146) is general and Wu's concept of entanglement variation with specific interactions can be easily incorporated into it. Since $F(G) \geq 0$, Eq (3.147) predicts a small NDB effect at $F(G) \rightarrow 0$.

As shown in Table 3.5 the log-additivity of $\eta_0$ vs. $\phi$ functions were reported for: polyvinylchloride/chlorinated polyvinylchloride (*Lehr,* 1986), polycarbonate/tetramethyl-Bis-A-polycarbonate (*Belaribi* et al., 1986), blends of two linear low density polyethylenes (*Utracki* and *Schlund,* 1987), etc. In these systems, the chemical and physical character of ingredients was similar.

TABLE 3.5 Examples of Polymer Alloys and Blends Showing Positive, Negative and Mixed Deviation from the Log-Additivity Rule. The Classification is Based on Viscosity vs. Composition Behavior, Where Viscosity was Taken at the Lowest Constant Stress.

| No. | Blend | Ref. |
|---|---|---|
| | I *Positive Deviating Blends (PDB)* | |
| | I A   Miscible Blends | |
| 1. | Poly(2,6-dimethylphenyleneether)/polystyrene | 1 |
| 2. | Polybutadiene fractions | 2 |
| 3. | Polydimethylsiloxane fractions | 3, 4 |
| 4. | Polystyrene fractions | 4 |
| 5. | Polymethylmethacrylate fractions | 4 |
| 6. | Linear low density polyethylenes blends | 5 |
| 7. | Polyisoprene/polyvinylethylene | 6 |
| | I B   Immiscible Blends | |
| 8. | High density polyethylene/poly(ethylene-co-vinylacetate) | 7 |
| 9. | High density polyethylene/low density polyethylene | 8, 9, 10 |
| 10. | Polyoxymethylene/polyamide-6/66 | 11, 12 |
| 11. | Polyamide-6/polyethylene | 13 |
| 12. | Polystyrene/polyethylene | 14 |
| 13. | Polycarbonate/tetramethylene polycarbonate | 15 |
| 14. | Linear low density polyethylene/low density polyethylene | 5 |
| | II *Negative Deviating Blends (NDB)* | |
| | II A   Miscible blends | |
| 15. | Polyethyleneoxide/polymethylmethacrylate | 16 |
| | II B   Immiscible blends | |
| 16. | High density polyethylene/polyamide-6 | 17 |
| 17. | Polystyrene/polyethylene | 18, 19 |
| 18. | Polystyrene/polypropylene | 18, 19 |
| 19. | Polystyrene/polymethylmethacrylate | 20 |
| 20. | Polyoxymethylene/poly(ethylene-co-vinylacetate) | 21 |
| 21. | Polyethyleneterephthalate/polyamide-6 | 22 |
| 22. | Polystyrene/polyoxymethylene | 23 |
| 23. | Polymethylmethacrylate/polyamide-12 | 24 |
| 24. | Low density polyethylene/polyoxymethylene | 24, 25 |
| 25. | Polystyrene/polycarbonate | 24, 25 |

| No. | Blend | Ref. |
|---|---|---|
|  | III *Positive-Negative Deviating Blends, PNDB* |  |
| 26. | Polyethyleneoxide/polyvinylacetate | 16 |
| 27. | Polybutadiene/polyisoprene | 2 |
| 28. | Low density polyethylene/polypropylene | 26 |
| 29. | Cellulose acetate butyrate/polyoxymethylene | 24, 28, 27 |
| 30. | Polyoxyethylene/polyoxypropylene | 24 |
| 31. | High density polyethylene/poly(ethylene-co-vinylacetate) | 24 |
| 32. | Low density polyethylene/polyoxymethylene | 30 |
| 33. | Polymethylmethacrylate/polyoxymethylene | 23 |
| 34. | Polyethyleneterephthalate/polyamide-6,6 | 31, 32, 33 |

*References:* 1. *W. M. Prest* and *R. S. Porter*, 1972; 2. *V. N. Kuleznev* et al., 1975; 3. *S. F. Christov* et al., 1978; 4. *T. U. Liu* et al., 1983; 5. *L. A. Utracki* and *B. Schlund*, 1987; 6. *C. M. Roland*, 1988; 7. *T. Fujimura* and *K. Iwakura*, 1974; 8. *H. W. Kammer* and *M. Socher*, 1982; 9. *V. Dobrescu*, 1981; 10. *D. Curto* et al., 1983; 11. *T. I. Ablazova* et al., 1975. 12. *M. V. Tsebrenko* et al., 1979; 13. *T. I. Zhila* et al., 1980; 14. *L. S. Bolotnikova* et al., 1982; 15. *C. Belaribi* et al., 1986; 16. *E. Martuscelli* et al., 1987; 17. *K. Hayashida* et al., 1970; 18. *C. D. Han*, and *T. C. Yu*, 1972; 19. *H.-K. Chuang* and *C. D. Han*, 1984; 20. *L. B. Kandyrin* and *V. N. Kuleznev*, 1974; 21. *N. M. Rezanova* and *M. V. Tsebrenko*, 1981; 22. *K. Dimov* and *M. Savov*, 1980; 23. *J. F. Carley* and *S. C. Crossan*, 1981; 24. *Yu. S. Lipatov* et al., 1982a; 25. *Yu. S. Lipatov*, 1983; 26. *A. P. Plochocki*, 1982; 27. *Yu. S. Lipatov* et al., 1979a; 28. *A. N. Gorbatenko* et al., 1982; 29. *Yu. S. Lipatov* et al., 1983a; 30. *Yu. S. Lipatov*, 1975, 1978; *Yu. S. Lipatov* et al., 1983b; 31. *L. A. Utracki* et al., 1981; 32. *L. A. Utracki* and *M. R. Kamal*, 1982; 33. *L. A. Utracki*, 1983a.

The number of miscible blends with NDB is increasing steadily. This behavior was reported for polystyrene/tetramethylpolycarbonate (*Wisniewski* et al., 1984), poly(styrene-co-maleicanhydride)/poly(styrene-co-acrylonitrile) (*Aoki*, 1984), polyethyleneoxide/polymethylmethacrylate (*Martuscelli*, 1984), polymethylmethacrylate/polyvinylidenefluoride (*Wu*, 1987) and others. In polyethyleneoxide/polyvinylacetate blends, mixed positive and negative deviations (PNDB), were observed (*Martuscelli* et al., 1987)

Judging from this incomplete listing of miscible blend behaviors it is evident that the PDB, expected on the basis of analysis of model systems, is not always observed. *Wu* (1987) tried to associate this with a decrease of entanglement density, writing:

$$G^0 = \phi_1^2 G_1^0 + \phi_2^2 G_2^0 + 2RT\phi_1\phi_2(\varrho_1\varrho_2)^{\frac{1}{2}}/M_{e_{12}} \tag{3.149}$$

where $M_{e12}$ is entanglement molecular weight for 1-2 contact. Since all parameters but $M_{e12}$ are experimental, the relations allow one to determine its numerical value. For the polymethymethacrylate/polyvinylidenefluoride NDB system $M_{e12} > M_{ei}$, i = 1,2. However, if the mechanism responsible for miscibility is based on specific interactions then the 1-2 pairs should be the preferred ones over 1-1 and 2-2. This should enhance the intertanglement, not reduce it. There is also a question of general validity of Eq (3.149). From Eq (3.146) for non-interactive blends:

$$G_N^0 = \phi_1^2 G_1^0 + \phi_2^2 G_2^0 + 2\phi_1\phi_2(G_1^0 G_2^0)^{\frac{1}{2}} \tag{3.150}$$

Since    $G_i^0 = RT\varrho_i/M_{ei}$    (3.151)

the $Me_{e12}$ in non-interactive systems is a geometric mean. If so, the increase of $M_{e12}$ calulated from Eq (3.149) is not necessarily caused by low entanglement density between 1-2 macromolecules, but a reflection of decrease of an average level of entanglement in the system involved in homo and hetero-interactions. Note that for non-interacting blends Eq (3.150) predicts $G_N^0 \geqslant G_i^0$; i.e., the plateau modulus of non-interactive $\chi_{12} = 0$, polymer blends is expected to be higher than that for neat resins.

The relation (3.150) can be generalized for three components: 1-1, 2-2, and 1-2, with concentrations $\phi_{ii} = \phi_i - \phi_{ij}/2$, i = 1,2. The derivation is straightforward, leading to a long algebraic expression. It can be shown that the excess plateau modulus, $G^0 - G_N$, is proportional to $\phi_{12}$ and to an expression containing $(\varrho_{ij}/M_{eij})$, i,j = 1,2. That indicates that the density is as important to the rheological response as the entanglements. Since in neat polymers the densities vary with T and P in a predictable manner rheologists have grown used to ignoring their influence. For multicomponent systems, this omission cannot be justified. To understand the blend behavior, one needs to separate the thermodynamic and rheological behavior, one has to know $\varrho$'s as much as $\eta$'s. For example, the recently published dilatometric data for blends of polystyrene with poly-2-chlorostyrene or with polyphenyleneether (*Tsujita* et al., 1987) confirm the densification of the blends expected from PDB, caused by the specific interactions. Not knowing how the volume changes on mixing makes interpretation of flow behavior speculative.

If the mechanism responsible for NDB is speculative, that leading to PNDB behavior is even more so. Here the knowledge of density variation with composition has to be first resolved (*Plochocki*, 1982). The phenomenon seem to be related to concentration dependent interactions. PNDB behavior was observed for blends of polyethyleneoxide/polyvinylacetate, but NDB for PEO blends with polymethylmethacrylate. Why would small amounts of PVAc cause enhancement of $\eta$ in respect to log-additivity while that of PMMA a depression? Formally, both sets of data can be described by *McAllister*'s Eq (3.83), treating the mix-index kinematic viscosities, $v_{12}$ and $v_{21}$, as experimental parameters. To generate PNDB, the third order dependence is required, indicating three-body interactions.

It is worth noting that the question of polymer miscibility has been a subject of vigorous debate. In most cases, blends are judged miscible on the basis of a single $T_g$. There are two arguments against this: (1) as discussed in Part 2.6.3 $T_g$ is a measure of degree of dispersion not of miscibility and (2) the rheological measurements are carried out at $T > T_g$. Even if the polymer were miscible at $T_g$, it does not necessarily mean that the thermodynamic miscibility exists under the rheological test conditions. Furthermore, since imposition of stresses affects the phase diagram, an immiscible system may become miscible. Finally, flow segregation/fractionation is a phenomenon well known for decades, affecting the flow behavior of polydispersed homopolymers. To build a base for understanding blend behavior, careful, multidisciplinary studies are required.

### 3.4.2    Critical Region

There are two facets of the issue: (i) how the vicinity of phase separation affects the flow behavior of single phase blends, and (ii) how the flow affects the phase equilibrium. The first aspect will be dealt with in this part, the second in the one to follow.

As indicated in Part 3.3.6, the steady state flow data of oligomers or solvents allowed observation of significant increase of viscosity due to proximity of the phase separation. The peak position is not necessarily related to critical conditions of phase separation; for solution of aniline and cyclohexane (*Brunet* and *Gubbins*, 1969) the peak appeared more than 21°C above the critical temperature. An increase of the volume of flow element in Eyring's expression for shear viscosity (*Glasstone* et al., 1941) could explain this deviation. The increase of thermal fluctuation of density (*de Gennes*, 1980; *Leibler*, 1980) would provide a justification. The flow properties near the phase separation have been subject to theoretical and experimental investigations. The effect of stress can cause either enhancement or decrease of miscibility (*Tirrell*, 1986). By the same token it is to be expected that the maximum on isothermal $\eta = \eta(\phi)$ dependence (across the spinodal) is not a universal truth.

*Manevich* et al. (1984) developed a theoretical relation for increase of shear viscosity due to density fluctuation near the spinodal, $\Delta\eta$. The derivation starts with Huggins - Flory

Eq (2.8) to which the de Gennes density fluctuation term was added. The resulting dependence is:

$$\Delta\eta = (\pi^2/20)\,\varrho f_0^2 b k_B T/\Lambda k \tag{3.152}$$

where $b = 18\phi_1\phi_2$ (3.153)

$$\Lambda = N_e\phi_1\phi_2/[N_1\phi_1 D_{M1} + N_2\phi_2 D_{M2}] \tag{3.154}$$

$$k^2 = (18/a^2)\,(\phi_1/N_1 + \phi_2/N_2 - 2\chi_{12}\phi_1\phi_2) \tag{3.155}$$

$f_0 \simeq 1$ is Onsager's coefficient for relation between diffusion and viscosity, $\varrho$ is the number of
monomers per unit volume, $k_B$ is the Boltzman constant, $D_{Mi}$ is the mutual diffusion coefficient, $a$ is the intersegmental distance, $N_i$ and $N_e$ are respectively degree of polymerization
of polymer i and its entanglement value. Eqs (3.152) to (3.155) allow one to predict the
enhancement of $\eta$ caused by the critical fluctuations. The criticality comes through k
dependence on $\chi_{12}$ with the rheological term $\Lambda$ acting as a multiplier. The effect of polydispersity has also been considered. Eq (3.152) indicates that enhancement of viscosity
increases with $N_i$ and the entanglement density, but it decreases with $D_{Mi}$. For $N_i = 10^4$ and
$N_e = 10^2$ the magnitude of the enhancement, $\Delta\eta$, is comparable to $\eta_0$.

More recently, *Fredrickson* and *Larson* (1987) derived a general expression for the
linear viscoelastic function (limited to low strains) near the critical conditions for phase
separation. The theory considers a Hamiltonian with a structure parameter. The free
energy, G, is then expressed as a sum of energetic (Hamiltonian) and entropic parts, both
being functions of an order parameter. At small strains, the stress:

$$\sigma(t) = \lim_{\gamma\to 0} \partial G(P,\gamma,t)/\partial\gamma \tag{3.156}$$

from which a general expression for storage and loss shear moduli, $G'(\omega)$ and $G''(\omega)$, were
derived. To apply these to a specific fluid, the structure (or time correlation) function has to
be known. This function is particularly well established for di-block copolymers. Thus the
first homogeneous, miscible blend analyzed theoretically was a di-block polymer melt. The
expressions for the dynamic shear moduli in the following paper (*Larson* and *Fredrickson*,
1987) were supplemented by the steady state predictions at the limit of low deformation
rates, $\dot{\gamma} \to 0$:

$$G'(\omega) \propto \omega^2 a^{-5/2}; \qquad\qquad \psi_1(\dot{\gamma}) \propto \psi_2(\dot{\gamma}) \propto a^{-5/2} \tag{3.157}$$

$$G''(\omega) \propto \omega a^{-3/2}; \qquad\qquad \eta(\dot{\gamma}) \propto a^{-3/2} \tag{3.158}$$

where the parameters $a \equiv 2[(\chi N)_s - \chi N]$ gives the thermodynamic distance from the
spinodal. At the spinodal, functions (3.157) and (3.158) become singular, indicating that
the block polymer melt no longer behaves as a linear viscoelastic body. It should be noted
that for di-blocks the appropriate dynamic and steady state functions have identical dependencies on the deformation rate and thermodynamic distance parameter. Numerically, near
the spinodal, the theory predicts that the ratio $\psi_2/\psi_1 \simeq -1.35$, instead of the usual $\psi_2/\psi_1 =
-0.05$ to $-0.20$. The results summarized in Eq (3.157) are valid for low strain viscoelastic
functions. For large strains, such as those encountered in steady state shear or extension, the
basic assumption, Eq (3.156), loses its validity. The system becomes perturbed and the
dependencies (3.157) and (3.158) probably overestimate the spinodal effect on flow. As
*Larson* and *Fredrickson* (1987) noted, their theory predicts much stronger influence of
thermodynamic criticallity for block polymers than the earlier mean field theories for small
molecule mixtures (*Oxtoby*, 1975; *Onuki*, 1977, 1986). Oxtoby's theory is conveniently
given as $\Delta\bar{\eta} = \Delta\bar{\eta}(\bar{x})$, where $\bar{x}$ is a dimensionless reduced variable:

$$\bar{x} = \sigma_{12}\zeta^3/k_B T \tag{3.159}$$

with the correlation length $\zeta$ being proportional to the critical temperature of miscibility:

$$\zeta = \zeta_0 (T/T_c - 1)^{-\nu} \tag{3.160}$$

($\zeta_0 \simeq 10^8$ and $\nu \simeq 1/2$ to $2/3$ are parameters). For larger values of $\bar{x}$, the predicted dependence is:

$$(\eta - \eta_0)/\eta_0 \equiv \tilde{\Delta}\eta \simeq (8/45\pi^2) \ln \bar{x}/\bar{x}_0 \tag{3.161}$$

where $\bar{x} \simeq 0.45$. It is important to note that the effects of shear stress and $\zeta^3$, are equivalent, e. g. $\Delta\eta$ will double either when $\sigma_{12}$ is increased by a factor of $e^2$ or when $(T-T_c)$ is decreased by a factor of e. The corollary conclusion is that the importance of shear stress increases when $T \to T_c$ (or $T_s$). The experimental data for mixtures of solvent give $\Delta\tilde{\eta} \leqslant 7\%$, i.e., significantly lower than that calculated from Eq (3.152) for polymer blends. Such a difference should be expected on the basis of different relaxation processes involved within the spinodal inter-connected structures for small and polymeric molecules.

*Cazabat* et al. (1982) discussed the critical effects on $\Delta\eta$ in terms of the relation:

$$\bar{\Delta}\eta = 1 + (Q\zeta)^x \tag{3.162}$$

with Q and x being adjustable parameters. For protein solutions, the exponent x was reported to vary from $x \leqslant 0.04$ (aqueous surfactant solution) to 2; for micro-emulsions, $x = 0.15$ was found.

In short, all the data for diverse miscible systems indicate that, approaching phase separation, the viscosity should increase with correlation length. Both the rate of the increase and the absolute magnitude, vary from one system to another. The effect is rate dependent and more pronounced in high molecular weight systems.

### 3.4.3    Flow-Induced Miscibility in Polymer Blends

In a sense, the situation discussed in this part is a mirror image of that treated in the preceding Part 3.4.2. Previously the question was how does approaching the critical conditions affect the flow properties of miscible blends, now it is how does shearing the phase-separated liquids affects the critical conditions.

The response of heterogenous systems to a stress field allows them to be placed in two categories (*Tirrell,* 1986): (i) those in which stress induces irreversible changes (e.g., precipitation, denaturation of protein, crystallization, etc.) and (ii) those in which the changes are reversible. The classification is not perfect, as the type and magnitude of stress field can be crucial, but it provides a guide: in most cases, miscibility in systems (i) is reduced by stress, that in systems (ii) is increased. In other words, if a system can be irreversibly modified by rheological means, its solubility will be reduced by flow. Prediction of which one of the reversible systems will show enhanced and which reduced miscibility is more difficult; e.g. solution of polystyrene in tert-butylacetate belongs to the first category, whereas that in dioctylphthalate to the second.

In sheared, phase separated blends in the vicinity of the critical region of miscibility there are local domains containing high concentration of each ingredient without interfacial tension barriers between them. *Onuki* (1986) discussed the flow problems near critical conditions in terms of another dimensionless number where, $\bar{\dot{\gamma}} \equiv \dot{\gamma}\tau_\zeta$, where $\tau_\zeta$ is the average lifetime of the density fluctuation:

$$\tau_\zeta = 6\,\pi\eta\zeta^3/k_B T \tag{3.163}$$

For $\bar{\dot{\gamma}} < 1$, the domains of dispersed phase are not strongly deformed and according to Eq (3.122), the diameter of a drop is of the order of $\nu/\sigma_{12}$. For $\bar{\dot{\gamma}} > 1$, the domains are continuously elongated and broken. Since the interfacial tension vanishes at the critical point, the effects of stress homogenization are largest near $T_c$ (*Wolf*, 1984). The theory also predicts that within the strong flow region, $\dot{\gamma} > 1$, the reduced viscosity $\Delta\tilde{\eta} \propto 1/\dot{\gamma}$. This has been observed for polystyrene/polyisoprene blends, where $\eta$ in the vicinity of phase separation decreased by a factor of 7 to 10 (*Klykova* and *Kuleznev*, 1981).

Due to the deformability of droplets, emulsions and immiscible blends show elasticity. The stored elastic energy is responsible for drops bursting and the resulting homogenization (*ver Strate* and *Philippoff*, 1974). Following this concept *Mazich* (1983) studied the effects of shear on variation of the spinodal temperature of polystyrene/polyvinylmethylether at constant storage modulus, $G'(\omega) = 400$ to 780 Pa. His results are summarized in Fig. 3.25. The effect amounts to an increase of the miscible region by $T_{sN_1} - T_s = 1$ to 7 °C ($T_{sN_1}$ is the $T_s$ value at constant normal stress, $N_1 \approx 2G'$). It can be shown that for stable compositional fluctuation under shear:

$$\partial\Delta\mu_2/\partial\phi_2 = \partial^2 N_1/2\partial\phi_2^2 \tag{3.164}$$

Expanding the left-hand side as a series of $(T-T_s)$ and measuring the right hand side, allowed calculation of the temperature $T^*$ at which the concentration fluctuations became stable. The predicted $T^*-T_s$ was found to be significantly smaller (by a factor of up to 4,000) than the experimental $T_{sN_1} - T_s$. There are several explications for the difference.

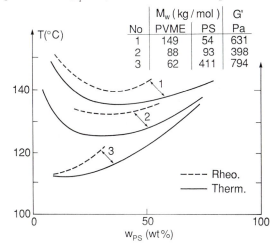

Fig. 3.25 Phase diagram for three polyvinylmethylether/polystyrene blends under equilibrium conditions (solid lines) and in dynamic shearing. Molecular weights and storage shear moduli used in the tests are indicated (*Mazich*, 1983).

A promising new theory of shear-induced miscibility is based on the nonequilibrium molecular dynamics concept (*Roming* and *Hanley*, 1986). Here, $\dot{\gamma}$ is directly incorporated in an extra-term for free energy describing the nonequilibrium. The phase diagram can be computed using the conditions given by Eqs (2.4) to (2.6). Computer simulation of real systems has led to excellent agreement with experiments.

The homogenizing effect of flow is not limited to shear. In a planar extensional flow at $\dot{\epsilon} = 0.013$ to 26 s$^{-1}$ the phase separated polystyrene/polyvinylmethylether were homogenized at temperatures 3 to 6°C above $T_s$ (*Katsaros* et al., 1986); the critical parameter of the homogenization process was the strain: $\epsilon_c \equiv \dot{\epsilon}t_c = 44\mp14$, where $t_c$ is the critical time to achieve miscibility at various $\phi$, T and $\dot{\epsilon}$. The constancy of $\epsilon_c$ indicates that the main mechanism of flow induced miscibility must be related to deformation of the system; after cessation of flow, the deformation dissipates and the homogenized blend reverts to phase separated morphology within 20 to 70 s. The same system in shear was studied by *Choplin* (1986).

This observation has a profound significance for understanding the mechanism of flow induced miscibility. The large values of $\varepsilon_c$ are non-attainable in dynamic small amplitude flow. The microrheological explanation of the phenomena should be able to propose a common mechanism for small and large strain flows. A help may come from direct observation of domain and macromolecular coil deformability in flow (*Lyngaae-Jorgensen*, 1985; *Hashimoto* et al., 1986; *Lyngaae-Jorgensen* and *Sondergaard*, 1987).

In Part 3.3.5, discussing block polymers, the flow-induced miscibility of these systems was mentioned and Eq (3.145) introduced. In the vicinity of the spinodal, homogenization is predicted at $a_0(T - T_s) \propto \sigma_{12}^2$, with $a_0$ being a characteristic parameter of the system. For block polymers $a_0 = 0.26$ $(kPa/K)^2$, for poly(styrene-co-acrylonitrile)/polymethylmethacrylate (*Lyngaae-Jorgensen* and *Sondergaard*, 1987) $a_0 = 0.53$ $(kPa/K)^2$, which may indicate that the homogenization mechanism is similar for blends and block polymers. On the other hand, if one assumes that in low strain dynamic testing:

$$\sigma_{12}^2 = G'/J_e^0 \tag{3.165}$$

($J_e$ is the steady state shear compliance) then the data on polystyrene/ polyvinylmethylether (*Mazich*, 1983) lead to $a_0 = 0.01$ to $0.04$, i. e. a value one order of magnitude smaller.

There is some question as to what the flow-induced homogenization means. Near the spinodal both $\chi_{12}$ and $v$ are small and co-deformation of the dispersed phase seems a reasonable assumption. If so, the homogenization requiring deformation of PAB by 44 Hencky strain units would reduce even centimeter-size drops into strands of atomic dimension. On the other hand if homogenization is evaluated only by turbidity under visible light, the dispersions with drop size $d \leq 0.2$ $\mu m$ are homogenous. Thus:

1. in spite of large overall strains required for stress homogenization the deformation of drops must have been much smaller than the matrix, i. e. *not* co-deformational;
2. the strains generated orientation in the system, decreasing the entropy and increasing the free energy, enhanced immiscibility of the system;
3. homogenization in flow most likely proceeded through a series of drop deformations and breaks, particularly effective near the spinodal temperature, $T_s$ (*Wolf*, 1980, 1984).

In both the aforementioned cases, flow induced immiscibility or miscibility, the process is identical and thermodynamically the flow energy contributes to the total free energy of the system in an analogous manner, but while in the first case the coalescence or aggregation leads to permanent structures the disaggregation or breaking provides mechanism for reduction of order and for the entropy increase, hence the interfacial properties and relative viscosity of the two phases are of critical importance.

### 3.4.4   Immiscible Blends

The relation between equilibrium thermodynamic functions, $\Delta H_m$ or $\Delta G_m$ as measured by inverse gas chromatography and the shear viscosity $\eta$ (determined in capillary viscometer) were studied by *Lipatov* et al. (1979, 1982, 1983), *Klykova* (1981), *Gorbatenko* et al. (1982), *Lipatov* (1983) and others (see Part 2.6.2). Examples of the generated data were shown in Fig. 3.26. It is obvious that miscibility in both systems is limited to low concentration regions. On the basis of the discussion in Part 3.4.2, as well as of the expectation based on the (Eyring) mirror image principle, PDB behavior should be expected up to spinodal. On the other hand, flow of the phase separated systems should follow the behavior defined by their own morphology, i.e. by stresses and interphase properties. These effects will be discussed in detail in the following text. The approximate location of spinodals is indicated in Fig. 3.26 by vertical lines. It is evident that only at high concentration of POM is the expected behavior observed. At the other concentration limits the viscosity initially follows

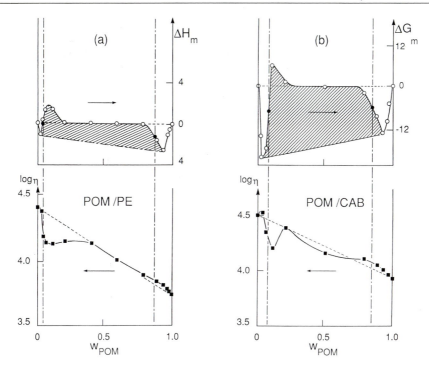

Fig. 3.26 Correlation between $\Delta H_m$ (or $\Delta G_m$) and $\log \eta$ plotted vs. weight fraction of polyoxymethylene, POM, for its blends with (a) polyethylene, PE, or (b) with celluloseacetatebutyrate, CAB. The shaded area under $\Delta H_m$ or $\Delta G_m$ represents the region of immiscibility (*Lipatov* et al., 1983).

PDB, but in the vicinity of the quiescent binodal (indicated by the lowest points on the thermodynamic functions) it becomes NDB. There is no independent information as to at which concentration the flowing system phase separates. If, as expected, separation takes place at higher than binodal concentration, then the only explanation for NDB can be volume dilatation occuring at $\phi \rightarrow \phi_s$. It is worth noting that in polyolefins blends, where miscibility at low concentration is expected, the specific volume vs. $\phi$ plot was non-monotonic (*Plochocki*, 1982).

There is another mechanism which may explain NDB near phase separation. Near the spinodal conditions $N\chi \rightarrow (N\chi)_s$ there are large fluctuation of density. In the absence of the interface tension (i.e. $v \rightarrow 0$) the flow causes severe deformation of the co-continuous forming domains. If $\lambda < 1$ then the developing morphology allows shear energy dissipation through the low viscosity layer. As the distance from the critical conditions increases, the co-continuity disappears and the resulting immiscible blend flows according to the laws governing its behavior. The thermodynamic arguments are relegated to the interphase.

The immiscible PAB can be modeled by suspensions ($\lambda \gg 1$), emulsions ($\lambda \simeq 1$) or block polymers (compatibilized alloys). The region of Newtonian flow is limited by inter-particle interactions and deformability of morphology. In some systems the linear viscoelastic region is limited to strains $\gamma < 1\%$. For this reason, frequently the $\eta_0$ is replaced by $\eta$ or $\eta'$ at constant stress level, $\sigma_{12}$ or $G''$.

Statistically, about 60% of PAB shows PDB, 30% NDB and the remaining 10% a mixed positive-negative deviating blend (PNDB) behavior (*Utracki* and *Kamal*, 1982). The classification of PAB based on the deviation from log-additivity is pertinent to the flow mechanism, but not to the chemical nature of blends; changing the molecular weight or test temperature may significantly alter the flow mechanism and the type of deviation from the log-additivity rule (*Romankevich* et al., 1982; *Bolotnikova* et al., 1982; *La Mantia* et al., 1986; *Santamaria* and *White*, 1986; *La Mantia*, 1987). Examples of PAB behavior are listed in Table 3.5.

Several mechanisms (expected on the basis of the model systems) can lead to PDB; in miscible blends dilatations was the only one which could explain NDB. In immiscible blends, if dilatation occurs it must do so at the interface, i. e. it may be expected in systems which show "antagonistic" tendencies towards each other. The examples listed above are in qualitative agreement with this concept. Furthermore, increasing MW of a component or decreasing T frequently either leads to NDB or deepens that deviation. The dilatation at the interface may result in an interlayer slip, i. e. a discontinuity of both $\dot{\gamma}$ and $\sigma_{12}$. *Lin* (1979), assuming interlayer slip in the telescopic flow of PAB through a tube, derived the following dependence:

$$1/\eta = \beta_1[w_1/\eta_1 + w_2/\eta_2]; \qquad \beta_1 = 1 - (\beta_{12}/\sigma_{12}) (\Pi w_1 w_2)^{\frac{1}{2}} \qquad (3.166)$$

where $\beta_1$ is the interlayer slip factor, $w_i$ is weight fraction of polymer i = 1,2 and $\beta_{12} \leq 0$ is the characteristic slip factor. Eq (3.166) formally allows prediction of NDB behavior. Note that for $\beta_{12} \rightarrow 0$ the fluidity-additivity rule is recovered (*Lees*, 1900; *Heitmiller* et al., 1964).

There are two possible explanations for PNDB: partial miscibility at low concentration, and concentration dependent change of the flow mechanism in the immiscible region. In the miscible region Eyring's "mirror image" can be expected: when $\Delta H_m$ decreases, the excess viscosity, $\eta^E$, should increase and vice versa. When critical concentration is approached, the viscosity is expected to increase sharply *before* the phase separation occurs. When the concentration exceeds the critical value the two-phase flow becomes controlled by structure: $\eta$ will increase further if a dispersion with rigid ellipsoids is created; it will stabilize for an emulsion-type system or decrease for lamellar morphology with interlayer slip. For immiscible systems the relation between $\Delta G_m$ and $\eta^E$ is a complex function, dependent on many variables. Furthermore, the conditions for phase separation in flowing systems differ from those considered by equilibrium thermodynamics (see Parts 3.4.2 and 3.4.3).

### 3.4.5  Phase Inversion

In emulsions or immiscible blends, there is a range of concentration, $\phi_i \pm \Delta\phi$, within which the role of two liquids inverts: the dispersed one becomes continuous and vice versa. In water/oil emulsions the emulsifier may have a profound effect on the $\phi_i$; in commercial emulsions the dispersed phase frequently constitutes well over 90 vol%. In organic immiscible systems the role of interfacial agent is considered less important, and as far as the PAB phase inversion is concerned, it is generally ignored.

*Paul* and *Barlow* (1980) in Fig. 6 of their review indicated that the condition for phase inversion can be expressed as:

$$\phi_{1i}/\phi_{2i} = \eta_1/\eta_2 \qquad (3.167)$$

The relation was found satisfactory to describe phase inversion in blends of polystyrene with either polybutadiene (*Jordhamo* et al., 1986), with high density polyethylene (*Elemans* et al., 1988), or with polymethylmethacrylate (*Miles* and *Zurek*, 1988).

A theory of phase inversion was proposed by *Metelkin* and *Blekht* (1984). The basic concept is shear flow generated formation of co-continuous phases subjected to the capillarity forces. The dynamic radius of the sinusoidally disturbed thread can be written as (*Tomotika*, 1935):

$$r^2 = r_0^2 - a^2/2 \qquad (3.168)$$

where $r_0$ is the radius of undisturbed thread and a is the amplitude of the disturbance:

$$a = a_{cr} \exp\{\dot\gamma \Omega t / \varkappa\} \tag{3.169}$$

where: $\Omega = \Omega(\theta,\lambda)$, $\theta$ is the distortion wavelength, $\lambda$ and $\varkappa$ functions defined in Eqs (3.121) and (3.122), respectively. Solving Eq (3.169) for $t_{bi}$ at which time the strand of phase i = 1,2 breaks and equating $t_{b_1} = t_{b_2}$ leads to:

$$\phi_{2i} = [1 + \lambda F(\lambda)]^{-1} \tag{3.170}$$

Where $F(\lambda)$ is a characteristic function of the system. For $F(\lambda) = 1$, Eqs (3.169) and (3.170) revert to Eq (3.167). Experiments with blends of low density polyethylene with rubber at 405 K allowed to estimate:

$$F(\lambda) = 1 + 2.25 \log \lambda + 1.81 (\log\lambda)^2 \tag{3.171}$$

Prediction of Eq (3.167) and that of Eqs (3.170) and (3.171) is shown in Fig. 3.27. For low values of $\lambda$ the low viscosity liquid-1 tends to englobe liquid-2 even when its (liquid-2) concentration is significantly higher. The situation is reversed at the point $\phi_{2i} = 0.5$, $\lambda = 1$. It is evident that the empirical Eq (3.167) with no adjustable parameters provides an excellent approximation. Eq (3.170) is more flexible, allowing for blend particularities reflected in $\lambda$, $\varkappa$ and $\theta$.

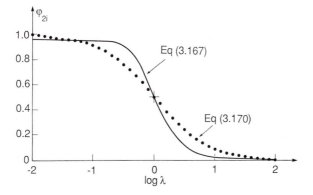

Fig. 3.27 Volume fraction of component-2 for the concentration inversion as a function of viscosity ratio $\lambda \equiv \eta_1/\eta_2$; solid line – Eq (3.167); dot-line – Eqs (3.170) – (3.171).

It is worth noting that $\lambda$ is defined at the employed level of shear stress. If the flow curves of liquids A and B intersect, within one range of $\sigma_{12}$ liquid A may show lower viscosity whereas in another region, on the other side of the intersection, the liquid B may be less viscous (*Southern* and *Ballman*, 1975). Accordingly, at one level of shear stress $\phi_{Bi} > 1/2$, whereas in another $\phi_{Bi} < 1/2$ must be expected. In a non-uniform stress field (which always exists in processing equipment and in most rheometers) predicting $\phi_{2i}$ can be frustrating. However, since the co-continuous structures at $\phi_{2i}$ result in enhancement of mechanical blend properties a successful optimization of processing can be very rewarding.

Equations (3.168) and (3.169) provide basis for determination of the interfacial tension coefficient, $\nu$, of industrial polymer blends. From the microscopie observation log a is plotted vs · time. The slope is proportional to $\nu$ (*Chappelear*, 1964; *Elmendorp*, 1988; *Carriere* et al., 1989); see Parts 2.7.1 and 3.5.1.

# 3.5    Microrheology

Microrheology aims to predict the macroscopic rheological properties of a dispersed system from a detailed description of changes in elemental volumes taking place during the flow. The principal systems of interest are dilute suspensions and emulsions. The interested reader should consult the basic work on liquid thread instability (*Tomotika*, 1935), the major review on the subject by *Goldsmith* and *Mason* (1967), a comprehensive report on liquid/liquid dispersions by *Grace* (1982) and recent work on microrheology of polymer blends by *Elmendorp* (1986).

The importance of microrheology for PAB is not that it provides a tool for better prediction of flow and processability, but mainly that it allows one to correlate rheology with morphology, which in turn determines the performance of the finished article.

The principles of microrheology have been formulated discussing flow of suspensions and emulsions (Parts 3.3.3 and 3.3.4) as well as the flow induced miscibility (Part 3.4.3). Here the microrheology of PAB is of concern. Two types of flow will be considered: shear (rotational) and elongational (irrotational). Since one of the mechanisms responsible for droplets dispersion in both of these flows is the formation and breakage of liquid fibrillas, a brief outline of principles governing the instability of a thread of one liquid in another seems to be a logical point of departure.

### 3.5.1    Instability of a Thread of Viscous Liquid

*Rayleigh* (1879) postulated that a varicose a column of liquid becomes unstable when the wavelength of the disturbance $\vartheta$ is larger than the circumference of the column. *Taylor* (1934) observed that during preparation of emulsions by shearing two liquids with $\lambda = 0.91$, the stable stationary threads of the minor phase liquid were formed. Once the shearing stopped, the threads gradually broke into small regularly spaced droplets. For Newtonian liquids ($N_1 = 0$) *Tomotika* (1935) developed a theory which quite successfully predicted the wavelength of instability and the resulting diameter of the secondary droplets. His general calculation of the critical ($\vartheta/2r_0$) ratio for maximum instability as a function of $\lambda$ is shown in Fig. 3.28. The time to break follows from Eq (3.169). The rate of disturbance growth, $\Omega$, depends on $\vartheta$ at maximum distortion and can be calculated from Tomotika's equation as a function of $\lambda$. These results are also shown in Fig. 3.28. The theoretical predictions were found to be valid for several pairs of Newtonian liquids (*Elmendorp*, 1986).

It is to be expected that Tomotika's theory will not be able to describe thread breaking in viscoelastic systems. Indeed, the presence of strain or stress causes variability in such rheological functions as shear or elongational viscosity and introduces unpredictable nonlinearity. In particular, deviations were noted due to strain hardening of the thread liquid as well as stabilization of distortions in blends with the yield stress, $\sigma_y$, e.g. for three-block copolymers. On the other hand, for such systems as polystyrene (PS), in polyethylene (PE), the Newtonian liquid theory was found to provide amazingly good predictions. The rationale was that the rates involved in the thread breakage were of the capillarity order i.e. $\dot{\varepsilon} \simeq 10^{-5}$ to $10^{-3}$ ($s^{-1}$). Under these conditions PS and PE behaved as viscous but Newtonian liquids (*Elmendorp*, 1986).

The discovery of the stabilizing effect of $\sigma_y$ has important commercial consequences – it allows one to design systems with or without yield and at will generate either discrete droplets or fibrillar morphology with the obvious implication vis-à-vis the performance. *Elmendorp* (1986) derived a useful criterion. The thread will not spontaneously break under capillary forces if:

$$\sigma_y > (4av/r_0^2)\{1/[2-3(a/r_0)^2] - \pi r_0/\vartheta\} \tag{3.172}$$

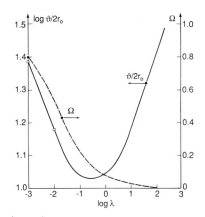

Fig. 3.28 Effect of viscosity ratio on the reduced wavelength of the disturbance, $\vartheta/2r_0$, and the rate of disturbance growth, $\Omega$ (*Tomotika, 1935*).

If stabilization of fibrils is the aim, then the relation provides several options: increase $\sigma_y$, decrease a (e.g. by quenching), decrease $v$, or select the blend ingredient in such a way that at the low rate of deformation viscosity ratio, $\lambda_0$, will require the wavelength of maximum instability (see Fig. 3.28) to be:

$$1/\vartheta_0 \leq \pi r_0[2 - 3(a/r_0)^2] \tag{3.173}$$

### 3.5.2 Shear Flow

Whereas there is a significant number of publications on the PAB morphology generated during compounding, processing or die flow, there is a definite paucity of information on microrheology in well controlled shear field.

In Part 3.3.4, the microrheology of Newtonian liquid emulsions has been briefly outlined. The principal information was presented in Figs. 3.18 and 3.19. The basic question is how that behavior is modified by the viscoelastic character of the liquid.

In the elegant work on Couette flow of viscoelastic drops in Newtonian liquid (*Elmendorp* and *Maalcke, 1985; Elmendorp, 1986*) there was a clear evidence for the stabilizing effect of $N_1$. Neither Taylor's Eq (3.123) nor Cox's Eq (3.123a) could predict deformability. On the other hand when the matrix was a viscoelastic liquid and the dispersed phase a Newtonian, the drop deformation was found to be larger than predicted. Calculating the conditions for drop burst was even more difficult.

In principle, the dependencies derived for Newtonian liquids, i. e. for systems characterized by a single characteristic rheological constant, $\eta_0$, should not be used for non-Newtonian ones in which $\eta$, $N_1$ and $N_2$ are functions of deformation rates. In derivation of relations valid for Newtonian fluids the terms which account for the non-Newtonian effects are dropped off. Assumption of $\eta = \eta(\dot{\gamma})$ variability in the remaining terms is unable to predict correct results, even if this "band-aid" solution may work in some cases.

Two effects of non-Newtonian character were relatively easy to incorporate: (1) The viscosity ratio $\lambda$ ought to be calculated for each set of $\eta_i = \eta_i(\dot{\gamma})$, i = 1,2. To do this $\dot{\gamma}$ has to be known on both sides of the interface. The equation for $\dot{\gamma}$ of liquid circulating within the drop was derived (*Elmendorp and Maalcke, 1985; Elmendorp, 1986*). Agreement between the computed and experimental $\dot{\gamma}$ still has to be demonstrated. (2) The interfacial tension, $v$, was predicted to depend on the difference in elasticity of two liquid components (*van Oene, 1972*):

$$v = v_0 + (d/12)(N_{1,1} - N_{1,2}) \tag{3.174}$$

where $N_{1,i} = N_{1,i}(\dot{\gamma})$, with $i = 1$ for the dispersed and $i = 2$ for the continuous phase. Incorporation of these corrections improved, but did not eliminate the observed deviations.

By contrast with earlier studies of drop deformability performed on a single droplet, the data for polymer blends were generated by calculating an average response in systems containing low, but finite concentration of the dispersed phase. It was observed that as the concentration decreased below 0.5 vol% the disagreement with predictions of Eq (3.123a) virtually disappeared (*Elmendorp* and *van der Vegt*, 1986). This led to the conclusion that the main source of deviation originated in drop coalescence, accompanying the shear dispersion at higher $\phi$. As discussed in Part 3.3.4 for emulsions, the dynamic coalescence/redispersion process leads to growth of average drop diameter as $\bar{d} \propto \phi^{2/3}$ (*Utracki*, 1973). In particular Eqs (3.134) to (3.136) provided alternative means for calculating the critical time for coalescence. Fig. 3.20 illustrates Taylor's and Elmendorp's predictions for variation of drop diameter with $\sigma_{12}/v$ ratio. It is expected that in real systems the drop diameters will be located between the two dependencies. The experimental results indicated that Eq (3.134) provides a good limitation for dilute systems with $\phi \leq 0.01$. At higher $\phi$ the assumption of concentration independent $t_c$ does not hold and Eqs (3.135) or (3.136) provide better agreement.

Of other publications on the subject, it is worth mentioning work by *Vinogradov* et al. (1982) and by *Plotnikova* and *Zabugina* (1984). The authors measured $\eta = \eta(T)$ at $\dot{\gamma} = 10^{-3}$ $(s^{-1})$ in a cone-and-plate geometry for three pairs of polystyrene/polyethylene blends. In Fig. 3.29 the abrupt increase of $\eta$(PE) near 120 °C indicates onset of crystallization. For the sake of clarity, only data for homopolymers and 30% PE blends are shown. It is evident that flow of blends is *dominated by the high fluidity components*. The authors reported similar morphology in all three systems. After extraction of polystyrene from quenched specimens for $w \geq 30$ wt% of PE the specimen shape was retained (i.e. continuity of PE phase) whereas for $w \leq 5\%$ PE, it was not. The constant rate of shear data in Fig. 3.29 indicate that in system I $\eta$(PE) is larger than $\eta$(PS) by nearly two decades, whereas in system III the reverse is true. In addition, the polymers were selected to have virtually identical melt elasticity. The invariant morphology was unexpected.

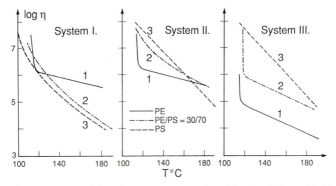

Fig. 3.29 Shear viscosity at $\dot{\gamma} = 10^{-3}$ $(s^{-1})$ vs. temperature for: (1) polyethylene, (2) 30 wt% polyethylene in polystyrene and (3) polystyrene (*Plotnikova* and *Zabugina*, 1984).

For Newtonian liquid emulsions $\lambda$ and $\varkappa$ in Eqs (3.121) and (3.122) are nonambiguously defined by ratios of Newtonian viscosities, and $\sigma_{12} = \eta_{0,2}\dot{\gamma}$ respectively. For non-Newtonian fluids, without interfacial slip, the continuity of shear stress across the interphase is usually assumed, $\sigma_{12} = $ constant, which leads to:

$$(\dot{\gamma}\eta)_1 = (\dot{\gamma}\eta)_2 \qquad \text{or} \qquad \dot{\gamma}_2 = \dot{\gamma}_1\lambda \tag{3.175}$$

i.e., the deformation rate should be higher in the less viscous phase. It follows that for immiscible blends without interlayer slip, the rate of deformation is an apparent quantity defined as a ratio: $\sigma_{12}/\eta(\sigma_{12} = \text{const.})$.

In a sense, the information in Fig. (3.29) is misleading; the stresses $(\eta\dot{\gamma})$ in blends $\neq (\eta\dot{\gamma})$ in homopolymer. To calculate $\lambda = \lambda(\sigma_{12})$ one has to know $\eta = \eta(\dot{\gamma},T)$; without this additional information $\lambda$ and $\varkappa$ cannot be calculated and the morphology cannot be predicted. However, the rate of shear in less viscous fluids is higher. Thus in shear thinning liquids the difference between viscosities of two components at constant stress is expected to be larger than that at constant rate, i.e. $\lambda$ will not be able to explain the relative invariance of morphology. To do that one must look at two related phenomena: means of stabilization of elongated liquid structures and extensional flow behavior of blends. The first phenomenon was discussed in Part 3.4.6.1, the second is the subject of the following part.

The assumption of stress continuity at the interface is in conflict with the assumption of interlayer slip on which Eq (3.166) is based. There is little doubt that in polymer blends the interlayer slip is not universal. In "antagonistic" systems with strong immiscibility of blend components interlayer slip can be expected. Example of such systems are the noncompatibilized blends of polyamide with polyolefin for which $\eta$ vs. $w_2$ shows NDB behavior (*Dumoulin* et al., 1985; *Utracki* et al., 1986). An elegant demonstration of interlayer slip in polystyrene/polymethylmethacrylate multilayer samples allowed the authors to calculate the interphase viscosity as at least ten times smaller than viscosity of the less viscous component (*Lyngaae-Jorgensen* et al., 1988).

### 3.5.3  Irrotational Flows

The velocity gradient tensor can be decomposed into the deformation and vorticity tensors respectively:

$$\partial v_i/\partial x_j = (\partial v_i/\partial x_j + \partial v_j/\partial x_i)/2 +$$
$$(\partial v_i/\partial x_j - \partial v_j/\partial x_i)/2 \qquad (3.176)$$

The flows where vorticity tensor $\boldsymbol{\omega} = \boldsymbol{\nabla} \times \mathbf{v} = 0$ are irrotational. For example, the simple shear can be represented as pure shear and rotation, the elongational flow as fully irrotational, etc. In die flow there is a strong irrotational element within the convergence and a rotational one inside the die.

For emulsions, the irrotational hyperbolic flow generated finer dispersions in broader range of $\lambda$ than the Couette shear flow (*Grace*, 1982). In Fig. 3.18 the minimum drop size for breakup in hyperbolic flow was about half of that in Couette flow.

The convergent flow to a die is of particular interest (*Petrie*, 1979). *Cogswell* (1972) derived the following relation between the extensional viscosity at the entrance to the die and the shear viscosity on the die wall

$$\eta_E/\eta = 2\tan^{-2}\alpha \qquad (3.177)$$

where $\alpha$ is the half-angle of free convergence given by the ratio of the respective deformation rates:

$$\alpha = \text{arc tan } (2\dot{\varepsilon}/\dot{\gamma}) \qquad (3.178)$$

It is interesting to note that from these equations the energy dissipated in shear $\eta\dot{\gamma}^2 = 2\eta_E\dot{\varepsilon}^2$, i.e. the entrance pressure loss due to extension is a significant part of the total. Analysis of entrance flow of polyethylenes gave the values of $\alpha$ in reasonable agreement with results from visual examination (*Catani* and *Utracki*, 1986):

LDPE        $\alpha = 1.24 \pm 0.03°$

HDPE        $\alpha = 20.6 \pm 1.6$

LLDPE       $\alpha = 30.0 \pm 0.2$

The later work (*Metzner* and *Metzner*, 1970) gave:

$$\dot{\varepsilon} = \dot{\gamma}\,\sin^3\alpha/4(1-\cos\alpha) \qquad (3.179)$$

Eqs (3.178) and (3.179) are identical at $\alpha \to 0$, diverging with increasing cone entrance angle. (For comparison of various $\eta_E$ measuring methods see *Laun* and *Schuch*, 1989). Provided that $\dot{\varepsilon}$ is known the droplet deformation can be calculated directly.

A more thorough theory for drop deformation in convergent flow was proposed by *Elmendorp* (1986). The derivation assumes that elemental straining follows the Kelvin-Voigt model. Drop deformation in Hencky strain can be expressed as:

$$\varepsilon(t) \equiv [l(t) - l(0)]/l(0) = \varkappa_E I(t)\,(19\lambda_E+16)/(16\lambda_E+16) \qquad (3.180)$$

where the time dependent integral:

$$I(t) = 1 - \exp\{-40\dot{\varepsilon}t/19\lambda_E\varkappa_E\}$$

$$\varkappa_E = \sigma_{11}d/v \qquad \text{and} \qquad \lambda_E = \eta_{E,1}/\eta_{E,2}$$

It can be seen that $0 \leqslant I(t) \leqslant 1$. For equilibrium stretching the deformation may be written as:

$$D_E = [(1+\varepsilon)^3-1]/[(1+\varepsilon)^3+1] \qquad (3.181)$$

where $D_E$ is defined in Eq (3.123) with the shear parameters replaced by the elongational ones. The theory was found to provide a reasonable approximation. For elastic Hookean spheres similar relations have been derived.

Comparing Eq (3.123b) with Eqs (3.180) and (3.181) gives:

$$D_E/D_c \approx 3.3[1+(1.9\lambda\varkappa)^2]^{\frac{1}{3}}/[1+1.5\varkappa] \qquad (3.182)$$

which, at limits: $\varkappa = \sigma_{11}d/v \to 0$ and $\varkappa \to \infty$, predicts that deformation in elongation will be larger than that in shear by a factor of 3.3, and $4.2\lambda$ respectively. These estimates based on Eq (3.123a) are expected to be valid within the region of small deformations.

Van der *Reijden-Stolk* et al. (1988) measured droplet deformation in elongational field using Newtonian, elastic and shear thinning systems. Plot of $D_E$ vs. $\sigma_{11}/E$ (where E is the elastic modulus) reduced data for each system into a single dependence, deviating from a straight line upwards for the Newtonian and downwards for the two other systems.

Generation of the fibrillar morphology in the die flow of PAB has been a widely discussed subject in the Russian literature (*Ablazova* et al., 1975; *Tsebrenko* et al., 1976, 1979, 1982). Strands containing up to $10^5$ fibrils, each 2-20µm in diameter and several millimeters

TABLE 3.6 Effect of the Viscosity Ratio, $\lambda$, in Polyoxymethylene/poly(ethylene-co-vinylacetate) Blends on Formation of POM Fibrils (*Tsebrenko* et al., 1982).

| $\lambda$ | $d \pm \sigma$ (µm) | Number of Fibrils in Crossection | POM forms (in wt%) Fibers | Plates |
|-----------|---------------------|----------------------------------|----------------------------|--------|
| 0.35 | 5.3 ± 2.5 | 61,500 | 83 | 17 |
| 0.91 | 4.2 ± 1.8 | 13,200 | 100 | 0 |
| 1.05 | 5.5 ± 3.6 | 6,800 | 100 | 0 |
| 1.70 | 6.2 ± 3.6 | 4,300 | 80 | 20 |
| 4.10 | 7.3 ± 5.8 | 4,400 | ~50 | 1.5 |

in length were generated. The optimum value of the viscosity ratio was found to be $\lambda \simeq 0.76$ to 0.91. An example is given in Table 3.6. This seems to contradict the frequent assumption that at $\lambda = 1$, the dispersing process is the most efficient (see also Fig. 3.18).

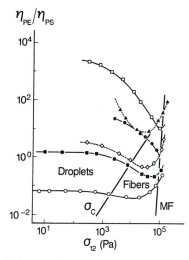

Fig. 3.30 Ratio of shear viscosity $\lambda = \eta_{PE}/\eta_{PS}$ for $\phi_{PE} \leq 0.3$ vs. shear stress. Points – experimental, solid straight lines: $\sigma_c$ – boundary between drops and fiber dispersion regions, MF – melt fracture (*Krasnikova* et al., 1981).

In another series of publications, the relation between the rheological parameters and morphology in polyethylene/polystyrene blends was investigated (*Krasnikova* et al., 1981, 1982, 1984; *Dreval* et al., 1983). These observations are summarized in Fig. 3.30. At $\phi(\text{HDPE}) \leq 0.3$ and at shear stress:

$$\sigma_{12} > \sigma_{12,c} = a\lambda^b \tag{3.183}$$

(where a and b are constants dependent on $\phi$ and type of blend, and the subscript c indicates a critical value) up to the melt fracture region (MF), formation of PE fibers was observed. At $\sigma_{12} < \sigma_{12,c}$ for $0.04 \leq \lambda \leq 2,000$ droplets were formed. Again, if only shear properties are considered, the data in Fig. 3.18 indicating impossibility of drop dispersion for $\lambda > 4$ seems to be in conflict with the results presented in Fig. 3.30. The information in the latter figure is particularly seminal. It was generated in a wide range of composition (venturing into the range of co-continuous morphology) using cone-and-plate as well as capillary flow and in wide range of absolute viscosities of the homopolymers. In both flow geometries fibers with diameter 2 to 5 μm were formed. Rapid quenching prevented them from desintegration into spheres under the influence of the capillarity forces. In a more detailed study *Krasnikova* et al. (1982) observed that in the region of drop formation ($\sigma_{12} < \sigma_{11,c}$) for $\lambda \leq 10$ the fibers appeared near the critical values of stress. However, as the ratio exceeds this value, only drops are visible. Furthermore, for $\sigma_{12}$ exceeding the melt fracture values, the fibers were disrupted.

In the third series of reports (*Yakovlev* et al., 1985, 1986; *Gerasimchuk* and *Romankevich*, 1986) the capillary flow of polyolefin/polyamide blends were studied using short capillaries of variable diameter. The data were evaluated using Eq (3.179). Defining $\sigma_{11} = \dot{\epsilon}\eta_E$, the results could be presented in the form of a morphological map; Fig. 3.31. The hyperbolas predict critical values of $\sigma_{11}d/v = \varkappa_E$; for $\varkappa_E < \varkappa_{E,1} \simeq 0.1$ drops remain undeformed, whereas for $\varkappa_E > \varkappa_{E,2} \simeq 0.5$ fibers were formed. The region "in between" defines the conditions for drops deformation into prolate ellipsoids.

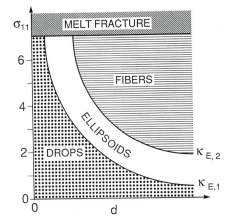

Fig. 3.31 Deformation map for convergent flow: extensional stress vs. initial droplet diameter. The critical values of $\varkappa_{E,2}$ are about 0.1 and 0.5, respectively (after *Yakovlev* et al., 1986).

In the full range of $\lambda$ the ratio $(19\lambda + 16)/(16\lambda + 16)$ varies from 1 to 1.19. Accordingly, Equation (3.180) predicts that at equilibrium the Hencky strain of the drops can be approximated by:

$$\varepsilon(\infty) \simeq 1.1\varkappa_E \tag{3.184}$$

with an error not exceeding 10%. Experimentally $\varkappa_{E,1}$ was estimated as about 0.1; indeed for this range of $\varkappa_E$ drop deformation is unnoticeable. The second limiting value of $\varkappa_E$ can be estimated as $0.5 < \varkappa_{E,2} < 2.3$, leading to axial ratios of the prolate ellipsoid $4 \leqslant b/a \leqslant 36$. How elongated has the ellipsoid to be to become a fiber?

In Fig. 3.32 the profile of flow pattern into a capillary are illustrated (*Miroshnikov*, 1984; *Ma* et al., 1985). The black and white material has the same rheological properties, the color being used only to observe the pattern. When considering the capillary flow of PAB, the telescopic character has to be kept in mind.

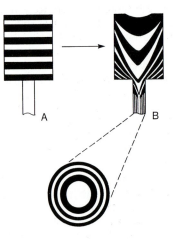

Fig. 3.32 Flow pattern into capillary; A – the initial state, B – during the flow (after *Miroshnikov*, 1984).

## 3.6    Small Strain Dynamic Shear Flow

The definitions and fundamental dependencies are given in Part 3.2.1. The small strain dynamic flow of PAB could be expected to follow a linear viscoelastic behavior. However, frequently the time effects, yield and strain/stress modification of morphology complicate the interpretation. These phenomena have been already discussed respectively in Parts 3.2.1 and 3.5 and the appropriate corrective procedures have been indicated. On the following pages, examples of more recent observations will be given.

### 3.6.1    Homologous Polymer Blends

The variation of $\eta_0$ with composition for homologous polymer blends was discussed in Part 3.3.2. The blending laws of linear viscoelastic behavior of these blends have been investigated during the last 30 years. Recently macromolecules have been synthesized in the form of most letters of the alphabet (B,H,I,K,O,P,R,T,X,Y). The studies of the rules of mixing of this "alphabet soup" will provide occupation for at least another 30; the blending rules for linear and non-linear macromolecules were found to be different (*McKenna* and *Plazek*, 1987).

Blends of linear, narrow molecular weight distribution polystyrene fractions were found to be rather well described, assuming the blending rule in the form of the extended Eq (3.88) (*Marin*, 1977; *Montfort* et al., 1978):

$$\eta^* = [(1-\alpha)\eta_1^{*1/a} + \alpha\eta_2^{*1/a}]^a \tag{3.185}$$

where:  $\alpha = [(1-\phi+\phi r^*)^{3.4/a} - 1]/(r^{*3.4/a} - 1)$

with:    $r^* \equiv M_{w2}/M_{w1} = (\eta_{02}/\eta_{01})^{1/3.4}$

Equation (3.185) provided good description for blends of PS fractions with $M_w > M_e \simeq$ 10kg/mol. An example of the data is shown in Fig. 3.33 where $\eta''/\eta_0$ vs. $\eta'/\eta_0$ is plotted for blends of narrow molecular weight fractions ($M_w/M_n < 1.1$) with $M_w = 110$ and 400. (In the original figure the theoretical line intersected the experimental points; for clarity these were omitted in Fig. 3.33).

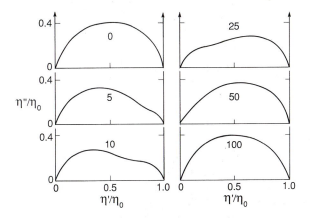

Fig. 3.33 The Cole-Cole plot of $\eta''/\eta_0$ vs. $\eta'/\eta_0$ for blends of narrow molecular weight distribution polystyrene ($M_w = 110$ kg/mol) with its homologue ($M_w = 400$); the numbers indicate weight percentage of the latter in blends (adopted from *Marin*, 1977).

The Cole-Cole dependence in Fig. 3.33 provides visual information on the distribution of relaxation times. The generalized dependence in the complex plane was given by (*Havriliak* and *Nagami*, 1967):

$$(\eta^* - \eta_\infty)/(\eta_0 - \eta_\infty) = [1 + (i\omega\tau)^{(1-\alpha)}]^{-\beta} \tag{3.186}$$

where $\alpha$ and $\beta$ are parameters.

When $\eta''$ is plotted vs. $\eta'$, there are two values of $\eta'$ corresponding to $\eta'' = 0$: $\eta' = \eta_\infty \simeq 0$ and $\eta' = \eta_0$. Substituting the first value into Eq (3.186) simplifies the calculations. A computer program makes use of the separate functions of the real and imaginary parts of the dynamic function (*Utracki* and *Schlund*, 1987):

$$\eta' = \eta_0 \, r^{-\beta} \cos\beta\Theta$$
$$\eta'' = \eta_0 \, r^{-\beta} \sin\beta\Theta \tag{3.187}$$

where:

$$r^2 = a^2 + b^2, \quad \Theta = \arctan(b/a)$$

with:

$$a \equiv 1 - (\omega\tau)^{1-\alpha} \sin(\alpha\pi/2)$$

and

$$b \equiv (\omega\tau)^{1-\alpha} \cos(\alpha\pi/2)$$

Similarly, substituting Eq (3.186) into the definition of $\tilde{H}_G$ in Eq (3.56) gives:

$$\tilde{H}_G = [\pi r^\beta]^{-1} \sin\beta\Theta = \eta''/\pi\eta_0 \tag{3.188}$$

From Eq (3.187) it follows that both parameters, $\alpha$ and $\beta$, affect the breadth of the relaxation spectrum. For $\alpha \to 0$ and $\beta \to 1$ the relation for a single Maxwell element is obtained. On the complex plane, $\eta''$ vs. $\eta'$, $\alpha$ is responsible for broadening the diagram, whereas $\beta$ for its skewness. Comparing Eqs (3.185) and (3.186) it is evident that the ability of the latter dependence to describe the viscoelastic properties hinges on a continuous distribution of the viscoelastic elements. In case of the discrete distribution, such as the one illustrated in Fig. 3.33, Eq (3.186) should be applied twice with different sets of parameters in the two regions.

*Montfort* (1984) investigated the viscoelastic properties of polystyrenes and their blends. Resins having a wide range of molecular weights $M_w = 2$ kg/mol to 3,800 with $M_w/M_n \leqslant 1.3$ have been used. Similarly as in Fig. 3.33 the Cole-Cole plot for the homologous blends indicated bimodality of relaxations. Since the investigation focused on the effects of addition of long chain molecules to melts of short chain homologues, the low concentration range $w_2 \leqslant 35\%$ was of a particular interest. The principal mixing rule assumed by the author was:

$$G(t) = G_N^0 \, \Sigma \, \phi_i^2 \exp\{ - t/\tau_i\}, \quad i = 1,2 \tag{3.189}$$

where $G_N^0$ is the plateau modulus and $\tau_i$ represents an average relaxation time:

$$1/\tau_i = 1/\tau_{rep,i} + 1/\tau_{mod,i}$$

with $\tau_{rep,i}$ and $\tau_{mod,i}$ representing the average time for reptation and tube modification, respectively. Eq (3.189) was used to derive blending rules for $\eta_0$ and $J_e$ assuming either discrete or continuous distribution of molecular weights. A reasonable agreement with experimental data has been demonstrated.

Another blending rule was more recently proposed by *Zang* et al. (1987b). The authors focused their attention on the compliance $J_e = \tau_w/\eta_0$ assuming that:

$$\tau_w = \Sigma \, w_i \tau_{wi} \tag{3.190}$$

and $\eta_0$ is given by Eq (3.84). The agreement between calculated and the experimental values of the zero shear recoverable compliance:

$$J_e^0 = \lim_{\omega \to 0} \; G'(\omega)/G''^2(\omega) \tag{3.191}$$

for PS blends was remarkable, considering that no adjustable parameters were used.

Another approach to blending rules directly considers the central relation of the linear viscoelasticity, the relaxation spectrum. The first, second and third order blending rules have been proposed:

$$H(\tau) = \sum_{ijk} P_{ijk} \, H_{ijk}(\tau/\Lambda_{ijk}) \tag{3.192}$$

where $P_{ijk}$ is the third order intensity function being given by concentration product of the specimens i, j and k, while $\Lambda_{ijk}$ is the third order relaxation time.

The generally complex expressions given by Eq (3.192) can be greatly simplified for the following two limiting cases (*Watanabe* et al., 1985). For large $r^* = M_{w_2}/M_{w_1}$ and for either (i) dilute blends with $w_2$ below the entanglement concentration, $w_e > w_2$:

$$H(\tau) \simeq w_1 H_1(\tau/\Lambda_{11}) + w_2[H_2(\tau) + H_{12}(\tau)] \tag{3.193}$$

or (ii) concentrated blends with $w_2 > w_e$:

$$H(\tau) \simeq w_1 H_1(\tau/\Lambda_{11}) + w_2 H_2(\tau) + f(w_2) H_{12}(\tau) + w_2^2 H_2(\tau/\Lambda_{22}) \tag{3.194}$$

where $f(w_2)$ is an intensity factor derived from the tube renewal process. (For discussion on the process see *Rubinstein* et al. (1987)).

For small $r^* \simeq 1$ Eq. (3.192) reduces to:

$$H(\tau) \simeq w_1 H_1(\tau) + w_2 H_2(\tau) \tag{3.195}$$

For blends with perfect interfacial interactions Eq (3.192) leads to *Bogue* et al. (1970) quadratic blending law. Eqs (3.192)-(3.195) provide a bridge between the linear viscoelastic functions and molecular parameters of the resins. In the more recent publication (*Watanabe* and *Kotaka*, 1987) the method has been extended to three component homologous blends.

In the limit of low deformation rates the blending rules must predict variation of the zero-shear viscosity and first normal stress difference with polydispersity. This problem has been frequently discussed in the literature. For more recent publication see *Liu* et al. (1983) or *Utracki* and *Schlund* (1987). The latter authors reported good agreement with Eq (3.85) provided that $M_w$ was replaced by $M_a$ (computed from Eq (3.86)) and K and $\alpha \simeq 3.5$ are taken as fitting parameters.

Experimental data on flow of several type of homologous polymer blends exists in the literature, viz.: polystyrene (*Akovali*, 1967; *Masuda* et al., 1970; *Marin*, 1977; *Frank* and *Meissner*, 1984; *Montfort*, 1984), polymethyl-methacrylate (*Onogi* et al., 1970), poly-dimethylsiloxane (*Prest* and *Porter*, 1973), polyamide-6 (*Hinrichsen* and *Green*, 1981), polypropylene (*Deopura* and *Kadam*, 1986), etc.

## 3.6.2  Miscible Blends

It should be of no surprise to note that the blending rules developed for homologous polymer blends are frequently valid for the miscible blends. For example, Eq (3.88) written in integral form:

$$[\eta^*(\omega)]^e = \int_0^\infty [\eta_i^*(\omega)]^e \, W(M)dM \tag{3.196}$$

[where e = 1/3.4, $\eta_i^*(\omega)$ is complex viscosity of monodispersed homopolymer at frequency

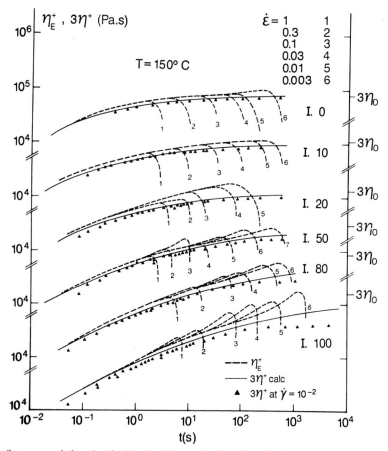

Fig. 3.34a Stress growth function for blends of linear low density polyethylene, LLDPE, with another type of LLDPE (miscible, Series I). The broken lines represent experimental data in elongation, the triangles indicate experimental data in steady state shearing at $\dot\gamma = 0.01s^{-1}$. The solid lines were computed from the relaxation spectrum (*Schlund* and *Utracki*, 1987c).

$\omega$ and $W(M)$ is the molecular weight distribution] can be applied to blends assuming the volume additivity:

$$\eta^*(\omega) = \Sigma \phi_i \eta_i^*(\omega, f_m) \tag{3.197}$$

Here all $\eta_i^*$ are taken at constant free volume, $f_m$ (*Wisniewsky* et al., 1984).

For broad molecular weight distribution linear low density polyethylene, LLDPE, blended with another type LLDPE the $\eta' = \eta'(\omega)$ dependence was found to follow Eq (3.62) (*Utracki* and *Schlund*, 1987). As a result the relaxation spectrum was computed using Eq (3.63), allowing calculation of other linear viscoelastic functions, viz. $G'$ or $\eta^+$ in good agreement with directly measured values (see Figs. 3.8a and 3.34a). Since the molecular weight dependence of various parameters of the linear viscoelastic functions are known (e.g. that of $\eta_0$) the compositional variations of these functions can be calculated from the basic molecular weights of the blend components:

$$M_n^{-1} = \Sigma w_i / M_{ni} \tag{3.198}$$

$$M_w = \Sigma w_i M_{wi} \tag{3.199}$$

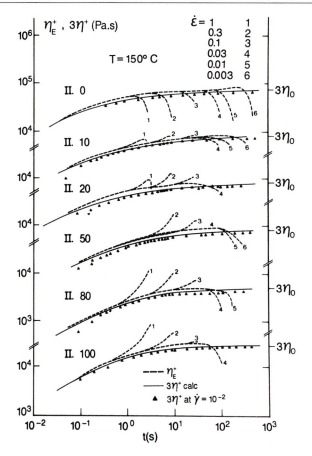

Fig. 3.34b The same dependence as in Fig. 3.34a, but for immiscible LLDPE/LDPE blends (*Schlund and Utracki*, 1987c).

$$M_z = \Sigma w_i M_{zi} M_{wi} / \Sigma w_i M_{wi}$$ (3.200)

Historically, the first flow measurements on miscible blends with significant specific interactions were reported by *Prest* and *Porter* (1972) for blends of poly-2,6-dimethylphenylene ether (PPE) with polystyrene. The blends were prepared by freeze-drying of benzene solutions. The dynamic data were determined in cone-and-plate geometry at $\omega = 0.19$ to 75 rad/ s and T = 220 ± 35 °C. All samples ($w_{PPE} \leqslant 40.3$ wt%) obeyed the time-temperature superposition principle within the indicated temperature range of 70 °C. The shift factor, $a_T$, was found to follow the WLF (*Williams, Landel* and *Ferry*, 1955) relation:

$$\log a_T = - c_1^0 (T - T_0) / (c_2^0 + T - T_0)$$ (3.201)

where $T_0$ is the reference temperature and $c_i^0$'s are equation constants related to the free volume fraction, f, and the thermal expansion coefficient, $\alpha$,; $c_1^0 = B/2.303f$ and $c_2^0 = f/\alpha$ (B $\simeq 1$ is a numerical constant). When $T_0 \simeq T_g + 50$ °C is selected $c_i^0$'s are becoming universal: $c_1^0 = 8.86$ and $c_2^0 = 101.6$ (*Ferry*, 1980). The plot of $\log\eta_0$ vs. composition was found to show positive deviation, expected on the basis of the Eyring mirror-image rule, Eq (3.81).

Miscible blends of polymethylmethacrylate with either polyvinylidenefluoride or poly-(styrene-co-acrylonitrile) were examined by *Wu* (1987). Again, the moduli, G' and G'', were smooth functions of frequency indicating that Eq (3.62) and the subsequent generalization via the frequency relaxation spectrum can be used. The author's analysis of the entanglement density was presented in Part 3.4.1.

The blends of polystyrene with polyvinylmethylether were analyzed by *Nishi* et al. (1981) and by *Ajji* et al. (1988). In both cases the isothermal frequency scans at T below and above $T_s$ showed suprisingly little difference. The tests were not conducted continously across the phase separation, but in the homogeneous and immiscible regions. It seems that the averaged, low strain material responses for molecular and macroscopic dispersions are quite similar, provided that the interfacial tension, $v$, is low. As $v$ increases, at low frequency, the phase separated systems show an apparent yield stress.

One of the methods of miscibility enhancement requires incorporation of ions (*Smith* et al., 1987). Blends of polystyrene with polyethylacrylate are immiscible. However, incorporation of $c \geq 5\%$ of styrenesulfonic acid mers into the first polymer and 4-vinylpyridine mers into the second changes the situation; the dynamic data superimpose on a master curve as expected for homogenous melts (*Bazuin* and *Eisenberg*, 1986). Due to ionic interactions the blends showed extended rubbery plateau and virtual absence of true flow even at T = 220 °C. The time-temperature shift factor, $a_T$, was found to follow the *Arrhenius* (1887) dependence:

$$\ln a_T = \ln A + \Delta E_\eta / RT \qquad (3.202)$$

with the pre-exponential factor A increasing with the ion content and the activation energy of flow $\Delta E_\eta \simeq 176$ kJ/mole.

### 3.6.3   Immiscible Blends

Here time effects (viz. Part 3.2.1.4), yield phenomena (viz. Part 3.2.1.5.3) and structural modifications (viz. Part 3.5) are important.

The time effects are related to variation of structure. For example, the crosslinked particles of polybutadiene in poly(acrylonitrile-co-styrene) matrix at higher temperatures (T $\simeq 245$ °C) aggregated causing an increase in the shear moduli, apparent especially at low test frequencies (*Aoki*, 1979; *Masuda* et al., 1984; *Aoki*, 1988). However, at lower temperatures (T $\leq 230$ °C) the morphology was found to be stable and at loadings of rubber up to 30 wt% the time-temperature principle was obeyed with independent of composition $a_T$ following Eq (3.201). At constant temperature, the aggregation was found to depend on acrylonitrile content in the matrix copolymer (*Aoki* and *Nakayama*, 1981). Formation of the aggregates lead to increase of the effective volume fraction of the filler (rubber) particles which in turn resulted in appearance of the yield stress. As a further consequence of the structure modification the agreement between dynamic and steady state data (G* $\simeq \sigma_{12}$ at $\omega \simeq \dot{\gamma}$) tended to disappear at loadings in excess of 15 wt% of rubber (*Aoki*, 1986).

Blends of polymethylmethacrylate with poly(acrylonitrile-co-styrene) grafted on polybutadiene particles (PMMA/ABS) gave similar information (*Han* and *Yang*, 1987). Unfortunately the authors did not study the morphology.

The general *Sprigg's* (1965) model allows one to expect:

$$\eta(\dot{\gamma}) = \eta'(\omega); \qquad \text{or} \qquad \sigma_{12}(\dot{\gamma}) = G''(\omega)/C \qquad (3.203)$$

$$\psi_1(\dot{\gamma}) = 2G'(\omega)/\omega^2; \qquad \text{or} \qquad N_1(\dot{\gamma}) = 2G'(\omega)/C^2 \qquad (3.204)$$

where

$$C \equiv \omega/\dot{\gamma} = [(2 - 2e - e^2)/3]^{\frac{1}{2}}$$

with e the model parameter. Eqs (3.203) and (3.204) provide a method for determining the equivalent rate of deformation ratio, C. For simple liquids C $\simeq 1$, which allows one to expect the well known equivalence: $N_1(\sigma_{12}) = 2G'(G'')$, for $\sigma_{12} = G''$.

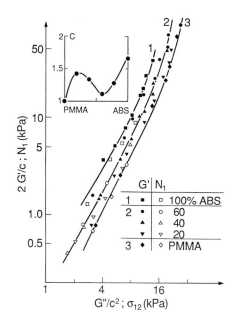

Fig. 3.35 Determination of Sprigg's parameter C = ω/γ̇ for superposition of dynamic and steady state shear stresses for poly(acrylonitrile-co-butadiene-co-styrene)/polymethylmethacrylate blends (data *Han and Yang*, 1987). Insert: compositional variation of C.

The *Han* and *Yang*'s (1987) data for PMMA/ABS blends were analyzed according to Eqs (3.203) and (3.204). Only for PMMA was C ≃ 1 found. The compositional variation of C is presented in the insert in Fig. 3.35. It seems reasonable to postulate that this dependence is a reflection of the morphological differences between the blend structure in the steady state and in the low strain dynamic shear flows. Plots of $N_1$ vs. $\sigma_{12}$ at γ̇ = ω/C and 2G'(ω)/C² vs. G''(ω)/C are also shown in Fig. 3.35. It can be seen that the steady state and dynamic data superimpose on constant composition master curves. Furthermore, the lower the ABS content, the lower the blend elasticity at the same shear stress. The consequent regularity of the dependence supports the basic concept of the Sprigg's model.

Blends of poly(styrene-b-butadiene) diblock copolymers (SB) with polybutadienes (PBD) were investigated by *Watanabe* and *Kotaka* (1983, 1984b). In spite of rather complex looking relaxation spectra the blends were found to obey the time-temperature superposition principle with $a_T$ independent of SB content. For low molecular weight PBD ($M_n$ = 2 kg/mol) $a_T$ followed the Arrhenius dependence (3.202). For high molecular weight PBD's ($M_n$ > 27.6) the data followed WLF relation (3.201).

By contrast, the time-temperature superposition principle fails in poly(styrene-b-butadiene-b-styrene) tri-block polymers. Here, the three dimensional structure depends on both deformation rate and temperature (*Diogo* et al., 1987).

The linear viscoelastic behavior of poly-2,6-dimethyl-phenyleneether (PPE) blended with 65 wt% of high impact polystyrene (HIPS) were studied by *Schmidt* (1979). The time-temperature superposition was obtained for the blend as well as for PPE and HIPS. However, $a_T$ plotted according to WLF Eq (3.201) required significantly different constants than the universal values. From the G'' plateau level, $G_p''$, the entanglement molecular weight was calculated (*Marvin*, 1960):

$$M_e = 0.32\varrho RT/G_p''$$

(3.205)

as 9.1, 20.7 and 30.1 kg/mol for PPE, the blend and HIPS, respectively. It was evident that in a similar manner as for polymethylmethacrylate/polyvinylidenefluoride NDB-miscible blends (*Wu*, 1987) also for PPE/HIPS, the entanglement molecular weight of blend is higher than could be expected on the basis of homopolymer $M_e$-values (see Part 3.4.1). However, it should be noted that $M_e$ from Eq (3.205) was calculated assuming melt density to be the same for all three systems, $\varrho \simeq 1000 \, kg/m^3$. The decrease of G'' by 9% below its average value may not be caused by a decrease of $M_e$ but rather that of $\varrho$.

Polystyrene/polyethylene (PS/PE) blends have been extensively studied either as a model of immiscible blends or for the purpose of development of economic method for plastics scrap recycling (*Frederix* et al., 1981). The steady state shear flow invariably led to shear segregation of phases and irreproducible results. The dynamic-oscillatory tests were reproducible, indicating the presence of the apparent yield stress – evidence of an interactive morphology. It seems that the concentration at which the yield stress was the largest depended on the method of sample preparation. This meant that morphology of the blends was not at equilibrium. The structure imposed by compounding was stabilized by the slow diffusion rate. This may explain why in spite of the apparent yield stress it was possible to construct time-temperature master curves. The more recent reports on dynamic flow of these materials are:

I. *Bolotnikova* et al. (1982) studied PS/PE blends at T = 150 to 220 °C. For $\lambda = \eta(PE)/\eta(PS) \simeq 0.7$ the maximum yield stress was observed at about 30 wt% of PE. The isothermal data followed the time-temperature master curves.

II. For $\lambda = \eta(PS)/\eta(PE) \simeq 45$ the maximum value of $\sigma_y$ was observed for about 20 wt% of PS (*Edel*, 1984). At the other end of the concentration scale, i.e. w = 20 wt% of PE, where $\lambda = 1/45$, only a small $\sigma_y$ could be deduced from the Cole-Cole plot. Again the data could be superimposed on a time-temperature master curve.

III. As a part of IUPAC Working Party 4.2.1 efforts the PS/PE blends have been studied (*Sammut* and *Utracki*, 1986a; *Utracki* and *Sammut*, 1988). Blends with and without hydrogenated poly(styrene-b-isoprene) di-block copolymer (SEB) were measured. The basic blend components were selected to secure $\lambda \simeq 1$ at high rates of shear expected during the blending. In dynamic tests at the stress levels, G'' = 1 to 10 kPa, $\lambda \simeq 0.3$ to 0.5 was determined for PS as the minor component. The low strain, $\gamma = 4\%$, data were reproducible within $\pm 2\%$. The apparent yield stress at low frequencies was the largest for sample containing w $\simeq 33$ wt% of PS. Addition of SEB (5 wt%) reduced this effect. The plot of G' vs. composition at G'' = 1 kPa indicated maximal PDB behavior at about 30 wt% of PS for samples with and without the block copolymer (Fig. 3.36).

The dynamic flow behavior of polymethylmethacrylate (PMMA) with polyethylene (PE) were studied by *Martinez* and *Williams* (1980). At the testing temperature T = 160 °C the viscosity ratio $\lambda_0 = \eta_0(PMMA)/\eta_0(PE) \simeq 5.9$ with $\eta(PMMA) > \eta(PE)$ in full range of $\dot{\gamma}$ and $\omega$. The plots of $\eta'$ vs. $\omega$ were quite regular without any evidence of flow induced morphological change within $\omega = 10^{-3}$ to 10. The zero shear viscosity vs. composition dependence showed small PDB behavior with a maximum at $\phi = 0.9$ of PMMA. The steady state rotational shearing provided different information. Invariably at $\dot{\gamma} \simeq 1 \, s^{-1}$ a sudden drop of $\eta$ was observed interpreted by the authors as due to "elastic instability" and loss of sample. At low limits, $\phi \leq 0.1$ of PMMA or PE, Einstein's Eq (3.96) with $\beta = 1$ and $\alpha = [\eta]_E$ calculated from Eq (3.118) provided a good approximation. This indicated that the emulsion model was valid and that the dispersed phase existed in a droplet form. The latter finding was verified by scanning electron microscopy. SEM also demonstrated that during high frequency tests the morphology changed only slightly.

Blends of PMMA with polyvinyldenefluoride (PVDF) or with polystyrene (PS) were analyzed by *Chuang* and *Han* (1984); the first blend was miscible, the second immiscible. For miscible systems: (i) $N_1(\sigma_{12}) \simeq 2G'(G'')$, independent of temperature; (ii) $\eta \simeq \eta'$ at low

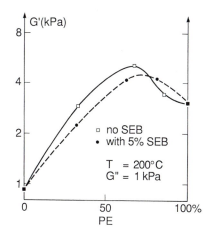

Fig. 3.36 Storage modulus vs. low density polyethylene content in its blend with polystyrene. Data at 4% strain, 200 °C and constant value of loss modulus G″ = 1kPa. The effect of 5 wt% block copolymer poly(styrene-b-3-butenemethyl-2) as compatibilizer is illustrated (*Sammut* and *Utracki, 1986a*).

deformation rates $\dot{\gamma} = \omega \leq 0.1$; and (iii) $\eta_0$ vs. composition showed NDB behavior. For immiscible blend: (i) for 30/70 ≤ PS/PMMA ≤ 70/30 at $\dot{\gamma} \simeq 0.2s^{-1}$ the flow curves indicated change of melt structure ; (ii) with the exception of 10/90 composition the plot of $N_1(\sigma_{12}) \simeq$ $2G'(G'')$ for all other samples at $\dot{\gamma} = \omega > 0.2$ was independent of T; (iii) shearing at $\dot{\gamma} = 2.7s^{-1}$ resulted in a severe change of morphology. For PS/PMMA = 10/90 or 90/10 an elongation or redispersion of droplets was obtained, for 30/70 ≤ PS/PMMA ≤ 70/30 the droplets were transformed into a co-continuous structure. Since $\lambda_0 = \eta_0(PS)/\eta_0(PMMA) \simeq$ 1.3 the extension of droplet was significantly higher for 90/10 than for 10/90 composition; (iv) the rheological behavior at low deformation rates in steady state and dynamic shear was quite different; (v) $\eta_0$ vs. composition showed PDB behavior with maximum at about 40/60.

Blends of bis-phenol-A polycarbonate (PC) have been frequently studied. Since PC can readily be quenched into amorphous state its blends with polystyrene (PS) are particularly attractive models. Not only the absence of crystallinity but also 40 °C difference in $T_g$, a difference in solubility and/or stainability, presence of $\pi - \pi$ interactions, etc., make them useful PAB paradigms. *Lipatov* et al. (1981) reported results of the dynamic shear measurements of 15 PS/PC solvent-cast compositions at three temperatures. Plots of $\eta_0$, $G'(\omega = 0.1)$ and $G''(\omega = 0.1)$ vs. PC content were similar, NDB-type. Three minima were observed at, 0.5, 10 and 99.5 wt%, and three local maxima at 5, 50 and 95 wt% of PC. The initial decrease of values of the rheological function upon addition of a small amount of the second component is evidence of miscibility at w ≤ 0.5%. The subsequent increase of the signal toward local maximum at w ≃ 10 (or 90) wt% indicates phase separation with increasing concentration of the dispersed phase. The strong NDB behavior at 10 ≤ wt% ≤ 90 may originate from the interlayer slip; note that at high frequency G'vs. composition reaches a local minimum of 50/50, in spite of the fact that the low frequency G' and G″ as well as $\eta_0$ go through a local maximum at this very composition (the latter observation is usually ascribed to a co-continuous structure). For all compositions at T = 180 to 260 °C the time-temperature master curves were obtained with $a_T$ following the WLF-type dependence. However, $\eta'/\eta_0$ vs. $\omega a_T$ was found to vary with composition.

*Bye* and *Miles* (1986) complemented the above information with measurements of the dynamic flow of PS/PC samples containing w ≤ 10% PC. The samples were prepared by three methods: (i) solvent casting at T = 90 °C, (ii) solvent casting in increasing T ≤ 110 °C, and (iii) melt blending at 200 °C. The low frequency data indicated increasing value of

$\eta'(\omega \leqslant 1)$ from (i) to (iii). Plot of $\eta_0$ vs. composition for blends (i) showed NDB, for blends (ii) near log-additivity and (iii) PDB. The authors reported that samples (i), dried to constant weight at $T < T_g$, contained entrapped solvent. The difference in the rheological behavior between (ii) and (iii) could be due to morphological differences.

An implication resulting from *Bye* and *Miles'* (1986) work was that the results found by *Lipatov* et al. (1981) may be affected by incomplete removal of solvent by vacuum drying at 20 °C, well below $T_g$ of PS or that of PC (105 and 140 °C, respectively). This may explain the different behavior reported for PS/PC system by these authors and by others, e.g. *Wisniewsky* et al (1985). However, even if this criticism is valid it does not detract from the general validity of *Lipatov*'s et al. data. Addition of a processing aid, low molecular weight antioxidant, stabilizer, etc. may have even more drastic effect on the flow behavior of an immiscible blend. In the author's laboratory, blends prepared from two batches of commercial polyethylene showed widely different rheological behavior at lower temperatures but identical at $T \geqslant 190$ °C. The cause was found to be a slightly different level of processing aid in the two PE batches. At lower temperatures the excess of processing aid phase separated, which led to die and interlayer slip, but at $T > 190$ °C that excess was absorbed by PE and blends regained the behavior observed for the original compositions prepared with the first batch of polyethylene.

There are many examples in the literature where blends prepared from the same type of polymer behave differently. Knowing how sensitive is the phase behavior to variation of temperature, composition, molecular weight, molecular weight distribution, type of deformational flow, etc., this is hardly surprising. The aim of the polymer blend scientist or engineer is first to understand, to correctly interpret the observed behavior, then to modify it for the maximum performance. Learning by rote is always dangerous, but particularly so in case of PAB science and technology.

The immiscible blends of polycarbonate with linear low density polyethylene (PC/LLDPE) were selected as a model system for international cooperative program of the VAMAS – Technical Working Party on Polymer Blends. The samples were prepared by melt blending, then extruded into sheets from which the rheological specimens were cut out. The dynamic flow results were found to be highly reproducible, leading to consistent results in the laboratories of seven cooperating countries. By contrast, the capillary flow data were very difficult to determine and results from different laboratories widely differed. This led to recommendation against the use of steady state flow as a method of immiscible blend characterization (*Kwok*, 1987). At frequencies $\omega < 5$ rads/s the yield stress was evident especially for PC/LLDPE = 25/75 and 50/50; setting F = G' or G'' in Eq (3.34) the apparent yield values for these two compositions were calculated as: $G'_y = 68$ and 202 Pa whereas $G''_y = 212$ and 90 Pa, respectively (*Sammut* and *Utracki*, 1986b). Plots G', G'' vs. $\omega$ are shown in Fig. 3.37 and 3.38. The Cole-Cole plot (Fig. 3.39) also clearly indicated an apparent yield stress. As a result of the extrusion/calendering process the LLDPE/PC samples had fibrillar morphology (*Utracki* et al., 1987). In capillary flow the morphology was quite different; SEM showed a significant degree of flow induced change of structure. The effects of morphological changes on the flow behavior are presented in Fig. 3.40, where constant stress $\eta'(G'' = \text{const.})$ and $\eta(\sigma_{12} = \text{const.})$ are plotted vs. PC content (*Utracki* and *Sammut*, 1987). In addition at $\sigma_{12} \simeq 10^5$Pa slip-type instabilities in capillary flow were observed.

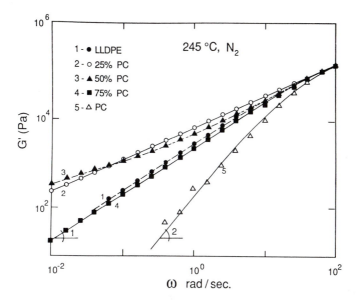

Fig. 3.37 Storage shear modulus vs. frequency at 245 °C for linear low density/polycarbonate blends (*Sammut* and *Utracki*, 1986b).

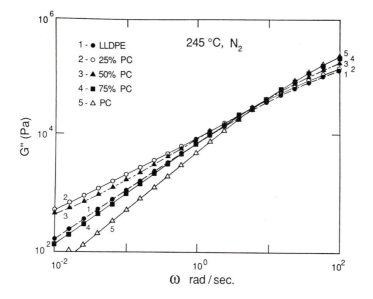

Fig. 3.38 Loss shear modulus vs. frequency for linear low density polyethylene/polycarbonate blends at 245 °C (*Sammut* and *Utracki*, 1986b).

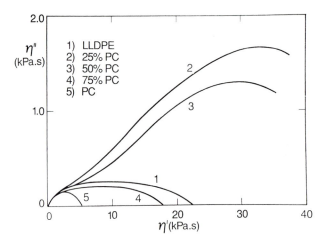

Fig. 3.39 Cole-Cole plot of $\eta''$ vs. $\eta'$ for linear low density polyethylene/polycarbonate blends at 245 °C (*Sammut* and *Utracki,* 1986b).

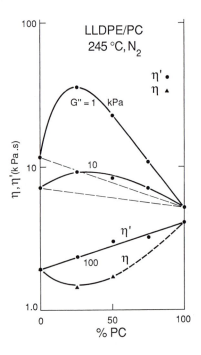

Fig. 3.40 Compositional dependence of constant stress dynamic and steady state viscosity of linear low density polyethylene/polycarbonate blends at 245 °C (*Sammut* and *Utracki,* 1986b).

# 3.7   Polyolefin Blends

The consumer market share of polyolefin resin is about 47% in Canada and 44% or about 9Mt per annum world-wide. To these polymers belong: polypropylene (PP) and a variety of polyethylenes (PE): ultra low density PE, $\varrho \simeq 885$ kg/m$^3$ (ULDPE), very low density PE, $\varrho \leq 910$ (VLDPE), low density (high pressure) PE, $\varrho \leq 920 \pm 10$ (LDPE), linear low density (copolymer) PE, $\varrho \simeq 920 \pm 10$ (LLDPE), and high density (low pressure) PE, $\varrho = 960 \pm 20$ kg/m$^3$ (HDPE) (*Allen,* 1987; *Utracki,* 1989). It is estimated that 60 to 70% of LLDPE enters the market as blends, primarily with other member of the polyolefin family, e.g. LDPE or PP. The blending may be mechanical using two commercial products, but equally well it may be in a reactor, merging two streams of LLDPE in solution/ suspension process using multi-site catalyst or changing the feedstock during the fluidized bed polymerization. Thousands of PE grades are being made to satisfy the growing variety of applications. In addition, there is an increasing tendency for post-reaction modification of PE's by blending, orientation, reactive processing, etc. From the molecular characteristic point of view all the diversity of PE-grades is due to a combination of four basic parameters: (i) molecular weight, MW, varying from about 1 (waxes) to over $10^4$ kg/mol (UHMWPE); (ii) molecular weight distribution, $M_w/M_n$ = 2 to 50, where $M_w$ and $M_n$ represent the weight and number average molecular weight, respectively; (iii) short chain branching (SCB), introduced either by a method of polymerization, type of catalyst and/or co-monomer type; and (iv) long chain branching (LCB), controlled primarily by the method of polymerization.

Linear low density polyethylene (LLDPE), was invented and commercialized in the late 1950's by DuPont-Canada. Its potential was not adequately explored until 1977 when the aggressively marketed Unipol process was announced. Due to severe market pressures, during the last years there have been a number of changes in the process, resulting in a variety of "new" LLDPE commercial grades. It has been found that a catalyst can modify the MWD, and that changing from one co-monomer to another (e.g. from butene to hexene) has a profound effect on the mechanical properties of the finished product. The combination of catalyst and feedstock composition allows for a binary control of MWD as well as of the composition of the growing macromolecules.

The temperature rising elution fractionation (TREF) maps the polyolefin sample as a function of molecular weight and copolymer content (*Wild* et al., 1982). An example is shown in Fig. 3.41. However, the main value of TREF may be in its ability to analyze and control polyolefin blends composition (*Kelusky* et al., 1987). Other methods of analysis were described by *Utracki* and *Schlund* (1987a).

The dynamic and steady state data were compared (*Schlund* and *Utracki,* 1987a). The instability in steady state capillary flow were also discussed (*Utracki* and *Dumoulin,* 1984; *Utracki* and *Gendron,* 1984). The influence of rheology on the extrusion of PE's has been considered by *Utracki* et al. (1984), *Utracki* and *Catani* (1985) and *Catani* and *Utracki* (1986). The extensional flow properties were found to be important in the die flow and essential for film blowing or blow molding (*Schlund* and *Utracki,* 1987b). The rheology of polyolefin blends has been reviewed by *Plochocki* (1978, 1982, 1986) and by *Utracki* (1984, 1985, 1989).

The polyolefin blends will be discussed under three subtitles: polyethylene/ polyethylene blends, polyethylene/polypropylene blends, and other polyolefin blends. While the main emphasis will be placed on the dynamic shear flow behavior, the steady state shear flow will also be discussed. As a result this part may be considered an introduction to Part 3.8 which deals specifically with the steady state shear flow. The extensional flow behavior of PAB, including the polyolefin blends, will be discussed in Part 3.9.

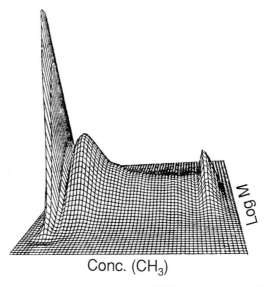

Conc. (CH₃)

Fig. 3.41 Temperature-rising elution fractionation (TREF). A typical three dimensional map: signal intensity vs. concentration of methyls and molecular weight for gas-phase linear low density polyethylene polymerized with Ti-based catalyst (courtesy BP).

### 3.7.1   Polyethylene/Polyethylene Blends

Blends of HDPE/HDPE and LDPE/LDPE are miscible and the constant shear stress viscosity vs. composition follows the log-additivity rule (*Dobrescu*, 1980; *Chuang* and *Han*, 1984). Due to the diversity of composition, molecular structure, molecular weight and distribution of molecular weights the LLDPE/LLDPE blends may or may not be miscible. For example, blend of two high molecular weight LLDPE's, a copolymer of butene prepared on titanium-based catalyst and the other a copolymer of hexene polymerized on vanadium based catalyst were found to be immiscible (*Utracki,* 1985c). On the other hand a very similar blend containing polymers of lower molecular weights was found to be miscible (*Utracki and Schlund,* 1987b). Both sets of blends were prepared in the same manner and tested under analogous conditions. In the first case the $\eta'(G'' = $ const.) vs. composition dependence followed a third order polynomial with local maximum and minimum at w $\simeq$ 25 and 75% of the hexene-copolymer, i.e. it showed a PNDB behavior. On the other hand for the second blend the log-additivity was observed (see Fig. 3.42).

Blends of two HDPE's of nearly identical density but with molecular weights differing by a factor of ten ($M_w$ = 280 and 2,800 kg/mol) were found to be only partially miscible (*Dumoulin* et al., 1984). The reason may be related to the slow dissolution rate of the ultra high molecular weight component (UHMWPE) rather than to the true equilibrium thermodynamic immiscibility. The blends behaved as a solution of two polymers containing suspended particles of undissolved high molecular weight component. The Cole-Cole plot was regular, without indication of yield stress or second relaxation mechanism. In a recent paper (*Vadhar* and *Kyu,* 1987) three methods of blending UHMWPE with LLDPE were used: "A" mechanical mixing of simultaneously loaded polymers, "B" mechanical mixing of LLDPE added to premelted UHMWPE, and "S" solvent mixed. The rheological [$\eta(\dot\gamma = $ const.) vs. w plot], crystallinity ($T_m$ vs. w, or lattice spacing vs. w) as well as mechanical test data indicated that only blends "A" were immiscible; miscibility and cocrystallinity were

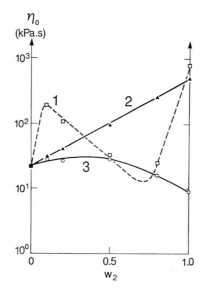

Fig. 3.42 Compositional dependence of the zero-shear viscosity for blends of a linear low density polyethylene (LLDPE) with: (1) and (2) different LLDPE resins, and (3) with low density polyethylene, LDPE.

claimed for "B" and "S". The rheological data were limited to capillary flow studied in a limited range of $1 < \dot{\gamma}_A < 30$. It is worth recalling that *Ree* (1987) from SANS also concluded miscibility of UHMWPE blended in solution with HDPE or LLDPE.

In the work on UHMWPE/HDPE (*Dumoulin* et al., 1984) the dynamic cross-point, defined as:

$$G_x(\omega_x) \equiv G'(\omega) = G''(\omega) \tag{3.206}$$

was found to be a sensitive measure of miscibility. Empirically, for polypropylenes, PP, *Zeichner* and *Patel* (1981) observed that $G_x$ and $\omega_x$ are inversely proportional, respectively, to polydispersity and molecular weight. It should be noted that the condition expressed in Eq (3.206) implies that $\omega\tau_p = 1$ or $\omega\tau = 1$ in Eqs (3.49)–(3.50) or Eqs (3.57)–(3.58) respectively. For a simple relaxation time, $p = 1$, the Rouse theory (see Eqs (3.49) and (3.52)) gives:

$$G'(\omega) = 6\eta_0\omega^2\tau_1/\pi^2[1 + (\omega\tau_1)^2] \tag{3.207}$$

whereas from the Maxwell model with single relaxation time:

$$G'(\omega) = \eta_0\omega^2\tau_1/[1 + (\omega\tau_1)^2] \tag{3.208}$$

Substituting the condition for the dynamic cross-point into these relations leads to:

$$G_x = A\eta_{0M}\omega_x \tag{3.209}$$

where $\eta_{0M}$ is the zero shear rate Maxwellian viscosity and the numerical constant $A = 3/\pi^2 \simeq 0.30$ and $A = 1/2$ for Rouse and single relaxation time Maxwell models, respectively. The Rouse model indicates that $A$ should increase with broadening of the relaxation spectrum. From Eqs (3.49)–(3.52) $A = 0.35$ can be calculated for $p \to \infty$. In Fig. 3.43 $\eta_{0M}$ calculated for LLDPE's and PE-blends from the cross-plot coordinates (using Eq (3.209) with $A = 1/2$) are plotted as function of experimental $\eta_0$. Surprisingly there is a good correlation for samples with $\eta_0 \leqslant 50$ kPa · s (*Utracki* and *Schlund,* 1987b). Similar results were found for polypropy-

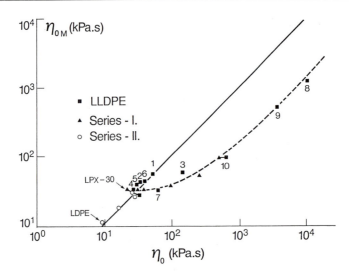

Fig. 3.43 Maxwellian zero-shear viscosity, $\eta_{0M}$, computed from cross-point coordinates vs. measured zero shear viscosity, $\eta_0$, for linear low density polyethylene, LLDPE, blends: Series-I (immiscible) and II (miscible) as well as for neat LLDPE resins (*Utracki* and *Schlund*, 1987b).

lene and its blends with PE (*Dumoulin* et al., 1986; *Dumoulin*, 1988). It can be seen that the Rouse theory prediction of an increase of A with broadening of the relaxation spectrum is correct, but the numerical value computed from Eq (3.52) is too small. To describe the data in Fig. 3.43 A should increase by a factor of seven, not 1.17. To accomplish that $p^2$ in Eq (3.52) should be replaced by $p^{2/\pi}$. Another interesting observation is that broadening of the spectrum should occur at $\eta_0 \simeq 50$ kPa $\cdot$ s, or at $M_w \simeq 450$, i. e. far above the entanglement molecular weight $M_e(PE) = 1.29$ kg/mol (*Utracki* and *Schlund*, 1987a). There is no explanation for this.

HDPE/LDPE blends of different molecular weight of the components were studied using a capillary rheometer (*Dobrescu*, 1980). In most cases the $\eta$ (at $\sigma_{12} = 30$kPa) vs. composition plot showed a positive deviation from the log-additivity rule (PDB-behavior). In general, the higher the viscosity ratio, the larger the PDB, which may indicate a decreasing miscibility. *Kammer* and *Socher* (1982) studied HDPE/LDPE blends in a cone-and-plate rotational rheometer. Plots of $\eta_0$, $\psi_0$ and $\tau$ vs. composition all indicated PDB. Immiscibility has been postulated. More recent works on these blends (*Curto* et al., 1983; *LaMantia* et al., 1984) indicated good superposition of capillary flow data for a series of HDPE/LDPE blends at T = 160 to 200 °C when plotted as:

$$\eta(\dot\gamma)/\eta_0 = f(\dot\gamma\tau) \tag{3.210}$$

Where according to Eq (3.52) $\tau \simeq \tau_1 \propto \eta_0/T$. The dependencies: $\eta_0$ or $\eta(\sigma_{12} = $ const.) vs. $\phi$ as well as the extrudate swell $B(\sigma_{12} = $ const.) vs. $\phi$ indicated PDB. In conclusion, in the absence of direct evidence, one may postulate that HDPE/LDPE blends are immiscible, but with either fine and/or stable morphology they may generate a time-temperature master curve in agreement with Eq (3.210).

The newest and most important commercial blends of the PE family are those of LLDPE/LDPE type (*Speed*, 1982; *Nancekivell*, 1985). The capillary viscosity and extrudate swell at $\sigma_{12} = $ const. showed similar PBD dependence on $\phi$ as that observed for HDPE/LDPE blends (*Acierno* et al., 1986; *LaMantia* et al., 1986; *Ghijsels* et al., 1988). Detailed rheological studies on LLDPE with another LLDPE or with LDPE were reported by *Utracki* and

*Schlund* (1987b). Several rheological functions including the frequency relaxation spectrum [$\bar{H}_G$, see Eq (3.62) to (3.67)] indicated that while the LLDPE/LLDPE blends are miscible LLDPE/LDPE ones are not. In spite of that Eq (3.62) provided an excellent description of $\eta'$ vs. $\omega$ dependence, allowing computation of $\bar{H}_G$ and subsequent calculations of several linear viscoelastic functions, viz. Figs. 3.8 and 3.34. The capillary flow data for single phase melts when corrected for the pressure effects lead to good agreement $\eta(\dot{\gamma}) = \eta'(\omega)$; for immiscible systems the correlation was less satisfactory. Furthermore, for single phase systems plot of $\eta_0$ vs. $M_a$ [see Eqs (3.86) to (3.88) and (3.194) to (3.196)] followed the homopolymer dependence, whereas that for LLDPE/LDPE blends did not. The main reason for addition of LDPE to LLDPE is modification of its extensional flow behavior, which in turn leads to amelioration of productivity of e.g. film blowing or wire coating, lines. This subject will be discussed in Part 3.9.

Effective blending can also be achieved by peroxide treatment of LLDPE. In one of the more recent patents (*Cordonnier* and *Kuhlburger*, 1985) LLDPE powder from a fluidized bed reactor was mixed with peroxide solution and extruded in a twin screw extruder. The peroxide caused formation of macromolecules with long branches resembling LDPE. During the reactive extrusion these were efficiently blended into the remaining non modified LLDPE. The treatment did not affect either the density or the gel content, but increased the degree of branching as well as the polydispersity. The shear and elongational viscosity were higher resulting in improved processability.

### 3.7.2  Polyethylene/Isotactic Polypropylene Blends

There is extensive literature on the subject (*Plochocki*, 1978; *Deanin* and *d'Isidoro*, 1980; *Utracki*, 1989). One of the reasons for addition of polyethylene to polypropylene is improvement of its low temperature impact and environmental stress cracking properties. Due to immiscibility, in order to enhance the ultimate properties, frequently a compatibilizer has to be used; e.g. in HDPE/PP blends 5% of ethylene-propylene rubber (EPR) was found necessary to ascertain linearity between the tensile impact strength and HDPE content (*Ho* and *Salovey*, 1981; *Bartlett* et al., 1982).

The melt flow of HDPE/PP blends was studied by *Alle* and *Lyngaae-Jorgensen* (1980) and *Alle* et al. (1981). The capillary viscosities at T = 180 to 210 °C plotted according to Eq (3.207) superimposed on time-temperature master curves with $\eta_0$ following the Arrhenius dependence (3.202). The plot of $\eta(\sigma_{12} = \text{const.})$ vs. $\eta$ indicated NDB behavior. To interpret these result the authors assumed that the difference originated in the viscosity ratio, $\lambda$. For $\lambda > 1$ the fibrils formed at the entrance to capillary were preserved in the fully developed flow region. For $\lambda < 1$ the elongated, low viscosity droplets either broke-up into smaller ones or re-formed into nearly spherical inclusions. For the first case the authors derived:

$$\eta(\sigma_{12}^0) = [\Sigma\phi_i/\eta_i(\sigma_{12}^0)]^{-1} \tag{3.211}$$

with $\sigma_{12}^0$ = constant. Eq (3.211) resembles Eq (3.167) in which $\beta_1 = 1$ was substituted and $w_i$ was replaced by $\phi_i$. In the second case the log-additivity was assumed. For $w_{PE} \geqslant 0.5$ Eq (3.211) was used; the additivity rule was assumed for $w_{PE} < 0.5$. Good agreement with the experimental data was obtained. However, the extrudate swell, B, indicated rather unusual behavior. While for homopolymers and blend containing 75 wt%PP (the higher viscosity polymer) the plot B vs. $\sigma_{12}$ was independent of T, that of 50 and 25%PP blends was highly temperature sensitive, indicating that the morphology of the latter blends changed with T. At low strain values the dispersed low viscosity PE phase was preferentially deformed, causing the extrudate swell to be nearly as large as that for pure PE. As the stress increased straining of both phases occured, causing an average response. In samples where PE is a continuous phase the swelling decreased with T as the interlayer slip became more important lowering the polymer viscosity.

Blends of PP/LDPE with approximately equal shear viscosities were investigated in capillary flow by *Santamaria* et al. (1985). The most dramatic was the shrinkage effect. For these measurements, the extrudate was quenched then placed in a silicone oil bath at 180 °C and allowed to relax for a period of about 1 hr. The Hencky strain was defined as:

$$\varepsilon = \ln(L_0/L_t) \tag{3.212}$$

where $L_0$ and $L_t$ indicate the initial length of the specimen and at time t, respectively. For t $\rightarrow \infty$ the dependence is illustrated in Fig. 3.44. Assuming that the shrinkage (due to residual stresses and to the oil-polymer interfacial tension) transforms a cylinder into a sphere, the terminal shrinkage strain can be expressed as:

$$\varepsilon(\infty) = -0.4055 + 2 \ln D/d \tag{3.213}$$

where d and D represent the diameter of cylinder and sphere respectively. Eq (3.213) indicates that the terminal shrinkage strain $\varepsilon(\infty)$ depends on the initial aspect ratio, p = L/d. In short, the data in Fig. 3.44 must be considered as indication of a relative magnitude of relaxed residual stresses: $\varepsilon(\infty) \leqslant 0.5$ for homopolymers and $\varepsilon(\infty) \simeq 3$ for 50/50 blend. Apparently, the co-continuous fibrillar morphology with weak interfacial interaction results in the largest shrinkage or in other words in the largest extrudate swell.

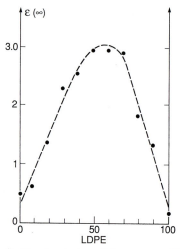

Fig. 3.44 Extrudate shrinkage (in Hencky strain units) vs. composition of polypropylene/low density polyethylene blends (*Santamaria* et al., 1985).

The LLDPE/PP systems have been discussed in more recent literature (*Dumoulin* et al., 1984, 1986; *Dumoulin*, 1988; *Tree* and *McHugh*, 1988). In the first paper a good correlation between dynamic and capillary viscosity, $\eta' \simeq \eta(ICR)$, was reported for 50/50 blends with and without the compatibilizing ethylene-propylene-ethylene block copolymer (EP). Addition of EP enhanced stability of flow and led to a Pe vs. $\sigma_{12}$ plot (Pe is the Bagley entrance-exit pressure drop correction) which was independent of the die diameter, i.e. indicating zero slip velocity. The Cole-Cole plot was regular, without any sign of either bimodality in the relaxation spectrum or the yield stress. The plot of $G_x$ vs. $\omega_x$ was linear, in accord with Eq (3.209). The most interesting aspect of that work was an observation that addition of compatibilizer was not needed; the 50/50 blends had high initial modulus and good ductility even at − 40 °C.

In the second more detailed analysis, (*Dumoulin* et al., 1986; *Dumoulin,* 1988) PP was blended with two LLDPE's, one having lower the other higher $\eta_0$ than that of PP. For both systems $\eta_0$ vs. $\phi$ plot indicated a local minimum for 95 wt% of PP. The plot of $\eta_{0M}$ vs. $\eta_0$ (see Eq (3.209)) was similar to that observed for LLDPE blends (*Utracki* and *Schlund,* 1987). The dynamic viscosity, $\eta'$ vs. $\omega$, was well described by relation (3.62). Consequently the parameters of reduced frequency relaxation spectrum ($\tilde{H}_{G,max}$, $\omega_{max}$) were determined, from which the limits of miscibility were estimated.

### 3.7.3 Other Polyolefin Blends

Addition of a small amount of polyolefin improves the processability and impact properties of engineering resins (*Utracki,* 1987a, b). The optimum performance is usually reached at 2 to 4 wt% level although in patent literature, up to 20 wt% is frequently claimed (*Rosenquist,* 1982). Polyolefins have also been used to "extend" the performance of more expensive polymers (*Sadova* et al., 1977; *Danesi* and *Porter,* 1978; *Akhtar* et al., 1987). However, of particular interest are blends in which polyolefin is the major component, modified by addition of another more expensive resin.

To this category belong the polyolefin blends with enhanced barrier properties. In particular addition of poly(ethylene-co-vinylalcohol), polyamides, polyvinylchloride or polyvinylidene chloride is well known in the industry. These blends are immiscible, although a degree of compatibilization is required. The immiscibility is precisely the reason for selecting the ingredients; if the blends were miscible only additive permeability could be expected. Since they are immiscible, the flow imposed morphology may generate overlapping lamellae creating surprisingly high barrier properties. This principle led to the development of proprietary DuPont technology where the custom tailored mixture of a polyamide with usually ionomeric compatibilizer is added to a polyolefin resin, blended and then blow molded into bottles or drums with high barrier properties. It is interesting to note that here not so much a product but rather the rheological/engineering know-how is being marketed. Depending on the customer's resin, processing equipment and product requirements a different mixture can be formulated and introduced at different concentration level (usually up to 20 wt%). Biaxial stretching of polyamide drops, dispersed in the polyolefin matrix and bound to it by appropriate compatibilizer is responsible for creating a multilayer overlapping lamellae, significantly reducing the oxygen and/or solvent permeability. The size of polyamide drops and the resulting lamellae thickness can be controlled by the amount of compatibilizer (*Willis* and *Favis,* 1988).

Permeability is a product of solubility of the penetrant and its diffusion through the barrier material; reduction of solubility or increase of the diffusion path (tortuosity) caused by the lamellar blend structure can decrease permeability. The semi-crystalline nature of both polyethylenes and polyamides also affects the barrier properties; the best pair was found to be the high density polyethylene, HDPE, blended with poly-$\varepsilon$-caprolactam, PA-6 (*Kamal* et al., 1984). The flow behavior and the flow-imposed morphologies in the HDPE/PA-6 system were studied by *Dumoulin* et al. (1985) and by *Utracki* et al. (1986). In these works compatibilizer was not used. The initial excellent superposition of dynamic and capillary flow data obtained for HDPE disappeared upon addition of PA-6. The dynamic data were highly reproducible and measurements at T = 150 to 250 °C could be superimposed on a time-temperature master curve. However, since $T_m(PA-6) = 219$ °C, the $a_T$ versus T plot did not follow any simple relation. Scanning electron micrography demonstrated that HDPE/PA-6 sample morphology was not affected by a low strain dynamic test.

In capillary flow the relative viscosity at 150 °C increased with PA-6 concentration according to Eq (3.95) whereas at 250 °C it decreased following the interlayer slip relation

(3.166). A similar dependence was also observed for polypropylene/PA-6 at 270 °C (*Haya-shida* and *Yoshida*, 1979). The melt fracture was observed at shear stress $\sigma_{12} \simeq 500$ kPa. Five different flow-induced morphological changes were reported (*Utracki* et al., 1986): (i) A shear-induced segregation of polymer domains, related to encapsulation in flow. At lower temperatures the high viscosity PA-6 migrated to the center of the extrudate, at 250 °C the lower viscosity PA-6 was found to concentrate on the outside of the strand. (ii) Dynamic dispersion/coalescence. For low concentration of disperse phases, it was observed that the average diameter of droplets decreased with $\sigma_{12}$ from its value in pre-blend. These dimensions were *not* related to equilibrium conditions determined by the thermodynamic interactions. (iii) The shear-induced interlayer slip responsible for a decrease of $\eta$ with increase of PA-6 concentration according with Eq. (3.166). (iv) Fibrillation. Formation of fibres is expected if $\lambda_E < 1$ (*Han*, 1981). However, PA-6 fibrillas were formed (see Fig. 3.45) at 150 °C, i.e. 69 °C below the melting point when $\lambda_E \gg 1$. As it was indicated before, $\lambda_E$ intervenes directly in the expression for drop formation, Eq (3.180), through the ratio: $1 \leqslant (19\lambda_E + 16)/(16\lambda_E + 16) \leqslant 19/16$, or in other words, $\varepsilon(t) \propto (\sigma_{11}d/v)I(t)$. When the extensional stress is sufficiently large and the residence time in the extensional field long enough, the drops will deform even if $\lambda_E \gg 1$. The fibrillation of PA-6 in HDPE at 150 °C took place because the extensional stress in the die entry zone, $\sigma_{11} = 50$ to 800 kPa, was larger than the tensile yield stress for plastic deformation of PA-6 at 150 °C, $\sigma \simeq 15$ kPa. The aspect ratio of PA-6 fibrillas developed at 150 °C was large, in excess of 1000. A knowledge of the average dimension of drops above the die and these of fibres in the extrudate led to the conclusion that the fibrillation was accompanied by drop coalescence. The coalescence of "solid" polyamides under the influence of an extensional field was the fifth observed flow induced morphological change.

To summarize, the dynamic flow measurements were found not to affect HDPE/PA-6 morphology, whereas the steady state flow through a capillary generated diverse structures, dependent on the flow conditions. These structures were different from the lamellar morphology expected in biaxial stretching of blends during e.g. blow molding operation. Complex morphologies of polypropylene/PA-6 have been also reported by *Liang* et al. (1983).

Further discussion of the flow-induced morphology will continue in Part 3.10. Here, it is appropriate to stress the non-intervening (in morphology) nature of the low strain, low frequency dynamic testing. As was the case for unstabilized low frequency emulsions, the morphology of an unstable blend may change during dynamic scans, but the change would originate in the thermodynamics, seldom in the rheological forces (although in such a case it may affect them). Recently a deformation of PS drops in an LDPE matrix during dynamic testing in a parallel plate geometry was reported (*Utracki* and *Sammut*, 1988). The deformation occured only at the highest frequencies, $\omega > 10$ rad/s, within a narrow annulus near the specimen edge. In spite of this the total signal, $G'$ and $G''$, was stable. The coalescence had the character of a critical phenomenon; at frequencies below a certain value the morphology remained stable even after a much longer test time. Similar behavior was also observed for polycarbonate/LLDPE blends.

In conclusion, dynamic response provides the best measure of the rheology of multiphase materials (including blends or composites) without artifacts of the flow-induced morphological changes dominant in the steady state flow. However, if the blend is well compatibilized and stable, with the average drop $d \leqslant 1$ $\mu$m, the morphology may not be seriously affected by flow within the low range of shear stresses. In that case the rheological responses in dynamic and steady state shear field are consistent, similar to those reported for neat polymers.

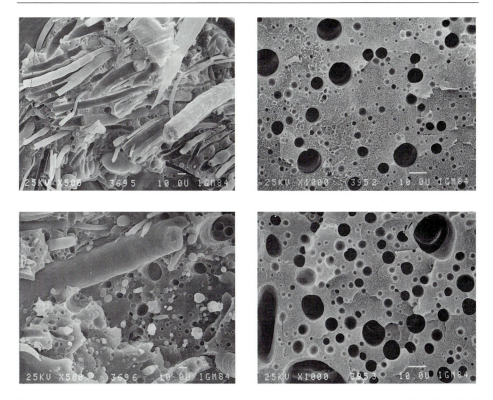

Fig. 3.45 Scanning electron micrograph of high density polyethylene with 30 wt% polyamide-6 extruded at: (1) T = 150 or (2) T = 250 °C. Micrographs: A – center, B – edge of the extrudate (*Utracki* et al., 1986).

## 3.8   Steady State Shear Flow

Steady state shear flow predominates in polymer processing. Flow through the extruder, dies and mold runners is controlled by the steady state shear behavior of the material. In rheometry the steady state shear viscosity, $\eta$, is measured either in capillary or rotational instruments. As indicated in Part 3.2, besides $\eta$ the two other functions: $N_1$ and $N_2 \simeq -0.1N_1$, characterize the flow. While in Part 3.6 the strains $\gamma = 2$ to 30% were applied, here hundreds or ever thousands of times higher strain values $\gamma = \dot{\gamma}t$ will be discussed. [In capillary flow: $\gamma \simeq 2(3 + 1/n)L/d$]. Due to these differences the structures in dynamic and steady state flows may be quite different which leads to differences in rheological responses (*Chang* and *Han*, 1984; *Dumoulin* et al., 1985; *Utracki* et al., 1986).

The most dramatic example of different shear behavior in capillary and dynamic flow is that reported for the blend of ethylenepropylene-1,4-hexadiene terpolymer (EPDM), with poly(vinylidene-co-hexafluoropropylene), Viton[R] (*Shih*, 1976, 1979; *Kanu* and *Shaw*, 1982). While Shih reported a six-fold reduction of shear viscosity in capillary flow upon addition of 2% or more of the other component Kanu and Shaw demonstrated that $\eta^*$ of EPDM and that of EPDM with 5% Viton are similar. The latter authors postulated accumulation of the second component at the capillary entrance, from where it periodically was fed into the capillary, lubricating the main stream by a sort of roll bearing effect. The difference between $\eta$ and $\eta^*$ was not related to material properties but rather to a flow segregation, enhanced by the geometry of the measuring device. It should be stressed that the $\eta$-reduction strongly depended on the shape of the die entry region; differences were observed not only for flat and tapered dies, but even when a tapered die became slightly chipped due to mishandling.

The experience with EPDM/Viton$^R$ blends can be considered a precursor of the recent modifications in linear low density polyethylene (LLDPE), technology. Addition of silane or fluoropolymers to LLDPE results in lubricated die flow and reduction of energy required. To maintain a layer of lubricant on the die surface, usually 250 to 3000 ppm of it should be added to the blend (*Rudin* et al., 1986; *Hedberg* and *Muschiatti*, 1986; *Nam*, 1987). Since the melt fracture occurs at nearly constant shear stress, $\sigma_{MF} \simeq 500$ kPa, the die lubrication allows smooth extrudates to be produced at higher rates of shear, i.e. at higher level of productivity (*Ruoff* et al., 1987; *Valenza* and *LaMantia*, 1988).

### 3.8.1   Shear Viscosity

The large strain shear viscosity within the low range of deformation rates, $\dot{\gamma} \leqslant 100(s^{-1})$, is usually measured in rotational rheometers, whereas that at $\dot{\gamma} > 1s^{-1}$ in capillary flow. To obtain good correlation between these two sets the capillary data have to be computed taking into account several correcting procedures (*Lee* and *White*, 1975; *Utracki* and *Schlund*, 1987b; *Utracki*, 1989).

The standard Rabinovitsch correction is given by the first term in Eq (3.37). For blends in which due to variation of $\phi$, T, P or $\sigma_{12}$ a phase separation may occur, the usual assumption of the pressure independent viscosity may lead to particularly large errors. However, if the data are to be corrected for pressure, first the shear heating effect must be taken into account (*Utracki*, 1986b; *Utracki* and *Schlund*, 1987b). The increase of temperature in capillary flow can be expressed as (*Daryanani* et al., 1973):

$$\Delta T \simeq kP/\varrho c_p \tag{3.214}$$

where $0 < k < 1$ is the adiabaticity factor, P is the driving pressure drop, $\varrho$ is the melt density and $c_p$ is the specific heat. Knowing the activation energy of flow and $\Delta T$ the experimental data determined at high stress can be corrected to constant temperature.

The pressure correction follows the free volume approach, where the free volume, f, computed from the conjugated Eqs (3.75) and (3.76) is related to the shear viscosity:

$$\ln \eta = a_0 + a_1 Y_s \tag{3.215}$$

where $Y_s$ is given by Eq (3.74). The easiest way to account for P is via the generalized Bagley expression:

$$P = \sum_{i=0}^{2} C_i (L/d)^i \tag{3.216}$$

where parameters $C_i$ are (*Utracki*, 1986b):

$C_0 = Pe$; the entrance-exit pressure drop.
$C_1 = 4\sigma_{12}$; the shear stress.
$C_2 \simeq a_1 b_1 C_1^2 / 2P^*$; where $b_1$ is a parameter in the dependence:

$$1/f = b_0(\tilde{T}) + b_1(\tilde{T})\tilde{P} \tag{3.217}$$

Note that $b_i$ are universal constants valid for any fluid at the reduced temperature $\tilde{T} = T/T^*$.

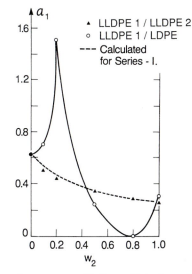

Fig. 3.46 The temperature and pressure sensitivity coefficient, $a_1$, for LLDPE-1 blended with either LLDPE-2 (triangles) or LDPE (circles). The broken line is theoretical, computed from Eqs (3.198) to (3.200) assuming miscibility.

If so, experimentally the parameter which expresses the temperature and pressure sensitivity of viscosity is proportional to the ratio of the polynomial constants:

$$a_1 \propto (C_2/C_1^2) \qquad (3.218)$$

where the proportionality factor is given by: $2P^*/b_1(\bar{T})$.

In Fig. 3.46 the variation of $a_1$ with composition is shown for two LLDPE blends. For the miscible LLDPE/LLDPE system the dependence can be calculated from blend polydispersity using Eqs. (3.198) to (3.200). However, for the immiscible system, LLDPE/LDPE, $a_1$ is strongly non-monotonic. In particular, near 20 wt% of either polymer the extremes of the $a_1 = a_1(w_2)$ may indicate limits of miscibility (*Utracki* and *Schlund,* 1987a, b).

At higher deformation stresses, the "power law", Eq (3.27), can be used to describe the local $\sigma_{12}$ vs $\dot{\gamma}$ dependence. In this case the plot of the power law exponent at constant shear stress $n_\sigma$ vs. $\phi$ may provide information on the morphological changes induced by both independent variables, $\sigma_{12}$ and $\phi$. The linearity of this dependence may be taken as evidence of relative insensitivity of the morphology, i.e. of miscibility or at least compatibility of the ingredients. For example, for polystyrene/low density polyethylene blends, $n_\sigma$ vs. $\phi$ at three levels of $\sigma_{12}$ showed a widely different dependence. For polypropylene/high density polyethylene blends the function was nearly linear at low $\sigma_{12}$ but sigmoidal at high stresses. For polycarbonate/polymethylmethacrylate blends at 250 °C it was nearly linear, suggesting miscibility, even at this temperature above LCST (*Kasajima* et al., 1981).

### 3.8.1.1 Miscible Blends

Dissolution of one high viscosity polymer in another is neither an easy nor a fast process. Consequently, the rheology of the same pair may differ with sample preparation (*Nishimura,* 1984; *Suprun* and *Romankevich,* 1984; *Romankevich* et al., 1984). Frequently, poor mixing leads to a sudden change of apparent viscosity from approximately the value characteristic for one ingredient to that of the other. The "jump" occurs at the concentration dependent on the shear stress. Similar behavior has also been observed for the extrudate swell, B vs. $\phi$.

These sudden changes in rheological functions are engendered by $\phi$ and $\sigma_{12}$ dependent morphology, which as discussed in Parts 3.4 and 3.5, can to a certain degree be predicted from properties of neat resins using the $\lambda$ and $\varkappa$ dimensionless parameters.

Blends of polyvinylidenefluoride with polymethylmethacrylate prepared by mechanical or solution blending methods exhibited significantly different rheological properties; while the mechanical blend showed the above described "jump", the solution blended system followed the dependence predicted by Eq (3.88). The extrudate swell, B, vs. $\phi$ dependence for the first blend also showed a step, whereas that for the second a regular, positive deviation from the additivity (*Romankevich* et al., 1984).

The capillary flow of polyarylate/polybutyleneterephthalate blends at 300 °C was studied by *Ausin* et al. (1987). At $\dot\gamma = 0.2$ to 250 s$^{-1}$ the behavior was Newtonian. A plot of $\eta_0$ vs. $w_i$ indicated NDB behavior, with the best description of data provided by the fluidity additivity Eq (3.166), in spite of the fact that no interlayer slip in miscible system could be postulated. The temperature dependence of $\eta_0$ followed the Arrhenius Eq (3.202) with $\Delta E_\eta$ following the additivity rule:

$$\Delta E_\eta = \sum_i \phi_1 \Delta E_{\eta i} \tag{3.219}$$

The NDB could have originated either in dilatation or chemical reaction. Unfortunately, neither the dilatometry of these blends nor the extent of ester exchange at 300 °C is known.

By contrast, the $\eta$ vs. $w_i$ plot for polyethyleneterephthalate/polybutyleneterephthalate showed a local maximum at $w_2 = 2$ wt% PBT. Since there is no reason to expect immiscibility, the most likely explanation is either a local increase of melt density or a chemical reaction (*Mishra* and *Deopura,* 1984).

### 3.8.1.2 Immiscible Blends

For immiscible blends with a well dispersed, compatibilized second polymer there can be a continuity of behavior in the wide range of $\dot\gamma$, T, P and $\phi$. Examples of these systems are: ABS (polybutadiene rubber particles grafted to styrene-acrylonitrile copolymer matrix) or ASA (similar to ABS with polybutadiene rubber replaced by a thermoplastic elastomer based on acrylic ester copolymers). These systems have been thoroughly characterized (*Münsted,* 1981; *Schuch* and *Wassmuth,* 1985). In spite of the apparent yield stress (increasing with the rubber content) the viscosity obeyed the time-temperature principle with $a_T$ following WLF dependence (3.201). The entrance-exit pressure drop correction $P_e$ vs. $\sigma_{12}$ relation was found to be independent of the rubber content, i.e. entirely defined by the rheological character of the matrix copolymer. On the other hand, the extrudate swell, B, depended on the rubber concentration; in the full range of shear stresses, B decreased with rubber content showing a composite-like behavior.

Neither the time-temperature superposition of shear viscosity nor of extrudate swell is observed for noncompatibilized immiscible blends, e.g. for polystyrene/polymethylmethacrylate (*Wang* and *Lee,* 1987), polycarbonate/ABS (*Dobrescu* and *Cobzaru,* 1978), polycarbonate/low density polyethylene (*Utracki* and *Sammut,* 1987), polyamide/linear low density polyethylene (*Utracki* et al., 1986), polyethylene/polypropylene (*Dumoulin,* 1988) etc. The lack of superposition (exemplified by data in Fig. 3.47) is a rule not an exception. There are several reasons for this. Since the temperature dependence of shear viscosity vary from one polymer to the next, in general $\lambda(T_1) \neq \lambda(T_2)$ for $T_1 \neq T_2$ which leads to different concentration for phase inversion, predicted by Eqs (3.167) or (3.171). The difference in $\lambda$ also results in variation of the extrudate morphology, i.e. different drop deformation, different degree of shear segregation, etc., which by reciprocity changes the rheological response of the system.

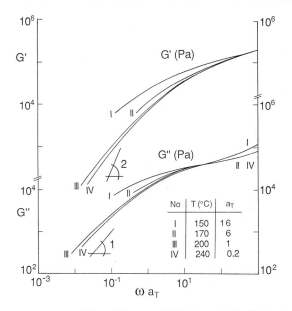

Fig. 3.47 Time-temperature superposition of shear moduli for immiscible blend of polystyrene with 33 wt% low density polyethylene (*Utracki* and *Sammut, 1988*).

Due to the diversity of morphology and rheological responses observed for immiscible blends any attempt at generalization must be viewed with suspicion. Nevertheless, on the basis of the available evidence it seems that the main condition for validity of time-temperature superposition principle, i.e. for relative stability of morphology in the full range of $\sigma_{12}$ and T, are good interphase interactions, either inherent or generated by a compatibilizer. Examples of the first type are the above mentioned ABS and ASA polymeric systems.

The blends of polyethyleneterephthalate/polyamide-6,6 can serve as an example of the second type (*Utracki* et al., 1981, 1982; *Utracki* and *Bata*, 1983). In spite of their immiscibility and coarse, dispersed morphology (PA-6,6 content did not exceed 35 wt%) apparently the ester-amide interactions were sufficiently strong to generate consistent responses from the dynamic and steady state shearing, as well as the time-temperature superposition within the full temperature range: $245 \leqslant T \leqslant 300\ °C$ (the lower limit was established by the PET "softening point", the upper by the thermal decomposition). Presence of the specific interactions between ester and amide groups could also be deduced from the miscibility of systems containing about 5 wt% of PA-6,6.

The capillary flow of polyethyleneterephthalate/polyamide-6 at 275 °C was studied by *Dimov* and *Savov* (1980). The authors reported that up to the phase inversion at $w \simeq 40$ wt% PA-6 the effective viscosity of blends was Newtonian for $\sigma_{12} \leqslant 100\ kPa$. This observation finds support in the previously cited work on PET/PA-6,6 (*Utracki* et al., 1982).

Blends of PET with either PA-6 or with PA-6,6 both showed NDB behavior in the dependence of $\eta$ (or $\Psi_1$) on composition. However, the depth of the negative deviation from the log-additivity rule was found to be nearly independent of the shear stress. By contrast, the NDB character in the $\eta$ vs. $\phi$ plot for antagonistically immiscible blends such as: polypropylene/polyamide-6, PP/PA-6, (*Yakovlev* et al., 1984) polyoxymethylene/poly(ethylene-co-vinylacetate), POM/EVAc, (*Rezanova* and *Tsebrenko*, 1981), polyoxymethylene/ polystyrene, POM/PS, (*Romankevich* et al., 1983) and others, significantly deepens with $\sigma_{12}$. This type of dependency is predicted by the interlayer slip model, Equation (3.166).

As indicated in Part 3.5.3, over the years fibrillation during the die flow of immiscible blends has been a subject of intensive studies in Kiev. Blends of POM/EVAc (*Tsebrenko* et al., 1980), POM/PS (*Romankevich* et al., 1982) and polyethylene/polyethyleneterephthalate (*Gerasimchuk* et al., 1986) were examined. Fibrillation was observed in all systems, independently of the type of $\eta - \phi$ dependence, and in a very wide range of the viscosity ratios $\lambda$, although it was found that near $1/3 < \lambda < 1$ it is easier to generate fibers. The diameter of the microfibers varied from sub-micron to as large as 100 µm, depending on the initial drop size, concentration range, parameter $\varkappa$ as defined in Eq (3.122), viscosity ratio $\lambda$ and the extrusion conditions. The average diameter vs. composition reached its maximum within the concentration range for phase inversion. As expected, for systems with $\lambda$ significantly different from unity, the flow encapsulation generated a non-uniform concentration of fibers across the extrudate, as well as a wide distribution of fiber diameters. Similarly, an increase in the wall shear stress increased nonuniformity of the deformational stress field, resulting in increased polydispersity of fiber diameters. The authors observed that at $\lambda > 10$ deformation of droplets was difficult to achieve. On the other hand for low viscosity system the capillary instability generated "defective fibers" and fine droplets with diameter 1 to 5 µm. An interesting observation was made that the presence of even a small amount of fibers led to an increase in the equilibrium extrudate swell, B.

Detailed studies of fibrillation during the capillary flow of either high density polyethylene (HDPE), or polypropylene (PP), dispersed in linear low density polyethylene (LLDPE), were reported by *Tree* and *McHugh* (1988). The authors related fibrillation to the stress-induced crystallization of the superheated dispersed phase. The stratified morphology observed at high stresses was found to be detrimental to the fibrillation process.

### 3.8.2    Melt Elasticity

Four measures of melt elasticity are commonly used: in steady state shearing $N_1$, in dynamic tests $G'$, and the two indirect and controversial ones, namely entrance-exit pressure drop (Bagley correction), $P_e$, and the extrudate swell, B. In homogeneous melts the four measures are in qualitative agreement. More complex behavior is expected for blends. If the blend can be regarded as an emulsion, in the absence of interlayer slip the PDB behavior for B is to be expected. In systems with $\lambda \simeq 1$, the deformation-and-recovery of the dispersed drops provides a potent mechanism for energy storage leading to an elastic response. On the other hand, in systems with $\lambda \gg 1$, where the dispersed phase is difficult to deform, B should be as small as that for suspensions.

There is a renewed interest in flow visualization studies by several techniques including birefringence. There is a linear relationship between the stress and birefringence tensors. The proportionality factor C, called the stress optical coefficient, was found to be independent either of strain or the strain rate. As long as C is constant the flow birefringence may be used to measure the stress tensor component in the melt, i.e. $\sigma_{12}$ and $N_1$ (*Janeschitz-Kriegl*, 1983).

Direct measurements of $N_1$ (*Thorton* et al., 1980; *Utracki* et al., 1981; *Plochocki*, 1982; *Dreval* et al., 1983; *Min*, 1984) indicate a parallel dependence on $\phi$ for both $\eta$ and $N_1$, even when these had a sigmoidal form. In dynamic testing isochronal $G'$ primarily show PDB behavior (*Lipatov*, 1975, 1978; *Bolotnikova* et al., 1982; *Dumoulin* et al., 1984) although NDB, similar to that observed for $\eta$, was also reported (*Murata* et al., 1981; *Utracki* and *Bata*, 1982).

In the steady state shear flow of a two phase system without interlayer slip it is more appropriate to consider the rheological functions in terms of stress than deformation rate (*Han*, 1981). Using a similar argument for the dynamic functions, $G'$ at constant $G''$ should be examined. To illustrate the point in Fig. 3.48 the isochronal $G'$ is plotted vs. weight

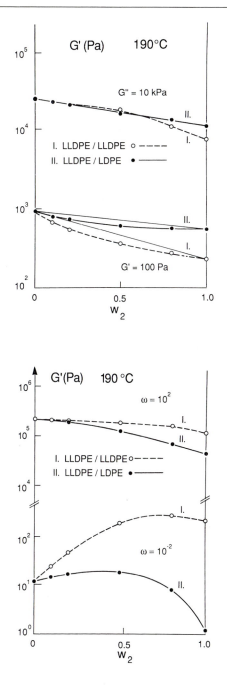

Fig. 3.48 Isochronal G′ at ω = $10^{-2}$ and $10^2$ rad/s vs. weight fraction of the second component for linear low density polyethylene, LLDPE, blended with either another LLDPE or low density polyethylene, LDPE.

Fig. 3.49 Storage modulus, G′, of linear low density polyethylene, LLDPE, blended with another LLDPE or with low density polyethylene, LDPE. The data points taken at T = 190 °C and at constant G″ = $10^2$ (bottom) and $10^4$ Pa. The same results as shown in Fig. 3.48 (*Utracki* and *Schlund,* 1987b).

fraction of the second component for linear low density polyethylene (LLDPE), blends with another LLDPE or with low density polyethylene (LDPE), whereas in Fig. 3.49 the same data are plotted at G″ = const. While in Fig. 3.48 strong PDB is observed, in Fig. 3.49 the data show either additivity or NDB, a behavior similar to that of η vs. $w_2$ (*Utracki* and *Schlund,* 1987b).

Another method of estimating the elastic contribution is via the Bagley entrance-exit pressure drop correction, $P_e$. The plot of $P_e$ vs. $\sigma_{12}$ for single phase liquids is independent of capillary diameter, temperature and molecular weight, but sensitive to changes in flow profile (*Utracki, 1985a*). Furthermore, for a series of polymers with an increasing degree of branching $P_e$ (at $\sigma_{12}$ = const) increases as expected from the network model. For immiscible PAB's the plot was reported useful for interpretation of the stress, temperature and composition-dependent morphological changes (*Dumoulin et al., 1985; Utracki et al., 1986b*). At low $\phi \leqslant 0.1$ $P_e$ was found to be independent of T and at constant shear stress it increased with loading. At higher concentrations $P_e$ behaved in a complex manner, dependent on $\phi$, T and $\sigma_{12}$.

There are two mechanisms for the extrudate swell:

1. related to the steady state, stress-induced straining in homogenous liquid (as treated by the continuum theories), and
2. generated by deformation of separated phases. While the first has been related to liquid elasticity, the latter to drop deformability, i.e. test conditions, $\lambda$ and $\varkappa$, viz. Eqs (3.126 and 3.2/3). The two should not be confused.

The extrudate swell, B, has been used to calculate the recoverable shear strain, $\gamma_R$, for single phase materials (*Tanner, 1970; Utracki et al., 1975*). Introduction of the interface negates the basic theoretical assumptions on which the calculation of $\gamma_R$ was based. In addition, presence of the yield stress prevents B from reaching its equilibrium value required to calculate $\gamma_R$. Nevertheless, B has been used as a qualitative measure of the elasticity of blends (*Tsebrenko et al., 1979*). Swelling of rubbers was reviewed by *Leblanc* (1981).

In most PAB's B passes through a maximum near 50 : 50 composition (*Zhila et al., 1980; Romankevich et al., 1982; Yakovlev et al., 1984; Gerasimchuk et al., 1984; La Mantia et al., 1984; Santamaria et al., 1985; Deri et al., 1985; Acierno et al., 1986*). It should be noted that the PDB of B has been reported for most immiscible PAB's, independently of the shape of the $\eta$ vs. $\phi$ curve. This behavior can be understood by considering the emulsion model for PAB; deformation of the dispersed phase provides a mechanism for energy storage in the system. By the same token, in systems with $\lambda \gg 1$, where the dispersed phase behaves like solid particles, B is expected to go through a minimum similar to that observed for filled, reinforced polymers or composites.

From the above discussion one may conclude that in multiphase systems the extrudate swell has little to do with the elasticity of the blend components or the system as measured by G' or $N_1$. In PAB's with emulsion-like behavior the shape recovery of the dispersed phase and the yield stress play the major role. In PAB systems with a certain degree of specific interactions between the two phases, as in the case of polyoxyethylene/copolyamide (*Tsebrenko et al., 1979*), the co-continuous structure seems to slow down the strain recovery leading to a local depression in the B vs. $\phi$ curve (PDB) at about 50 : 50 composition. The molecular mechanism responsible for extrudate swell in homopolymers plays only a secondary role in PAB's.

It can be shown that a plot of the extrudate swell vs. composition is similar to the concentration dependence of the total strain recovery. In Fig. 3.44 the extrudate shrinkage during annealing was plotted as a function of PP/LLDPE composition; $\epsilon$ vs. $\phi$, reaches the maximum value at about 50 : 50 composition. The mechanism responsible for both B and $\epsilon$ is the same; the tendency of molten fibrillas to contract into spherical domains, desired for minimization of the interfacial energy of the system.

Similar information was obtained from measurements of strain recovery, $\gamma_r$, for PS/PMMA blends (*Thornton et al., 1980*). A maximum of $\gamma_r$ was reported at 58 wt% of PMMA, coinciding with the longest recovery time. The plot of $\gamma_r$ vs. $w_2$ (see Fig. 3.50) indicated two steps at $w_2 \simeq 27$ and 78 wt%, interpreted by the authors as evidence of the boundary concentration at which the dispersed and co-continuous morphologies met. It is unfortunate that this test procedure is not more widely used in PAB research.

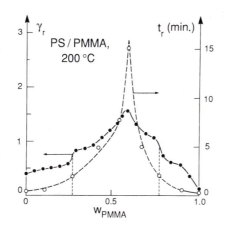

Fig. 3.50 Strain recovery of polystyrene/polymethylmethacrylate blends at 200 °C; the total recoverable strain, $\gamma_r$, and the time for recovery, $t_r$, are plotted vs. the weight fraction of the second component. The vertical broken lines indicate concentrations at which the minor phase changes from discrete dispersion into co-continuous (*Thornton* et al., 1980).

If deformation of the disperse phase occurs mainly in the die entrance region, than a correlation between $P_e$ and B is to be expected. However, since the die entrance deformation is elongational while the shear flow in the die allows a certain recovery to take place, the correlation can be only approximate. Within the limits of experimental uncertainty the literature seems to confirm this hypothesis (*Nishimura*, 1984; *Utracki* and *Schlund*, 1987b).

In conclusion, only G' and $N_1$ (and indirectly the flow birefringence) provide information on PAB elasticity whereas both $P_e$ and B are primarily a measure of the stored deformational energy related to the dispersed, multiphase character of these materials.

## 3.9    Elongational Flow

The constant rate of straining, $\dot{\varepsilon} \equiv \dot{\varepsilon}_{11}$, of incompressible fluids can be described in terms of the rate of deformation tensor as (*Meissner* et al., 1982):

$$\dot{\varepsilon}_{ij} = 0 \quad \text{for} \quad i \neq j, \quad \Sigma \dot{\varepsilon}_{ii} = 0$$

$$\text{and} \quad \dot{\varepsilon}_{22} = m\varepsilon = m\dot{\varepsilon}_{11}$$

(3.220)

where m defines the type of extensional deformation. For m = −1/2 Eq(3.220) describes uniaxial elongational flow (see Part 3.2.1.3), for m = 1 the deformation is equibiaxial and for m = 0 planar. Most instruments are designed to provide one type of deformation with m = const. However, Meissner's rotary clamps rheometer can be operated at variable stretch ratio, e.g. changing from m = $\frac{1}{2}$ to 2 (*Meissner*, 1985, 1987). Since to date the elongational behavior of PAB has been measured only in uniaxial deformation (m = −$\frac{1}{2}$) the following text will be restricted to this mode.

## 3.9.1    Uniaxial Extensional Rheometry

To determine the uniaxial elongational properties a molten specimen with a simple geometry has to be uniformly stretched either at constant rate, $\dot{\varepsilon}$, stress, $\sigma_{11}$, velocity or force.

In general three types of instruments can be identified: (i) limited total strain rheometer, (ii) rheometer with rotary clamp(s), and (iii) uncontrolled stretching methods and devices (see Fig. 3.51).

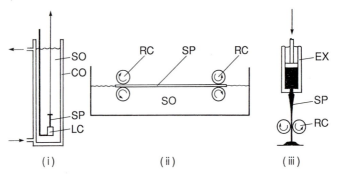

Fig. 3.51 Three types of extensional rheometers: (i) limited strain, (ii) rotary clamp and (iii) melt spinning type; SO – stationary thermostating oil, CO – circulating oil, SP – specimen, LC – load cell, RC – rotary clamps attached to load cell, and EX – extruding device.

Type (i) represents the only commercially available rheometer where the temperature and stretching history are well controlled (*Dealy*, 1982; *Meissner*, 1985, 1987). In this case the specimen is immersed in thermostatted oil (although home-made instruments with floating specimens are known) and after melting it is stretched at a specified $\dot{\varepsilon}$ or $\sigma_{11}$ to strains usually limited to $\varepsilon_{max} \leq 3.2$ (stretch ratio $L/L_0 \leq 25$).

In rheometers of type (ii) the specimen usually floats on a thermostatted oil of slightly higher than the sample density and it is stretched by one or two rotating clamps. In this case the maximum strain is limited by instrument sensitivity, operator skill (in preparing a flawless specimen) and the material properties; strains in excess of $\varepsilon = 7$ (i.e. stretch ratio $L/L_0 \leq 1100$) were obtained for low density polyethylenes.

Measurements by methods and/or instruments of type (iii) suffer from lack of total control of the experiment. To this type belong *Metzner* and *Metzner* (1970) or *Cogswell* (1972) methods of $\eta_E$ estimation from pressure drop in the die entrance region; see Eqs (3.174) to (3.176), as well as the melt-spinning type measuring devices. The measurements are frequently done under non-isothermal condition and in non-uniform deformational field. The calculated $\eta_E$ represents an average response, which nevertheless can well stimulate material response in processing.

During polymer blending and processing the material undergoes complex deformation including elongation. For example, during convergent flow a strong extensional element is present with the elongational rate of straining $\dot{\varepsilon} = (\partial v_2/\partial z)$ being usually time dependent. Similarly, in twin screw or twin roller mixers the variable elongational fields are responsible for the blending/dispersing process. There is a relation between the equilibrium droplet size and the extensional stress or strain rate existing in the machine. Due to the complexity of the field and time history there is no analytical solution to the drop deformability problem available, although the microrheology résuméed in Part 3.5.3 provides a guidance.

From the conceptual point of view the uniaxial extensional flow is the simplest of all types. In practice the measurements are tedious. First of all the specimens have to be molded into a defined geometrical form and the stresses imposed by the forming process must be relaxed without alternating the form. Next, the specimen has to be attached to the rheometer toolings, immersed in a neutral buoyancy, inert fluid and melted. Only then may the test start.

For homogenous specimens the procedure is time consuming; for immiscible blends sometimes it cannot be done. The basic problem is the morphological stability of the blend during all the stages of specimen forming, relaxing and testing. Only well stabilized blends can be expected to give interpretable data. In any case, since there is always a suspicion of morphological change on annealing the extensional flow measurements should always be supported by results of morphological and dynamic tests.

### 3.9.2   Elongational Flow of Polymers

It is convenient to distinguish between two contributions to the tensile stress growth function, $\eta_E^+$, one due to linear viscoelastic response, $\eta_{EL}^+$, and the other originating in the structural change of the specimen during deformation, $\eta_{ES}^+$. The first can be calculated from any linear viscoelastic principles e.g. from the dynamic shear behavior (*Schlund* and *Utracki*, 1987b,c):

$$\eta_{EL}^+(t) = 3\eta_L^+(t) = 3\eta_0 \int_{-\infty}^{\infty} \tilde{H}_G \, [1-\exp\{-\omega t\}]d\ln\omega \qquad (3.221)$$

where $\tilde{H}_G$ is the reduced frequency relaxation spectrum, given by Eq (3.63).

The second component, $\eta_{ES}^+$, originates in the intermolecular interactions or entanglements and its value depends on both the total strain, $\varepsilon = \dot{\varepsilon}t$, and either strain rate $\dot{\varepsilon}$ or straining time, t. Due to the industrial importance of strain hardening, $SH \equiv \eta_E^+(t)/\eta_{EL}^+(t)$, a large body of literature focuses on optimization of PAB composition to maximize SH. Since SH depends on the entanglement density, blending even a small quantity of branched polymers usually increases SH.

In homologous polymer blends the linear viscoelastic behavior, $\eta_{EL}^+$, should be defined by Eq (3.221) in which $\tilde{H}_G$ is calculated from the appropriate blending rule, Eq (3.192). Similar correlation is also expected for miscible polymer blends.

There is a useful empirical observation (*Dumoulin* et al., 1984; *Schlund* and *Utracki*, 1987b) that the initial slope of the stress growth function:

$$S_i = \lim_{t \to 0} \, [d\ln\eta_E^\pm/d\ln t] \qquad (3.222)$$

correlates with the polydispersity index $M_z/M_n$ (Fig. 3.52). The observation is in agreement with the *Gleissle* (1978, 1980) "mirror image" principle:

$$\eta(\dot{\gamma}) = \eta^+(t); \qquad \psi_1(\dot{\gamma}) = \psi_1^+(t) \qquad (3.323)$$

valid for $t \propto 1/\dot{\gamma}$. Accordingly, $S_i$ as an analog of the power law index n, should reflect sample polydispersity. Once the relation between $S_i$ and polydispersity is determined, then it can be used for evaluation of blend miscibility.

A comprehensive review of polymer behavior in elongation can be found in *Petrie's* (1979) monograph. During the last few years the extensional flow has enjoyed increased interest, caused on one hand by the availability of commercial rheometers (*Dealy*, 1982; *Meissner*, 1985, 1987) and on the other by the demand for better understanding and control of polymer processing. Extensional flow plays important role in any process in which streamlines are not parallel (*Cogswell*, 1972; *Pearson* and *Conelly*, 1982; *Kwack* and *Han*, 1983; *Utracki* et al., 1984; *Kanai* and *White*, 1984) e.g. fiber spinning, film blowing, die flow, injection and blow molding, stretch or squeeze flows. An extensive collaborative study was

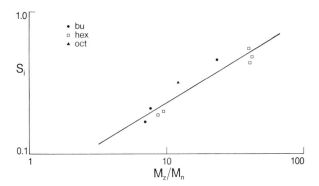

Fig. 3.52 The initial slope of the stress growth function in uniaxial extension of linear low density polyethylene (with comonomer: bu = butene, hex = hexene, and oct = octene) vs. polydispersity index $M_z/M_n$ (*Schlund* and *Utracki*, 1987b).

carried out on the processability and rheology of polyethylenes by IUPAC Working Party 4.2.1 (*Meissner*, 1975; *Winter*, 1983).

The literature on the extensional flow of polyethylenes is particularly voluminous. For example, since 1979 the flow behavior of low density and high density polyethylenes (LDPE and HDPE, respectively) were compared (*Astarita* et al., 1980; *Münstedt* and *Laun*, 1981; *Shaw*, 1981; *Münstedt* and *Middleman*, 1981; *Attalla* and *Romanini*, 1983; *Utracki* and *Lara*, 1983; *Utracki* et al., 1983; *Utracki*, 1985; *Schlund* and *Utracki*, 1987b; *Minoshima*, 1983; *Laun* and *Schuch*, 1987). The extensional flow of LDPE (*Raible* and *Meissner*, 1980; *Laun*, 1980; *Prokunin*, 1980; *Raible* et al., 1982; *Koyama* and *Ishizuka*, 1983; *Leonov* and *Prokunin*, 1983; *Montes*, 1984) of HDPE (*Garcia-Rejon* et al., 1981; *Koyama* and *Ishizuka*, 1982; *La Mantia* and *Acierno*, 1985) linear low density polyethylene (LLDPE) (*Attalla* et al., 1980; *Utracki* and *Lara*, 1983; *Attalla* and *Romanini*, 1983; *Utracki* et al., 1983; *Attalla* and *Bertinotti*, 1983; *Constantin*, 1984; *Utracki*, 1985; *Schlund* and *Utracki*, 1987b) were also measured.

### 3.9.3   Uniaxial Elongation of PAB

Since both the miscible polymer blends and extensional flow measurement are rare the data on $\eta_E$ behavior of miscible blends are scarce. The melt creep flow and recovery of homologous polystyrene blends at 150.9 °C were reported by *Franck* and *Meissner* (1984). For polymers with a narrow molecular weight distribution, linear viscoelastic behavior was observed at $\sigma_{11} = 10$ kPa and $\varepsilon \leq 3.5$. For blends the linearity was found to be determined by the molecular weights of the original components, not by their ratio. The elongational behavior of miscible blends of linear low density polyethylenes, LLDPE, will be discussed later.

An interesting study of the extensional flow effect on polystyrene/ polyvinylmethylether, PS/PVME, was reported by *Katsaros* et al., (1986). When the immiscible blend was pumped through a device generating planar extension optical clarity was observed for strains above the critical strain: $\varepsilon_c = \dot{\varepsilon}t \simeq 44 \pm 14$ (see Part 3.4.3).

Most of the work on the uniaxial extensional flow of immiscible polymer blends has focused on systems containing polyethylene. The main reasons for this preocupation are the needs for better, easier to process film resins and the stability of polyolefin blend morphology. Film blowing involves two engineering operations: extrusion and blowing. For most production lines the latter limits the productivity. For low density resins (LDPE) the strain hardening (SH) provides a self-regulating, self-healing mechanism. For high density (HDPE) and the new, linear low density (LLDPE) polyethylenes, slight SH can be obtained only for the high MW and MWD resins. As a result, 60 to 70% of LLDPE on the market are blends. For film blowing applications, LLDPE is blended with either LDPE, rubber, elastomeric copolymer or with another type of LLDPE resin. In all cases improvement in SH resulted in improved film bubble stability and increased output (*Utracki, 1987a*). Strain hardening was also found to be an important resin characteristic in wire-coating (*Utracki et al., 1984*). Here, the surface finish and uniformity of the deposited layer were superior for blends with high strain hardening and low shear viscosity. The uniaxial elongational flow of LLDPE/LDPE blends have been studied by several research groups (*Utracki et al., 1984; Utracki, 1984a,b, 1985c, 1987a; La Mantia et al., 1986; Acierno et al., 1986; Schlund and Utracki, 1987c; LaMantia et al., 1988; Ghijsels et al. 1988*). Melt flow of PE-blends (including the extensional) was recently reviewed by *Utracki* (1989).

The non-linear viscoelastic behavior of polymers in uniaxial extension manifests itself as strain/stress hardening, SH. It originates in the physical or interactive entanglements. SH implies a broad spectrum of relaxation times (*Petrie, 1979*). The first qualitative agreement between the measured and computed SH behavior of LDPE was based on the network model (*Chang* and *Lodge, 1972*). Addition of LDPE to LLDPE generates entanglements in the system. Since the mechanical properties of LLDPE are better than those of LDPE the aim is to add a necessary minimal amount of LDPE. Such a minimum depends not only on molecular parameters of blend ingredients but also on the compounding as well as on the test methods. Experimentally SH is a function of two parameters: $\dot{\varepsilon}$ and t or $\dot{\varepsilon}$ and $\varepsilon = \dot{\varepsilon}t$.

The need for entanglement enhancement implies that the enhancing polymer (LDPE, rubber, etc.) must be soluble in LLDPE, at least at low but sufficient concentration. For good mechanical properties of the film the molecular weight (MW) of LLDPE must be high. On the other hand to ascertain adequate miscibility the MW of LDPE should be low. In short, there are two industrially important questions which should be answered by the product development engineer: (i) what is the minimum level of LDPE necessary for SH, and (ii) what is the miscibility of the system.

Blending LDPE($M_w = 220$ kg/mol) with LLDPE($M_w = 110$) resulted in SH only at w(LDPE) $\geq 50$ wt%, i.e. when LDPE in the immiscible blend commenced to form a continuous phase (*La Mantia et al., 1986*). However, blending of LDPE($M_w = 80$) with LLDPE($M_w = 100$) resulted in strain hardening observable at w(LDPE) = 10% (*Schlund and Utracki, 1987c*). Moreover, for the same blends flow visualization of the die entry region demonstrated dramatic changes in the flow streamlines after addition of as little as 2 to 5 wt% of LDPE (*Tremblay* and *Utracki, 1988*). In Fig. 3.34b the stress growth function in uniaxial elongation is shown for LLDPE/LDPE blends; the numbers 0 to 100 indicate wt% of LDPE in the blends. The triangles represent $3\eta^+$, where the stress growth function in steady state shearing, $\eta^+$, was determined at $\dot{\gamma} = 10^{-2}\,s^{-1}$. The solid line was computed from the frequency relaxation spectrum by means of Eq (3.221).

Determination of LLDPE/LDPE blend miscibility in the melt is not an easy task. Since the refractive index of these two polymers is nearly identical the turbidity method cannot be used. Similarly, due to rapid crystallization it is impossible to quench the sample preserving the morphology of the melt. However, analysis of the rheological behavior provides indirect information of blend miscibility (*Utracki* and *Schlund, 1987b; Schlund* and *Utracki, 1987c; Utracki, 1987, 1989*):

(i) Since the initial slope $S_i$ in Eq (3.222) depends on sample polydispersity one can experimentally determine the $S_i$ vs. $M_z/M_n$ relation (see Fig. 3.52). From the molecular weights of the ingredients the blend polydispersity can be calculated by means of Eqs (3.198) to (3.200) and then from the experimental correlation can be determined what should be the $S_i$ value, provided the blend is miscible. Comparison of the calculated and measured $S_i$ gives a good indication of the blend miscibility. An example of this approach is

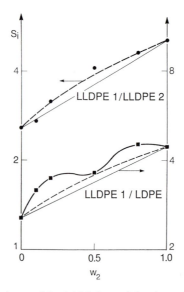

Fig. 3.53 Compositional dependence of the initial slope of the elongational stress growth function for LLDPE-1/LLDPE-2 (top) and LLDPE-1/LDPE (bottom). The broken lines were computed assuming miscibility.

shown in Fig. 3.53 where the points are experimental and the broken line is calculated assuming miscibility. It is evident that by contrast with LLDPE-1/LLDPE-2 the LLDPE-1/LDPE blend indicates lack of predicted behavior, i.e. immiscibility.

ii) The second measure of miscibility based on the elongational flow behavior is more qualitative. It has been observed that deformation of immiscible blends is frequently irregular, leading to a decrease in the maximum strain at break, $\varepsilon_b$. Sometimes in the range of 50:50 blend composition the co-continuous morphology may lead to an average $\bar{\varepsilon}_b$ value (*Min*, 1984) but outside that range $\varepsilon_b$ is significantly below the average. However, due to limitations of the instrument $\varepsilon_b > 3.2$ cannot be determined in commercial extensional rheometers of the type schematically presented in Fig. 3.51 (i).

(iii) It is expected that an onset of immiscibility should result in a change of the relaxation spectrum. Since coordinates of the maximum of relaxation spectrum are a sensitive measure of polydispersity, a plot of $\check{H}_{G,max}$ vs. $M_n/M_w$ provides direct evidence (see Fig. 3.54) of miscibility extending to about 10 wt% of LDPE.

(iv) The steady state capillary flow of LLDPE-1/LDPE blends furnished other corroborative evidences of limited miscibility: (a) the unpredicted increase of the temperature and pressure sensitivity coefficient, $a_1$, shown in Fig. 3.45 may indicate the limit of LLDPE/LDPE miscibility under shear stress as $w \leqslant 20$ wt% and (b) the extrudate swells, B, for LLDPE-1 and LDPE were determined as 1.29 and 1.27, respectively, whereas B = 1.51 for their 50:50 blend. This large increase is more typical for the strain recovery of dispersed fibers than the extrudate swell of homogenous melts.

There is no doubt that the investigated LLDPE-1/LDPE blends were immiscible. However, in polyethylenes the diffusion is slow. There is mounting evidence that it takes several hours at 180 °C for LLDPE to achieve equilibrium entanglement (*Teh* et al., 1984; *Schlund* and *Utracki*, 1987b). If so, it is possible that melt blending in a twin-screw extruder produced two-phase blends not because the two components were immiscible but because the time required for the intermolecular diffusion was orders of magnitude longer than the residence time of the compounding operation. On the other hand, it is worth pointing out

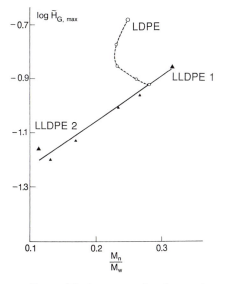

Fig. 3.54 Correlation between ordinate of the frequency relaxation spectrum maximum and the molecular weights ratio $M_n/M_w$ for LLDPE-1/LLDPE-2 blends (triangles) and LLDPE-1/LDPE (open circles). The results for the three neat resins are indicated by larger symbols (*Utracki* and *Schlund*, 1987b).

that under analogous conditions blending the LLDPE-1 with another type, high molecular weight LLDPE-2, resulted in blends which rheologically indicated total miscibility. Since the molecular weight MW(LLDPE-2) > MW(LDPE) the difference in miscibility of these polymers with LLDPE-1 determined by rheological means should reflect their true thermodynamic behavior.

The measurements of LLDPE/LDPE melt strength by a melt spinning method indicated a local maiximum at about 70 wt% of LDPE (*Acierno* et al., 1987; *Ghijsels* et al., 1988). For a given LDPE the maximum value of the melt strength was found to increase with LLDPE molecular weight and tended to shift to lower concentration. The maximum strain at break showed an opposite tendency (*LaMantia* et al., 1988).

Blends of two types of LLDPE have been frequently mentioned. The blends LLDPE-1/LLDPE-2 were found to be miscible with the rheological functions calculable from molecular weight averages. However, blends of another pair of the same polymers showed quite a different behavior (*Utracki*, 1985c). As illustrated in Fig. 3.55 the elongational viscosity at constant rate of straining plotted as a function of composition show a sigmoidal dependence. Plot of $S_i$ vs. $w_2$ resulted in nearly identical dependence allowing one to postulate partial miscibility. Since the resins were supposed to be quite similar to the LLDPE-1/LLDPE-2 pair the possible explanation for the different behavior in extension lies in differences of either polymerization or post-polymerization processes. Again, there is a possibility of non-equilibrium behavior.

The changes in the $\eta_E^+$ vs. t dependence of LLDPE blends observed in the rheological laboratory were found to correlate directly with bubble stability on the commercial film blowing line. The "line processability index" interrelated very well with SH for all three series of differently behaving blends (see Fig. 3.42): LLDPE-1/LLDPE-2, LLDPE-1/LDPE and LLDPE-3/LLDPE-4. In short, the miscibility of these systems affected the extensional flow behavior in the rheometer the same way as it did the film blowing process.

Melt blending of an LLDPE-type medium density polyethylene with ultra high molecular weight polyethylene (UHMWPE) resulted in incomplete mixing (*Dumoulin* et al., 1984).

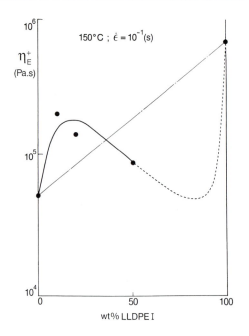

Fig. 3.55 Steady state extensional viscosity of a mixture of two different linear low density polyethylenes vs. composition. Points – experimental, curve – third order polynomial (*Utracki*, 1985c).

The strain hardening in uniaxial elongational flow was found to be a sensitive measure of the degree of dissolution of UHMWPE in an LLDPE matrix.

The elongational properties of HDPE/LDPE blends were studied using the die entrance pressure drop method (*Cogswell*, 1972). The method did not allow control of the straining time and the results represented neither equilibrium nor constant strain values. Nevertheless, the method provided a gradation of the relative performance. The authors reported that for a series of HDPE blends with LDPE, $\eta_E$ varied systematically with composition: "When the shear viscosity of the LDPE is much higher than that of HDPE all blends show a behavior very similar to that of LDPE" (*La Mantia* et al., 1982). The melt spinning tests demonstrated that the melt strength goes through a maximum at concentration determined by the ratio of molecular weight of the blend components. As usual, the minimum of the strain at break occurred at about the same concentration (*La Mantia* and *Acierno*, 1985). The miscibility of the system was not discussed.

The elongational flow of polypropylene (PP) blends has also been studied (*Sebastian* and *Chen*, 1983; *Dumoulin* et al., 1984 b,c). The first authors reported on PP/elastomer while the second ones on PP/LLDPE. Both PP and LLDPE were found to display a purely linear viscoelastic stress growth function in extension and in shear:

$$\eta_E^+(t) = 3\eta^+(t); \quad t \leqslant 10^3 s, \quad \dot{\varepsilon} = 0.01 \text{ to } 1 \text{ s}^{-1}$$

Plot of $\eta_E$ vs. $\dot{\varepsilon}$ showed a slower rate of viscosity decrease than that of $\eta$ vs. $\dot{\gamma}$ or $\eta^*$ vs. $\omega$.

### 3.9.4 Yield Stress

The influence of the rubber phase copolymerized with the thermoplastic matrix was studied by *Münstedt* (1981), *Saito* (1982) and *Dreval* et al. (1983). Münstedt analyzed the elongational behavior of poly(butadiene-styrene-acrylonitrile) (ABS) and poly(acrylicester-styrene-acrylonitrile) (ASA) melts. Both copolymers were found to show strong yield stress behavior in shear and elongation. As illustrated in Fig. 3.56 the yield stress in extension $\sigma_{yE} \simeq \sqrt{3}\sigma_y$ in accord with the von Mieses criterion. Similar relation was observed for polymer composites in the molten state (*Utracki*, 1986a).

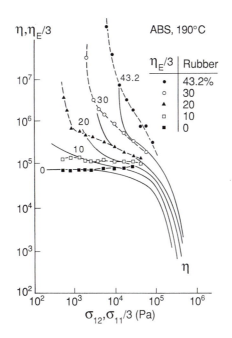

Fig. 3.56 The stress dependence of shear (solid lines) and extensional (points) viscosity for ABS at 190 °C. The numbers indicate the polybutadiene content in the same SAN matrix (*Münstedt*, 1981).

*Saito* (1982), using a vertical elongational rheometer with rotary clamps measured properties of ABS and those of matrix polystyreneacrylonitrile (SAN) at 120 to 150 °C at strains $\varepsilon \leqslant 30$. The linear viscoelastic behavior was observed for $\varepsilon \leqslant 0.54$ regardless of SAN molecular weights; above this limit $\eta_E^+$ was found to depend on the morphology of the rubber particles, their concentration and the molecular characteristics of the matrix. A small evidence of yield stress was reported, but the data could be superimposed on a time-temperature master curve with the horizontal shift factor, $a_T \propto M^{4.0}$, obeying WLF Eq (3.201) with the universal constants $C_i^0$. For both SAN and ABS the strain hardening was large, exceeding one order of magnitude.

There is no conflict between these two reports. As shown in Fig. 3.56 the yield stress in ABS becomes strong for more than 20 wt% of rubber; the ABS studied by Saito contained about 15% of rubber. The difference again points out the difficulties in drawing sweeping generalizations for blend behavior.

Blends of polystyrene (PS) with poly(styrene-b-butadiene-b-styrene) (SBS) were prepared by *Dreval* et al., (1983). The main question the authors tried to answer was at what concentration of SBS $\eta_E$ does reach a maximum. The results did not allow an assesment of whether the enhancement was due to apparent yield stress or other rheological effects. The minimum was found to depend on molecular weight (MW) of SBS; the higher it was, the more of it was required and the effect was more pronounced; C $\simeq$ 10 and 4 wt% for MW = 83 and 53 kg/mol, respectively.

*Min* (1984) reported $\eta_E$ vs. $w_2$ dependence for blends of HDPE with either PS, poly-amide-6 (PA-6) or polycarbonate (PC). Three HDPE samples of different MW blended with PS showed either positive or negative deviation from the log-additivity rule (PDB or NDB), the blend with PA-6 showed NDB, that with PC a PDB behavior. The author reported that increase of steady state shear stress viscosity occurred when droplet formation was observed and a decrease when layered structures were noted.

In "antagonistically" immiscible blends of PA-6 in HDPE a sharp decrease of the maximum strain at break, $\varepsilon_b$, in the investigated range of $w_{PA} \leqslant 35$ wt% was observed (*Utracki* et al., 1986). In a series of PS/LDPE blends with and without hydrogenated poly(styrene-b-isoprene) (SEB) a similar decrease in $\varepsilon_b$ was observed. In Fig. 3.57 $\eta_E^+$ at 150°C for LDPE:PS:SEB = 100:0:0, 63:32:5, 32:63:5 and 0:100:0 is shown. The strain hardening visible in the figure originated primarily from compatibility between the two phases caused by addition of SEB (see Fig. 3.58). In spite of immiscibility of the non-compatibilized PS/LDPE samples good correlation was found between low deformation rate part of the stress growth function in shear and elongation: $3\eta^+ \simeq \eta_{EL}^+$ for all samples. The rate of deformation dependence, $\eta' = \eta'(\omega)$ and $\eta_E/3 = \eta_E(\dot{\varepsilon})$, of dynamic and elongational viscosities is presented in Fig. 3.59. It can be seen that the Trouton rule, Eq (3.16), is valid. Blends containing 5% of compatibilizer showed lower values of $\varepsilon_b$ caused by high viscosity of the SEB (*Sammut* and *Utracki*, 1987).

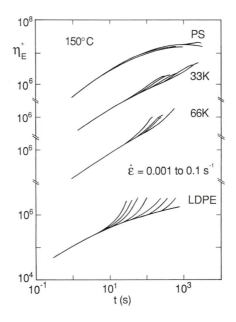

Fig. 3.57 Stress growth function in uniaxial extension vs. straining time at 150 °C for polystyrene (PS) low density polyethylene (LDPE) and their blends containing 5 wt% SEB. For clarity the traces for each sample are displaced vertically by one decade. The numbers indicate LDPE content in wt% (*Sammut* and *Utracki*, 1987).

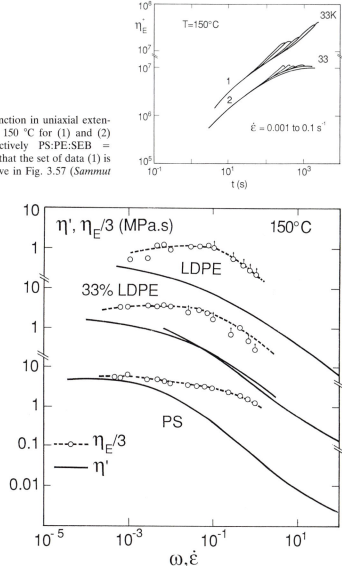

Fig. 3.58 Stress growth function in uniaxial extension vs. straining time at 150 °C for (1) and (2) blends containing respectively PS:PE:SEB = 63:32:5 and 67:33:0. Note that the set of data (1) is identical with the 33K curve in Fig. 3.57 (*Sammut* and *Utracki*, 1987).

Fig. 3.59 The rate of deformation dependence of dynamic viscosity, $\eta'$ vs. $\omega$ (solid line) and uniaxial elongational viscosity $\eta_E/3$ vs. $\dot{\varepsilon}$ (points and broken line) at T = 150 °C for: (1) LDPE, (2) LDPE:PS = 33:67 and (3) PS. For clarity the data are displaced vertically each by two decades. The arrows indicate that at $\varepsilon \simeq 3.1$ the stress growth function did not reach its equilibrium value (*Sammut* and *Utracki*, 1987).

### 3.9.5  Flow Modeling

There are several ways one may model the elongational flow of PAB melts: I. Since the linear viscoelastic behavior can be predicted from the relaxation spectrum only the non-linear part of $\eta_E^+$ is unknow. Several empirical and semi-empirical methods described in the

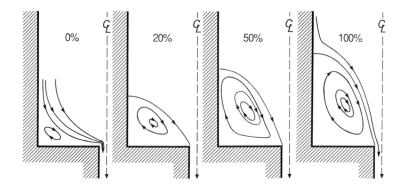

Fig. 3.60 Flow pattern at the entrance to capillary for linear low density/low density polyethylene blend (LLDPE/LDPE) at 190 °C and $\dot{\gamma} = 125$ (s$^{-1}$). From the left hand side: 0, 20, 50 and 100% of LDPE (*Tremblay* and *Utracki, 1988a*).

literature for determination of $\eta^+_{ES}$ or SH for homopolymers can be adopted for PAB (*Laun,* 1978; *Meissner* et al., 1982; *Raible* et al., 1982; *Koyama* and *Ishizuka,* 1983; *Leblans,* 1985). II. Several constitutive relations can be expressed as series in terms of the empirical relaxation times, $\tau_p$, usually with p $\leqslant$ 5. These can be related to molecular parameters, providing in principle a semi-empirical description of systems (*Ishizuka* and *Koyama,* 1980; *Sebastian* and *Chen,* 1983). III. A more promising approach is the use of closed-form constitutive equations with a small number of adjustiable material constants (viz. *Bogue* et al, 1970; *Larson,* 1985). Again, the value of the material constants can be correlated with molecular parameters providing a means for predicting the flow behavior (*Tremblay* and *Utracki,* 1988a). IV. By analogy with the mechanical properties of multicomponent systems (blends or composites) one may attempt to use various mixing rules to simulate blend behavior. As an input the flow description of neat components is required. The drawback of this approach is the need to change the mixing rule with composition and method of blend preparation (*Sebastian* and *Chen,* 1983). The diversity of approaches is a sign that the problem of PAB flow modeling is far from being solved.

In principle, modeling of miscible or well compatibilized blend should be the easiest; for these systems assumption of stable morphology simplifies the calculation. However, even here the situation is complex enough. Particularly challenging are those blends in which polymer-1 shows strong strain hardening effect, whereas in polymer-2 SH = 0. Use of a close-form constitutive equation, as discussed in case III above, seems to be the most promising.

Modeling of immiscible blends will provide employment for decades to come. The presence of the interphase introduces a set of parameters which depend on blend morphology, concentration and age of the blend, i.e. it cannot be a priori calculated from the properties of the neat resin.

However, model we must. One needs mathematical description of the system to predict its flow pattern during processing. For example, a commercially available finite element program was found to generate not only a good description of the vorticity at the die entrance for linear low density or low density polyethylenes but also for their blends. The flow pattern presented in Fig. 3.60 illustrate variation of the flow lines determined by flow visualization technique. Modeling not only provided a good agreement with the observed flow behavior but also allowed quantification of strain hardening effects on vorticity at the die entrance (*Tremblay* and *Utracki,* 1988b).

# 3.10  Flow-Induced Morphology

Morphology is a science of form and structure, some aspects of which have been discussed in Parts 2.4 (Mechanism of Phase Separation), 2.6 (Determination of Polymer/Polymer Miscibility), 3.5 (Microrheology), as well as in Parts 3.6, 3.7 and 3.9. Now the effects of flow-imposed deformation will be outlined.

The deformation field in compounding or processing equipment is usually complex, leading to a multitude of PAB morphological forms. To understand these it is preferable proemially to study the morphologies created under well controlled stress-field conditions. In this part the effects of a simple deformational field, shear or extensional, will be considered.

Most of the theoretical works on flow-imposed morphology assume that: (i) the system consists of dispersed, non-interacting droplets, (ii) the flow is at steady state, (iii) the stress field is uniform, (iv) the time effects on rheological and thermodynamic parameters can be neglected, and (v) the deformations are free from interference by other factors, viz. phase homogenization, ripening, stress-induced crystallization, etc. Effects of processing on PAB morphology was recently reviewed by *White* and *Min* (1988).

There are several types of flow-induced morphological changes in which: flow encapsulation, fiber or platelet formation, shear-induced coalescence, interlayer slip and shear-controlled SD or NG are well documented (*Ablazova* et al., 1975; *Tsebrenko* et al., 1979; *Rezanova* and *Tsebrenko,* 1981; *White* et al., 1981; *Han,* 1981; *Min,* 1984; *Min* et al., 1984; *Han* et al., 1984; *White* and *Min,* 1985; *Dumoulin* et al., 1985; *Utracki* et al., 1986; *Endo* et al., 1986; *Kozlowski* and *Piglowski,* 1986; *Lyngaae-Jorgensen* and *Sondergaard,* 1987; *Utracki,* 1988).

There are numerous illustrations of the fact that the morphology of PAB strongly depends on the method of its initial preparation; mechanical or solution blending may lead to very different blends (*Razinskaya* et al., 1979). In a limit, the same blend prepared by these two methods may appear miscible or immiscible. Since the miscibility is determined by the equilibrium thermodynamics such a diversity of structure can only be due to slow equilibration process. For example, in blends of polyolefins both the conformational entropy and specific interactions are small; there are no strong forces to drive the macromolecules. On the other hand, due to high entanglement density in these systems, $N_e = M/M_e$, the rate of thermal (self)diffusion is low (*Fleischer,* 1987).

Mechanical blending is done in several types of compounding machines. In each of these the shearing and extensional modes differ in their intensity and preponderance. As a result one must expect different degrees of entanglement, and different morphologies resulting from mixing for the same period of time the same ingredients in different mixers. Experimental data on highly entangled blends without strong repulsive forces certainly confirm this expectation. However in systems with low entanglement (high mobility) and high immiscibility the rate of phase separation is dominated by non-equilibrium thermodynamics (viz. Part 2.4.1). In this case separation of phases occurs quite rapidly (*Shaw* and *Somani,* 1984) and the blend morphology is insensitive to the type of compounding equipment (*Valsamis* et al., 1987; *Karian* and *Plochocki,* 1987). It is expected that noncompatibilized blends will show large differences in morphology for specimens processed by different methods, viz. extrusion and molding (*van Gisbergen* et al., 1988; *Utracki* and *Sammut,* 1989).

Another effect complicating the analysis of flow induced morphology is related to chemical modification of macromolecules during blending. Shear or oxidative reactions are common (*Schlund* and *Utracki,* 1987a). However, the ester exchange reactions have a more serious effect on morphology (co-reactive compatibilization was discussed in Part 2.7.2). To several engineering blends a crystalline polymer has been added for enhancement of mechanical properties and solvent/chemical resistance. Since transreaction leads to randomization of the mer sequence and reduction of crystallinity, frequently these systems were stabilized to prevent extensive transreaction. As an example polycarbonate/polybuty-leneterephthalate (PC/PBT) blend is stabilized by addition of tri-n-octadecylphosphite deactivating the PBT titanium complex catalyst. Nevertheless blending for 30 min at 260 °C changed the 60/40-blend morphology from PBT-continuous phase to PC-continuous phase (*Delimoy* et al., 1984, 1988). In accord with Eq (3.168) one may expect that such a prolonged mixing resulted in degradation of PC and in turn in an increase of the relative viscosity ratio: $\lambda = \eta(PBT)/\eta(PC)$.

Blends of liquid crystal polymers (LCP) are known to be susceptible to flow orientation (*Ciferri* et al., 1982; *Frayer*, 1987; *Kiss*, 1987). Here also the transreactions can be expected, affecting the morphology and properties of the finished product (*Ramanathan* et al., 1987).

When discussing the flow-induced morphology the aforementioned two effects, (i) the non-equilibrium degree of miscibility and entanglement, (ii) as well as the chemical effects, are usually neglected.

The steady state shearing or elongation causes deformation of a flow element measured in shear or extensional strain units, $\gamma = \dot{\gamma}t$ or $\varepsilon = \dot{\varepsilon}t$, respectively. To interpret the morphological changes during shear blending *Starita* (1972) used the concept of relative viscosity, $\lambda$, defined in Eq (3.121). In systems with $\lambda \leqslant 1$ a fine dispersion, in those with $\lambda \geqslant 1$ a coarse one was obtained. The relative elasticity was considered to affect only the strain recovery; for $\lambda \simeq 1$ and $N_{1,1}, > N_{1,2}$ strain recovery of the dispersed phase was expected but not for $N_{1,1} \leqslant N_{1,2}$. In the first case a coarsening of morphology toward spherical dispersion was expected, in the second preservation of a fibrillar structure. The dissymetric variation of PAB morphology with concentration was later reported by *Plochocki* (1983ab, 1984).

The dissymmetry in blend morphology at low concentration of component A in B vs. B in A was theoretically justified by *van Oene* (1972), viz. Eq (3.174). In this case again the elasticity was supposed to control the type of dispersion, but rather by affecting the dynamic interfacial tension coefficient. However, it is worth noting that in accord with Starita's (1972) reasoning, Eq (3.174) for $N_{1,1} \geqslant N_{1,2}$ also predicts a dispersed, whereas for $N_{1,1} < N_{1,2}$ a continuous structure. The relation is only approximative and as shown in Fig. 3.61 the predicted morphological dissymmetry is not always observed (*Heikens* and *Barentsen*, 1977; *Favis* and *Chalifoux*, 1987; *Favis* et al., 1987). For more detail see *Elmendorp* (1986).

*Han* (1981) discussed the two mechanisms leading to flow encapsulation during flow through a long pipe: (i) for two liquids with the viscosity ratio $\lambda \equiv \eta_1/\eta_2 < 1$ and the normal

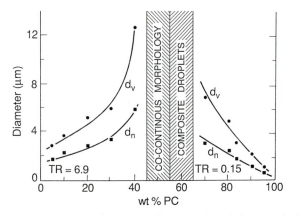

Fig. 3.61 Number and volume average droplet diameter, $d_n$ and $d_v$ respectively, as a function of composition for polypropylene/polycarbonate (PP/PC) uncompatibilized blends. TR stands for torque ratio of the dispersed to matrix polymer (*Favis* et al., 1987).

stress ratio $\lambda_N \equiv N_{1,1}/N_{1,2} \simeq 1$ the less viscous liquid 1 migrates toward the wall eventually encapsulating liquid 2; (ii) for systems with $\lambda \simeq 1$ but $\lambda_N > 1$ the more elastic liquid 1 encapsulates liquid 2. Mechanism (ii) is not always observed (*White*, 1985; *Endo* et al., 1986).

*Plochocki* (1986) used the concept of $\lambda$ and $\lambda_N$ for development of blends with desired morphology. The author plotted $\lambda$ and $\lambda_N$ vs. shear stress, $\sigma_{12}$. To minimize the dispersing energy the mixing stress was selected as that at which $\lambda \simeq 1$. Under these circumstances the value of $\lambda_N$ was used to predict the type of dispersion from Eq (3.171). However, it should be pointed out that in principle this method may be used only at low concentration of the dispersed phase. As the concentration increases the conditions for phase inversion, Eqs (3.167) to (3.171), dominate the blend behavior.

A further complication is to be expected in systems near the phase separation. Here, the level of stress, fluctuation of temperature and pressure may significantly affect the resulting morphology (see Part 3.4.3). It is to be noted that improvement of compatibility, either via the co-reaction or addition of a compatibilizer may enhance sensitivity of the blend to morphological changes (*Breuer* et al., 1977; *Hobbs* et al., 1987). Exceptions are fine, well stabilized dispersions at low concentration.

Contrary to the theoretical predictions, the minimum droplet diameter, d, for a given type of polymer A blended with polymer B was more frequently observed at $\lambda \simeq 0.3$ than $\lambda = 1.0$ (*Berger* et al., 1984; *Utracki*, 1984b; *Favis* and *Chalifoux*, 1987). As the latter authors indicated the minimum in the d vs. $\lambda$ depends on concentration of the dispersed phase, suggesting that coalescence may be an important factor.

In capillary flow the shear stress decreases monotonically from the maximum value at the wall to zero in the center of the stream. Excepting the rare polymer pairs in which $\lambda$ is independent of $\sigma_{12}$, for most blends $\lambda$ changes with $\sigma_{12}$, i.e. with the radial position inside the die. The ratio of viscosity, $\lambda$, determines both, the flow encapsulation as well as the phase inversion. In systems in which $\lambda = \lambda(\sigma_{12})$ and whose concentration is near the phase inversion, one may expect the extrudate morphology to vary with the radial position. Some of these expectations were experimentally proven for blends of poly(ethylene-co-vinylacetate) with co-polyamide (*Tsebrenko* et al., 1985) or for polyethylene with either polystyrene, polyamide-6 or with polycarbonate (*Min*, 1984).

The elongational field is more efficient in deforming the dispersed phase than the shear field. The intensity of the extensional field in the convergent zone was shown to be sufficient to cause coalescence and fibrillation of polyamide-6 spheres at the temperature 79 °C below the melting point (see Fig. 2.45). It was shown in ingenious experiments (*Sakellarides* and *McHugh*, 1987; *Tree* and *McHugh*, 1988) that the extensional field can produce fibrous crystals of high density polyethylene in its blend with linear low density polyethylene at 160 °C, i.e. 27 °C above the equilibrium melting temperature. Extensional field fibrilation of the dispersed phase was also discussed in Part 3.5.3.

# 3.11  Viscoelasticity of PAB

The basic concepts of viscoelasticity and its fundamental relations were presented in 3.2.2. As before, the discussion will be limited to the linear viscoelastic region (*Ferry*, 1980).

From the fundamental point of view it is important to determine variation of the dynamic moduli in as wide a range of independent variables as possible. The principal variables are frequency (or its inverse – time, t), temperature, T, and pressure, P. Since there are experimental limitations for measuring the moduli in a wide range of each of these variables, there is a significant interest in constructing tTP-master curves by shifting the experimental data.

For simple fluids, the procedure involves e.g. isobaric and isothermal scans of the storage and loss shear moduli, $G'$ and $G''$, within at least three decades of frequency. (If the range of frequency is too narrow it is impossible to detect deviation from the "master curve"; in this case use of the curve outside the investigated range of variables may lead to serious error). To construct the master curve $G'b_T$ and $G''b_T$ are plotted as functions of frequency, $\omega$, and then by horizontal shifting the parameter $a_T$ is determined; see Eqs (3.68) to (3.73). If the measurements are carried out at different temperature and pressure, then two-step shifting may be necessary. For some systems associations at low temperatures may lead to network formation which also necessitates a double shifting (*Saunders* et al., 1959). The stated interest in "variation of moduli" refers to their absolute value as well as to the transitions, separating various structures of the material. For isobaric tests an example of the transition map is given in Fig. 3.7. The "map" simply indicates variation of structure with both frequency (or time) and temperature. It is important to recognize that the structure of a viscoelastic material is the same within the bounds of the neighboring lines or, in other words, that, for example, the material in the $\alpha$ to $\beta$ transition region behaves differently than that in any other region.

The tTP-principle works if the relaxation spectrum of the material can be "shifted" uniformly when T or P changes, or more simply if a change of e.g. temperature, modifies the frequency of all the vibrating units by the same factor, $a_{TP}$. This implies that the T,P-effects should be a simple thermal activation type, not involving chemical or structural changes. In short, for tTP-superposition to work the material structure must remain stable; a corollary: an attempt tof generate the tTP-superposition should be restricted to one region at a time on the transition map. In particular one should not expect superposition within the transition zones, $T_m$, $T_g$ or $T_i$, $i = \beta, \gamma...$ (*Cavaille* et al., 1987, 1988; *Perez* et al., 1988).

Experimentally, if data were collected within a narrow frequency range, one may force superposition across the transition region, but this not only obscures the true behavior of the system, but also leads to complications, when variation of $a_T$ or $a_P$ with independent variables, is examined.

So far, the discussion has been limited to the rheologically simple bodies, e.g. amorphous glass/liquid system constituting but a fraction of the polymeric materials. Most polymers are semicrystalline and the crystallinity adds another set of difficulties in generating the tTP-master curve. From the discussion on RTP-NMR studies on crystallization (*Tanaka* and *Nishi*, 1986) in Part 2.5.2, it is apparent that the chain mobility (at least within the crystallization zone) in all three regions: amorphous, intermediate and crystalline is kinetically controlled. In short, the crystallization and melting depends not only on $\omega$, T and P but also on the time and history of the specimen. This makes generation of the tTP-master curve more difficult (*Miki*, 1970; *Fesko* and *Tschoegl*, 1971; *Stein* et al., 1974).

If the specimens are carefully prepared, e.g. by annealing them near the melting point for an adequate period of time (to release the stresses and at the same time to ascertain the maximum crystallinity), then superposition is possible. However, in this case besides $a_T$ and $b_T$ the third (vertical) shift factor, $v_T$, is usually needed. The procedure for calculating $a_T$, $b_T$ and $v_T$ was proposed by *Arai* and *Ferry* (1986). Since $b_T$ and $v_T$ are identical for $G'$ and $G''$, they cancel out when the moduli are plotted as $G''/G' = \tan\delta$ vs. $\omega$. Thus horizontal shifting of $\tan\delta$ vs. $\omega$ allows calculation of $a_T$. The shift factor $b_T$ is calculated directly from the temperature variation of density, Eq. (3.68). Then plotting $G'b_T$ (or $G''b_T$) vs. $\omega a_T$ permits calculation of $v_T$ from vertical shifts of the isothermal portions. Note that this procedure assumes a pseudo-equilibrium structure at each temperature. The isothermal frequency sweep of three decades takes about 10 minutes. The time allowed for stepping from one temperature to another should be sufficiently long for equilibration; the heating rates $r \leqslant 0.2\,°C/min$ are usually required (*Dumoulin*, 1988). As a result about 30 hours are needed for the frequency sweep from $-150$ to $+150\,°C$ with adequate care needed for tT-superposition.

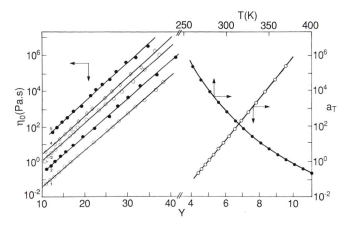

Fig. 3.62 Linearization of the temperature dependence of: (left) zero-shear viscosity of epoxy resins (*Utracki* and *Ghijsels*, 1987), and (right) the time-temperature shift factor of poly-n-octylmethacrylate (*Utracki*, 1980) by means of Eq (3.225).

The temperature variation of isobaric $a_T$, $b_T$ and $v_T$ differs. It also changes from one tT-zone of the transition map to another. For example, $a_T$ below and above $T_g$ usually follows Arrhenius Eq(3.202) and WLF Eq(3.201), respectively. Note that:

$$\ln a_T = \ln \eta_0/\eta_{0,R} + \ln b_T \tag{3.224}$$

where the subscript R indicates the reference condition. The first term on the right-hand-side of Eq (3.224) can be calculated from (*Utracki*, 1974, 1980, 1982; *Utracki* and *Simha*, 1981; *Utracki* and *Ghijsels*, 1987):

$$\ln \eta_0 = B_0 + B_1 Y \tag{3.225}$$

where   $Y \equiv 1/[h \exp\{0.11515(T/T_g)^{3/2}\} - 1]$

with $B_i$ - the parameters and $0.9 \le h \le 1.0$ – the shielding factor.

An example of linearization of the log $\eta_0$ (or log $a_T$) vs. Y in accord with Eq (3.225) is shown in Fig. 3.62. It was found that for some systems (e.g. see Fig. 3.63) Eq (3.225) provides a better, easier to interpret description of $a_T$ or $\eta_0$ dependence on T than either the Arrhenius or WLF relation (*Utracki*, 1982; *Sammut* and *Utracki*, 1988; *Dumoulin*, 1988). The second term on the right hand side of Eq (3.224), $\ln b_T$, can be calculated from the statistical thermodynamics dependence:

$$\ln b_T = \ln(\varrho T/\varrho_R T_R) = S(T_R^{3/2} - T^{3/2}) + \ln T/T_R \tag{3.226}$$

where $S = S_1 T^{*-3/2}$, with $S_1 = 23.8345$ being a universal constant for linear polymers and $T^*$ the temperature reducing parameter characteristic for a given fluid. The dependence is based on the *Simha* and *Somcynsky* (1969) theory, discussed in Parts 2.3.4 and 3.3.

The tT-superposition of dynamic shear moduli of the linear low density polyethylene, polypropylene and their blends indicated that in most cases (*Dumoulin*, 1988):

$$v_T \simeq v_0 + v_1 T \tag{3.227}$$

where $v_i$ are parameters. This observation may suggest that at least in polyolefins the population of vibrating units, changes linearly with temperature at $T < T_m$. For rubbers $v_T$ was found to follow the Arrhenius Eq (3.202) (*Arai* and *Ferry*, 1986).

While for semicrystalline polymers construction of tTP-master curves is difficult, for PAB it is sometimes impossible. For immiscible blends of two semi-crystalline polymers the temperature range within which the morphology of both resins is constant may be too narrow for determination of $a_T$, $b_T$ and $v_T$. Furthermore, there may be so many of these "stable" regions, that the resulting master curve becomes too complex for use. Under these circumstances the viscoelastic analysis of PAB is usually restricted to the temperature scans at constant frequency. The main purpose of these scans is not the construction of a tT-master curve, but rather that part of the transition map which is of interest in a specific application of the blend. The minimum information required is a single temperature sweep at usually low frequency in which the transition temperatures and magnitudes of storage and loss moduli can be determined. Accordingly, the discussion of the viscoelastic behavior of PAB will be divided into two parts: 1. dealing with tT-superposition and 2. with the temperature scans.

### 3.11.1  Time-Temperature Superposition

The homologous polymer mixtures are good model systems for miscible polymer blends. Over the years many of these have been studied, providing an invaluable source of information (e.g. *Prest* and *Porter*, 1972a; *Ferry*, 1980).

The tT-superposition for polystyrene/polyphenyleneether (PS/PPE) was shown to be well obeyed for all investigated compositions, $w_2 \leq 40.3$ wt% at T = 140 to 235 °C and $0.19 \leq \omega(\text{rad/s}) \leq 75.0$ (*Prest* and *Porter*, 1972b). Only one horizontal shift factor, $a_T$, was used, indicating the same relaxation mechanism in G' and G" for both polymers. This lead to the conclusion of blend miscibility. The $a_T$ vs. T dependence was found to follow the WLF Eq (3.201) with $c_i^0$ parameters generalized for composition variation by assuming additivity of both the free volume fraction and the thermal expansion coefficient:

$$f = \sum_{i=1}^{2} \phi_i[f_{gi} + \alpha_i(T - T_{gi})] \tag{3.228}$$

and:   $\alpha = \sum_{i=1}^{2} \phi_i\alpha_i$

where $\phi_i$ and $T_{gi}$ are respectively volume fraction and glass transition temperature for component i = 1, 2. At the iso-free volume state, f = 0.115, the effective segmental friction coefficient was found to be constant, independent of the blend composition. Excellent tT-superposition was recently reported for miscible blends of cis-1,4-polyisoprene and atactic polyvinylethylene (*Roland*, 1988).

There is extensive literature on tT-superposition for block copolymers. Since these materials are good models for compatibilized blends a short summary is in order. The poly(1,4-butadiene-b-1,4-isoprene) di-block copolymers were found to be miscible (*Ramos*, 1977; *Ramos* and *Cohen*, 1977, 1979), even though blends of polybutadiene/polyisoprene of similar molecular weights are immiscible. The tT-superposition was achieved with $a_T$ calculated from WFL Eq (3.201) assuming additivity of the homopolymer constants. The measurements were conducted at T < $T_g$. A molecular theory for these systems was proposed by *Liu* and *Soong* (1980). The theory combines the transient network concept and a homogeneous block copolymer model of beads and springs with a frictional coefficient due to viscous retardation. A numerical solution of the derived matrices allowed computation of the relaxation time spectrum, from which the storage and loss shear moduli, G'($\omega a_T$) and G"($\omega a_T$) were calculated in good agreement with Ramos and Cohen experimental data.

Poly(styrene-b-butadiene) di-block copolymers (SB) and their blends with homopolymers are immiscible. Within the rubbery-terminal zones the tT-superposition was obtained with $a_T$ following either the Arrhenius Eq (3.202) (low molecular weights) or WLF Eq (3.201) (*Watanabe* et al., 1982; *Watanabe* and *Kotaka*, 1983, 1984).

The thermorheologically complex three-block SBS copolymers have been extensively studied (*Fesko* and *Tschoegl*, 1971, 1974; *Cohen* and *Tschoegl* 1972, 1974, 1976). At temperatures below $T_g$ of the polystyrene block the material behaved as filled rubber. However, even in this region the viscoelasticity reflected the three-phase nature of the block polymer; different temperature dependencies of the polystyrene and polybutadiene phase had to be accounted for, and the effect of the interphase necessitated a correction. Empirically $a_T$ was found to follow the WLF dependence at $T < 15\ °C$ and Arrhenius relation at $T > 15\ °C$.

For the creep compliance of thermorheologically complex materials *Fesko* and *Tschoegl* (1971) wrote:

$$(\partial \ln J(t)/\partial \ln t)_T = (\partial \ln J[t/a_T(t)]/\partial \ln[t/a_T(t)])_{T_R} \times [1 - (\partial \ln a_T(t)/\partial \ln t)_T] \qquad (3.229)$$

where $T_R$ is the reference temperature. By definition, for the thermorheologically simple materials $\partial a_T/\partial t = 0$ and the last square bracket on the right hand side of Eq (3.229): $[\ ] = 1$. On the basis of experimental evidence additivity of compliances was postulated for SBS system:

$$J = \Sigma w_i J_i \qquad (3.230)$$

from which:

$$(\partial \ln a_T(t)/\partial T)_t = \sum_i N_i(t) d\ln a_{Ti}/dT \qquad (3.231)$$

with $N_i(t)$ being the population coefficents defined as:

$$N_i(t) = w_i L_i(\tau)/\sum_i w_i L_i[\tau/a_T(t)] \Big|_{\tau = t}$$

$L_i(\tau) = [\partial J_i(T)/\partial \ln t]T$ is the first approximation of the retardation spectrum. Eq (3.231) can be written in terms of the dynamic variables, $J'(\omega)$ and $J''(\omega)$, with $\omega = 1/\tau$. The model predicts that the shift factors for $J(t)$ and $J'(\omega)$ should be the same within the experimental uncertainty, but different from that of $J''(\omega)$.

For SBS the tT-master curve was constructed using Eq (3.230) and assuming that the neat components are thermorheologically simple. By shifting onto this curve the discreet $J(t,T)$ functions a set of horizontal shift factors, $a_T(t)$, was generated. The plot of $a_T(t)$ was found to depend on $t = 1/\omega$; at lower temperature and higher frequency $a_T$ was dominated by polybutadiene, at the other end by polystyrene. The authors warned that for multiphase materials the empirical shifting procedure, even when generating good superposition, does not necessarily lead to a valid master curve (*Fesko* and *Tschoegl*, 1971).

The tT-superposition of poly(styrene-co-acrylonitrile) grafted on polybutadiene rubber particles (ABS) was observed for a wide range of compositions, rubber content and rubber particle diameters within the rubbery and terminal zones. The horizontal shift factor was found to follow WLF dependence (3.201) with the universal $c_i^0$ constants and $T_s = 130$ to $134\ °C$, depended on composition. At high rubber content and low frequency, $G'(\omega a_T)$ showed a positive deviation from the tT-master curve caused by the yield stress. In this region the relaxation spectrum calculated from $G''$ did not agree with that computed from $G'$, indicating different value of yield stress of these two functions.

Within the $T = -60$ to $+80\ °C$ the dynamic tensile properties of miscible polybutene-1/polypropylene (PB/PP) blends were measured at frequency: $\nu = 3.5$ to $110$ Hz. The shift factor $a_T$ was found to follow WLF relation with the universal constants, $c_i^0$, and $T_s$ was taken as $T_g + 50$, where $T_g = -275$ to $-11°C$ for composition changing from 0 to 100% PP (*Piloz* et al., 1976).

The stress relaxation, $E = E(t,T)$, of polypropylene/block copolymer of styrene and butadiene (PP/SBS) or PP/polyisobutylene (PP/PIB) blends, were studied at $T = -60$ to 80 °C (*Goldman* et al., 1977). The data were superimposed on master curves by horizontal shifting, $E(t,T) = E[ta(t,T)]$. Following Fesko and Tschoegl the authors assumed that blend components are thermorheologically simple, which led to the following relations:

$$(\partial E(t,T)/\partial T)_t = (\partial E(t,T)/\partial \ln t)_T \, d\ln a(T)/dT \tag{3.232}$$

and     $d\ln a(t,T)/dT = \sum_i N_i(t) d\ln a_i(T)/dT; \qquad i = 1,2 \tag{3.233}$

where   $N_i(t) = \phi_i L_i(t,T)/[\phi_1 L_1(t,T_0) + \phi_2 L_2(t,T_0)]$

with    $L_i(t,T) = \partial E_i(\ln t,T)/\partial \ln t$

Numerical integration of Eq (3.233) allowed calculation of $a(t,T)$ for the blend from $a(T)$ of blend components and their volume fractions, $\phi_i$. The tT-superposition worked quite well for PP/SBS, but not for PP/PIB.

Polycarbonate/ABS blends were analyzed for the shear stress relaxation, $G = G(t,T)$, behavior as a function of the physical aging time, $t_a$ (*Maurer* et al., 1985):

$$G(t,T) = G_0(t/t_r)^b \exp\{-(t/t_r)^a\} \tag{3.234}$$

where: $G_0$ is an elastic constant, which slightly decreases with T and increases (from 0 to 3%) with $t_a$, $t_r = t_r(t_a,T)$ is the characteristic relaxation time, a and b are numerical constants; $a = 0.4$ and 0.45, $-b \times 10^4 = 88$ and 14 respectively for ABS and PC at the reference temperature $T_R = 50°C$ and for $t_a = 1hr$. At temperatures well below $T_g$ the slope $\partial \ln t_r/\partial \ln t_a = 0.9$ for both ABS and PC independent of T; at $T \to T_g$ the slope decreased to zero. Consequently the tT-superposition for the blends can be expected only within the low temperature region below $T_g(ABS) < T_g(PC)$. For the higher temperatures $G(t,T)$ can be calculated from properties of the immiscible blend components and their concentration using a suitable morphological model.

*Cavaille* et al. (1987b) investigated the dynamic behavior of the polystyrene/polyvinylmethylether (PS/PVME) miscible blends containing 10 and 20% PVME at $v = 10^{-5}$ to $10^5$ Hz and $T = 100$ to 450K. In spite of a secondary relaxation peak at $T < T_g$, good tT-superposition was obtained by horizontal shifting. Within the glass transition region, similarly as reported previously for neat PS (*Cavaille* et al., 1987a), no tT-superposition was possible. The lack of superposition was particularly apparent for the loss tangent – frequency dependence at different temperatures; tan$\delta$ tended to be broader and lower as the temperature increased. The lack of superposition within the glass transition region is related to the fact that the polymer structure on the two sides of the transition are different. The transition is kinetic in nature with the rate constant dependent on T. Even if the tT-superposition were forced to occur (e.g. by virtue of narrow range of scanned frequencies and/or large temperature steps) the temperature dependence of the shift factor, $a_T = a_T(T)$, would show discontinuity in the vicinity of the glass transition temperature $T_g$; at $T > T_g$ the plot as usual would follow the WLF Eq (3.201) whereas at $T \le T_g$ the $a_T$ values would fall below the WLF predicted dependence. The kinetic nature of the discontinuity can be demonstrated by physically aging the specimens within the $T < T_g$ region (*Hunston*, 1987).

The relaxation moduli of polyvinylacetate (PVAc) with lightly crosslinked polymethylmethacrylate, $\phi = 0.5$, at $T = 29.6$ to 163.2°C and within two decades of the relaxation times were determined by *Horino* et al. (1965). The lack of superposition was noted. The method of data treatment developed by *Fesko* and *Tschoegl* (1971, 1974) for SBS was later used by *Kaplan* and *Tschoegl* (1974). The authors constructed the $E(t)$ vs. $t/a_T$ master curve using the *Takayanagi* et al. (1964) model:

$$E(t,T) = (1-\lambda)E_2 + \lambda/[(1-v)/E_2 + v/E_1] \tag{3.235}$$

where λ and v are parameters defining the system morphology; $\lambda v = \phi_1$. Fitting the model necessitated the use of three values of λ in three temperature ranges. The limiting temperatures depended on the time scale, t. The analysis indicated that PVAc constituted the matrix. *Kaplan* and *Tschoegl* (1974) observed that $a_T$ depends on both time and temperature, i.e. that independently of the constructed superposition the singular master curve for the system does not exist.

Blends of polystyrene/low density polyethylene (PS/LDPE) with and without the compatibilizing, partially hydrogenated poly(styrene-b-isoprene) were studied by *Utracki* and *Sammut* (1988). As shown in Fig. 3.47 the tT-superposition was limited to T ⩾ 200 °C; below this limit $a_T = a_T(T,\omega)$ was observed. Superposing the loss modulus data at $\omega = 100$ rad/s the $a_T$ was generated. Plot of this parameter vs. T is shown in Fig. 3.63. Of the three tested relations: Arrhenius Eq (3.202), WLF Eq (3.201) and Utracki Eq (3.225) the latter one, with h and $T_g$ parameters of the matrix PS, best fitted the data.

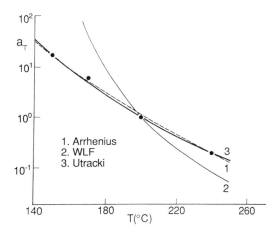

Fig. 3.63 Temperature dependence of the time-temperature shift factor for polystyrene/low density polyethylene blends. Points – experimental, lines 1 to 3 calculated form Eqs (3.202), (3.201) and (3.225), respectively (*Utracki* and *Sammut*, 1988).

In Fig. 3.64 the tT-superposition as well as the temperature dependence of the horizontal, $a_T$, and vertical, $v_T$, shift factors for LLDPE/PP = 75/25 blend are shown (*Dumoulin*, 1988). Since for LLDPE a strong transition peak was detected at T ≃ − 20 °C (see Fig. 3.65) and for PP at T ≃ 0 °C arbitrarily the master curve was constructed using the isothermal data (spanning the frequency range from 0.03 to 10 Hz) at T = −90 to 0 °C ($T_R = $ −50 °C) and T = 0 to 100 °C ($T_R = $ + 50 °C). The temperature dependence of $a_T$ followed either WLF Eq (3.201) with adjustable (non-universal) parameters or Eq (3.225); $v_T$ was found to increase linearly with T, in accord with Eq (3.227).

There is a question as to how useful such a forced tT-superposition is. Obviously the constructed master curves do not reflect inherent superposability of the system but rather allow for generalization of data within a limited range of experimentally accessible variables, v and T. In consequence the curve should not be used outside this range. This in principle negates the main purpose of the tT-procedure.

It has been mentioned that the rheological functions of immiscible polymer blends without interlayer slip should be plotted as a function of stress not deformation rate or frequency. However, the tT-superposition procedure considers mainly the frequency dependent moduli. Defining the $a_T$ shift factors taken at constant stress and constant deformation

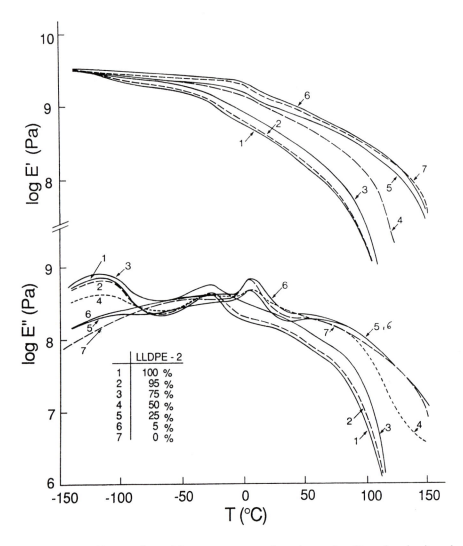

Fig. 3.64 Storage and loss tensile modulus vs. temperature for polypropylene/linear low density poly-ethylene blends at frequency 1Hz (*Dumoulin* et al., 1987).

rate as $a_{T\sigma}$ and $a_{T\gamma}$, respectively, the correlation between these two was written by *Kasajima* (1978):

$$(\partial \ln a_{T\gamma}/\partial \ln a_{T\sigma})_P = (\partial \ln \sigma/\partial \ln \gamma)_{P,T} = n_{P,T} \qquad (3.236)$$

where $n_{PT}$ is the local power-law index, and the subscripts P,T indicate isobaric and isothermal conditions, respectively. Similar dependence was derived for the pressure shift factors:

$$(\partial \ln a_{P\gamma}/\partial \ln a_{T\sigma})_T = n_{P,T} \qquad (3.237)$$

In summary, the tT-superposition for miscible or immiscible blends can be found only within a range of stable morphology. Variation of the morphology, during either sample

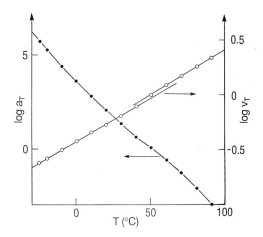

Fig. 3.65 Temperature dependence of the vertical, $v_T$, and horizontal, $a_T$, time-temperature shift factors for polypropylene/linear low density polyethylene blends (*Dumoulin*, 1988).

preparation, aging or testing leads to different rheological responses and at best an apparent master curve. If the morphology does not change during the test, then analysis of the viscoelastic data can furnish valuable information on the effects of interfacial interactions on the blend structure.

The above conclusions are general, independently of whether the viscoelastic spectrum is obtained by mechanical or other means. For example, the dielectric studies of polystyrene/polymethylmethacrylate within the sub-$T_g$ region of β-dispersion at frequency 50 Hz to 100 kHz were reported by *Balda* et al. (1987). For blends the tT-superposition could not be obtained.

### 3.11.2 Temperature Scans

In view of the complexity of the tTP-superposition for PAB the temperature scans at one or several frequencies are a popular method of blend analysis. The scans allow determination of the transition temperatures, $T_T$, as well as absolute magnitude of the dynamic moduli between $T_T$'s.

In Part 2.6.3 the viscoelastic measurements were listed as suitable and popular methods of $T_g$ determination. From the concentration dependence of storage and loss moduli in the $T_g$ region one can deduce the blend miscibility. However, note that as shown in Fig. 1.3 a single transition temperature does not necessarily indicate miscibility. Since methods of specimen preparation for the viscoelastic and thermal (DSC/DTA) measurements differ, the morphology of immiscible blends may also vary, leading to differences in $T_g$. As was indicated in Part 2.6.3 the $T_g$ is a measure of degree of dispersion; for fine particles with dimension d ≤ 2 to 15 nm a single $T_g$ is expected. However, as will be discussed on the following pages, the temperature scans can provide more information than $T_g$.

The model tri-block SBS copolymer and its blends with co- and homopolymers have been extensively studied. Low frequency ($v = 0.5$ Hz) scan of SBS and SBS/PS blends allowed determination of the microstructure of these systems (*Diamant*, 1982; *Diamant* et al., 1982). Following *Nielsen's* (1974) work on composites, the authors derived the following microstructural model for the blend shear modulus:

$$G/G_2 = (1 - A\psi R\phi_1)/(1 + R\phi_1) \tag{3.238}$$

where    $A = [\eta]-1$

$\psi = 1 + (1-\phi_{max})\phi_1/\phi_{max}$

and    $R = (G_2-G_1)/(AG_2+G_1)$

with subscripts 1 and 2 indicating respectively the dispersed and matrix phase, and $\phi_{max}$ being the maximum packing volume fraction. Fitting Eq (3.238) to the experimental G', G'' data allowed determination of an average composition profile in the system. The method can be used for analyzing dynamic behavior of any PAB.

An addition of a homopolymer (polystyrene (PS) or polybutadiene (PB)) to SBS affects the corresponding glass transition region as well as, in the case of PS, the absolute value of moduli at $T > T_g(PB)$. The behavior depends on concentration and molecular weight of the homopolymer (*Diamant*, 1982; *Hsiue* and *Ma*, 1984; *Shyu* and *Hsu*, 1984). When the specimens are prepared by solvent casting the dynamic mechanical behavior depends strongly on solvent and physical aging (*Hsiue* and *Ma*, 1984). Since viscoelastic performance is affected by the specimen morphology, *eo ibso* the morphology changes with solvent and thermal history. The effect of mixed solvent (ethyl acetate/tetrahydrofuran) was particularly pronounced. The effect of molecular weight of the block copolymer has also been studied (*Kraus* and *Rollman*, 1976).

The dynamic mechanical properties, reflecting on the specimen morphology, frequently provide a powerful tool for analyzing complex systems, where other methods fail. The viscoelasticity has been also used for examination of interpenetrating polymer networks (IPN). For example *Rosovizky* et al. (1979) conducted systematic analysis of polyurethane-IPN using the *Takayanagi* et al. (1964) model (see Eq (3.235)) for dynamic tensile moduli:

$$E' = (1-\lambda)E_2' + \lambda X/(X^2+Y^2) \qquad (3.239)$$

$$E'' = (1-\lambda)E_2'' + \lambda X/(X^2+Y^2)$$

where:    $X = (1-v)E_2'/(E_2'^2+E_2''^2) + vE_1'/(E_1'^2+E_1''^2)$

$Y = (1-v)E_2''/(E_2'^2+E_2''^2) + vE_1''/(E_1'^2+E_1''^2)$

with $\lambda$ and $v$ being the model parameters, $\lambda v = \phi_1$. The temperature-induced changes in IPN morphology were evidenced by variation of $v = v(T)$ parameter, while its microheterogeneity in breadth of the E'' (or tan$\delta$) peak in the glass transition region (*Suzuki* et al., 1980; *Li* et al., 1988).

The Takayanagi model was also used by *Eastmond* and *Haraguchi* (1983) for calculating the dynamic moduli of polycarbonate blends with polystyrene. The blends were cast from 1,1,1-trichloro-bis-2-p-hydroxyphenylethane. The calculations were in good accord with experimental data.

Dynamic mechanical testing in extensional mode allowed optimization of polyurethane/epoxy/unsaturated polyester-type IPN elastomers and foams (*Klempner* et al., 1988).

Polycarbonate (PC), blends properties have been studied by thermal and dynamic mechanical methods. In Fig. 3.66 the complex shear modulus, G* and tan$\delta$ of PC/polybutyleneterephthalate (PBT), are plotted vs. T (*Heuschen*, 1986). The tan$\delta$ peak corresponding to the PC glass-rubber dispersion changed with PBT content from 150 to 141 and 136 °C for w(PBT) = 45 and 80 wt%, respectively. Similarly, the PBT loss peak position changed with composition from 51 to 63 and 55 °C for w(PBT) = 100, 80 and 45 wt%, respectively. On the other hand the melting point of PBT, $T_m$ = 225 °C, was found to be constant, independent of the blend composition. *Wahrmund* et al. (1978) reported three loss peaks for PC/PBT blends containing 30 to 50 wt% PBT; in addition to the characteristic peaks of the homopolymers an intermediate was observed. The latter relaxation may have originated in transesterified PC-PBT copolymer, absent in the well stabilized blends studied by *Heuschen* (1986).

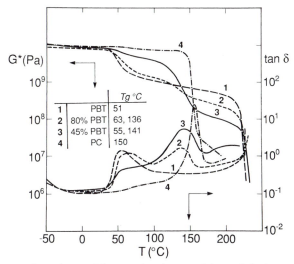

Fig. 3.66 Temperature dependence of the complex shear modulus and the loss tangent for polycarbonate/polybutyleneterephthalate blends (*Heuschen*, 1986).

The analysis of PC/PET blends by dynamic-mechanical means allowed miscibility of these polymers in the amorphous phase in PET-rich blends to be postulated, whereas PC-rich blends seperated into two amorphous regions. According to the authors the prepared blends contained little if any transesterification products (*Nassar* et al., 1979). Miscibility of PC with either poly(1,4-cyclohexanedi- methanol-co-terephthalic acid), its analog in which a part of terephthalic acid was replaced by isophthalic acid, or poly-ε-caprolactone was observed in temperature scans at single frequency (*Mohn* et al., 1979; *Cruz* et al., 1979).

Blends of rigid polyphenyleneterephthalamide (PPTA) and flexible ABS was studied by *Takayanagi* and *Goto* (1984). A systematic increase of $T_g$ with PPTA content as well as that of tensile storage modulus ,E', was observed.

Polyhydroxyether of bisphenol-A (Phenoxy) exhibits strong specific interactions with other polymers either through the hydrogen bonding or π−π interactions. As a result it is miscible with numerous resins; e.g. polybutyleneterephthalate, partially transesterified polyethyleneterephthalate (*Robeson* and *Furtek*, 1979; *Eguiazabal* and *Iruin*, 1987), poly-butyleneterephthalate/polytetrahydrofuran copolymer (Hytrel), polyethyleneoxide, polyvinylmethylether, polyvinylpyrollidone, poly-1,4cyclohexylenedimethylene-tere/isophthalate, poly-1,4butyleneadipate, poly-2,2dimeth-1,3propyleneadipate (or succinate), poly-ε-caprolactone, polyethyloxazoline, linear polyurethanes based on polyesters and ethyleneoxide/epichlorydrin copolymer (partial miscibility) (*Merriam* and *Robeson*, 1985). Because of its high miscibility Phenoxy has been used as an interphasing ingredient in blends and composites. Temperature scanning at low frequency, ν = 1Hz, provided evidence of miscibility, transesterification, morphological modification, etc.

The viscoelasticity of polyvinylchloride (PVC), blends have been extensively studied for information on miscibility, dispersion and morphology. PVC/Hytrel blends were studied by *Hourston* and *Hughes* (1977, 1981). On the basis of tanδ peak position the miscibility between Hytrel's soft segments (polytetrahydrofuran glycol terephthalate) and PVC was postulated. On the other hand PVC/chlorosulfonated PE blends were found to be immiscible (*Hourston* and *Hughes*, 1979). Miscibility of PVC blends with polyurethanes (PU), depends on the chemical nature of PU segments (*Wang* and *Cooper*, 1981). An excellent review of PVC modification by blending and copolymerization with emphasis on the mechanical performance was published by *Manson* (1981).

The miscibility and morphology of chlorinated-PVC (CPVC), and PU were studied by thermal and dynamic mechanical methods (*Garcia*, 1986). The CPVC contained 67% Cl and PU contained end-capped soft polytetramethyleneadipate segments. Addition of about 5% PU caused an increase of G' of CPVC by about 50% (antiplasticization). Both DSC and torsion pendulum tests indicated a single $T_g$ which in the full range of composition followed the Gordon-Taylor Eq (2.93) with K $\simeq$ 3. Both the width of the loss peak as well as large K-value indicated immiscibility in spite of the fact that only a single $T_g$ peak for the blends was observed. Transmission electron microscopy revealed two-phase structure, with domain size varying from d = 0.1 to 1.5 μm.

Blends of polystyrene (PS), with low density polyethylene (LDPE), are immiscible (*Han*, 1971–1974). Torsion pendulum measurements indicated that transition temperatures of homopolymers are independent of composition while the intensity of loss peaks systematically varies with their content (*Huppenthal* and *Kasperczuk*, 1977). These observations were confirmed by *Sjoerdsma* et al. (1980). The authors demonstrated that addition of 1% of di-block PS-PE copolymer has a profound effect on morphology and the low temperature dynamic mechanical spectrum.

*Class* and *Chu* (1985) used the dynamic tests for studying the miscibility of natural (NR), and styrene-butadiene (SBR), rubbers with low molecular weight resins: polystyrene (PS), polyvinylcyclohexane (PVCH), and polytertbutylstyrene (PTBS). The authors reported that the viscoelastic properties correlated quite well with the morphological observations under light microscope; i.e. that the dynamic-mechanical tests provided adequate information on blend compatibility. PS was found to be compatible with SBR, but not with NR. By contrast PVCH was reported to be compatible with NR but not with SBR. The aromato-aliphatic PTBS was compatible with both rubbers. The miscibility was found to change dramatically with molecular weight; the system became non-compatible when the weight average molecular weight was increased to $M_w \geq 1$ kg/mole. The effect of concentration was also examined.

Blends of polypropylene (PP), with either ethylene-propylene-diene copolymer (EPDM), or its sulfonated and metal-neutralized derivative were studied at ν = 1 Hz at T = 173 to 473 K (*Duvdevani* et al., 1982). Both blend series showed multiple transitions consistent with the two-phase structure observed by scanning electron microscopy. However, while morphology of the two blend series was similar, the mechanical properties of the ones containing ionomer were superior. Blends of PP with EPDM, ethylene-propylene copolymers (EPR), polyethylenes of different type, or with combinations of any three polymers from the above list, are of commercial interest. The mechanical performance of these blends depends on both the thermodynamic miscibility and morphology of the crystalline form of the polymeric components. Both factors affect the dynamic mechanical spectrum. The blends are compatible but immiscible and the transition temperatures observed in the temperature scans are invariants of composition (*Dumoulin* and *Utracki*, 1984; *Kolarik* et al., 1986; *Goldman* et al., 1986; *Kallitsis* and *Kalfoglu*, 1987; *Karger-Kocsis* and *Kiss*, 1987; *Dumoulin* et al., 1987; *Dumoulin*, 1988). An example of the dynamic spectra for PP/LLDPE is shown in Fig. 3.65. The glass transition temperature of LLDPE and PP is characterized by peaks on the E" vs. T curve at − 115 and + 3 °C. While the position of these peaks does not change with composition their intensity does; the relaxation disappears when the polymer content falls below 25 wt%. Since for PP/LDPE or PP/HDPE addition of the compatibilizing copolymer, EPR or EPDM, was reported to be necessary, but not so for blends of PP with LLDPE; it seems that the miscibility of PP with LLDPE is better than that with either LDPE or HDPE. As LLDPE is a copolymer containing 11 to 19 mol percent of a comonomer (*Schlund* and *Utracki*, 1987a) the higher miscibility with PP could be expected. The use of *Takayanagi* et al. (1964) of Eqs (3.235), (3.239) for describing the compositional variation of either G, G* or G', G" provides information on blend morphology. Other models have also been used, i.e. Kerner (1956), *Hill* (1965), *Tsai* (1968), *Halpin* (1969), *Dickie* (1973), *Nielsen* (1974), *Levin* (1976) as well as *McGee* and *McCullough* (1981).

When blends are cast from a solvent their morphology, and in consequence the dynamic mechanical behavior, is solvent dependent. This observation, mentioned for block copolymers, is true as well for blends of two polymers (*Miyata* and *Hata*, 1970; *Shultz* and *Young*, 1980). Blends which were either dried rapidly or freeze-dried tended to preserve their molecular dispersion in a mutually good solvent. As a result these mixtures showed only one loss peak on a dynamic spectrum. By contrast, when the solvent was good for one but poor for another blend component or when the drying was slow enough to allow phase ripening, then two loss peaks were obtained. The kinetics of the process depended on concentration, temperature, and molecular weights of the blend components. This led to a whole spectrum of possible dynamic behaviors from apparent miscibility to immiscibility. In Fig. 3.67 the storage and loss tensile moduli are shown for polymethylmethacrylate/ polyvinylacetate, 50/50-blend cast from several solvents. The distribution function, F, can be computed comparing the experimental values of dynamic moduli with the values given by (*Miyata* and *Hata*, 1970):

$$E' = \int_0^1 F(\phi) \sum_i^j \phi_i E_i' \{t,T + [k\phi_j(T_{gi} - T_{gj})/(\phi_i + k\phi_j)]\}d\phi \qquad (3.240)$$

where for two component blends $\phi_i + \phi_j = 1$ and $k \equiv \Delta\alpha_i/\Delta\alpha$ with $\Delta\alpha_i$ being the difference between volume expansion coefficients in the rubbery and the glassy state.

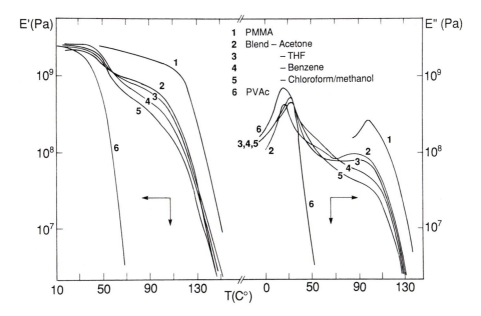

Fig. 3.67 Temperature dependence of the storage, E', and loss, E", tensile modulus for polymethylmethacrylate, polyvinylacetate and their 50:50 blend cast from acetone, tetrahydrofuran, benzene, or a mixture of chloroform with methanol (data from *Miyata* and *Hata*, 1970).

During the last decade new micromechanical methods were introduced for analysis of the origin of the relaxation processes. Two of these methods have been succesfully adopted for PAB: thermally simulated creep (TSC), and the thermally simulated current method (TSCM). TSC is particularly well suitable for non-polar polymers, such as polyolefins and their blends, while TSCM for systems with dipoles. Both methods are based on the same principle: the sample is subjected to mechanical or electrical stress, then cooled down to temperature where molecular motion is hindered. When subsequently the material is warmed up the stresses relax with rates characteristic for the molecular mobility at a given temperature. For TSC the strain variation, for TSCM the depolarization current is measured.

Blends and copolymers of polyethylene (LDPE), and polypropylene (PP), were studied by means of TSC (*Demont* et al., 1984). The method was sensitive enough for detecting the difference in TSC spectrum upon addition of 5% LDPE to PP. The difference was more pronounced in annealed samples. Furthermore, the peaks were observed to be complex. Using a discrete stressing method their fine structure was resolved into the Arrhenius-type activated stress relaxation and Vogel-type volume expansion.

The TSCM was used in studies of poly(ether-b-amide), the PEBAX block copolymer of polytetramethyleneglycol (PTMG, $M_n$ = 2 kg/mole) and polyamide-12 (PA-12, $M_n$ = 0.9). The TSCM spectrum strongly depended on the rate of cooling. Changing the system viscosity allowed a conclusion that phase coarsening was diffusion controlled. PEBAX, in a similar manner to other commercially important block copolymers, was found to be a two phase system. The amorphous phase was found to be PTMG unchanged by the presence of PA–12, whereas the hard-phase PA–12 was found to be plastified by PTMG (*Faruque* and *Lacabanne, 1986*).

## 3.12  Summary

The key to efficient utilization of multiphase materials is optimization of structure. Permeability, weathering, electrical conductivity, mechanical properties, etc. all depend on the developed morphology. While fibrillar reinforcement is desirable for monofilaments, platelets oriented normally in respect to the flux direction are required for enhancement of the barrier properties. Thus the processing engineer must select the material, process and processing parameters which will generate the desired structure in a fabricated piece.

In Part 2, the morphology was discussed in terms of both the equilibrium thermodynamics and the dynamics of phase separation. The equilibrium thermodynamics can be used as a guide for predicting the ultimate blend structure as determined by the intensive and extensive material properties of the ingredients. Depending on the interaction and/or interfacial parameters, the phases may separate into two chemically homogeneous layers or into a structured dispersion whose form is controlled by the concentration. By analogy with block copolymers, the idealized, compatibilized blend is expected to have either a drop ($\phi <$ 0.12), fiber ($0.12 \leq \phi \leq 0.38$) or lamellar structure ($0.38 < \phi < 0.62$).

The dynamics of phase separation allow for two incipient morphologies: dispersed (NG) and co-continuous (SD). The structure is mainly controlled by the depth of quench. The initial size of segregated regions also depends on quench depth, decreasing with its increase from about 100 to 10 nm. With time these initial structures grow in size tending toward the ultimate morphology as predicted by the equilibrium thermodynamics.

In Part 3, the flow and flow-imposed structures were discussed. Inherently these are non-equilibrium morphologies. Under the well-controlled flow conditions, e.g. in hyperbolic or pure shear, several simple geometries can be generated.

In immiscible diluted blends the flow dispersion process is controlled by: viscosity ratio ($\lambda$), capillarity parameter ($\varkappa$), prehistory, deformational field and concentration. At relatively low concentration, $\phi \simeq 0.02$, the flow coalescence begins to become responsible for increase in the drop size, $d \propto \phi^{2/3}$. As the concentration increases two other factors intervene: (i) the apparent yield stress, $\sigma_y$, and (ii) the phase inversion.

The apparent yield stress stabilizes the morphology to the extent that the structure predicted by the equilibrium thermodynamics may not be attainable within the experimentally accessible time limit. The value of $\sigma_y$ increases with $\phi$, but surprisingly it is not a symmetrical function. Even for $\lambda \simeq 1$ diluting polymer A with B generates a different value of $\sigma_y$ from that obtained at analogous concentration generated by diluting polymer B with A, i.e. $\sigma_y(\phi = \phi_B) \neq \sigma_y(\phi = \phi_A)$ for $\phi_B = \phi_A$. It seems that the interface is asymmetric and a single interfacial tension coefficient is not sufficient for its characterization.

The second complication is the phase inversion. In the blend literature this phenomenon is taken to be dependent only on $\lambda$. However, there are numerous indications that in some systems the inversion concentration, $\phi_i$, is insensitive to even drastic changes in $\lambda$. It is worth recalling that in emulsions, $\phi_i$ depends not on $\lambda$ but rather on the type and amount of emulsifier. This again implies dissymmetry of the interface. The phase inversion is a thermodynamic phenomenon. On the two sides of $\phi_i$ the role of the two liquids is reversed; what was the matrix phase at $\phi < \phi_i$ becomes the disperse one at $\phi > \phi_i$, and vice versa. The ultimate structure is determined by the equilibrium thermodynamics. However, shearing polymer blends in the vicinity of $\phi_i$ usually leads to development of co-continuous morphology. The breadth of the concentration range within which this structure is generated depends on: $\lambda$, the absolute value of $\eta$ and the flow field. Again, the co-continuous structure is inherently unstable, but owing to $\sigma_y$ it may remain unchanged for a long time (*Thornton* et al., 1980).

In systems with a marginal miscibility, i.e. those in the vicinity of binodal, there is a strong coupling between flow and thermodynamics; on the one hand, the flow may affect phase separation and on the other, phase separation changes the rheological functions and their sensitivity to independent variables such as temperature and pressure. The control of flow provides a means for generation of interesting morphologies originating from superposition of either NG or SD phase separation and flow deformation.

During the last four years there has been a significant improvement in understanding of the origins and mechanisms responsible for structure formation in liquid/liquid mixtures. In particular, the dynamics of drop deformation in a dilute Newtonian system has been well documented both theoretically and experimentally. The deformation of drops in a steady state flow field is promoted by extension but inhibited by vorticity. At low deformation, D, the interfacial tension acts as an inhibiting, mending factor, whereas at high D-values, where the drop is elongated into a thread, it causes its disintegration into secondary droplets. Formation of the threads is promoted by low $\lambda$ and low viscosity. At $\lambda \geq 3.7$ the vorticity prevents the drop from bursting. Only in extensional fields can they be extended and broken. The rate of deformation depends on the absolute value of the viscosity; the higher the $\eta$, the slower the process (*Rallison*, 1984).

Blending polymers is more complex than mixing Newtonian liquids. Not only does the viscoelastic character of the ingredients complicate the process but the complex flow field in the compounding and processing equipment does as well. Consequently, PAB's show secondary morphological features, viz. complex drops (with droplets of phase A dispersed in drops of phase B, dispersed in phase A), mixtures of drops, fibers and ribbons, flow-induced composition heterogeneity, etc. We are a long way from being able to fully predict blend morphology.

The main emphasis of Part 3 was on PAB flow behavior. The discussion commenced with a résumé of basic rheological relations, then a flow of model systems was summarized, followed by presentation of more recent PAB rheological data. It was assumed that the model systems will facilitate understanding of blend behavior and provide a guide for systematization of information. At the end of this section, the question arises as to the extent of predictability of PAB flow behavior. The answer should address miscible and immiscible systems separately.

The miscible, athermal blends can be modeled as homologous mixtures. On mixing, the theory predicts a decrease of the free volume fraction below the additivity line as reflected in the well predicted PDB behavior of $\eta_0$ seen in Fig. 3.10. Thus, rheology of athermal mixtures can be predicted from the components' behavior. However, the majority of PAB's are not athermal. The specific interactions must generate negative heat of mixing, $\Delta H_m < 0$, which in turn also leads to expectation of PDB. For mixtures of solvents the magnitude of deviation from the log-additivity rule is controlled by $\Delta H_m$. However, for PAB with negative heat of mixing not only resulted in PDB but NDB and PNDB have been reported as well. Two, not necessarily exclusive, explanations can be offered: (i) an increase of the free volume fraction, or (ii) a low value of the interaction viscosity (viz. Eq. (3.83)). To determine independently which one is valid for predicting the flow behavior of the interacting miscible blends, it is necessary to know not only the properties of the constituents but also two interaction parameters (*McAllister*, 1960; *Stroeks* and *Nies*, 1988). Unfortunately, so far there has been no systematic study of the validity of mixing rules for miscible, interacting blends based on a constitutive equation.

The situation becomes more complicated for immiscible blends. Since, as indicated above, there are no valid methods for predicting development of blend morphology there is no basis for derivation of a general constitutive equation which could describe their flow behavior. However, it is fair to ask how far we are on the way toward development of such a constitutive theory.

One may seek an answer to this question by examining the progress of theoretical work on model systems, viz. suspensions and emulsions. The recent reviews in these areas provide an excellent guide (*Rowlinson* and *Swinton*, 1982; *Rallison*, 1984; *Utracki*, 1988; *Barthes-Biesel*, 1988).

For uniform suspension of particles in incompressible, Newtonian liquid, where the diameter of the particle is much smaller than the flow length scale and the system may be considered homogeneous, the average stress tensor components can be written as:

$$\sigma_{ij} = - P\delta_{ij} + 2\eta e_{ij} + \Sigma(S_{ij}^{\alpha} - x_i^{\alpha}F_j^{\alpha})/V \qquad (3.241)$$

where P is the pressure, $\delta_{ij}$ ist the Kronecker delta, $\eta$ is viscosity of the suspending liquid, $e_{ij}$ are local rate of strain tensor components, $S_{ij}^{\alpha}$ is the deviatoric dipole strength, $x_i^{\alpha}$ is the particle position, $F_j^{\alpha}$ represents the non-hydrodynamic force and V is the representative volume of suspension. In the absence of non-hydrodynamic forces such as electric, magnetic, steric and gravitational ones $F_j^{\alpha} = 0$ and Eq (3.241) can be solved provided an exact expression for $S_{ij}^{\alpha}$ is known. In the latter expression both the hydrodynamic and colloidal forces as well as their orientation must be considered. The problem is difficult with exact solutions available only for special simplified cases.

Three simplifications are frequently used: (i) where the inertial forces can be neglected, (ii) where the particles are identical, i.e. $\Sigma$ can be replaced by $\langle \ \rangle$, and (iii) where particles are non-interacting, the problem can be reduced to consideration of a single particle in an infinite volume of liquid. Most theories concentrate on suspension of ellipsoidal solid particles, but deformable drops, either homogeneous elastic bodies or liquid capsules (e.g. blood cells) have also been treated. Even with these simplifications Eq (3.241) was solved only for a few simple flows: simple shear, plane shear, orthogonal rheometer flow, as well as hyperbolic and uniaxial, axisymmetric purely extensional ones. The exact solutions are known for either small or large deformations with the intermediate range accessible only via numerical methods. Where available, the theoretical results give good agreement with the experiment and most of all they provide an invaluable insight into the mechanism of flow, as well as that of drop deformation and burst.

Extension of the theories into the non-dilute region poses enormous problems. Flow in this region simultaneously causes deformation and redistribution of particle orientation. At relatively low concentration, $\phi \geqslant 0.02$, doublets, then aggregates are formed with properties dependent not only on the nature of the interface but also on prehistory and the type of flow field. Three approaches have been used: a polynomial extension to include binary interaction, i.e. $0(\phi^2)$ term, a numerical solution and the uniform cell approximation for the high concentration region. So far, only shear flow of solid spheres was considered. Formation of clusters with the size and $\eta_r$ both scaling with $1/[1 - (\phi/\phi_m)^{1/3}]$ reconfirmed the earlier work (*Simha*, 1952). For obvious reasons there is no theoretical derivation of a constitutive equation for a concentrated system with deformable droplets.

In concluding, one wishes to express both satisfaction with developments in the search for a rheological equation of state for multiphase systems and, at the same time, regret that the outlook for an early derivation of one valid for PAB is bleak indeed. The problem is complex and at present only partial, approximative solutions may be expected. Since in principle flow, deformation and orientation are mutually dependent and frequently non-linear it is appropriate to ask: under what condition does the problem have a unique solution. An answer to this may have a profound significance for the manufacture and utilization of polymer alloys and blends.

# APPENDIX I

# COMMERCIAL POLYMER ALLOYS AND BLENDS

## Appendix I.A – Commercial Blends in Alphabetical Order by Name

| No. | Blend | Manufacturer | Composition | Rein-forced | Properties and Typical Uses |
|---|---|---|---|---|---|
| 1. | Abson | Abtec Chem. Co. | ABS/PVC | – | thermoformable sheets |
| 2. | Acrylivin | Gen. Tire & Rubber Co. | PVC/Acrylic | – | impact resistant |
| 3. | Albis | Albis Plastics | PA-6/PO (10%) | – | flow, mold release |
| 4. | Alcryn | Du Pont | PO/EPDM | – | processable, TPO |
| 5. | Alphon | Custom M.P. | Elast./PTFE | – | |
| 6. | Alton | Intl. Polym. Corp. | PPS/PTFE | – | |
| 7. | Ardel | Union Carbide | PAr/PET | | |
| 8. | Ariloks | USSR | PPE/HIPS | ? | |
| 9. | Arloy 1000 | Arco Chem. Co. | PC/SMA | – | automotive, medical |
| 10. | Arloy 2000 | Arco Chem. Co. | SMA/PET | – | food grade, transp. |
| 11. | Arylon | US Steel/Uniroyal | ABS/PSO | – | (no longer commercial) |
| 12. | Aspect | Phillips 66 | PET based blends | yes | |
| 13. | Azloy | Azdel Inc. | PC/PBT, reinf. | yes | automobile, electronics |
| 14. | Bayblend | Mobay/Bayer | PC/ABS | GF, Al | high impact strength, dimensional stability |
| 15. | Benvic | Solvay | PVC/ABS, NBR, MBS or CPE | yes | |
| 16. | Bexel | Bakelite Xylonite | SAN/Acrylic | yes | |
| 17. | Bexloy C | Du Pont | PA-amorphous/Elast. | – | blow, inject. molding |
| 18. | Bexloy J | Du Pont | PBT/Elast. | | car bumpers |
| 19. | Bexloy M | Du Pont | PAr/PA-toughened | | vertical panels |
| 20. | Bexloy V | Du Pont | TPO blends | | automotive fascias |
| 21. | Bexloy W | Du Pont | Ionomeric alloys | | automobile bumper |
| 22. | BR | Phillips | PPS/PTFE | – | |
| 23. | Brilion BT 40 | EMS | PA Alloy | – | |
| 24. | Bristrend | Polymers Inc. | PVC/PVAc | | extrudable |
| 25. | Cadon | Monsanto | SMA/ABS | – | moldability, paintability |
| 26. | C-Flex | Concept | SEBS/PDMS | – | medical applications |
| 27. | Capron | Allied Corp. | PA-6/PE | – | flexibility, impact strength |
| 28. | Carloy | Cary Chem. Inc. | PVC/Elast. | | |
| 29. | Celanese Nylon | Celanese Eng. Resin | PA-6,6/TPU | GF | automotive application |
| 30. | Celanex | Celanese Eng. Resin | PBT/PET/Elast. | GF | mechanical properties |
| 31. | Celcon | Celanese Eng. Resin | POM/Copol./Elast. or PDMS (2%) | – | impact resistance |
| 32. | Cladlux | Richard Daleman Group | Acrylic/PVC | – | cladding |

| No. | Blend | Manufacturer | Composition | Rein-forced | Properties and Typical Uses |
|---|---|---|---|---|---|
| 33. | CP | Continental Polym Inc. | PMMA/Elast. | – | lighting fixtures |
| 34. | Cycolac EHA | Borg-Warner | ABS/PC | – | automotive applications |
| 35. | Cycoloy | Borg-Warner/Ube | ABS/PC or TPU | – | heat, impact resistance |
| 36. | Cycoloy EHA | Borg-Warner/Ube | PC/ABS | – | automotive applications |
| 37. | Cycovin | Borg-Warner/Ube | ABS/PVC | – | flame retardancy |
| 38. | Decoloy | Borg-Warner/Ube | Acrylic/PVC | yes | |
| 39. | Defsan | USSR | PC/PET | ? | |
| 40. | Delrin | Du Pont | POM/Elast. or PTFE | – | impact resistance |
| 41. | Denka HS | Denki Kagaku | ABS/PC | – | automotive, electronic |
| 42. | Denka LCS | Denki Kagaku | PVC/NBR | – | |
| 43. | Denka Taimelan | Denki Kagaku | ABS/PVC | – | electronics housing |
| 44. | Dexcarb | Dexter Corp. | PC/PA | GF (≤ 30%) | |
| 45. | Dexlon | Dexter Corp. | PA/PP | | |
| 46. | Dexpro | Dexter Corp. | PP/PA | | |
| 47. | Dia Alloy | Mitsubishi Rayon | ABS/PC | – | automotive, electronics |
| 48. | Diacon | ICI | Acrylic/Elast. | – | clear |
| 49. | DIC-PPS X 7000 | Dainippon Ink & Chem. | PPS blends | GF | electronic, auto-parts |
| 50. | DKE | Du Pont | Acrylic/PVC | – | |
| 51. | Duralex | Dexter Plastics | PVC/TPU/NBR | – | |
| 52. | Duraloy/Vandar | Celanese/Hoechst | POM/TPU or PBT | GF | automotive, electronics |
| 53. | Durel | Celanese | PAr/PBT | – | |
| 54. | Durethan | Bayer AG | PA-6/PO or Elast. | – | household appliances |
| 55. | Dynyl | Rhne Poulenc | PA-6,6 - modified block | GF | low T impact, flex prop., sports goods |
| 56. | Ektar MB | Eastman Kodak | PCTG/PC or SMA | – | electronic, appliances |
| 57. | Elemid | Borg-Warner | ABS/PA | – | auto, high T application |
| 58. | Envex | Rogers Corp. | PI/PTFE | – | continuous use T = 225°C |
| 59. | Estane | B.F. Goodrich | TPU/SAN | – | chemical/oil resistance |
| 60. | ETA-Polymer | Republic Plast. | PO/EPDM | – | automotive application |
| 61. | ETP | DuPont | PA/Acrylic rubber | – | |
| 62. | Ethavin | Vichem Corp. | PVC/PE | yes | |
| 63. | FerroFlex | Ferro Corp. | PP/EPDM | – | automotive, electric |
| 64. | Flo-Well | Air Prod. & Chem. | PP/PVC copol. | – | moldability |
| 65. | Fiberfil TN | Wilson-Fiberfil | PA-6,12/PO | GF | |
| 66. | Formaldafil | Wilson-Fiberfil | POM/PTFE | GF | |
| 67. | Freshtuff | American Can Co. | Ionomer/PA | – | extruded sheets |
| 68. | Formion | A. Schulman Inc. | PE-ionomer alloys | – | bumpers, adhesion to metal |
| 69. | Fulton KL | LNP Corp. | POM/PTFE (20%) | – | moving parts, automotive applications |
| 70. | Gafite/Celanex | GAF Corp./ Hoechst | PBT/Elast. | GF, mica | electronics |
| 71. | Gaftuf/Vandar | GAF Corp./ Hoechst | PBT/Elast. | GF | high impact resistance |
| 72. | Geloy XP 4001 | General Electric | ASA/PC | – | automotive |

| No. | Blend | Manufacturer | Composition | Rein-forced | Properties and Typical Uses |
|-----|-------|--------------|-------------|-------------|-----------------------------|
| 73. | Geloy XP 2003 | General Electric | ASA/PVC | – | sidings, impact strength |
| 74. | Geloy SCC 1320 | General Electric | ASA/PMMA | – | gloss, surface hardness |
| 75. | Gemax | General Electric | PPE/PBT | yes | automotive applications |
| 76. | Geolast | Monsanto Polym. Prod. | NBR/EPDM | CB | heat, oil resistance |
| 77. | Geon | B.F. Goodrich | PVC/NBR | – | coating, binding |
| 78. | Grilamid | EMS-Chem. AG | PA-12/arom.-aliph. PA | – | eye-glasses frames |
| 79. | Grilon | EMS-Chem. AG | PA-6/Elast. | GF ($\leqslant 30\%$) | moldability, low T strength |
| 80. | Grilon BT | EMS-Chem. AG | PA-6/arom.-aliph. PA | – | impact, moisture resistance |
| 81. | GX-200 | General Electric Co. | ASA/PC | | |
| 82. | Himod PU GL | Polymer Compos. Inc. | TPU alloys | yes | |
| 83. | Hostadur X | Hoechst AG | PBT/PET | GF | computer, appliances |
| 84. | Hostaform | Hoechst AG | POM/TPU | $MoS_2$, PTFE | impact strength |
| 85. | Hostalen | Hoechst AG | PP/EPDM | GF, talc | automotive applications |
| 86. | Hostyren | Hoechst AG | PS/Elast. | – | high impact PS |
| 87. | Hytrel | Du Pont | TPEs Elast. | – | for blow molding |
| 88. | Idemitsu SC-250 | Idemitsu Pet-rochem. | PC/ABS, PES, Elast. | – | automotive, housings |
| 89. | Illen | Dr. Illing GmbH | PBT/Elast. ($\sim 25\%$) | yes | automotive |
| 90. | Iupilon Polym. Alloy | Mitsubishi Gas Chem. | PC/ABS | – | excellent moldability |
| 91. | JSR Excelloy CB | Japan Synth. Rubb. | ABS/PC | GF | automobile, electric |
| 92. | JSR Excelloy GE | Japan Synth. Rubb. | PC/AES | – | automotive parts |
| 93. | JSR NV | Japan Synth. Rubb. | NBR/PVC (15 to 35%) | – | oil, chemical and low-T resistance |
| 94. | JSR NE | Japan Synth. Rubb. | NBR/EPDM (30 to 40%) | – | automotive parts |
| 95. | Kaneka Enplex N | Kanagafuchi Chem. | ABS/PVC | – | electronic parts |
| 96. | Kelburon | DSM | PP/EPDM | – | bumpers, suitcases |
| 97. | Keltan | DSM | PP/EPDM | – | automotive parts |
| 98. | Koroseal | B.F. Goodrich | PVC/PVF | – | linings |
| 99. | Kralastic | Uniroyal/Sumito-mo | ABS/PVC | – | moldability |
| 100. | Kraton D | Shell Chem. Co. | SBS, SIS, SEP alloys | – | automotive, sport |
| 101. | Kraton D2103 | Shell Chem. Co. | SBS/HIPS | – | food containers |
| 102. | Kraton G | Shell Chem. Co. | SEBS blends | – | thermoplastic rubber |
| 103. | Krynac NV | Polysar Inc. | NBR/PVC (30 to 50%) | – | weather, low T flex |
| 104. | Kydene | Rohm and Haas | PVC/PMMA | – | thermoformable sheets |

| No. | Blend | Manufacturer | Composition | Rein-forced | Properties and Typical Uses |
|-----|-------|--------------|-------------|-------------|------------------------------|
| 105. | Kydex100 | Rohm and Haas | PVC/Acrylic | – | thermoformable sheets |
| 106. | Lexan 100 | General Electric | PC/PO | – | electrical, housings |
| 107. | Lexan 500, 3000 | General Electric | PC/PO | GF | glass/metal replacement |
| 108. | Lomod | General Electric | PBT/SBS/ASA | – | sporting, safety equip. |
| 109. | Luranyl | BASF | PPE/HIPS | GF, mineral | housings, electronics |
| 110. | Lustran | Monsanto Polym. Prod. | ABS or PVC/SAN | – | glass, impact resistance |
| 111. | Mablex | Mazzucchelli Cell. | ABS/PC | – | electrical, automotive parts |
| 112. | Makroblend PR | Bayer/Mobay | PC/PET or PBT | – | bumpers |
| 113. | Makroblend | Bayer/Mobay | PBT/Elast. | yes | automotive parts |
| 114. | Makroblend UT, DP | Bayer/Mobay | PC/PET | GF ($\leq 30\%$) | car bumpers, sport |
| 115. | Maranyl | ICI | PA-6 or PA-6,6/ Elast. | GF, mineral | sport, automotive parts |
| 116. | Merlon | Bayer/Mobay | PC/PO | – | toughened PC |
| 117. | Mertex | Mobay | TPU blends | | |
| 118. | Metamarble | Teijin Chem. Ltd. | PC/PMMA | – | decorative use |
| 119. | Milkon | Tribol Ind. Inc. | PPS/PTFE | – | |
| 120. | Mindel A | Amoco Chem. Co. | PSO/ABS | – | hot water resistance |
| 121. | Mindel B | Amoco Chem. Co | PSO/PET | GF(40%) | high heat resistance |
| 122. | Minlon | Du Pont | PA-6,6/ionomer | mineral | low T impact strength |
| 123. | Modylen | Tiszai Vegyi Komb. | PP copol./EPDM | $CaCO_3$ | low T impact strength |
| 124. | MPPE | Asahi Chem. Ind. | PPE/PA | CF, GF | automotive parts |
| 125. | Multilon | Teijin Chem. Ltd. | PC/ABS | GF | for injection molding |
| 126. | N5 | Thermofil Inc. | PA/ABS | GF (15&30%) | dimensional stability |
| 127. | Nipeon AL | Zeon Kasei Co. | ABS/PVC (50%) | – | good weatherability |
| 128. | Nipol | Nippon Zeon Co. | NBR/PVC (30%) | – | fuel hoses |
| 129. | Nitrilene | Rhein-Chemie | PVC/BR/ABS | – | |
| 130. | Nitrovin | Vichem Corp. | TPU/PVC | – | |
| 131. | Noryl | General Electric | PPE/HIPS | yes | processability, impact |
| 132. | Noryl FN | General Electric | PPE/HIPS | foamable | equipment housing |
| 133. | Noryl GFN | General Electric | PPE/HIPS | GF ($\leq 30\%$) | continuous use T = 100°C |
| 134. | Noryl-GTX (Noryl Plus) | General Electric | PA/PPE (30%) | yes | auto panels, wheels, fenders |
| 135. | Novalloy | Daicel Chem. Ind. | ABS/PC | – | automotive, electrical |
| 136. | Novamate A | Mitsubishi Chem. Ind. | AAS/PC | GF (15%) | electrical, electronic |
| 137. | Novamate B | Mitsubishi Chem. Ind. | ABS/PC | – | automotive application |
| 138. | Novamid ST | Mitsubishi Chem. Ind. | PA/Elast. | – | processability, impact |
| 139. | NovarexAM | Mitsubishi Chem. Ind. | PC/Elast. | – | car instrument panels |
| 140. | Novolen KR | BASF | PP/EPR | – | self-supporting bumpers |
| 141. | Nycoa | Nylon Corp. | PA/PO or iono-mer | – | |

| No. | Blend | Manufacturer | Composition | Rein-forced | Properties and Typical Uses |
|-----|-------|--------------|-------------|-------------|------------------------------|
| 142. | Nydur | Bayer/Mobay | PA/Elast. | GF (15%) | low-T impact strength |
| 143. | Nylafil | Wilson-Fiberfil Intl. | PA-6,6/Elast. | GF ($\leq$ 43%) | stiffness, impact resist. |
| 144. | Nylon | Celanese Eng. Resins | PA-6,6/Elast. TPU or PE | GF ($\leq$ 33%) | automotive parts |
| 145. | Ontex ABX, APE | Dexter Crop. | PP/Elastom./ Binder | – | paintable alloy |
| 146. | Orgalloy | Atochem | PA-6/PP | – | automobile body, underhood |
| 147. | Orgater | Atochem | PBT/EVA/PEBA | | |
| 148. | Oxyblend | Occidental Chem. | PVC blends | | |
| 149. | Oxytuf | Occidental Chem. | PVC/EPDM | | |
| 150. | Pantalast | Pantasote Inc. | PVC/EVA | | |
| 151. | Paracril OZO | Uniroyal Chem. | NBR/PVC alloy | – | |
| 152. | Paxon Pax Plus | Allied Corp. | PE/Elast. | – | for film applications |
| 153. | Pebax | CdF Chimie | PEther/PA block polym. | GF ($\leq$ 20%) | sports goods |
| 154. | Pellethane | Dow Chemical | ABS/TPU | – | automobile bumpers |
| 155. | Pocan-KÜ1 | Mobay/Bayer | PBT/PC | – | bumper |
| 156. | Pocan-S | Mobay/Bayer | PBT/Elast. | – | automotive applications |
| 157. | Polycomp | LNP Corp. | PPS or PET/ PTFE | CF, GF | bearings, cams, gears |
| 158. | Polymer XE 3055 | Ems Chemie AG | PA blends | – | electric/electronic |
| 159. | Polyloy | Dr. Illing GmbH | PA-6 or PA-6,6/ PO or TPO | | low-T impact strength |
| 160. | Polyman 506 | A. Schulman Inc. | PVC/ABS | – | housings, appliances |
| 161. | Polyman 552 | A. Schulman Inc. | SAN/PO | – | recreational applications |
| 162. | Polypur | A. Schulman Inc. | TPU alloys | yes | automotive applications |
| 163. | Polysar | Polysar Inc. | PS/PB (4–8%) | – | food containers |
| 164. | Polytrope | A. Schulman Inc. | EPR/PO | – | automotive applications |
| 165. | Prevex | Borg-Warner Chem. | PPE copol./HIPS | GF $\leq$ 30% | low-T impact strength |
| 166. | Prevex S33 | Borg-Warner Chem. | PA/PPE copol. | GF | automotive market |
| 167. | Pro-Fax | Himont | PP/EPR | – | automotive, houseware |
| 168. | Proloy | Borg-Warner Chem. | ABS/PC | – | appliance housings |
| 169. | Propathene | ICI | PP/Elast. | GF | automotive applications |
| 170. | Pulse | Dow Chem Co. | PC/ABS (30%) | yes | auto panels, wheel covers |
| 171. | R2-9900 | Thermofil Inc. | PC/PBT | GF $\simeq$ 20% | tensile str., flex modulus |
| 172. | R4-9900 | Thermofil Inc. | PC/SMA | yes | |
| 173. | Reichold TPR | Reichold Chem. | PO/EPDM | – | thermoplastic rubber |
| 174. | Rimplast | LNP Corp. | PA-6,6 or PA-12/ Silicone | GF $\leq$ 30% | short shelflife time; low warpage |
| 175. | Rislan | Atochem | PA-6,6/PEBA | – | sports goods |
| 176. | Riteflex BP | Hoechst-Celanese | TPEs alloys | – | golf carts, athletic shoes, spoilers |
| 177. | Ronfalin | DSM | ABS/PC | – | computer housings |
| 178. | Ronfaloy V | DSM | ABS/PVC | – | business machines |
| 179. | Ropet | Rohm and Haas | PET/PMMA | | (discontinued) |
| 180. | Rovel | Dow Chem. Co. | PC/AES | – | |

| No. | Blend | Manufacturer | Composition | Rein-forced | Properties and Typical Uses |
|---|---|---|---|---|---|
| 181. | Rovel | Uniroyal Chem. | ABS/Elast. | GF | weather., impact strength |
| 182. | Royalene | Uniroyal Chem. | EPDM/HDPE | | impact modifier |
| 183. | Royalite R 11 | Uniroyal Chem. | PC/ABS | | |
| 184. | RPI | Research Polym. Intl. | PO/EPDM | GF | automotive applications |
| 185. | RPI 507 EP | Research Polym. Intl. | PP/EPDM | GF | stiffness, impact strength |
| 186. | RPS | Dow Chem. Co. | PS-Reactive | – | (contains oxazoline) |
| 187. | RTA-Polymer | Republic Plast. Co. | Rigid TP alloys | – | (replaces HIPS or ABS) |
| 188. | RTP 200H | RTP Co. | PA/PTFE (≤ 20%) | GF (≤ 30%) | uses impact-modified PA |
| 189. | RTP 200C | RTP Co. | PA-11/PTFE (20%) | GF (20%) | low water absorption, lubricity |
| 190. | RTP 200D | RTP Co. | PA-6,12/PTFE (≤ 20%) | GF (≤ 30%) | electronic, sport |
| 191. | RTP 200 TFE | RTP Co. | PA-6,6/PTFE/ PDMS | GF, CF | many formulations |
| 192. | RTP 300 TFE | RTP Co. | PC/PTFE/PDMS | GF (≤ 30%) | gears and cams |
| 193. | RTP 600 | RTP Co. | ABS/PTFE or PDMS | – | pumps, automotive |
| 194. | RTP 800 | RTP Co. | POM/PTFE or PDMS | GF (≤ 30%) | cams and gears |
| 195. | RTP 900 | RTP Co. | PSO/PTFE (15%) | GF (≤ 30%) | appliance parts |
| 196. | RTP 1000 | RTP Co. | PBT/PTFE (15%) | GF, CF (≤ 30%) | electrical parts |
| 197. | RTP 1300 | RTP Co. | PPS/PTFE (≤20%) | GF, CF (≤ 40%) | high-T, chem. resistance |
| 198. | RX | Intl. Polym. Corp. | PPS/PTFE (≤ 60%) | GF, Grafite | bearings |
| 199. | Rynite SST | Du Pont | PET/Elast. | GF (35%) | automotive body parts |
| 200. | Ryulex C | Dainippon Ink & Chem. | PC/ABS | GF, CF (≃ 15%) | electronics, medical parts |
| 201. | Santoprene | Monsanto Polym. Prod. | PP/EPDM | – | thermoplastic rubbers |
| 202. | Saranex | Dow Chem. Co. | PVDC/PE | – | film applications |
| 203. | Selar | Du Pont | PA/PO | – | blow molding |
| 204. | Shutane | Reichold Chem. | PVC/TPU | – | impact resistance |
| 205. | Shuvinite | Reichold Chem. | PVC/ABR | – | extrudable |
| 206. | SPX | Mitsubishi Petrochem. | PP/EPR | – | extrusion, injection molding |
| 207. | ST-801 | Du Pont | PA/Elast. | | high-T applications |
| 208. | ST-Nylon | Toray | PA/Ionomer(?) | GF | winter sports goods |
| 209. | Stanyl | DSM | PA-4,6 blends | | |
| 210. | Stilon | USSR | ABS/PC | ? | |
| 211. | Stycone | United Compos. Inc. | PS-alloys | | |
| 212. | Styron XL | Dow Chem. Co. | PS/Elast. | – | electronic |
| 213. | Sumiploy | Sumitomo | PES, PEEK-Modified | yes | high-T applications |

| No. | Blend | Manufacturer | Composition | Rein-forced | Properties and Typical Uses |
|-----|-------|--------------|-------------|-------------|------------------------------|
| 214. | Sunloid KD | Tsusunaka Plast. Ind. | PVC/PMMA | – | sheets |
| 215. | Supec | General Electric | PPS alloys | – | high-T applications |
| 216. | Superec P | Mitsubishi-Monsanto | ABS/PC | – | excellent moldability |
| 217. | Surlyn HP | Du Pont | Ionomer (modified) | – | film, coatings applications |
| 218. | Taflite | Mitsui Toatsu Chem. | PS/EPDM | – | |
| 219. | Techniace | Sumitomo Naugatuck | ABS/PC | – | dimensional stability |
| 220. | Technyl A | Rhône Poulenc | PA-6,6/Elast. | | auto, recreational |
| 221. | Technyl B | Rhône Poulenc | PA-6,6/Elast. | GF ($\leq 50\%$) | auto, recreational |
| 222. | Techster | Rhône Poulenc | PBT/PET | – | |
| 223. | Techster T | Rhône Poulenc | PBT/Elast. | GF 30% | mech., electr. properties |
| 224. | Telcar | Teknor Apex Co. | PO/EPDM | – | automotive applications |
| 225. | Tenneco | Tenneco Polymers | PVC/EVA | – | building industry |
| 226. | Terblend-B | BASF | ABS/PC | – | low-T impact |
| 227. | Terblend-S | BASF | ASA/PC | yes | auto, household applications |
| 228. | Texin | Mobay | PC/TPU | – | thermoplastic rubber |
| 229. | Thermalloy | CdF Chimie | ABS Blends | | heat, impact resistance |
| 230. | Thermocomp DL | LNP Corp. | PC/PTFE 13%/silicone 2% | – | for moving parts |
| 231. | Thermocomp PDX | LNP Corp. | PEEK/PTFE (20%) | – | moving parts |
| 232. | Thermocomp RFL | LNP Corp. | PA-6,6/Silicone 5% | GF ($\leq 30\%$) | for injection molding |
| 233. | Thermocomp RL | LNP Corp. | PA-6,6/PTFE 13%/Rimplast | – | gears and cams |
| 234. | Thermolan 2000 | Mitsubishi Petrochem. | PP/EPDM | – | auto, construction |
| 235. | Thermolan 3000 | Mitsubishi Petrochem. | EPDM/PP | | thermoplastic rubber |
| 236. | Torlon | Amoco Chem. Corp. | PAI/PTFE (3%) | graphite 30% CF, GF | strength, thermal resist. |
| 237. | TPO 900 | Reichold Chem. | PP/EPDM | – | thermoplastic rubber |
| 238. | Triax 1120 | Monsanto Co. | PA-6/ABS | | impact, heat, chem. resistance |
| 239. | Triax 2000 | Monsanto Co. | PC/ABS | – | automotive market |
| 240. | Triax 1125 | Monsanto Co. | PA -6,6($\sim 50\%$)/ABS | – | IPN type morphology |
| 241. | Triax 1180 | Monsanto Co. | PA-6,6.6/ABS | – | molding |
| 242. | Tribolon | Tribol. Ind. Inc. | PI/PTFE | – | aerospace parts |
| 243. | Tribolon XT | Tribol. Ind. Inc. | PPS/PTFE | – | moving parts |
| 244. | Triplus TPR 178 | General Electric | Silicone-based | – | paints and coatings |
| 245. | Tufrex VB | Mitsubishi Monsanto | ABS/PVC | – | electronics housings |

| No. | Blend | Manufacturer | Composition | Rein-forced | Properties and Typical Uses |
|---|---|---|---|---|---|
| 246. | Tylac | Standard Brands Chem. | PVC/BR/AN | – | |
| 247. | Ube Nylon | Ube Inc. | PA modified | – | low-T impact |
| 248. | Ube Alloy CA 700 | Ube Inc. | PP/PA | – | heat resist., auto parts |
| 249. | Ucardel P4174 | General Electric | PSO/SAN | – | single phase, transparent |
| 250. | Ultem | General Electric | PEI/PC | ≤ 40% | |
| 251. | Ultem | General Electric | PEI/TP | GF | |
| 252. | Ultrablend KR | BASF | PBT or PET/PC/Elast. | | bumpers, auto parts |
| 253. | Ultrablend S | BASF | PBT/ASA or SAN | GF (≤ 30%) | electronic, automotive |
| 254. | Ultraform N254OX | BASF | POM/Elastom. | – | low-T impact strength |
| 255. | Ultramid/Lurans | BASF | PA/ASA | mineral | resistance to environmental |
| 256. | Ultramid/Terluran | BASF | PA/ABS | mineral | stress cracking |
| 257. | Ultranyl | BASF | PPE/PA | yes | automotive |
| 258. | Ultrason | BASF | PSO Alloys | | electr., appliances |
| 259. | Ultrastryr OSA | Montedipe | SAN-EPDM/ABS or PC | – | light, weather resistance |
| 260. | UP | Unitika | PAr/PET | | |
| 261. | Uravin | Vichem Corp. | TPU/PVC | | |
| 262. | Valox 500 or 700 | General Electric Co. | PBT/PET or PBT/PC/Elast. | GF (≤ 45%) | dimensional stability |
| 263. | Vandar 8001 | Hoechst-Celanese | PBT blend | yes | exterior auto. body panels |
| 264. | Vectra | Celanese | LCP blends | | high-T mech. properties |
| 265. | Verton | Hüls AG | PPE alloys | | mechanical, electrical |
| 266. | Vestoblend | Hüls/Nuodex Inc. | PA/PPE | | automotive applications |
| 267. | Vestolen | Hüls AG | PP/EPDM | – | automotive, sport |
| 268. | Vestoran | Hüls/Nuodex Inc. | HIPS/PPE/Elast. | – | automotive |
| 269. | Victrex VKT | ICI | PEEK/PTFE (7.5 to 30%) | – | moving parts, bearings |
| 270. | Victrex VST | ICI | PES/PTFE | – | bearing applications |
| 271. | Vifnen VN | Hitachi Chem. | AAS/PVC | – | electrical appliances |
| 272. | Viniproz | USSR | PVC/PMMA Copolymer | – | |
| 273. | Voloy 680 | ComAlloy | PA-6,6 based blends | GF | |
| 274. | Vynite | Alpha Chem. Plast. | PVC/Nitrile Rubber | – | |
| 275. | Vyhene | Alpha Chem. Plast. | PVC/TPU | – | |
| 276. | Wellamid MR | Wellman Inc. | PA-6,6/PA-6 | mineral 25% | automotive applications |
| 277. | Wellamid 22 LHI | Wellman Inc. | PA-6,6/Elast. | GF (15%) | |
| 278. | Xenoy 1000 | General Electric | PC/PBT (50%) | yes | low-T prop., car bumpers |
| 279. | Xenoy 2000 | General Electric | PC/PET/MBA (10%) | GF | good weldline |
| 280. | Xenoy 3000 | General Electric | PC/TPEs | GF | replace glassware |
| 281. | Xenoy 6000 | General Electric | PC/TPEs | GF (≤ 30%) | mech., electr. properties |

| No. | Blend | Manufacturer | Composition | Rein-forced | Properties and Typical Uses |
|-----|-------|--------------|-------------|-------------|------------------------------|
| 282. | XT | American Cy-anamid | Acrylic(multi-) | – | |
| 283. | XT 3055 | Ems Chem. | PA alloys | – | |
| 284. | XU | Dow Chem. Co. | TPU/ABS | – | experimental (bumper) |
| 285. | Xycon | Amoco Chem. | TPEs/TPU | | bumper beams, electr. |
| 286. | Xyron 200 | Asahi Chem. Ind. | PPE/HIPS | – | office equipment |
| 287. | Xyron A | Asahi Chem. Ind. | PPE/PA | – | electric, automotive |
| 288. | Xyron G | Asahi Chem. Inc. | PPE/PA | GF,CF (≤ 30%) | high-T resistant |
| 289. | Zerlon | Dow Chem. Co. | PS/PMMA | – | |
| 290. | Zytel 300, 400 | Du Pont | PA-6,6/Ionomer | – | tubing, cables |
| 291. | Zytel 71G | Du Pont | PA-6,6/Ionomer | GF (35%) | moldability |
| 292. | Zytel 3100 | Du Pont | PA-6/PA-6,6 | – | moldability, toughness |
| 293. | Zytel 77G | Du Pont | PA-6,12/Ionomer | GF | low water absorption |
| 294. | Zytel ST | Du Pont | PA-6,6/Elast. | GF (35%) | many grades available |
| 295. | Zytel ST-350 | Du Pont | PA-6,12/Elast. | – | automotive applic. |

## Appendix I.B – Commercial Blends in Alphabetical Order by Composition

| No. | Composition | Blend | Manufacturer | Rein-forced | Properties and Typical Uses |
|-----|-------------|-------|--------------|-------------|------------------------------|
| 1. | AAS/PC | Novamate A | Mitsubishi Chem. Ind. | GF (15%) | electrical, electronic |
| 2. | AAS/PVC | Vifnen VN | Hitachi Chem. | – | electrical appliances |
| 3. | ABS Blends | Thermalloy | CdF Chimie | | heat, impact resistance |
| 4. | ABS or PVC/ SAN | Lustran | Monsanto Polym. Prod. | – | glass, impact resistance |
| 5. | ABS/Elast. | Rovel | Uniroyal Chem. | GF | weather., impact strength |
| 6. | ABS/PA | Elemid | Borg-Warner | – | auto, high-T application |
| 7. | ABS/PC | Terblend-B | BASF | – | low-T impact |
| 8. | ABS/PC | Proloy | Borg-Warner | – | appliance housings |
| 9. | ABS/PC | Cycolac EHA | Borg-Warner | – | automotive |
| 10. | ABS/PC | Novalloy | Daicel Chem. Ind. | – | automotive, electrical |
| 11. | ABS/PC | Denka HS | Denki Kagaku | – | automotive, electronic |
| 12. | ABS/PC | Ronfalin | DSM | – | computer housings |
| 13. | ABS/PC | JSR Excelloy CB | Japan Synth. Rubb. | GF | automobile, electric |
| 14. | ABS/PC | Mablex | Mazzucchelli Cell. | – | electrical, automotive parts |
| 15. | ABS/PC | Dia Alloy | Mitsubishi Rayon | – | automotive, electronics |
| 16. | ABS/PC | Novamate B | Mitsubishi Chem. Ind. | – | automotive application |
| 17. | ABS/PC | Techniace | Sumitomo Nauga-tuck | – | dimensional stability |
| 18. | ABS/PC | Stilon | USSR | ? | |

| No. | Composition | Blend | Manufacturer | Rein-forced | Properties and Typical Uses |
|-----|-------------|-------|--------------|-------------|------------------------------|
| 19. | ABS/PC | Superec P | Mitsubishi-Monsanto | – | excellent moldability |
| 20. | ABS/PC or TPU | Cycoloy | Borg-Warner/Ube | – | heat, impact resistance |
| 21. | ABS/PSO | Arylon | US Steel/Uniroyal | – | (no longer commercial) |
| 22. | ABS/PTFE or PDMS | RTP 600 | RTP Co. | – | pumps, automotive |
| 23. | ABS/PVC | Abson | Abtec Chem. Co. | – | thermoformable sheets |
| 24. | ABS/PVC | Cycovin | Borg-Warner/Ube | – | flame retardancy |
| 25. | ABS/PVC | Denka Taimelan | Denki Kagaku | – | electronics housings |
| 26. | ABS/PVC | Ronfaloy V | DSM | – | business machines |
| 27. | ABS/PVC | Kaneka Enplex N | Kanagafuchi Chem. | – | electronics parts |
| 28. | ABS/PVC | Tufrex VB | Mitsubishi Monsanto | – | electronics housings |
| 29. | ABS/PVC | Kralastic | Uniroyal/Sumitomo | – | moldability |
| 30. | ABS/PVC (50%) | Nipeon AL | Zeon Kasei Co. | – | good weatherability |
| 31. | ABS/TPU | Pellethane | Dow Chemical | – | automobile bumpers |
| 32. | Acrylic(multi-) | XT | American Cyanamid | – | |
| 33. | Acrylic/Elast. | Diacon | ICI | – | clear |
| 34. | Acrylic/PVC | Decoloy | Borg-Warner/Ube | yes | |
| 35. | Acrylic/PVC | DKE | Du Pont | – | |
| 36. | Acrylic/PVC | Cladlux | Richard Daleman Group | – | cladding |
| 37. | ASA/PC | Geloy XP 4001 | General Electric | – | automotive |
| 38. | ASA/PC | Terblend-S | BASF | yes | auto, household applications |
| 39. | ASA/PC | GX-200 | General Electric | | |
| 40. | ASA/PMMA | Geloy SCC 1320 | General Electric | – | gloss, surface hardness |
| 41. | ASA/PVC | Geloy XP 2003 | General Electric | – | sidings, impact strength |
| 42. | Elast./PTFE | Alphon | Custom M.P. | – | |
| 43. | EPDM/HDPE | Royalene | Uniroyal Chem. | | impact modifier |
| 44. | EPDM/PP | Thermolan 3000 | Mitsubishi Petrochem. | | thermoplastic rubber |
| 45. | EPR/PO | Polytrope | A. Schulman Inc. | – | automotive application |
| 46. | HIPS/PPE/Elast. | Vestoran | Hüls/Nuodex Inc. | – | automotive |
| 47. | Ionomer (modified) | Surlyn HP | Du Pont | – | film, coatings applications |
| 48. | Ionomer/PA | Freshtuff | American Can | – | extruded sheets |
| 49. | Ionomeric alloys | Bexloy W | Du Pont | | automobile bumper |
| 50. | LCP blends | Vectra | Celanese | | high-T mech. properties |
| 51. | NBR/EPDM | Geolast | Monsanto Polym. Prod. | CB | heat, oil resistance |
| 52. | NBR/EPDM (30 to 40%) | JSR NE | Japan Synth. Rubb. | – | automotive parts |
| 53. | NBR/PVC (15 to 35%) | JSR NV | Japan Synth. Rubb. | – | oil, chemical and low-T resistance |
| 54. | NBR/PVC (30 to 50%) | Krynac NV | Polysar Inc. | – | weather, low-T flex |
| 55. | NBR/PVC (30%) | Nipol | Nippon Zeon Co. | – | fuel hoses |

| No. | Composition | Blend | Manufacturer | Rein-forced | Properties and Typical Uses |
|---|---|---|---|---|---|
| 56. | NBR/PVC alloy | Paracril OZO | Uniroyal Chem. | – | |
| 57. | PA -6,6(~ 50%)/ ABS | Triax 1125 | Monsanto Co. | – | IPN type morphology |
| 58. | PA Alloy | Brilion BT 40 | EMS | – | |
| 59. | PA alloys | XT 3055 | Ems Chem. | – | |
| 60. | PA blends | Polymer XE 3055 | Ems Chemie AG | – | electric/electronics |
| 61. | PA modified | Ube Nylon | Ube Inc. | – | low-T impact |
| 62. | PA-11/PTFE (20%) | RTP 200C | RTP Co. | GF (20%) | low water absorption, lubricity |
| 63. | PA-12/arom.-aliph. PA | Grilamid | EMS-Chem. AG | – | spectacle frames |
| 64. | PA-4,6 blends | Stanyl | DSM | | |
| 65. | PA-6 or PA-6,6/ Elast. | Maranyl | ICI | GF, mineral | sports, automotive parts |
| 66. | PA-6 or PA-6,6/ PO or TPO | Polyloy | Dr. Illing GmbH | | low-T impact strength |
| 67. | PA-6,12/Elast. | Zytel ST-350 | Du Pont | – | automotive applic. |
| 68. | PA-6,12/Ionomer | Zytel 77G | Du Pont | GF | low water absorption |
| 69. | PA-6,12/PO | Fiberfil TN | Wilson-Fiberfil | GF | |
| 70. | PA-6,12/PTFE (≤20%) | RTP 200D | RTP Co. | GF (≤ 30%) | electronic, sport |
| 71. | PA-6,6 – modi-fied block | Dynyl | Rhône Poulenc | GF | low-T impact, flex prop., sports goods |
| 72. | PA-6,6 based blends | Voloy 680 | ComAlloy | GF | |
| 73. | PA-6,6 or PA-12/ Silicone | Rimplast | LNP Corp. | GF (30%) | short shelflife; low warpage |
| 74. | PA-6,6/ABS | Triax 1180 | Monsanto Co. | – | molding |
| 75. | PA-6,6/Elast TPU or PE | Nylon | Celanese Eng. Re-sins | GF (≤ 33%) | automotive parts |
| 76. | PA-6,6/Elast. | Zytel ST | Du Pont | GF (35%) | many grades available |
| 77. | PA-6,6/Elast. | Technyl B | Rhône Poulenc | GF (≤ 50%) | auto, recreational |
| 78. | PA-6,6/Elast. | Technyl A | Rhône Poulenc | – | auto, recreational |
| 79. | PA-6,6/Elast. | Wellamid 22 LHI | Wellman Inc. | GF (15%) | |
| 80. | PA-6,6/Elast. | Nylafil | Wilson-Fiberfil Intl. | GF (≤ 43%) | stiffness, impact resist. |
| 81. | PA-6,6/Ionomer | Minlon | Du Pont | mineral | low-T impact strength |
| 82. | PA-6,6/Ionomer | Zytel 300, 400 | Du Pont | – | tubing, cables |
| 83. | PA-6,6/Ionomer | Zytel 71G | Du Pont | GF (35%) | moldability |
| 84. | PA-6,6/PA-6 | Wellamid MR | Wellman Inc. | mineral 25% | automotive applications |
| 85. | PA-6,6/PEBA | Rislan | Atochem | – | sports goods |
| 86. | PA-6,6/PTFE 13%/Rimplast | Thermocomp RL | LNP Corp. | – | gears and cams |
| 87. | PA-6,6/PTFE/ PDMS | RTP 200 TFE | RTP Co. | GF, CF | many formulations |
| 88. | PA-6,6/Silicone 5% | Thermocomp RFL | LNP Corp. | GF (≈ 30%) | for injection molding |
| 89. | PA-6,6/TPU | Celanese Nylon | Celanese Eng. Resin | GF | automotive application |

| No. | Composition | Blend | Manufacturer | Rein-forced | Properties and Typical Uses |
|-----|-------------|-------|--------------|-------------|------------------------------|
| 90. | PA-6/ABS | Triax 1120 | Monsanto Co. | | impact, heat, chem. resistance |
| 91. | PA-6/arom.-aliph. PA | Grilon BT | EMS-Chem. AG | – | impact, moisture resistance |
| 92. | PA-6/Elast. | Grilon | EMS-Chem. AG | GF ($\approx$ 30%) | moldability, low-T strength |
| 93. | PA-6/PA-6,6 | Zytel 3100 | Du Pont | – | moldability, toughness |
| 94. | PA-6/PE | Capron | Allied Corp. | – | flexibility, impact strength |
| 95. | PA-6/PO or Elast. | Durethan | Bayer AG | – | household appliances |
| 96. | PA-6/PO (10%) | Albis | Albis Plastics | – | flow, mold release |
| 97. | PA-6/PP | Orgalloy | Atochem | – | automobile body and under-hood |
| 98. | PA-amorphous/Elast. | Bexloy C | Du Pont | | blow, inject. molding |
| 99. | PA/ABS | Ultramid/Terluran | BASF | mineral | stress cracking |
| 100. | PA/ABS | N5 | Thermofil Inc. | GF (15& 30%) | dimensional stability |
| 101. | PA/Acrylic rubber | ETP | DuPont | – | |
| 102. | PA/ASA | Ultramid/Lurans | BASF | mineral | resistance to environmental |
| 103. | PA/Elast. | Nydur | Bayer/Mobay | GF (15%) | low-T impact strength |
| 104. | PA/Elast. | Zytel ST-801 | Du Pont | | high-T applications |
| 105. | PA/Elast. | Novamid ST | Mitsubishi Chem. Ind. | – | processability, impact |
| 106. | PA/Ionomer(?) | ST-Nylon | Toray | GF | winter sporting goods |
| 107. | PA/PO or ionomer | Nycoa | Nylon Corp. | – | |
| 108. | PA/PP | Dexlon | Dexter Corp. | – | |
| 109. | PA/PPE | Vestoblend | Hüls/Nuodex Inc. | | automotive applications |
| 110. | PA/PO/Ionomer | Selar | Du Pont | – | blow molding |
| 111. | PA/PPE (30%) | Noryl-GTX | General Electric | yes | auto panels, wheels, fenders |
| 112. | PA/PPE copol. | Prevex S33 | Borg-Warner Chem. | GF | automotive market |
| 113. | PA/PTFE ($\leqslant$ 20%) | RTP 200H | RTP Co. | GF ($\leqslant$ 30%) | uses impact-modified PA |
| 114. | PAI/PTFE ($\approx$ 3%) | Torlon | Amoco Chem. Corp. | graphite 30% CF, GF | strength, thermal resist. |
| 115. | PAr/PA-toughened | Bexloy M | Du Pont | | vertical panels |
| 116. | PAr/PBT | Durel | Celanese | | |
| 117. | PAr/PET | Ardel | Union Carbide | | |
| 118. | PAr/PET | UP | Unitika | | |
| 119. | PBT blend | Vandar 8001 | Hoechst-Celanese | yes | exterior autobody panels |
| 120. | PBT/ASA or SAN | Ultrablend S | BASF | GF ($\leqslant$ 30%) | electronic, automotive |
| 121. | PBT/Elast. | Makroblend | Bayer/Mobay | yes | automotive parts |
| 122. | PBT/Elast. | Bexloy J | Du Pont | | car bumpers |
| 123. | PBT/Elast. | Gafite/Celanex | GAF Corp./Hoechst | GF, mica | automotive, electronics |
| 124. | PBT/Elast. | Gaftuf/Vandar | GAF Corp./Hoechst | GF | high impact resistance |

| No. | Composition | Blend | Manufacturer | Rein-forced | Properties and Typical Uses |
|---|---|---|---|---|---|
| 125. | PBT/Elast. | Pocan-S | Mobay/Bayer | – | automotive application |
| 126. | PBT/Elast. | Techster T | Rhône Poulenc | GF ($\approx 30\%$) | mech., electr. properties |
| 127. | PBT/Elast. ($\leq 25\%$) | Illen | Dr. Illing GmbH | yes | automotive |
| 128. | PBT/EVAL/ PEBA | Orgater | Atochem | | |
| 129. | PBT/PC | Pocan-KÜ1 | Mobay/Bayer | – | bumper |
| 130. | PBT/PET | Hostadur X | Hoechst AG | GF | computer, appliances |
| 131. | PBT/PET | Techster | Rhône Poulenc | – | |
| 132. | PBT/PET or PBT/PC/Elast. | Valox 500 or 700 | General Electric | GF ($\leq 45\%$) | dimensional stability |
| 133. | PBT/PET/Elast. | Celanex | Celanese Eng. Resin | GF | mechanical properties |
| 134. | PBT/PTFE (15%) | RTP 1000 | RTP Co. | GF,CF ($\leq 30\%$) | electrical parts |
| 135. | PBT/SBS/ASA | Lomod | General Electric | – | sports, safety equip. |
| 136. | PC/ABS | Cycoloy EHA | Borg-Warner/Ube | – | automotive application |
| 137. | PC/ABS | Ryulex C | Dainippon Ink & Chem. | GF,CF ($\leq 15\%$) | electronics, medical parts |
| 138. | PC/ABS | Bayblend | Mobay/Bayer | GF, Al | high impact strength, dimensional stability |
| 139. | PC/ABS | Triax 2000 | Monsanto Co. | – | automotive market |
| 140. | PC/ABS | Multilon | Teijin Chem. Ltd. | GF | for injection molding |
| 141. | PC/ABS | Royalite R 11 | Uniroyal Chem. | | |
| 142. | PC/ABS | Iupilon Polym. Alloy | Mitsubishi Gas Chem. | – | excellent moldability |
| 143. | PC/ABS (30%) | Pulse | Dow Chem Co. | yes | auto panels, wheel covers |
| 144. | PC/ABS, PES, Elast. | Idemitsu SC-250 | Idemitsu Petrochem. | – | automotive, housings |
| 145. | PC/AES | Rovel | Dow Chem. Co. | – | |
| 146. | PC/AES | JSR Excelloy GE | Japan Synth. Rubb. | – | automotive parts |
| 147. | PC/Elast. | Novarex AM | Mitsubishi Chem. Ind. | – | car instrument panels |
| 148. | PC/PA | Dexcarb | Dexter Corp. | GF ($\leq 30\%$) | |
| 149. | PC/PBT | R2-9900 | Thermofil Inc. | GF ($\approx 20\%$) | tensile str., flex modulus |
| 150. | PC/PBT (50%) | Xenoy 1000 | General Electric | yes | low-T prop; car bumpers |
| 151. | PC/PBT, reinf. | Azloy | Azdel Inc. | yes | automobile, electronics |
| 152. | PC/PET | Makroblend UT, DP | Bayer/Mobay | GF ($\leq 30\%$) | car bumpers, sport |
| 153. | PC/PET | Defsan | USSR | ? | |
| 154. | PC/PET or PBT | Makroblend PR | Bayer/Mobay | – | bumpers |
| 155. | PC/PET/Elast. MBA (10%) | Xenoy 2000 | General Electric | GF | good weldline |
| 156. | PC/PMMA | Metamarble | Teijin Chem. Ltd. | – | decorative use |
| 157. | PC/PO | Merlon | Bayer/Mobay | – | toughened PC |
| 158. | PC/PO | Lexan 100 | General Electric | – | electrical, housings |

| No. | Composition | Blend | Manufacturer | Rein-forced | Properties and Typical Uses |
|-----|-------------|-------|--------------|-------------|------------------------------|
| 159. | PC/PO | Lexan 500, 3000 | General Electric | GF | glass/metal replacement |
| 160. | PC/PTFE 13%/ silicone 2% | Thermocomp DL | LNP Corp. | – | for moving parts |
| 161. | PC/PTFE/PDMS | RTP 300 TFE | RTP Co. | GF ($\approx 30\%$) | gears and cams |
| 162. | PC/SMA | Arloy 1000 | Arco Chem. Co. | – | automotive, medical |
| 163. | PC/SMA | R4-9900 | Thermofil Inc. | GF | |
| 164. | PC/TPEs | Xenoy 3000 | General Electric | GF | substitute glassware |
| 165. | PC/TPEs | Xenoy 6000 | General Electric | GF ($\approx 30\%$) | mech., electr. properties |
| 166. | PC/TPU | Texin | Mobay | – | thermoplastic rubber |
| 167. | PCTG/PC or SMA | Ektar MB | Eastman Kodak | – | electronic, appliances |
| 168. | PE-ionomer alloys | Formion | A. Schulman Inc. | – | bumpers, adhesion to metal |
| 169. | PE/Elast. | Paxon Pax Plus | Allied Corp. | – | for film application |
| 170. | PEEK/PTFE (20%) | Thermocomp PDX | LNP Corp. | – | moving parts |
| 171. | PEEK/PTFE (7.5 to 30%) | Victrex VKT | ICI | – | moving parts, bearings |
| 172. | PEI/PC | Ultem | General Electric | $\leq 40\%$ | |
| 173. | PEI/TP | Ultem | General Electric | GF | |
| 174. | PBT or PET/PC/ Elast. | Ultrablend KR | BASF | | bumpers, auto parts |
| 175. | PES, PEEK – modified | Sumiploy | Sumitomo | yes | high-T applications |
| 176. | PES/PTFE | Victrex VST | ICI | – | bearing applications |
| 177. | PET based blends | Aspect | Phillips 66 | yes | |
| 178. | PET/Elast. | Rynite SST | Du Pont | GF (35%) | automotive body parts |
| 179. | PET/PMMA | Ropet | Rohm and Haas | | (discontinued) |
| 180. | PEther/PA block polym. | Pebax | CdF Chimie | GF ($\approx 20\%$) | sports goods |
| 181. | PI/PTFE | Envex | Rogers Corp. | – | continuous use T = 225°C |
| 182. | PI/PTFE | Tribolon | Tribol. Ind. Inc. | – | aerospace parts |
| 183. | PMMA/Elast. | CP | Continental Polym Inc. | – | lighting fixtures |
| 184. | PO/EPDM | Alcryn | Du Pont | – | processable, TPO |
| 185. | PO/EPDM | Reichold TPR | Reichold Chem. | – | thermoplastic rubber |
| 186. | PO/EPDM | ETA-Polymer | Republic Plast. | – | automotive applications |
| 187. | PO/EPDM | RPI | Research Polym. Intl. | GF | automotive applications |
| 188. | PO/EPDM | Telcar | Teknor Apex Co. | – | automotive applications |
| 189. | POM/Copol./ Elast. | Celcon | Celanese Eng. Resin | – | impact resistance or PDMS (2%) |
| 190. | POM/Elast. or PTFE | Delrin | Du Pont | – | impact resistance |
| 191. | POM/Elastom. | Ultraform N254OX | BASF | – | low-T impact strength |

| No. | Composition | Blend | Manufacturer | Rein-forced | Properties and Typical Uses |
|-----|-------------|-------|--------------|-------------|------------------------------|
| 192. | POM/PTFE | Formaldafil | Wilson-Fiberfil | GF | |
| 193. | POM/PTFE (20%) | Fulton KL | LNP Corp. | – | moving parts application |
| 194. | POM/PTFE or PDMS | RTP 800 | RTP Co. | GF ($\leqslant 30\%$) | cams and gears |
| 195. | POM/TPU | Hostaform | Hoechst AG | $MoS_2$, PTFE | impact strength |
| 196. | POM/TPU or PBT | Duraloy/Vandar | Celanese/Hoechst | GF | automotive, electronics |
| 197. | PP copol./EPDM | Modylen | Tiszai Vegyi Komb. | $CaCO_3$ | low-T impact strength |
| 198. | PP/Elast. | Propathene | ICI | GF | automotive applications |
| 199. | PP/Elast./Binder | Ontex ABX, APE | Dexter Corp. | – | paintable alloy |
| 200. | PP/EPDM | Keltan | DSM | – | automotive parts |
| 201. | PP/EPDM | Kelburon | DSM | – | bumpers, suitcases |
| 202. | PP/EPDM | FerroFlex | Ferro Corp. | – | automotive, electric |
| 203. | PP/EPDM | Hostalen | Hoechst AG | GF, talc | automotive applications |
| 204. | PP/EPDM | Vestolen | Huls AG | – | automotive, sport |
| 205. | PP/EPDM | Thermolan 2000 | Mitsubishi Petro-chem. | – | auto, construction |
| 206. | PP/EPDM | Santoprene | Monsanto Polym. Prod. | – | thermoplastic rubbers |
| 207. | PP/EPDM | TPO 900 | Reichold Chem. | – | thermoplastic rubber |
| 208. | PP/EPDM | RPI 507 EP | Research Polym. Intl. | GF | stiffness, impact strength |
| 209. | PP/EPR | Novolen KR | BASF | – | self-supporting bumpers |
| 210. | PP/EPR | Pro-Fax | Himont | – | automotive, houseware |
| 211. | PP/EPR | SPX | Mitsubishi Petro-chem. | – | extrusion, injection molding |
| 212. | PP/PA | Dexpro | Dexter Corp. | – | |
| 213. | PP/PA | Ube Alloy CA 700 | Ube Inc. | – | heat resist., auto parts |
| 214. | PP/PVC copol. | Flo-Well | Air Prod. & Chem. | – | moldability |
| 215. | PPE alloys | Verton | Hüls AG | | mechanical, electrical |
| 216. | PPE copol. /HIPS | Prevex | Borg-Warner Chem. | GF ($\leqslant 30\%$) | low-T impact strength |
| 217. | PPE/HIPS | Xyron 200 | Asahi Chem. Ind. | – | office equipment |
| 218. | PPE/HIPS | Luranyl | BASF | GF, mineral | housings, electronics |
| 219. | PPE/HIPS | Noryl FN | General Electric | foamable | equipment housings |
| 220. | PPE/HIPS | Noryl | General Electric | yes | processability, impact |
| 221. | PPE/HIPS | Noryl GFN | General Electric | GF ($\leqslant 30\%$) | continuous use T = 100 °C |
| 222. | PPE/HIPS | Ariloks | USSR | ? | |
| 223. | PPE/PA | MPPE | Asahi Chem. Ind. | CF, GF | automotive parts |
| 224. | PPE/PA | Xyron G | Asahi Chem. Inc. | GF,CF ($\simeq 30\%$) | high-T resistant |
| 225. | PPE/PA | Xyron A | Asahi Chem. Ind. | – | electrical, automotive |
| 226. | PPE/PA | Ultranyl | BASF | yes | automotive |

| No. | Blend | Manufacturer | Composition | Rein-forced | Properties and Typical Uses |
|---|---|---|---|---|---|
| 227. | PPE/PBT | Gemax | General Electric | yes | automotive applications |
| 228. | PPS alloys | Supec | General Electric | – | high-T applications |
| 229. | PPS blends | DIC-PPS X 7000 | Dainippon Ink & Chem. | GF | electronic, auto-parts |
| 230. | PPS or PET/ PTFE | Polycomp | LNP Corp. | CF, GF | bearings, cams, gears |
| 231. | PPS/PTFE | Alton | Intl. Polym. Corp. | – | |
| 232. | PPS/PTFE | BR | Phillips | – | |
| 233. | PPS/PTFE | Milkon | Tribol Ind. Inc. | – | |
| 234. | PPS/PTFE | Tribolon XT | Tribol. Ind. Inc. | – | moving parts |
| 235. | PPS/PTFE (≤20%) | RTP 1300 | RTP Co. | GF,CF (≤ 40%) | high-T, chem. resistance |
| 236. | PPS/PTFE (≤ 60%) | RX | Intl. Polym. Corp. | GF, Grafite | bearings |
| 237. | PS-alloys | Stycone | United Compos. Inc. | | |
| 238. | PS/Elast. | Hostyren | Hoechst AG | – | high impact PS |
| 239. | PS - reactive | RPS | Dow Chem. Co. | – | (contains oxazoline) |
| 240. | PS/Elast. | Styron XL | Dow Chem. Co. | – | electronic |
| 241. | PS/EPDM | Taflite | Mitsui Toatsu Chem. | – | |
| 242. | PS/PB (4 - 8%) | Polysar | Polysar Inc. | – | food containers |
| 243. | PS/PMMA | Zerlon | Dow Chem. Co. | – | |
| 244. | PSO Alloys | Ultrason | BASF | | electr., appliances |
| 245. | PSO/ABS | Mindel A | Amoco Chem. | – | hot water resistance |
| 246. | PSO/PET | Mindel B | Amoco Chem. | GF(40%) | high heat resistance |
| 247. | PSO/PTFE (15%) | RTP 900 | RTP Co. | GF (≤ 30%) | appliance parts |
| 248. | PSO/SAN | Ucardel P4174 | General Electric | – | single phase, transparent |
| 249. | PVC blends | Oxyblend | Occidental Chem. | | |
| 250. | PVC/ABR | Shuvinite | Reichold Chem. | – | extrudable |
| 251. | PVC/ABS | Polyman 506 | A. Schulman Inc. | | housings, appliances |
| 252. | PVC/ABS, NBR, MBS or CPE | Benvic | Solvay | yes | |
| 253. | PVC/Acrylic | Acrylivin | Gen. Tire & Rubber Co. | – | impact resistant |
| 254. | PVC/Acrylic | Kydex 100 | Rohm and Haas | – | thermoformable sheets |
| 255. | PVC/BR/ABS | Nitrilene | Rhein-Chemie | – | |
| 256. | PVC/BR/AN | Tylac | Standard Brands Chem. | – | |
| 257. | PVC/Elast. | Carloy | Cary Chem. Inc. | | |
| 258. | PVC/EPDM | Oxytuf | Occidental Chem. | | |
| 259. | PVC/EVA | Pantalast | Pantasote Inc. | | |
| 260. | PVC/EVA | Tenneco | Tenneco Poly-mers | – | building industry |
| 261. | PVC/NBR | Geon | B.F. Goodrich | – | coating, binding |
| 262. | PVC/NBR | Denka LCS | Denki Kagaku | – | |
| 263. | PVC/Nitrile Rubber | Vynite | Alpha Chem. Plast. | – | |

| No. | Blend | Manufacturer | Composition | Rein-forced | Properties and Typical Uses |
|-----|-------|--------------|-------------|-------------|----------------------------|
| 264. | PVC/PE | Ethavin | Vichem Corp. | yes | |
| 265. | PVC/PMMA | Kydene | Rohm and Haas | – | thermoformable sheets |
| 266. | PVC/PMMA | Sunloid KD | Tsusunaka Plast. Ind. | – | sheets |
| 267. | PVC/PMMA Copolymer | Viniproz | USSR | – | |
| 268. | PVC/PVAc | Bristrend | Polymers Inc. | extrudable | |
| 269. | PVC/PVF | Koroseal | B.F. Goodrich | – | linings |
| 270. | PVC/TPU | Vyhene | Alpha Chem. Plast. | – | |
| 271. | PVC/TPU/NBR | Duralex | Dexter Plastics | – | |
| 272. | PVDC/PE | Saranex | Dow Chem. Co. | – | film applications |
| 273. | PVC/TPU | Shutane | Reichold Chem. | – | impact resistance |
| 274. | Rigid TP alloys | RTA-Polymer | Republic Plast. | – | (replaces HIPS or ABS) |
| 275. | SAN-EPDM/ABS or PC | Ultrastryr OSA | Montedipe | – | light, weather resistance |
| 276. | SAN/Acrylic | Bexel | Bakelite Xylonite | yes | |
| 277. | SAN/PO | Polyman 552 | A. Schulman Inc. | – | recreational applications |
| 278. | SBS, SIS, SEP alloys | Kraton D | Shell Chem. Co. | – | automotive, sport |
| 279. | SBS/HIPS | Kraton D2103 | Shell Chem. Co. | – | food containers |
| 280. | SEBS blends | Kraton G | Shell Chem. Co. | – | thermoplastic rubber |
| 281. | SEBS/PDMS | C-Flex | Concept | – | medical applications |
| 282. | Silicone-based | Triplus TPR178 | General Electric | – | paints and coatings |
| 283. | SMA/ABS | Cadon | Monsanto | – | moldability, paintability |
| 284. | SMA/PET | Arloy 2000 | Arco Chem. Co. | – | food grade, transp. |
| 285. | TPEs alloys | Riteflex BP | Hoechst-Celanese | – | golf carts, athletic shoes, spoilers |
| 286. | TPEs Elast. | Hytrel | Du Pont | – | for blow molding |
| 287. | TPEs/TPU | Xycon | Amoco Chem. Corp. | | bumper beams, electr. |
| 288. | TPO blends | Bexloy V | Du Pont | | automotive fascias |
| 289. | TPU alloys | Polypur | A. Schulman Inc. | yes | automotive applications |
| 290. | TPU alloys | Himod PU GL | Polymer Compos. Inc. | yes | |
| 291. | TPU blends | Mertex | Mobay | | |
| 292. | TPU/ABS | XU | Dow Chem. Co. | – | experimental (bumper) |
| 293. | TPU/PVC | Uravin | Vichem Corp. | | |
| 294. | TPU/PVC | Nitrovin | Vichem Corp. | – | |
| 295. | TPU/SAN | Estane | B.F. Goodrich | – | chemical/oil resistance |

# Appendix I.C – Commercially Interesting Polymer Pairs

I.  **Polyolefin blends**
Polypropylene/EPDM, EPR or polyethylene
Butyl rubber/polyethylene
Polybutylene or polyisobutylene/olyolefin
Polyethylene/linear low density polyethylene
Polyolefin/ionomer
Thermoplastic olefinic rubbers
Poly(styrene-co-acrylonitrile)/EPDM (SAN/EPDM)

II.  **Polyvinyl chloride (PVC) blends**
PVC/acrylates, acrylate elastomers or methacrylates
PVC/ethylene-vinylacetate copolymer
PVC/chlorinated-polyethylene, chloroprene or chlorinated PVC
PVC/polystyrene
Nitrile rubber/PVC or PVC/nitrile rubber
EPDM, EPR or polyethylene/PVC
Poly(ethylene-vinylacetate-carbon monoxide)/PVC
Thermoplastic polyurethane/PVC or PVC/TPU

III.  **Polystyrene (PS) blends**
Toughened (or high impact) PS
Polycarbonate/ABS or ABS/PC
PC/poly(styrene-co-maleic anhydride)
SAN/EPDM
SMA/HIPS
SBS/many thermoplastics
Polypropylene/PS
Polytetrafluoroethylene/PS
Poly-α-methylstyrene/PS

IV.  **Acrylonitrile-butadiene-styrene (ABS) blends**
ABS/PVC with or without third polymer (e.g. PET)
ABS/polycarbonate or polysulfone
ABS/PA
ABS/AB or ABA hydrogenated styrene block copolymers
ABS/EPDM or EPR
ABS/ethylene-vinylacetate copolymer
ABS/chlorinated polyethylene
ABS/acrylates and their copolymers
ABS/thermoplastic polyurethane

V.  **Acrylonitrile-styrene-acrylate (ASA) blends**
ASA/polycarbonate
ASA/polyvinylchloride
ASA/polymethylmethacrylate

VI.  **Polyamide (PA) blends**
Impact modified PA with polyolefins, TPO and ionomers
Polyolefin/PA and PA/PO-maleic anhydride
Elastomer/PA
PA/PA/EPDM-acid
PA-11 or PA-12/nitrile rubber
PA/polytetrafluoroethylene
Polyesteramide/PA

VII.  **Polyphenyleneether (PPE) blends**
PPE/PS and/or styrene-based copolymers, e.g. HIPS
PPE/PA or PA/PPE
PPE/polyolefins
PPE/polyester

**VIII.**     **Thermoplastic polyester (TPE) blends**
Polybuthyleneterephthalate/polyethyleneterephthalate (PBT/PET)
PBT or PET/elastomer
PET/polymethylmethacrylate
PBT/polycarbonate/MBS
PET/polysulfone
PBT/polytetrafluoroethylene
TPEs/elastomer
TPEs/thermoplastic polyurethane
TPEs/polyarylate

**IX.**     **Polycarbonate (PC) blends**
PC/ABS or ASA
Impact modified PC with PO, TPO or rubber
PC/PBT or PET
PC/thermoplastic polyurethane
PC/polytetrafluoroethylene
PC/poly(styrene-co-maleicanhydride)
PC/PA or polysulfone

**X.**     **Polyoxymethylene (POM) blends**
Impact modified POM with PO, TPO or elastomer
POM/polytetrafluoroethylene
POM/thermoplastic polyurethane
PA/POM

**XI.**     **Polysulfone (PSO) blends**
PSO/ABS
PSO/TPEs
PSO/polytetrafluoroethylene

**XII.**     **Polyarylate (PAr) blends**
PAr/toughened-PA
PAr/TPEs
PAr/PC

**XIII.**     **Polyphenylenesulfide (PPS) blends**
PPS/polytetrafluoroethylene
PPS/polyethersulfone

**XIV.**     **Thermoplastic polyurethane (TPU) blends**
TPU/PC or PC/TPU
TPU/styrenic copolymers (ABS, SAN, ASA, . . .) or reverse
TPEs/TPU or TPEs/PC/TPU
PVC/TPU or TPU/PVC
POM/TPU
PA/TPU
Polyolefin/TPU

# Appendix I.D – Binary Blends of Engineering and Speciality Resins

**I. Polyamide blends with:**

| No. | Polymer | PAB-name | Manufacturer |
|-----|---------|----------|--------------|
| 1. | Elastomer/PO | Albis | Albis Plastics |
| | | Bexloy C | DuPont |
| | | Brilion BT-40 | Emser Ind. |
| | | Capron | Allied |
| | | Durethan | BASF |
| | | Grilon | Emser Ind. |
| | | Novamid | Mitsubishi Chem. Ind. |
| | | Nycoa | Nylon Corp. |
| | | Nydur | Bayer/Mobay |
| | | Polyloy | Dr Illing GmbH |
| | | Polymer XE 3055 | EMS Chemie AG |
| | | Technyl | Rhône Poulenc |
| | | Zytel | DuPont |
| 2. | PU-elastomer | Celanese Nylon | Celanese |
| | Acrylic rubber | ETP | DuPont |
| 3. | ABS | Elemid | Borg-Warner |
| | | N5 | Thermofil Inc. |
| | | Triax 1000 | Monsanto |
| | | Ultramid/Terluran | BASF |
| 4 | ASA | Ultramid/Luran | BASF |
| 5. | Ionomer/PO | Freshtuff | American Can Co. |
| | | Nycoa | Nylon Corp. |
| | | Orgalloy | Atochem |
| | | Selar | DuPont |
| | | Zytel/Minlon | DuPont |
| 6. | Silicone | Rimplast | LNP |
| 7. | PEBA | Rislan | Atochem |
| 8. | PP | Dexlon/Dexpro | Dexter Corp. |
| | | Orgalloy | Atochem |
| | | Ube Alloy CA700 | Ube Inc. |
| 9. | PA | Dynyl | Rhone Poulenc |
| | | Grilon | EMS-Chem. AG |
| | | Maranyl | ICI |
| | | Stanyl | DSM |
| | | Stapron | DSM |
| | | Zytel | DuPont |
| 10. | PC | Dexcarb | Dexter Corp. |
| 11. | Polyarylate | Bexloy M | DuPont |
| 12. | PPE | MPPE | Asahi |
| | | Noryl-GTX | General Electric Co. |
| | | Prevex S33 | Borg-Warner |
| | | Ultranyl | BASF |
| | | Vestoblend | Hüls/Nuodex Inc. |
| | | Xyron A,G | Asahi Chem. Ind. |
| 13. | PTFE | RTP 200C, 200TFE | RTP Co. |
| | | Thermocomp RL | LNP Corp. |

**II. Polycarbonate blends with:**

| No. | Polymer | PAB-name | Manufacturer |
|-----|---------|----------|--------------|
| 1. | ABS | Bayblend | Bayer/Mobay |
|    |     | Cycolac | Borg-Warner |
|    |     | Cycoloy | Borg-Warner |
|    |     | Denka HS | Denki Kagaku |
|    |     | Dia Alloy | Mitsubishi Rayon Co. |
|    |     | Idemitsu SC-250 | Idemitsu Petrochem. |
|    |     | Iupilon | Mitsubishi Gas Chem. |
|    |     | JSR Excelloy | Japan Synth. Rub. Co. |
|    |     | Mablex | Mazzucchelli Cell. |
|    |     | Multilon | Teijin Chem. Co. |
|    |     | Novalloy | Daicel Chem. Ind. |
|    |     | Novamate B | Mitsubishi Chem. Ind. |
|    |     | Proloy | Borg-Warner |
|    |     | Pulse | Dow Chem. Co. |
|    |     | Royalite | Uniroyal |
|    |     | Ronfalin | DSM |
|    |     | Ryulex | Dainippon Ink & Chem. |
|    |     | Stilon | USSR |
|    |     | Terblend-B | BASF |
|    |     | Triax 2000 | Monsanto |
| 2. | ASA | BX-200/Geloy XP 4001 | General Electric Co. |
|    |     | Terblends | BASF |
| 3. | AES | JSR Excelloy GE | Japan Synth. Rub. |
|    |     | Rovel | Dow Chem. Co. |
| 4. | SMA | Arloy | Arco |
|    |     | Ektar MB | Eastman Kodak Co. |
|    |     | R4-9900 | Thermofil Inc. |
| 5. | PE | Merlon | Bayer/Mobay |
|    |     | Lexan | General Electric Co. |
| 6. | PEI | Ultem | General Electric Co. |
| 7. | PMMA | Metamarble | Teijin Chem. Ltd. |
| 8. | TPU | Texin | Bayer/Mobay |
| 9. | PA | Dexcarb | Dexter Corp. |
| 10. | PET | Defsan | USSR |
|    |     | Macroblend | Bayer/Mobay |
|    |     | Ultrablend | BASF |
|    |     | Xenoy 2000 | General Electric Co. |
| 11. | PBT | Azloy(reinforced) | Azdel Inc. |
|    |     | Pocan | Mobay/Bayer |
|    |     | R2-9900 | Thermofil Inc. |
|    |     | Ultrablend | BASF |
|    |     | Valox | General Electric Co. |
|    |     | Xenoy 1000 | General Electric Co. |
| 12. | TPEs | R2-9900 | Thermofil Inc. |
|    |     | Ultrablend | BASF |
|    |     | Xenoy 3000 | General Electric Co. |

## III. Polyoxymethylene blends with:

| No. | Polymer | PAB-name | Manufacturer |
|-----|---------|----------|--------------|
| 1. | Elastomer | Celcon | Celanese |
| | | Delrin | DuPont |
| | | Ultraform N254OX | BASF |
| 2. | TPU or PBT | Duraloy/Vandar | Hoechst-Celanese |
| 3. | TPU | Hostaform | Hoechst AG |
| 4. | PTFE | Formaldafil | Wilson-Fiberfil |
| | | RTP 800 | RTP Co. |
| | | Thermocomp/Fulton | LNP |

## IV. Polyphenyleneether blends with:

| No. | Polymer | PAB-name | Manufacturer |
|-----|---------|----------|--------------|
| 1. | HIPS | Ariloks | USSR |
| | | Luranyl | BASF |
| | | Noryl | General Electric Co. |
| | | Prevex | Borg-Warner |
| | | Verton | Hüls |
| | | Vestoran | Hüls/Nuodex Inc. |
| | | Xyron 200 | Asahi |
| 2. | PBT | Gemax | General Electric Co. |
| 3. | PA | MPPE/Xyron A,G | Asahi Chem. Ind. |
| | | Noryl-GTX | General Electric Co. |
| | | Prevex-S33 | Borg-Warner |
| | | Ultranyl | BASF |
| | | Vestoblend | Hüls/Nuodex Inc. |

## Va. Polyethyleneterephthalate blends with:

| No. | Polymer | PAB-name | Manufacturer |
|-----|---------|----------|--------------|
| 1. | Elastomer | Rynite SST | DuPont |
| 2. | PMMA | Ropet | Rohm and Haas |
| 3. | PTFE | Polycomp | LNP |
| 4. | PBT | Celanex | Celanese |
| | | Hostadur-X | Hoechst |
| | | Techster | Rhône Poulenc |
| | | Valox | General Electric Co. |
| 5. | PC | Defsan | USSR |
| | | Macroblend | Mobay/Bayer |
| | | Ultrablend | BASF |
| | | Xenoy-2000 | General Electric Co. |
| 6. | PAr | Ardel | Union Carbide |
| | | UP | Unitika |
| 7. | PSO | Mindel B | Amoco Chem. Corp. |
| 8. | SMA | Arloy 2000 | Arco Chem. Co. |
| 9. | TPU | Xycon | Amoco Chem. Corp. |

**Vb. Polybutyleneterephthalate blends with:**

| No. | Polymer | PAB-name | Manufacturer |
|-----|---------|----------|--------------|
| 1. | Elastomer | Bexloy J. | DuPont |
| | | Gafite/Gaftuf | GAF |
| | | Macroblend | Mobay/Bayer |
| | | Pocan-S | Mobay/Bayer |
| | | Techster T | Rhône Poulenc |
| 2. | ASA | Ultrablend-S | BASF |
| 3. | SBS/ASA | Lomod | General Electric Co. |
| 4. | PET | Celanex | Celanese |
| | | Hostadur-X | Hoechst |
| | | Techster | Rhône Poulenc |
| | | Valox | General Electric Co. |
| 5. | PC | Azloy (reinf.) | Azdel Inc. |
| | | Macroblend/Pocan | Bayer/Mobay |
| | | R2-990 | Thermofil Inc. |
| | | Ultrablend | BASF |
| | | Valox | General Electric Co. |
| | | Xenoy-1000 | General Electric Co. |
| 6. | POM | Duraloy/Vandar | Hoechst-Celanese |
| 7. | PAr | Durel | Celanese |
| 8. | PPE | Gemax | General Electric Co. |
| 9. | PEBA/EVAl | Orgater | Atochem |

**VI. Blends of speciality resins:**

| No. | Speciality resin | Other polymer | PAB Name | Manufacturer |
|-----|------------------|---------------|----------|--------------|
| 1. | PPS | PTFE | Alton | Intl. Polym. Corp. |
| | | " | BR | Phillips |
| | | " | Milkon | Tribol Ind. Inc. |
| | | " | Polycomp | LNP |
| | | " | RTP 1300 | RTP Co. |
| | | " | Tribolon-XT | Tribol Ind. Inc. |
| 2. | PSO | ABS | Arylon | US Steel/Uniroyal |
| | | SAN | Ucardel P4174 | General Electric Co. |
| | | ABS | Mindel A | Amoco Chem. Corp. |
| | | PET | Mindel B | Amoco Chem. Corp. |
| | | PTFE | RTP 900 | RTP Co. |
| 3. | Polyarylate | PET | Ardel | Union Carbide |
| | | PET | UP | Unitika |
| | | PA | Bexloy M | DuPont |
| | | PBT | Durel | Celanese |
| 4. | Ionomer | ? | Bexloy W | DuPont |
| | | PA (olefins) | Surlyn HP | DuPont |
| | | PA | Freshtuff | American Can Co. |
| | | PA | Nycoa | Nylon Corp. |
| | | PA | Zytel-ST-801 | DuPont |

# APPENDIX II

# SURVEY OF PATENT LITERATURE ON ENGINEERING BLENDS

## Appendix II.A – Selected Recent Patents on Polyamide Blends

| No. | US. Patent No./ Date | Assignee | Composition | Advantages |
|---|---|---|---|---|
| 1. | 3,920,602/ Nov. 18, 1975 | Celanese | PA-66/ 5 to 60wt% GF/0.5 to 3wt% Phenoxy | Tensile strength and Izod Impact |
| 2. | 4,242,470/ Dec. 30, 1980 | Shell | PA's/1 to 29wt% Block Polymer, e.g. SEBS with viscosity ratio at $\dot{\gamma} = 100s^{-1}$ from 0.8 to 1.2 | Dry impact strength |
| 3. | 4,283,502/ Aug. 11, 1981 | Du Pont | PA-66/1% of adduct maleic or fumaric acid | Enhanced crystallinity leading to improved tensile strength and dimensional stability. |
| 4. | 4,287,315/ Sept. 1, 1981 | Krefeld, FRG | PA-6 or PA 66/1 to 30wt% copolymer of ethylene, acrylamide and acrylic acid ester | Impact strength |
| 5. | 4,292,416/ Sept. 29, 1981 | Phillips | PA's/0.01 to 10wt% polyarylene sulfide | Moldability, impact strength and warpage resistance |
| 6. | 4,317,891/ Mar. 2, 1982 | Sumitomo, Japan | 1 to 10wt% PA/(PC + ABS, MBS or ABSM in 1:1 to 4:1 ratio) | Moldability, solvent resistance, paintability and impact strength |
| 7. | 4,320,213/ Mar. 16, 1982 | Monsanto | PA/3 to 50wt%hydroxyl functional elastomer/0.1 to 10wt% succinic functional copolymer | High impact strength, moldability |
| 8. | 4,335,223/ Jun. 15, 1982 | Allied | 60 to 98wt% PA with acid/ ester $\alpha$-olefin copolymer and 0.05 to 1 wt% of metal oxide $(MgO, Sb_2O_3, \dots)$ | Notched Izod impact strength |
| 9. | 4,346,194/ Apr. 24, 1982 | Du Pont | PA-66 blend with PA-6 in ratio 1:4 to 4:1/3 with 40 wt% EPDM-furamic acid | Low temperature toughness |
| 10. | 4,346,024/ Aug. 24, 1982 | Rhône-Poulenc, France | 55 to 99 wt% PA with polyesteramide | Enhanced mechanical properties (moduli, impact) |
| 11. | 4,347,332/ Aug. 31, 1982 | American Can Co. | PA-6 with 10 to 80 wt% EVOH copolymer and 2 to 25 wt% plasticizer (e.g. PA-11) | Low temperature film extrudability, improved adhesion between layers, high strength, toughness and oxygen barrier properties |
| 12. | 4,348,502/ Sept. 7, 1982 | Monsanto | 40 to 65 wt% PA with EVA rubber | Enhanced tensile strength and modulus |
| 13. | 4,381,371/ Apr. 26, 1983 | Bayer, FRG | Amorphous PA with 5 to 30 wt% ABS | Toughness, rigidity, impact and high tracking resistance (for automobile and E/E application) |

| No. | US. Patent No./ Date | Assignee | Composition | Advantages |
|-----|----------------------|----------|-------------|------------|
| 14. | 4,383,084/ May 10, 1983 | Standard Oil | Amorphous PA with 2.5 to 5 wt% polyolefin | Elongation at break, tensile and impact strength |
| 15. | 4,391,956/ Jul. 5, 1983 | Polymer Corp. | PA-6 with 5 to 50 wt% polyester elastomer (Hytrel) | Impact strength, increased viscosity and melt strength for enhanced processability |
| 16. | 4,404,317/ Sept. 13, 1983 | Du Pont | Semicrystalline PA (e.g. PA-66) with 2 to 95 amorphous co-polyamide based on phthalic acids | Transparency, low flammability, solvent/acid resistance, high flexural modulus at 50%RH, etc. |
| 17. | 4,404,325/ Sept. 13, 1983 | Allied | 46 to 94 wt% PA with 5 to 44 wt% ionomer (Surlyn) and 1 to 12% ester copolymer and a metallic cation ($Mg^{2+}$, $Sb^{3+}$, ...) | Impact strength, flexural modulus |
| 18. | 4,427,825/ Jan. 24, 1984 | Allied | 1 to 65 wt% PA-6 with ethylenevinylalcohol copolymer having 15 to 65 mol% ethylene and dispersed to domain size less than 50 nm | Transparency, toughness, reduction of $O_2$ permeability (for films, fibers or lamination) |
| 19. | 4,429,076/ Jan. 31, 1984 | Asahi, Japan | 1 to 99% wt% PA with 1 to 99% of modified block copolymers containing neutralized ionic groups (e.g. SB or SBS modified with maleic anhydride, Surlyn, Copolene, etc.) | Tensile, Izod impact strength, heat and oil resistance, flexibility |
| 20. | 4,438,236/ Mar. 20, 1984 | ICI | PA-66 with 0.5 to 5 wt% LCP (broad claims for most engineering and blends) | Processability (at lower temperature at least 10% lower shear viscosity) |
| 21. | 4,461,808/ Jul. 24, 1984 | Du Pont, Canada | PA-66 blends with other PA's in a ratio 94:6 to 10:90 | (For oriented films, lamination) Printability, clarity, $O_2$-permeability, dimensional stability |
| 22. | 4,501,861/ Febr. 26, 1985 | Monsanto | PA-6 with 15 to 85 wt% block polymer of ε-carolactam with either propylene oxide, isoprene, dialkyl silane or other flexible polymer | Impact strength, flex modulus HDT |
| 23. | 4,562,228/ Dec. 31, 1985 | UpJohn | Aromatic-aliphtic co-polyamide with 5 to 30 wt% impact modifying acrylonitrile-butadiene copolymer | Impact resistance |
| 24. | 4,579,914/ Apr. 1, 1986 | Dow Chem. Co. | Segmented, partially aromatic polyesteramide with 5 to 40 wt% of linear aliphatic PA | Increased hardness, solvent resistance and elongational at break |
| 25. | 4,602,058/ Jul. 22, 1986 | Dow Chem. Co. | 70 to 90 wt% PA with 10 to 30 wt% of ethylene acrylic (or methacrylic) acid copolymer, 3 to 5 pph of di-carboxylic acid compatibilizer and 0.5 to 1.0 pph free radicals scavenger | Compatibilization of polymeric blend leading to stability of thermal and rheological properties |

| No. | US. Patent No./ Date | Assignee | Composition | Advantages |
|---|---|---|---|---|
| 26. | 4,612,353/ Sept. 16, 1986 | Dow Chem. Co. | 25 to 75 wt% of aromatic-aliphatic polyamide and 75 to 25% of a polyethyerimide (Ultem) | Enhanced tensile and impact strength and resistance to industrial solvents |
| 27. | 4,670,522/ June 2, 1987 | Union Camp Corp. | Low MW PA with 5 to 75 wt% polyetherester (Hytrel) | For hot melt adhesives, encapsulation; low melt viscosity, good toughness |

| No. | European Patent Office No./Date Publ. | Assignee | Composition | Advantages |
|---|---|---|---|---|
| 28. | 31,287/ Jul. 1, 1981 | Rhône-Poulenc France | 55 to 99 wt% PA with 1 to 45 wt% immiscible polyesteramide | HDT, modulus |
| 29. | 34,704/ Sept. 2, 1981 | Du Pont | 60 to 97 wt% PA-6 or PA-66 with 3 to 40 wt% Zn-neutralized ionomer | Low temperature toughness |
| 30. | 51,471/ May 12, 1982 | Monsanto | 55 to 99 wt% PA with 1 to 45 wt% multiphase polymer with elastomeric core and rigid, ionic shell | High impact resistance and ductility |
| 31. | 60,579/ Sept. 22, 1982 | Akzo, Netherlands | 75 to 99% of PA-6 or PA-66 with 1 to 25 wt% of segmented poly (ether-b-amide) | Moldability, elongation at low and ambiant temperature, Charpy impact strength |
| 32. | 70,001/ Jan. 19, 1983 | Du Pont | 5 to 40 wt% semicrystalline PA with 60 to 95 wt% of amorphous copolyamide of iso- and terephthalic acid and hexamethylene diamine with cyclohexane diamine | Transparent, solvent and water resistant molded articles. Readily adjustable properties by blend composition. Compatibilization via transamidation |
| 33. | 72,480/ Feb. 23, 1983 | Asahi, Japan | 50 to 95 wt% PA, with 1 to 45 wt% of ionomer and 0.5 to 40 wt% of ethylenic elastomer | High impact strength at ambiant and low temperatures |
| 34. | 73,036/ Mar. 2, 1983 | Du Pont | Blend of semicrystalline and amorphous PA (see case 29 above) can be further toughened by acid grafted olefinic elastomer | Notched Izod impact strength |
| 35. | 82,020/ June 22, 1983 | Du Pont | 60 to 99 wt% PA with 1 to 40 wt% of acrylic rubber containing carboxylic groups | Notched Izod impact strength |
| 36. | 86,069/ Aug. 17, 1983 | Uniroyal | 40 to 95 wt% PA with 5 to 60 wt% (plasticized 8 to 10%) neutralized sulfonated EPDM | Tensile and impact strenght |
| 37. | 122,305/ Oct. 24, 1984 | General Electric | 40 to 60 wt% PA-66 or PA-12 with 40 to 60 wt% polyetherimide | Tensile, flexural and impact strength, HDT |

| No. | European Patent Office No./Date Publ. | Assignee | Composition | Advantages |
|---|---|---|---|---|
| 38. | 140,372/ May 8, 1985 | Toyoda Gosei, Japan | 30 to 80 wt% PA with 20 to 70 wt% of rubber compound containing acrylonitrile, butadiene, epichlorohydrin and carboxylic acid functional groups | Improved resistance to ozone, to stress whitening and to gasoline |
| 39. | 140,377/ May 8, 1985 | Toyoda Gosei, Japan | Same as above but the carboxylic acid requirement is replaced by addition of 0.1 wt% polyepoxy compound (Epicote 828). | (same as above) |
| 40. | 191,548/ Aug. 20, 1986 | Du Pont | 75 to 85 wt% amorphous PA and ≥ 15% of toughener particles with diameter ≤ 360 nm, composed of neutralized ionomer | High impact at low temperature |
| 41. | 219,973/ Apr. 29, 1987 | Asahi, Japan | 65 to 85 wt% PA-6 or PA-66 with 3 to 30 wt% Kraton-G and 3 to 30 wt% of (maleated) carboxylic acid groups containing ethylene-α-olefin copolymer (Perhexa or Perbutyl) | High impact strength with well balanced properties such as: stiffness, HDT, weld zone strength, moldability and appearance |
| 42. | 225,039/ | Toyo Boseki, Japan | PA mixed and reacted with block copolymer (e.g. SEBS) + butyl rubber + maleic anhydride + dicumyl peroxide | Moldability, elongation; low temperature impact strength and whitening resistance |
| 43. | 234,819/ Sept. 2, 1987 | Sumitomo | 5 to 59 wt% PA with ethylene copolymer containing carboxylic acid ester and maleic anhydride groups | Cold abrasion and chemical resistance, impact strength esp. at low temperature |

| No. | Patent Cooperation Treaty No.; Date | Assignee | Composition | Advantages |
|---|---|---|---|---|
| 44. | WO84/03894; Oct. 11, 1984 | General Electric | 20 to 60 wt% PA-66 with polyetherimide | Tensile, flexural, impact strength, HDT |
| 45. | WO87/05304; Sept. 11, 1987 | General Electric | 20 to 95% wt% PA, 80 to 5 wt% PPE and 0.1 to 10% of the total of 1,2 substituted olefinic compound with carboxyl or acid anhydride, radically correacted | For molding; surface appearance, impact strength, low warpage, heat resistance |

| No. | French Patent No./Date Publ. | Assignee | Composition | Advantages |
|---|---|---|---|---|
| 46. | 2,582,659/ Jul. 31, 1987 | Isover Saint-Gobain S.A. | 25 to 50 wt% PA with 75 to 50 wt% PS and 2 to 10 wt% on total of a diblock copolymer: poly(styrene-b-acrylic ester), e.g. PS-PMMA partially hydrolyzed | Fine morphology with dispersion ca. 0.5 to 1μm; toughness, elongation |
| 47. | 2,592,388/ Febr. 26, 1988 | Atochem | 30 to 94.8 wt% PA with 0.2 to 65% polyetheramide and 5 to 50% elastomer (e.g. EPDM, NBR, ABS, MBS, Acrylic) | Low-T impact strength |

# Appendix II.B – Selected Recent Patents on Polycarbonate Blends

| No. | US. Patent No./ Date | Assignee | Composition | Advantages |
|---|---|---|---|---|
| 1. | 4,122,131/ Oct. 24, 1978 | General Electric | PC with 1 to 40 wt% PE and 0 to 20 SEBS | Flowability, stress crack resistance and impact strength |
| 2. | 4,188,314/ Febr. 12, 1980 | General Electric | PC with 25 to 75 wt% poly-cyclohexane dimethanol phthalic esters | Solvent resistance, transparency, impact strength, with stable dimensions and lower processing temperature |
| 3. | 4,201,703/ May 6, 1980 | Ethyl Corp. | 10 to 40 wt% PC with polypivalolactone | Low warpage |
| 4. | 4,218,544/ Aug. 19, 1980 | Dow Chem. Co. | PC with 10 to 62 wt% anhydride copolymer, 2 to 50 wt% SAN and 5 to 25 wt% butadiene | Flowability, impact strength and heat resistance |
| 5. | 4,226,961/ Oct. 7, 1980 | General Electric | PC with 10 to 85 wt% of PET (and/or PBT) and 5 to 50 wt% aromatic polyester carbonate | Processability, ductility and transparency |
| 6. | 4,243,764/ Jan. 6, 1981 | Dow Chem. Co. | PC with 10 to 60 wt% ABS | Melt flow properties, impact strength and heat resistance |
| 7. | 4,317,891/ Mar. 2, 1982 | Sumitomo, Japan | 50 to 80 wt% PC with conjugated diene rubber and 1 to 10 wt% PA | Solvent resistance, paintability, moldability |
| 8. | 4,335,032/ Jun. 15, 1982 | General Electric | PC with 2 to 7 wt% PE and 0.2 to 2 wt% PDMS | Melt flow and impact strength |
| 9. | 4,350,799/ Sept. 21, 1982 | Mobay | PC with 0.5 to 80 wt% polyphosphonate and polyurethane | Flame resistance |
| 10. | 4,358,563/ Nov. 9, 1982 | General Electric | PC - aliphatic ester terminated with 4 to 6 wt% PE or PP | Thick section impact strength |
| 11. | 4,358,569/ Nov. 9, 1982 | General Electric | PC or copolyester carbonate/ polysulfone in a ratio 1:3 to 3:1 | High impact strength and flame retardancy |

| No. | US. Patent No./ Date | Assignee | Composition | Advantages |
|-----|---------------------|----------|-------------|------------|
| 12. | 4,367,310/ Jan. 4, 1983 | Dow Chem. Co. | PC with 5 to 25 wt% butadiene, 10 to 62 wt% SMA and 2 to 50 wt% ABS | Melt flow properties, impact strength and heat resistance |
| 13. | 4,388,443/ Jun. 14, 1983 | Atlantic Richfield | 5 to 70 wt% PC with 2 to 5% polylactone and 25 to 93 wt% of styrene-maleic anhydride copolymer (Dylark) | Impact strength, moldability |
| 14. | 4,390,657/ Jun. 28, 1983 | General Electric | PC with 5 to 45 wt% ABS and 0.5 to 40 wt% MBS (Acryloid) | Impact strength, ductibility, improved aging characteristics, high welding strength |
| 15. | 4,393,161/ Jul. 12, 1983 | General Electric | PC with 35 to 95 wt% PS, 0.05 to 4% hydrogen siloxane and 5 to 65% glass fibers | Modulus, impact strength, moldability |
| 16. | 4,393,169/ Jul. 12, 1983 | General Electric | PC with 5 to 95 wt% SMA and 1 to 20 wt% styrene-diallyl maleate-buti-diene-methyl methacrylate co-polymer (Cevien) | Impact and heat resistance (for business machines, cars, E/E and helmets) |
| 17. | 4,397,973/ Aug. 9, 1983 | General Electric | PC with 0.4 to 1% siloxyoxyalkylene copolymer | Reduction of melt viscosity, high impact strength |
| 18. | 4,397,982/ Aug. 9, 1983 | General Electric | PC with 2 to 8 wt% LLDPE and 2 to 4 wt% of MBS (Acryloid) | Low temperature impact, weld line strength, low viscosity, heat stability, chemical resistance and reprocessability |
| 19. | 4,410,662/ Oct. 18, 1983 | Mobay | PC with 0.1 to 50 wt% polyanhydride or its imidized derivative (e.g. PA-18) | Impact strength |
| 20. | 4,430,476/ Feb. 7, 1984 | General Electric | 35 to 90 wt% PC with 0.5 to 20% LDPE ($\varrho$ = 915 to 945 kg/m$^3$) and 9.5 to 45% ABS | Weld line strength, heat stability, hydrolytic stability and solvent resistance |
| 21. | 4,439,582/ Mar. 27, 1984 | Dow Chem. Co. | 25 to 88 wt% PC with 10 to 70% acid copolymer (e.g. of alkyl acrylate), 0 to 35% compatible copolymer and 2 to 30% rubber | Processability, economy without loss of final properties |
| 22. | 4,469,843/ Sep. 4, 1984 | Atlantic Richfield | PC with 3 to 10.5 wt% of styrenemaleic anhydride-rubber copolymer (K-resin TM BDS Polymer-KROX) | Impact strength |
| 23. | 4,472,554/ Sept. 18, 1984 | Mobay | PC with 5 to 95 wt% ABS and/or SAN and 0.1 to 15 wt% acidic polymer or copolymer (e.g. AC540 ethylene-acrylic acid copolymer) | Flowability, tensile and impact strength, elongation and stability |
| 24. | 4,482,672/ Nov. 13, 1984 | Bayer, FRG | PC with 1 to 99 wt% PBT or PET, 1 to 30 wt% SAN or ABS and 4 to 15 wt% ethylene-acrylic acid copolymer | High multiaxial impact strength, high HDT (Vicat B > 110°C) |
| 25. | 4,489,181/ Dec. 18, 1984 | – | 1 to 99 wt% PC with polysulfone carbonate and filler (e.g. mica, glass or carbon fibers). | HDT and high modulus without loss of electrical properties |

| No. | US. Patent No./ Date | Assignee | Composition | Advantages |
|-----|---------------------|----------|-------------|------------|
| 26. | 4,491,647/ Jan. 1, 1985 | Atlantic Richfield | 20 to 80 wt% PC with methylmethacrylate N-phenylmaleimide copolymer or with such copolymer grafted onto EPDM | Tensile and flexural strength modulus, notched Izod |
| 27. | 4,491,648/ Jan. 1. 1985 | Shell Oil | 10 to 80 wt% PC with 10 to 85% hydrogenated block polymer ABA and/or $(AB)_x$ BA type, and 10 to 80% SMA | Good low temperature properties, low distortion and shrinkage, tensile strength |
| 28. | 4,493,920/ Jan. 15, 1985 | Atlantic Richfield | 1 to 99 wt% PC with random terpolymer of styrene, N-phenylmaleide and maleic anhydride | Dependent on composition total or partial miscibility |
| 29. | 4,493,921/ Jan. 15, 1985 | Uniroyal | 5 to 60 wt% PC with 20 to 90% PBT and 5 to 50% EPDM grafted with polar monomers (e.g. styrene, acrylonitrile and methylmethacrylate) | Notched Izod impact strength at low and ambient temperatures |
| 30. | 4,507,434/ Mar. 26, 1985 | Occidental Chem. | 40 to 60 wt% PC with vinylchloride polyolefin graft polymer | Weld line strength, surface properties, impact strength, flame resistance |
| 31. | 4,520,164/ May 28, 1985 | General Electric | PC containing 10.5 to 45 wt% of polyolefin mixed with 20 to 80% of copolymer of butylacrylate, butyldiacrylate, diallylmaleate and methylmethacrylate (Acryloid KM330) | Stress cracking resistance, good ductility, gasoline resistance |
| 32. | 4,548,997/ Oct. 22, 1985 | General Electric | 0 to 100 wt% PC with polyetherimide | HDT, flexural and tensile strength, impact resistance |
| 33. | 4,560,722/ Dec. 24, 1985 | General Electric | PC with PBT blend stabilized by addition of 0.01 to 1 wt% boric acid | Improved stability of the composition by increased resistance toward trans-esterification |
| 34. | 4,560,725/ Dec. 24, 1985 | DSM, Netherlands | 5 to 95 wt% PC with two types of ABS and SN copolymer | Flow properties, impact strength, hardness, stiffness and energy absorbance |
| 35. | 4,562,222/ Dec. 31, 1985 | General Electric | 60 to 89 wt% PC with 5 to 20% SB block copolymer (KR03), 5 to 20% ethylene ethyl acrylate copolymer (DPD6169) and not more than 10% LLDPE | Improved environmental stress crazing and cracking, impact and solvent resistance |
| 36. | 4,564,655/ Jan. 14, 1986 | General Electric | PC with 2 to 20 wt% $A((BA)_nB)_m$ block polymer (e.g. SBS) and 1 to 20% ethylene propylene ethylidene norbornene terpolymer (Vistalon 3708) | Improved resistance to organic solvents, environmental stress cracking, ductility, impact strenght |
| 37. | 4,568,712/ Feb. 4, 1986 | General Electric | PC with PET (and/or PBT) and 5 to 65 wt% siloxane coated glass fibers | High impact strength and modulus molding composition |

| No. | US. Patent No./ Date | Assignee | Composition | Advantages |
|---|---|---|---|---|
| 38. | 4,568,723/ Feb. 4, 1986 | Mobil Oil | 1 to 40 wt% PC with 50 to 98.5% PP and 0.5 to 10% SEBS | High Elmendorf tear strength, elongation and tensile strength |
| 39. | 4,579,909/ Apr. 1, 1986 | General Electric | 5 to 90 wt% PC with 10 to 90% PMMA and 10 to 90% ASA (Geloy 1020) | Impact and flexural properties |
| 40. | 4,579,910/ Apr. 1, 1986 | General Electric | 10 to 96 wt% PC with 2 to 35% olefin vinylester copolymer (DPD-6169) and 2 to 35% ethylene vinyl alcohol copolymer or 2 to 90% polyolefin | Resistance to solvents |
| 41. | 4,607,079/ Aug. 19, 1986 | General Electric | 68 to 90 wt% PC with 8 to 25% Phenoxy and 3 to 7% acrylate elastomer (Acryloid KM330) | Retention of impact strength and ductility after exposure to primary ethers and alcohols |
| 42. | 4,608,417/ Aug. 26, 1986 | General Electric | PC and PP ($\geq$ 70 wt%) with olefin acrylate copolymer (EEA,DPD 6169) | A tie material for PC/polyolefin multilayer clear film |
| 43. | 4,624,986/ Nov. 25, 1986 | Dow Chem. Co. | 20 to 95 wt% PC with rubber modified copolymer (ABS) | Low temperature performance, low gloss |
| 44. | 4,629,760/ Dec. 16, 1986 | General Electric | 51 to 84 wt% PC with 5 to 15% acrylate elastomer (Acryloid KM330), 8 to 20% linear polyester (PET) and 3 to 14% Phenoxy | Retention of notched impact strength after immersion in alcohols and ethers (break fluids) |
| 45. | 4,645,802/ Feb. 24, 1987 | Eastman Kodak | 5 to 95 wt% PC with polyesterimides and polyesterimideamide | Compatible transparent moldings with single $T_g$, good impact strength and HDT |
| 46. | 4,645,804/ Feb. 24, 1987 | General Electric | 10 to 90 wt% mixed polycarbonate (including sulfonated units) and polyetherimide | Compatible blend with good mechanical properties |
| 47. | 4,654,400/ Mar. 31, 1987 | Electric Electric | 40 to 60 wt% PC with 30 to 50% aromatic polyester (PBT) and 8 12% acrylate elastomer | Good mechanical properties, no solvent stress whitening |
| 48. | 4,677,148/ Jan. 30, 1987 | Mobay Corp. | 15 to 85 wt% PC with 85 to 15% TPEs (e.g. PET) and 5 to 30% on total of butadiene and acrylate copolymer impact modifier (e.g. ABS, Akryloid KM, Polysar S1006) | Low melt viscosity, low-T impact strength, tensile strength and elongation at break |
| 49. | 4,698,390/ Oct. 6, 1987 | Amoco Corp. | Polycarbonate of tetramethylene-bis-sulfone and bisphenol-A with PVC | Compatible blend with good impact mechanical and HDT properties |
| 50. | 4,710,548/ Dec. 1, 1987 | Dow Chem. Co. | 10 to 90 wt% PC with 90 to 10 wt% polyester carbonate | Low-T thoughness, hydrolytic stability, good HDT |
| 51. | 4,737,545/ Apr. 12, 1988 | General Electric | 76 to 92 wt% PC with 4 to 12% of each: (i) teleblock copolymer (e.g. Kraton G), and (ii) ethylene-ethylacrylate copolymer, EEA | Environmental stress crazing and cracking, solvent resistance |

| No. | US. Patent No./ Date | Assignee | Composition | Advantages |
|-----|----------------------|----------|-------------|------------|
| 52. | 4,749,738/ June 7, 1988 | General Electric | PC or PEC with 3 to 70 wt% polyolefin (LLDPE), 3 to 7% fluorinated polyolefin (PTFE), 0.05 to 0.5% silicone fluid (polymethyl-hydrogensiloxane) and GF | Wear resistance |

| No. | European Patent Office No./Date Publ. | Assignee | Composition | Advantages |
|-----|----------------------------------------|----------|-------------|------------|
| 53. | 44,175/ Jan. 20, 1982 | Celanese Corp. | 5 to 75 wt% PC with aromatic polyester (LCP) forming anisotropic melt phase [see also USP 4,489,190] | Tensile/flexural strength and modulus, impact strength and HDT |
| 54. | 56,247/ Jul. 21, 1982 | Dow Chem. Co. | 25 to 88 wt% PC with 10 to 70% acid copolymer (styrene-acrylic acid copolymer) and up to 35% compatible copolymer with rubber (KM 611, SBS or SAN) [see also USP 4,439,582] | Processability, good mechanical properties for electrical appliances housing and auto parts |
| 55. | 80,767/ Jun. 8, 1983 | Stamicarbon, Netherlands | 5 to 95 wt% PC with ABS and SAN [see also USP, 4,560,725] | Processability, impact strength |
| 56. | 106,096/ Apr. 25, 1984 | General Electric | 84 to 96 wt% PC with 2 to 8 % polyolefin (PP) and 2 to 8% LLDPE [see also USP 4,430,476] | Extraordinary resistance to environmental stress crazing and cracking |
| 57. | 107,048/ May 2, 1984 | General Electric | 51 to 97 wt% PC with 3 to 49% PET and 3 to 20% multiphase acrylic elastomer (Acryloid KM330); optional: flame retardent | Processability, notched impact strength and weatherability |
| 58. | 111,851/ Jun. 27, 1984 | General Electric | PC with ≥ 10 wt% polyolefin or copolyolefin (e.g. PP, EPR, . . .) and 10 to 45% acrylic interpolymer (Acryloid MK330) [see also USP 4,520,164] | Resistance to gasoline soaking |
| 59. | 119,531/ Sept. 26, 1984 | General Electric | 55 to 93 wt% PC with 3.5 to 30% polyolefin and/or copolyolefin (e.g. PP, EPDM) and 3.5 to 15% olefin-acrylate copolymer (e.g. Polybond 1016). | Resistance to gasoline, weld line strength |

| No. | European Patent Office No./Date Publ. | Assignee | Composition | Advantages |
|---|---|---|---|---|
| 60. | 122,601/ Oct. 24, 1984 | Idemitsu, Japan | 20 to 94.6 wt% PC with 5 to 50% saturated polyester (PET), 0.2 to 15% polyolefin (LDPE or LLDPE) and 0.2% to 15% acrylate rubber (e.g. methylmethacrylate/butyl acrylate/styrene copolymer, MBS, Metablend W-529 or Acryloid KM 330) | Low temperature impact, chemical resistance, fluidity, colorability, coating and plating properties. Use in car bumpers, instruments panels, appliances, etc. |
| 61. | 122,759/ Oct. 24, 1984 | Henkel Corp., USA | PC with 0.01 to 1 wt% of lubricating linear ester | Mold release, clarity of molded parts |
| 62. | 133,657/ Mar. 6, 1985 | General Electric | Reactive processing leading to grafting during the extrusion of two thermoplastic polymers by addition of e.g. sulfonylazide: $R(SO_2N_3)_x$. In particular PC/polyolefin, ABS or SBS | Prevented delamination, lower gloss |
| 63. | 135,492/ Mar. 27, 1985 | Monsanto Co. | 5 to 70 wt% PC with 5 to 70% styrene-maleicanhydride-methyl methacrylate copolymer and 5 to 70% ABS | Izod impact strength and dart impact |
| 64. | 173,358/ Mar. 5, 1986 | General Electric | 86 to 99 wt% PC with 0.5 to 4% hydrogenated block polymer (Kraton G) and 0.5 to 10% graft copolymer with elastomeric core (Acryloid KM653) | Increased resistance to organic solvents, low temperature impact strength |
| 65. | 186,089/ Jul. 2, 1986 | Idemitsu, Japan | PC with 5 to 67 wt% copolyester carbonate (PC-PET type) | Fluidity, solvent cracking resistance, transparency, impact strength |
| 66. | 192,065/ Aug. 27, 1986 | Idemitsu, Japan | 30 to 90 wt% PC with 4 to 45% polyester ether elastomer (based on terephthalic acid), 1 to 25% rubber-like elastomer (e.g. Acryloid KM330 or MABS resin HIA 15) and 2 to 40% PET | Rigidity, solvent resistance, moldability, impact strength |
| 67. | 239,157/ Sept. 30, 1987 | General Electric | Blend of PC:PBT = 2.5 to 0.9 with 5 to 30 wt% of total of a coreshell toughening agent: butadiene-co-styrene-co-alkylmethacrylate, e.g. MBS | Melt flow, impact strength, low $T_g$, elongation at break |
| 68. | 254,054/ Jan. 27, 1988 | General Electric | 86 to 97 wt% PC with 2 to 6% graft copolymer having an elastomeric core (e.g. Acryloid KM 653) and 1 to 8% of block copolymer build up form PC and PDMS parts (e.g. Copel LR 3320) | Melt viscosity, impact strength, elongation at fracture after dipping in Fuel C |

| No. | Patent Coopera-tion Treaty No./Date | Assignee | Composition | Advantages |
|---|---|---|---|---|
| 69. | WO80/00027/ Jan. 10, 1980 | General Electric | PC with 7 to 80 wt% PS and 0 to 25 wt% MBS | Flowability, processability, tensile strenght |
| 70. | WO80/00084/ Mar. 29, 1984 | General Electric | PC with poly(carbonate-co-organo siloxane) in an amount of about up to 50% by weight of PC | Flame retardance, ductility, solsolvent resistance |
| 71. | WO84/01164/ Mar. 29, 1984 | General Electric | 70 to 99.5 wt% PC with LLDPE (density 890 to 960 kg/m$^3$) [see US Pat. 4,430,014] | Weld line, impact strength low shear degradability, thermal stability |
| 72. | WO84/04104/ Oct. 25, 1984 | Union Carbide | 5 to 95 wt% PC (containing bishydroxy sulfone units) and styrenic copolymers (SAN, ABS, . . .) | Compatible, transparent moldings with good mechani-cal properties |
| 73. | WO84/04752/ Dec. 6, 1984 | General Electric | PC with 50-95 wt% poly-ether imide | HDT, flexural impact and tensile strenght |

# Appendix II.C – Selected Recent Patents on POM Blends

| No. | Patent No./ Date | Assignee | Composition | Advantages |
|---|---|---|---|---|
| N 1. | US 4,181,685/ Jan. 1, 1980 | Hoechst, FRG | POM with 0.001 to 10 wt% branched or crosslinked POM | Small spherulites, hardness, stiffness and tensile strength |
| 2. | US 4,351,916/ Sept. 28, 1982 | Du Pont | POM with 0.1 to 10 wt% PEO and 0.15 to 3 wt% PA-66 | Thermal stability |
| 3. | US 4,424,308/ Jan. 3, 1984 | Celanese | POM with 1 to 20 wt% PB (3% optimum) | Tensile and impact strength |
| 4. | US 4,526,921/ Jul. 2, 1985 | Mitsubishi Gas, Japan | 38 to 99.9 wt% POM with 0.1 to 20% low molecular weight PC ([$\mu$] = 0.2 dl/g) | Surface gloss and weather resistance |
| 5. | US 4,556,690/ Dec. 3, 1985 | Mitsui Petrochem, Japan | POM with 1 to 67 wt% of graftmodified polyolefin (e.g. maleic anhydride modified ethylene-butene-1 copolymer) | Rigidity, toughness, impact and flexural strength, heat resistance, moldability, lack of delamination |
| 6. | US 4,730,015/ Mar. 8, 1988 | Polyplastics Co. Ltd. Japan | POM with 0.01 to 2 wt% of benzotriazole and 0.01 to 2% of hindered amine (piperidine) | Crack resistance, weather-ability |
| 7. | EPO 38,881/ Nov. 4, 1981 | Cyanamid | 2 to 20 wt% POM with ther-moplastic polyurethane elas-tomer | Melt strength, no sagging of parison in bottle blowing |
| 8. | EPO 47,529/ Mar. 17, 1982 | Du Pont | POM with 0.4 to 2 wt% poly-ethyleneglycol and 0.4 to 2% PA | Thermal stability |

| No. | Patent No./ Date | Assignee | Composition | Advantages |
|-----|------------------|----------|-------------|------------|
| 9. | EPO 124,879/ Nov. 14, 1984 | Mitsui Petrochem, Japan | [See US 4,556,690] | |
| 10. | EPO 242,037/ Oct. 21, 1987 | Polyplastics Co. Ltd., Japan | 90 to 99.5 wt% POM (or polyester or polyamide) and 0.5 to 10% liquid organopolysiloxane of viscosity 5 to 10,000 St | For hinge materials |
| 11. | PCT WO84/ 04103 Oct. 25, 1984 | Union Carbide | 45 to 95 wt% POM (containing 20% bishydroxyphenyl sulfone units) and styrene copolymer (e.g. ABS) and/or PVC | Moldable, compatible blends |

## Appendix II.D – Selected Recent Patents on Polyphenylene Ether Blends

| No. | US Patent No./ Date | Assignee | Composition | Advantages |
|-----|---------------------|----------|-------------|------------|
| 1. | 4,196,116/ Apr. 1, 1980 | General Electric | PPE with 20 to 80 wt% EPDM-modified PS and 1 to 20 wt% hydrogenated SB block polymer | Impact strength, moldability |
| 2. | 4,277,575/ Jul. 7, 1981 | General Electric | PPE with 35 wt% PS and 15 wt% hydrogenated SB and SBS type block copolymers (e.g. Shellvis and Kraton G) | Impact strength |
| 3. | 4,284,735/ Aug. 18, 1981 | ARCO | PPE with 50±15 wt% terpolymer of rubbery block polymer + maleimide + styrene | Impact strength |
| 4. | 4,309,514/ Jan. 5, 1982 | General Electric | PPE with 1 to 50 wt% teleblock polymer of styrene and saturated butadiene units (Solprene) | Impact strength |
| 5. | 4,313,864/ Feb. 2, 1982 | General Electric | PPE with 10 to 30 wt% aromatic phosphate plasticizer/10 wt% Solprene | Melt flow, fire retardancy, impact strength and gloss |
| 6. | 4,322,506/ Mar. 30, 1982 | Phillips | PPE with conjugated diene-mono-vinylarene copolymer (Solprene) | Solution blending process leading to improved mechanical properties |
| 7. | 4,360,618/ Nov. 23, 1982 | Monsanto | PPE with 10 to 90 wt% of SAN or ABS, containing 2 to 8% AN | HDT and impact strength |
| 8. | 4,371,672/ Feb. 1, 1983 | Atlantic Richfield | PPE with phosphorus containing alternating copolymer of styrene and propylene oxide | At least partially miscible blends with excellent fire retardancy |
| 9. | 4,387,189/ Jan. 7, 1983 | BASF | PPE reacted with reactive copolymers of S, AA and MA/PS or HIPS | Processability, impact strength and HDT |

| No. | US Patent No./ Date | Assignee | Composition | Advantages |
|---|---|---|---|---|
| 10. | 4,389,511/ Jun. 21, 1983 | Monsanto | PPE with 10 to 90 wt% poly-(styrene-co-4-tertbutylsty-rene) modified with rubber | Miscible blends of good ductility, tensile strength, impact strength and HDT |
| 11. | 4,405,753/ Sept. 20, 1983 | Monsanto | PPE with 10 to 30 wt% SAN or ABS and 10 to 30 wt% SMA | Impact strength and HDT |
| 12. | 4,444,934/ Apr. 24, 1984 | Asahi, Japan | 50 wt% PPE with 10 to 40% mixed, neopentyl fatty acid polyester and 10 to 40% PS | HDT, processability, solvent and crack resistance |
| 13. | 4,454,271/ Jun. 12, 1984 | General Electric | 10 to 90 wt% PPE with copolymer of styrene and tertbutylstyrene | HDT, tensile, impact strength, ductility; miscible blends |
| 14. | 4,480,073/ Oct. 30, 1984 | Mobil Oil | PPE with 20 to 99 wt% poly-(butadiene-g-methylethyl-benzene) | Compatible blends with excellent processability |
| 15. | 4,481,332/ Nov. 6, 1984 | Kanegafuchi, Japan | 1 to 99 wt% copolymer of phenylene ether and indole (or imidazole) with styrene copolymer (e.g. HIPS, PMS, PAS, PS, PMMA...) | HDT, flowability, transparency, improved oxydative degradation resistance |
| 16. | 4,491,649/ Jan. 1, 1985 | Borg-Warner | PPE copolymers with 2 to 25 wt% ABA and 5 to 50 wt% PC | Toughness, reduced notch sensitivity and HDT |
| 17. | 4,537,925/ Aug. 27, 1985 | General Electric | 5 to 95 wt% PPE with 4 to 95% PS + sulfonated PS and 1 to 15% antistatic agent | Melt flow, permanent antistatic properties of molded articles |
| 18. | 4,555,538/ Nov. 26, 1985 | General Electric | 5 to 95 wt% PPE with HIPS and UV-stabilizers (ben-zophenone + dipiperidinyl ester) | UV-stability |
| 19. | 4,556,685/ Dec. 3, 1985 | Mitsubishi Gas, Japan | 60 to 90 wt% PPE with 10 to 30% HIPS, 2 to 15% nitrile rubber, 2 to 10% elastomer (EPDM), and 2 to 10% aromatic phosphate | Impact strength, HDT, fire retardancy |
| 20. | 4,579,901/ Apr. 1, 1986 | General Electric | PPE with an alkenyl aromatic resin (HIPS) and aromatic polyester plasticizer (e.g. Admex) | Melt flow properties, processability |
| 21. | 4,600,741/ Jul. 15, 1986 | General Electric | 5 to 95 wt% PPE with PA and 1 to 95% on PPE + PA of a compatibilizing PPE-modified with acyl functional groups | Improved compatibility, elongation, impact properties and processability |
| 22. | 4,617,346/ Oct. 14, 1986 | Mitsubishi Gas, Japan | 10 to 90 wt% PPE with 5 to 88% PS or rubber-modified PS, and 1 to 25% alkyl acry-late core/shell graft copolym-er (HIA-15, HIA-28 or HIA-30) | Impact resistance, weatherability, moldability, HDT |
| 23. | 4,618,637/ Oct, 21, 1986 | General Electric | 5 to 95 wt% PPE with PA and 0.05 to 5% oxalyldihyd-razide | Resistance to oxydation |

| No. | US Patent No./ Date | Assignee | Composition | Advantages |
|-----|---------------------|----------|-------------|------------|
| 24. | 4,659,760/ Apr. 21, 1987 | General Electric | 1 to 99 wt% PPE with PA and 0.01 to 10% oxidized polyolefin wax (Hoechst Wachs PED 136 or 153) | Mechanical properties, especially notched Izod impact, dart impact, maximum strain at break |
| 25. | 4,659,763/ Apr. 21, 1987 | General Electric | 30 to 70 wt% PPE with PA and 0.1 to 4% quinone | Quinone induced grafting PPE on PA chains, leading to improved impact strength, elongation, chemical resistance, processability and HDT |
| 26. | 4,678,839/ Jul. 7, 1987 | General Electric | 10 to 97 wt% PPE (hydroxy or hydroxy amine terminated), at least one lactam (e.g. ε-caprolactam) and a catalyst. PS or PS-copolymers, EPDM and others can be added | The reaction product consists of blend and/or graft or block copolymer of PPE and PA with high thermal stability solvent resistance |
| 27. | 4,681,915/ Jul. 21, 1987 | General Electric | At least 35 wt% PA with PPE and core-shell impact modifier with crosslinked acrylate core and IPN type styrenic shell | Thermal stability, impact strength, tensile elongation |
| 28. | 4,684,681/ Aug. 4, 1987 | General Electric | PPE with 10 to 90% HIPS or hydrogenated SBS and thiodiphenol | Low melt viscosity |
| 29. | 4,684,696/ Aug. 4, 1987 | General Electric | PPE with or not HIPS at a ratio 10:90 to 90:10 and core/shell impact modifying polyacrylate copolymer | Impact strength, thermal stability, elongation |
| 30. | 4,687,799/ Aug. 18, 1987 | Enichem S.p.A. Italy | PPE with styrene or α-methyl styrene polymer or copolymer and 0.1 to 3% of a mixture of 2,4-bis(n-octylthio)-6-(4-hydroxy 3,5-di tertbutylanilino)-1,3,5-triazine and dilauryl thiopropanoate | High melt fluidity and thermal stability |
| 31. | 4,690,978/ Sept. 1, 1987 | Hüls AG FRG | 15 to 95 wt% PPE with 0 to 70% styrenic resin (HIPS), 3 to 15% styrene-butadiene emulsion copolymer, 3 to 15% SBR | Simple to prepare blend with high impact strength and HDT |

| No. | European Patent Office No./Date Publ. | Assignee | Composition | Advantages |
|-----|---------------------------------------|----------|-------------|------------|
| 32. | 044,703/ Jan. 27, 1982 | Asahi-Dow, Japan | PPE with 5 to 95 wt% poly-(styrene-co-N-phenylmalein imide) and 0 to 90 wt% hydrogenated or not S-B, SEBS | Impact strength |
| 33. | 046,040/ Feb. 17, 1982 | Asahi-Dow, Japan | 10 to 70 wt% PPE with 2 to 50% SMA, 5 to 70% PA and 0 to 70% impact resistant copolymer (HIPS, SBS, . . .) | HDT, chemical/solvent resistance |

| No. | European Patent Office No./Date Publ. | Assignee | Composition | Advantages |
|-----|---------------------------------------|----------|-------------|------------|
| 34. | 083,049/ Jul. 6, 1983 | General Electric | PPE with 1 to 25 wt% PS grafted EPDM, 0 to 20 wt% PS and 1 to 35 wt% triaryl-phosphate | Improved integrity of mold-ings (lack of delamination), gloss, ductility and tensile strength |
| 35. | 086,448/ Aug. 24, 1983 | General Electric | PPE + HIPS with 20 to 80 wt% terpolymer of styrene, butadiene and caprolactone | Impact strength, elongation, processability |
| 36. | 088,293/ Sept. 14, 1983 | General Electric | PPE with or without HIPS and 0.1 to 5 wt% poly(ethy-lene-co-methyl-acrylate) | Impact and tensile strength, elongation |
| 37. | 129,825/ Jan. 2, 1985 | General Electric | PPE with 30 wt% PA and 1 to 20 wt% organic phosphate | Compatible, flame retardant blends |
| 38. | 133,487/ Feb. 27, 1985 | General Electric | PPE with 20 wt% PE modi-fied by, SB, SBS or hydroge-nated SB | Tensile and impact strength, ductility, absence of delami-nation |
| 39. | 138,599/ Apr. 24, 1985 | Mitsubishi Gas, Japan | PPE with 10 to 30 wt% PS, 2 to 15 wt% nitrile rubber, 2 to 10 wt% butyl rubber and 5 to 20 wt% aromatic phosphate | Impact strength, HDT and flame retardancy |
| 40. | 168,652/ Jan. 22, 1986 | General Electric | 75 to 98 wt% PPE, 2 to 25% ionic elastomer (Uniroyal IE-2590 sulfonated EPDM) and 3 to 30% plasticizer (e.g. triphenylphosphate) | Impact resistance |
| 41. | 171,826/ Feb. 19, 1986 | General Electric | 1 to 50 wt% PPE (with or without HIPS) with 50 to 99% PC and 0.1 to 2% poly-hydrogen siloxane | Low melt instability, good notch impact strength |
| 42. | 191,326/ Aug. 20, 1986 | Dow Chem. Co. | 1 to 99 wt% PPE with poly-(styrene-co-α-methylstyrene) | Tensile modulus, tenacity, elongation |
| 43. | 226,851/ Jul. 1, 1987 | General Electric | 5 to 95 wt% PPE and HIPS with 1 to 40% copolymer of ethylene and methacrylic acid, (Nucrel 403), 1 to 20% SEBS (Kraton-G 1651) and 0.1 to 10% styrene-glycidyl methacrylate copolymer (Nippon-Oils GS20); with or without fillers | Chemical resistance, good tensile and impact properties, moldability without delami-nation |
| 44. | 226,910/ Jul. 1, 1987 | Borg-Warner Chem. | 5 to 75 wt% carboxylated-PPE with PA | Impact strength, elongation, tensile strength |
| 45. | 234,060/ Sept. 2, 1987 | General Electric | PPE, PA, SBS or HIPS with 0.01 to 5% pentaerythrityl-tetrastearate | Heat stability, consistent im-pact strength |
| 46. | 234,063/ Sept. 2, 1987 | General Electric | 5 to 94% PPE with 5 to 94 PA (PA-6,6) and 1 to 50% core-shell compatibilizer im-pact modifier (core = buty-lacrylate, methyl-methacry-late and/or styrene, shell = maleicanhydride) | Impact resistance, [reactive processing] |

| No. | European Patent Office No./Date Publ. | Assignee | Composition | Advantages |
|---|---|---|---|---|
| 47. | 237,948/ Sept. 23, 1987 | General Electric | Two step melt compounding of PPE with PA-66 and poly-functional compatibilizer (e.g. citric acid) then down-stream in the extruder addi-tion of 0 to 80 wt% of PA (e.g. PA-6, -6,9, -10, -11, -12, -4,6 or amorphous PA) | Improved impact strength, ductility and HDT |
| 48. | 244,090/ Nov. 4, 1987 | Japan Synthetic Rubber Co. | 4 to 95 wt% PPE, 4 to 95% PA, 1 to 50% elastomer (e.g. SBS), not more than 91% styrene-glycidyl-methacrylate or styrene-acrylic acid copolymer, 0.001 to 10% un-saturated compound and 0.001 to 5% peroxide | Melt flow, moldability, heat and impact resistance |
| 49. | 268,981/ June 1, 1988 | Mitsubishi Petrochem. Co. | PPE with 1 to 80 wt% sty-rene polymer blended with 25% to 85% polar thermo-plastic resin (PA, PC or TPEs) and 10 to 30% hyd-rogenated block copolymer (Kraton G-1652) | Compatible blend with excellent impact strength and solvent resistance for auto-motive and appliance applications |

| No. | Patent Coopera-tion Treaty No./Date | Assignee | Composition | Advantages |
|---|---|---|---|---|
| 50. | W082/01885/ Jun. 10, 1982 | General Electric | PPE with 17 to 83 wt% PS and 3 to 15 wt% butadiene membrane | Impact strength |
| 51. | WO82/04056/ Nov. 25, 1982 | Western Electric | PPE-PC copolymer with 5 to 95 wt% PS or HIPS | Thermal/oxidative/dimen-sional stability, electrically insulating, mechanical prop-erties |
| 52. | WO83/03422/ Oct. 13, 1983 | General Electric | PPE with 10 to 90 wt% polyetherimide | Impact strength and mechan-ical properties |
| 53. | W085/05372/ Dec. 5, 1985 | General Electric | 30 to 70 wt% PPE with PA, 4% of polycarboxylic acid and impact modifiers (e.g. HIPS) | Impact strength, elongation, chemical resistance, proces-sability, heat resistance, low water absorption |
| 54. | WO 87/00850/ Feb. 12, 1987 | General Electric | 10 to 45 wt% PPE with 10 to 45% polyalkylenedicarboxy-late (PBT or PET), 8 to 25% impact modifier (SBS, SEBS, hydrogenated SB, . . .) 3 to 40% PC and 0.1 to 1% cyanurate. | Impact, solvent resistance, compatible blends |
| 55. | W087/05311/ Sept. 11, 1987 | General Electric | 3 to 95 wt% PPE com-patibilized with PA (continu-ous phase) and 1 to 20% hyd-rogenated SB copolymer (with or without glass fiber) | Improved low temperature ductility |

| No. | Other Patents No./Date | Assignee | Composition | Advantages |
|---|---|---|---|---|
| 56. | Can. 1,065,091/ Oct. 23, 1979 | General Electric | PPE with 30 to 65 wt% SBS and 5 to 25 wt% hydrogenated SBS (e.g. Kraton) | Impact strength and flame retardance |
| 57. | Fr.2,483,444/ May 27, 1981 | General Electric | PPE with 15 to 85 wt% poly-(styrene-co-bromostyrene) | Flammability, UV-stability |
| 58. | Can. 1,220,591/ Apr. 14, 1987 | General Electric | 5 to 95 wt% PPE with poly-α-methyl styrene or rubber modified poly-α-methyl styrene | Tensile, impact strength, HDT |

# Appendix II.E – Selected Recent Patents on Thermoplastic Polyester Blends

| No. | US Patent No./ Date | Assignee | Composition | Advantages |
|---|---|---|---|---|
| 1. | 3,937,757/ Feb. 10, 1976 | BASF, FRG | PBT with 10 to 30 wt% polyolefin | Tracking resistance |
| 2. | 4,011,285/ Mar. 8, 1977 | Eastman Kodak | 70 to 96 wt% PBT with 2 to 15% polyetherester and 2 to 15% radial teleblock copolymer (Solprene 411C) | Notched Izod impact strength and good overall mechanical properties |
| 3. | 4,020,126/ Apr. 26, 1977 | Du Pont | 95 to 99 wt% PET with 1 to 5% ethylene-vinylacetate-methacrylic acid terpolymer | Impact strength of thermoformed containers, durability, mold release, moldability |
| 4. | 4,119,607/ Oct. 10, 1978 | Shell Oil | PBT with 10 to 35 wt% block copolymer (SEBS) and 8 to 20% engineering thermoplastic (preferably PA) | Stabilization of blend morphology leading to improvement of properties and processability |
| 5. | 4,126,602/ Nov. 21, 1978 | Hooker Chem. | Linear amorphous aromatic polyester with 10 to 30 wt% of rubber modified copolymer of styrene, maleic anhydride and butadiene | Hydrolytic stability |
| 6. | 4,157,997/ Jun. 12, 1979 | General Electric | PBT with 10 to 25 wt% of poly(siloxane-b-carbonate) and 10 to 25% CaCO$_3$ | Low warpage, processability |
| 7. | 4,184,997/ Jan. 22, 1980 | Du Pont | 20 to 80 wt% PET with 5 to 50% glass fiber and 6 to 60% copolyetherester | Surface smoothness |
| 8. | 4,187,259/ Feb. 5, 1980 | Hooker Chem. | Linear aromatic polyester with 5 to 20 wt% crosslinked acrylate-methacrylate copolymer | Hydrolytic stability with good mechanical and chemical properties |

| No. | US Patent No./ Date | Assignee | Composition | Advantages |
|-----|---------------------|----------|-------------|------------|
| 9. | 4,195,134/ Mar. 25, 1980 | GAF Corp. | PBT with 0.1 to 15 wt% diepoxy and 5 to 20% of multiphase, elastomeric acrylate (7709-XP) | Hydrolytic stability evidenced by good impact strength after 4 days in boiling water |
| 10. | 4,208,322/ Jun. 17, 1980 | Pennwalt Corp. | Polyester, PA or polyesteramide with 2.5 to 20 wt% polymetalphosphinates | Flame retardancy |
| 11. | 4,219,628/ Aug. 26, 1980 | Eastman Kodak | 70 to 90 wt% polyester with 5 to 25% EPR and 5 to 25% poly(ethylene-co-acrylic acid) (Surlyn) | Balance of physical properties (e.g. impact, modulus, elongation at break) |
| 12. | 4,283,326/ Aug. 11, 1981 | GAF Corp. | PBT with 1 to 40 wt% mica and 5 to 30% multiphase elastomeric copolymer (e.g. Acryloid KM330) | Low warpage |
| 13. | 4,290,937/ Sept. 22, 1981 | General Electric | PBT with 0.25 to 4.5% PE or PE-copolymer and 0.02 to 0.5% talc | Mold releasability |
| 14. | 4,303,573/ Dec. 1, 1981 | Du Pont | PET with 2 to 20 wt% ionomer poly(ethylene-co-methacrylic acid-co-isobutyl acrylate) neutralized with Zn and 2 to 20% poly(ethylene-co-propylene-co-1,4 hexadiene-co-norbornadiene) | Improvement of high velocity impact strength |
| 15. | 4,317,764/ Mar. 2, 1982 | Du Pont | 20 to 95 wt% PBT with 0.1 to 10% polyalkylene oxide or PA-66 and 5 to 35% fumaric acid grafted copolyolefin | Impact resistance |
| 16. | 4,324,869/ Apr. 13, 1982 | Union Carbide | Polyarylate derived from dihydric phenol and dicarboxylic acid (e.g. PET), poly (ethylene-co-alkylacrylate and other polymer (e.g. PA) | Good balance of mechanical properties and hydrolytic stability |
| 17. | 4,338,243/ Jul. 6, 1982 | Du Pont | 20 to 90 wt% PET with 1 to 12% ionomer 1 to 12% organic compound and flame retardants, including $SbBr_3$ | Thermal stability, low flammability and good impact strength |
| 18. | 4,342,846/ Aug. 3, 1982 | Stauffer Chem. | 10 to 90 wt% PET or PBT with interpolymer of methacrylate, styrene and acrylonitrile (e.g. SCC 1004) | Elongation at break, flexural, tensile and impact strength |
| 19. | 4,346,195/ Aug. 24, 1982 | Ethyl Corp. | 20 to 80 wt% PET with rubber modified graft copolymer of polyvinyl with maleic anhydride, SMA, (Dylark 338 or 350) | Thermal properties, especially HDT |
| 20. | 4,351,758/ Sept. 18, 1982 | Celanese Corp. | 40 to 95 wt% of PET/PBT mixture at a ratio 1:1 to 1:9 with 4 to 65% fillers and 0.1 to 20% nucleating agent | glossy surface, HDT |
| 21. | 4,369,280/ Jan. 18, 1983 | General Electric | PBT with 0.1 to 4.5% EVA and 0.1 to 4.5 PE | Impact strength and low density |

| No. | US Patent No./ Date | Assignee | Composition | Advantages |
|-----|---------------------|----------|-------------|------------|
| 22. | 4,370,438/ Jan. 25, 1983 | Celanese Corp. | 35 to 85 wt% PET and PBT with 5 to 60% glass fiber, 4 to 15% decabromodiphenylether and 2 to 10 Sb-compound | Suppression of PET/PBT transesterification, non-flammability |
| 23. | 4,388,446/ June 14, 1983 | Ethyl Corp. | 20 to 80 wt% PET with rubber modified styrene-maleimide copolymer (Dylark DKB 162 or 176) | HDT |
| 24. | 4,397,986/ Aug. 9, 1983 | Ethyl Corp. | PET with 5 to 75 wt% SAA | HDT |
| 25. | 4,408,022/ Oct. 4, 1983 | Celanese Corp. | 50 to 75 wt% PET or PBT with wholy aromatic polyester (LCP), post polymerized to enhance interactions between the two polymers | Mechanical properties not significantly reduced below the weighted averages of the two components, anisometry |
| 26. | 4,414,230/ Nov. 8, 1983 | Sumitomo, Japan | 20 to 50 wt% PET with polyester-carbonate | Improved barrier properties against gases and water vapor |
| 27. | 4,472,553/ Sept. 18, 1984 | Ethyl Corp. | 20 to 80 wt% PET with rubber modified styrene-maleimide copolymer (Dylark DKB 162 or 176) [see USP 4,388,446] | HDT |
| 28. | 4,483,949/ Nov. 20, 1984 | Ethyl Corp. | 10 to 90 wt% PET with SMA (Dylark 338) as well as 1 to 10% glass fiber and 0.1 to 5% of nucleating agent (sodium stearate) | HDT, surface appearance, flexural modulus |
| 29. | 4,485,204/ Nov. 27, 1984 | Phillips Petroleum | 50 to 90 wt% PET with rubbery block copolymer (Solprene 414P) and a dessicant (e.g. CaO, MgO, $Al_2O_3$) | Upgrading the mechanical (impact) properties of recycled PET |
| 30. | 4,485,212/ Nov. 27, 1984 | Uniroyal Inc. | PBT with 25 to 55 wt% EPDM rubber grafted with styrene and acrylonitrile | Hardness and impact strength |
| 31. | 4,493,921/ Jan. 15, 1985 | Uniroyal Inc. | PBT with 20 to 40% PC and 20 to 30% copolymer of styrene and acrylonitrile on EPDM | Hardness, stiffness and impact strength |
| 32. | 4,526,923/ Jul. 2, 1985 | Ethyl Corp. | 20 to 80 wt% PET with SMA (Dylark 332, 350 or Dow XP 5272.07) [see USP 4,472,553] | Thermal properties, esp. HDT |
| 33. | 4,551,368/ Nov. 5, 1985 | Goodyear Tire & Rubber Co. | 10 to 90 wt% polyethylene isophthalate with PET (or PBT) | Reduction of $O_2$ permeability film or container |
| 34. | 4,554,314/ Nov. 19, 1985 | Mobay Chem. | 50 to 80 wt% PET with PC and methylmethacrylate-styrene graft butadiene copolymer (Acryloid KM653) | Impact strength |
| 35. | 4,558,096/ Dec. 10, 1985 | Goodyear Tire & Rubber Co. | 10 to 90 wt% PET with EPR or EPDM rubber containing 0.001 to 2% alkyl succinic anhydride | Impact strength |

| No. | US Patent No./ Date | Assignee | Composition | Advantages |
|-----|---------------------|----------|-------------|------------|
| 36. | 4,578,295/ Mar. 25, 1986 | Owens-Illinois Inc. | 80 to 90 wt% PET with amorphous copolyester of iso- and terephthalic acids with bis(hydroxyethoxy/benzene) and bis(hydroxyethoxy phenyl)sulfone | Barrier properties to $CO_2$ and $O_2$ permeability, mechanical properties and processability |
| 37. | 4,680,344/ Jul. 14, 1987 | Du Pont | 15 to 40 wt% PET with ionomer (ethylene-methacrylic acid copolymer 5 to 80% neutralized with Zn) | Heat and impact rsistance |
| 38. | 4,687,819/ Aug. 18, 1987 | General Electric | 25 to 50 wt% TPEs (PET), 20 to 60% polyterephthalate-carbonate and 20 to 60% polyetherimide | Low melt viscosity and low processing temperature |
| 39. | 4,725,651/ Feb. 16, 1988 | Dow Chem. Co. | 25 to 40 wt% thermoplastic copolyester (Kodar PETG) and vinylchloride-co-vinyl-didene chloride interpolymer (Saran) | Miscible, transparent blend with good oxygen barrier properties |

| No. | European Patent Office No./Date Publ. | Assignee | Composition | Advantages |
|-----|---------------------------------------|----------|-------------|------------|
| 40. | 25,920/ Sept. 4, 1980 | Rohm and Haas | PET with 1 to 50% PC and 4 to 25% core-shell butyl acrylate based impact modifier | Impact strength |
| 41. | 39,155/ Apr. 8, 1981 | Asahi, Japan | PET with 0.05 to 10% PA or polyhydrazine as nucleating agent | Rapid crystallization of PET |
| 42. | 42,724/ Dec. 30, 1981 | Ethyl Corp. | PET with 10 to 90% SMA or rubber modified SMA (e.g. Dylark) | HDT |
| 43. | 42,737/ Dec. 30, 1981 | | | |
| 44. | 71,773/ July 7, 1982 | General Electric | PBT with 10% PB and 5% LDPE/5% PC | Impact strength |
| 45. | 79,477/ May 25, 1983 | General Electric | 30 to 80 wt% PBT with 10 to 30% Acryloid KM653, 10 to 40% PC and 1.5% PE | Impact strength |
| 46. | 88,263/ Feb. 19, 1983 | General Electric | PBT with 1 to 20% Poly(2-methyl-1,3-propyl terephthalate) | Moldability, crystallization rate, uniformity and gloss |
| 47. | 95,189/ Nov. 30, 1983 | Toyo Boseki, Japan | 5 to 98 wt% PBT with polyester block copolymer (PBT-PCL type) | Moldability, impact, heat and water resistance |
| 48. | 105,826/ Apr. 18, 1984 | Goodyear Tire and Rubber Co. | Polyethyleneisophthalate with PET or PBT [see USP 4,551,368] | Oxygen barrier property |
| 49. | 107,048/ Sept. 22, 1983 | General Electric | PET with 51 to 97% PC and 3 to 20% poly(methyl-n-butylacrylate), e.g. Acryloid, 0.5% LLDPE and (optionally) a flame retardant | Moldability, impact strength, flammability |

| No. | European Patent Office No./Date Publ. | Assignee | Composition | Advantages |
|---|---|---|---|---|
| 50. | 107,303/ May 2, 1984 | Uniroyal | 60 to 80 wt% PBT with 10 to 20% PC and 10 to 20% graft copolymer of styrene and acrylonitrile on EPR or EPDM [see USP 4,485,212 and 4,493,921] | High impact strength |
| 51. | 108,996/ May 23, 1984 | Mobay Chem. | 20 to 80 wt% PET with 30 to 60% PC and 3 to 40% ABS [see USP 4,554,314] | Impact strength upon addition of a modifying oil |
| 52. | 113,096/ Dec. 19, 1983 | General Electric | PET with 60% impact modifier: 10 to 15% polyacrylate rubber and 10 to 15% PC | Impact strength, tensile strength and tensile strain. Recyclable |
| 53. | 135,904/ Sept. 17, 1984 | Mobay | PET with 5 to 61.5% PC and 5 to 50% butadiene copolymer (e.g. MBS), 0.1 to 4% talc | Low warpage and high impact strength |
| 54. | 135,677/ Jun. 23, 1984 | General Electric | PET and/or PBT with 5 to 95% ABS (Rovel) | Gloss and solvent resistance |
| 55. | 171,161/ Feb. 12, 1986 | Owens-Illinois | PET with copolyester of iso- and terephthalic acid with bis(hydroxy-ethoxy)benzene [see USP 4,578, 295] | High gas and water vapour transmission barrier |
| 56. | 181,141/ Jun. 4, 1986 | Eastman Kodak | Polyester of terephthalic acid, trans-4,4 stilbenedicarboxylic acid and 1,4 cyclohexanedimethanol (5 to 95 wt%) with PC | Transparency, compatibility and high impact strength at low-T |
| 57. | 187,416/ Jul. 16, 1986 | General Electric | 70 to 90 wt% of PET or PBT with 5 to 80% polyterephthalatecarbonate and 5 to 80% polyetherimide | Processability, low melt viscosity, DUTL, impact strength, flex modulus |
| 58. | 230,703/ Aug. 5, 1987 | Atlantic Richfield | 50 to 99 wt% PBT with elastomer grafted with acrylics (e.g. EPDM-g-ethyl methacrylate/methacrylic acid) | Impact resistance and thermal stability |
| 59. | Canad. Pat. No. 1,123,534/ May 11, 1982 | General Electric | PBT and/or PET with 2.5 to 50% of PC and butylacrylate rubber (e.g. | Impact, tensile strength, modulus and HDT |
| 60. | German Pat. No. DE 3,167,070A1/ Nov. 26, 1987 | BASF AG FRG | 10 to 89 wt% of polyester blend (20 to 98% PET + 80 to 2% bisphenol-A-polycarbonate of isoand terephthalic acid) with 10 to 89% PC and 1 to 30% acrylic elastomer with $T_g$ < -30°C (e.g. poly-(ethylene-co-n-butylacrylate-co-acrylic acid) | low-T impact strength, HDT |

# Appendix II.F – Selected Recent Patents on Speciality Polymer Blends

## 1. With liquid crystal polymers (LCP)

| No. | Patent No./ Publication Date | Assignee | Composition | Advantages |
|---|---|---|---|---|
| 1. | US 4,207,407/ Jun. 10, 1980 | USAF | 10 to 30% rod-like aromatic polymer with coil-like heterocyclic polymer | Self-reinforcing (on molecular level) blends |
| 2. | Eur. 051,933/ May 19, 1981 | ICI | LCP with 0.5 to 99.5% PTFE | Processability, lubricity |
| 3. | US 4,408,022/ Oct. 4, 1983 | Celanese Corp. | LCP with 50 to 75% PET or PBT | High anisotropy/self reinforcement, economy |
| 4. | US 4,438,236/ Mar. 20, 1984 | ICI | LCP(0.5 to 5%) with thermoplastic resin (e.g. PES, PPE, PC, PVC, PA) | Processability |
| 5. | US 4,489,190/ Dec. 18, 1984 | Celanese Corp. | LCP with 5 to 50% PET or PBT | Synergistic mechanical properties, economy |
| 6. | Eur. 169,947/ Feb. 5, 1986 | Celanese Corp. | 20 to 75 wt% isotropic aromatic polyester with 25 to 80% anisotropic aromatic polyester | Good mechanical properties, HDT, processability, economy |
| 7. | US 4,581,399/ Apr. 8, 1986 | Celanese Corp. | LCP with 0.1 to 5 wt% liquid crystalline compound with molecular weight $\simeq$ 1 kg/mol | Processability |

## 2. With polyetherimide (PEI)

| No. | Patent No./ Publication Date | Assignee | Composition | Advantages |
|---|---|---|---|---|
| 1. | US 4,387,193/ Jun. 7, 1983 | General Electric | PEI with poly(carbonate-b-siloxane) | Impact strength, flexural properties |
| 2. | US 4,390,665/ Jun. 28, 1983 | General Electric | PEI with EPDM | Impact strength |
| 3. | US 4,393,168/ Jul. 12, 1983 | General Electric | PEI with ABS or MBS | HDT, impact strength, flexural and tensile properties |
| 4. | US 4,395,518/ Jul. 26, 1983 | General Electric | PEI with acrylate copolymers (e.g. Acryloid) | Processability, impact strength with high flexural, tensile strength and HDT |
| 5. | (PCT)W083/ 03416/ Oct. 13, 1983 | General Electric | PEI with PEI of different type | High performance, high $T_g$; application in aerospace and transport |
| 6. | US 4,427,830/ Jan 24, 1984 | General Electric | PEI with 1 to 20% PP or PP-copolymer | Notched Izod strength (maximum at 10% PP) |
| 7. | US 4,455,410/ Jun. 19, 1984 | General Electric | PEI with polysulfide(e.g. Ryton) | Flexural strength |
| 8. | US 4,468,506/ Aug. 28, 1984 | General Electrics | Blend of two or more PEI's | Glass transition temperature 125 to 210°C suitable for automobile and aerospace application |
| 9. | Eur. 117,326/ Sept. 5, 1984 | General Electrics | PEI with polyarylate | Processability, impact strength, flexural strength and modulus |

| No. | Patent No./ Publication Date | Assignee | Composition | Advantages |
|---|---|---|---|---|
| 10. | Eur. 117,327/ Sept. 5, 1984 | General Electric | PEI with polyarylate and polycarbonate | HDT, flame resistance |
| 11. | (PCT)W084/ 03894/ Oct. 11, 1984 | General Electric | PEI with (40 to 80%) PA's | Tensile, flexural strength |
| 12. | (PCT)W084/ 04752/ Dec. 6, 1984 | General Electric | PEI with PC | HDT, flexural strength, tensile strength, impact strength and flame resistance |
| 13. | Eur. 141,347/ May 15, 1985 | General Electric | 85 to 97 wt% PEI with polyacrylate elastomer (Hycar 4004 or 4051CG) | Impact strength, transparency |

## 3. With Polyestercarbonate (PEC)

| No. | Patent No./ Publication Date | Assignee | Composition | Advantages |
|---|---|---|---|---|
| 1. | US 4,346,197/ Aug. 24, 1982 | PPG Industries Inc. | Polymerization of bisallylcarbonate in presence of other polymers | Processability, transparency |
| 2. | Fr. 2,535,332/ Nov. 3, 1982 | General Electric | PEC with 0.1 to 20% LLDPE | Enhanced stability against hydrolysis |
| 3. | US 4,401,785/ Aug. 30, 1983 | General Electric | 80 to 99.1 wt% PEC with LDPE ($\varrho$ = 915 to 945 kg/m$^3$) | Stabilization against hydrolysis |
| 4. | US 4,430,484/ Feb. 7, 1984 | General Electric | 30 to 70 wt% PEC with aromatic PA, aromatic polyamideimide or polyimide | HDT, flexural strength and modulus |
| 5. | US 4, 464, 512/ Aug. 7, 1984 | General Electric | PEC with 0.1 to 20 wt% LLDPE ($\varrho$ = 915 to 945 kg/m$^3$) | Hydrolytic stability |
| 6. | US 4,559,388/ Dec. 17, 1985 | General Electric | 20 to 85 wt% PEC with 10 to 75% PC, 2 to 25% polyol and 3 to 10% impact modifier (polyolefin, EEA, ...) | Solvent resistance, notched Izod impact strength |
| 7. | US 4,579,903/ Apr. 1, 1986 | General Electric | 20 to 85 wt% PEC with 10 to 75% PC, 2 to 25% hydrogenated block copolymer (e.g. SEBS) and 1 to 20% olefin acrylate copolymer, EPDM, etc. | Impact strength, solvent, heat resistance |
| 8. | US 4,598,130/ Jul. 1, 1986 | Union Carbide | 30 to 70 wt% PEC with polyarylate | Improved light transmission, low haze, good mechanical properties |

**4. With Polysulfone (PSO)**

| No. | Patent No./ Publication Date | Assignee | Composition | Advantages |
|---|---|---|---|---|
| 1. | Fr. 2,535,332/ Nov. 3, 1982 | Electricité de France | PSO with 20 to 40% PTFE | Processability, chemical and thermal stability (application in electrochemical cells) |
| 2. | US 4,360,636/ Nov. 23, 1982 | Stauffer Chem. | PSO with 5 to 50% mixture of crosslinked and not SAN | Processability, tensile, flexural, impact properties and HDT |
| 3. | Eur. 090,404/ Oct. 5, 1983 | Union Carbide | 20 to 85 wt% polyarylether sulfone with styrene or acrylic copolymer (e.g. ABS, ASA, SMA, Akryloid KM611) and 0.5 to 20% polyhydroxyether | Weld line strength, elongation, tensile properties |
| 4. | (PCT)W084/ 04104/ Oct. 25, 1984 | Union Carbide | PSO with 5 to 95% SAN | Compatible blend with high moldability and high $T_g$ |
| 5. | US 4,493,917/ Jan. 15, 1985 | Electricité de France | PSO (or polyphenyl sulfide) with 20 to 40 wt% fluorocarbon polymer (e.g. PTFE) | Processability, chemical and thermal stability in aggressive environment |
| 6. | US 4,562,231/ Dec. 31, 1985 | Atlantic Richfield | 1 to 99 wt% PSO with styrene-N-phenylmaleimide | Mechanical properties, processability |
| 7. | Eur. 176,989/ Apr. 9, 1986 | Union Carbide | PSO with polyarylether-ketone | Mechanical properties, environmental stress cracking resistance |
| 8. | US 4,614,767/ Sept. 30, 1986 | Atlantic Richfield | Polyestersulfone with impact modified styrene copolymer (e.g. Kraton-G) | Heat and impact resistance, fire retardancy |
| 9. | Eur. 224,236/ Jun. 3, 1987 | Sumitomo Chem Japan | 5 to 80 wt% PSO with poly-ether-ketone | Chemical resistance, moldability |

**5. With Polyphenylene Sulfide (PPS)**

| No. | Patent No./ Publication Date | Assignee | Composition | Advantages |
|---|---|---|---|---|
| 1. | Eur. 062,830/ Oct. 30, 1982 | Union Carbide | PPS with 10 to 90% polyaryl-ketone (e.g. PEEK). PC, PSO or Phenoxy can also be added | Processability, synergistically high flexural and tensile strength |
| 2. | US 4,395,512/ Jul. 12, 1983 | Shin-Etsu Chem., Japan | PPS with 1 to 50% fluoro-rubber (e.g. Viton) and filler | Moldability, mechanical properties, crack and heat resistance |
| 3. | US 4,451,607/ May 29, 1984 | Phillips Petroleum | 10 to 90 wt% PPS with hydrogenated diene monovinyl aromatic block copolymer (SEBS) | Increase of PPS crystallinity, processability, economy |
| 4. | US 4,476,284/ Oct. 9, 1984 | Phillips Petroleum | PPS with 1 to 30% hydrogenated SB block polymer (e.g. Solprene) | Mechanical properties, economy |
| 5. | US 4,497,928/ Febr. 5, 1985 | Atlantic Richfield | PPS with 1 to 99% copolymer of styrene and maleimide | Moldability, tensile strength and elongation |

| No. | Patent No./ Publication Date | Assignee | Composition | Advantages |
|---|---|---|---|---|
| 6. | Eur. 189,895/ Aug. 6, 1986 | Kureha, Japan | 25 to 90 wt% poly-p-phenylene sulfide with poly-m-phenylene sulfide and 5 to 50% block copolymer of these two types | Compatible blends, transparency, tensile strength, modulus, processability |
| 7. | US 4,607,078/ Aug. 19, 1986 | Dow Chem. | Polysulfide with elastomer (e.g. SBS, SIS, SB, NBR) and polymer (e.g. PS, LDPE) or copolymer (e.g. EVA, EPR, Saran) | Tensile properties, resilience |
| 8. | Eur. 241,019/ Oct. 14, 1987 | Phillips Petroleum | 10 to 90 wt% PPS with 5 to 40% polyamideimide and 5 to 80% polyarylketone (PEEK) or polyarylsulfone (PES) (Victrex) | Balance of thermal and mechanical properties, homogenous blends |
| 9. | US 4,708,983/ Nov. 24, 1987 | Phillips Petroleum | 100 parts PPS with 0.1 to 25 parts polysiloxane (PDMS, $MW \simeq 300$ kg/mol), 0.01 to 5 parts trialcoxysilate and 0.05 to 20 parts polyolefin (PE or PP) | Processability, impact strength |
| 10. | Eur. 257,228/ Mar. 2, 1988 | Tohpren Co., Ltd. | 70 to 97 wt% of para-PPS with 30 to 3% meta-PPS or pPPS blended with (p-co-m)PPS block or random copolymer | Low crystallization temperature while retaining high melting point for film or fiber extrusion |

## 6. Polyaryletherketones (PAEK), polyimides (PI) and others

| No. | Patent No./ Publication Date | Assignee | Composition | Advantages |
|---|---|---|---|---|
| 1. | Eur. 090,404/ Oct. 5, 1983 | Union Carbide | 20 to 85 wt% PAE (e.g. polyarylether sulfone or ketone with styrenic or acrylic copolymer (e.g. ABS, ASA, SMA, Akryloid KM611) and 0.5 to 20% polyhydroxyether (Phenoxy) | Weld line strength, elongation, tensile properties, surface finish |
| 2. | Eur. 163,464/ Dec. 4, 1985 | Raychem Corp. | At least 40 wt% PAEK (e.g. PEEK) with PEI (Ultem) and optionally PAS | Miscible blends with high tensile strength at high temperatures, elongation |
| 3. | Eur. 166,450/ Jan 2, 1986 | Union Carbide | 5 to 95 wt% PAEK (e.g. PEEK) or PPS with poly-amideimide | Solvent resistance and hydrolytic stability |
| 4. | Eur. 170,067/ Feb. 5, 1986 | Union Carbide | 5 to 95 wt% PAEK (e.g. PEEK) with polyarylate (Ardel D-100, Lexan 3250 or 4450, LCP, etc.) | Elongation, impact strength, tensile strength, environmental stress cracking |
| 5. | US 4,255,322/ Mar. 10, 1981 | Rohm and Hass Co. | 5 to 95% polyglutarimide with vinylchloride polymer (PVC, CPVC or PVC-Ac) | Compatible blends with high HDT transparency, impact resistance |

| No. | Patent No./ Publication Date | Assignee | Composition | Advantages |
|-----|------------------------------|----------|-------------|------------|
| 6. | Eur. 216,505/ Apr. 1, 1987 | Rohm and Hass Co. | 1 to 99 wt% PI with thermoplastic polymer (SAN, PA, PVC, PET, ABS, PC, POM, SMA, PPS, PEI, Phenoxy, $PVF_2$, CPVC, PE, PP, EVA $PVCl_2$, . . .) | Processability, weatherability, compatibility |
| 7. | Eur. 108,738/ May 16, 1984 | Monsanto Co. | 3 to 20 wt% thermoplastic copolyetherester, 15 to 75% SMA, 12 to 60% ABS or MBS and 3 to 20% NR | Impact properties, esp. at low temperature |
| 8. | US 4,508,870/ Apr. 2, 1985 | Monsanto Co. | 1 to 15 wt% thermoplastic copolyetherester elastomer (Hytrel) with ABS or MBS | Ductility, chemical resistance |
| 9. | US 4,324,869/ Apr. 13, 1982 | Union Carbide | Polyarylate e.g. PET with 1 to 5% ethylene-alkyl acrylate copolymer (e.g. EEA, EVA) and 5 to 45% thermoplastic polymer (e.g. TPE, PC, PS, PMMA, etc.) | Good hydrolytic stability, notched Izod, tensile strength and elongation |
| 10. | US 4,346,024/ Aug. 24, 1982 | Rhone-Poulenc, France | Polyesteramide with PA | Mechanical properties, especially strength |
| 11. | US 4,585,581/ Apr. 29, 1986 | USA, Dept. Energy | Polypyrrole (or poly-N-p-nitrophenylpyrrole) with PEO (or PPO) complexed with NaI or KI | Electrical conductivity |
| 12. | US 4,617,337/ Oct. 14, 1986 | Exxon R & E Co. | Neutralized sulfonated polymer (e.g. sulfonated EPDM, copolymer of butadiene and zinc sulfonated styrene) with pyridine co-polymer | Low melt viscosity and high mechanical properties of elastomeric blends |
| 13. | US 4,642,267/ Feb. 10, 1987 | Hydromer Inc. | Thermoplastic polyurethane with poly-N-vinyl lactam | Slipperiness in aqueous environment |
| 14. | Fr. 2,591,607/ June 19, 1987 | Atochem France | 0.1 to 99.9 wt% of block copolyetheramide with 99.9% to 0.1% styrene-diene copolymer, e.g. PA-PTMG/ SBS blends | Miscible blends for molding or extrusion into flexible but strong with a spectrum of properties |
| 15. | WO88/00605/ Jan. 28, 1988 | Amoco Corp. | PAEK, PAE, or PPE blended with LCP prepared in the presence of preformed PAEK, PAES or PPE | Mechanical properties, high T stability, solvent resistance and processability |
| 16. | Eur. 257,150/ Mar. 2, 1988 | Amoco Corp. | PAEK with PI in a ratio 4:1 to 1:4 | Miscible blends with high $T_g$ and controllable crystallinity for film, fiber and other formed articles |
| 17. | Eur. 257,862/ Mar. 1, 1988 | Amoco Corp. | PAEK or PAES (PSO) with polyalkylene-terephthalate (PET) and a nucleating agent for PET, with or without GF | Combination of best properties of PSO and PET resulting in warp free moldings without blisters when exposed to humid conditions |

# APPENDIX III

## Abbreviations for Thermoplastics

(Based on H.-G. Elias, *Polym News, 9,* 101 (1983); ibid. *10,* 169 (1984)

| | |
|---|---|
| AAS | Copolymer of acrylonitrile, acrylate (ester) and styrene |
| ACRYLIC | Poly- or copolymethylmethacrylate |
| ABR | Elastomeric copolymer from an acrylate (ester) and butadiene; acrylate-butadiene rubber |
| ABS | Acrylonitrile-butadiene-styrene copolymer |
| ACS | Thermoplastic blend of a copolymer from acrylonitrile and styrene with chlorinated polyethylene |
| AES | Thermoplastic quaterpolymer from acrylonitrile, ethylene, propylene, and styrene |
| AMMA | Thermoplastic copolymer from acrylonitrile and methyl methacrylate |
| ASA | Thermoplastic copolymer from acrylonitrile, styrene, and acrylates |
| BR | Elastomeric polybutadiene; butadiene rubber |
| CA | Cellulose acetate |
| CF | Carbon fiber |
| CN | Cellulose nitrate |
| CPE | Chlorinated polyethylene |
| CPVC | Chlorinated polyvinylchloride |
| CR | Elastomeric polychloroprene |
| CTFE | Polychlorotrifluoroethylene |
| EC | Ethyl cellulose |
| EEA | Ethylene-acrylic acid copolymers |
| EAM | Elastomeric copolymer of ethylene and vinyl acetate |
| EEA | Elastomeric copolymer from ethylene and ethyl acrylate |
| ELAST. | Elastomer |
| EMA | Ethylene methacrylate copolymer |
| EPDM | Elastomeric terpolymer from ethylene, propylene, and a non-conjugated diene |
| EPM | Ethylene-propylene copolymer |
| EPR | Elastomeric copolymer of ethylene and propylene |
| EVA | Copolymer from ethylene and vinyl acetate |
| FEP | Fluorinated EPM |
| GF | Glass fiber |
| HDPE | High density polyethylene (ca. 960 kg/m$^3$) |
| HIPS | High impact polystyrene |
| IIR | Isobutene-isoprene rubber (Butyl Rubber) |
| IPN | Interpenetrating polymer network |
| IR | Synthetic cis-1,4-polyisoprene |
| LCP | Liquid crystal polymer |
| LDPE | Low density polyethylene (ca. 918 kg/m$^3$) |
| LLDPE | Linear low density polyethylene |
| MBS | Copolymer from methylmethacrylate, butadiene, and styrene |
| MDPE | Polyethylene of medium density (ca. 930 – 940 kg/m$^3$) |
| NBR | Elastomeric copolymer from butadiene and acrylonitrile; nitrile rubber |
| NR | Natural rubber |
| PA | Polyamide, the abbreviation PA is normally followed by a number, a combination of numbers, a letter or a combination of letters and numbers. A single number refers to the polyamide from an $\alpha$, $\omega$-amino acid or its lactam. A combination of two numbers is often separated by a comma. The first number following the symbol PA indicates the number of methylene groups of aliphatic diamines, the second number the number of carbon atoms of aliphatic dicarboxylic acids. An I stands for isophthalic acid, a T for terephthalic acid. |

| PAA | Polyacrylic acid |
|---|---|
| PAE | Polyarylether |
| PAEK | Polyaryletherketone |
| PAES | Polyarylethersulfone |
| PAI | Polyamide-imide |
| PAMS | Poly-α-methylstyrene |
| PAN | Polyacrylonitrile |
| PAr | Polyarylate |
| PAS | Polyarylsulfide |
| PB | Poly-1-butene |
| PBT | Polybutyleneterephthalate |
| PC | Bisphenol-A polycarbonate |
| PCTG | Poly(cyclohexaneterephthalate-glycol) |
| PDMS | Polydimethylsiloxane |
| PE | Polyethylene |
| PEBA | Polyether-block-amide |
| PEC | Polyestercarbonate |
| PEEK | Polyetheretherketone |
| PEI | Polyetherimide |
| PEO | Polyethyleneoxide |
| PEG | Polyethyleneglycol |
| PES | Polyethersulfone |
| PET | Polyethyleneterephthalate |
| PFEP | Copolymer from tetrafluoroethylene and hexafluoropropylene |
| PI | Polyimide |
| PIB | Polyisobutene |
| PMMA | Polymethylmethacrylate |
| PMA | Polymethylacrylate |
| PMP | Poly-4-methyl-1-pentene |
| PO | Polyolefin |
| POM | Polyoxymethylene (Acetal) |
| PP | Polypropylene |
| PPE | Polyphenyleneether |
| PPG | Polypropylene glycol |
| PPS | Polyphenylenesulfide |
| PS | Polystyrene |
| PSO | Polysulfone |
| PSU | Polyphenylenesulfone |
| PTFE | Polytetrafluoroethylene |
| PTMG | Polyoxytetramethylene glycol |
| PTR | Polysulfide rubber |
| PU | Polyurethane |
| PVAc | Polyvinyl acetate |
| PVAl | Polyvinyl alcohol |
| PVB | Polyvinyl bytyrate |
| PVC | Polyvinyl chloride |
| PVDC | Polyvinylidene chloride |
| PVDF | Polyvinylidene fluoride |
| PVF | Polyvinyl fluoride |
| PVME | Polyvinylmethylether |
| PVP | Poly-N-vinylpyrrolidene |
| SAN | Thermoplastic copolymer from styrene and acrylonitrile |
| SBR | Elastomeric copolymer from styrene and butadiene |
| SBS | Styrene-butadiene-styrene block copolymer |
| S-EPDM | Sulfonated ethylene-propylene-diene terpolymers |
| SEBS | Styrene-ethylene-butylene-styrene block copolymer (hydrogenated SIS) |
| SEP | Styrene-ethylene-propylene block copolymer |
| SI | Silicones |

| SIN | Simultaneous interpenetrating network |
| SIS | Styrene-isoprene-styrene block copolymer |
| SMA | Copolymer from styrene and maleic anhydride |
| SMS | Copolymer from styrene and α-methylstyrene |
| TPE | Thermoplastic elastomer |
| TPEs | Thermoplastic polyesters, e.g. PBT, PET, ... |
| TPO | Thermoplastic olefinic elastomer |
| TPU | Thermoplastic polyurethanes (linear) |
| TPX | Poly-4-methyl-1-pentene |
| UHMWPE | Polyethylene with ultrahigh molar weight (molar mass over 3 Mg/mol) |
| ULDPE | Ultra low density polyethylene (ca. 900 to 915 $kg/m^3$) |
| VLDPE | Very low density polyethylene (ca. 885 $kg/m^3$) |

# APPENDIX IV

## Appendix IV.A – Selected Monographies on Polymer Rheology

*I Fundamental approach*

I.1      *F. R. Eirich*, "Rheology: Theory and Application", Academic Press, New York (1956); five volumes.

I.2      *A. S. Lodge*, "Elastic Liquids", Academic Press, New York (1964).

I.3      *B. D. Coleman, H. Markovitz* and *W. Noll*, "Viscometric Flows of Non- Newtonian Fluids", Springer-Verlag, New York (1966).

I.4      *S. Middleman*, "The Flow of High Polymers", Interscience Publ., New York (1968).

I.5      *G. Astarita* and *G. Marrucci*, "Principle of Non-Newtonian Fluid Mechanics", McGraw-Hill, London (1974).

I.6      *J. L. Leblanc*, "Rhéologie Expérimentale des Polymères à l'État Fondu", Éditions *Cebedoc*, Liège, (1974).

I.7      *R. Darby*, "Viscoelastic Fluids", M. Dekker, New York (1976).

I.8      *L. E. Nielsen*, "Polymer Rheology", M. Dekker, New York (1977).

I.9      *J. Harris*, "Rheology and Non-Newtonian Flow", Longman, London (1977).

I.10      *R. B. Bird, R. C. Armstrong* and *O. Hassager*, "Dynamics of Polymeric Liquids: Volume 1, Fluid Mechanics"; *R. B. Bird, O. Hassager, R. C. Armstrong* and *C. F. Curtis*, "Dynamics of Polymeric Liquids: Volume 2, Kinetic Theory". John Wiley & Sons, New York (1977). The second thoroughly revised edition was published in 1987; Vol. 2 was co-authored by R. B. Bird, C. F. Curtis, R. C. Armstrong and O. Hassager.

I.11      *W. B. Schowalter*, "Mechanics of Non-Newtonian Fluids", Pergamon Press, New York (1978).

I.12      *R. S. Lenk*, "Polymer Rheology", Applied Science Publishers Ltd., London (1978).

I.13      *C. J. S. Petrie*, "Extensional Flows", Pittman, London (1979).

I.14      *J. D. Ferry*, "Viscoelastic Properties of Polymers", 3rd Ed., John Wiley & Sons, New York (1980).

I.15      *J. A. Brydson*, "Flow Properties of Polymer Melts", Godwin, London (1981).

I.16      *G. V. Vinogradov* and *A. Y. Malkin*, "Polymer Rheology", Khimya, Moscow (1977). [English translation by G. V. Vinogradov, Springer-Verlag, Berlin, New York (1981)].

I.17      *H. Janeschitz-Kriegl*, "Polymer Melt Rheology and Flow Birefringence", Springer-Verlag, Berlin (1983).

I.18      *N. W. Tschoegl*, "The Phenomenological Theory of Linear Viscoelastic Behavior", Springer-Verlag, Berlin (1989).

*II Experimental approach*

II.1      *J. R. van Wazer, J. W. Lyons, K. Y. Min* and *R. E. Colwell*, "Viscosity and Flow Measurements", Intersci. Publ., New York (1963).

II.2      *P. Sherman*, "Industrial Rheology", Academic Press, London (1970).

II.3      *K. Walters*, "Rheometry", Chapman & Hall, London (1975).

II.4      *C. D. Han*, "Rheology in Polymer Processing", Academic Press, New York (1976).

II.5      VDI-Gesellschaft Kunststofftechnik, "Praktische Rheologie der Kunststoffe", VDI-Verlag, Duesseldorf (1978).

II.6      *R. W. Whorlow*, "Rheological Techniques", Ellis Horwood (distributed by John Wiley & Sons), New York (1979).

II.7      *F. N. Cogswell*, "Polymer Melt Rheology: A Guide for Industrial Practice", G. Godwin, London (1981).

II.8      *C. D. Han*, "Multiphase Flow in Polymer Processing", Academic Press, New York (1981).

II.9      *J. M. Dealy*, "Rheometers for Molten Plastics: A Practical Guide to Testing and Property Measurement", Van Nostrand Reinhold, New York (1982).

II.10      *P. Avenas, J.-F. Agassant,* and *J.-Ph. Sergent*, "La Mise en Forme des Matières Plastiques", Lavoisier, Paris (1982).

II.11      *A. I. Malkin*, "Experimental Methods of Polymer Physics: (Measurement of Mechanical Properties, Viscosity, and Diffusion)", Prentice-Hall Englewood Cliffs, NJ (1983).

II.12      *R. Tanner*, "Engineering Rheology", Clarendon Press, Cambridge UK (1985).

II.13      *A. A. Collyer* and *D. W. Clegg*, Eds., "Rheological Measurements", Elsevier Sci. Publ., London (1988).

# Appendix IV.B – Selected Rheological Terminology
# (after British Standards Institution publication BS 5168 of 1975)

| | |
|---|---|
| *Anisotropic* | Not having the same properties in all directions. |
| *Anti-thixotropy* | Negative thixotropy. |
| *Apparent viscosity* | Uncorrected shear stress divided by uncorrected rate of shear mainly in capillary experiment. |
| *Bingham model* | A model with the behaviour of an elastic solid up to the yield stress. Above the yield stress the rate of shear is directly proportional to the shear stress minus the yield stress. |
| *Bulk modulus* | The isotropic stress divided by the elastic volume strain. The reciprocal of compressibility. |
| *Bulk viscosity* | The viscosity associated with changes in volume i.e. the isotropic stress divided by volume strain rate. |
| *Coefficient of interfacial viscosity* | The constant value of the force per unit length acting along a line lying in the plane of the interface divided by the rate of shear in the plane of the interface for steady flow. Its dimensions are the same as those of viscosity times length. |
| *Complex compliance* | The sum of a real and an imaginary part. The real part is sometimes called storage compliance and the imaginary part loss compliance. |
| *Complex modulus* | The sum of a real and an imaginary part. The real part is sometimes called storage modulus and the imaginary part loss modulus. |
| *Complex viscosity* | The sum of a real and an imaginary part. The real part is usually called dynamic viscosity, the imaginary part is related to the real part of the complex modulus. |
| *Compliance* | The strain divided by its corresponding stress. The reciprocal of elastic modulus. |
| *Compressibility* | The relative volume decrease caused by an increase of pressure. The reciprocal of bulk modulus. |
| *Constitutive equation* | An equation relating stress, strain, time and (sometimes) other variables, such as temperature or pressure; also rheological equation of state. |
| *Continuum rheology* | The rheology that treats a material as a continuum without explicit consideration of microstructure. Also called macrorheology or phenomenological rheology. |
| *Couette flow* | Shear flow in the annulus between two co-axial cylinders in relative rotation. |
| *Creep* | The slow deformation of a material measured under constant stress. |
| *Deborah number* | The ratio of a relaxation time of a material to the duration of the observation; the ratio of a time characteristic of a material to a characteristic time of observation. |
| *Deformation* | A change of shape or volume or both. |
| *Dilatancy* | Shear thickening. |
| *Dynamic viscosity* | 1. A synonym of coefficient of viscosity used to distinguish this quantity from kinematic viscosity. The reciprocal of fluidity. 2. The part of the stress in phase with the rate of strain divided by the rate of strain under sinusoidal straining. |
| *Elastic modulus* | The stress divided by the corresponding elastic strain (see bulk modulus or shear modulus). The reciprocal of compliance. |
| *Elongational viscosity* (Trouton viscosity) | The quotient of the tensile stress divided by the rate of extension. |
| *Extrudate swell* (Barus effect) | A post-extrusion swelling. |
| *Flow* | A deformation, of which at least part is nonrecoverable in the rheological use of the term. |
| *Flow curve* | A curve relating stress (or sometimes viscosity) to rate of shear. |
| *Fluid* | A liquid or a gas. |

| | |
|---|---|
| *Fluidity* | The reciprocal of viscosity. |
| *Hencky strain* | The natural logarithm of the ratio of the final to the initial length in tension or in compression. |
| *Hooke model* | A model representing Hooke's law of elasticity; e.g. a spring. |
| *Huggins constant* | The slope at zero concentration of a plot of reduced viscosity against concentration, divided by the square of the intrinsic viscosity. |
| *Hysteresis* | The property of a body whereby different velues of a response are produced for the same value of the corresponding stimulus, according to whether that value has been reached by a continuously increasing or by a continuously decreasing stimulus. *Note.* In the field of rheology, it usually applies to stress/strain or stress/rate of strain functions. |
| *Interfacial rheology* | The two-dimensional rheology at an interface. |
| *Intrinsic viscosity* | The limiting value of the reduced viscosity as the concentration approaches zero; also "limiting viscosity number". |
| *Kelvin-Voigt model* | A model consisting of a Hooke model and a Newtonian fluid model in parallel. |
| *Kinematic viscosity* (viscosity/density ratio) | The quotient of dynamic viscosity divided by the density of the material. |
| *Laminar flow* | Flow without turbulence. |
| *Linear viscoelasticity* | Viscoelasticity characterized by a linear relationship between stress, strain and the time derivatives of strain. |
| *Liquid* | That phase of matter which flows under even vanishingly small shear stresses so as ultimately to assume the shape of the containing vessel up to a certain definite level called the surface of the liquid. |
| *Loss compliance* | The imaginary part of the complex compliance. |
| *Loss modulus* | The imaginary part of the complex modulus. |
| *Macrorheology* | The rheology that treats of material as a continuum without explicit consideration of microstructure. Also called continuum rheology or phenomenological rheology. |
| *Maxwell model* | A Hooke model and a Newtonian fluid model in series. |
| *Melt fracture* | The irregular distortion of a polymer extrudate on passing through a die. |
| *Microrheology* | The rheology in which account is taken of the microstructure of material. |
| *Modulus* | In rheology the ratio of stress to strain. |
| *Necking* | The non-uniform local reduction of the cross-sectional area of a test piece under extension. |
| *Negative thixotropy* (anti-thixotropy, rheopexy) | An increase of the apparent viscosity under shear stress followed by a gradual recovery when the stress is removed. The effect is time dependent. |
| *Newtonian fluid model* | A model characterized by a constant value for the shear stress divided by the rate of shear in a simple shear flow and with zero normal stress differences. |
| *Normal force* | A force acting at right-angles to an applied shear stress. |
| *Normal stress* | The component of stress at right-angles to the area considered. |
| *Overshoot* | The transient rise of a stress above an equilibrium value in the initial stages of flow at constant rate. |
| *Pascal second* (Pa·s) | The SI unit of dynamic viscosity; $1 \text{ Pa·s} = 1 \text{ N s/m}^2 = 1 \text{ kg/(m·s)}$. |
| *Plastic flow* | A flow above the yield stress. |
| *Plastic viscosity* | For a Bingham model the excess of the shear stress over the yield stress divided by the rate of shear. The reciprocal of mobility. |
| *Plug flow* | Movement along a pipe of material with a core having zero velocity gradient, Bingham flow. |
| *Poiseuille flow* | Laminar flow in a pipe of circular cross-section under a constant pressure gradient. |
| *Power-law fluid model* | A model characterized by a linear relationship between the logarithm of the shear stress and the logarithm of the rate of shear in simple shear flow. |
| *Pseudoplasticity* | A time-independent shear thinning with no yield stress. |

| | |
|---|---|
| *Pure shear* | A shear that is not accompanied by rotation of the element of which it is applied, with respect to the body of the material. |
| *Rate of shear* | The change of shear strain per unit time. |
| *Rate of strain* | The change of strain per unit time. |
| *Recovery* | The version to an earlier rheological condition usually on the removal of stress. |
| *Reduced viscosity* | The specific viscosity per unit of concentration. |
| *Relative viscosity* | The ratio of the viscosity of a solution to that of the solvent or of a dispersion to that of its continuous phase. |
| *Relaxation time* | The time taken in a Maxwell model for the stress to decrease to $e^{-1}$ of its initial value under constant strain. Many materials have a multiplicity of relaxation times. |
| *Retardation time* | The time taken in a Kelvin model for the strain to decrease to $e^{-1}$ of its original value after the removal of stress. |
| *Rheopexy* | Negative thixotropy. |
| *Secondary flow* | A creep at constant rate. |
| *Shear* | The movement of a layer relative to parallel adjacent layers. |
| *Shear modulus* | The shear stress divided by the corresponding elastic shear strain. |
| *Shear strain* | Relative deformation in a shear. |
| *Shear stress* | The component of stress tangential to the area considered. |
| *Shear thickening* | An increase of viscosity with increasing rate of deformation in steady flow (dilatancy). |
| *Shear thinning* | A reduction of the viscosity with increasing rate of shear in steady flow (pseudoplasticity). |
| *Simple shear* | A shear caused by the parallel relative displacement of parallel planes (viscometric flow). |
| *Solid* | A material that does not flow under a vanishingly small stress. |
| *Specific viscosity* | Relative viscosity minus one. |
| *Steady flow* | A flow in which the velocity at every point does not vary with time. |
| *Storage compliance* | The part of the strain in phase with the stress divided by the stress under sinusoidal conditions. |
| *Storage modulus* | The part of the stress in phase with the strain divided by the strain under sinusoidal conditions. |
| *Strain* | The measurement of deformation relative to the reference configuration of length, area or volume. |
| *Strain hardening* (work hardening) | Increase of viscosity with strain above its value predicted by the linear viscoelastic behavior. |
| *Stress* | The force per unit area. |
| *Stress tensor* | A matrix of the stress components representing the state of stress at a point in a body. |
| *Thermoplastic* | A plastic material capable of being softened by heating and hardened by cooling. |
| *Thixotropy* | A decrease of the apparent viscosity under shear stress, followed by a gradual recovery when the stress is removed. The effect is time-dependent. |
| *Time-temperature superposition principle* | The principle of scaling the results of experiments carried out at different temperatures to fit onto a single curve. |
| *Ultimate tensile strength* | The maximum attainable load acting on a specimen in a tensile test divided by the original cross-sectional area of the specimen. |
| *Viscoelasticity* | Having both viscous and elastic properties. |
| *Viscometric flow* | A laminar flow in which the rate of shear history has been constant for a long time. Such a flow can be completely determined by a maximum of three materials functions: the viscosity and two normal stress functions. |
| *Viscosity* | Qualitatively, the property of a material to resist deformation. Quantitatively, the shear stress divided by rate of shear in steady flow (often used synonymously with coefficient of viscosity). |
| *Volumetric flow rate* | The volume of fluid passing through any cross-sectional area of a duct in unit time. |

| | |
|---|---|
| *Weissenberg effect* | An effect found in some non-Newtonian fluids manifested for example, in the climbing of the fluid up a rod rotating in it. |
| *Weissenberg number* | The product of the relaxation time, or some other characteristic time of a material, and the rate of shear. |
| *Yield point* | The point on the stress/strain or stress/rate of strain curve corresponding to the transition from elastic to plastic deformation. |
| *Yield stress* (yield value) | The stress corresponding to a yield point. |

# ABBREVIATIONS AND NOTATION

*1 – Abbreviations*

| | |
|---|---|
| A | – amorphous polymer |
| BC | – block copolymer |
| C | – crystalline polymer |
| CH | – centrifugal homogenizer |
| CMC | – critical micelle concentration |
| CPC | – cloud point curve |
| CST | – critical solution temperature |
| CTM | – cavity transfer mixer |
| DR | – draw ratio |
| DSC | – differential scanning calorimetry |
| EP | – engineering polymer |
| EPB | – engineering polymer blends |
| FTIR | – Fourier transform IR |
| GPC | – gel permeation chromatography |
| HPB | – homologous polymer blend |
| im | – immiscible |
| IR | – infrared |
| IUPAC | – International Union of Pure and Applied Chemistry |
| LALLS | – low angle laser light scattering |
| LCB | – long chain branching |
| LCST | – lower critical solution temperature |
| m | – miscible |
| MPB | – miscible polymer blend |
| MTT | – melt titration technique |
| MW | – molecular weight |
| MWD | – distribution of MW |
| NDB | – negatively deviating blends |
| NG | – nucleation-and-growth |
| NI | – notched Izod impact strength |
| NIRT | – NI at room temperature |
| NMR | – nuclear magnetic resonance |
| NRET | – non-radiative energy transfer |
| OM | – optical microscopy |
| PA | – polymer alloy |
| PAB | – polymer alloys and blends |
| PB | – polymer blend |
| PDB | – positively deviating blends |
| PICS | – pulse induced critical scattering |
| pm | – partially miscible |
| PNDB | – positively and negatively deviating blends (sigmoidal) |
| PRC | – particular rheological composition |
| SANS | – small angle neutron scattering |
| SAXS | – small angle X-ray scattering |
| SCB | – short chain branching |
| SD | – spinodal decomposition |
| SEC | – size exclusion chromatography |
| SEM | – scanning electron microscope |
| SH | – strain hardening |
| SIS | – solvent-induced shift |
| TEM | – transmission electron microscopy |
| TREF | – temperature rising elution fractionation |
| TW | – glass temperature width (°C) |
| UCST | – upper critical solution temperature |
| WAXS | – wide angle X-ray scattering |

*2 – Notation*

| | |
|---|---|
| $A_2$ | – second virial coefficient; Eq 2.74 |
| $A_i$ | – equation constants |
| a | – drop curvature; Eq 2.113 |
| a | – distance from SD condition; Eqs 3.157, 3.158 |
| $a_c$, $a_T$ | – concentration and temperature shift factor |
| $a_i$ | – equation constant |
| B | – interaction parameter; Eq 2.66 |
| B, $B_0$ | – extrudate swell and its value for Newtonian liquid |
| $B_{11}$ | – second virial coefficient of solvent probe; Eq 2.89 |
| $b_i$ | – equation constant |
| $b_T$ | – vertical time-temperature shift factor; Eq 3.68 |
| C | – cost in \$; Eq 1.1 |
| $C = \omega/\dot{\gamma}$ | – Sprigg's constant in Eqs 3.203, 3.204 |
| c×3, (3c) | – number of external degress of freedom per macromolecular segment |
| $C_i$ | – equation constants; Eqs 3.71 to 3.73 |
| $C_p$ | – heat capacity |
| $c_i^0$ | – universal constants in WLF; Eq 3.201 |
| $c_2$, C | – concentration (g/dl) |
| D | – derivative; Eq 2.5 |
| D | – droplet deformability defined in Eq 3.123 |
| D | – self diffusion coefficient; Eq 2.117 |
| $D^c$ | – Cahn-Hilliard diffusion constant |
| $D_c$ | – Cox deformability function; Eqs 3.123 |
| $D_c$, $D_e$ | – capillary and extrudate diameter, respectively |
| $D_E$ | – droplet deformability in extensional flow; Eqs 3.181, 3.182 |
| $D_r$ | – rotational Brownian diffusion coefficient |
| $D_t$ | – diffusion coefficient |
| d, $d_i$ | – diameter, diameter of i-th generation of particles in polydisperse suspensions |
| $d_{v/s}$ | – volume-to-surface average particle diameter |
| $\bar{d}$ | – average value of d |
| E | – elasticity of interphase in Eq 3.131 |
| E | – tensile modulus |
| $E_i$ | – activation energy; Eq 3.40 |
| $E_{ij}$ | – exchange energy of i-j contact |
| $E^+$ | – threshold energy of coagulation; Eqs 3.125; 3.136 |
| $E^*$ | – interaction energy, Eq 2.15 |
| e | – exponent in Eq 3.84 |
| F | – function in Eq 2.3 |
| F, $F_y$, $F_m$ | – function, its yield value and that of a matrix; Eq 3.34 |
| f | – free volume fraction |
| $f_O$ | – Onsager coefficient; Eq 3.152 |
| f(x) | – function of a parameter x |
| G | – free energy |
| G, G', G'' | – shear modulus, and storage and loss dynamic shear moduli |
| $G'_y$, $G''_y$ | – yield values for G' and G'' |
| g | – acceleration due to gravity in Eq 2.113 |
| g | – functional in SIS determination; Eq 2.103 |
| g* | – concentration gradient at the interface; Eq 2.104 |
| H | – enthalpy |
| $\tilde{H}_G$ | – reduced Gross relaxation spectrum in Eq 3.63 |
| $H_G(s)$ | – Gross frequency relaxation spectrum |
| H(t) | – relaxation spectrum |
| h | – hydrodynamic shielding parameter; Eq 3.225 |
| $h_c$ | – critical separation distance for drop coalescence |
| I | – scattering intensity ratio, Eq 2.47 |
| $I_D$, $I_M$ | – intensity of emission of the excimer and monomer |

| | |
|---|---|
| Im | – imaginary part of a complex function |
| $J, J_0, J_e^0$ | – creep compliance, its value at t = 0 and at steady state |
| K | – bulk modulus; Eq 2.80 |
| K | – compounding cost in \$/kg; Eq 1.1 |
| K | – energy gradient term in Eq 2.42 |
| $K = 1/K^*$ | – equation constant; Eqs 2.97, 2.98 |
| k | – adiabacity factor; Eq 3.214 |
| $k_B$ | – Boltzman constant |
| $k_H, k_M$ | – Huggins, Martin constants |
| $k_i$ | – equation parameters, viz. Eq 2.23 |
| $k = 1/k^*$ | – equation constant; Eqs 2.93, 2.96 |
| L | – length of a dispersed particle |
| $L, L^*$ | – lamellar thickness in Eqs 2.58, 2.59 |
| $L(t)$ | – retardation spectrum |
| $l, \tilde{l}$ | – droplet half length and dimensionless half length; Eq 3.128 |
| M | – mobility constant |
| $M, M_w, M_n$ | – molecular weight and its weight and number averages |
| $M_e$ | – entanglement molecular weight |
| $m_i$ | – degree of polymerization |
| $m_i$ | – equation parameters |
| $N_e$ | – number of polymer segments between entanglements |
| $N_i$ | – number of macromolecules in Eq 2.37 |
| $N_1, N_2$ | – first and second normal stress difference, Eqs 3.5, 3.6 |
| $N_1^+, N_2^+$ | – normal stress growth functions |
| n | – number of moles; Eq 2.2 |
| n | – "power law" exponent; Eq 3.27 |
| $n_c$ | – coarsening exponent in Ostwald Eq 2.41 |
| $n_e$ | – entanglement degree of polymerization |
| $n_i$ | – number of particles |
| $n_i$ | – refractive index; Eq 2.103 |
| P | – pressure |
| Pe | – Péclet number; Eq 3.109 |
| $P_e$ | – entrance-exit pressure drop in capillary flow |
| $P_{ijk}$ | – third order intensity function; Eq 3.192 |
| $P(q)$ | – one-particle scatter function |
| $p_1^0$ | – vapour pressure; Eq 2.89 |
| p | – counter in Eq 3.52 |
| $p, p^*$ | – aspect ratio and its generalized value |
| Q | – function of specific surface in Eq 2.23 |
| Q | – functional in Eq 2.111 |
| $Q_A$ | – distribution function of polymer A |
| q | – wavevector |
| q | – equation constant; Eq 2.99 |
| R | – capillary radius; Eq 3.37 |
| R | – gas constant; 8.31432 J/mol deg |
| $R_d$ | – hard spheres diameter ratio, Eq 3.98 |
| $R_c$ | – particle diameter-to-capillary diameter ratio |
| Re | – real part of complex function |
| Re | – Reynolds number |
| $R_g$ | – radius of gyration |
| $R_R$ | – Rao constant; Eq 2.79 |
| $R_T, R_T^0$ | – Trouton ratio and its limit at vanishing deformation rate |
| $R(\beta)$ | – functional defined in Eq 2.44 |
| r | – position variable radius in Eq 2.43 |
| r | – molar volume ratio $\simeq$ degree of polymerization; Eqs 2.9, 2.64 |
| $r, r_c$ | – radial position of a particle and its critical value |
| $\langle r^2 \rangle$ | – mean square end-to-end distance |
| S | – entropy |

| | |
|---|---|
| $S_i$ | – initial slope of the stress growth function in uniaxial extension |
| s | – effective slip velocity; Eq. 3.37 |
| s | – material parameter |
| s | – number of statistical segments per macromolecule |
| $s_i$ | – slip equation constants; Eq 3.38 |
| $s_i$ | – specific surface area of i-th particle |
| T | – temperature |
| $T_i$ | – nuclear spin constants; Eq 2.102 |
| $T_m, T_g$ | – melting point; glass transition temperature |
| $T_s$ | – separation temperature in Eq 3.145 |
| t | – time |
| $t_p$ | – period of rotation for anisometric particles; Eq 3.108 |
| $t_c$ | – critical time for droplet coalescence |
| U | – particle velocity in Eq 3.125 |
| U | – total energy of the system |
| V | – volume |
| $V_i$ | – volume of i-th fraction of particles |
| $V_i$ | – partial molar volume of ingredient i |
| $V_L, V_S$ | – ultrasonic velocity; transverse and shear |
| v | – specific volume |
| $v_i$ | – velocity in direction i; Eq 3.3 |
| w | – interaction energy in Eq 2.11 |
| w | – weight fraction |
| $w_i$ | – weight fraction of specimen i |
| $X_{ij}^k$ | – energetic interaction parameter |
| $X_{12}$ | – interactional parameter in Eq 2.17 |
| x | – variable |
| $x_i$ | – mole fraction |
| $Y_S$ | – packing functional; Eq 3.74 |
| $Z_i$ | – degree of polymerization |
| z | – coordination number |
| $\alpha, \alpha_i$ | – equation parameters; see Eqs 2.25, 2.26 |
| $\alpha_i$ | – thermal expansion coefficient, Eq 3.228 |
| $2\alpha$ | – convergence angle in Eqs 3.178, 3.179 |
| $\beta$ | – exponent in Eq 2.57 |
| $\beta$ | – parameter |
| $\beta$ | – wave number in Eq 2.43 |
| $\beta_i$ | – functional in Eqs 2,109, 2.110 |
| $\beta_1, \beta_{12}$ | – slip factor in Lin's Eq 3.166 |
| $\Gamma_{ij}$ | – non-randomness parameter for ij segment placement |
| $\Gamma_0$ | – critical parameter for droplet break-up |
| $\gamma$ | – reduced segmental surface difference in Eq 2.23 |
| $\gamma$ | – shear strain |
| $\dot{\gamma}$ | – rate of shear |
| $\dot{\gamma}_c, \dot{\gamma}_y$ | – critical value of $\dot{\gamma}$ for onset of dilatancy or yield |
| $\dot{\gamma}$ | – dimensionless $\gamma'$ defined in Eq 3.128 |
| $\gamma_R$ | – recoverable shear strain |
| $\Delta$ | – increment |
| $\Delta$ | – parameter in Eq. 3.74 |
| $\Delta_c$ | – supercooling index |
| $\Delta E_\eta$ | – activation energy of flow |
| $\Delta G_m, \Delta G_{el}$ | – Gibbs free energy of mixing and an elastic contribution |
| $\Delta H_m$ | – heat of mixing |
| $\Delta_l$ | – thickness of the interphase |
| $\Delta n_i$ | – population of nuclei; Eq 2.102 |
| $\Delta V$ | – overlapping volume |
| $\delta$ | – segmental density |
| $\delta$ | – solubility parameter |

| | |
|---|---|
| $\varepsilon$ | – dielectric parameter |
| $\varepsilon$ | – extensional Hencky strain |
| $\dot{\varepsilon}$ | – strain rate in uniaxial extension |
| $\varepsilon_b$ | – maximum strain at break |
| $\varepsilon_{max}$ | – maximum filament shrinkage; Eq (3.212) |
| $\zeta$ | – correlation length; Eqs 3.159, 3.160 |
| $\zeta$ | – domain size in NG |
| $\eta, \eta_0, \eta_\infty$ | – shear viscosity and its upper and lower Newtonian plateau value |
| $\eta', \eta'', \eta^*$ | – dynamic, loss and complex viscosity, respectively |
| $\eta_E, \eta_E^+$ | – elongational viscosity, stress growth function in extension at $\dot{\varepsilon}$ = const |
| $\eta_r, \eta_{sp}$ | – relative, specific viscosity |
| $\eta_r^0, \eta_{E,r}$ | – zero-shear relative viscosity, relative viscosity in elongation |
| $[\eta], [\eta]_s, [\eta]_a$ | – intrinsic viscosity, intrinsic viscosity of suspensions and that for anisometric particle suspensions |
| $[\eta]_E, [\eta]_{E,d}$ | – emulsion and deformable droplet emulsion intrinsic viscosity, respectively |
| $\eta_p, \eta_m$ | – viscosity of dispersed and matrix liquid; Eq 3.118 |
| $\eta_i, \eta_{si}, \eta_{ei}$ | – interface viscosity and its shear and extensional components |
| $\eta_{r, i}$ | – relative viscosity of the i-th generation of particles in polydisperse suspension |
| $\eta^+, \eta_E^+$ | – time dependent viscosity (or the stress growth function) in shear and uniaxial extension |
| $\eta_{app}$ | – apparent viscosity |
| $\eta_{0,M}$ | – Maxwellian viscosity; Eq 3.209 |
| $\theta$ | – functional; Eq 3.65 |
| $\theta$ | – scattering angle; Eq 2.72 |
| $\theta$ | – surface interaction ratio in Eq 2.15 |
| $\theta_h$ | – parameter |
| $\vartheta$ | – distortion wavelength in capillary instability |
| $\varkappa$ | – ratio of rheological to interface forces; capillarity factor, Eq 3.122 |
| $\Lambda$ | – wavelength |
| $\Lambda, \lambda$ | – viscosity ratios defined in Eqs 3.120 and 3.121, respectively |
| $\Lambda_{ijk}$ | – third order relaxation time; Eq 3.192 |
| $\lambda$ | – functional in Eq 2.33 |
| $\mu$ | – chemical potential |
| $\mu$ | – Poisson ratio |
| $\mu_0$ | – microscopic mobility; Eq 2.52 |
| $\nu$ | – interfacial tension coefficient |
| $\nu, \nu_0$ | – dynamic interfacial tension coefficient and its equilibrium value |
| $\nu, \nu_e$ | – side and interfacial energies; Eq 2.55 |
| $\nu_{ij}$ | – kinetic viscosity coefficient; Eq 3.83 |
| $\varrho$ | – density |
| $\sigma$ | – stress |
| $\sigma, \sigma^*$ | – shape constant in Eqs 3.111, 3,112 and Lennard-Jones constant, respectively |
| $\sigma_{ij}$ | – i, j component of the stress tensor |
| $\sigma_y, \sigma_{y, c}, \sigma_{y, E}$ | – yield shear stress, its value in compression and extension |
| $\sigma_{ij}^+$ | – stress growth function in shear (ij=12) or elongation (ij=11) |
| $\sigma_c$ | – critical shear stress for droplet break-up |
| $\sigma_m$ | – critical shear stress for melt fracture |
| $\tau$ | – dimensionless half length of a drop |
| $\tau$ | – reduced temperature difference in Eq 2.18 |
| $\tau$ | – reduced time; Eq 2.49 |
| $\tau$ | – relaxation time |
| $\tau_p$ | – discrete relaxation time; Eqs 3.49 – 3.52 |
| $\tau_y$ | – characteristic time for yield cluster |
| $\tau_\zeta$ | – lifetime of the density fluctuation |
| $\Phi$ | – Farris volume fraction as defined in Eqs 3.104 to 3.106 |
| $\phi, \phi_m$ | – volume fraction; maximum packing – $\phi$ |
| $\phi_{m, N}$ | – $\phi_m$ for N generations of spheres, Eqs 3.100 to 3.102 |
| $\phi_{m0}, \phi_{m\infty}$ | – maximum packing volume fraction at shear stress $\sigma \to 0$ and $\sigma \to \infty$ |

| | |
|---|---|
| $\phi_F$ | – effective volume of a flock |
| $\chi$ | – thermodynamic interaction parameter |
| $\chi_{ij}$ | – thermodynamic interaction coefficient between species i and j |
| $\Psi(t)$ | – retardation function |
| $\psi_1, \psi_2$ | – first and second normal stress difference coefficients |
| $\Omega$ | – distortion wavelength; Eq 3.169 |
| $\Omega$ | – vorticity |
| $\omega$ | – frequency (rad/s) |
| $\omega$ | – rotational speed; Eq 2.116 |
| $\omega_i$ | – conformational entropy in Eq 2.37 |

## SUBSCRIPTS

| | |
|---|---|
| app, a | – apparent |
| B | – binodal |
| E | – uniaxial extension |
| g | – glass |
| i | – counting subscript, inversion or dispersed phase |
| L | – linear viscoelastic |
| m | – mixing, melt, matrix |
| R | – reference variable |
| S | – strain hardening |
| S | – spinodal |
| s | – suspension |
| y | – yield |

## SUPERSCRIPTS

| | |
|---|---|
| E | – excess value |
| L | – lattice gas model |
| + | – stress growth function |
| − | – relaxation function |
| ~ (tilde) | – reduced variable |
| * | – complex or reducing variable |

## MATHEMATICAL SYMBOLS

| | |
|---|---|
| <> | – average |
| $\Pi$ | – multiplication |
| $\pi$ | – 3.1415926536..... |
| $\Sigma$ | – summation |

# REFERENCES/AUTHOR INDEX

Citation page

**Ablazova,** T. I., M. V. Tsebrenko, A. V. Yudin, G. V. Vinogradov and B. V. Yarlykov, *J. Appl. Polym. Sci.*, **19**, 1781 (1975).　173, 186, 229

**Acierno,** D., D. Curto, F. P. La Mantia and A. Valenza, NRCC/IMRI symposium *"Polyblends-'85"*, Boucherville, Qubec, Canada, April 16–17, 1985; *Polym. Eng. Sci.*, **26**, 28 (1986).　204, 216, 221, 223

**Acrivos,** A., and T. S. Lo, *J. Fluid Mech.*, **86**, 641 (1978).　163

**Adachi,** H., S. Nishi and T. Kotaka, *Polym. J.*, **14**, 985 (1982).　118

**Addonizio,** M. L., E. Martuscelli and C. Silvestre, *Polymer*, **28**, 183 (1987).　56, 61

**Agarwal,** P. K., I. Duvdevani, D. G. Peiffer, and R. D. Lundberg, *J. Polym. Sci., Part B, Polym. Phys.*, **25**, 839 (1987).　128

**Aharoni,** S. M., *J. Macromol. Sci., Phys.*, **B22**, 813 (1983–84).　98

**Aharoni,** S. M., in *Integration of Fundamental Polymer Science and Technology*, L. A. Kleitjens and P. J. Lemstra, Eds., Elsevier, London and New York (1985).　127

**Aifantis,** E. C. in *Phase Transformations*, J. Gittus, Ed., Inst. Metals, Brookfield, VT (1986).　43

**Aifantis,** E. C., *Math. Modelling*, **8**, 306 (1987).　43

**Ajji,** A., L. Choplin and R. E. Prud'homme, NRCC/IMRI Symposium *"Polyblends-'88"*, Boucherville, Que., Canada, April 5 and 6, 1988; *J. Polym. Sci., Part B, Polym. Phys.*, **26**, 2279 (1988).　194

**Akhtar,** S., B. Kuriakose, P. P. De and S. K. De, *Plast. Rubber Process. Appl.*, **7**, 11 (1987).　207

**Akitt,** J. W., *NMR and Chemistry*, 2-nd ed., Chapman and Hall, London, (1983).　105

**Akovali,** G., *J. Polym. Sci.*, **A–2**, 5, 875 (1967).　199

**Albert,** B., R. Jerome, P. Teyssie and J. Selb, *J. Polym. Sci., Polym. Chem. Ed.*, **24**, 537 (1986a).　81, 82

**Albert,** B., R. Jerome, P. Teyssie and B. Baeyens-Volant, *J. Polym. Sci., Polym. Chem. Ed.*, **24**, 551, 2577 (1986b).　112, 125

**Alexandrovich,** P. S., *PhD thesis,* Univ. of Massachusetts, Amherst (1978).　98, 100, 101

**Alle,** N., and J. Lyngaae-Jorgensen, *Rheol. Acta*, **19**, 94, 104 (1980).　205

**Alle,** N., F. E. Andersen and J. Lyngaae-Jorgensen, *Rheol. Acta*, **20**, 222 (1981).　205

**Allen,** G., G. Gee and J. P. Nicholson, *Polymer*, **2**, 8 (1961).　67

**Allen,** G., *Polym. J.*, **19**, 1 (1987).　201

**Allport,** D. C., and W. H. Jones, Eds., *Block Copolymers*, Appl. Sci. Publ., London (1973).　167

**Amrani,** F., J. M. Hung and H. Morawetz, *Macromolecules*, **13**, 649 (1980).　80, 82

**Anastasiadis,** S. H., J. K. Chen, J. T. Koberstein, J. E. Sohn and J. A. Emerson, *Polym. Eng. Sci.*, **26**, 1410 (1986).　122

**Anon.,** *Res. Discl.* (UK), 229, 182 (1983).　98, 102

**Antonietti,** M., J. Coutandin, R. Grütter and H. Sillescu, *Macromolecules*, **17**, 789 (1984).　81

**Aoki,** Y., *J. Soc. Rheol.* (Japan)., **7**, 20 (1979).　194

**Aoki,** Y., and K. Nakayama, *J. Soc. Rheol.* (Japan), **9**, 39 (1981).　194

**Aoki,** Y., and K. Nakayama, *Polym. J.*, **14**, 951 (1982).　194

**Aoki,** Y., *Polym. J.*, **16**, 431 (1984).　152, 173

**Aoki,** Y., *J. Non-Newtonian Fluid Mech.*, **22**, 91 (1986).　194

**Aoki,** Y., *Nihon Reor. Gak.*, **16**, 136 (1988).　194

**Arai,** K., and J. D. Ferry, *Rubber Chem. Technol.*, **59**, 592 (1986).　232, 233

**Ardell,** A. J., *Acta Metal.*, **20**, 601 (1972).　47

**Arman,** J., A. Lahrouni and Ph. Monge, *Eur. Polym. J.*, **19**, 647 (1983); **22**, 955 (1986).　84

**Arnold,** K. R., and D. J. Meier, *J. Appl. Polym. Sci.*, **14**, 427 (1970).　167, 169

**Arrhenius,** S., *Z. Phys. Chem.* (Leipzig), **1**, 285 (1887).　194

**Astarita,** G., G. Marrucci and L. Nicolais, Eds., *Rheology*, Plenum Press, New York (1980).　220

Citation page

**Atkin**, E. L., L. A. Kleintjens, R. Koningsveld and L. J. Fetters, *Makromol. Chem.*, 78
**185**, 377 (1984).

**Attalla**, G., G. Corrieri and D. Romanini, in *Rheology*, G. Astarita, G. Marrucci and 220
L. Nicolais, Eds., Plenum Press, New York, **2**, 407 (1980).

**Attalla**, G., and F. Bertinotti, *J. Appl. Polym. Sci.*, **28**, 3505 (1983). 220

**Attalla**, G., and D. Romanini, *Rheol. Acta*, **22**, 471 (1983). 220

**Atwood**, B. T., *PhD thesis*, Princeton Univ. (1982). 140

**Aubin**, M., and R. E. Prud'homme, *Macromolecules*, **13**, 365 (1980). 85, 86

**Aubin**, M., Y. Bedard, M.-F. Morrissette and R. E. Prud'homme, *J. Polym. Sci.*, 85, 86
*Polym. Phys. Ed.*, **21**, 233 (1983).

**Aubin**, M., and R. E. Prud'homme, *Polym. Eng. Sci.*, **24**, 350 (1984). 86, 98, 102

**Ausin**, A., I. Eguiazabal, M. E. Munoz, J. J. Pena and A. Santamaria, *Polym. Eng.* 212
*Sci.*, **27**, 529 (1987).

**Avrami**, M., *J. Chem. Phys.*, **7**, 1103 (1939); ibid., **8**, 212 (1940). 55

**Aylwin**, P. A., and R. H. Boyd, *Polymer*, **25**, 323 (1984). 56


**Baba**, Y., N. Noethiger, K. Fujioka and C. L. Beatty, *A. C.S., Org. Coat. Plast.* 98, 102
*Chem.*, **45**, 73 (1981).

**Bagchi**, S., and R. P. Singh, *Acustica*, **51**, 68 (1982). 83

**Bair**, H. E., and P. C. Warren, *J. Macromol. Sci., Phys.*, **B20**, 381 (1981). 93

**Baïtoul**, M., H. Saint-Guirons, P. Xans and Ph. Monge¦ *Eur. Polym. J.*, **17**, 1281 85
(1981); ibid., **19**, 651 (1983).

**Baker**, W. E., and A. M. Catani, NRCC/IMRI symposium "Polyblends-'84", 124
Boucherville, Que., Canada, April 17, 1984; *Polym. Eng. Sci.*, **24**, 1348 (1984).

**Balda**, R., M. A. Perez-Jubindo, M. R. de la Fuente and I. Katime, *Mater. Chem.* 239
*Phys.*, **18**, 359 (1987).

**Balizer**, E., and H. Talaat, *J. Physique*, **C6**, 131 (1983). 113, 114

**Balzas**, A. C., I. C. Sanchez, I. R. Epstein, F. E. Karasz and W. J. MacKnight, *Mac-* 40
*romolecules*, **18**, 2188 (1985).

**Barbee**, J., *Trans. Soc. Rheol.*, **17**, 413 (1973). 136

**Barlow**, J. W., and D. R. Paul, *Ann. Rev. Mater. Sci.*, **11**, 299 (1981). 65

**Barlow**, J. W., and D. R. Paul, *Polym. Eng. Sci.*, **24**, 525 (1984). 124

**Barlow**, J. W., and D. R. Paul, NRCC/IMRI symposium "Polyblends-'87", Boucher- 40, 84, 87
ville, Que., Canada, April 28–29 1987; *Polym. Eng. Sci.*, **27**, 1482 (1987).

**Barnum**, R. S., *PhD thesis*, Univ. Texas, Austin (1981). 61

**Barry**, B. W., *Adv. Coll. Interf. Sci.*, **5**, 37 (1977). 160, 162

**Bartczak**, Z., A. Galeski and E. Martuscelli, *Polym. Eng. Sci.*, **24**, 1155 (1984). 116

**Bartczak**, Z., and A. Galeski, *Polymer*, **27**, 544 (1986). 62

**Bartczak**, Z., A. Galeski and M. Pracella, *Polymer*, **27**, 537 (1986). 61

**Bartczak**, Z., and E. Martuscelli, *Makromol. Chem.*, **188**, 445 (1987). 61

**Barthes-Biesel**, D., and A. Acrivos, *Int. J. Multiph. Flow*, **1**, 1 (1973). 163

**Barthes-Biesel**, D., in *Rheological Measurements*, A. A. Collyer and D. W. Clegg, 246
Eds., Elsevier Appl. Sci., London and New York (1988).

**Bartlett**, D. W., J. W. Barlow and D. R. Paul, *J. Appl. Polym. Sci.*, **27**, 2351 (1982). 205

**Bashforth**, S., and J. C. Adams, *An Attempt to Test the Theory of Capillary Action*, 122
Cambridge Univ. Press, London (1882).

**Bates**, F. S., *Macromolecules*, **17**, 2067 (1984). 168

**Bates**, F. S., G. D. Wignall and W. C. Koehler, *Phys. Rev. Lett.*, **55**, 2425 (1985). 78

**Bates**, F. S. and G. D. Wignall, *Phys. Rev. Lett.*, **57**, 1429 (1986); *Macromolecules*, 78
**19**, 932 (1986).

**Bates**, F. S., S. B. Dierker and G. D. Wignall, *Macromolecules*, **19**, 1938 (1986). 78

**Bauer**, B. J., *Polym. Eng. Sci.*, **25**, 1081 (1985). 40

**Bauer**, R. F., NRCC/IMRI symposium "Polyblends-'81", Montreal, Que. Canada, 118
April 28, 1981; *Polym. Eng. Sci.*, **22**, 130 (1982).

**Baumgärtner**, A. and D. W. Heermann, *Polymer*, **27**, 1777 (1986). 50

Citation page

**Bazuin,** C. G., and A. Eisenberg, *J. Polym. Sci., Part B: Polym. Phys.*, **24**, 1021,    194
1121, 1137, 1155 (1986).

**Bedeaux,** D., *Physica*, **121A**, 345 (1983).    154

**Bedeaux,** D., *J. Colloid Interface Sci.*, **118**, 80 (1987).    154

**Belaribi,** C., G. Marin and Ph. Monge, *Eur. Polym. J.*, **22**, 487 (1986).    172, 173

**Belorgey,** G. and R. E. Prud'homme, *J. Polym. Sci., Polym. Phys. Ed.*, **20**, 191    98, 101
(1982).

**Berger,** W., H. W. Kammer, and C. Kummerlöwe, *Makromol. Chem., Suppl.*, **8**, 101    231
(1984).

**Berry,** V. K., *46th Ann. Meet. EMSA; Proceeds.* pg 220 (1988).    117

**Berry,** V. K., *Scanning*, **10**, 19 (1988).    117

**Bersted,** B. H., *J. Appl. Polym. Sci.*, **31**, 2061 (1986).    144, 151

**Berticat,** Ph., G. Boiteux, J.-C. Dalloz, A. Douillard, J. Guillet and G. Seytre, *Eur.*    98
*Polym. J.*, **16**, 479 (1980).

**Beyer,** R. T., and S. V. Letcher, *Physical Ultrasonics*, Academic Press, New York    83
(1969).

**Biagini,** E., E. Gattiglia, E. Pedemonte, A. Turturro, P. Lanzani and G. Modini,    86
*Conv. Ital. Sci. Macromol., (Atti)*, **2**, 163 (1983).

**Binder,** K., *Colloid. Polym. Sci.*, **265**, 273 (1987).    43

**Bingham,** E. C., and H. Green, *Proc. Am. Soc. Test. Mat. II*, **19**, 640 (1919).    137

**Bird,** R. B., R. C. Armstrong and O. Hassager, *Dynamics of Polymeric Liquids,* Vol.    134, 151
1: Fluid Mechanics, 2nd ed., J. Wiley and Sons, Inc., New York (1987).

**Birley,** A. W., and X. Y. Chen, *Brit. Polym. J.*, **16**, 77 (1984).    102, 113

**Blahovici,** T. F., G. R. Brown and L. E. St-Pierre, NRCC/IMRI symposium, *"Poly-*    98
*blends-'82"*, Montreal, April 20, 1982; *Polymer Eng. Sci.*, **22**, 1123 (1982).

**Blum,** F. D., *Spectroscopy*, **1(5)** 32 (1986).    105

**Bogue,** D. C., T. Masuda, Y. Einaga and S. Onogi, *Polymer J.*, **1**, 563 (1970).    191, 228

**Boiteux,** G., J.-C. Dalloz, J. Guillet and G. Seytre, *Europ. Polym. J.*, **16**, 489 (1980).    98, 104

**Bolotnikova,** L. S., A. K. Evseer, Yu.N. Panov and S. Ya. Frenkel, *Vysokomol.*    173, 180, 196, 214
*Soed.*, **B24**, 154 (1982).

**Bonardelli,** P., G. Moggi and A. Turturro, *Polymer*, **27**, 905 (1986).    93

**Bondi,** A., in *Rheology, Theory and Applications*, Vol. 4, F. R. Eirich, Ed.,    148, 149
Academic Press, New York (1967).

**Booij,** H. C., and J. H. M. Palmen, *Rheol. Acta*, **21**, 376 (1982).    140

**Boyer,** R. F., *J. Polym. Sci., Part C*, **14**, 267 (1966).    93

**Brandt,** A., and G. Bugliarello, *Trans. Soc. Rheol.*, **10**, 229 (1966).    161

**Bredimas,** M., M. Veyssie, D. Barthes-Biesel and V. Chhim, *J. Coll. Interf. Sci.*, **93**,    163
513 (1983).

**Brenner,** H., *Int'l. J. Multiphase Flow*, **1**, 195 (1974).    152, 158

**Brenner,** H., and D. W. Condiff, *J. Coll. Interf. Sci.*, **47**, 199 (1979).    158

**Breuer,** H., F. Haff and J. Stabenow, *J. Macromol. Sci.,* - Phys., **B14**, 387 (1977).    231

**Brinkman,** H. C., *J. Chem. Phys.*, **20**, 571 (1952).    154

**Brochard,** F., J. Jouffroy and P. Levinson, *Macromolecules*, **16**, 1638 (1983).    120

**Brochard,** F., and P. G. de Gennes, *Physica*, **118A**, 289 (1983).    50

**Brooks,** N. M., *J. Ind. Irradiat. Technol.*, **1**, 237 (1983).    127

**Brunet,** J., and K. E. Gubbins, *Trans. Faraday Soc.*, **65**, 1255 (1969).    170, 174

**Buckingham,** A. D., and H. G.E. Hentschel, *J. Polym. Sci., Polym. Phys. Ed.*, **18**,    78
853 (1980).

**Bucknall,** C. B., *Toughened Plastics*, Appl. Sci. Publ., London (1977).    117

**Bucknall,** C. B., and W. W. Stevens, *J. Mater. Sci.*, **15**, 2950 (1980).    117

**Bucknall,** C. B., and C. J. Page, *J. Mater. Sci.*, **17**, 808 (1982).    117

**Bucknall,** C. B., and I. K. Partridge, in *Toughening of Plastics* PRI, London (1985).    117

**Burchell,** D. J., J. E. Lasch, R. J. Farris and S. L. Hsu, *Polymer*, **23**, 965 (1982).    113

**Burchell,** D. J., and S. L. Hsu, *A. C.S. Adv. Chem. Ser.*, **203**, 533 (1983).    113

**Bye,** D. J., and I. S. Miles, *Europ. Polym. J.*, **22**, 185 (1986).    197, 198

Citation page

**Cabasso,** I., *A. C.S. Org. Coating Plast. Chem.*, **40**, 669 (1979).  126, 128

**Cahn,** J. W., and J. E. Hilliard, *J. Chem. Phys.*, **28**, 258 (1958).  43, 46

**Cahn,** J. W., in *Segregation to Interfaces*, J. J. Blakely and W. C. Johnson (Eds.),  43, 120
A. S.M. Semin. Ser., Cleveland (1978).

**Calahorra,** M. E., J. I. Eguizabal, M. Cortazar and G. M. Guzman, *Polym. Com-*  127
*mun.*, **28**, 39 (1987).

**Callaghan,** P. T., C. M. Trotter and K. W. Jolley, *J. Magn. Reson.*, **37**, 247 (1980).  105

**Cangelosi,** F., *PhD thesis*, Univ. of Connecticut, Storrs (1982).  112, 128

**Cantow,** M. J.R., Ed., *Polymer Fractionation*, Academic Press, New York (1967).  170

**Caravatti,** P., P. Neuenschwander and R. R. Ernst, *Macromolecules*, **18**, 119 (1985);  105, 112
ibid., **19**, 1889 (1986).

**Carley,** J. F., and S. C. Crossan, *S. P.E. Techn. Papers*, **26**, 285 (1980); *Polym. Eng.*  149, 150, 173
*Sci.*, **21**, 249 (1981).

**Carley,** J. F., *Polym. Eng. Sci.*, **25**, 1017 (1985).  150

**Carlin,** D. M., *S. P. E. Techn. Papers*, **35**, 1447 (1989).  114

**Carmesin,** H.-O., D. W. Heermann and K. Binder, *Z. Phys. B.-Condensed Matter.*,  50
**65**, 89 (1986).

**Carreau,** P. J., *Trans. Soc. Rheol.*, **16**, 99 (1972).  136

**Carriere,** C. J., A. Cohen and C. B. Arends, *J. Rheol.*, **33**, 681 (1989).  181

**Casper,** R., and L. Morbitzer, *Ang. Makromol. Chem.*, **58/59**, 1 (1977).  100, 102

**Casson,** N., in *Rheology of Disperse Systems*, C. C. Mill, Ed., Pergamon Press,  138
Oxford (1959).

**Catani,** A. M., and L. A. Utracki, *Proceed. Ann. Meet. Polymer Processing Society*,  185, 201
Akron, Oh., March 28–29, 1985; *J. Polym. Eng.*, **6**, 23 (1986).

**Cavaille,** J. Y., C. Jourdan, J. Perez, L. Monnerie and G. P. Johari, *J. Polym. Sci.,*  232, 236
*Part B: Polym. Phys.*, **25**, 1235 (1987a).

**Cavaille,** J. Y., J. Perez, C. Jourdan and G. P. Johari, *J. Polym. Sci.; Part B: Polym.*  232, 236
*Phys.*, **25**, 1847 (1987b).

**Cavaille,** J. Y, C. Jourdan and J. Perez, *Makromol. Chem., Macromol. Symp.*, **16**,  232
341 (1988).

**Cazabat,** A. M., D. Langevin and O. Sorba, *J. Phys. Lett.*, **43**, L505 (1982).  176

**Chalykh,** A. Ye., I. N. Sapozhnikova and A. D. Aliyev, *Vysokomol. Soed.*, **A21**,  98
1664 (1979).

**Chalykh,** A. Ye., I. N. Sopozhnikova, *Dokl. Akad. Nauk SSSR*, **270**, 382 (1983).  98

**Chalykh,** A. Ye, and N. N. Avdeyev, *Vysokomol. Soed.*, **A27**, 2467 (1985).  42

**Chang,** H., and A. S. Lodge, *Rheol. Acta*, **11**, 127 (1972).  221

**Chang,** L. P., and H. Morawetz, *Macromolecules*, **20**, 428 (1987).  81, 82

**Chappelear,** D. C., *A. C. S., Div. Chem. Polym. Prepr.*, **5(2)**, 363 (1964).  181

**Chen,** C.-Y., and S.-A. Chen, *Proc. Nat. Sci. Counc. B., Republ. China*, **6**, 292  103, 104
(1982).

**Chen,** C. C., E. Fontan, K. Min and J. L. White, *Polym. Eng. Sci.*, **28**, 69 (1988).  115

**Chen,** Y.-L., M. Kawaguchi, H. Yu and G. Zografi, *Langmuir*, **3**, 31 (1987).  123

**Chii,** N. V., A. I. Isayev, A. Ya. Malkin, G. V. Vinogradov and I. Yu. Kirchevskaya,  167
*Vysokomol. Soed.*, **A17**, 983 (1975).

**Chiou,** J. S., J. W. Barlow and D. R. Paul, *J. Polym. Sci., Part B: Polym. Phys.*, **25**,  129
1459 (1987).

**Chiu,** S.-Ch., and T. G. Smith, *J. Appl. Polym. Sci.*, **29**, 1781, 1797 (1984).  86, 98, 104

**Choplin,** L., *Report to VAMAS-TWP-PB*, Boucherville, Quebec, Canada, April 7–8  177
(1986).

**Chow,** T. S., *Macromolecules*, **14**, 1386 (1981).  54

**Christov,** S. F., I. I. Skorokhodov and Z. V. Shuralava, *Vysokomol. Soed.*, **A20**,  151, 173
1699 (1978).

**Chuang,** H.-K., and C. D. Han, *Adv. Chem. Ser.*, **204**, 171 (1984a).  127, 173, 196, 202, 209

**Chuang,** H.-K., and C. D. Han, *J. Appl. Polym. Sci.*, **29**, 2205 (1984b).  127

**Chung,** C. I., and J. C. Gale, *J. Polym. Sci. Phys. Ed.*, **14**, 1149 (1976).  168

**Cielo,** P., L. A. Utracki and M. Lamontagne, *Can. J. Phys.*, **64**, 1172 (1986).  69

Citation page

**Cielo,** P., B. D. Favis and X. Maldague, NRCC/IMRI Symposium *"Polyblends-'87"*,    69
Boucherville, Que., Canada, April 28–29, 1987; *Polym. Eng. Sci.*, **27**, 1601
(1987).

**Ciferri,** A., W. R. Krigbaum and R. W. Meyer, Eds., *Polymer Liquid Crystals*,    230
Academic Press, New York (1982).

**Class,** J. B., and S. G. Chu, *J. Appl. Polym. Sci.*, **30**, 805, 815, 825 (1985).    242

**Cogswell,** F. N., *Trans. Soc. Rheol.*, **16**, 383 (1972).    185, 218, 219, 224

**Cogswell,** F. N., and D. E. Hanson, *Polymer*, **16**, 936 (1975).    168

**Cohen,** R. E., and N. W. Tschoegl, *Intl. J. Polym. Mater.*, **2**, 49, 205 (1972); ibid., **3**,    235
3 (1974).

**Cohen,** R. E., and N. W. Tschoegl, *Trans. Soc. Rheol.*, **20**, 153 (1976).    235

**Cohen,** R. E., and A. R. Ramos, *Macromolecules*, **12**, 131 (1979).    126

**Cohen,** R. E., and D. E. Wilfong, *Macromolecules*, **15**, 370 (1982).    126

**Coleman,** M. M., and D. F. Varnell, *J. Polym. Sci. Polym. Phys. Ed.*, **18**, 1403    112
(1980).

**Coleman,** M. M., D. F. Varnell and J. P. Runt, in *Polymer Alloys III*, D. Klempner    112
and K. C. Frisch, Eds., Plenum Press, New York (1981).

**Coleman,** M. M., and D. F. Varnell, *Macromolecules*, **15**, 937 (1982).    113

**Coleman,** M. M., and E. J. Moskala, *Polymer*, **24**, 251 (1983).    113

**Coleman,** M. M., D. F. Varnell and J. P. Runt, *Polym. Sci. Technol.*, **20**, 59 (1983a).    112

**Coleman,** M. M., E. J. Moskala, P. C. Painter, D. J. Walsh and S. Rostami, *Polymer*,    112
**24**, 1410 (1983b).

**Coleman,** M. M., and P. C. Painter, *Appl. Spectrosc. Rev.*, **20**, 255 (1984a).    112

**Coleman,** M. M., D. J. Skrovanek and P. C. Painter, *Appl. Spectrosc.*, **38**, 448    114
(1984b).

**Coleman,** M. M., D. F. Varnell and J. P. Runt, *Contemp. Topics Polym. Sci.*, **4**, 807    113
(1984c).

**Coleman,** M. M., D. J. Skrovanek, J. Hu and P. C. Painter, *Macromolecules*, **21**, 59    105, 112
(1988).

**Composto,** R. J., J. W. Mayer, E. J. Kramer and D. M. White, *Phys. Rev. Lett.*, **57**,    120
1312 (1986).

**Composto,** R. J., E. J. Kramer and D. M. White, *Macromolecules*, **21**, 2580 (1988).    120

**Cong,** G., Y. Huang, W. J. MacKnight and F. E. Karasz, *Macromolecules*, **19**, 2765    30
(1986).

**Constantin,** D., *Polym. Eng. Sci.*, **24**, 268 (1984).    220

**Cook,** H. E., *Acta. Metall.*, **18**, 297 (1970).    47

**Coppola,** F., R. Greco, E. Martuscelli, H. W. Kammer and C. Kummerlowe, *Poly-*    116
*mer*, **28**, 47 (1987).

**Coran,** A. Y., R. Patel and D. Williams-Headd, *Rubber Chem. Technol.*, **58**, 1014    127
(1985).

**Cordonnier,** M., and J. J. Kuhlburger, Intl. Patent Appl., No. Wo85/04664, to B. P.    205
Chem. Ltd., 24 Oct. 1985.

**Couchman,** P. R., *Macromolecules*, **11**, 1156 (1978).    94

**Couchman,** P. R., D. J. Woan and J. I. Scheinbeim, *A. C.S. Div. Polym. Mat. Sci.*    105
*Eng.*, **51**, 379 (1984).

**Couchman,** P. R., *Polym. Eng. Sci.*, **27**, 618 (1987).    105

**Coumans,** W. J., D. Heikens and S. D. Sjoerdsma, *Polymer*, **21**, 103 (1980).    126

**Cousin,** P., and R. E. Prud'homme, *Eur. Polym. J.*, **18**, 957 (1982).    98, 102

**Cousin,** P., and R. E. Prud'homme, *A. C.S. Div. Polym. Mat. Sci. Eng.*, **51**, 291    110, 112
(1984).

**Cox,** R. G., *J. Fluid Mech.*, **37**, 601 (1969).    162

**Cox,** R. G., and S. G. Mason, *Ann. Rev. Fluid Mech.*, **3**, 291 (1971).    162

**Cross,** M. M., *J. Coll. Sci.*, **20**, 417 (1965); ibid., **33**, 30 (1970); ibid., **44**, 175    136, 137
(1973).

**Cross,** M. M., A. Kaye, J. L. Stanford and R. F. T. Stepto, *A. C. S. Polym. Mater.*    159
*Sci. Eng. Div., Preprints*, **49**, 531 (1983).

**Cruz,** C. A., D. R. Paul and J. W. Barlow, *J. Appl. Polym. Sci.*, **23**, 589 (1979).    40, 241

|                                                                                                                                                                                 | Citation page |
| ------------------------------------------------------------------------------------------------------------------------------------------------------------------------------- | ------------- |
| **Cruz,** C. A., J. W. Barlow and D. R. Paul, *Macromolecules*, **12**, 726 (1979).                                                                                             | 40, 241       |
| **Cumberland,** D. J., and R. J. Crawford, *The Packing of Particles*, Elsevier, Amsterdam (1987).                                                                              | 154           |
| **Curro,** J. G., R. R. Lagasse and R. Simha, *Macromolecules*, **15**, 1621 (1982).                                                                                            | 38            |
| **Curto,** D., F. P. La Mantia and D. Acierno, *Rheol. Acta*, **22**, 197 (1983).                                                                                               | 173, 204      |
| **Dalal,** E. N., and P. J. Phillips, *Macromolecules*, **16**, 890 (1983).                                                                                                     | 105           |
| **Danesi,** S., and R. S. Porter, *Polymer*, **19**, 448 (1978).                                                                                                                | 207           |
| **Daryanani,** R., H. Janeschitz-Kriegl, R. van Donselaar and J. van Dam, *Rheol. Acta*, **12**, 19 (1973).                                                                     | 210           |
| **Das,** S., R. P. Singh, and S. Maiti, *Polym. Bull.*, **2**, 403 (1980).                                                                                                      | 83            |
| **Datta,** N. K., and A. W. Birley, *Plast. Rubb. Proc. Appl.*, **2**, 237 (1982).                                                                                              | 85            |
| **Davidse,** P. D., H. I. Waterman and J. B. Westerdijk, *J. Polym. Sci.*, **59**, 389 (1962).                                                                                  | 82            |
| **Davis,** D. D., and T. K. Kwei, *J. Polymer Sci., Polym.Phys. Ed.*, **18**, 2337 (1980).                                                                                      | 31, 67        |
| **De Bruijn,** H., *Rec. Trav. Chim. Pays Bas*, **61**, 863 (1942).                                                                                                             | 154           |
| **De Bruijn,** H., *Discuss. Faraday Soc.*, **11**, 86 (1951).                                                                                                                  | 154           |
| **de Gennes,** P. G., *J. Chem. Phys.*, **55**, 572 (1971).                                                                                                                     | 41            |
| **de Gennes,** P. G., *Scaling Concepts in Polymer Physics*, Cornell University Press, Ithaca, N. Y. (1979).                                                                     | 41, 50        |
| **de Gennes,** P. G., *J. Chem. Phys.*, **72**, 4756 (1980).                                                                                                                    | 50, 174       |
| **De Kee,** D., P. Mohan and D. S. Soong, *J. Macromol. Sci. Phys.*, **B25**, 153 (1986).                                                                                       | 168           |
| **Dealy,** J. M., *Rheometers for Molten Plastics*, Van Nostrand Reinhold Co., N. Y. (1982).                                                                                    | 218, 219      |
| **Dealy,** J. M., *J. Rheol.*, **28**, 181 (1984).                                                                                                                              | 131           |
| **Deanin,** R. D., and G. E. D'Isidoro, *A. C.S. Div. Org. Coat. Plast. Prepr.*, **43**, 19 (1980).                                                                             | 205           |
| **Del Giudice,** L., R. E. Cohen, G. Attalla, and F. Bertinotti, *J. Appl. Polym. Sci.*, **30**, 4305 (1985).                                                                   | 125           |
| **Delimoy,** P., C. Bailly, R. Legras and J. P. Mercier, in *Polymer Alloys: Structure and Properties*, Intl. Symp., Bruges, Belgium, June 4–7, (1984).                         | 230           |
| **Delimoy,** D., C. Bailly, J. Devaux and R. Legras, *Polym. Eng. Sci.*, **28**, 104 (1988).                                                                                    | 116, 230      |
| **Demont,** P., D. Chatain, C. Lacabanne, D. Ronarc'h and J.-L. Moura, NRCC/IMRI symposium *"Polyblends-'83"*, Montreal, Que., Canada, 12 April 1983; *Polym. Eng. Sci.*, **24**, 127 (1984). | 244 |
| **Deopura,** B. L., and S. Kadam, *J. Appl. Polym. Sci.*, **31**, 2145 (1986).                                                                                                  | 191           |
| **Derham,** K. W., J. Goldsbrough and M. Gordon, *Pure Appl. Chem.*, **38**, 97 (1974).                                                                                         | 71            |
| **Deri,** F., R. Genillon and J. F. May, *Angew. Makromol. Chem.*, **134**, 11 (1985).                                                                                          | 216           |
| **Derinovskii,** V. S., I. N. Zakirov, V. M. Lantsov, V. P. Volkov and B. A. Rozenberg, *Vysokomol. Soed.*, **A24**, 2390 (1982).                                               | 105, 107, 109 |
| **Devaux,** J., P. Godard, J. P. Mercier, R. Touillaux and J. M. Dereppe, *J. Polym. Sci., Polym. Phys. Ed.*, **20**, 1881 (1982).                                              | 127           |
| **Devaux,** J., P. Godard and J. P. Mercier, *J. Polym. Sci., Polym. Phys. Ed.*, **20**, 1875, 1895, 1901 (1982).                                                               | 127           |
| **Devaux,** J., 16th Europhysics Conf. Macromol. Phys., June 4–7, 1984, Brugge, Belgium.                                                                                        | 127           |
| **Diamant,** J., *PhD thesis*, Univ. California, Berkeley (1982).                                                                                                               | 239, 240      |
| **Diamant,** J., D. Soong, and M. C. Williams, *Polym Eng. Sci.*, **22**, 673 (1982).                                                                                           | 239           |
| **Dickie,** R. A., *J. Appl. Polym. Sci.*, **17**, 45 (1973).                                                                                                                   | 242           |
| **Dimarzio,** E. A., C. M. Guttman and J. D. Hoffman, *Polymer*, **21**, 1379 (1980).                                                                                           | 56            |
| **Dimarzio,** E. A., and C. M. Guttman, *Polymer*, **21**, 733 (1980).                                                                                                          | 56            |
| **Dimov,** K., and M. Savov, *Vysokomol. Soed.*, **A22**, 65 (1980).                                                                                                            | 173, 213      |
| **Diogo,** A. C., G. Marin and Ph. Monge, *J. Non-Newtonian Fluid Mech.*, **23**, 435 (1987).                                                                                   | 195           |
| **DiPaola-Baranyi,** G., *Macromolecules*, **14**, 683 (1981); ibid., **15**, 622 (1982).                                                                                       | 90            |
| **DiPaola-Baranyi,** G., and P. Degre, *Macromolecules*, **14**, 1456 (1981).                                                                                                   | 90, 91        |
| **DiPaola-Baranyi,** G., S. J. Fletcher and P. Degre, *Macromolecules*, **15**, 885 (1982).                                                                                     | 90            |
| **DiPaola-Baranyi,** G., J. Richer and W. M. Prest, Jr., *Can. J. Chem.*, **63**, 223 (1985).                                                                                   | 90            |

Citation page

**Djakovic,** L., P. Dokic, P. Radivojevic and V. Kler, *Coll. Polym. Sci.*, **254**, 907    166
(1976).

**Djomo,** H., R. Colmenares and G. C. Meyer, *Eur. Polym. J.*, **17**, 521 (1981).    118

**Djordjevic,** M. B., and R. S. Porter, *A. C. S. Polym. Prepr.*, **22(2)**, 323 (1981).    65, 110, 111

**Djordjevic,** M. B., and R. S. Porter, NRCC/IMRI symposium *"Polyblends-'82"*,    65, 110, 111
Montreal, April 20, 1982; *Polym. Eng. Sci.*, **22**, 1109 (1982).

**Djordjevic,** M. B., and R. S. Porter, *Polym. Eng. Sci.*, **23**, 650 (1983).    65, 110, 111

**Doan,** M. H., and J. Brunet, *Ind. Eng. Chem. Fundam.*, **11**, 356 (1972).    170

**Dobrescu,** V., and V. Cobzaru, *J. Polym. Sci., Polym. Symp.*, **64**, 27 (1978).    212

**Dobrescu,** V., in *Rheology*, G. Astarita, G. Marrucci and L. Nicolais, Eds., Plenum    202, 204
Press, New York, Vol. 2, 555 (1980).

**Dobrescu,** V., *Polym. Bull.*, **5**, 75 (1981).    173

**Doi,** M., and S. F. Edwards, *J. Chem. Soc., Faraday Trans. II*, **74**, 560, 918 (1978).    159

**Douglass,** D. C., and V. J. McBrierty, *Macromolecules*, **11**, 766 (1978).    65, 105, 107, 109

**Douglass,** D. C., *A. C.S. Polym. Prepr.*, **20(2)**, 251 (1979).    109

**Dreval,** V. Ye., G. V. Vinogradov, E. P. Plotnikova, M. P. Zabugina, N. P. Kras-    187
nikova, E. V. Kotova and Z. Pelzbauer, *Rheol. Acta*, **22**, 102 (1983).

**Dreval,** V. Ye., A. Kassa, Ye. K. Borisenkova, M. L. Kerber, G. V. Vinogradov and    214, 225
M. S. Akutin, *Vysokomol. Soed.*, **A25**, 156 (1983).

**Dufour,** D. L., and W. J. Jones, U. S. Pat. 4,508,870 to Monsanto Co., Apr. 2,    11
1985.

**Dumoulin,** M. M., and L. A. Utracki, Colloq. *"Characterization of Plastics and Rub-*    219, 242
*bers"*, Hamilton, Ont. Canada, 21–22 June, 1984.

**Dumoulin,** M. M., and L. A. Utracki, C. S.Ch.E. Meeting, Quebec, Que., Canada,    219
Sept. 30 - Oct. 3, 1984.

**Dumoulin,** M. M., L. A. Utracki and J. Lara, NRCC/IMRI symposium *"Polyblends-*    53, 114, 202, 203,
*'83"*, Montreal, April 12, 1983; *Polym. Eng. Sci.*, **24**, 117 (1984a).    206, 223

**Dumoulin,** M. M., L. A. Utracki and C. Farha, *S. P.E. Techn. Pap.*, **30**, 443 (1984b).    53, 114, 202, 214,
    223, 224

**Dumoulin,** M. M., C. Farha and L. A. Utracki, NRCC/IMRI symposium *"Poly-*    114, 202, 203, 206,
*blends-'84"*, April 17, 1984 Boucherville, Qu., Canada; *Polym. Eng. Sci.*, **24**,    223, 224
1319 (1984c).

**Dumoulin,** M. M., P. Toma, L. A. Utracki, I. A. Jinnah and M. R. Kamal, *S. P.E.*    114, 185, 207, 209,
*Techn. Papers*, **31**, 534 (1985).    216, 229

**Dumoulin,** M. M., L. A. Utracki and P. J. Carreau, paper no. 186, 36th Conference    204, 206
of the Canad. Soc. Chem. Eng., Sarnia, Ont., Canada, Oct. 5–8, 1986.

**Dumoulin,** M. M., P. J. Carreau and L. A. Utracki, NRCC/IMRI Symposium    59, 85, 117, 238, 242
*"Polyblends-'87"*, Boucherville, Que., Canada, 28–29 April, 1987; *Polym. Eng.*
*Sci.*, **27**, 1627 (1987).

**Dumoulin,** M. M., *PhD thesis*, École Polytechnique, Montral (1988).    59, 62, 87, 117, 204,
    206, 207, 212, 232,
    233, 237, 239, 242

**Duvdevani,** I., P. K. Agarwal and R. D. Lundberg, *Polym. Eng. Sci.*, **22**, 499 (1982).    242

**Dymond,** J. H., K. J. Young and J. D. Isdale, *Intl. J. Thermophys.*, **1**, 345 (1980).    148

**Dymond,** J. H., J. Robertson and J. D. Isdale, *Int. J. Thermophys.*, **2**, 133 (1981).    148

**Eastmond,** G. C., and K. Haraguci, *Polymer*, **24**, 1171 (1983).    240

**Eastmond,** G. C., and D. G. Phillips, *Polym. Commun.*, **26**, 98 (1985).    115

**Echte,** A., *Angew. Makromol. Chem.*, **58/59**, 175 (1977).    116

**Edel,** P., *PhD thesis* (3e cycle), Univ. Pau (1984).    196

**Edwards,** S. F., *Inst. Phys. Conf. Ser. Sect.* **4**, **64**, 329 (1983).    78

**Egan,** L. S., and M. A. Winnik, NRCC/IMRI Symposium *"Polyblends-'85"*,    78
Boucherville, Que., Canada, Apr. 16–17, 1985; *Polym. Eng. Sci.*, **26**, 15 (1986).

**Eguiazabal,** J. I., M. E. Calahorra, M. M. Cortazar and J. J. Iruin, *Polym. Eng. Sci.*,    98, 126, 127
**24**, 608 (1984).

**Eguiazabal,** J. I., and J. J. Iruin, *Mater. Chem. Phys.*, **18**, 147 (1987).    241

**Eichinger,** B. E. and P. J. Flory, *Trans. Faraday Soc.*, **64**, 2035 (1968).    34

Citation page

**Einstein**, A., *Ann. Phys.*, **17**, 549 (1905); ibid., **19**, 289 (1906); ibid., **34**, 591 — 153
(1911).

**Einstein**, A., *Kolloid-Z.*, **27**, 137 (1920). — 153

**Eisenberg**, A., P. Smith and Z.-L. Zhou, NRCC/IMRI symposium, *"Polyblends-* — 103, 118, 126, 128
*'82"*, Montreal, April 20, 1982; *Polymer Eng. Sci.*, **22**, 1117 (1982).

**Eisenberg**, A., and M. Hara, NRCC/IMRI symposium, *"Polyblends-'84"*, Boucher- — 118, 126, 128
ville, Que., Canada, April 17, 1984; *Polym. Eng. Sci.*, **24**, 1306 (1984).

**Ekka**, P. A.K., G. V. Reddy and R. P. Singh, *Acustica*, **46**, 341 (1980). — 83

**Elbirli**, B., and M. T. Shaw, *J. Rheol.*, **22**, 561 (1978). — 136

**Elemans**, P. H.M., J. G.M. van Gisbergen and H. E.M. Meijer, in *Integration of* — 115, 180
*Fundamental Polymer Science and Technology - 2*, P. J. Lemstra and L. A. Kleintjens, Eds., Elsevier Appl. Sci., London (1988).

**Ellis**, T. S., *Macromolecules*, **22**, 742 (1989). — 40

**Elmendorp**, J. J., and R. J. Maalcke, *Polym. Eng. Sci*, **25**, 1041 (1985). — 183

**Elmendorp**, J. J., *Polym. Eng. Sci.*, **26**, 418 (1986). — 161, 164, 183

**Elmendorp**, J. J., and A. K. van der Vegt, *Polym. Eng. Sci.*, **26**, 1332 (1986). — 161, 184

**Elmendorp**, J. J., and G. de Vos, *Polym. Eng. Sci.*, **26**, 415 (1986). — 123, 161, 165

**Elmendorp**, J. J., *PhD thesis*, Techn. Hogesch., Delft (1986). — 124, 161, 165, 182, 186

**Elmendorp**, J. J., *Report to IUPAC WP 4.2.1*, May 10, 1988. — 181

**Elmquist**, C., *Eur. Polym. J.*, **13**, 95 (1977). — 109

**Elorza**, J. M., M. J. Fdz-Berridi, J. J. Iruin and G. M. Guzman, *Polym. Eng. Sci.*, **24**, — 91
287 (1984).

**Endo**, S., K. Min. J. L. White and T. Kyu, NRCC/IMRI symposium *"Polyblends-* — 229, 231
*'85"*, Boucherville, Quebec, Canada, April 16 and 17, 1985; *Polym. Eng. Sci.*, **26**,
45 (1986).

**Endres**, B., R. W. Garbella and J. H. Wendorff, *Coll. Polym. Sci.*, **263**, 361 (1985). — 64

**Eshuis**, A., E. Roerdink and G. Challa, *Polymer*, **23**, 735 (1982). — 54

**Eshuis**, A., and J. Mellema, *Colloid Polym. Sci.*, **262**, 159 (1984). — 163

**Esmukhanov**, M. M., Yu.V. Pridatchenko and Yu. I. Shmakov, *Priklad. Mekh.*, **21**, — 163
110 (1985).

**Estes**, G. M., S. L. Cooper and A. V. Tobolsky, *J. Macromol. Chem.*, **C4**, 313 — 167
(1970).

**Eveson**, G. F., in *"Rheology of Dispersed Systems"*, C. C. Mill, Ed., Pergamon Press, — 155
London (1959).

**Fahrenholtz**, S. R., and T. K. Kwei, *Macromolecules*, **14**, 1076 (1981). — 113

**Fahrenholtz**, S. R., *Macromolecules*, **15**, 937 (1982). — 113

**Farris**, J., *Trans. Soc. Rheol.*, **12**, 281 (1968). — 157

**Faruque**, H. S., and C. Lacabanne, *Jap. J. Appl. Phys.*, **25**, 473 (1986). — 244

**Favis**, B. D., and J. P. Chalifoux, NRCC/IMRI symposium *"Polyblends-'87"*, — 230, 231
Boucherville, Que., Canada, April 28–29, 1987; *Polym. Eng. Sci.*, **27**, 1591
(1987).

**Favis**, B. D., J. P. Chalifoux and P. Van Gheluwe, *S. P.E. Techn. Pap.*, **33**, 1326 — 230
(1987).

**Favis**, B. D. and J. P. Chalifoux, *Polymer*, **29**, 1761 (1988). — 115

**Fayt**, R., R. Jerome and Ph. Teyssie, *J. Polym. Sci., Polym. Letters Ed.*, **24**, 25 — 16
(1986).

**Fernandes**, A. C., *PhD thesis*, Univ. Texas, Austin (1986). — 40

**Fernandes**, A. C., J. W. Barlow and D. R. Paul, *J. Appl. Polym. Sci.*, **32**, 5357 — 40
(1986).

**Fernandes**, A. C., J. W. Barlow and D. R. Paul, *Polymer*, **27**, 1788 (1986). — 40

**Ferry**, J. D., *Viscoelastic Properties of Polymers*, 3rd. ed., J. Wiley and Sons, New — 142, 193, 231, 234
York (1980).

**Fesko**, D. G., and N. W. Tschoegl, *J. Polym. Sci.*, **C35**, 51 (1971). — 232, 235, 236

**Fesko**, D. G., and N. W. Tschoegl, *Intl. J. Polym. Mater.*, **3**, 51 (1974). — 235, 236

**Fisa**, B., and L. A. Utracki, *Polym. Compos.*, **5**, 36 (1984). — 158, 159, 160

**Fleischer**, G., *Coll. Polym. Sci.*, **265**, 89 (1987). — 71, 129, 229

Citation page

**Fleming,** W. W., J. R. Lyerla and C. S. Yannoni, *A. C.S. Symp. Ser.*, **247**, 83 (1984).   110

**Flory,** P. J., *J. Chem. Phys.*, **9**, 660 (1941).   34

**Flory,** P. J., *Principles of Polymer Chemistry*, Cornell Univ. Press, Ithaca, N. Y.   34
(1953).

**Flory,** P. J., R. A. Orwoll and A. Vrij, *J. Amer. Chem. Soc.*, **86**, 3515 (1964).   34, 36

**Folkes,** M. J., Ed., *Processing, Structure and Properties of Block Copolymers*,   167
Elsevier Appl. Sci. Publ., London (1985).

**Förster,** T., *Discuss. Faraday Soc.*, **27**, 7 (1959).   80

**Fortelny,** I., J. Kovar, A. Sikora, D. Hlavata, Z. Krulis, Z. Novakova, Z. Pelzbauer,   117
and P. Cefelin, *Angew. Makromol. Chem.*, **132**, 111 (1985).

**Fowkes,** F. M., D. O. Tischler, J. A. Wolfe, L. A. Lannigan, C. M. Ademu-John and   65
M. Holliwell, *J. Polym. Sci., Polym. Chem. Ed.*, **22**, 547 (1984).

**Fowler,** M. E., *PhD thesis*, Univ. Texas, Austin (1986).   127

**Fowler,** M. E., J. W. Barlow and D. R. Paul, *Polymer*, **28**, 1177 (1987).   127

**Fox,** D. W., R. B. Allen, J. I. Kroschwitz, "Compatibility" in *Encyclop. Polym. Sci.*   129
*Eng.*, J. Wiley and Sons, New York (1985).

**Fox,** T. G., *Bull. Am. Phys. Soc.*, **1**, 123 (1956).   94

**Fox,** T. G., *J. Polym. Sci., Part C*, **9**, 35 (1965).   151

**Frank,** A., and J. Meissner, *Rheol. Acta*, **23**, 117 (1984).   151, 191, 220

**Frank,** C. W., M.-A. Garshgari, P. Chutikamontham and V. J. Haverly, *Stud. Phys.*   79, 82
*Theor. Chem.*, **10**, 187 (1980).

**Frank,** C. W., *Plastics Comp.*, Jan./Feb. 1981, pp. 67–74.   78, 82

**Franklin Associates Ltd.** (Prairie Village, KS, USA). Report to US EPA: *"Charac-*   17
*terization of Municipal Solid Waste in the USA, 1960 to 2000";* March 30 1988.

**Frayer,** P. D., NRCC/IMRI Symposium *"Composites-'86"*, Boucherville, Que.,   230
Canada, Nov. 25–26, 1986; *Polym. Compos.*, **8**, 379 (1987).

**Frederix,** H., R. Fayt and A. Gilliquet, *"Comportement Industriel des Alliages Poly-*   114, 128, 196
*meriques - Analyse et Perspectives Nouvelles"*, internal report No. PL 15 CRIF,
Bruxelles, Belgium, July (1981).

**Fredrikson,** G. H., and R. G. Larson., *J. Chem. Phys.*, **86**, 1553 (1987).   175

**Freeman,** P. I. and J. S. Rowlinson, *Polymer*, **1**, 20, (1960).   34

**Fried,** J. R., F. E. Karasz and W. J. MacKnight, *Macromolecules*, **11**, 150 (1978).   94, 98, 100

**Friedman,** E. M., and R. S. Porter, *Trans. Soc. Rheol.*, **19**, 493 (1975).   151

**Frisch,** K. C., D. Klempner And H. L. Frisch, NRCC/IMRI symposium *"Polyblends*   93, 98, 118
*-'82"*, Montreal, April 20, 1982; *Polym. Eng. Sci.*, **22**, 1143 (1982).

**Frish,** H. L., and R. Simha, in *Rheology, Theory and Applicatoins*, Vol. 1, F. R.   152
Eirich, Ed., Academic Press, New York (1956).

**Fujimura,** R., and K. Iwakura, *Int. Chem. Eng.*, **10**, 683 (1970); *Kobunshi Ronbun-*   171, 173
*shu*, **31**, 617 (1974).

**Fulcher,** G. S., *J. Am. Chem. Soc.*, **8**, 339, 789 (1925).   169


**Galli,** P., G. Foschini and A. Moro, Intl. Symp. on Polymer Alloys, Brugge, Bel-   124
gium, June 4–7, 1984.

**Garcia,** D., *J. Polym. Sci., Part B: Polym. Phys.*, **24**, 1577 (1986).   242

**Garcia,** D., in *Current Topics in Polymer Science*, R. M. Ottenbrite, L. A. Utracki   65, 113
and S. Inoue, Eds., Hanser Verlag, München, (1987).

**Garcia-Rejon,** A., J. M. Dealy and M. R. Kamal, *Can. J. Chem. Eng.*, **59**, 76 (1981).   220

**Garlund,** Z. G., *A. C.S. Adv. Chem. Ser.*, **206**, 129 (1984).   103, 104

**Garroway,** A. N., W. B. Moniz and H. A. Resing, *Chem. Soc. Faraday Symp.*, **13**, 63   105
(1978); *A. C.S. Symp. Ser.*, **103**, 67 (1979).

**Garton,** A., M. Aubin and R. E. Prud'homme, *J. Polym. Sci., Polym. Lett. Ed.*, **21**,   110, 112
45 (1983).

**Garton,** A., P. Cousin and R. E. Prud'homme, *J. Polym. Sci., Polym. Phys. Ed.*, **21**,   110, 112
2275 (1983).

**Garton,** A., *Polym. Eng. Sci.*, **23**, 663 (1983).   112, 113

**Garton,** A., and J. H. Daly, Canadian Aeronautics Space Inst. Conf., Ottawa, Ont.,   113
Canada, June 1984.

Citation page

**Garton,** A., NRCC/IMRI symposium, *"Polyblends-'83"*, Montreal, April 12, 1983; 65, 113
*Polym. Eng. Sci.*, **24**, 112 (1984a).

**Garton,** A., NRCC/IMRI symposium *"Composites-'83"*, Boucherville, Que. 113
Canada, Nov. 29, 1983; *Polym. Compos.*, **5**, 258 (1984b).

**Gashgari,** M.-A. D., *PhD thesis*, Stanford Univ., CA (1983). 79, 82

**Gelles,** R., and C. W. Frank, *Macromolecules*, **16**, 1448 (1983). 50, 79, 80

**Gelles,** R., *S. P. E. RETEC Proceed.*, Chicago IL, Sept. 23–24, 75(1987). 8

**Genillon,** R., and J. F. May, 5th Conf. Europ. Plast. Caoutch., Paris (1978). 149

**Gerasimchuk,** A. A., A. V. Yudin, O. V. Romankevich and E. M. Aizenshtein, 216
*Khim. Volokna*, **5**, 14 (1984).

**Gerasimchuk,** A. A., O. V. Romankevich and E. M. Aizenshtein, *Khim. Volok.*, **2**, 214
21 (1986).

**Gerasimchuk,** A. A., and O. V. Romankevich, *Khim. Tekhnol. (Kiev)*, **3**, 22 (1986). 187

**Ghaffar,** A., C. Sadrmohaghegh and G. Scott, *Eur. Polym. J.*, **17**, 941 (1981). 125, 126

**Ghijsels,** A., J. J. S. M. Ente and J. Raadsen, in *Integration of Fundamental Polymer* 204, 221
*Science and Technology-2*, P. J. Lemstra and L. A. Kleintjens, Eds., Elsevier
Appl. Sci. Amsterdam (1988).

**Giacomin,** A. J., and J. M. Dealy, *S. P. E. Techn. Pap.*, **32**, 711 (1986). 140

**Gifford,** K. R., D. R. Moore and R. G. Pearson, *Plast. Rubber Mat. Appl.*, Nov., 129
161–4 (1980).

**Gillespie,** T., *J. Coll. Interf. Sci.*, **22**, 554 (1966). 136

**Gilmer,** J., N. Goldstein and R. S. Stein, *J. Polym. Sci., Polym. Phys. Ed.*, **20**, 2219 31
(1982).

**Gladwell,** N., R. R. Rahalkar and P. Richmond, *Rheol. Acta*, **25**, 55 (1986). 163

**Glasstone,** S., K. L. Laidler and H. Eyring, *Theory of Rate Processes*, McGraw-Hill, 148, 174
New York (1941).

**Gleissle,** W., *Dr.-Ing. thesis*, Univ. Karlsruhe (1978). 219

**Gleissle,** W., in *Rheology*, G. Astarita, G. Marruci and L. Nicolais, Eds., Plenum 219
Press, New York, **2**, 457 (1980).

**Goh,** S. H., D. R. Paul and J. W. Barlow, *J. Appl. Polym. Sci.*, **27**, 1091 (1982). 31, 67, 98

**Goh,** S. H., D. R. Paul and J. W. Barlow, *Polym. Eng. Sci.*, **22**, 34 (1982). 31, 67

**Goh,** S. H., K. S. Siow, T. T. Nguyen and A. Nam, *Eur. Polym. J.*, **20**, 65 (1984). 67

**Goh,** S. H., and S. Y. Lee, *Eur. Polym. J.*, **23**, 315 (1987). 101

**Goh,** S. H., S. Y. Lee, K. S. Siow and C. L. Pua, *J. Appl. Polym. Sci.*, **33**, 353 (1987). 40, 126

**Goldman,** A. Ya., G. Kh. Murzakhanov and O. A. Soshina, *Mekhan. Polim.*, **4**, 614 236
(1977).

**Goldman,** A. Ya., I. I. Perepechko, L. T. Kudryavtseva, V. V. Nizhegorodov and 242
M. A. Butuzova, *Mekh. Kompoz. Meter.*, **2**, 207 (1986).

**Goldsmith,** H. L., and S. G. Mason, in *Rheology, Theory and Applications*, F. R. 152, 158, 161, 162,
Eirich, Ed., Vol. 4, Academic Press, New York (1967). 182

**Golovoy,** A., M.-F. Cheung, and H. van Oene, NRCC/IMRI symposium *"Poly-* 87
*blends-'87"*, Boucherville, Que., Canada, April 28–29, 1987; *Polym. Eng. Sci.*,
**27**, 1642 (1987).

**Gorbatenko,** A. N., T. D. Ignatova, V. F. Shumskii, A. Ye. Nesterov, Yu. S. Lipatov, 91, 173, 178
L. S. Bolotnikova and Yu. N. Panov, *Kompoz. Polim. Mater.*, **15**, 18 (1982).

**Gordon,** M., and J. S. Taylor, *J. Appl. Chem.*, **2**, 493 (1952). 94, 100

**Gordon,** M., J. Goldsbrough, B. W. Ready and K. Derham, in *Industrial Polymers*, 71
J. H. S. Green and R. Dietz, Eds., Transcripta Books, London, (1973).

**Gordon,** M., and B. W. Ready, U. S. Pat. 4,131,369, Dec. 26, 1978. 71

**Gordon,** M., L. A. Kleintjens, B. W. Ready, and J. A. Torkington, *Br. Polym. J.*, **10**, 71
170 (1978).

**Goto,** H., and H. Kuno, *J. Rheol.*, **26**, 387 (1982), ibid., 28, 197 (1984). 155

**Grace,** H. P., Eng. Found. 3rd Res. Conf. Mixing, Andover N. H. (1971). 163

**Grace,** H. P., *Chem. Eng. Commun.*, **14**, 225 (1982). 164, 165, 182, 185

**Greassley,** W. W., and S. F. Edwards, *Polymer*, **22**, 1329 (1981). 146

**Green,** P. F., and B. L. Doyle, *Macromolecules*, **20**, 2471 (1987); *Phys. Rev. Lett.*, 78
**57**, 2407 (1986).

Citation page

**Green,** P. F., P. J. Mills and E. J. Kramer, *Polymer,* **27,** 1063 (1986).                    129

**Groeninckx,** G., and M. Vandermarliere in *Polymer Alloys: Structure and Properties,*    103
16th Europhysics Conf. Macromol. Phys., Bruges, Belgium, June 4–7, 70–72
(1984).

**Gross,** B., *Mathematical Structure of the Theories of Viscoelasticity,* 2nd ed., Her-    143
man, Paris (1968).

**Guggenheim,** E. A., *Mixtures,* Clarendon Press, Oxford (1952).                    40

**Guillet,** J. E., in *Progress in Gas Chromatography,* J. H. Purnell, Ed., J. Wiley and    89
Sons, New York (1973).

**Gupta,** R. K., I. D. Gaba, C. D. Pande and R. P. Singh, *Polym. Bull.,* **8,** 443 (1982).    83

**Haaf,** F., H. Breuer, A. Echte, B. J. Schmitt and J. Stabenow, *J. Sci. Ind. Res.,* **40,**    116
659 (1981).

**Haber,** S., and H. Brenner, *J. Coll. Interf. Sci.,* **97,** 496 (1984).                    158

**Hadziioannou,** G., R. S. Stein and J. Higgins, *Polym. Prepr.,* **24,** 213 (1983).    74

**Hage,** E. Jr., *PhD thesis,* North Carolina State Unv., Raleigh, NC (1983).    118

**Hahn,** B. R., O. Herrmann-Schönherr and J. H. Wendorff, *Polymer,* **28,** 201 (1987).    31, 63

**Halpin,** J. C., *J. Compos. Mater.,* **3,** 732 (1969).                    242

**Hamielec,** L. A., *Polym. Eng. Sci.,* **26,** 111 (1986).                    15

**Han,** C. C. in *Molecular Conformation and Dynamics of Macromolecules in Con-*    43
*densed Systems,* M. Nagasawa (Ed.), Elsevier Sci. Publ., Amsterdam (1988).

**Han,** C. D. and T. C. Yu, *Polym. Eng. Sci,* **12,** 81 (1972).                    173

**Han,** C. D., *J. Appl. Polym. Sci.,* **15,** 1163, 2579 (1971); ibid., **17,** 1289 (1973);    242
ibid., **18,** 481 (1974).

**Han,** C. D., *Multiphase Flow in Polymer Processing,* Academic Press, New York    131, 160, 208, 214,
(1981).                    229, 230

**Han,** C. D., Y. J. Kim and H.-K. Chuang, *Polym. Eng. Rev.,* **3,** 1 (1983).    131

**Han,** C. D., Y.-J. Kim and H. B. Chin, *Polym. Eng. Rev.,* **4,** 177 (1984).    129

**Han,** C. D., and H.-K. Chuang, *J. Appl. Polym. Sci.,* **30,** 2431, 2457 (1985).    52

**Han,** C. D., and H.-H. Yang, *J. Appl. Polym. Sci.,* **33,** 1199, 1221 (1987).    194, 195

**Handlin,** D. L., W. J. MacKnight, and E. L. Thomas, *Macromolecules,* **14,** 795    117
(1980).

**Hanrahan,** B. D., S. R. Angeli and J. Runt, *Polym. Bull.,* **14,** 399 (1985); ibid., **15,**    87, 102
455 (1986).

**Hansen,** R. S., and J. A. Mann Jr., *J. Appl. Phys.,* **35,** 152 (1964).    123

**Hansen,** P. J., and M. C. Williams, *Polym. Eng. Sci.,* **27,** 586 (1987).    168

**Hara,** M., D. Wollmann and A. Eisenberg, *A. C.S. Polym. Prepr.,* **25,** 280 (1984).    126, 128

**Hara,** M., and A. Eisenberg, *Macromolecules,* **17,** 1335 (1984).    126, 128

**Harris,** J. B., and J. F.T. Pittman, *Trans. Inst. Chem. Eng.,* **54,** 73 (1976).    161

**Harris,** J. E., *PhD thesis,* U. Texas (1981).                    92

**Harris,** J. E., S. H. Goh, D. R. Paul and J. W. Barlow, *J. Appl. Polym. Sci.,* **27,** 839    85, 92, 98
(1982).

**Harris,** J. E., D. R. Paul and J. W. Barlow, *Polym. Eng. Sci.,* **23,** 676 (1983).    40, 65, 84, 86, 92

**Harris,** J. E., D. R. Paul and J. W. Barlow, *A.C.S. Adv. Chem. Ser.,* **206,** 43 (1984).    92

**Harris,** J. E., and L. M. Robeson, *J. Polym. Sci., Phys. Ed.,* **25,** 311 (1987).    61, 62, 85

**Harrison,** I. R., and J. Runt, *J. Macromol. Sci., Phys.,* **B17,** 83 (1980).    56

**Hartmann,** B., *Encyclopedia Polym. Sci. Eng.,* 2nd ed., J. Wiley and Sons Inc., New    82
York (1984).

**Hartmann,** B., and M. A. Haque, *J. Appl. Phys.,* **58,** 2831 (1985).    39

**Hartmann,** B., R. Simha and A. E. Berger, Am. Phys. Soc. Meeting, New York,    39
March 16–20, 1987.

**Hartney,** M. A., and R. E. Cohen, *O. N.R. Techn. Rept. No. 10,* Aug. 22, 1983; AD-    126
A132–832.

**Hasegawa,** H., T. Shiwaku, A. Nakai and T. Hashimoto, in *Dynamics of Ordering*    50
*Processes in Condensed Matter,* S. Kamura and H. Furukawa, Eds., Plenum Publ.
Co., New York (1988).

**Hashimoto,** T., T. Takebe and S. Suehiro, *Polym. J.,* **18,** 123 (1986a).    44, 178

Citation page

**Hashimoto,** T., M. Itakura and H. Hasegawa, *J. Chem. Phys.*, **85**, 6118 (1986b).   48

**Hashimoto,** T., in *Current Topics in Polymer Science*, R.M. Ottenbrite, L.A.   43, 47
Utracki and S. Inoue, Eds., Hanser Verlag, Munich (1987).

**Hashimoto,** T., *Phase Transitions*, **12**, 47 (1988).   43, 44, 48

**Havriliak,** S., and S. Nagami, *Polymer*, **8**, 161 (1967).   190

**Hay,** I.L., J.R. Shaner and P.K. Sullivan, *AFOSR Techn. Rept.*, No. 0954, March   128
1979; ADA-080–068.

**Hay,** J.N., in *Flow Induced Crystallization*, R.L. Miller, Ed., Gordon and Breach   55
Sci. Publ. Ltd., London (1979).

**Hayashida,** K., J. Takahashi and M. Matsui, *Proceed. Intl. Congress Rheology,*   173
*Tokyo, Japan, 1968*; S. Onogi, Ed., Tokyo Press (1970).

**Hayashida,** K., and T. Yoshida, *Bull. Faculty Textile Sci., Kyoto U.*, **9**, 65 (1979).   208

**Hedberg,** J.G., and L.C. Muschiatti, U.S. Pat. No. 4,581,406 to DuPont, 8 Apr.   110
1986.

**Heermann,** D.W., *Phys. Rev. Let.*, **52**, 1126 (1984a).   47

**Heermann,** D.W., *Z. Phys. B – Condensed Matter.*, **55**, 309 (1984b).   47

**Heermann,** D.W., *Z. Phys. B – Condensed Matter.*, **61**, 311 (1985).   47

**Heikens,** D., and W. Barentsen, *Polymer*, **18**, 69 (1977).   230

**Heitmiller,** R.F., R.Z. Naar and H.H. Zabusky, *J. Appl. Polym. Sci.*, **8**, 873 (1964).   180

**Helfand,** E., and Y. Tagami, *J. Polym. Sci., Polym. Lett.*, **9**, 741 (1971).   120

**Helfand,** E., and Y. Tagami, *J. Chem. Phys.*, **56**, 3593 (1972).   123

**Helfand,** E., and A.M. Sapse, *J. Chem. Phys.*, **62**, 1327 (1975).   120

**Helminiak,** T.E., U.S. Pat. Appl., 902,525; May 3 (1978).   128

**Henderson,** D.E., U.S. Pat. 2,330,353 to B.F. Goodrich, Sept. 28 (1943).   31

**Henderson,** C.P., and M.C. Williams, *J. Polym. Sci., Polym. Lett. Ed.*, **17**, 257   168
(1979).

**Herkt-Maetzky,** C., and J. Schelten, *Phys. Rev. Lett.*, **51**, 896 (1983).   50

**Herkt-Maetzky,** C., D294 *PhD thesis,* Univ. Bochum, C., Kernforschunganlage   43, 50
Juelich Gmbh, March (1984).

**Hess,** W.R., *Kolloid-Z.*, **27**, 1 (1920).   154

**Heuschen,** J.M., Am. Chem. Soc., Symp. History Eng. Polym., New York, April   240, 241
(1986).

**Hill,** R., *J. Mech. Phys. Solids*, **13**, 213 (1965).   242

**Hinch,** E.J., and A. Acrivos, *J. Fluid Mech.*, **91**, 401 (1979).   163

**Hindmarch,** R.S., and G.M. Gale, A.C.S. Rubber Div. Meet., Philadelphia PA,   17
May 4–8, 1982.

**Hinrichsen,** G., and W. Green, *Kunststoffe*, **71**, 99 (1981).   191

**Hiramatsu,** N., S. Hashida, M. Yasuniwa and S. Hirakawa, *Fukuoka Daigaku*   42, 67
*Rigaku Shuho*, **13**, 39 (1983).

**Hirata,** Y., and T. Kotaka, *Polymer J.*, **13**, 273 (1981).   85, 103

**Ho,** W.-J., and R. Salovey, *Polym. Eng. Sci.*, **21**, 839 (1981).   205

**Hobbs,** S.Y., and V.H. Watkins, *J. Polym. Sci., Polym. Phys. Ed.*, **20**, 651 (1982).   114

**Hobbs,** S.Y., R.C. Bopp and V.H. Watkins, *Polym. Eng. Sci.*, **23**, 380 (1983).   52

**Hobbs,** S.Y., M.E.J. Dekkers and V.H. Watkins, *Polym. Bull.*, **17**, 341 (1987).   231

**Hobbs,** S.Y., M.E.J. Dekkers and V.H. Watkins, *J. Mater. Sci.*, **23**, 1219, 1225   127
(1988).

**Hoffman,** J.D., and J.I. Lauritzen, *J. Res. N.B.S.*, **A65**, 297 (1961).   54

**Hoffman,** J.D., and J.J. Weeks, *J. Res. N.B.S.*, **A66**, 13 (1962).   54

**Hoffman,** R.L., *Trans. Soc. Rheol.*, **16**, 155 (1972).   136

**Hoffman,** R.L., *J. Coll. Interf. Sci.*, **46**, 491 (1974).   136

**Holden,** G., E.T. Bishop and N.R. Legge, *J. Polym. Sci.*, **C26**, 37 (1969).   167

**Holden,** G., Chapter 6 in *Block and Graft Copolymerization*, R.J. Ceresa, Ed., J.   169
Wiley and Sons, London (1973).

**Holste,** J.C., C.J. Glover, K.C.B. Dangayach, T.A. Powel and D.T. Magnuson,   128
*AFWAL Techn. Rept.*, No. 4138, June 1980; ADA-097–929.

**Hong,** K.M., and J. Noolandi, *Macromolecules*, **14**, 727 (1981a); ibid., **14**, 736   41, 120
(1981b); ibid., **14**, 1229 (1981c).

Citation page

**Horikiri,** S., and K. Kodera, *Polymer J.*, **4**, 213 (1973).    59

**Horino,** T., Y. Ogawa, T. Soen and H. Kawai, *J. Appl. Polym. Sci.*, **9**, 2261 (1965).    236

**Horsfield,** H. T., *J. Soc. Chem. Ind.*, **107T–115T** (1934).    156

**Hourston,** D. J., and I. D. Hughes, Intl. Rubber Conf., Brighton, UK, **1**, 13/1 - 13/11    241
(1977).

**Hourston,** D. J., and I. D. Hughes, *Polymer*, **20**, 823 (1979).    241

**Hourston,** D. J., and I. D. Hughes, *J. Appl. Polym. Sci.*, **21**, 3099 (1977); ibid., **26**,    241
3467 (1981).

**Hsiue,** G.-H., and M.-Y. M. Ma, *Polymer*, **25**, 882 (1984).    240

**Hsu,** C. C., and P. H. Geil, NRCC/IMRI Symposium *Polyblends-'87*, Boucherville,    115
Que., Canada, April 28–29, 1987; *Polym. Eng. Sci.*, **27**, 1542 (1987).

**Hsu,** S. L., L. D. Coyne, D. J. Burchell, X. Li and F. J. Lu, 16th Europhysics Conf.    113
Macromol. Phys., June 4–7, 1984, Brugge, Belgium.

**Hu,** S.-R., T. Kyu and R. S. Stein, *J. Polym. Sci., Part B, Polym. Phys.*, **25**, 71    62
(1987).

**Huang,** Z. H., and L. H. Wang, *Makromol. Chem., Rapid Commun.*, **7**, 255 (1986).    113

**Huggins,** M. L., *J. Chem. Phys.*, **9**, 440 (1941).    34

**Huggins,** M. L., *J. Phys. Chem.*, **80**, 1317 (1976).    37

**Huh,** W., R. A. Weiss and L. Nicolais, *Polym. Eng. Sci.*, **23**, 779 (1983).    98

**Hunston,** D. L., paper presented at *"Dynamic Mechanical Characterization of Poly-*    236
*mer Composites"* symposium, Michigan State University, East Lansing, MI, USA,
13–14 July, 1987.

**Huppenthal,** L., and Z. Kasperczuk, *Polimery*, **22**, 231 (1977).    242

**Illers,** K.-H., W. Heckmann and J. Hambrecht, *Coll. Polym. Sci.*, **262**, 557 (1984).    102

**Illin,** M. I., Yu. V. Sharikov, A. A. Zhitinkin and P. V. Chernyavskii, *Theor. Osnovy*    56
*Khim. Tekhnol.*, **17**, 44 (1983).

**Imken,** R. L., D. R. Paul and J. W. Barlow, *Polym. Eng. Sci.*, **16**, 593 (1976).    85

**Inaba,** N., K. Sato, S. Suzuki and T. Hashimoto, *Macromolecules*, **19**, 1960 (1986).    63

**Inoue,** T., T. Kobayashi, T. Hashimoto, T. Tanigami and K. Miyasaka, *Polym.*    21
*Commun.*, **25**, 148 (1984).

**Inoue,** T., T. Ougizawa, O. Yasuda and K. Miyasaka, *Macromolecules*, **18**, 57    21, 31, 50
(1985).

**Inoue,** T., T. Ougizawa and K. Miyasaka, in *Current Topics in Polymer Science* R. M.    50
Ottenbrite, L. A. Utracki and S. Inoue, Eds. Hanser Verlag, Munich (1987).

**Ishizuka,** O., and K. Koyama, *Polymer*, **21**, 164 (1980).    228

**Iskandar,** M., C. Tran, L. M. Robeson and J. E. McGrath, *Polym. Eng. Sci.*, **23**, 682    112
(1983).

**Ivanov,** Y., and T. G.M. van de Ven, *J. Rheol.*, **26**, 231 (1982).    157

**Ivanov,** Y., T. G.M. van de Ven and S. G. Mason, *J. Rheol.*, **26**, 213 (1982).    157, 160

**Ivin,** K. J. Ed., *Structural Studies of Macromolecules by Spectroscopic Methods*, J.    105
Wiley & Sons, London, Uk (1976).

**Izumitani,** T., and T. Hashimoto, *J. Chem. Phys.*, **83**, 3694 (1985).    31, 48

**Jager,** H., E. J. Vorenkamp and G. Challa, *Polym. Comm.*, **24**, 290 (1983).    31, 67

**Jain,** R. K., and R. Simha, *Macromolecules*, **13**, 1501 (1980).    38, 148

**Jain,** R. K., and R. Simha, *J. Chem. Phys.*, **72**, 4909 (1980).    38, 148

**Jain,** R. K., and R. Simha, *J. Phys. Chem.*, **85**, 2182 (1981).    38

**Jain,** R. K., R. Simha and P. Zoller, *J. Polym. Sci., Polym. Phys. Ed.*, **20**, 1399    38, 87, 105
(1982).

**Jain,** R. K., and R. Simha, *Macromolecules*, **17**, 2663 (1984).    38, 42

**Janeschitz-Kriegl,** H., *Polymer Melt Rheology and Flow Birefringence*, Springer V.,    214
Berlin (1983).

**Janik,** R., and J. Plucinski, *Przemysl Chem.*, **59**, 555 (1980).    110

**Jeffrey,** D. J., and A. Acrivos, *A. I.Ch.E. J.*, **22**, 417 (1976).    135

**Jelenic,** J., R. G. Kirste, B. J. Schmitt and S. Schmittstrecker, *Makromol. Chem.*,    74, 77
**180**, 2057 (1979).

Citation page

**Jelenic,** J., R. G. Kirste, R. C. Oberthür, S. Schmittstrecker and B. J. Schmitt, *Makromol. Chem.*, **185**, 129 (1984).   74, 77

**Jelinski,** L. W., J. J. Dumais, F. C. Schilling and F. A. Bovey, *A. C.S. Symp. Ser.*, **191**, 345 (1982).   105, 109

**Jiang,** M., X.-Y. Huang and T.-Y. Yu, *Polymer*, **24**, 1259 (1983); ibid., **26**, 1689 (1985).   115, 124

**Joanny,** J.-F., *C. R. Acad. Sci. Paris*, **286B**, 89 (1978).   41

**Joanny,** J.-F., *PhD thesis* (3e cycle), Univ. Paris 6, 1978; *J. Phys. A: Math. Gen.*, **11**, L117 (1978).   41, 50

**Joanny,** J.-F., and L. Leibler, *J. Physique*, **39**, 951 (1978).   50, 118

**Joanny,** J.-F., and F. Brochard, *J. Physique*, **42**, 1145 (1981).   50

**Jones,** R. A.L., J. Klein and A. M. Donald, *Nature*, **321**, 161 (1986).   120

**Jordan,** E. A., R. C. Ball, A. M. Donald, L. F. Fetters, R. A.L. Jones and J. Klein, *Macromolecules*, **21**, 235 (1988).   120

**Jordhamo,** G. M., J. A. Manson and L. H. Sperling, *Polym. Eng. Sci.*, **26**, 517 (1986).   180

**Joseph,** E. A., M. D. Lorenz, J. W. Barlow and D. R. Paul, *Polymer*, **23**, 112 (1982).   98, 104

**Juliano,** P., NRCC/IMRI symposium *Polyblends-'84*, Panel Discussion, Boucherville, Que. Canada, April 17, 1984; *Polymer Eng. Sci.*, **24**, 1359 (1984).   117


**Kalfoglou,** N. K., *J. Polym. Sci., Polym. Phys. Ed.*, **20**, 1259 (1982).   85, 86, 98

**Kallitsis,** J. K., and N. K. Kalfoglu, *Europ. Polym. J.*, **23**, 117 (1987).   242

**Kamal,** M. R., M. A. Sahto and L. A. Utracki, NRCC/IMRI symposium *Polyblends-'82*, Montreal, April 20, 1982; *Polym. Eng. Sci.*, **22**, 1127 (1982).   54, 126, 128

**Kamal,** M. R., M. A. Sahto and L. A. Utracki, S. P. E.-NATEC, Bal Harbour, FA, Oct. 25–27, 1982; *Polym. Eng. Sci.*, **23**, 637 (1983).   54, 126, 128

**Kamal,** M. R., and P. G. Lafleur, NRCC/IMRI symposium *Modeling-'83*, Montreal, Febr. 9th 1983; *Polym. Eng. Sci.*, **24**, 692 (1984a).   56, 207

**Kamal,** M. R., I. A. Jinnah and L. A. Utracki, NRCC/IMRI symposium *Polyblends-'84*, Boucherville, Que. Canada, April 17, 1984; *Polym. Eng. Sci.*, **24**, 1337 (1984b).   114

**Kamal,** M. R., and P. G. Lafleur, *Polym. Eng. Sci.*, **26**, 103 (1986).   56

**Kambour,** R. P., R. C. Bopp, A. Maconnachie and W. J. MacKnight, *Polymer*, **21**, 133 (1980).   74, 77

**Kamide,** K., and Y. Miyazaki, *Polym. J.*, **13**, 325 (1981).   50, 89

**Kammer,** H. W., and M. Socher, *Acta Polym.*, **33**, 658 (1982).   173, 204

**Kammer,** H. W., *Acta Polym.*, **37**, 1 (1986).   40

**Kanai,** T., and J. L. White, *Polym. Eng. Sci.*, **24**, 1185 (1984).   219

**Kandyrin,** L. B., and V. N. Kulezney, *Kolloid. Zh.*, **36**, 473 (1974).   173

**Kanu,** R. C., and M. T. Shaw, *Polym. Eng. Sci.*, **22**, 507 (1982).   209

**Kaplan,** D., and N. W. Tschoegl, *Polym. Eng. Sci.*, **14**, 43 (1974).   236

**Kaplan,** D. S., *J. Appl. Polym. Sci.*, **20**, 2615 (1976).   93

**Kaplan,** S., and J. J. O'Malley, *Polym. Prepr.*, **20**(2), 266 (1979); *Polymer*, **22**, 221 (1981).   105, 109

**Kaplan,** S., *A. C.S. Polym. Prepr.*, **25**(1), 356 (1984).   105, 109

**Karasz,** F. E., and W. J. MacKnight, *Pure Appl. Chem.*, **52**, 409 (1980).   89

**Karger-Kocsis,** J., A. Kallo and V. N. Kulezney, *Polymer*, **25**, 279 (1984).   114, 115, 117

**Karger-Kocsis,** J., L. Kiss and V. N. Kulezney, *Polym. Commun.*, **25**, 122 (1984).   114, 115, 117

**Karger-Kocsis,** J., Z. Balajthy and J. Kollar, *Kunststoffe*, **74**, 104 (1984).   114, 115, 117

**Karger-Kocsis,** J., and I. Csikai, *Polym. Eng. Sci.*, **27**, 241 (1987).   117

**Karger-Kocsis,** J., and L. Kiss, *Polym. Eng. Sci.*, **27**, 254 (1987).   115, 242

**Karian,** H. G., and A. P. Plochocki, *S. P. E. Techn. Pap.*, **33**, 1334 (1987).   229

**Kasajima,** M., *Bull. Hosei Univ., College Eng.*, **14**(3), 13, 25 (1978).   238

**Kasajima,** M., K. Ito, A. Suganuma and D. Kunti, *Kobun. Robunshu*, **38**, 239, 245 (1981).   211

**Kato,** K., *J. Polym. Sci., Polym. Lett.*, **4**, 35 (1966).   114

Citation page

Kato, K., *Polym. Eng. Sci.*, **8**, 38 (1967).   114

Katsaros, J. D., M. F. Malone and H. H. Winter, *Polym. Bull.*, **16**, 83 (1986).   177, 220

Katz, M., P. W. Lobo, A. S. Minano and H. Solimo, *Can. J. Chem.*, **49**, 2605 (1971).   149

Kausch, H. H., and N. W. Tschoegl, private communication (1986).   156

Kausch, H. H., and M. Tirrell, *Ann. Rev. Mater. Sci.*, **19**, 341 (1989).   71, 120

Kawasaki, K., and T. Ohta, *Prog. Theoret. Phys.*, **59**, 362 (1978).   47

Kehlen, H., and M. T. Rätzsch, *Z. Phys. Chem (Leipzig)*, **264**, 1153 (1983); ibid. **265**, 191 (1984).   41

Keller, A., *Inst. Phys. Conf. Ser.*, **64**, 317 (1983).   74

Kelusky, E. C., C. T. Elston and R. E. Murray, NRCC/IMRI symposium *"Poly-blends-'87"*, Boucherville, Quebec, Canada, April 28–29, 1987; *Polym. Eng. Sci.*, **27**, 1562 (1987).   201

Kelvin, L., *Philos. Mag. Ser. 4*, **42**, 368 (1871).   123

Kenig, S., and M. R. Kamal, *S. P.E. J.*, **26**, 50 (1970).   56

Kennedy, J. W., M. Gordon and G. Alvarez, *Polimery*, **20**, 463 (1975).   71

Kerner, E. H., *Proc. Phys. Soc.*, **69B**, 808 (1956).   242

Keskkula, H., Plast, *Rubb. Mater. Appl.*, **16(5)**, 66 (1979).   116

Khambatta, F. B., *PhD thesis*, Univ. Massachusetts, Amherst (1976).   72

Kimura, M., and R. S. Porter, *A. C.S. Org. Coating Plast. Chem.*, **45**, 84 (1981).   127

Kimura, M., R. S. Porter and G. Salee, *J. Polym. Sci., Polym. Phys. Ed.*, **21**, 367 (1983).   98, 126, 127

Kimura, M., G. Salee and R. S. Porter, *J. Appl. Polym. Sci.*, **29**, 1629 (1984).   98, 102

Kirianov, G. D., R. M. Vasenin amd B. N. Dinzburg, *Vysokomol. Soed.*, **B17**, 492 (1975).   170

Kirste, R. G., and B. R. Lehnen, *Makromol. Chem.*, **177**, 1137 (1976).   74, 77

Kiss, G., NRCC/IMRI symposium, *"Polyblends-'86"*, Montreal, April 4, 1986; *Polym. Eng. Sci.*, **27**, 410 (1987).   230

Kita, M., H. Tanaka and T. Shimada, *Seni. Gak*, **40**, T411 (1984).   116

Klein, J., D. Fletcher and L. J. Fetters, *Nature*, **304**, 526 (1983).   71

Kleintjens, L. A., and R. Koningsveld, *Coll. Polym. Sci.*, **258**, 711 (1980).   37

Kleintjens, L. A., M. H. Onclin and R. Koningsveld, *Symp. EFCE Publ. Ser. 11*, Part II, Berlin 521 (1980).   37, 72

Kleintjens, L. A., private communication (1986).   50

Klempner, D., B. Mum and M. Okoroafor, in *"Recent Developments in Polyuretha-nes and Interpenetrating Polymer Networks"*, K. C. Frisch Jr. Ed., Technomic Publ. Co., Lancaster, Pa (1988).   240

Klopffer, W., *"Introduction to Polymer Spectroscopy"*, Springer-Vlg., Berlin (1984).   112

Klykova, V. D., and V. N. Kuleznev, *Kolloid. Zh.*, **43**, 22 (1981).   177

Klykova, V. D., *Mash. Tekhnol. Pererab. Kauch. Polim. Rezin. Smesei*, **15** (1981).   178

Koberstein, J. T., B. Morra and R. S. Stein, *J. Appl. Cryst.*, **13**, 34 (1980).   122

Koenig, J. L., and M. J.M. Tovar-Rodriguez, *Appl. Spectrosc.*, **35**, 543 (1981).   113

Koenig, J. L., *Adv. Polym. Ser.*, **54**, 87 (1983).   114

Kohler, J., G. Riess and A. Banderet, *Eur. Polymer J.*, **4**, 173, 187 (1968).   67

Kolarik, J., G. L. Agarwal, Z. Krulis and J. Kovar, *Polym. Compos.*, **7**, 463 (1986).   242

Kolarik, J., J. Velek, G. L. Agarwal and J. Fortelny, *Polym. Compos.*, **7**, 472 (1986).   242

Koningsveld, R., and A. J. Staverman, *J. Polym. Sci., Part A–2*, **6**, 349 (1968).   66

Koningsveld, R., L. A. Kleintjeans and H. M.Schoffaleers, *Pure Appl. Chem.*, **39**, 1 (1974).   37, 42, 67, 89

Koningsveld, R., and L. A. Kleintjens, *J. Polym. Sci., Polym. Symp.*, **61**, 221 (1977).   37, 67

Koningsveld, R., L. A. Kleintjens and M. H. Onclin, *J. Macromol. Sci., - Phys.*, **B18**, 363 (1980).   21, 37

Koningsveld, R., M. H. Onclin and L. A. Kleintjens, in *Polymer Compatibility and Incompatibility*, K. Solc, Ed., MMI Press, New York, (1982).   37, 38, 72

Koningsveld, R., private communication (1986).   38

Kosfeld, R., and L. Zumkley, in *Polymer Compatibility and Incompatibility*, K. Solc, Ed., Harwood Acad. Publ., Chur, Switzerland (1982).   105

Citation page

**Kosfeld,** R., and L. Zumkley, *Colloid Polym. Sci.*, **260**, 198 (1982).    109

**Kotaka,** T., and H. Watanabe, in *Current Topics in Polymer Science*, R. M. Otten-    167, 169
brite, L. A. Utracki and S. Inoue, Eds., Hanser Publ., München (1987).

**Koyama,** K., and O. Ishizuka, *Sen-i Gakkaishi*, **38**, 41 (1982).    220

**Koyama,** K., and O. Ishizuka, *Polym. Process. Eng.*, **1**, 55 (1983).    220, 228

**Kozlowski,** M., and J. Piglowski, in *Morphology of Polymers*, B. Sedlacek, Ed., W.    229
de Gruyer & Co., Berlin (1986).

**Kramer,** E. J., P. Green and C. J. Palmstron, *Polymer*, **25**, 473 (1984).    120

**Krapez,** J. C., P. Cielo, X. Maldague and L. A. Utracki, NRCC/IMRI symposium    69
*Composites-'86*, Boucherville, Que., Canada Nov.25–26, 1986; *Polym. Compos.*,
**8**, 396 (1987).

**Krasnikova,** N. P., V. E. Dreval, E. V. Kotova and Z. Pelzbauer, *Vysokomol. Soed.*,    187
**B23**, 378 (1981).

**Krasnikova,** N. P., V. E. Dreval, E. V. Kotova, E. P. Plotnikova, G. V. Vinogradov,    187
B. P. Below and Z. Pelzbauer, *Vysokomol. Soed.*, **A24**, 1423 (1982).

**Krasnikova,** N. P., E. V. Kotova, E. P. Plotnikova, M. P. Zabugina, G. V. Vinog-    187
radov, V. E. Dreval, and Z. Pelzbauer, *Kompoz. Polim. Mater.*, **21**, 37 (1984).

**Kraus,** G., and J. T. Gruver, *J. Appl. Polym. Sci.*, **11**, 2121 (1967).    167

**Kraus,** G., and K. W. Rollman, *J. Polym. Sci., Polym. Phys. Ed.*, **14**, 1133 (1976).    240

**Krause,** S., *5th Conveg. Ital. Sci. Macromol.*, (1981).    118

**Krause,** S., *Pure Appl. Chem.*, **58**, 1553 (1986).    74, 129

**Krieger,** I. M., and T. J. Dougherty, *Trans. Soc. Rheol.*, **3**, 137 (1959).    136, 154

**Krieger,** I. M., *Coll. Interf. Sci.*, **3**, 111 (1972).    136

**Kruse,** W. A., R. G. Kirste, J. Haas, B. J. Schmitt and D. J. Stein, *Makromol.*    31, 77
*Chem.*, **177**, 1145 (1976).

**Kuleznev,** V. N., O. L. Melnikova, V. D. Klykova, V. P. Skvortsov and V. S.    127, 173
Glukhovskoi, *Kolloid. Zh.*, **37**, 273 (1975).

**Kuleznev,** V. N., A. E. Chalykh, V. D. Klykova and L. V. Vershinin, *Kolloid. Zh.*,    30
**47**, 30 (1985).

**Kumaki,** J., and T. Hashimoto, *Macromolecules*, **19**, 763 (1986).    31, 47, 50

**Kuo,** C.-C. E., *PhD thesis*, Univ. Akron, Ohio (1981).    85

**Kuznetsov,** V. L., E. A. Dorokhova, V. Yu. Erofeev and B. K. Basov, *Kolloid. Zh.*,    166
**47**, 806 (1985).

**Kwack,** T. H., and C. D. Han, *J. Appl. Polym. Sci.*, **28**, 3419, 3399 (1983).    219

**Kwei,** T. K., T. Nishi and R. F. Roberts, *Macromolecules*, **7**, 667 (1974).    109

**Kwei,** T. K., G. D. Patterson and T. T. Wang, *Macromolecules*, **9**, 780 (1976).    85

**Kwei,** T. K., and T. T. Wang, Ch. 4 in *Polymer Blends*, D. R. Paul and S. Newman,    43
Eds., Academic Press, New York (1978).

**Kwei,** T. K., E. M. Pearce and B. Y. Min, *Proc. 28th IUPAC, Macromol. Symp.*,    113
Amherst, MA; July 12–16, 667 (1982).

**Kwei,** T. K., *J. Polym. Sci., Lett. Ed.*, **22**, 307 (1984).    100

**Kwei,** T. K., E. M. Pearce, J. R. Pennacchia and M. Charton, *Macromolecules*, **20**,    100
1174 (1987).

**Kwok,** J., *Minutes of VAMAS TWP-PB meeting*, Berlin, 13 April, 1987.    198

**Kyotani,** M., and H. Kanetsuna, *J. Macromol. Sci. Phys.*, **B26**, 325 (1987).    115

**Kyu,** T. S., S.-R. Hu and R. S. Stein, *J. Polym. Sci., Part B, Polym. Phys.*, **25**, 89    62
(1987).


**Lafleur,** P. G., and M. R. Kamal, *Polym. Eng. Sci.*, **26**, 92 (1986).    56

**La Mantia,** F. P., *Rheol. Acta*, **16**, 302 (1977).    140

**La Mantia,** F. P., D. Acierno and D. Curto, *Rheol. Acta*, **21**, 452 (1982).    224

**La Mantia,** F. P., D. Curto and D. Acierno, *Acta Polym.*, **35**, 71 (1984).    204, 216

**La Mantia,** F. P., and D. Acierno, *Plast Rubber Process. Appl.*, **5**, 183 (1985a).    220, 224

**La Mantia,** F. P., and D. Acierno, *Polym. Eng. Sci.*, **25**, 279 (1985b).    220, 224

**La Mantia,** F. P., A. Valenza and D. Acierno, *Europ. Polym. J.*, **22**, 647 (1986a).    180, 204, 221

**La Mantia,** F. P., A. Valenza and D. Acierno, *Polym. Bull.*, **15**, 381 (1986b).    180, 221

**La Mantia,** F. P., *Mater. Chem. Phys.*, **16**, 115 (1987).    180

Citation page

**La Mantia**, F. P., A Valenza and D. Acierno, *Polym Eng. Sci.*, **28**, 90 (1988).     221, 223

**Lambla**, M., *A. C.S. Polym. Materials Sci. Eng. Div. Preparings*, **58**, 879 (1988).     129

**Landel**, R. F., B. G. Moser and A. Bauman, Proceed. 4th Intl. Congress Rheol.,     154
USA (1963).

**Langer**, J. S., *Physica (Utrecht)*, **73**, 61 (1974).     47

**Langer**, J. S., M. Baron and H. D. Miller, *Phys. Rev.*, **A11**, 1417 (1975).     47

**Langer**, J. S., in *Fluctuations, Instabilities and Phase Transitions*, T. Riste, Ed.,     44
Plenum Press, New York (1977); "Kinetics of Metastable States", *Lect. Notes
Phys.*, **132**, 12 (1980).

**Langevin**, D., *J. Coll. Interf. Sci.*, **80**, 412 (1981).     123

**Lapp**, A., C. Picot and H. Benoit, *Macromolecules*, **18**, 2437 (1985).     78

**Larbi**, F. B.C., S. Leloup, J. L. Halary and L. Monnerie, *Polym. Commun.*, **27**, 23     78
(1986).

**Lars**, G., J. Bohse, R. Stephan and J. Sachse, *Plast. Kautsch.*, **30**, 458 (1983).     115

**Larson**, R. G., *Rheol. Acta,* **24**, 443 (1985).     228

**Larson**, R. G., and G. H. Fredrikson, *Macromolecules*, **20**, 1897 (1987).     175

**Lau**, S.-F., J. Pathak and B. Wunderlich, *Macromolecules*, **15**, 1278 (1982).     94, 98, 101

**Lau**, W. W.Y., C. M. Burns and R. Y.M. Huang, *J. Appl. Polym. Sci.*, **29**, 1531     92
(1984); ibid., **30**, 1187 (1985).

**Laun**, H. M., *Rheol. Acta*, **17**, 1 (1978).     228

**Laun**, H. M., in *Rheology*, G. Astarita, G. Marrucci and L. Nicolais, Eds., Plenum     220
Press, New York, **2**, 419 (1980).

**Laun**, H. M., and H. Schuch, *J. Rheol.*, **33**, 119 (1989).     186, 220

**Lauritzen**, J. I., and J. D. Hoffman, *J. Appl. Phys.*, **44**, 4340 (1973).     54

**Lavengood**, R. E., A. F. Harris and A. R. Padwa, Eur. Pat. Appl. EP 202,214 to     52
Monsanto, Nov. 20, 1986.

**Lavengood**, R. E., and F. M. Silver, *S. P.E. Techn. Pap.*, **33**, 1369 (1987); *S. P.E.*     52
*RETEC*, Dearborn, MI, Nov. 2–4, 1987; pap. No. 17–2.

**Lavengood**, R. E., and A. R. Padwa, Eur. Pat. Appl., EP 272,241 to Monsanto,     52
June 22, 1988.

**Leal**, L. G., *Ann. Rev. Fluid Mech.*, **12**, 435 (1980).     162

**Leary**, D. F., and M. C. Williams, *J. Polym. Sci., Part B*, **8**, 335 (1970); *J. Polym.*     169
*Sci., Phys. Ed.*, **11**, 345 (1973); ibid. **12**, 265 (1974).

**Leblanc**, J. L., *Rubb. Chem. Technol.*, **54**, 905 (1981).     216

**Leblans**, P., *PhD thesis*, Univ. Antwerpen (1985).     140, 228

**Lee**, B.-L., and J. L. White, *Trans. Soc. Rheol.*, **19**, 481 (1975).     210

**Lee**, D. I., *J. Paint. Technol.*, **42**, 579 (1970).     154

**Lee**, M.-S., and S.-A. Chen, *J. Polym. Sci., Part C, Polym. Letters*, **25**, 37 (1987).     62

**Lees**, C., *Proc. Phys. Soc.*, **17**, 460 (1900).     23, 180

**Lehr**, M. H., *Polym. Eng. Sci.*, **25**, 1056 (1985).     102

**Lehr**, M. H., *Polym. Eng. Sci.*, **26**, 947 (1986).     172

**Leibler**, L., *Macromolecules*, **13**, 1602 (1980).     49, 174

**Leibler**, L., *Makromol. Chem., Rapid Commun.*, **2**, 393 (1981).     125

**Leibler**, L., *Macromolecules*, **15**, 1283 (1982).     119

**Leibler**, L., *Makromol. Chem., Macromol. Symp.*, **16**, 1 (1988).     119, 125

**Leonard**, C., J. L. Halary, L. Monnerie, D. Broussoux, B. Servet and F. Micheron,     112
*Polym. Comm.*, **24**, 110 (1983).

**Leonov**, A. I., and A. N. Prokunin, *Rheol. Acta*, **22**, 137 (1983).     220

**Letz**, J., *J. Polym. Sci.*, **A28**, 1415 (1979).     61

**Levin**, V. M., *Izv. Akad. Nauk SSSR, Mekh. Tverd. Tela*, **6**, 137 (1976).     242

**Levy**, G. C., Ed., *NMR Spectroscopy: New Methods and Applications*, A. C.S.     105
Symp. Series, Vol. 191, Washington, D. C. (1982).

**Li**, C., J. G. Homan, R. A. Phillips, and S. L. Cooper, in *Recent Developments in*     240
*Polyurethanes and Interpenetrating Polymer Networks*, K. C. Frisch Jr. Ed., Technomic Publ. Co., Lancaster, PA (1988).

**Li**, H.-M., and A. H. Wong, in *Polymer Compatibility and Incompatibility*, K. Šolc,     103
Ed., Harwood Acad. Publ., Chur, Switzerland (1982).

Citation page

Liang, B.-R., J. L. White, J. E. Spruiell and B. C. Goswami, *J. Appl. Polym. Sci.*, **28**,    208
2011 (1983).

Liégeois, J. M., and F. Terreur, 16 Europhysics Conf. Macromol. Phys., June 4–7,    126, 127
1984, Brugge, Belgium.

Lifshitz, I. M., A. Yu. Grosberg and A. R. Khokholov, *Rev. Mod. Phys.*, **50**, 685    41
(1978).

Lifshitz, I. M., and V. V. Slyozov, *J. Phys. Chem. Solids, Lett. Sect.*, **19**, 35 (1961).    47

Lin, C.-C., *Polym. J.*, **11**, 185 (1979).    23, 180

Lin, T. S., *PhD thesis*, Virginia Polytechnic Inst., Blacksburg (1983).    105, 107

Lin, T. S., and T. C. Ward, *A. C.S. Polym. Prepr.*, **24**(2), 136 (1983).    107, 109

Lipatov, Yu. S., *Pure Appl. Chem.*, **43**, 273 (1975).    173, 214

Lipatov, Yu. S., *Vysokomol. Soed.*, **A20**, 3 (1978a).    118, 214

Lipatov, Yu. S., *J. Appl. Polym. Sci.*, **22**, 1895 (1978b).    118

Lipatov, Yu. S., V. F. Shumskii, Ye. V. Lebedev and A. Ye. Nesterov, *Dokl. Akad.*    90, 173, 178
*Nauk SSSR*, **244**, 148 (1979a).

Lipatov, Yu. S., A. Ye. Nesterov and T. D. Ignatova, *Vysokomol. Soed.*, **A21**, 2659    90, 178
(1979b).

Lipatov, Yu. S., V. F. Shumsky, A. N. Gorbatenko, Yu.N. Panov and L. S. Bolot-    197
nikova, *J. Appl. Polym. Sci.*, **26**, 499 (1981).

Lipatov, Yu.S., A. Ye. Nesterov, T. D. Ignatova, V. F. Shumskii and A. N. Gor-    91, 173, 178
batenko, *Eur. Polym. J.*, **18**, 981 (1982a).

Lipatov, Yu. S., A. Ye. Nesterov, T. D. Ignatova, V. F. Shumskii and A. N. Gor-    91, 178
batenko, *Vysokomol. Soed.*, **A24**, 549 (1982b).

Lipatov, Yu.S., V. F. Shumskii, A. N. Gorbatenko and I. P. Gietmanchuk, *Fiz.*    173, 178, 179
*Khim. Mekh. Disp. Struktur*, **117** (1983a).

Lipatov, Yu.S., *Mekh. Kompoz. Mater.*, **3**, 499 (1983).    173, 178

Lipatov, Yu. S., E. V. Lebedev and V. F. Shumskii, *Dopov. Akad. Nauk URSR*, Ser.    173
B, **9**, 39 (1983b).

Lipatov, Yu. S., A. Ye. Nesterov, T. D. Ignatova, N. P. Gudima and O. T. Grit-    91, 118, 127
senko, *Eur. Polym. J.*, **22**, 83 (1986a).

Lipatov, Yu. S., O. P. Grigorieva, L. M. Sergeyeva and V. V. Shilov, *Vysokomol.*    91, 118, 127
*Soed.*, **A28**, 335 (1986b).

Liu, T. Y., and D. S. Soong, *Macromolecules*, **13**, 853 (1980).    234

Liu, T. Y., D. S. Soong and M. C. Williams, *J. Rheol.*, **27**, 7 (1983).    151, 173

Liu, T. Y., D. S. Soong and D. De Kee, *Chem. Eng. Commun.*, **22**, 273 (1983).    168, 169, 191

Lohse, D. J., *Polym. Eng. Sci.*, **26**, 1500 (1986).    77

Lord, F. W., UK Pat. 1,364,675 to ICI, Aug. 29 (1974); appl. July 5, 1971.    156

Loutfy, R. O., Proceed. Intl. Coll. *"Quantitative Characterization of Plastics and*    81
*Rubber"*, Hamilton, Ont. Canada, June 21–22, 1984.

Lu, F. J., D. J. Burchell, X. Li and S. L. Hsu, *Polym. Eng. Sci.*, **23**, 861 (1983a).    113

Lu, F. J., E. Benedetti and S. L. Hsu, *Macromolecules*, **16**, 1525 (1983b).    113, 114

Lyngaae-Jorgensen, J., in *Processing, Structure and Properties of Block Copolymers*,    167, 169, 178
M. J. Folkes, Ed., Elsevier Appl. Sci. Publ., London (1985).

Lyngaae-Jorgensen, J., and K. Sondergaard, NRCC/IMRI symposium *"Polyblends*    50, 178, 229
*-'86"*, Montreal, Que. Canada, April 4, 1986; *Polym. Eng. Sci.*, **27**, 344, 351
(1987).

Lyngaae-Jorgensen, J., L. Dahl Thomsen, K. Rasmussen, K. Sondergaard and F. E.    185
Andersen, *Intl. Polym. Proc.*, **2**, 123 (1988).


Ma, C.-Y., J. L. White, F. C. Weissert and K. Min, *Polym. Compos.*, **6**, 215 (1985).    188

Macchi, E. M., S. A. Liberman and A. S. Gones, *Ann. Asoc. Quim. Argent.*, **74**, 75    101
(1986).

MacKnight, W. J., F. E. Karasz and J. R. Fried, Chapter 5 in *Polymer Blends*, D. R.    53
Paul and S. Newman, Eds., Academic Press, New York (1978).

Maconnachie, A., R. P. Kambour and R. C. Bopp, *Polymer*, **25**, 357 (1984).    74, 75, 77

Maeda, J., F. E. Karasz and W. J. MacKnight, *J. Appl. Polym. Sci.*, **32**, 4432 (1986).    42

Malik, T. M., and R. E. Prud'homme, *Macromolecules*, **16**, 311 (1983).    98, 104

Citation page

**Malik,** T. M., and R. E. Prud'homme, NRCC/IMRI symposium *"Polyblends-'83"*, 98, 101, 104
Montreal, April 12, 1983; *Polym. Eng. Sci.*, **24**, 144 (1984).
**Manevich,** L. I., V. S. Mitlin and Sh.A. Shaginyan, *Khim. Fiz.*, **3**, 283 (1984). 174
**Manley,** R. S.J., and S. G. Mason, *J. Colloid Sci.*, **7**, 354 (1952). 154
**Manson,** J. A., *Pure Appl. Chem.*, **53**, 471 (1981). 241
**Marin,** G., *PhD thesis*, Universit de Pau (1977). 189, 191
**Maron,** S. H., and P. E. Pierce, *J. Colloid Sci.*, **11**, 80 (1956). 154
**Maron,** S. H., *J. Polym. Sci.*, **38**, 329 (1959). 34
**Martinez,** C. B., and M. C. Williams, *J. Rheol.*, **24**, 421 (1980). 196
**Martuscelli,** E., C. Silvestre, and G. A. Bate, *Polymer*, **23**, 229 (1982). 54
**Martuscelli,** E., G. Demma, E. Rossi and A. L. Segre, *Polym. Compos.*, **24**, 266 105, 109
(1983).
**Martuscelli,** E., *Macromol. Chem., Rapid Commun.*, **5**, 255 (1984). 54, 152, 173
**Martuscelli,** E., M. Pracella, and W. P. Yue, *Polymer*, **25**, 1097 (1984). 86
**Martuscelli,** E., C. Sellitti, and C. Silvestre, *Makromol. Chem., Rapid Commun.*, **6**, 61
125 (1985).
**Martuscelli,** E., L. Vicini and S. Seves, *Makromol. Chem.*, **188**, 607 (1987). 173
**Marvin,** R. S., in *Viscoelasticity – Phenomenological Aspects*, J. T. Bergen, Ed., 195
Academic Press, New York (1960).
**Masi,** P., D. R. Paul and J. W. Barlow, in *Rheology*, G. Astarita, G. Marrucci and 92, 98, 104
L. Nicolais, Eds., Plenum Press, New York (1980); *J. Polym. Sci., Polym. Phys.
Ed.*, **20**, 15 (1982).
**Mason, D.,** Ed. *The Story of the Plastics Industry*, S. P.I., New York (1972). 4
**Masuda,** T., K. Kitagawa, T. Inoue and S. Onogi, *Macromolecules*, **3**, 116 (1970). 191
**Masuda,** T., A. Nakajima, M. Kitamura, Y. Aoki, N. Yamauchi and A. Yoshioka, 194
*Pure Appl. Chem.*, **56**, 1457 (1984).
**Matsumoto,** S., and P. Sherman, *J. Coll. Interf. Sci.*, **30**, 525 (1969). 161
**Maurer,** F. H.J., J. H.M. Palmen and H. C. Booij, *Rheol. Acta*, **24**, 243 (1985). 236
**Maxwell,** B., and A. J. Scalora, *Mod. Plast.*, **37**, 107 (1959). 18
**Maxwell,** B., E. J. Dormier, P. F. Smith and P. P. Tong, *Polym. Eng. Sci.*, **22**, 280 128
(1982).
**Maxwell,** B., and G. L. Jasso, *Polym. Eng. Sci.*, **23**, 614 (1983). 128
**Mazich,** K. A., *PhD thesis*, Northwestern Univ. (1983). 177, 178
**McAllister,** R. A., *A. I.Ch.E. J.*, **6**, 427 (1960). 149, 170, 174
**McBrierty,** V. J., D. C. Douglass and T. K. Kwei, *Macromolecules*, **11**, 1265 (1978). 31, 105, 109
**McBrierty,** V. J., D. C. Douglass and P. J. Barham, *J. Polym. Sci., Polym. Phys. Ed.*, 105, 109
**18**, 1561 (1980).
**McCarthy,** S. P., and C. E. Rogers, *Polym. Eng. Sci.*, **27**, 647 (1987). 8
**McCrum,** N. G., B. E. Read and G. Williams, *Anelastic and Dielectric Effects in* 83
*Polymeric Solids*, J. Wiley and Sons, New York (1967).
**McGeary,** R. K., *J. Amer. Ceram. Soc.*, **44**, 513 (1961). 155
**McGee,** S., and R. L. McCullough, *Polym. Compos.*, **2**, 149 (1981). 242
**McHugh,** A. J., *Polym. Eng. Sci.*, **22**, 15 (1982). 56
**McIntyre,** D., N. Rounds and E. Campos-Lopez, *A. C.S. Polym. Prepr.*, **10**, 531 37
(1969).
**McKenna,** G. B., and D. J. Plazek, *A. C.S. Polym. Prepr.*, **28(1)**, 325 (1987). 189
**McKinney,** J. E., and R. Simha, *Macromolecules*, **9**, 430 (1976). 38
**McMaster,** L. P., *Macromolecules*, **6**, 760 (1973). 31, 66
**McMaster,** L. P., *Adv. Chem. Ser.*, **142**, 43 (1975). 31
**McMaster,** L. P., and O. Olabisi, *ACS, Div. Org. Coat. Plast. Chem. Prepr.*, **35**, 322 31
(1975).
**Meakin,** P., and S. Reich, *Phys. Lett.*, **92**, 247 (1982). 49
**Meakin,** P., H. Metiu, R. G. Petschek and D. J. Scalapino, *J. Chem. Phys.*, **79**, 1948 49
(1983).
**Meakin,** P., and J. M. Deutch, *J. Chem. Phys.*, **80**, 2115 (1984). 55
**Meijer,** H. E.M., P. J. Lemstra and P. H.M. Elemans, *Makromol. Chem., Macromol.* 115
*Symp.*, **16**, 113 (1988).

Citation page

Meissner, J., *Pure Appl. Chem.*, **42**, 553 (1975).     220

Meissner, J., S. E. Stephenson, A. Demarels and P. Portmann, *J. Non-Newtonian Fluid Mech.*, **11**, 221 (1982).     217, 228

Meissner, J., *Ann. Rev. Fluid Mech.*, **17**, 45 (1985).     217–219

Meissner, J., *Polym. Eng. Sci.*, **27**, 537 (1987).     217, 218

Mendelson, R. A., *J. Polym. Sci., Polym., Phys., Ed.*, **23**, 1975 (1985).     127

Menzheres, I. Ya., and E. G. Moisya, *Kompoz. Polim. Mater.*, **17**, 14 (1983).     79, 82

Merriam, C. N., and L. M. Robeson, *S. P. E. Techn. Papers*, **31**, 373 (1985).     241

Metelkin, V. I., and V. S. Blekht, *Kolloid. Zh.*, **46**, 476 (1984).     180, 181

Metzner, A. B., and M. Whitlock, *Trans. Soc. Rheol.*, **2**, 239 (1958).     136

Metzner, A. B., and A. P. Metzner, *Rheol. Acta*, **9**, 174 (1970).     186, 218

Metzner, A. B., *J. Rheol.*, **29**, 739 (1985).     152, 154

Mewis, J., *J. Non-Newtonian Fluid Mech.*, **6**, 1 (1979).     135

Mewis, J., in *Rheology*, G. Astarita, G. Marrucci and L. Nicolais, Eds., Vol. 1, pos. 149–68, Plenum Press, New York (1980).     152

Meyer, R., M. Meyer, J. Metzger and A. Peneloux, *J. Chim. Phys., Physico-chim. Biol.*, **68**, 406 (1971).     149, 150

Michler, G. H., *Ultramicroscopy*, **15**, 81 (1984).     114

Mikes, F., H. Morawetz and K. S. Dennis, *Macromolecules*, **13**, 969 (1980); ibid., **17**, 60 (1984).     80–82, 98, 102

Miki, K., *Polym. J.*, **1**, 432 (1970).     232

Miles, I. S., *Report to VAMAS Technical Working Party on Polymer Blends*, 10 Nov., 1986.     122, 124

Miles, I. S., and Z. Zurek, *Polym. Eng. Sci.*, **28**, 796 (1988).     180

Mill, C. C., Ed.; *Rheology of Dispersed Systems*, Pergamon Press, London (1959).     135

Min, B. Y., and E. M. Pearce, *A. C. S. Org. Coat. Plast. Chem.*, **45**, 58 (1981).     98, 101

Min, K., J. L. White and J. F. Fellers, NRCC/IMRI symposium *"Polyblends-'84"*, Boucherville, Quebec, Canada, April 17, 1984; *Polym. Eng. Sci.*, **24**, 1327 (1984).     214, 229

Min, K., *PhD thesis*, Univ. Tenessee, Knoxville (1984).     226, 229, 231

Minana-Perez, M., P. Jarry, M. Perez-Sanchez, M. Ramirez-Gouveia and J. L. Salager, *J. Disp. Sci. Technol.*, **7**, 331 (1986).     167

Minoshima, W., *PhD thesis*, Univ. Tennessee, Knoxville (1983).     220

Miroshnikov, Yu. P., *Mekh. Kompoz. Mater.*, **20**, 104 (1984).     188

Mishra, S. P., and B. L. Deopura, *Rheol. Acta*, **23**, 189 (1984).     212

Miya, M., R. Iwamoto and S. Mima, *J. Polym. Sci., Polym. Phys. Ed.*, **22**, 1149 (1984).     113

Miyata, S., and T. Hata, *Intl. Congr. Rheol., Tokyo Press*, **3**, 71 (1970).     243

Mohn, R. N., D. R. Paul and J. W. Barlow, *J. Appl. Polym. Sci.*, **23**, 575 (1979).     241

Mondragon, I., M. Cortazar and G. M. Guzman, *Makromol. Chem.*, **184**, 1741 (1983).     85

Montandu, G., P. Maravigna, P. Finocchiaro and G. Centineo, *J. Polym. Sci., Polym. Chem. Ed.*, **11**, 65 (1973).     62

Montes, S. A., *Polym. Eng. Sci.*, **24**, 259 (1984).     220

Montfort, J. P., G. Marin, J. Arman and Ph. Monge, *Polymer*, **19**, 277 (1978).     151

Montfort, J. P., *Doctorat d'Etat*, Universit de Pau (1984).     190, 191

Moonan, W. K., and N. W. Tschoegl, *Int. J. Polym. Mater.*, **10**, 199 (1984).     146

Mooney, M., *J. Colloid Sci.*, **6**, 162 (1951).     152

Moore, M. A., *J. Phys. A, Math. Gen.*, **10**, 305 (1977).     41

Morawetz, H., and F. Amrani, *Macromolecules*, **11**, 281 (1978).     80–82

Morawetz, H., *Pure Appl. Chem.*, **52**, 277 (1980).     80–82

Morawetz, H., *Ann. N. Y. Acad. Sci.*, **366**, 404 (1981).     80–82

Morawetz, H., *Polym. Eng. Sci.*, **23**, 689 (1983).     78

Morawetz, H., *Polymers: Their Origins and Growth of a Science*, J. Wiley and Sons, New York (1985).     4

Morel, G., and D. R. Paul, *J. Membrane Sci.*, **10**, 273 (1982).     92

Morgan, R. J., *Trans. Soc. Rheol.*, **12**, 511 (1968).     136

Citation page

Morra, B. S., and R. S. Stein, *J. Polym. Sci., Polym. Phys. Ed.*, **20**, 2243 (1982).     59, 85, 112

Morra, B. S., and R. S. Stein, *Polym. Eng. Sci.*, **24**, 311 (1984).     59, 61

Moskala, E. J., and M. M. Coleman, *Polym. Commun.*, **24**, 206 (1983).     113

Moskala, E. J., *PhD thesis*, Pennsylvania State Univ. (1984).     112

Moskala, E. J., D. F. Varnell and M. M. Coleman, *Polymer*, **26**, 228 (1985).     112

Mucha, M., *Polimery*, **27**, 153 (1982).     102

Mucha, M., *Coll. Polym. Sci.*, **264**, 859 (1986).     102

Mukherji, A. K., M. A. Butler and D. L. Evans, *J. Appl. Polym. Sci.*, **25**, 1145     113
(1980).

Münstedt, H., *Polym. Eng. Sci.*, **21**, 259 (1981).     212

Münstedt, H., and S. Middleman, *J. Rheol.*, **25**, 29 (1981).     220, 225

Münstedt, H., and H. M. Laun, *Rheol. Acta*, **20**, 211 (1981).     220

Murakami, Y., T. Inui and Y. Takegami, *Polymer*, **24**, 1596 (1983).     91

Murata, K., K. Nakashima, K. Funatsu and H. Shinohara, *Kagaku Kogaku* Robun.,     214
**7**, 549 (1981).


Nadkarni, V. M., and J. P. Jog, *J. Appl. Polym. Sci.*, **32**, 5817 (1986).     62

Nagarajan, S., and Z. H. Stachurski, *J. Polym. Sci., Polym. Phys. Ed.*, **20**, 989     109
(1982).

Nagata, I., *PhD Thesis*, Polytechnic Institute of New York (1980).     80

Nagata, I., and H. Morawetz, *Macromolecules*, **14**, 87 (1981).     80

Naito, K., G. E. Johnson, D. L. Allara and T. K. Kwei, *Macromolecules*, **11**, 1260     31
(1978).

Naito, K., and T. K. Kwei, *J. Polym. Sci., Polym. Chem. Ed.*, **17**, 2935 (1979).     81

Naito, K., and T. K. Kwei, *Polym. Eng. Sci.*, **19**, 841 (1979).     81

Nakafuku, C., *Polym. J.*, **15**, 641 (1983).     61

Nakamura, Y., A. Watanabe, K. Mori, K. Tamura and H. Miyazaki, *J. Polym. Sci.,*     127
*Part C., Polym. Lett.*, **25**, 127 (1987).

Nam, S., *Intl. Polym. Process.*, **1**, 98 (1987).     210

Nancekivell, J., *Canad. Plast.*, **43**(1), 28 (1985); **43**(9), 27 (1985).     204

Nandi, A. K., B. M. Mandal and S. N. Bhattacharyya, *Macromolecules*, **18**, 1454     91
(1985).

Narasimhan, V., D. R. Lloyd and C. M. Burns, *J. Appl. Polym. Sci.*, **23**, 749 (1979).     92

Narasimhan, V., R. Y.M. Huang and C. M. Burns, *J. Polym. Sci., Polym. Phys. Ed.*,     92
**21**, 1993 (1983).

Narasimhan, V., C. M. Burns, R. Y.M. Huang and D. R. Lloyd, *A. C.S. Adv. Chem.*     92
*Ser.*, **206**, 3 (1984).

Nassar, T. R., D. R. Paul and J. W. Barlow, *J. Appl. Polym. Sci.*, **23**, 85 (1979).     241

Natansohn, A., *J. Polym. Sci., Polym. Letter Ed.*, **23**, 305 (1985).     66, 87

Natansohn, A., M. Rutkowska and A. Eisenberg, NRCC/IMRI Symposium *"Poly-*     128
*blends-'87"*, Boucherville, Que., Canada, April 28–29, 1987; *Polym. Eng. Sci.*,
**27**, 1504 (1987).

Natta, G., G. Allegra, I. W. Bassi, D. Sianesi, G. Caporico and E. Torti, *J. Polym.*     62
*Sci., Part A*, **3**, 4263 (1965).

Natta, G., G. Allegra, I. W. Bassi, C. Carlino, E. Chiellini and G. Montagnoli,     62
*Macromolecules*, **2**, 311 (1969).

Nauman, E. B., S.-T. Wang and N. P. Balsara, *Polymer*, **27**, 1637 (1986).     50

Nawab, M. A., and S. G. Mason, *Trans. Faraday Soc.*, **54**, 1712 (1985).     160

Newman, S. B., in *Analytical Chemistry of Polymers*, O. M. Klein, Ed., J. Wiley and     114
Sons, New York, (1962).

Nielsen, L. E., *Mechanical Properties of Polymers and Composites*, M. Dekker, New     239, 242
York (1974).

Nielsen, L. E., *Polymer Rheology*, Marcel Dekker Inc., New York (1977).     160, 162

Nies, E., R. Koningsveld and L. A. Kleintjens, presented at IUPAC meeting,     37, 38
Bucharest, Sept. 1983a.

Nies, E., L. A. Kleintjens, R. Koningsveld, R. Simha and R. K. Jain, *Fluid Phase*     37, 39
*Equil.*, **12**, 12 (1983b).

Citation page

**Nies,** E., R. Koningsveld and L. A. Kleintjens, Proceed. 5th Intl. Conf. *"Interactions in Liquids",* Halle, April 1983c.　　37, 39

**Nishi,** M., H. Watanabe and T. Kotaka, *Nihon Reor. Gak.*, **9**, 23 (1981).　　194

**Nishi,** T., and T. K. Kwei, *Polymer*, **16**, 285 (1975).　　31, 67

**Nishi,** T., T. T. Wang and T. K. Kwei, *Macromolecules*, **8**, 227 (1975).　　31, 67, 109

**Nishi,** T., and T. T. Wang, *Macromolecules*, **8**, 909 (1975); ibid. **10**, 421 (1977).　　57, 85, 91

**Nishi,** T., *Rubber Chem. Technol.*, **51**, 1075 (1978).　　62

**Nishi,** T., *J. Macromol. Sci., Phys.*, **B17**, 517 (1980).　　62

**Nishi,** T., *CRC Crit. Rev. Solid State Mat. Sci.*, **12**, 329 (1985).　　30, 54, 62

**Nishimura,** T., *Rheol. Acta*, **23**, 617 (1984).　　211, 217

**Noel,** O. F. Iii, and J. E. Carley, *Polym. Eng. Sci.*, **24**, 488 (1984).　　59, 114

**Nojima,** S., K. Tsutsumi and T. Nose, *Polym. J.*, **14**, 225, 289, 907 (1982).　　31

**Noolandi,** J., and K. M. Hong, *Macromolecules*, **15**, 482 (1982).　　41, 120, 122

**Noolandi,** J., and K. M. Hong, *Polym. Bull.*, **7**, 561 (1982b).　　41

**Noolandi,** J., NRCC/IMRI symposium *"Polyblends-'83"*, Montreal, April 12, 1983; *Polym. Eng. Sci.*, **24**, 70 (1984).　　41, 120

**Noolandi,** J., *Ber. Bunsenges. Phys. Chem.*, **89**, 1147 (1985).　　41

**Nose,** T., *Phase Transitions*, **8**, 245 (1987).　　43

**Noshay,** A., and J. E. McGrath, *Block Copolymers; Overview and Critical Survey*, Academic Press, New York (1977).　　167


**Ogawa,** E., N. Yamaguchi and M. Shima, *Polym. J.*, **18**, 903 (1986).　　88

**Ohta,** T., and K. Kawasaki, *Phys. Lett.*, **A64**, 404 (1978).　　47

**Okagawa,** A., R. G. Cox and S. G. Mason, *J. Coll. Interf. Sci.*, **45**, 303 (1973).　　160

**Okagawa,** A., and S. G. Mason, *Can. J. Chem.*, **53**, 2689 (1975).　　161

**Olabisi,** O., and R. Simha, *J. Appl. Polym. Sci.*, **21**, 149 (1977).　　38

**Olabisi,** O., L. M. Robeson and M. T. Shaw, *Polymer-Polymer Miscibility*, Academic Press, New York (1979).　　31, 43, 53, 66, 89, 92, 105, 112

**Olabisi,** O., and A. G. Farnham, *A. C. S. Adv. Chem. Ser.*, **176**, 559 (1979).　　126, 128

**Olabisi,** O., "Polyblends" in Kirk-Othmer, *Encyclop. Chem. Technol.*, Third Ed., J. Wiley and Sons, New York (1982).　　129

**Oldroyd,** J. C., *Proc. Roy. Soc.*, **A218**, 122 (1953); **A232**, 567 (1955).　　160, 161

**Onclin,** M. H., L. A. Kleintjens and R. Koningsveld, *Makromol. Chem. Suppl.*, **3**, 197 (1979).　　72

**Onclin,** M. H., *PhD thesis*, Antwerp (1980).　　72

**Onclin,** M. H., L. A. Kleintjens and R. Koningsveld, *Brit. Polym. J.*, **12**, 221 (1980).　　72

**Onogi,** S., T. Masuda, N. Noda, and K. Koga, *Polym. J.*, **1**, 542 (1970).　　191

**Onogi,** S., and T. Matsumoto, *Polym. Eng. Rev.*, **1**, 45 (1981).　　138, 140

**Onuki,** A., *Phys. Lett.*, **64A**, 115 (1977).　　175

**Onuki,** A., *Physica*, **140A**, 204 (1986).　　175, 176

**Oosterbroek,** M., J. S. Lopulissa And J. Mellema, in *Rheology*, G. Astarita, G. Marruci and L. Nicolais, Eds., Vol. 2, 601; Plenum Press, New York (1980).　　162

**Oosterbroek,** M., J. Mellema and J. S. Lopulissa, *J. Coll. Interf. Sci.*, **84**, 27 (1981).　　163

**Oosterbroek,** M., and J. Mellema, *J. Coll. Interf. Sci.*, **84**, 14 (1981).　　163

**Ostwald,** W., *Z. Phys. Chem.*, **34**, 495 (1900).　　44, 47

**Ougizawa,** T., T. Inoue, and H. W. Kammer, *Macromolecules*, **18**, 2089 (1985).　　30, 31

**Ougizawa,** T., and T. Inoue, *Polym. J.*, **18**, 521 (1986).　　30, 31

**Ouhadi,** T., R. Fayt, R. Jerome and Ph. Teyssie, *J. Appl. Polym. Sci.*, **32**, 5647 (1986); *J. Polym. Sci., Part B: Polym. Phys.*, **24**, 973 (1986); *Polym. Commun.*, **27**, 212 (1986).　　125

**Oxtoby,** D. W., *J. Chem. Phys.*, **62**, 1463 (1975).　　175


**Padday,** J. F., in *Surface and Colloid Science*, Vol. 1, E. Matijevic, Ed., J. Wiley and Sons, New York (1969).　　122

**Painter,** P. C., Y. Park and M. M. Coleman, *Macromolecules*, **21**, 66 (1988).　　105, 112

**Pal,** R., S. N. Bhattacharya and E. Rhodes, *Canad. J. Chem. Eng.*, **64**, 3 (1986).　　166

**Panayiotou,** C., and J. H. Vera, *Fluid Phase Equil.*, **5**, 55 (1980).　　40

Citation page

**Parker,** M. A., and D. Vesely, *J. Polym. Sci., Part B Polym. Phys.*, **24**, 1869 (1986).    120

**Parkinson,** C., S. Matsumoto and P. Sherman, *J. Coll. Interf. Sci.*, **33**, 150 (1970).    157

**Patfoort,** G. A., *Plastica*, **3**, 22, 95 (1969); *Plast. Machin. Equip.*, Feb., 52 (1981);    18, 128
Jun., 53 (1981).

**Patterson,** D., *Macromolecules*, **2**, 672 (1969).    34

**Patterson,** D., and A. Robard, *Macromolecules*, **11**, 690 (1978).    3, 34, 36, 42

**Patterson,** D., NRCC/IMRI mini-symposium, *"Thermodynamics of Liquids and their*    32, 33, 34
*Blends"*, Montreal, November 21, 1980; *Polym. Eng. Sci.*, **22**, 64 (1982).

**Patterson,** G. D., *A. C.S. Adv. Chem. Ser.*, **176**, 529 (1979).    114

**Paul,** D. R., and S. Newman, Eds., *Polymer Blends*, Academic Press, New York,    124, 127
(1978).

**Paul,** D. R., in *Polymer Blends*, D. R. Paul and S. Newman Eds., Academic Press,    124
New York, (1978).

**Paul,** D. R., and J. W. Barlow, *A. C.S., Div. Org. Coat. Plast. Chem. Prepr.*, **40**, 745    60
(1979).

**Paul,** D. R., and J. W. Barlow, *J. Macromol. Sci., Rev. Macromol. Chem.*, **C18**, 109    65, 129, 180
(1980).

**Paul,** D. R., and J. W. Barlow, Final Report, Sept. 30, 1981; A. R.O.-15466.5-C.    98, 104

**Paul,** D. R., *"Phase Equilibria in Polymer Blends"*, presented at symposium under    65
the same title, Inst. Mat. Sci., Univ. Connecticut, Storrs, CT, May 1, 1981.

**Paul,** D. R., and J. W. Barlow, Proceed. 28th IUPAC Meeting, Amherst, MA, July    65
12–16, 1982, pg. 684.

**Paul,** D. R., and J. W. Barlow, *Polymer*, **25**, 487 (1984).    40, 125

**Paul,** D. R., J. W. Barlow and H. Keskkula, in *Encyclopedia of Polymer Science and*    116
*Engineering*, J. I. Kroschwitz, Ed., J. Wiley and Sons, New York (1985).

**Pearson,** G. H., and R. W. Connelly, *J. Appl. Polym. Sci.*, **27**, 969 (1982).    219

**Pennacchia,** J., *PhD thesis*, Polytechnic Inst., New York (1986).    112

**Perez,** J., J. Y. Cavaille, S. Etienne and C. Jourdan, *Revue Phys. Appl.*, **23**, 125    232
(1988).

**Pethrick,** R. A., *J. Macromol. Sci., Rev. Macromol. Chem.*, **C9**, 91 (1973).    82

**Petrie,** C. J.S., *Elongational Flows*, Pitman, London (1979).    185, 219, 221

**Petschek,** R., and H. Metiu, *J. Chem. Phys., 79*, 3443 (1983).    49

**Phillips,** D. W., and R. A. Pethrick, *J. Macromol. Sci., Rev. Macromol. Chem.*, **C16**,    82
1 (1977–8).

**Piche,** L., *Polym. Eng. Sci.*, **24**, 1354 (1984).    82, 84

**Pico,** E. R., and M. C. Williams, *Nature*, **259**, 388 (1976).    168

**Piglowski,** J., J. Kressler and H. W. Kammer, *Polym. Bull.*, **16**, 493 (1986).    50

**Piglowski,** J., and M. Kozlowski, *Angew. Makromol. Chem.*, **153**, 187 (1987).    66

**Pilati,** F., and G. Pezzin, *Polym. Eng. Sci.*, **24**, 618 (1984).    114

**Pillon,** L. Z., and L. A. Utracki, NRCC/IMRI mini-symposium *Polyblends-'84*,    110, 126
Boucherville, Que., Canada, April 17, 1984; *Polym. Eng. Sci.*, **24**, 1300 (1984).

**Pillon,** L. Z., and L. A. Utracki, NRCC/IMRI symposium *"Polyblends-'85"*,    54, 85, 87, 110, 114,
Boucherville, Que. Canada, April 16, (1985).    126, 127

**Pillon,** L. Z., and L. A. Utracki, Proceedings of Third Intl. Conf. "Reactive Proces-    54, 85, 87, 113, 114,
sing of Polymers", Sept. 5–7, 1984 Strasbourg, France; *Polym. Proc. Eng.*, **4**, 375    126, 127
(1986).

**Piloz,** A., J.-Y. Decroix, and J.-F. May, *Angew. Makromol. Chem.*, **54**, 77 (1976).    235

**Pincus,** P., *J. Chem. Phys.*, **75**, 1996 (1981).    50

**Pivinski,** Y. E., *Kolloid. Zhurn.*, **35**, 286 (1973).    136

**Plans,** J., W. J. MacKnight and F. E. Karasz, *Macromolecules*, **17**, 1100 (1984).    59, 84

**Plochocki,** A. P., *Kolloid Z. Z. Polym.*, **208**, 168 (1966).    61

**Plochocki,** A. P., in *Polymer Blends*, D. R. Paul and S. Newman, Eds., Academic    201, 205
Press, New York (1978).

**Plochocki,** A. P., NRCC/IMRI symposium *"Polyblends-'82"*, Montreal, Que.,    173, 174, 179, 201,
Canada, April 20, 1982; *Polym. Eng. Sci.*, **22**, 1153 (1982).    214

**Plochocki,** A. P., *Adv. Polym. Technol.*, **2**, 267 (1983a); ibid. **3**, 405 (1984).    230

**Plochocki,** A. P., *Polym. Eng. Sci.*, **23**, 618 (1983b).    230

Citation page

**Plochocki,** A. P., NRCC/IMRI symposium *"Polyblends-'85"*, Boucherville, Quebec,    27, 149, 201, 231
Canada, April 16–17, 1985; *Polym. Eng. Sci.*, **26**, 82 (1986).
**Plotnikova,** E. P., and M. P. Zabugina, *Mekh. Kompoz. Mater.*, **5**, 937 (1984).    184
**Poser,** C. I., and I. C. Sanchez, *J. Coll. Interf. Sci.*, **69**, 539 (1979).    120, 121
**Poser,** C. I., and I. C. Sanchez, *Macromolecules*, **14**, 361 (1981).    120, 121
**Powell,** R. L., and W. H. Schwarz, *J. Rheol.*, **23**, 323 (1979).    140
**Prest,** W. M. Jr., and R. S. Porter, Interamerican Conf. Mater. Technol., Mexico    149, 171, 173, 193,
(1972a).    234
**Prest,** W. M. Jr., and R. S. Porter, *J. Polym. Sci., Part A–2*, **10**, 1639 (1972b).    149, 193
**Prest,** W. M., and R. S. Porter, *Polym. J.*, **4**, 154 (1973).    191
**Princen,** H. M., *J. Coll. Interf. Sci.*, **91**, 160 (1983).    163
**Princen,** H. M., *J. Coll. Interf. Sci.*, **105**, 150 (1985).    163
**Privalko,** V. P., Yu. S. Lipatov, Yu. D. Besklubenko and G. Ye. Yarema, *Vyso-*    87
*komol. Soyed.*, **A27**, 1021 (1985).
**Prokunin,** A. V., *Intern. J. Polym. Mater.*, **8**, 303 (1980).    220
**Prud'homme,** R. E., NRCC/IMRI symposium *"Polyblends-'81"*, Montreal, April 28,    86, 101, 104
1981; *Polym. Eng. Sci.*, **22**, 90 (1982a).
**Prud'homme,** R. E., NRCC/IMRI symposium *"Polyblends-'82"*, Montreal, April 20,    86, 101, 112
1982; *Polym. Eng. Sci.*, **22**, 1138 (1982b).
**Pugh,** C., and V. Percec, *Macromolecules*, **19**, 65 (1986).    128
**Pugh,** C., J. M. Rodriguez-Parada and V. Percec, *J. Polym. Sci., Polym. Chem. Ed.*,    128
**24**, 747 (1986).

**Quate,** C. F., *Phys. Today*, **39**(8), 26 (1986).    114
**Quemada,** D., *Rheol. Acta*, **16**, 82 (1977).    154

**Rafailovich,** M. H., J. Sokolov, R. A. L. Jones, G. Krausch, J. Klein and R. Mills,    120
*Europhys. Lett.*, **5**, 657 (1988).
**Rahimian,** D. E., *M. S. thesis*, Univ. Lowell, MA (1982).    129
**Raible,** T., and J. Meissner, in *Rheology*, G. Astarita, G. Marrucci and L. Nicolais,    220
Eds., Plenum Press, New York, **2**, 425 (1980).
**Raible,** T., S. E. Stephenson, J. Meissner and M. H. Wagner, *J. Non-Newtonian*    220, 228
*Fluid Mech.*, **11**, 239 (1982).
**Rallison,** J. M., *Ann. Rev. Fluid Mech.*, **16**, 45 (1984).    160, 245, 246
**Ramahathan,** R., K. G. Blizard and D. G. Baird, *S. P. E., Techn. Pap.*, **33**, 1399    230
(1987).
**Ramos,** A. R., and R. E. Cohen, *Polym. Eng. Sci.*, **17**, 639 (1977).    234
**Ramos,** A. R., *Sc. D. thesis*, Massachusetts Inst. Technol., Cambridge, MA (1977).    234
**Ramos,** A. R., and R. E. Cohen, *Am. Chem. Soc., Adv. Chem. Ser.*, **176**, 237 (1979).    234
**Randall,** J. C., Ed., "NMR and Macromolecules", *A. C. S. Symp. Ser.*, Vol. 247,    105
Washington, D. C. (1984).
**Rao,** M. R., *Indian J. Phys.*, **14**, 109 (1940).    82
**Rao,** M. R., *J. Chem. Phys.*, **9**, 683 (1941); ibid. 14, 699 (1946).    82
**Ratke,** L., and W. K. Thieringer, *Acta Metall.*, **33**, 1793 (1985).    47
**Rätzsch,** M. T., and H. Kehlen, *J. Macromol. Sci.*, **A22**, 323 (1985a).    41
**Rätzsch,** M. T., H. Kehlen and D. Browarzik, *J. Macromol. Sci.*, **A22**, 1679,    41
(1985b).
**Rätzsch,** M. T., H. Kehlen and D. Thieme, *J. Macromol. Sci.*, **A23**, 811 (1986a).    41
**Rätzsch,** M. T., H. Kehlen, D. Browarzik, and M. Schirutschke, *J. Macromol. Sci.*,    41
**A23**, 1349 (1986b).
**Rätzsch,** M. T., and H. Kehlen, *Prog. Polym. Sci.*, **14**, 1 (1989).    41
**Rayleigh,** J. W. S., *Proc. London Math. Soc.*, **10**, 4 (1879).    182
**Razinskaya,** I. N., B. P. Shtarkman, L. I. Batuyeva, B. S. Tyves and M. N. Shlykova,    229
*Vysokomol. Soed.*, **A21**, 1860 (1979).
**Read,** B. E., and G. D. Dean, *The Determination of Dynamic Properties of Polymers*    83
*and Composites*, A. Hilger Ltd. Bristol (1978).
**Reault,** J., M. Sotton, C. Rabourdin and E. Robelin, *J. Physique*, **41**, 1459 (1980).    56

Citation page

**Reckinger,** C., F. B.C. Larbi and J. Rault, *J. Macromol. Sci., Phys.*, **B23**, 511 (1984–5).   73

**Reddy,** G. V., and R. P. Singh, *Acustica*, **46**, 229 (1980).   83

**Reddy,** G. V., S. Majumdar and R. P. Singh, *Acustica*, **47**, 343 (1981).   82, 83

**Reddy,** G. V., S. Chattopadhyay, Y. P. Singh and R. P. Singh, *Acustica*, **48**, 347   83
(1981).

**Ree,** M., *PhD thesis*, Univ. Massachusetts, Amherst (1987).   62, 74, 128, 203

**Ree,** M., T. Kyu and R. S. Stein, *J. Polym. Sci., Part B, Polym. Phys.*, **25**, 105   62
(1987).

**Reed,** M. C., *Mod. Plast.*, **27**, 117 (1949).   31

**Rehage,** G., and W. Brochard, in *The Physics of Glassy Polymers*, R. N. Haward,   93
Ed., Appl. Sci., Publ. Ltd., London (1973).

**Reich,** S., *Phys. Lett.*, **114A**, 90 (1986).   31, 45

**Reiner,** M., *J. Rheol.*, **1**, 250 (1930); ibid., **2**, 337 (1931).   139

**Remizova,** A. A., S. A. Kuptsov and F. G. Gilimyanov, *Plast. Massy*, **4**, 12 (1983).   58

**Rezanova,** N. M., and M. V. Tsebrenko, *Kampoz. Polym. Materialy*, **11**, 47 (1981).   173, 213, 229

**Riedl,** B., and R. E. Prud'homme, NRCC/IMRI symposium *"Polyblends-'84"*,   57, 84
Boucherville, Que., Canada, April 17, 1984; *Polym. Eng. Sci.*, **24**, 1291 (1984).

**Riedl,** B., and R. E. Prud'homme, *J. Polym. Sci., Polym. Phys.*, **B24**, 2565 (1986).   65, 92

**Riess,** G., M. Schilienger and S. Marti, *J. Macromol. Sci., Phys.*, **B17**, 355 (1980).   116

**Rietveld,** B. J., *Br. Polym. J.*, **6**, 181 (1974).   71

**Rim,** P. B., *PhD thesis*, Pennsylvania State Univ., Philadelphia (1983).   84, 85

**Ritter,** J., *Appl. Polym. Symp.*, **15**, 239 (1971).   156

**Rizzo,** G., G. Spadaro, D. Acierno and E. Calderaro, *Radiat. Phys. Chem.*, **21**, 349   126, 127
(1983).

**Robelin,** E., F. Rousseaux, M. Lemonnier and R. Rault, *J. Phys.*, **41**, 1469 (1980).   56

**Robeson,** L. M., and A. B. Furtek, *J. Appl. Polym. Sci.*, **23**, 645 (1979).   241

**Robeson,** L. M., in *Polymer Compatibility and Incompatibility* K. Solc (Ed.), Har-   65, 112, 117, 129
wood Acad. Publ., New York, (1980).

**Robeson,** L. M., W. F. Hale and C. N. Merriam, *Macromolecules*, **14**, 1644 (1981).   101

**Robeson,** L. M., *J. Appl. Polym. Sci.*, **30**, 4081 (1985).   127

**Robeson,** L. M., private communications (1989).   65, 117

**Roche,** E. J., and E. L. Thomas, *Polymer*, **22**, 333 (1981).   114, 117

**Rodriguez-Parada,** J. M., and V. Percec, *J. Polym. Sci., Polym. Chem. Ed.*, **24**, 579   65, 99, 100, 128
(1986).

**Rodriguez-Parada,** J. M., and V. Percec, *Macromolecules*, **19**, 55 (1986).   65, 99, 128

**Roe,** R.-J., and W.-Ch. Zin, *Macromolecules*, **17**, 189 (1984).   41, 67, 72

**Roe,** R.-J., *Polym. Eng. Sci.*, **24**, 1103 (1985).   41

**Roerdink,** E., and G. Challa, *Polymer*, **19**, 173 (1978); ibid. **21**, 1161 (1980).   31, 67, 68, 85

**Roland,** C. M., *J. Polym. Sci., Part B Polym. Phys.*, **26**, 839 (1988).   149, 171, 173, 234

**Romankevich,** O. V., T. I. Zhila, S. E. Zabello, N. A. Sklyar and S. Ya. Frenkel,   180, 216
*Vysokomol. Soed.*, **A24**, 2282 (1982).

**Romankevich,** O. V., and S. Ya. Frenkel, *Kompoz. Polim. Mater.*, **14**, 6 (1982).   214

**Romankevich,** O. V., T. I. Zhila, N. A. Sklyar and S. E. Zabello, *Khim. Tekhnol.*   213
*(Kiev)*, 1, 9 (1983).

**Romankevich,** O. V., K. V. Yakovlev, S. E. Zabello, T. I. Zhila and V. S. Rudchuk,   211
*Khim. Volokna*, **1**, 21 (1984 a).

**Romankevich,** O. V., N. P. Suprun and S. Ya. Frenkel, *Vysokomol. Soed.*, **A26**, 748   211, 212
(1984b).

**Roming,** K. D., and H. J.M. Hanley, *Intl. J. Thermophys.*, **7**, 877 (1986).   177

**Ronca,** G., and T. P. Russell, *Macromolecules*, **18**, 665 (1985).   121

**Roscoe,** R., *Brit. J. Appl. Phys.*, **3**, 267 (1952).   154

**Rosenquist,** N. R., U. S. Pat. 4,335,032 to General Electric Co., Jun. 15, 1982.   207

**Rosovizky,** V. F., M. Ilavsky, J. Hrouz, K. Dusek and Yu. S. Lipatov, *J. Appl.*   240
*Polym. Sci.*, **24**, 1007 (1979).

**Rostami,** S., and D. J. Walsh, *Macromolecules*, **17**, 315 (1984); ibid., **18**, 1228   42, 66, 67, 87, 129
(1985).

**Rouse,** P. E. Jr., *J. Chem. Phys.*, **21**, 1272 (1953).   143

Citation page

**Rowlinson,** J. S., and F. L. Swinton, *Liquids and Liquid Mixtures*, Butterwords Sci.,    246
London, (1982).

**Rubinstein,** M., E. Helfand and D. S. Pearson, *Macromolecules*, **20**, 822 (1987).    191

**Rudin,** A., D. A. Loucks and J. M. Goldwasser, *Polym. Eng. Sci.*, **20**, 741 (1980).    126, 128

**Rudin,** A., S. Nam, A. T. Worm and J. E. Blacklock, *S. P.E. Techn. Pap.*, **32**, 1154    210
(1986).

**Rummens,** F. H.A., *J. Chim. Phys.*, **72**, 448 (1975); *Chem. Phys. Lett.*, **31**, 596    110
(1975); *Can. J. Chem.*, **54**, 254 (1976).

**Rummens,** F. H.A., and F. H. Mouritz, *Can. J. Chem.*, **55**, 302 (1977).    110

**Rumscheidt,** F. D., and S. G. Mason, *J. Colloid. Sci.*, **16**, 210 (1961).    164

**Runt,** J., I. R. Harrison and S. Dobson, *J. Macromol. Sci. Phys.*, **B17**, 99 (1980).    56

**Ruoff,** M., H.-G. Fritz and K. Geiger, *Kunststoffe*, **77**, 480 (1987).    210

**Russell,** T. P., *Ph.D. thesis*, Univ. Massachusetts, Amherst (1979).    73, 74

**Russell,** T. P., and R. S. Stein, *J. Polym. Sci., Polym. Phys.*, **20**, 1593 (1982); ibid.,    72
**21**, 999 (1983).

**Rutgers,** R., *Rheol. Acta*, **2**, 305 (1962).    152, 154, 155

**Rutkowska,** M., and A. Eisenberg, *Macromolecules*, **17**, 821 (1984).    126, 128

**Ryan,** Ch. L. Jr., *PhD thesis*, Univ. Massachusetts, Amherst (1979).    89, 94, 98, 99, 100

**Rybnikar,** F., *J. Appl. Polym. Sci.*, **30**, 1949 (1985).    115


**Sadova,** L. P., B. V. Yarlykov, M. L. Kerber, M. S. Akutin, T. I. Sogolova and T. V.    207
Babkina, *Izv. Vuz, Khim. Khim. Tekhn.*, **4**, 540 (1977).

**Sadrmohaghegh,** C., G. Scott and E. Setoudeh, *Europ. Polym. J.*, **19**, 81 (1983).    124, 125

**Saeki,** S., J. C. Holste and D. C. Bonner, *J. Polym. Sci., Polym. Phys. Ed.*, **19**, 307    88
(1981).

**Saeki,** S., J. M.G. Cowie and I. J. McEwen, *Polymer*, **24**, 60 (1983).    98, 101, 102

**Saeki,** S., S. Tsubotani, H. Kominami, M. Tsubokawa and T. Yamaguchi, *J. Polym.*    88
*Sci., Polym. Phys. Ed.*, **24**, 325 (1986).

**Saito,** H., Y. Fujita and T. Inoue, *Polym. J.*, **19**, 405 (1987).    31, 65, 112

**Saito,** Y., *Nihon Reor. Gakk.*, **10**, 123, 128, 135 (1982).    225

**Sakanishi,** A., and Y. Takano, *Jap. J. Appl. Phys.*, **13**, 882 (1974).    162

**Sakellarides,** S. L., and A. J. McHugh, *Rheol. Acta*, **26**, 64 (1987).    231

**Sakiadis,** B. C., and J. C. Coates, Louisiana State Univ., Eng. Experim. Station,    82
Bull. No. 46, 1 (1954).

**Salager,** J. L., M. Minana-Perez, J. M. Anderez, J. L. Grosso and C. I. Rojas, *J.*    166
*Disp. Sci. Technol.*, **4**, 161 (1983).

**Sammut,** P., and L. A. Utracki, IUPAC Working Party No. 4.2.1. Meeting, Düssel-    196
dorf, Nov. 3–6, 1986 a.

**Sammut,** P., and L. A. Utracki, *Rapport to VAMAS TWP-PB*, March, 1986 b.    197, 198, 199, 200

**Sammut,** P., and L. A. Utracki, IUPAC W. P. No. 4.2.1. Meeting, Montreal, 1 - 4    226, 227, 233
Nov. 1987.

**Sanchez,** I. C., Ch. 3 in *Polymer Blends*, D. R. Paul and S. Newman, Eds., Academic    42
Press, New York (1978).

**Sanchez,** I. C., and R. H. Lacombe, *J. Phys. Chem.*, **80**, 2352 (1976); *J. Polym. Sci.,*    34
*Polym. Lett. Ed.*, **15**, 71 (1977).

**Sanchez,** I. C., *Ann. Rev. Mater. Sci.*, **13**, 387 (1983).    31, 34, 43, 120

**Sanchez,** I. C., NRCC/IMRI symposium *"Polyblends-'83"*, Montreal, April 12,    34, 120
1983; *Polym. Eng. Sci.*, **24**, 79 (1984); ibid., **24**, 598 (1984).

**Sano,** M., M. Kawaguchi, Y.-L. Chen, R. J. Skarlupka, T. Chang, G. Zografi and H.    123
Yu, *Rev. Sci., Instrum.*, **57**, 1158 (1986).

**Santamaria,** A., M. E. Munoz, J. J. Pena and P. Remiro, *Angew. Makromol. Chem.*,    206, 216
**134**, 63 (1985).

**Santamaria,** A., and J. L. White, *J. Appl. Polym. Sci.*, **31**, 209 (1986).    180

**Sato,** T., and C. C. Han, *J. Chem. Phys.*, **88**, 2057 (1988).    46

**Sauer,** B. B., H. Yu, C.-F. Tien and D. F. Hager, *Macromolecules*, **20**, 393 (1987).    123

**Saunders,** P. R., D. M. Stern, S. F. Kurath, C. Sakoonkim, and J. D. Ferry, *J. Col-*    232
*loid. Sci.*, **14**, 222 (1959).

Citation page

**Schaaf,** P., B. Lotz and J. C. Wittman, *Polymer*, **28**, 193 (1987).    63

**Schaefer,** J., M. D. Sefcik, E. O. Stejskal and R. A. McKay, *Macromolecules*, **14**,    105, 109
188 (1981).

**Schalek,** E., and A. Szegvary, *Kolloid Z.*, **32**, 318 (1923).    135

**Schelten,** J., G. D. Wignall, D. G.H. Ballard and G. W. Longnian, *Polymer*, **18**,    78
1111 (1977).

**Scheraga,** H. A., *J. Am. Chem. Soc.*, **23**, 1526 (1955).    158, 160

**Schichtel,** T. E., and K. Binder, *Macromolecules*, **20**, 1671 (1987).    43

**Schlund,** B., and M. Lambla, *Polym. Compos.*, **6**, 272 (1985).    11

**Schlund,** B., and L. A. Utracki, *Polym. Eng. Sci.*, **27**, 359, 380 (1987 a,b).    201–203,    219–222,
229, 242

**Schlund,** B., and L. A. Utracki, NRCC/IMRI Symposium *"Polyblends-'87"*,    192, 193, 219–221
Boucherville, Que. Canada, 28–29 April, 1987; *Polym. Eng. Sci.*, **27**, 1523
(1987 c).

**Schmidt,** L. R., *J. Appl. Polym. Sci.*, **23**, 2463 (1979).    195

**Schmitt,** B. J., *Angew. Chem.*, **91**, 286 (1979).    74, 77

**Schmitt,** B. J., *Angew. Chem., Int. Ed. Engl.*, **18**, 273 (1979).    74, 77

**Schmitt,** B. J., R. G. Kirste and J. Jelenic, *Makromol. Chem.*, **181**, 1655 (1980).    74, 77

**Schneider,** H. A., H.-J. Cantow, U. Massen and H. Northfleet-Neto, *Polym. Bull.*,    128
**7**, 263 (1982).

**Schneider,** H. A., H.-J. Cantow, P. Lutz and H. Northfleet-Neto, *Makromol. Chem.*    128
*Suppl.*, **8**, 89 (1984).

**Schowalter,** W. R., C. E. Chaffey and H. Brenner, *J. Coll. Interf. Sci.*, **26**, 152    162
(1968).

**Schuch,** H., and G. Wassmuth, Intl. Conf. Toughening Plast., London, July, 1985.    212

**Schuyer,** J., *J. Polym. Sci.*, **36**, 475 (1959).    82

**Schwahn,** D., K. Mortensen and H. Yee-Madeira, *Phys. Rev. Lett.*, **58**, 1544 (1987).    73

**Schwartz,** S. S., and S. H. Goodman, *Plastics Materials and Processes*, Van Nostrand    4
Publ. Co., New York (1982).

**Scott,** C. D., *Nature*, **188**, 908 (1960).    154

**Sebastian,** D. H., and Y.-T. Chen, *J. Elastom. Plast.*, **15**, 135 (1983).    224

**Semerak,** S. N., and C. W. Frank, *Macromolecules*, **14**, 443, (1981); **17**, 1148    79, 82
(1984).

**Semerak,** S. N., *PhD thesis*, Stanford Univ., CA (1983).    79, 82

**Seymour,** R. B., Ed., *History of Polymer Science and Technology*, M. Dekker, New    4
York (1982).

**Shah,** V. S., J. D. Keitz, D. R. Paul and J. W. Barlow, *J. Appl. Polym. Sci.*, **32**, 3863    40
(1986).

**Shao-Cheng,** Ch., *PhD thesis*, Univ. Maryland (1981).    67, 68, 85, 86, 98, 104

**Sharma,** B. K., *Acustica*, **48**, 118 (1981).    82

**Shaw,** M. T., *J. Appl. Polym. Sci.*, **18**, 449 (1974).    31

**Shaw,** M. T., *Rheol. Acta*, **20**, 231 (1981).    220

**Shaw,** M. T., NRCC/IMRI mini-symposium, *"Polyblends-'81"*, Montreal, April 28,    69, 70
1981; *Polym. Eng. Sci.*, **22**, 115 (1982).

**Shaw,** M. T., and R. H. Somani, *Polym. Eng. Sci.*, **24**, 601 (1984).    69, 70, 229

**Shaw,** M. T., in *Polymer Blends and Mixtures*, D. J. Walsh, J. S. Higgins and A.    114
Maconnachie, Eds., NATO Series E No. 89, Martinns Nijhoff Publ., Dordrecht
(1985).

**Shaw,** S., and R. P. Singh, *Europ. Polym. J.*, **23**, 547 (1987).    83

**Shenoy,** A. V., D. R. Saini and V. M. Nadkarni, *Intl. J. Polym. Mater.*, **10**, 213    151
(1984).

**Sherman,** P., in *Rheology of Emulsions*, P. Sherman, Ed., Pergamon Press, Oxford    135, 160
(1963).

**Sherman,** P., Ed., *Rheology of Emulsions*, Pergamon Press, Oxford (1963).    135

**Sherman,** P., in *Emulsion Science*, P. Sherman, Ed., Academic Press, London    135, 160
(1968).

**Sherman,** P., Ed., *Emulsion Science*, Academic Press, London (1968).    135

Citation page

**Sherwood,** C. H., F. P. Price and R. S. Stein, *J. Polym. Sci., Polym. Symp.*, **63**, 77    55
(1978).

**Shiah,** T. Y.-J., and H. Morawetz, *Macromolecules*, **17**, 792 (1984).    81

**Shih,** C. K., *Polym. Eng. Sci.*, **16**, 198 (1976).    209

**Shih,** C. K., in *Science and Technology of Polymer Processing*, N. P. Suh and N.-H.    209
Sung, Eds., MIT Press, Cambridge, MA (1979).

**Shih,** K. S., and C. L. Beatty, *A. C. S. Org. Coat. Plast. Chem. Div. Prepr.*, **45**, 65    66
(1981).

**Shilov,** V. V., V. V. Tsukruk and Yu. S. Lipatov, *Vysokomol. Soed.*, **A26**, 1347    118, 123
(1984).

**Shiomi,** T., K. Kohno, K. Yoneda, T. Tomita, M. Mia and K. Imai, *Macromolecules*,    88
**18**, 414 (1985).

**Shiomi,** T., F. E. Karasz and W. J. MacKnight, *Macromolecules*, **19**, 2274 (1986).    40

**Shultz,** A. R., and A. L. Young, *Macromolecules*, **13**, 663 (1980).    93, 243

**Shyu,** S. S., and G. P. Hsu, *Hua Hsueh*, **42**, 1 (1984).    240

**Siegfried,** D. L., *Ph.D. thesis*, Lehigh Univ., Bethlehem, PA (1980).    118

**Siegfried,** D. L., D. A. Thomas and L. H. Sperling, *J. Appl. Polym. Sci.*, **26**, 177    118
(1981); *Polym. Eng. Sci.*, **21**, 39 (1981).

**Siggia,** E. D., *Phys. Rev.*, **A20**, 595 (1979).    45, 47

**Silvestre,** C., S. Cimmino, E. Martuscelli, F. E. Karasz and W. J. MacKnight, *Poly-*    129
*mer*, **28**, 1190 (1987).

**Simha,** R., *J. Phys. Chem.*, **44**, 25 (1940); *J. Chem. Phys.*, **13**, 188 (1945).    158

**Simha,** R., *J. Res. Nat. Bur. Stand.*, **42**, 409 (1949); *J. Colloid Sci.*, **5**, 386 (1950).    158

**Simha,** R., *J. Appl. Phys.*, **23**, 1020 (1952).    152, 247

**Simha,** R., and R. F. Boyer, *J. Chem. Phys.*, **37**, 1003 (1962).    98

**Simha,** R., and T. Somcynsky, *Macromolecules*, **2**, 342 (1969).    38, 146, 148, 233

**Simha,** R., *Macromolecules*, **10**, 1025 (1977).    99

**Simha,** R., *Polym. Eng. Sci.*, **22**, 74 (1982).    148

**Simha,** R., J. C. Curro and R. E. Robertson, *Polym. Eng. Sci.*, **24**, 1071 (1984 a).    38

**Simha,** R., and R. K. Jain, NRCC/IMRI symposium *"Polyblends-'84"*, Boucherville,    38, 148
Que., Canada, April 17th, 1984; *Polym. Eng. Sci.*, **24**, 1284 (1984 b).

**Singh,** R. P., G. V. Reddy, S. Majumdar and Y. P. Singh, in *Rheology*, G. Astarita,    83
G. Marrucci and L. Nicolais, Eds., Plenum Press, New York, **2**, 309 (1980).

**Singh,** V. B., and D. J. Walsh, *J. Macromol. Sci., Phys.*, **B25**, 65 (1986).    87

**Singh,** Y. P., and R. P. Singh, *Europ. Polym. J.*, **19**, 529 (1983 a); ibid., **19**, 535    83, 84, 152
(1983 b); ibid., **20**, 201 (1984 a).

**Singh,** Y. P., and R. P. Singh, *J. Appl. Polym. Sci.*, **29**, 1653 (1984 b).    83, 84, 152

**Sivashinsky,** N., T. J. Moon and D. S. Soong, *J. Macromol. Sci., Phys.*, **B22**, 213    169
(1983).

**Sjoerdsma,** S. D., J. Dalmolen, A. C. A. M. Bleijenberg and D. Heikens, *Polymer*,    242
**21**, 1469 (1980).

**Slagowski,** E. L., E. P. Chang and J. J. Tkacik, *Polym. Eng. Sci.*, **21**, 513 (1981).    85, 86, 98, 104

**Smith,** B. J., and R. G. Kirste, Iupac International Symposium on Macromolecular    74
Chemistry, Tashkent 1978, Abstracts of short communications, Vol. 7, p. 24.

**Smith,** P., and A. Eisenberg, *J. Polym. Sci., Polym. Phys. Ed.*, **21**, 223 (1983).    126, 128

**Smith,** P., M. Hara and A. Eisenberg in *Current Topics in Polymer Science*, R. M.    65, 118, 128, 194
Ottenbrite, L. A. Utracki and S. Inoue, Eds., Hanser Verlag, München (1987).

**Smith,** T. L., *J. Paint Technol.*, **44**, 71 (1972).    162

**Smoluchowski,** M., *Kolloid-Z.*, **18**, 190 (1916).    154

**Snyder,** H. L., and P. Meakin, *A. C. S. Polym. Prepr.*, **24**, 411 (1983 a).    46, 48, 67, 70

**Snyder,** H. L., and P. Meakin, *J. Chem. Phys.*, **79**, 5588 (1983 b).    46, 67, 70

**Snyder,** H. L., P. Meakin and S. Reich, *J. Chem. Phys.*, **78**, 3334 (1983 a).    46, 67, 70

**Snyder,** H. L., P. Meakin and S. Reich, *Macromolecules*, **16**, 757 (1983 b).    46, 67, 70

**Snyder,** H. L., and P. Meakin, *J. Polym. Sci., Polym., Symp.*, **73**, 217 (1985).    47

**Somani,** R. H., *M. Sc. thesis*, Univ. Connecticut (1981).    69, 70

**Somani,** R. H., and M. T. Shaw, *Macromolecules*, **14**, 886, 1549 (1981).    69, 70

**Soong,** D. S., *Rubber Chem. Technol.*, **54**, 641 (1981).    140

Citation page

**Southern,** J. H., and R. L. Ballman, *J. Polym. Sci., Polym. Phys. Ed.*, **13**, 863 (1975).  181

**Speed,** C. S., *Plast. Eng.*, **38**, 39 (1982).  204

**Sperling,** L. H., *Mod. Plast.*, **58**, 74 (1981).  127

**Sperling,** L. H., *Interpenetrating Polymer Networks and Related Materials*, Plenum  118
Press, New York (1981).

**Sperling,** L. H., and J. M. Widmaier, *Polym. Eng. Sci.*, **23**, 693 (1983).  118

**Sperling,** L. H., J. M. Widmaier, J. K. Yeo and J. Michel, *Polym. Sci. Technol.*, **20**,  118
191·(1983).

**Sperling,** L. H., *Polym. Eng. Sci.*, **24**, 1 (1984).  74

**Spriggs,** T. W., *Chem. Eng. Sci.*, **20**, 931 (1965).  194

**Starita,** J. M., *Trans. Soc. Rheol.*, **16**, 339 (1972).  230

**Starkweather,** H. W. Jr., *J. Appl. Polym. Sci.*, **25**, 139 (1980).  124

**Starkweather,** H. W. Jr., *Macromolecules*, **13**, 892 (1980).  59

**Stein,** R. S., R. S. Finkelstein, D. Y. Yoon and C. Chang, *J. Polym. Sci., Symp.*, **46**,  232
15 (1974).

**Stein,** R. S., G. Hadziioannou, M. Wai, J. Gilmer, F. Herold and B. Morra, *A. C.S.*  73, 74
*Org. Coat. Plast. Chem. Div. Prepr.*, **45**, 80 (1981).

**Stejskal,** E. O., J. Schaefer, M. D. Sefcik and R. A. McKay, *Macromolecules*, **14**,  105, 109
275 (1981).

**Strobl,** G. R., J. T. Bendler, R. P. Kambour and A. R. Shultz, *Macromolecules*, **19**,  31, 37
2683 (1986).

**Stroeks,** A., and E. Nies, NRCC/IMRI symposium *"Polyblends-'88"*, Boucherville,  38, 39, 42
Que., Canada, April 5–6, 1988; *Polym. Eng. Sci.*, **28**, 1347 (1988).

**Struglinski,** M. J. and W. W. Graessley, *Macromolecules*, **18**, 2630 (1985).  171

**Suess,** M., J. Kressler and H. W. Kammer, *Polymer*, **28**, 957 (1987).  40

**Suprun,** N. P., and O. V. Romankevich, *Khim. Tekhnol. (Kiev)*, **2**, 29 (1984).  152, 211

**Suresh,** R., Y. P. Singh, G. D. Nigam and R. P. Singh, *Europ. Polym. J.*, **20**, 739  83
(1984).

**Suzuki,** Y., T. Fujimoto, S. Tsunoda and K. Shibayama, *J. Macromol. Sci., Phys.*,  240
**B17**, 787 (1980).

**Suzuki,** Y., Y. Miyamoto, H. Miyaji and K. Asai, *J. Polym. Sci., Polym. Lett. Ed.*,  42
**20**, 563 (1982).

**Szulenyi,** F., and J. Mokry, *Plast. Kauch.*, **20**, 299 (1983).  129


**Takahashi,** M., S. Kinoshita and T. Nose, *Polym. Prepr. Jpn.*, **34**, 2421 (1985).  31

**Takahashi,** M., H. Horiuchi, S. Kinoshita and T. Nose, *J. Phys. Soc. Jpn.*, **55**, 2687  31
(1986).

**Takayanagi,** M., S. Uemura and S. Minami, *J. Polym. Sci.*, **8**, 2147 (1964).  236, 240, 242

**Takayanagi,** M., and K. Goto, *J. Appl. Polym. Sci.*, **29**, 2547 (1984).  241

**Talstoguzov,** V. B., A. I. Mzhel'Sky and V. Ya. Gulov, *Coll. Polym. Sci.*, **252**, 124  166
(1974).

**Tanaka,** H., and T. Nishi, *J. Fac. Eng. Univ. Tokyo*, **A–21**, 36 (1983).  60

**Tanaka,** H., and T. Nishi, *Phys. Rev. Lett.*, **55**, 1102 (1985).  63

**Tanaka,** H., T. Ikeda and T. Nishi, *Appl. Phys. Lett.*, **48**, 393 (1986).  60

**Tanaka,** H., and T. Nishi, *J. Appl. Phys.*, **59**, 1488 (1986); *J. Chem. Phys.*, **85**, 6197  57, 60
(1986).

**Tanaka,** H., and T. Nishi, *Phys. Rev. Lett.*, **59**, 692 (1987).  45

**Tanner,** R. I., *J. Polym. Sci.*, **A–2**, 8, 2067 (1970).  216

**Taylor,** G. I., *Proc. Roy. Soc.*, **A138**, 41 (1932); ibid., **A146**, 501 (1934).  160, 162, 182

**Teh,** J. W., A. Rudin and H. P. Schreiber, *Plast. Rubb. Proc. Appl.*, **4**, 149, 157  222
(1984).

**Tekely,** P., *Polimery*, **27**, 137 (1982).  105

**Tekely,** P., F. Laupretre and L. Monnerie, *Polymer*, **26**, 1081 (1985).  61

**ten Brinke,** G., A. Eshuis, E. Roerding and G. Challa, *Macromolecules*, **14**, 867  31, 67, 68
(1981).

**ten Brinke,** G., E. Roerdink and G. Challa, in *Polymer Compatibility and Incompati-*  31, 67
*bility*, K. Šolc, Ed., Harwood Acad. Publ., New York (1982).

Citation page

**ten Brinke,** G., F. E. Karasz and W. J. MacKnight, *Macromolecules*, **16**, 1827 (1983).    40, 98

**ten Brinke,** G., and F. E. Karasz, *Macromolecules*, **17**, 815 (1984).    39

**Teyssie,** Ph., R. Fayt and R. Jerome, *A. C.S. Polym. Materials Sci. Eng. Div. Preprints*, **58**, 622 (1988).    16

**Thomas,** D. G., *J. Colloid Sci.*, **20**, 267 (1965).    114, 152, 153, 154

**Thomas,** D. A., *J. Polym. Sci., Polym. Symp.*, **60**, 189 (1977).    114

**Thornton,** B. A., R. G. Villasenor and B. Maxwell, *J. Appl. Polym. Sci.*, **25**, 653 (1980).    98, 128, 214, 217

**Ting,** S.-P., *PhD thesis*, Polytechnic Inst. New York (1980).    84, 98, 101, 112

**Ting,** S.-P., E. M. Pearce and T. K. Kwei, *J. Polym. Sci., Polym. Lett. Ed.*, **18**, 201 (1980).    86, 98, 112

**Tirrell,** M., *Fluid Phas. Equil.*, **30**, 367 (1986).    174, 176

**Tomita,** M., K. Takano and T. G.M. van de Ven, *J. Coll. Interf. Sci.*, **92**, 367 (1983).    136

**Tomita,** M., and T. G.M. van de Ven, *J. Coll. Interf. Sci.*, **99**, 374 (1984).    136

**Tomotika,** S., *Proc. Roy. Soc.*, **150**, 322 (1935).    45, 180, 182

**Tompa,** H., *Polymer Solutions*, Butterwords Sci. Publ., London (1956).    30, 66

**Trapeznikov,** A. A., G. G. Petrzhik and T. I. Korotina, *Dokl. Akad. Nauk*, **176**, 378 (1967).    136

**Traugott,** T. D., J. W. Barlow and D. R. Paul, *J. Appl. Polym. Sci.*, **28**, 2947 (1983).    124

**Tree,** D. A., and A. J. McHugh, *Intl. Polym. Proces.*, **2**, 223 (1988).    204, 214, 231

**Tremblay,** B., and L. A. Utracki, Polymer Processing Society 4th Annual Meeting, Orlando, FA, 8 to 11 May (1988 a).    221, 228

**Tremblay,** B., and L. A. Utracki, *A. C.S. Polym. Mater. Sci. Eng.*, **58**, 708 (1988 b).    221, 228

**Trostyanskaya,** E. B., M. B. Zemskov and O. Ya. Mikhasenok, *Plast. Massy*, **11**, 28 (1983).    125, 126

**Trouton,** F. T., *Proc. Roy. Soc.*, **A77**, 426 (1906).    135

**Tsai,** S. W., U. S. Dept. Commerce Rep. No. AD834,851 (1968).    242

**Tsebrenko,** M. V., A. V. Yudin, T. I. Ablazova and G. V. Vinogradov, *Polymer*, **17**, 831 (1976).    186

**Tsebrenko,** M. V., T. I. Ablazova, G. V. Vinogradov and A. V. Yudin, *Vysokomol. Soed.*, **A18**, 420 (1976).    186

**Tsebrenko,** M. V., A. I. Benzar, A. V. Yudin and G. V. Vinogradov, *Vysokomol. Soed.*, **A21**, 830 (1979).    173, 186, 216, 229

**Tsebrenko,** M. V., N. M. Rezanova and G. V. Vinogradov, *Polym. Eng. Sci.*, **20**, 1023 (1980).    214

**Tsebrenko,** M. V., N. M. Rezanova and G. V. Vinogradov, *Nov. Reol. Polim., 11th Mater. Vses. Simp. Reol.*, **2**, 136 (1982).    186

**Tsebrenko,** M. V., N. M. Rezanova and I. N. Siplivets, *Vysokomol. Soed.*, **B27**, 544 (1985).    231

**Tsenoglou,** C., *A. C.S. Polym. Prepr.*, **28(2)**, 185 (1987).    171

**Tsenoglou,** C., and S. Bhakuni, *A. C.S. Polym. Prepr.*, **28(2)**, 187 (1987).    171

**Tsenoglou,** C., *PhD thesis*, Northwestern Univ., Evanston, IL (1985).    172

**Tsuchida,** E., Y. Osada and H. Ohno, *J. Macromol. Sci., Phys.*, **B17**, 683 (1980).    65

**Tsujita,** Y., K. Iwakiri, T. Kinoshita, A. Takizawa and W. J. MacKnight, *J. Polym. Sci., Part B*, **25**, 415 (1987).    174

**Tung,** M. A., and L. J. Jones, *Scanning Electron Microscopy*, **3**, 523 (1981).    117

**Turnbull,** D., and J. C. Fisher, *J. Chem. Phys.*, **17**, 71 (1949).    54

**Ubrich,** J. M., F. B.C. Larbi, J. L. Halary, L. Monnerie, B. J. Bauer and C. C. Han, *Macromolecules*, **19**, 810 (1986).    31

**Utracki,** L. A., *J. Appl. Polym. Sci.*, **6**, 399 (1962).    34, 35, 66

**Utracki,** L. A., Gulf Oil Corp., *Internal Reports* (1970); (1971).    156, 161

**Utracki,** L. A., *J. Polym. Sci., A–1*, **10**, 2115 (1972).    127

**Utracki,** L. A., *J. Coll. Interf. Sci.*, **42**, 185 (1973).    136, 161, 165, 166, 184

**Utracki,** L. A., *J. Macromol. Sci. Phys.*, **B10**, 477 (1974).    150, 233

Citation page

**Utracki,** L. A., Z. Bakerdjian and M. R. Kamal, *Trans. Soc. Rheol.*, **19**, 173 (1975).   139, 140, 216

**Utracki,** L. A., M. R. Kamal and Z. Bakerdjian, *J. Appl. Polym. Sci.*, **19**, 487 (1975).   139

**Utracki,** L. A., *J. Macromol. Sci., Phys.*, **B18**, 731 (1980).   150, 152, 233

**Utracki,** L. A., and R. Simha, *J. Rheol.*, **25**, 329 (1981).   152, 233

**Utracki,** L. A., G. L. Bata, V. Tan and M. R. Kamal, *Preprints of the 2nd World Congress of Chemical Engineering*, Montreal, Quebec, October 5, 1981, **6**, 428 (1981).   173, 213, 214

**Utracki,** L. A., and B. Fisa, *Polym. Compos.*, **3**, 193 (1982).   152, 153

**Utracki,** L. A., and G. L. Bata, Proceedings, CANPLAST meeting, Montreal, October 25, 1981; *Matériaux Techn.*, **70**, 223, 290 (1982).   128, 160, 214

**Utracki,** L. A., A. Catani, G. L. Bata, M. R. Kamal and V. Tan, *J. Appl. Polym. Sci.*, **27**, 1913 (1982).   128, 213

**Utracki,** L. A., *Polym. Eng. Sci.*, **22**, 1166 (1982a).   15, 179

**Utracki,** L. A., and M. R. Kamal, NRCC/IMRI symposium *"Polyblends-'81"*, Montreal, April 1981; *Polym. Eng. Sci.*, **22**, 96 (1982).   138, 160, 173

**Utracki,** L. A., and G. L. Bata, in *Polymer Alloys III*, D. Klemper and Frisch, K. C., Eds., Plenum Press, New York (1982).   160, 213

**Utracki,** L. A., *Polym., Eng. Sci.*, **22**, 81 (1982b).   150, 152, 233

**Utracki,** L. A., and J. Lara, *"Table Ronde Internationale Ecoulement Elongationnels"*, La Bresse, France, Jan. 23–28, 1983.   220

**Utracki,** L. A., *Proceedings S. P.E. NATEC,* Bal Harbour, Florida, October 25–27, 1982; *Polym. Eng. Sci.*, **23**, 602 (1983 a).   146, 160, 173

**Utracki,** L. A., *Canad. J. Chem. Eng.*, **61**, 753 (1983b).   146, 150

**Utracki,** L. A., *A. C.S. Polym. Prepr.*, **24(2)**, 113 (1983c).   146, 150

**Utracki,** L. A., *Polym. Eng. Sci.*, **23**, 446 (1983d).   146, 150

**Utracki,** L. A., *Rubber Chem. Technol.*, **57**, 507 (1984a).   136, 152, 158, 221

**Utracki,** L. A., A. M. Catani, J. Lara and M. R. Kamal; Proceedings of European Meeting on Polymer Processing and Properties, Capri, Italy, June 13–16, 1983; in *Polymer Processing and Properties*, G. Astarita and L. Nicolais, Eds., Plenum Press, New York (1984).   138, 201, 220, 221

**Utracki,** L. A., and M. M. Dumoulin, *Polym.-Plast. Technol. Eng.*, **23**, 193 (1984).   201

**Utracki,** L. A., and R. Gendron, *J. Rheol.*, **28**, 601 (1984).   201

**Utracki,** L. A., *Polym-Plast. Technol. Eng.*, **22**, 27 (1984b).   201, 231

**Utracki,** L. A., and J. A. Jukes, *J. Vinyl Technol.*, **6**, 85 (1984).   98

**Utracki,** L. A., in *Advances in Rheology*, B. Mena, A. Garcia-Rejon and C. Rangel-Nafaile, Eds., Univ. Natl. Autonom. Mexico, **3**, 567 (1984c).   201, 220

**Utracki,** L. A., M. R. Kamal and N. M. Al-Bastaki, *S. P.E. Techn. Pap.*, **30**, 417 (1984a).   159, 201, 219

**Utracki,** L. A., B. D. Favis and B. Fisa, NRCC/IMRI symposium *"Composites-'83"*, Boucherville, Que., Canada, Nov. 29, 1983; *Polym. Compos.*, **5**, 277 (1984b).   159, 221

**Utracki,** L. A., *Proceedings, 1984–International Chemical Congress of Pacific Basin Societies,* Honolulu, Hawaii, USA, Dec. 16–21, 1984d.   201

**Utracki,** L. A., 9th Intl. Congr. Rheology, Acapulco, Mexico, Oct. 8–13, 1984; *Advances in Rheology*, B. Mena, A. Garcia-Rejon and C. Rangel- Nafaile, Eds., Univ. Natl. Aut. Mexico Press, **3**, 467 (1984e).   150

**Utracki,** L. A., *Adv. Polym. Technol.*, **5**, 33 (1985a).   150, 215

**Utracki,** L. A., NRCC/IMRI symposium *"Modeling-'84"*, Boucherville, Que., Canada, Jan. 24, 1984; *Polym. Eng. Sci.*, **25**, 655 (1985b).   38, 39, 98, 146, 150

**Utracki,** L. A., and A. M. Catani, *Polym. Eng. Sci.*, **25**, 690 (1985).   201

**Utracki,** L. A., *Adv. Polym. Technol.*, **5**, 41 (1985c).   146, 150, 201, 202, 221–224

**Utracki,** L. A., *Polym. Compos.*, **7**, 274 (1986a).   146

**Utracki,** L. A., 36th annual CSCHE meeting, Sarnia, Ont., Canada, Oct. 5 to 8, 1986b.   146, 185, 210, 214

**Utracki,** L. A., M. M. Dumoulin and P. Toma, NRCC/IMRI symposium *"Polyblends-'85"*, Boucherville, Que., Canada, April 16, 1985; *Polym. Eng. Sci.*, **26**, 34 (1986).   114, 207–209, 212, 226, 229

Citation page

Utracki, L. A., *J. Rheol.*, **30**, 829 (1986c).    38, 39, 146, 147, 151
Utracki, L. A., and P. Sammut, VAMAS TWP-PB Meeting, Berlin, 13 April 1987.    198
Utracki, L. A., and A. Ghijsels, *Adv. Polym. Technol.*, **7**, 35 (1987).    150, 233
Utracki, L. A., and B. Schlund, *Polym. Eng. Sci.*, **27**, 367 (1987a).    144, 155, 172, 173, 190, 204, 211

Utracki, L. A., and B. Schlund, NRCC/IMRI symposium *"Polyblends-'87"*, Boucherville, Quebec, Canada, April 28–29, 1987; *Polym. Eng. Sci.*, **27**, 1512 (1987b).    144, 155, 172, 192, 201–203, 205, 207, 210, 211, 215, 217, 223

Utracki, L. A., Polymer Processing Society Regional Meeting, Buffalo, NY, 28–30 Sept., 1987b.    144, 207

Utracki, L. A., in *Current Topics in Polymer Science*, R. M. Ottenbrite, L. A. Utracki and S. Inoue, Eds., Hanser Publ., München, (1987a).    127, 131, 144, 152, 159, 160, 207

Utracki, L. A., P. Sammut and B. D. Favis, *S. P. E. Techn. Pap.*, **33**, 1343 (1987).    212
Utracki, L. A., *Intl. Polym. Process.*, **2**, 3 (1987b).    127
Utracki, L. A., C. S.Ch.E. 37th conference, Montreal, Que., Canada, 18–22 May, 1987c, p. 214–217.    127

Utracki, L. A., in *Rheological Measurements*, A. A. Collyer and D. W. Clegg, Eds., Elsevier Sci. Publ., London (1988).    127, 131, 140, 229

Utracki, L. A., and P. Sammut, NRCC/IMRI symposium *Polyblends-'88*, Boucherville, Que., Canada, 5–6 April, 1988,; *Polym. Eng. Sci.*, **28**, 1405 (1988).    196, 208, 237, 246

Utracki, L. A., in *Multiphase Polymeric Materials*, L. A. Utracki and R. A. Weiss, Eds., ACS Books, Washington DC, (1989).    131, 144, 201, 205, 210, 221

Utracki, L. A., and P. Sammut, 5th Annual Polym. Processing Soc. Meeting, Kyoto, Japan, April 11–14, 1989.    229


Vadhar, P., and T. Kyu, *Polym. Eng. Sci.*, **27**, 202 (1987).    202
Valenza, A., and F. P. La Mantia, *Intl. Polym. Proces.*, **2**, 220 (1988).    210
Valsamis, L. N., M. R. Kearney, S. S. Dagli, D. D. Merhta, and A. P. Plochocki, *S. P. E. Techn. Pap.*, **33**, 1316 (1987); Adv. Polym. Technol., 8, 115 (1988).    115, 229
van de Ven, T. G.M., NRCC/IMRI symposium, *"Composites-84"*, Boucherville, Que. Canada, November 20, 1984; *Polym. Compos.*, **6**, 209 (1985).    158
van der Reijden-Stolk, C., A. S. van Heel, J. Schut and J. van Dam, in *Integration of Fundamental Polymer Science and Technology–2*, P. J. Lemstra and L. A. Kleintjens, Eds., Elsevier Appl. Sci., Amsterman (1988).    186
van Gisbergen, J. G.M., J. I. Meijerink and N. Overbergh, 3rd Chem. Congress of North America, Toronto, Ont., Canada, June 5–10, 1988.    229
Van Krevelen, D. W., and P. J. Hoftyzer, *Properties of Polymers*, Elsevier Publ. Co., Amsterdam (1976).    83
Van Oene, H., and H. K. Plummer, *A. C.S. Org. Coat. Plast. Chem. Prepr.*, **37**, 498 (1977).    123
Van Oene, H., *J. Colloid. Interface Sci.*, **40**, 448 (1972).    183, 230
Vand, W., *Nature*, **155**, 364 (1954).    154
Varnell, D. F., J. P. Runt and M. M. Coleman, *Macromolecules*, **14**, 1350 (1981).    113
Varnell, D. F., and M. M. Coleman, *Polymer*, **22**, 1324 (1981).    112
Varnell, D. F., *PhD thesis*, Pennsylvania State Univ., University Park (1982).    112
Varnell, D. F., E. J. Moskala, P. C. Painter and M. M. Coleman, *Polym. Eng. Sci.*, **23**, 658 (1983a).    112
Varnell, D. F., J. P. Runt and M. M. Coleman, *Polymer*, **24**, 37 (1983b).    112
ver Strate, G., and W. Philippoff, *J. Polym. Sci., Polym. Lett.*, **12**, 267(1974).    177
Vesely, D., and H. Lindberg, *Inst. Phys. Conf. Ser.*, **61**, 7 (1982).    114
Vesely, D., and D. S. Finch, *Makromol. Chem., Macromol. Symp.*, **16**, 329 (1988).    117
Vinogradov, G. V., and A. Ya. Malkin, *Rheologia Polimerov*, Khimia, Moscow (1977).    146, 151
Vinogradov, G. V., N. P. Krasnikova, V. E. Dreval, E. V. Kotova, E. P. Plotnikova and Z. Pelzbauer, *Intern. J. Polym. Mater.*, **9**, 187 (1982).    184

Citation page

**Voigt-Martin,** I. G., K.-H. Leister, R. Rosenau, and R. Koningsveld, *J. Polym. Sci.,*    31, 45
*Polym. Phys. Ed.*, **24**, 723 (1986).

**Volkova,** A. V., *Nauch. Tr. Kursk. Gos. Pedagog. Inst.*, **214**, 104 (1981).    84

**Vonnegut,** B., *Rev. Sci. Instr.*, **13**, 6 (1942).    123


**Wagner,** C., *Z. Electrochem.*, **65**, 581 (1961).    47

**Wahrmund,** D. C., D. R. Paul and J. W. Barlow, *J. Appl. Polym. Sci.*, **22**, 2155    240
(1978).

**Walker,** J. S., and C. A. Vouse, in "Eight Symposium on Thermophysical Proper-    39
ties", J. V. Sengers Ed., *Am. Soc. Mech. Eng.*, **1**, 411 (1982).

**Walsh,** D. J., and J. G. McKeown, *Polymer*, **21**, 1330, 1335 (1980).    67, 90, 91, 103

**Walsh,** D. J., S. Lainghe and Ch. Zhikuan, *Polymer*, **22**, 1005 (1981).    66, 67

**Walsh,** D. J., J. S. Higgins and Ch. Zhikuan, *Polymer*, **23**, 336 (1982).    31, 66

**Walsh,** D. J., J. S. Higgins and S. Rostami, *Macromolecules*, **16**, 388 (1983a).    66, 67

**Walsh,** D. J., J. S. Higgins, S. Rostami and K. Weeraperuma, *Macromolecules*, **16**,    66, 67
391 (1983b).

**Walsh,** D. J., and V. B. Singh, *Makromol. Chem.*, **185**, 1979 (1984).    31, 58

**Walsh,** D. J., and G. L. Cheng, *Polymer*, **25**, 445 (1984).    126, 127

**Walsh,** D. J., and S. Rostami, *Adv. Polym. Sci.*, **70**, 119 (1985).    31, 42, 129

**Walsh,** D. J., S. Rostami and V. B. Singh, *Makromol. Chem.*, **186**, 145 (1985).    87

**Walsh,** D. J., and S. Rostami, *Macromolecules*, **18**, 216 (1985).    31, 42, 129

**Walsh,** D. J., and P. Zoller, *Makromol. Chem.*, **188**, 2193 (1987).    42, 105

**Wang,** C. B., and S. L. Cooper, *J. Appl. Polym. Sci.*, **26**, 2989 (1981).    242

**Wang,** C. B.-S., *PhD thesis*, Univ. of Wisconsin, Madison (1982).    115

**Wang,** K. J., and J. L. Lee, *J. Appl. Polym. Sci.*, **33**, 431 (1987).    212

**Wang,** L. H., and R. S. Porter, *J. Polym. Sci., Polym. Phys. Ed.*, **21**, 1815 (1983).    113

**Wang,** Y.-Y., and S.-A. Chen, *Polym. Eng. Sci.*, **20**, 823 (1980); ibid., **21**, 47    85, 86, 98, 104
(1981).

**Wapner,** P. G., and W. C. Forsman, *Trans. Soc. Rheol.*, **15**, 603 (1971).    142

**Ward,** I. M., *Developments in Oriented Polymers–1*, Appl. Sci. Publ., Barking, UK    129
(1982).

**Ward,** I. M., *Adv. Polym. Sci.*, **70**, 1 (1985).    129

**Ward,** T. C., and T. S. Lin, *A. C.S., Adv. Chem. Ser.*, **206**, 59 (1984).    107, 109

**Warfield,** R. W., and B. Hartmann, *Polymer*, **21**, 31 (1980).    93

**Watanabe,** H., S. Yamao and T. Kotaka, *Nihon Reoroji Gak.*, **10**, 24 (1982).    234

**Watanabe,** H., and T. Kotaka, *Macromolecules*, **16**, 769 (1983).    169, 194, 234

**Watanabe,** H., and T. Kotaka, *Macromolecules*, **17**, 342 (1984a).    144, 169, 234

**Watanabe,** H., and T. Kotaka, *Macromolecules*, **17**, 2316 (1984b).    144, 169, 194, 234

**Watanabe,** H., T. Sakamoto and T. Kotaka, *Macromolecules*, **18**, 1008, 1985    191
(1985).

**Watanabe,** H., and T. Kotaka, *Macromolecules*, **20**, 530, 535 (1987).    191

**Weeks,** N. E., F. E. Karasz and W. J. MacKnight, *J. Appl. Phys.*, **48**, 4068(1977).    89

**Wefer,** J. M., U. S. Pat. 4,493,921 to Uniroyal Inc., Jan. 15, 1985.    12

**Wendorff,** J. H., *J. Polym. Sci., Polym. Lett. Ed.*, **18**, 439 (1980); *Polymer*, **23**, 543    50, 73, 74, 84, 85
(1982).

**Wenig,** W., and K. Meyer, *Coll. Polym. Sci.*, **258**, 1009 (1980).    61

**White,** H. E., and S. F. Walton, *J. Amer. Ceram. Soc.*, **20**, 155 (1937).    154, 156

**White,** J. L., A. P. Plochocki and H. Tanaka, *Polym. Eng. Rev.*, **1**, 217 (1981).    131, 229

**White,** J. L., and K. Min, in *Polymer Blends and Mixtures*, I. J. Walsh, J. S. Higgins    229, 231
and A. Maconnachie, Eds., NATO ASI series E., Appl. Sci. No 89, pp. 413–28,
Martinus Nijhoff Publ., Dordrecht (1985).

**White,** J. L., in Discussion Period during NRCC/IMRI symposium, "*Polyblends-*    231
*'85*", Boucherville, Qc, Canada, April 16–17, 1985.

**White,** J. L., and K. Min, *Makromol. Chem. Macromol. Symp.*, **16**, 19 (1988).    229

**White,** J. R., and E. L. Thomas, *Rubber Chem. Technol.*, **57**, 457 (1984).    114, 117

**Whitmore,** M. D., and J. Noolandi, *Polym. Eng. Sci.*, **25**, 1120 (1985).    41

**Wignall,** G. D., H. R. Child and F. Li-Aravena, *Polymer*, **21**, 131 (1980).    74, 77

Citation page

**Wild,** L., T. R. Ryle, D. C. Knobeloch and I. R. Peat, *J. Polym. Sci., Polym. Phys. Ed.*, **20**, 441 (1982). 201

**Wildemuth,** C. R., and M. C. Williams, *Rheol. Acta*, **23**, 627 (1984). 168

**Williamson,** R. V., *J. Rheol.*, **1**, 283 (1930). 136

**Williams,** M. L., R. F. Landel and J. D. Ferry, *J. Amer. Chem. Soc.*, **77**, 3701 (1955). 169, 193

**Williams,** M. C., *A. I. Ch. E., J.*, **12**, 1064 (1966). 136

**Willis,** J. M., and B. D. Favis, *Polym. Eng. Sci.*, **28**, 1416 (1988). 207

**Wilusz,** E. B., *PhD thesis*, Univ. Massachusetts, Amherst (1976). 85

**Winding,** C. C., and G. D. Hiatt, *Polymeric Materials*, McGraw-Hill Book Co. New York (1961). 4

**Winnik,** M. A., NRCC/IMRI symposium *"Polyblends-'83"*, Montreal, April 12, 1983; *Polym. Eng. Sci.*, **24**, 87 (1984). 78, 79, 81

**Winnik,** M. A., O. Pekcan, L. Chen and M. D. Croucher, *Macromolecules*, **21**, 55 (1988). 79, 81

**Winter,** H. H., *Pure Appl. Chem.*, **55**, 943 (1983). 220

**Wisniewski,** C., G. Marin and Ph. Monge, *Eur. Polym. J.*, **20**, 691 (1984). 173, 192

**Wisniewski,** C., G. Marin and Ph. Monge, *Eur. Polym. J.*, **21**, 479 (1985). 151

**Witten,** T. A., and L. M. Sander, *Phys. Rev. Lett.*, **47**, 1400 (1981). 55

**Wolf,** B. A., *Makromol. Chem. Rapid. Comm.*, **1**, 231 (1980). 178

**Wolf,** B. A., *Macromolecules*, **17**, 615 (1984). 177, 178

**Woo,** E. M., J. W. Barlow and D. R. Paul, *Polymer*, **26**, 763 (1985). 40

**Wood,** L. A., *J. Polym. Sci.*, **28**, 318 (1958). 94

**Wu,** S., in *Polymer Blends*, D. R. Paul and S. Newman, Eds., Academic Press, New York (1978). 118, 123, 124

**Wu,** S., *Polymer Interfaces and Adhesion*, M. Dekker Inc., New York (1979). 123

**Wu,** S., *J. Polym. Sci., Polym. Phys. Ed.*, **21**, 699 (1983). 52

**Wu,** S., *J. Polym. Sci., Part B*, **25**, 557 (1987). 173, 195

**Wu,** S., *Polymer*, **28**, 1144 (1987). 127, 171, 193

**Wu,** W., *Polymer*, **24**, 43 (1983). 78

**Wunderlich,** B., *Macromolecular Physics*, Vol. 2: "Crystal Nucleation, Growth and Annealing", 1976, Vol. 3: "Crystal Melting", 1980, Academic Press, New York. 27, 53, 55, 58

**Yakovlev,** K. V., R. I. Zhitomirets, O. V. Romankevich, S. E. Zabello and A. V. Yudin, *Khim. Tekhnol. (Kiev)*, **5**, 14 (1984). 213, 216

**Yakovlev,** K. V., O. V. Romankevich, A. V. Yudin and T. I. Zhila, *Ukr. Khim. Zh.*, **51**, 540 (1985). 187

**Yakovlev,** K. V., A. S. Shevchenko and O. V. Romankevich, *Ukr. Khim. Zh.*, **52**, 771 (1986). 187, 188

**Yang,** D., B. Zhang, Y. Yang, Zh. Fang, G. Sun and Zh. Feng, *Polym. Eng. Sci.*, **24**, 612 (1984). 114, 115

**Yang,** H., G. Hadziioannou and R. S. Stein, *J. Polym. Sci., Polym. Phys. Ed.*, **21**, 159 (1983). 78

**Yang,** H., R. S. Stein, C. C. Han, B. J. Bauer and E. J. Kramer, *Polym. Commun.*, **27**, 132 (1986). 78

**Yano,** O. and Y. Wada, *J. Polym. Sci.*, A–2, **9**, 669 (1971). 142

**Yasuda,** K., *PhD thesis*, Massachussetts Institute of Technology, Cambridge, U. S. A. (1979). 136

**Yee,** A. F., and M. T. Takemori, *J. Polym. Sci., Polym. Phys. Ed.*, **20**, 205 (1982). 142

**Yeo,** J. K., L. H. Sperling and D. A. Thomas, *Polymer*, **24**, 307 (1983). 118

**Yerukhimovich,** I. Ya., *Vysokomol. Soed.*, **A24**, 1942, 1950 (1982). 49

**Yip,** C. W., "Plasticon '81", Symposium 4, Sept. 14–16, Univ. Warwick, U. K., Plast. Rubb. Inst., London (1981). 54, 59

**Yoshida,** S., and Y. Tsunekawa, *Intl. Progress Urethanes*, **3**, 181 (1981). 128

**Yoshimura,** D. K., and W. D. Richards, *Mod. Plast.*, **64(3)**, 64 (1987). 168

**Zacharius,** S. L., G. ten Brinke, W. J. MacKnight and F. E. Karasz, *Macromolecules*, **16**, 381 (1983). 31, 89

|  | Citation page |
|---|---|
| **Zang,** Y. H., R. Muller and D. Froelich, *Polymer*, **28**, 1577 (1987). | 190 |
| **Zeichner,** G. R., and P. D. Patel, 2nd World Congress Chem. Eng., Montreal, Que., Canada, **6**, 333 (1981). | 203 |
| **Zhang,** Y. H., and R. E. Prud'homme, *J. Polym. Sci., Part B, Polym. Phys.*, **24**, 723 (1987). | 42 |
| **Zhikuan,** C., and D. J. Walsh, *Eur. Polym. J.*, **19**, 519 (1983a). | 87, 90 |
| **Zhikuan,** C., and D. J. Walsh, *Eur. Polym. J.*, **19**, 519 (1983b); *Makromol. Chem.*, **84**, 1459 (1983c). | 87, 90 |
| **Zhikuan,** C., S. Ruona, D. J. Walsh and J. S. Higgins, *Polymer*, **24**, 263 (1983). | 87, 90 |
| **Zhila,** T. I., V. I. Mazurenko, O. V. Romankevich, S. E. Zabello and V. V. Anokhin, *Khim. Tekhnol. (Kiev)*, **5**, 35 (1980). | 173, 216 |
| **Zhou,** Z.-L., and A. Eisenberg, *J. Polym. Sci., Polym. Phys. Ed.*, **21**, 595 (1983). | 126, 128 |
| **Ziabicki,** A., *Coll. Polym. Sci.*, **252**, 433 (1974). | 56 |
| **Zimm,** B. H., *J. Chem. Phys.*, **24**, 269 (1956). | 143 |
| **Zin,** W.-Ch., *PhD thesis*, Univ. Cincinnati, OH (1983). | 67, 72, 73 |
| **Zin,** W.-Ch., and R.-J. Roe, *Macromolecules*, **17**, 183 (1984). | 67, 72 |
| **Zoller,** P., and P. Bolli, *J. Macromol. Sci., Phys.*, **B18**, 555 (1980). | 54 |
| **Zoller,** P., and H. H. Hoehn, *J. Polym. Sci., Polym. Phys. Ed.*, **20**, 1385 (1982). | 105 |
| **Zosel,** A., *Rheol. Acta*, **21**, 72 (1982). | 162 |
| **Zuzovsky,** M., Z. Priel and S. G. Mason, *J. Rheol.*, **24**, 705 (1980). | 160 |

# BLEND INDEX (see also Appendix I and II)*

---

* Abbreviations for thermoplastics are listed in Appendix III. In the adopted notation: A/B, A is the matrix, B is the dispersed phase polymer.

# SUBJECT INDEX (see also Blend Index)